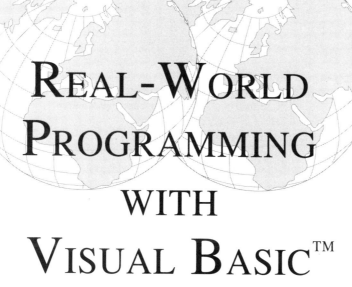

REAL-WORLD
PROGRAMMING
WITH
VISUAL BASIC™

ANTHONY T. MANN

SAMS
PUBLISHING

201 West 103rd Street
Indianapolis, Indiana 46290

I dedicate this book to my beautiful wife, Alison. Without her love and support, this book would not be possible.

OVERVIEW

CONTENTS

ACKNOWLEDGMENTS

I would like to thank and acknowledge the following people and organizations:

Richard Swadley, Publisher, and Cindy Morrow, Managing Editor, at Sams Publishing for their belief in this series and that I would be the one to set the stage.

Chris Denny, Acquisitions Editor at Sams Publishing, for allowing me write this book, for having the confidence in me, and for keeping this project under control.

Brad Jones, Development Editor at Sams Publishing (AKA: Brad!), for conceiving of the concept of this series. I would also like to thank Brad for sticking with me, keeping my spirits up, and having the confidence that additional authors were not necessary. Thanks Brad! Angelique Brittingham, Development Editor at Sams Publishing, for her help in developing this book.

Anne Owen, Freelance Editor, for keeping me laughing during the grueling review process and doing a great job in editing this book.

Keith Brophy, Technical Editor, for PUTTING me through the grueling review process. But seriously, Keith has done an outstanding job in making sure that this book is technically accurate and keeping me on my toes. Steve Flatt at Sams Publishing for doing a great job preparing the CD in the back of this book.

Guy Bryant at Philip Morris for his unbelievable support and belief that this could be done, even when I wasn't sure (and for stopping me from throwing the manuscript out the window). Doug LaDuke and Brenda Wassum in the I.S. department at Philip Morris for their encouragement in moving forward with this project. Mark and Lisa Spenik for their help and insight into the future, technology, and consulting! Mark Pruett for his insight into the publishing world. Pat Gervasio for introducing me to Visual Basic, back in the version 1.0 days.

My two sets of parents, Bryant and Eve Hanke, and David and Janice Mann, for all of their love and support.

My brother, Ed Mann, who has always been there for me. I wish him the best of luck!

Andrew Coupe at Microsoft, for his help with obtaining the VB4 beta and cutting through all the red tape. Allison Watson at Microsoft, for her help and support with the Developer Network CDs which helped immensely in making sure this book was technically accurate. Becky Kaske at Microsoft, for her help with obtaining SQL Server, and Visual C++.

Bill Gates, president and CEO of Microsoft, for his vision of the future and, ultimately, making this book possible.

Most importantly, a very special thanks to my wife, Alison, who has stood by me through thick and thicker and watched me bury myself under reams of paper, cover myself in toner, put up with my eat-and-run lifestyle for six months, and never doubted me for a second.

ABOUT THE AUTHOR

Anthony T. Mann is a professional software engineer and consultant with the Maxim Group on contract at Sara Lee Knit Products in Winston-Salem, North Carolina. Prior to that he was a consultant with IPC Technologies on contract for two years at Philip Morris in Richmond, Virginia. He specializes in developing client-server database systems and technology such as Sybase, Microsoft SQL Server, and Oracle in conjunction with Visual Basic and Visual C++. He also is certified by Microsoft in Visual Basic, SQL Server, and Windows NT. Mr. Mann is a registered Beta tester for the next version of Visual Basic (either VB 4.0 or VB '95, whichever it will be called).

Mr. Mann is the founder of SoftHouse, a specialized software engineering company, which markets and sells a custom control for Visual Basic for writing home automation applications. For more information about this custom control, the VBX-10 home automation custom control, refer to the advertisement in the back of this book. Anthony Mann can be reached via CompuServe at 75141,2522.

INTRODUCTION

Real-World Programming with Visual Basic is the first book in an exciting new series that shows tips and techniques in creating applications you can apply in the Real World. This book doesn't show silly examples, leaving you to wonder how they will help you as a developer on the job. It shows entire real-world applications (13 to be exact), from start to finish, and explains how to relate the concepts to your application. This allows you to develop better and faster applications.

This book is geared toward an intermediate to advanced level developer of Visual Basic applications. A novice level developer may not understand some of the examples presented here. It makes assumptions that the reader is at least of an intermediate level.

This book is divided into two parts as follows:

> Part I: Concepts in Action

> Part II: Applications for the Real World

Let's start with Part II. Part II is comprised of Chapters 20 through 32, which are the application chapters. One complete application is presented in each chapter in its entirety. Each of these chapters contains complete code listings and explanations regarding an entire application. The source code is also provided on the CD accompanying this book. Part I, on the other hand, takes selected real-world topics from those that are illustrated in Part II and expounds on them. Part I gives detailed information that can be applied in the Real World, as well as cross references to where the code comes from in Part II.

I'd like to answer some of the questions that may arise as you read this book. As you may know, there have long been different opinions about object and variable naming conventions. Therefore, these conventions are used in the book:

◆ If an object WILL be referenced in code, the default Visual Basic control name is changed to reflect a Microsoft recommended standard naming convention.

◆ If an object WILL NOT be referenced in code, such as a static label, the default Visual Basic control name is used.

◆ All variables use the type identifiers, such as %-Integer, &-Long, $-String, and so on, instead of explicitly declaring them as, for example:

```
Dim sTemp As String
```

Neither is right or wrong, but in a single user environment, I believe that the type identifiers are easier to read and to demonstrate in the book.

◆ String concatenation is performed by using the "+" symbol instead of the "&" symbol. Again, there is no right or wrong answer to this. I feel that it maintains consistency to use the "+" symbol.

◆ The message boxes within this book that allow for the user to select "Yes" or "No" use an argument of 292, instead of a string of constants. This allows for less code and limits the possibility for the word to be wrapped to the next line. For example, this statement

```
res% = MsgBox(cmd$, 292, "Warning")
```

is used in the book over its equivalent statement:

```
res% = MsgBox(cmd$, MB_YESNO + MB_ICONQUESTION + MB_DEFBUTTON2, "Warn-
ing")
```

There are some places in the book where you may notice that code can be made more efficient than presented. It is presented this way for clarity and ease of understanding, not optimization.

You will notice two flags used throughout the book: `Populating%` and `FormLoading%`. If you are not familiar with why they are used, it is because some of the applications will generate a flag that a Save is needed (or a change is made) upon the changing of some field or control. This means that when the form is populating with data, the code is flagged that you must save the change. Setting the `Populating%` or `FormLoading%` flag is a way around this.

Many places in the book appear to have `Resume` statements that will never be executed because there is an `Exit Sub` statement preceding it. Although this is true, the Visual Basic design-time environment can generate an error, `No Resume`, if this is not in place.

All of the chapters include at least one control (`SSPanel`) which is only included with the Professional Edition of Visual Basic version 3.0. Although the DLLs and VBXs are provided on the CD accompanying this book in the RESOURCE subdirectory, it is strongly advised to use the Professional Edition.

One final note is that for these applications to correctly load with Visual Basic, you must either have Visual Basic in your DOS path or create a Visual Basic icon for each one of the applications and specify each of the working directories as the name of the directory where the source files are.

CONVENTIONS USED IN THIS BOOK

The following typographic conventions are used in this book:

- ◆ Code lines, commands, statements, variables, and any text you see on the screen appears in a `computer` typeface.
- ◆ Command output and anything that you type appears in a bold **`computer`** typeface.
- ◆ Placeholders in syntax descriptions appear in an *`italic computer`* typeface. Replace the placeholder with the actual filename, parameter, or whatever element it represents.
- ◆ *Italics* highlight technical terms when they first appear in the text, and are sometimes used to emphasize important points.
- ◆ Pseudocode, a way of explaining in English what a program does, also appears in *italics*.

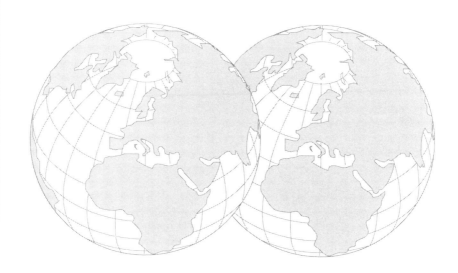

CONCEPTS
IN ACTION

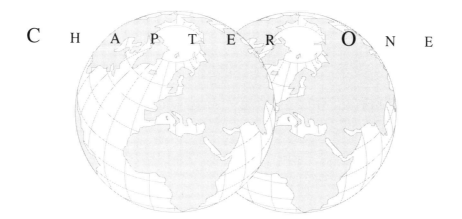

DEBUGGING

DEBUGGING IS ONE OF THE MOST IMPORTANT STEPS IN CREATING A QUALITY VISUAL BASIC APPLICATION. MOST VISUAL BASIC PROGRAMMERS HAVE PERFORMED AT LEAST SOME DEBUGGING. SOME INFORMATION IN THIS CHAPTER MAY NOT BE NEW TO YOU; HOWEVER, THIS BOOK WOULD NOT BE COMPLETE WITHOUT COVERING DEBUGGING BECAUSE IT'S SO IMPORTANT. DEBUGGING CAN ALSO BE ONE OF THE MOST DIFFICULT ASPECTS OF DEVELOPMENT BECAUSE BUGS CAN BE VERY ELUSIVE, THEREBY INCREASING THE TIME IT TAKES TO BUILD AN APPLICATION. THIS CHAPTER SHOWS SOME PROCEDURES, TIPS, AND TECHNIQUES USED IN DEBUGGING APPLICATIONS.

See Chapter 2, "Error Handling," for more information.

Of the three Visual Basic modes of operation (Run, Break, and Design), you can only perform debugging in Break mode. Figure 1.1 shows the Visual Basic CD Player application presented in Chapter 27 in Break mode. You can enter the Break mode in one of the five following ways:

◆ Press CTRL-BREAK while in Run mode. This doesn't work in any other mode.

◆ Enter a STOP command in the code. Listing 1.1 shows an example of the STOP command in a fragment of code from Chapter 27.

◆ Set a breakpoint on a line of code. When the program encounters this line, Visual Basic enters Break mode.

◆ Click the Break command button on the Visual Basic toolbar.

◆ Enter Break mode by satisfying a condition of a watch. For more information on watches, refer to "Watch Expression," later in the chapter.

◆ Enter an Error statement.

◆ Single step through code from Design mode by pressing F8 or by selecting the Debug->Single Step menu option.

◆ Procedure step through code from Design mode by pressing SHIFT-F8 or by selecting the Debug->Procedure Step menu option.

FIGURE 1.1.
*CD Player application
in Break mode.*

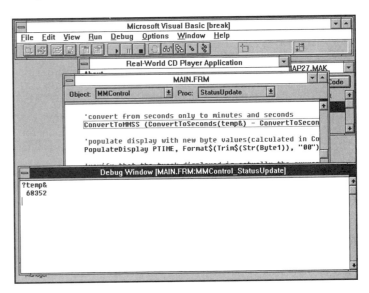

Listing 1.1. Code fragment showing STOP command.

```
FirstDigit% = Val(Mid$(temp$, 4, 1))
pictTime(0).Picture = pictSource(FirstDigit%).Picture
Stop
SecondDigit% = Val(Mid$(temp$, 3, 1))
pictTime(1).Picture = pictSource(SecondDigit%).Picture
```

When the program encounters and executes the STOP command, program execution pauses, Visual Basic enters Break mode, and the Debug window (or immediate pane) appears. Figure 1.2 shows the Debug window after it encounters this command. At the time the Debug window appears, it must be made active to begin debugging your application. To make the window active, simply click anywhere in the window.

REM The STOP command must either be removed or commented out before compiling. This command is for troubleshooting and debugging purposes only. If the command is not removed or commented out, running the executable file generates a runtime error that is not trapable. It generates the error Stop Statement Encountered and terminates the program. For a list of the most common trapable errors, refer to the Visual Basic User's Manual or on-line help.

FIGURE 1.2.
Debug window after executing a STOP command.

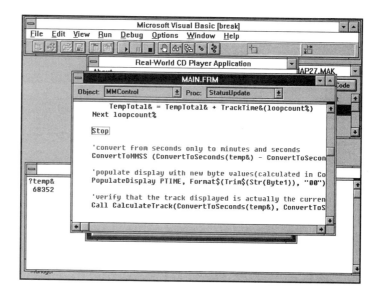

You can perform debugging in one of two ways: By using breakpoints and Step functions to track the flow of program execution, or by using the Debug/Watch windows to actually check and modify program variables.

There are three main differences between using the STOP command and using breakpoints. For example, you compile an executable file and you find out there is a bug that needs to be tracked. The first difference is that if you run Visual Basic and either enter a STOP command or un-comment a STOP command, Visual Basic recognizes the change and prompts for saving. On the other hand, setting a breakpoint does not cause Visual Basic to prompt for saving. The second difference is that a STOP command is saved in the source code (as are all commands). A breakpoint is not saved. If you exit Visual Basic and re-enter, you have to reset the breakpoints. The third difference is that a breakpoint allows for you to clear all breakpoints at once with the Debug->Clear All Breakpoints menu option. You cannot remove all Stop statements at once. (For more information on breakpoints, see the following section, "Design Mode.") Visual Basic provides many ways to access different modes and functions. Table 1.1 lists these ways.

TABLE 1.1. VISUAL BASIC DEBUGGING HOTKEYS AND OPTIONS.

Hotkey	Menu Option	Command Button	Action
CTRL-B	Window->Debug	No	Invokes Debug window
F5	Run->Start	Yes	Runs the application
SHIFT-F5	Run->Restart (from Break mode)	No	Stops and restarts the application
F8	Debug->Single Step	Yes	Single steps through all lines of code
SHIFT-F8	Debug->Procedure Step	Yes	Single steps through code, skipping procedures
F9	Debug->Toggle Breakpoint	Yes	Toggles breakpoints on and off
N/A	Debug->Clear All Breakpoints	No	Clears all Breakpoints in application
SHIFT-F9	Debug->Instant Watch	Yes	Shows value of currently selected code variable
N/A	Debug->Add Watch	No	Allows possibility to add a new watch
CTRL-W	Debug->Edit Watch	No	Allows possibility to edit, add, or delete watches
CTRL-L	Debug->Calls List	Yes	Shows list of procedures that are not completed
N/A	Debug->Set Next Statement	No	Tells Visual Basic which line of code to execute next

Hotkey	Menu Option	Command Button	Action
N/A	Debug->Show Next Statement	No	Tells Visual Basic to show next line of code

DESIGN MODE

In Design mode, you can set breakpoints, watches, or enter Stop statements into the code. You cannot actually perform debugging in Design mode. You receive errors from Visual Basic that can only be detected at runtime. Certain errors are only detected when you try to run the program or even when a certain line is encountered. These errors are *runtime errors*. For more information on runtime errors, see the section "Run Mode," later in the chapter. For more information on watches, see the following section, "Break Mode."

To set a breakpoint, position the cursor on the line where the desired breakpoint is to be located and press F9 or select the Debug->Toggle Breakpoint menu option. Note that you can change the color of the breakpoint by selecting the Options->Environment menu option and by selecting the Breakpoint Background option to change the background color. When this line of code is encountered, Visual Basic is immediately in Break mode and brings up the Debug window. If the Debug window is not the active window, you can make it active by pressing CTRL-B or by selecting the Window->Debug menu option. For more information on Break mode, see the following section, "Break Mode."

There are some situations where you can't place a breakpoint on the line, and Visual Basic generates a design time error Breakpoint not allowed on this line. You cannot place a breakpoint on a line under the following conditions:

◆ On a blank line

◆ In the (declarations) section of a form or module

◆ On a line containing the Case clause (as part of a select case structure)

◆ On a line containing the End Select statement

◆ On a line containing a non-numeric line label

BREAK MODE

To enter Break mode manually (without a STOP command, breakpoint, or watch) from Run mode, either press CTRL-BREAK, select the Break button on the Visual Basic toolbar, or select the Run->Break menu option. If the program execution is in the middle of a procedure, the procedure is paused immediately at the point in time where Break mode is entered.

REM An exception to the program pausing immediately is if a process that is waiting for the results of another process is occurring, which ties up 100 percent of the CPU's time. For example, if you are waiting for the results of a query from SQL Server, you won't enter Break mode until the process returns.

Visual Basic brings up the Code window for the particular module that contains the currently executing code. This procedure is a call that has not completed execution. To view a list of all the calls that have not completed execution, press CTRL-L or select the Debug->Calls menu option. This only works if the Code window is active. From this list of calls, you can view any of them by highlighting the desired procedure and clicking the Show button. Figure 1.3 shows the Calls list from Visual Basic, using the CD Player application.

FIGURE 1.3.
CD Player application,
Calls list.

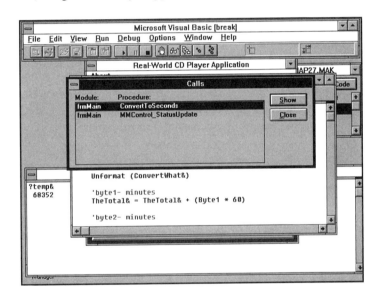

After the program is in Break mode, you can begin debugging. If you want to step through the program line by line to see exactly how the logic flows, you must single step into each line of code by pressing F8, by selecting the Debug->Single Step menu option, or by clicking on the Step Into command button on the Visual Basic toolbar. This command button is represented by a single footprint. Single stepping causes Visual Basic to step through each and every line of code, one line at a time, on each step operation. This means that if a line of code is encountered that calls another procedure, Visual Basic shows that procedure (and adds it to the Calls list). If you don't want to enter the procedure but return to Break mode only after the procedure is finished (the line after where the procedure is called), you must procedure step over a line of code by pressing Shift-F8, by selecting the Debug->Procedure Step menu option, or by clicking on the Step Over command button on the Visual Basic toolbar. This command button is represented by a double footprint.

Debugging really is the procedure of finding out why a program does not perform as expected. The only way to do this is to track the flow of execution and to determine what values are in which variables and compare these to the way you know the program must flow. The preceding sections describe how to track the flow of execution. To determine the value of a variable, open the Debug window from Run mode by pressing CTRL-B or by selecting the Window->Debug menu option. You can perform almost all Visual Basic commands immediately from the Debug window. This is why Microsoft calls the Debug window the "Immediate Pane." Following is a listing of the commands and statements that cannot be performed from the Debug window:

- Global declarations
- Const declarations
- Declare declarations
- Def declarations
- Type declarations
- Dim declarations
- Function declarations
- Sub routine declarations
- Option Base statement
- Option Explicit statement
- Option Compare statement
- Redim declarations
- Static declarations

If any of the preceding actions is attempted in the Debug window, Visual Basic generates the error Invalid in Immediate Pane. As long as you don't use the preceding listed statements, you can either determine the value of a variable or assign new values to variables. To determine the value of a variable, type ? or **Print** in the Debug window (both are equivalent in most basic languages), type the variable name, and press Enter. Visual Basic returns the value on the next line. You can even use a Visual Basic function to test for certain conditions. For example, if you want to know what is in the string variable Temp$, type **?Temp$**. Visual Basic returns Microsoft Visual Basic. You now know the value of Temp$, but what if you need to know the length? You can simply type **?Len(Temp$)**. Visual Basic returns 22. You can use any statement, except for the ones listed earlier, to test different conditions before putting them into your actual code.

Another way you can check the value of a variable instantly is with an *instant watch*. To use this method, click on the variable in the code window to check and invoke the instant watch by pressing Shift-F9, by selecting the Debug->Instant Watch menu option, or by clicking the Instant Watch button on the Visual Basic toolbar. Figure 1.4 shows the instant watch form in checking the value of a variable.

FIGURE 1.4.
CD Player application, instant watch.

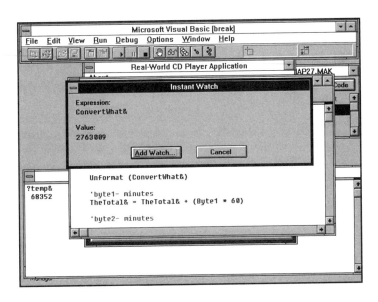

You can either overwrite a previous line in the Debug window by clearing the contents of the line and typing your statement, or by continuing statement after statement and having the Debug window scroll through your statements. You can also print the contents of a variable by typing **Printer.Print**, followed by a space and the name of the variable, and then pressing Enter. If you want to have the value of a variable printed to the Debug window in your code, you can enter **Debug.Print** in your code listing, followed by a space and the name of the variable, and then press Enter.

If you change the value of a variable in the Debug window, you can enter Run mode by pressing F5 and continue with the newly assigned value. You can also step through the code and check the values of additional variables that are dependent on the value of the modified variables.

Suppose that you want to watch for a certain change in a variable or for a variable to equal a certain value. You can add the watch to a list of watches and assign it an action. For example, consider the following code fragment:

```
For x% = 0 To 1000
        Select Case (x%)
            Case 105:
                y% = x% * Val(text1.Text)
        End Select
Next x%
```

If you need to debug the value of x%, you do not want to single step through this code until the value of x% equals 105. You'll be there all day! You can add a watch of the variable x% and set an action to break when the value equals 105 (or even 104 and then single step). To do this, from

Break mode select the Debug->Add Watch menu option. This action brings up the Add Watch form. Figure 1.5 shows the Visual Basic Add Watch form. Select the appropriate options to break when the value is equal to 105. The possible options are listed next.

FIGURE 1.5.
CD Player application,
Add Watch form.

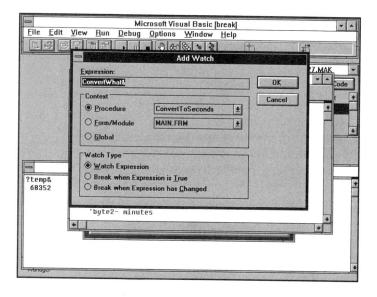

The Add Watch form allows for three possible watch types. They are:

◆ Watch Expression

◆ Break when Expression is True

◆ Break when Expression has Changed

WATCH EXPRESSION

The first watch type, Watch Expression, simply adds the expression to the Watch list. If you enter Break mode and click on the Watch command button, the watch appears at the top of the Debug window with the value assigned to it. It does not put Visual Basic into Break mode automatically.

BREAK WHEN EXPRESSION IS TRUE

The next option, Break when Expression is True, automatically puts Visual Basic into Break mode when the expression listed in the Expression text box is true. For example, consider the following expression:

```
x% = 75
```

At the point where x% equals 75, as long as the variable is within the scope of the context selected, Visual Basic goes into Break mode. It is very important to consider the context of the variable, or scope. For example, suppose that the context is selected for all procedures and all modules, and the watch expression is set to break when the value is true. The context is then, in effect, global. It is also assumed that the variable x% is declared as global. At any point in the program, Visual Basic breaks when x% = 75. If under the same conditions, the context is limited to a certain procedure, Visual Basic breaks only in the procedure selected, not anywhere else. The possible context scopes are:

◆ Procedure

◆ Form/Module

◆ Global

BREAK WHEN EXPRESSION HAS CHANGED

The third option, Break when Expression has Changed, acts the same as the Break when Expression is True option, except that the expression entered in the expression list is only a variable name and Visual Basic breaks upon any change of the variable. For example, suppose that you want to find out when the variable x% has changed. In the expression list, simply enter **x%** and select the Break when Expression has Changed option.

If you want to cause program execution to jump to a certain location (only in Break mode), place the cursor on the line you want to jump to and select the Debug->Set Next Statement menu option. The next line of code executed is this line—the line you've placed the cursor on. The lines of code to be executed before this line are skipped. This enables you to skip a procedure that is known to have a bug. You can then go back later and use the methods described earlier to debug that procedure.

 You can single step through a command button procedure without setting a breakpoint or watch. To do this, enter Break mode by pressing CTRL-BREAK. Notice that nothing happens. There are no events triggered, and there is no code currently processing; therefore, pressing F8 to single step has no effect. Click on the Command button and press F8. This action allows you to single step through the procedure.

RUN MODE

After you're in Run mode, you cannot perform debugging. Depending on the severity of the bug, it could produce a runtime error. If the problem is simply that the value of a variable is not as expected, it does not cause a runtime error. This is assuming that the unexpected value is within the limits of the datatype used.

Refer to Chapter 2, "Error Handling," for more information on runtime errors.

SPECIAL CONSIDERATIONS

Sometimes situations arise for which it helps to have a thorough knowledge and understanding of Visual Basic in order to help debug problems. For example, you want to drag/drop an item from one list box to another. You need to add the item to the second list box, but remove it from the first. Consider the following code fragments:

```
'ADD
    'loop through all items in List 1
    For LoopCount% = 0 To list1.ListCount - 1
        'if List1 item is selected-add to list 2
        If list1.Selected(LoopCount%) = True Then
            list2.AddItem list1.List(LoopCount%)
        End If
    Next LoopCount%

'REMOVE
    'loop through all items in List 1
    For LoopCount% = 0 To list1.ListCount - 1
        'if List1 item is selected-remove
        If list1.Selected(LoopCount%) = True Then
            list1.RemoveItem LoopCount%
        End If
    Next LoopCount%
```

The first loop certainly adds the contents to list2, but the problem occurs in the second loop. It loops through all the items in the list box and removes them if they are selected. Seems easy enough, but if any items are actually removed, the number of items in the list changes. Even though the value of list1.ListCount is changed, the value calculated from List1.ListCount -1 is set at the moment the loop is entered and isn't recalculated just because an item is removed. This presents a problem because if an item is removed when LoopCount% equals the highest possible value, this generates a runtime error. This is because if there are five items in the list, the loop expects to cycle from zero to four. If the second item in the list is removed, there are now only four items in the list (zero to three). When LoopCount% gets to four, the index no longer exists.

One way around problems such as this is to understand the way Visual Basic works and determine a work-around. Many of these types of situations will definitely arise. There is a very simple work-around for this particular case. All you have to do is reverse the order of the loop. The following code fragment represents the "fix" for the problem in the REMOVE loop:

```
'REMOVE
'loop through all items in List 1
For LoopCount% = list1.ListCount - 1 To 0 Step -1
    'if List1 item is selected-remove
    If list1.Selected(LoopCount%) = True Then
```

```
         list1.RemoveItem LoopCount%
      End If
   Next LoopCount%
```

This works because if the second item in the list is removed, it affects the total number of indexes in the listcount, but Loopcount would have already looped through the highest index number first. This way, the program can loop through all indexes and remove the ones selected without error.

Thorough knowledge of Visual Basic can save many hours of debugging time. The rest of this book provides detailed code examples and insight into how to do certain things and how Visual Basic works.

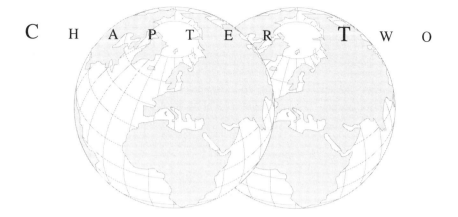

ERROR HANDLING

HANDLING RUNTIME ERRORS PROMPTLY IS VERY IMPORTANT BECAUSE IF YOU DON'T, THE PROGRAM EXITS ABRUPTLY WHEN A RUNTIME ERROR OCCURS. THE USER MAY HAVE ENTERED DATA BUT NOT SAVED IT. THIS CAN RESULT IN DATA LOSS. ERROR HANDLING IS NOT DIFFICULT, AND IT'S IMPORTANT THAT IT'S INCORPORATED. THIS CHAPTER POINTS OUT HOW TO INCORPORATE ERROR HANDLING.

To handle errors, the error handling code is placed into your code *before* the expected (or unexpected) error occurs. The general syntax of an error handler is

```
ON ERROR xxx
```

where *xxx* can be one of the following:

◆ RESUME NEXT
◆ GOTO label
◆ GOTO line

Any of these error handling techniques is sufficient enough to stop Visual Basic from coming to a crashing halt when a runtime error is encountered—unless the error is handled in such a way that causes an error. However, it is possible to have Visual Basic stuck in an endless loop. It's important to anticipate errors and handle all possibilities. For example, if you consider a routine that opens files, you probably don't need to consider printing errors.

When an error occurs, you need to feed information back to the user in an understandable form. For example, you don't want to put up a message box that says Printer Error. You want to give more detailed information if possible, such as Printer Not Ready. Give only the necessary information. For example, you probably don't need to provide information about system resources if the printer is not ready. You don't want to overload the user with too much information.

It can also be useful to allow support staff to have access to some information that is not relevant for the general user but can be helpful in troubleshooting. You may want to provide certain system information in an error handler only to a person who logged in with a certain authority.

 There is no one solution to handling errors. The purpose of this chapter is to suggest some possibilities.

WORKING WITH ERROR HANDLING

To turn error handling off, enter the following line of code into your procedure:

```
On Error Goto 0
```

This code works because the syntax indicates that if an error occurs, Visual Basic jumps to line 0. However, line 0 doesn't exist. This effectively turns the error handling off.

It is important to note that if you have a routine that contains an error handler but no error occurs, Visual Basic steps through each line of code until it reaches End Sub or End Function. What this means is that the lines of code that constitute the error handler are executed unless you place an Exit Sub or Exit Function statement above the error handling label.

For example, consider the following function taken from Chapter 22, "Icon Printing Application," MAIN.FRM, `FindFont()`:

```
1    Function FindFont () As Integer
2
3    'declare variables
4    Dim loopcount%          'looping variable
5
6    'there could be a printer font error
7    On Error GoTo fonterror
8
9    'find out which fonts exist for printer, and use first available in size 6
10   For loopcount% = 0 To printer.FontCount - 1
11       'assign to first available font
12       printer.FontName = printer.Fonts(loopcount%)
13
14       'assign to size 6
15       printer.FontSize = 6
16
17       'test to see if 6 is still assigned, if so, exit loop
18       If printer.FontSize = 6 Then
19
20          'set variable flag to print text in print routine
21          FontFound% = True
22
23          'exit function
24          FindFont = True
25          Exit Function
26       End If
27
28   Next loopcount%
29
30   'font was not found
31   FindFont = False
32   Exit Function
33
34   fonterror:
35   'an error occurred
36    Resume Next
37
38   End Function
```

REM The line numbers shown in the preceding code are not part of the code. They are shown for instructional purposes only. This also applies to line numbers in the rest of the code examples in this chapter.

If there is no error and line 32 doesn't exist, Visual Basic tries to execute lines 34, 35, and 36. The Exit Function code in line 32 insures that the code following this line is only executed if there is an error.

Based on the preceding, it is possible to have more than one level of error handlers in one procedure. You may need to incorporate multi-level error handling in the same routine in your application. You use the same basic techniques of exiting the procedure if an error doesn't occur, as in the preceding code list. Consider the following code taken from Chapter 26, "Communications Terminal Application," MAIN.FRM, cbComPort_Click():

```
1    Sub cbComPort_Click ()
2
3    'declare variables
4    Dim m$          'message constructor
5
6    'this routine is only valid if auto is selected
7    If InStr(cbComPort.Text, "Auto") > 0 Then
8        'enable test button
9        cmdTest.Enabled = True
10
11       'turn auto answer off-can't auto detect ringing on all ports at once
12       cbRecMode.ListIndex = 1
13
14       Exit Sub
15   End If
16
17   'handle errors
18   On Error GoTo porterrorclose
19
20   'test to see if there is a selection
21   If cbComPort.ListIndex = -1 Then Exit Sub
22
23   'first close port
24   mscomm.PortOpen = False
25
26   'handle error
27   On Error GoTo porterroropen
28
29   'assign port
30   mscomm.CommPort = Val(Right$(cbComPort.List(cbComPort.ListIndex), 1))
31
32   'open port if NOT set to "No Answer"
33   If cbRecMode.Text <> "No Answer" Then
34       If Not (mscomm.PortOpen = True) Then
35           'open port
36           mscomm.PortOpen = True
37
38           'enable test button
39           cmdTest.Enabled = True
40
41           'configure to answer on first ring
42           SendToModem ("ATS0=1" + Chr$(13))
43
44           'enable menus
45           menu_terminal.Enabled = True
46       End If
```

```
47    End If
48
49    'exit
50    Exit Sub
51
52    PortErrorClose:
53     Resume Next
54
55    PortErrorOpen:
56     'build message
57     m$ = "Can't open port!"
58     MsgBox m$
59
60     'disable test button
61     cmdTest.Enabled = False
62
63     'disable menu options
64     menu_terminal.Enabled = False
65
66     'blank com port display
67     cbComPort.ListIndex = -1
68
69    Exit Sub
70    'avoid errors
71    Resume
72
73    End Sub
```

There are two error handler labels: one at line 52 and one at line 55. The error handler at line 52, PortErrorClose, is called when the com port can't be closed. It is not a critical error because the port must have been previously closed.

The error handler at line 55, PortErrorOpen, is called when the com port can't be opened. This is a critical error because it affects all further operations. It is for this reason that the message box is displayed and the sub is exited, instead of the code resuming to the line where the error occurred.

It is important to note that, theoretically, even though there is an exit sub in an error handler, such as in line 69, the routine is exited. In reality, Visual Basic expects some type of RESUME command in every error handler. That's why the RESUME command in line 71 exists, even though Visual Basic never gets to this line. If you don't enter this command, you receive a No Resume error. It is also possible that this error only shows up at runtime. To avoid all of these problems, simply make sure that this line exists.

You may want to customize an error handler routine by taking an action based on a certain error. Do this by using a Select Case statement. You test for the actual error number by using the ERR command. It holds the last error number, which is a number between 1 and 32767.

Following is a code fragment taken from Chapter 26, "Communications Terminal Application," MAIN.FRM, `cmdTest_Click()`, which demonstrates how to take an action based on a certain error number:

```
TestError:
    'error occurred

    Select Case (Err)
        Case 68: '(device unavail)
            m$ = cbComPort.List(cbComPort.ListIndex) + " is invalid." + Chr$(13)
            m$ = m$ + "It could be the mouse port."

            'change cursor
            screen.MousePointer = DEFAULT

            'show message
            MsgBox m$

            'exit
            Exit Sub

            'avoid errors
            Resume
        Case Else:
            Resume Next
    End Select
```

The preceding code fragment tests for the error 68, which is `device unavailable`. The default, `Case Else`, is used as a catchall. It simply resumes at the next statement after the statement that causes the error.

PROCEDURAL ERROR HANDLING

You generally handle errors at the procedure level. Any procedure called by another procedure uses the calling procedure's error handler, unless one of the following happens:

- ◆ The called procedure has its own error handler
- ◆ The calling procedure ends

Any procedure that is currently active uses its own error handler, if it has one. If it doesn't, the procedure uses the error handler from the calling procedure. However, if the calling procedure that has an error handler ends, there are no more error handlers in effect. There are two types of procedural error handling. They are *in-line* and *multi-line* error handlers. Both are described in the following sections.

IN-LINE ERROR HANDLING

With *in-line error handling*, you can handle the error in one line. You don't need to instruct the program to jump to another location to handle the error. You can invoke an in-line error handler by typing the following at the beginning of the procedure:

```
On Error Resume Next
```

By typing the preceding, you are insured that *any* error that occurs in the procedure immediately executes the line of code after the line in which the error occurred. Why jump around the procedure with an error handling routine if it is not necessary?

Typically, an in-line error handler is incorporated to avoid only runtime errors and not to provide useful information back to the user, or to anticipate specific errors.

Consider the following code fragment as an example of how to incorporate an in-line error handler:

```
1     'handle error
2     On Error Resume Next
3
4     'loop through file list
5     For LoopCount% = 0 To List1.ListCount - 1
6         'open the file
7         Open List1.List(LoopCount%) For Output As #1
8
9         'write string
10        Print #1, TestString$
11
12        'close the file
13        Close #1
14
15    Next LoopCount%
```

The error is handled by line 2. This fragment loops through all items in the listbox List1, opens a file by that name, writes a string, and closes the file. If any step fails, the code resumes to the next line of code. If, in turn, another step fails, the code resumes to the next line, and so on, until the loop is finished. With this code example, the user may lose data if an error occurs.

MULTI-LINE ERROR HANDLING

Multi-line error handling consists of invoking the error handler on one line, but referencing a line that starts the error handling routine. This routine must be located in the same procedure and must be unique within a module or form. Following is a code fragment for a multi-line error handler:

```
1     'handle error
2     On Error GoTo Handler1
3
4     Open "LPT1" For Output As #1
5
```

```
6    Exit Sub
7
8 Handler1:
9    MsgBox Error$
10   Resume Next
```

Line 2 invokes the error handler but instructs Visual Basic to jump to the label Handler1 when an error is encountered. The statement in line 9 simply displays the string text of the error. Line 6 serves two purposes. First, if there is no error, Visual Basic never gets to line 7 and later because it exits the subroutine first. If this line is not entered, the message box appears anyway. The second purpose for line 6 is that if there is an error in this particular code fragment, the error may have only occurred in line 4. In which case, Visual Basic goes through Handler1 and returns to the line after the error-causing line. In this case, the error-causing line is line 6, which exits the subroutine.

It's possible to generate your own errors to test the flow of execution from the error and to test for all possible situations. To generate an error, use the Error statement. Do not confuse Error with Error$. The Error$ statement is used in the preceding listing to display the text message of the error. Make sure not to compile the program with the Error statement in your program. This action generates an error every time the procedure is executed.

GLOBAL ERROR HANDLING

There is really no built-in global error handling in Visual Basic because the error handler routine invoked terminates when the procedure that called it terminates.

The only possible way to work around the lack of a global error handling routine is to start the application from a routine you define, called sub_main(). Set the startup form as sub_main() in the project menu option and enter your error handling routine into the sub_main procedure, as listed in the preceding sections.

Theoretically, if you can find a way to enter into sub_main procedures that call other procedures, error handling will work on a global scale. In reality, this is impossible because of the event-driven nature of Visual Basic.

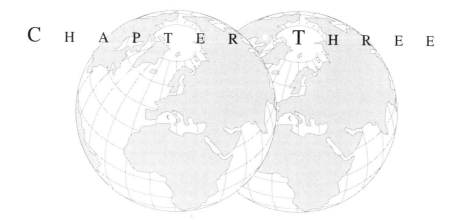

CALLING WINDOWS APIS AND DLLS

CALLING A WINDOWS *APPLICATION PROGRAMMING INTERFACE (API)* IS A VERY EASY WAY FOR A VISUAL BASIC PROGRAMMER TO EXTEND THE LANGUAGE OF VISUAL BASIC BY USING FUNCTIONS THAT ARE NOT BUILT INTO VISUAL BASIC DIRECTLY. THERE ARE OVER 600 WINDOWS API FUNCTIONS. YOU CAN USE MOST OF THESE WITHOUT PROBLEMS FROM VISUAL BASIC, BUT THERE ARE SOME DEFINITE RULES TO FOLLOW. THESE RULES ARE DISCUSSED LATER IN THIS CHAPTER. VISUAL BASIC IS A VERY EXTENSIBLE LANGUAGE BECAUSE IF YOU NEED A FUNCTION THAT DOESN'T EXIST, YOU CAN WRITE IT YOURSELF IN C OR C++ IN THE FORM OF A *DYNAMIC LINK LIBRARY (DLL)*, AND THEN USE IT AS ANY API FUNCTION. YOU CANNOT USE VISUAL BASIC TO WRITE A DLL.

Although C and C++ are the most common languages to write DLLs, there are many third-party tools and languages that are emerging in the marketplace.

 For more information on writing DLLs, refer to Chapter 19, "Writing DLLs and VBXs."

 Because Windows APIs are contained inside of DLLs, the terms are sometimes used interchangeably. However, technically they are not the same. Windows APIs are contained inside DLLs (and are declared as such) and refer to a specific set of functions designed for use with Windows. You do not write an API; you write a DLL.

Declaring a Function from a DLL

To declare a function from a DLL, you must declare the function so that Visual Basic knows where to find it, what parameters the function expects, and what the function returns. Declaring a function follows this general syntax:

```
DECLARE FUNCTION function LIB "dll" [ALIAS "alias name"]([argument list]) AS return type
```

where the following variables are used:

function: The name of the API function used inside your Visual Basic code.

dll: The name of the DLL file. Note that the name of the DLL is in quotes.

alias name: Aliases are used only if the function name referenced inside Visual Basic code is different from the function name the DLL expects. If the alias name is omitted, Visual Basic expects the function name used inside the code to be the same name as the function inside the DLL itself. If you use an alias name, this is where you enter the name the DLL itself expects. Note that the name of the alias is in quotes.

argument list: The name of the arguments passed into the function. If there are none, empty set parentheses are needed.

return type: The datatype variable returned from the function.

You do not have to actually supply the return type or parameter type if the name of the function includes a Visual Basic datatype variable. For example, the following two declarations are equivalent:

```
Declare Function ShowCursor% Lib "User" (ByVal bShow%)

Declare Function ShowCursor Lib "User" (ByVal bShow%) As Integer
```

Likewise, these declarations are equivalent:

```
Declare Function ShowCursor% Lib "User" (ByVal bShow%)

Declare Function ShowCursor% Lib "User" (ByVal bShow As Integer)
```

 The declarations for applications are not case sensitive. Any of the parameters or function names can be uppercase, lowercase, or any mixture. In the future, this may not be true. It is highly recommended that you treat the declarations as if they are case sensitive. You should pass all parameters and function names exactly as the API expects them to be passed.

DECLARING A SUBROUTINE FROM A DLL

To declare a subroutine from a DLL, you must declare the subroutine so that Visual Basic knows where to find the subroutine and what parameters the subroutine expects. There is no return value from a subroutine. Declaring a subroutine follows the general syntax

```
DECLARE  SUB sub LIB "dll" [ALIAS "alias name"]([argument list])
```

where the following variables are used:

sub: The name of the API routine used inside your Visual Basic code.

dll: The name of the DLL file. Note that the name of the DLL is in quotes.

alias name: Aliases are used only if the subroutine name referenced inside Visual Basic code is different from the subroutine name the DLL expects. If the alias name is omitted, Visual Basic expects the subroutine name used inside the code to be the same name as the subroutine inside the DLL itself. If you use an alias name, this is where you enter the name the DLL itself expects. Note that the name of the alias is in quotes.

argument list: The name of the arguments passed into the function. If there are none, empty set parentheses are needed.

The vast majority of all DLL calls will be functions. There is only one DLL subroutine procedure in this entire book.

 A DLL subroutine procedure is presented in Chapter 25, "Dynamic Hotspot Application," and is used for playing a sound at a specified frequency. Chapter 25 is also the only chapter that uses a custom DLL instead of a Windows-supplied DLL.

For more information on creating DLLs, see Chapter 19, "Writing DLLs and VBXs."

You'll find that you use the same API functions over and over. This really is only a small fraction of the API functions available. As an example, Table 3.1 lists the API functions used in this book. Notice how many of the same functions are used in multiple chapters. For a complete reference of the API functions available, refer to the help file, WIN31WH.HLP, that comes with Visual Basic.

TABLE 3.1. API/DLL FUNCTIONS USED IN THIS BOOK.

Chapter(s)	Function	Declaration
20	sndPlaySound	Declare Function sndPlaySound Lib "MMSYSTEM.DLL" (ByVal lpszSoundName$, ByVal wFlags%) As Integer
	GetSystemMenu	Declare Function GetSystemMenu Lib "User" (ByVal hWnd%, ByVal bRevert%) As Integer
	DestroyMenu	Declare Function DestroyMenu Lib "User" (ByVal hMenu As Integer) As Integer
21	ShowCursor%	Declare Function ShowCursor% Lib "User" (ByVal bShow%)
	ClipCursor	Declare Sub ClipCursor Lib "User" (lpRect As Any)
	SetCursorPos	Declare Sub SetCursorPos Lib "User" (ByVal X As Integer, ByVal Y As Integer)
	GetWindowRect	Declare Sub GetWindowRect Lib "User" (ByVal hWnd As Integer, lpRect As RECT)
20, 23, 24, 25, 28	GetPrivateProfileString	Declare Function GetPrivateProfileString Lib "Kernel" (ByVal lpAppName As String, ByVal lpKeyName As String, ByVal lpDefault As String, ByVal lpReturnedString As String, ByVal nSize As Integer, ByVal lpFileName As String) As Integer

Chapter(s)	Function	Declaration
21, 23, 25, 28	WritePrivateProfileString	Declare Function WritePrivateProfileString Lib "Kernel" (ByVal lpApplicationName As String, ByVal lpKeyName As String, ByVal lpString As String, ByVal lpFileName As String) As Integer
25	LoadCursorByString	Declare Function LoadCursorByString Lib "User" Alias "LoadCursor" (ByVal hInstance As Integer, ByVal lpCursorName As String) As Integer
	LoadLibrary	Declare Function LoadLibrary Lib "Kernel" (ByVal lpLibFileName As String) As Integer
	SetClassWord	Declare Function SetClassWord Lib "User" (ByVal hWnd As Integer, ByVal nIndex As Integer, ByVal wNewWord As Integer) As Integer
	DestroyCursor	Declare Function DestroyCursor Lib "User" (ByVal hCursor As Integer) As Integer
	INP	Declare Function INP Lib "INOUT.DLL" (ByVal address&) As Integer
	OUT	Declare Sub OUT Lib "INOUT.DLL" (ByVal address&, ByVal value%)
29	FindWindow	Declare Function FindWindow Lib "User" (ByVal lpClassName As Any, ByVal lpWindowName As Any) As Integer

Rules

There are some definite rules you need to follow when declaring DLL functions in Visual Basic. Generally, if you find a list of API declarations from a help file or text file, you can usually cut and paste the declarations into your Visual Basic Application, and everything will be fine. There are some times, however, when you need to be wary. The following sections list some points to watch out for.

Using *Any* as a Parameter Type

An instant clue that you need to change the declaration is if the argument datatype uses the Visual Basic datatype `Any`. The `FindWindow` declaration listed in Table 3.1 under Chapter 29 shows `lpClassName As Any`. It actually works in this case, but it is left here as an example. Use this as a flag that you need to change this declaration. Keeping the `Any` datatype can cause *General Protection Faults (GPFs)*. The `Any` datatype turns off all Visual Basic type checking. This is the main cause of crashes when using DLLs. The `Any` keyword in an API declaration is sometimes used instead of the specific datatype because it allows for different kinds of datatypes to be passed into the function or subroutine to provide multifunctionality.

 The `Any` keyword itself does not cause GPFs. The use of the `Any` keyword turns off all Visual Basic type checking and thus exposes DLL calls to errors, causing GPFs.

It is the preferred method to declare a separate function in Visual Basic using an alias, and then supplying the appropriate datatypes. Consider the following API declaration taken directly out of the WIN31API.HLP help file that comes with Visual Basic:

```
Declare Function LoadCursor Lib "User" (ByVal hInstance As Integer, ByVal lpCursorName As
Any) As Integer
```

Notice the `lpCursorName As Any` parameter. This parameter is declared by Microsoft in this way because it can accept multiple datatypes. The preferred method is to supply two API declarations (one of which is listed in Table 3.1) like this:

```
Declare Function LoadCursorByString Lib "User" Alias "LoadCursor" (ByVal hInstance As
Integer, ByVal lpCursorName As String) As Integer

Declare Function LoadCursorByID Lib "User" Alias "LoadCursor" (ByVal hInstance As
Integer, ByVal lpCursorName As Long) As Integer
```

Both of these functions use the same "LoadCursor" function in the USER.DLL Windows API, but they both perform different functions. At the same time, Visual Basic allows for type checking because the `Any` datatype is not used.

PASSING BY VALUE OR REFERENCE

Visual Basic, by default, passes all parameters by reference. This means that the values of variables are not passed, but a 32-bit pointer to the variable is passed. This method is not always desirable. As a matter of fact, you find that most parameters passed into a DLL function or subroutine are passed by value. The only true exceptions are for strings, arrays, and user-defined types. For more information on strings and arrays, see the section "Exercise Caution when Using Strings and Arrays," later in this chapter. For more information about structures, see the section "API Structures," later in this chapter. Because variables default to being passed by reference, you have to explicitly declare that the value is being passed by value with the keywords By Val. The following shows a *fictitious* declaration by reference:

```
Declare Function LoadCursorByID Lib "User" Alias "LoadCursor" (hInstance%, lpCursorName&)
As Integer
```

This is what the declaration looks like as declared by value:

```
Declare Function LoadCursorByID Lib "User" Alias "LoadCursor" (ByVal hInstance%,ByVal
lpCursorName&) As Integer
```

 Generally, if you forget to declare the parameter type as ByVal, you only get a Bad DLL Calling Convention error. You can, however, get a General Protection Fault. The worst case is that Windows locks up entirely! All of these problems can be avoided by declaring your API functions correctly.

 As a general rule, if you are not sure whether to pass the variable by value or reference, it is safer to pass by value than by reference. The very worst that can happen is that an unexpected value is passed. If you blindly pass by reference, you can modify a value in memory that has nothing to do with your program. It's not advised to blindly pass by value than by reference. You should first consult the documentation or help file concerning the DLL you are trying to use.

DETERMINE THE SCOPE OF DECLARATION

You can only enter Visual Basic DLL declarations in a module or in the (declarations) section of a form.

The *scope* of a variable is a term that describes its lifetime—in other words, how long the values given to a variable will be valid. Making a variable *global* means that its scope is valid throughout the entire project. Making a variable *confined* to a module or procedure means that the scope of the variable is limited to that module or procedure. You don't necessarily want to make the declaration global by default. This eats up memory. Granted, one declaration is not significant, but many of them can be.

If you determine that an API function only needs to be called from one form, why not place the declaration in that form only and declare it to be local to that form? Many programmers prefer to have the declarations all in one place. Some programmers even have a separate module for these declarations only, without any procedure code at all.

There is no right or wrong way to decide where to place the declarations, except for the conditions mentioned earlier. It is a matter of convenience versus potential resources.

SAVE YOUR WORK

While this may seem like a very basic statement, it can't be stressed enough: *Save your work before trying out a new DLL function.* Many times the DLL causes the computer to crash, in which case your work is lost!

EXERCISE CAUTION WHEN USING STRINGS AND ARRAYS

It is important to exercise caution when you use strings and arrays, mainly because most DLLs are written in C or C++. The C convention for strings and arrays is to always pass them by reference. If you attempt to pass a variable by value when the DLL expects it to be passed by reference, the variable tries to access a memory location that is used for something else. This case will almost certainly cause a General Protection Fault.

There is no way to handle the errors caused by incorrect DLL declarations. You cannot use an On Error Goto statement simply to catch the error if you incorrectly declare an API.

Visual Basic handles strings differently than C or C++. C and C++ use *null terminated* strings (to determine where the end of the string is), and Visual Basic doesn't. This method can cause many problems when passing a string. An example of such a problem is with perhaps the most commonly used API function, GetPrivateProfileString. The declaration of this API is as follows:

```
Declare Function GetPrivateProfileString% Lib "Kernel" (ByVal lpAppName$, ByVal
lpKeyName$, ByVal lpDefault$, ByVal lpReturnedString$, ByVal nSize%, ByVal lpFileName$)
As Integer
```

Many strings are being passed into and out of the function. The only string we need to be concerned with is lpReturnedString$. It is the string that is returned from the function. A way to get around the problem of null-termination is to declare the string to be a certain length. Notice that in all of the applications included with this book that use this function (see Chapters 20, 23, 24, 25, and 28), there is a line preceding the function. This line sets the string to a certain length using the Visual Basic Space$() function. The line basically looks like this:

```
c1Temp$ = Space$(1028)
```

The reason 1028 is used is because no more than this number of characters is expected to be returned. You can change this number to suit your needs. The minimum number is 1, and the maximum number is around 32K.

MOST COMMONLY USED APIS

API functions are an integral part of the way Windows operates. Microsoft provides the functions as part of the environment. Windows 3.1 has over 600 functions. Because there are so many, Table 3.2 lists only the most commonly used API functions. For declaration information, refer to the WIN31WH.HLP help file.

TABLE 3.2. COMMON API FUNCTIONS.

API Function	Group	Purpose
BitBlt	Bitmap Functions	Copies a bitmap between two device contexts
StretchBlt	Bitmap Functions	Sets the mode for bitmap stretching
DestroyCursor	Cursor Functions	Destroys a cursor resource
GetCursorPos	Cursor Functions	Retrieves a cursor's position
LoadCursor	Cursor Functions	Loads a cursor resource
CreateCompatibleDC	Device Context Functions	Creates a device context compatible with the current device context
BringWindowToTop	Display Functions	Uncovers an overlapped window
GetWindowText	Display Functions	Copies window text to a buffer
IsWindowVisible	Display Functions	Determines the visibility of a window
SetWindowPos	Display Functions	Sets a window's position and z-order
ShowWindow	Display Functions	Sets a window's visibility state
CreatePen	Drawing Functions	Creates a pen with specified attributes
DeleteObject	Drawing Functions	Deletes an object from memory
ExtFloodFill	Drawing Functions	Fills an area of the screen with the current brush

continues

TABLE 3.2. CONTINUED

API Function	Group	Purpose
FillRect	Drawing Functions	Fills a specified rectangle
RoundRect	Drawing Functions	Draws a rectangle with rounded corners
SelectObject	Drawing Functions	Selects an object into a device context
GetPrivateProfileInt	File Functions	Gets an integer value from an INI file
GetPrivateProfileString	File Functions	Gets a string value from an INI file
GetProfileInt	File Functions	Gets an integer value from WIN.INI
GetProfileString	File Functions	Gets a string value from WIN.INI
GetSystemDirectory	File Functions	Returns the path of the Windows System directory
GetTempFileName	File Functions	Creates a temporary file
GetWindowsDirectory	File Functions	Returns the path of the Windows directory
WritePrivateProfileString	File Functions	Writes a string value to an INI file
WriteProfileString	File Functions	Writes a string value to WIN.INI
DrawIcon	Icon Functions	Draws an icon in a specified device context
LoadIcon	Icon Functions	Loads an icon from an icon resource
FindWindow	Information	Returns a handle to a certain window class or name
GetDesktopWindow	Information Functions	Returns a handle to the desktop window
GetParent	Information Functions	Returns the handle to a parent window
IsWindow	Information Functions	Determines if a window's handle is valid

API Function	Group	Purpose
GetActiveWindow	Input Functions	Returns a handle to the active window
SetCapture	Input Functions	Sets the mouse capture to a window
SetSysModalWindow	Input Functions	Makes a window the system modal window
GetFreeSpace	Memory Management Functions	Returns the number of bytes of memory available
GetWinFlags	Memory Management Functions	Returns the current system flags
SendMessage	Message Functions	Sends a message to a window
GetModuleFileName	Module Functions	Returns the file name for a module
GetModuleHandle	Module Functions	Returns the handle for a specified module
GetModuleUsage	Module Functions	Returns a module's reference count
GetVersion	Module Functions	Returns the versions of DOS and Windows
GetPaletteEntries	Palette Functions	Returns the range of palette entries
GetSystemMetrics	System Functions	Returns system metrics
GetWindowLong	Window Functions	Retrieves a long value from extra window memory
SetWindowLong	Window Functions	Sets a long value to extra window memory

VARIABLE NAMING CONVENTIONS

APIs use many standard variable naming conventions. For example, a handle to a window is an *integer*. Theoretically, any name assigned to the integer variable will work. However, there is a standard naming convention adopted. For example, a handle to a window is always noted as hWnd. This makes it easy for another programmer to read your code and modify it. Consider the following API declaration:

```
Declare Function SetClassWord Lib "User" (ByVal hWnd As Integer, ByVal nIndex As Integer,
ByVal wNewWord As Integer) As Integer
```

Three parameters are passed into the function: hWnd, nIndex, and wNewWord. The first hWnd, according to Table 3.3, is the handle to a window. nIndex is an int with the name Index. wNewWord is a WORD with the name NewWord. Table 3.3 lists the naming conventions. The prefix type is the type of variable used in a C or C++ declaration. The *base* type is the type you most likely will see as the base (beginning) part of a variable in an API declaration. Table 3.3 lists the most common of these standard Windows naming conventions.

TABLE 3.3. COMMON STANDARD NAMING CONVENTIONS.

Prefix Type	Base Type	Description
BOOL	f	16-bit boolean value
BYTE	b	8-bit unsigned integer
BYTE FAR*	lpb	32-bit byte pointer
DLGPROC	dlgprc	32-bit pointer to dialog box procedure
DWORD	dw	32-bit unsigned integer or segment offset address
DWORD FAR*	lpdw	32-bit pointer to offset address
HBITMAP	hbm	16-bit bitmap handle
HBRUSH	hbr	16-bit brush handle
HCURSOR	hcur	16-bit cursor handle
HDC	hdc	16-bit device context handle
HFILE	hf	16-bit file handle
HFONT	hfont	16-bit font handle
HICON	hicon	16-bit icon handle
HINSTANCE	hinst	16-bit instance handle
HMODULE	hmod	16-bit module handle
HWND	hwnd	16-bit window handle
int	n	16-bit signed integer
LONG	l	32-bit signed integer
LPARAM	lParam	32-bit signed parameter value
LPBYTE	lpb	32-bit byte pointer
LPCSTR	lpsz	32-bit pointer to nonmodifiable character string
LPSTR	lpsz	32-bit pointer to a character string
LPVOID	lpv	32-bit pointer to an unspecified type
LPWORD	lpw	32-bit pointer to a 16-bit unsigned value
UINT	u	16-bit unsigned value

Prefix Type	Base Type	Description
WNDPROC	wndprc	32-bit pointer to window procedure
WORD	w	16-bit unsigned value
WPARAM	wParam	16-bit signed value passed as a parameter to window procedure

API STRUCTURES

API structures are sometimes used to pass data to and from an API. Structures provide a way to pass data in one nice, neat little data package. You can transfer many pieces of related data all at once. An example of a Windows structure is called RECT. The API declaration looks like this:

```
Declare Function FillRect Lib "User" (ByVal hDC As Integer, lpRect As RECT, ByVal hBrush
As Integer) As Integer
```

where the structures are used for the purposes listed in Table 3.4. To use a structure, however, you must declare its type by using the same scope as the API declaration. You can find these structure type definitions in the WIN31API.HLP help file. For example, the type definition for the RECT structure is

```
Type RECT
    left As Integer
    top As Integer
    right As Integer
    bottom As Integer
End Type
```

API structure type definitions are usually passed by reference. This allows you to pass the address of the entire type definition at one time.

TABLE 3.4. WINDOWS STRUCTURES.

Structure	Used For
ABC	TrueType font character width
BITMAP	Logical bitmap characteristics
BITMAPCOREHEADER	DIB bitmap characteristics
BITMAPCOREINFO	DIB bitmap and color characteristics
BITMAPFILEHEADER	DIB file characteristics
BITMAPINFO	DIB bitmap and color characteristics
BITMAPINFOHEADER	DIB bitmap characteristics
CBT_CREATEWND	WH_CBT hook data

continues

TABLE 3.4. CONTINUED

Structure	Used For
CBTACTIVATESTRUCT	WH_CBT hook data
CHOOSECOLOR	Color dialog box
CHOOSEFONT	Font dialog box
CLASSENTRY	Windows Class
CLIENTCREATESTRUCT	First MDI child window
COMPAREITEMSTRUCT	Data for sorted combo box
COMSTAT	Data for communications device
CONVCONTEXT	Language data for DDE
CONVINFO	Data about DDE
CPLINFO	Resource data for Control Panel
CTEATESTRUCT	Window initialization parameters
CTLINFO	Class name/version of selected control
CTLSTYLE	Attributes of selected control
CTLTYPE	Width/height/style of control
DCB	Settings for communications device
DDEACK	Status flags for WM_DDE_ACK message
DDEADVISE	Flags for WM_DDE_ADVISE message
DDEDATA	Data from WM_DDE_DATA message
DDEPOKE	Data from WM_DDE_POKE message
DEBUGHOOKINFO	Debugging
DELETEITEMSTRUCT	Deleted owner-drawn item
DEVMODE	Data about printer environment
DEVNAMES	Device data for print dialog box
DOCINFO	Document file names (I/O)
DRAWITEMSTRUCT	Painting data for owner-drawn control
DRIVERINFOSTRUCT	Data about installable driver
DRVCONFIGINFO	Driver configuration data
EVENTMSG	Journalling hook data
FINDREPLACE	Find/Replace dialog box data
FIXED	Integral and fractional parts of a number
FMS_GETDRIVEINFO	File Manager drive data

Structure	Used For
FMS_GETFILESEL	File Manager file data
FMS_LOAD	File Manager custom menu data
GLOBALENTRY	Memory object on global heap
GLOBALINFO	Global heap
GLYPHMETRICS	Placement of a glyph in character cell
HANDLETABLE	GDI handles (array)
HARDWAREHOOKDSTRUCT	Nonstandard hardware data
HELPWININFO	Journalling message information
HSZPAIR	DDE service name and topic
KERNINGPAIR	Kerning pair
LOCALENTRY	Memory object on local heap
LOCALINFO	Local heap
LOGBRUSH	Characteristics of logical brush
LOGFONT	Attributes of logical font
LOGPALETTE	Logical color palette
LOGPEN	Logical pen
MAT2	Transformation matrix
MDICREATESTRUCT	Initialization data for MDI child
MEASUREITEMSTRUCT	Dimensions of owner-drawn control
MEMMANINFO	Virtual Memory Manager
MENUITEMTEMPLATE	Menu item
MENUITEMTEMPLATEHEADER	Header data for menu template
METAFILEPICT	Clipboard metafile picture format
METAHEADER	Metafile data
METARECORD	Metafile record
MINMAXINFO	Window size and tracking data
MODULEENTRY	Module data in module list
MONCBSTRUCT	DDE transaction data
MONCONVSTRUCT	DDE conversation data
MONERRSTRUCT	DDE error data
MONHSZSTRUCT	DDE string handle data
MONLINKSTRUCT	DDE advise loop data

continues

TABLE 3.4. CONTINUED

Structure	Used For
MONMSGSTRUCT	DDE message data
MOUSEHOOKSTRUCT	Mouse event data
MSG	Message information
MULTIKEYHELP	Keyword data for Windows Help
NCCALCSIZE_PARAMS	Client area data calculations
NEWCPLINFO	Control Panel Resource data
NEWTEXTMETRIC	Physical font data
NFYLOADSEG	Segment loaded
NFYLOGERROR	Validation error
NFYLOGPARAMERROR	Parameter-validation error
NFYRIP	RIP exit code and relevant registers
NFYSTARTDLL	DLL data
OFSTRUCT	Open file data
OLECLIENT	State information
OLECLIENTVTBL	Client's Callback function
OLEOBJECT	Object function pointers
OLEOBJECTVTBL	Object manipulation functions
OLESERVER	Server-function pointers
OLESERVERDOC	Document-function pointers
OLESERVERDOCVTBL	Document manipulation functions
OLESERVERVTBL	Server manipulation functions
OLESTREAM	Server-function pointers
OLESTREAMVTBL	Stream operations functions
OLETARGETDEVICE	Client target device
OPENFILENAME	Open dialog box data
OUTLINETEXTMETRIC	TrueType font metrics
PAINTSTRUCT	Client area painting data
PALETTEENTRY	Logical color palette
PANOSE	Panose values for TrueType fonts
POINT	Coordinates of a point
POINTFX	Point in a character outline

Structure	Used For
PRINTDLG	Print dialog box data
RASTERIZER_STATUS	TrueType installation data
RECT	Coordinates of a rectangle
RGBQUAD	DIB color data
RGBTRIPLE	DIB color data
SEGINFO	Code or data segment information
SIZE	Function extents
STACKTRACEENTRY	Stack frame
SYSHEAPINFO	User and GDI modules
TASKENTRY	Task data
TEXTMETRIC	Physical font data
TIMERINFO	Task elapsed time data
TTPOLYCURVE	Curve in a character outline
TTPOLYGONHEADER	Starting point of a curve in a character outline
VX_FIXEDFILEINFO	File version information
WINDEBUGINFO	System debugging information
WINDOWPLACEMENT	Window placement information
WINDOWPOS	Window size and position information
WNDCLASS	Window class data

The most commonly used API structures listed in this table are RECT, POINT, and DEVMODE.

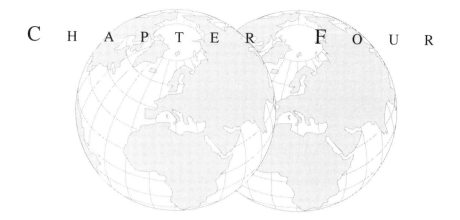

CHAPTER FOUR

THE MOUSE

WINDOWS AND VISUAL BASIC PROVIDE AN EASY INTERFACE THAT USES THE MOUSE SEAMLESSLY. AS A VISUAL BASIC PROGRAMMER, YOU HARDLY NEED TO KNOW ANYTHING ABOUT THE MOUSE. THIS IS BECAUSE THE APPROPRIATE MOUSE DRIVER THAT WINDOWS AND VISUAL BASIC INSTALL PROCESSES MOUSE EVENTS FOR YOU. YOU DON'T HAVE TO WORRY ABOUT WINDOWS MESSAGES BEING SENT TO VISUAL BASIC. THERE ARE TIMES, HOWEVER, WHEN YOU MAY WANT TO MANIPULATE THE MOUSE IN A MANNER NOT INCORPORATED INTO THE DESIGN OF VISUAL BASIC. FOR EXAMPLE, WHAT IF YOU WANT TO RESTRICT THE MOUSE'S MOVEMENT TO A CERTAIN AREA OF THE SCREEN? THIS CHAPTER addresses this question and demonstrates some techniques that can help you develop professional applications for the Real World.

RESTRICTING MOUSE MOVEMENT

Sometimes you may want to restrict the mouse to a certain area of the screen. You want to restrict the mouse movement to make it impossible for any other action to take place while a process is going on. For example, you may want to restrict the mouse movement to a certain area of the screen while a file is copying to avoid the possibility of error.

 That is precisely what the application in Chapter 21, "File Copy Application," does. It demonstrates a technique that restricts the mouse to a certain area of the screen while copying, moving, or deleting files.

Chapter 21's application uses Windows APIs to perform the mouse restriction. Table 4.1 lists the Windows APIs that deal with mouse usage. There are some additional APIs for drag/drop operations; however, Visual Basic handles that functionality for you, so they are not included in the table.

 For more information on using Windows APIs, refer to Chapter 3, "Calling Windows APIs and DLLs."

TABLE 4.1. APIs FOR MOUSE USAGE.

API	Use
ClipCursor	Confines the mouse cursor to a specified rectangle
CreateCursor	Creates a mouse cursor with specified dimensions
DestroyCursor	Destroys a custom mouse cursor
GetCursorPos	Returns the mouse cursor coordinates
LoadCursor	Loads a mouse cursor resource
SetCursor	Changes the mouse cursor
SetCursorPos	Sets the mouse cursor to a specific point
ShowCursor	Shows or hides the mouse cursor

The basic technique for restricting the mouse while some other process is going on is to do the following:

◆ Define an area of the screen for restriction

◆ Start the process for which restriction is necessary

◆ Restrict the mouse movement

◆ Complete the process

◆ Unrestrict the mouse movement

 Consider the following code fragment from CHAP21.BAS, CursorClip() function, which restricts the mouse:

```
'Get current window position (in pixels) and compute width & height
GetWindowRect f.hWnd, CopyRect

'clip the cursor
ClipCursorRect CopyRect

'move cursor to center of form
SetCursorPos ((CopyRect.Right - CopyRect.Left) / 2) + CopyRect.Left,
((CopyRect.Bottom - CopyRect.Top) / 2) + CopyRect.Top
```

 The ClipCursorRect subroutine is an alias for the ClipCursor API subroutine declared like this:

```
Declare Sub ClipCursorRect Lib "User" Alias "ClipCursor" (lpRect As RECT)
```

The first step in restricting the mouse cursor is to get the Windows coordinates for the window to which you want to restrict the mouse. Use the GetWindowRect API function for this. It uses the handle of the window to determine its coordinates and assigns them into a RECT structure, CopyRect.

 The RECT structure format is

```
Type RECT
    left   As Integer
    top    As Integer
    right  As Integer
    bottom As Integer
End Type
```

The next step is to limit the cursor to the area of the RECT structure. To do this, use the ClipCursorRect user-defined Visual Basic function, which is an alias for the ClipCursor API function. It needs only the RECT structure passed to it.

Then set the cursor position to the middle of the RECT region. This is necessary because you need to ensure that the cursor is not stuck outside of the region where the cursor is limited. The cursor position is set using the SetCursorPos API function. It only needs the x and y positions to move to.

The key to being able to restore the mouse to the full screen is that the `ClipCursor` API function is declared using an alias because it can accept two types of arguments. One is used to restrict the cursor, and one is used to restore the cursor. The two declarations look like this:

```
Declare Sub ClipCursorRect Lib "User" Alias "ClipCursor" (lpRect As RECT)
Declare Sub ClipCursorClear Lib "User" Alias "ClipCursor" (ByVal lpRect&)
```

Both declarations use the `ClipCursor` API function, but because they perform different functions based on what data type is passed to them, they use an alias for the routine name used in Visual Basic. After this declaration is made, Visual Basic refers to `ClipCursorRect` and `ClipCursorClear`, respectively, and expects the data types declared. Although the application in Chapter 21 declared the names listed, you can alter the names to suit your application. The `ClipCursor` API, however, must be used to perform the function of limiting the mouse cursor.

You can now restore the cursor back to the full screen with calling the subroutine you declared earlier. The only argument you have to pass to the subroutine is `0&`. The Windows API function expects this to restore the cursor. In the case of Chapter 21, you call the `ClipCursor` subroutine. Consider the following code fragment to demonstrate how to restore the cursor to the full screen:

```
ClipCursorClear Cl&
```

Just in case the application crashes while the cursor is restricted, you can run a program, located on the CD accompanying this book in the CHAP21 subdirectory, called UNCLIP.EXE. It is a program that really only uses the `ClipCursorClear` function.

USING THE RIGHT MOUSE BUTTON IN YOUR APPLICATIONS

Using the right mouse button is actually very simple. All you need to do is query which button is pressed on any one of the following events in an object containing these events:

◆ `MouseDown`

◆ `MouseMove`

◆ `MouseUp`

You can determine which mouse buttons have been pressed because the button parameter contains values corresponding to the following constants:

```
Global Const LEFT_BUTTON = 1
Global Const RIGHT_BUTTON = 2
Global Const MIDDLE_BUTTON = 4
```

The preceding listed constants are available in the CONSTANT.TXT file, which comes with Visual Basic.

To make popup menus appear when the right mouse button is pressed, you first design a menu as you would design a regular menu. The only difference is that you must keep in mind that the popup menu will be specified from any point in the menu, but all lower-level menus in a hierarchical tree will be in the popup. To specify where the popup menu will occur, simply use the PopupMenu method, but specify the name of the menu item that will appear as the top-most menu item in the popup. Figure 4.1 shows the Menu Design window used in Chapter 20's application, "MDI File Search Application," to show the hierarchical relationship. As an example, refer to the same chapter to see how to invoke the Popup method:

```
'if user presses the right mouse button, display popup
    If Button = RIGHT_BUTTON Then
        'make sure form has focus
        Me.SetFocus
        'invoke popup menu
        Me.PopupMenu menu_popup
    End If
```

REM It is possible to control where the popup menu is displayed. You can specify this by using optional arguments when calling the PopupMenu method. Without using optional arguments, the popup menu appears at the cursor location. By using optional arguments, you can specify the x and y coordinates for the placement of the menu. Most of the time, you want the popup menu to be displayed at the cursor location.

FIGURE 4.1.
*Menu Design window
showing popup.*

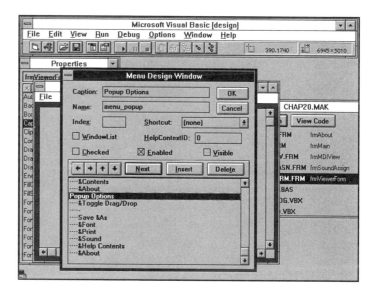

If you don't want to have the menu items displayed in the menu at the top of the form but only in the popup, you must make the top-most level of popup menu invisible. Calling the popup method using the top-most level menu name shows the menu as a popup, and also makes it visible.

DETERMINING MOUSE POSITION WITHIN A CONTROL

For most applications, you don't need to know the actual coordinates of the mouse. There are some times, however, where Visual Basic does not provide properties that you want. An example of this is in Chapter 21, "File Copy Application." The application allows the user to drag a file to a directory listed in a directory list box.

The problem is that this application shows which item in the list box the mouse is positioned over by highlighting it as the mouse moves over the item. There is a `ListIndex` property that can be accessed, but it is only accurate when an item is clicked. It is for this reason that you may need to determine what the x and y coordinates of the mouse are. It allows you to show a visual representation of which item in the list box the cursor is over.

 A way around this is to determine where the mouse is inside the directory List Box control and to manually assign the `ListIndex` accordingly. The key to doing this is to use the `DragOver` event. It occurs when the mouse is placed over a control and it is currently involved in a drag operation. The following code is taken from the directory List Box control's `DragOver` event in Chapter 21:

```
Sub lbDirectory_DragOver (Index As Integer, Source As Control, X As Single, y As
Single, State As Integer)
    TheIndex% = DecodeRow(Index, y)
    On Error GoTo indexerror
    If TheIndex% < lbDirectory(Index).ListCount Then
        lbDirectory(Index).ListIndex = TheIndex%
    End If
    'exit
    Exit Sub
indexerror:
    TheIndex% = TheIndex% + 1
    Resume
End Sub
```

The preceding code calls a user-defined function, `DecodeRow()`, and assigns it to the variable, `TheIndex%`. Unless there is an error, this is the calculated `ListIndex` property to use. It is unlikely that an error will occur; but if it does, it won't terminate the application.

 For more information on error handling, refer to Chapter 2, "Error Handling."

Following is the DecodeRow() function from Chapter 21, which actually determines where the cursor is inside the list box.

```
Function DecodeRow (Index As Integer, y As Single) As Single

    'declare variables
    Dim m$                  'message constructor
    Dim TheHeight%          'height of listbox
    Dim ProposedIndex%      'current index

    'force positive values
    If y < 0 Then y = 0

    'determine the height of each item in list
    TheHeight% = TextHeight(lbDirectory(Index).List(0))

    '25 allows for the area above and below the actual text, but still
    'in the index area
    ProposedIndex% = (Int(y / (TheHeight% + 25))) - 3

    'since directory list box can have listindexes of -1,-2, or -3
    'test to see if this particular index, shows the root.  If not
    'add 2 to it-this allows the selected text to be in line with the icon
    If lbDirectory(Index).List(-2) = "" Then
        ProposedIndex% = ProposedIndex% + 2
    End If
    DecodeRow = ProposedIndex%
End Function
```

 Depending on your monitor resolution, you may need to adjust the value of the constant of 25 in the preceding listing. You only need to adjust it by a couple of numbers. If you don't adjust it, the wrong item in the list box may be selected.

In the DecodeRow() function listed here, the x coordinate is ignored. You are only concerned with the y coordinate to determine the ListIndex property.

Although every list box has a ListIndex property, the directory list box is unique in that it can have a ListIndex of -1, -2, or -3. These indexes are used for the root and parent directories. In your application, you need to test for the ListIndex of -2 because it indicates a root directory. If it is not the root directory, add 2 to it. This way the correct ListIndex is calculated.

Basically, you calculate the ListIndex position in the following manner: Divide the y value passed into the function by the TextHeight of the entries in the directory list box and add 25 to it to allow for spacing between entries. This figure, 25, is not a hard and fast rule. It is used as an average. If you use a considerably larger font, this number has to be adjusted.

CREATING A CUSTOM CURSOR

It may become necessary to display a cursor in Visual Basic that is not a Standard Visual Basic cursor. Table 4.2 lists all of the standard cursors available in Visual Basic and the constants associated with them.

TABLE 4.2. VISUAL BASIC CURSORS.

Constant	Cursor
0	Default
1	Arrow
2	Cross-Hair Pointer
3	I-Beam
4	Icon
5	Size indicator pointing North, South, East, and West
6	Size indicator pointing Northeast and Southwest
7	Size indicator pointing North and South
8	Size indicator pointing Northwest and Southeast
9	Size indicator pointing East and West
10	Up Arrow
11	Hourglass
12	No Drop

 If you need a custom cursor, such as a hand cursor, it's important to know that it is possible. Although not covered here, this information is covered in Chapter 19, "Writing DLLs and VBXs."

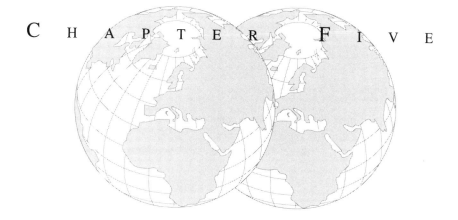

GRAPHICS

GRAPHICS ARE AN IMPORTANT PART OF WINDOWS APPLICATIONS AND VISUALLY ENHANCE THE WAY USERS INTERACT WITH THE SYSTEM. THERE ARE MANY TECHNIQUES DEMONSTRATED THROUGHOUT THIS CHAPTER THAT SHOW HOW TO DISPLAY AND MANIPULATE GRAPHICS, SUCH AS USING THE Screen OBJECT, GRAPHIC HOTSPOTS, AND ANIMATING ICONS.

THE *SCREEN* OBJECT

Visual Basic provides a Screen object with many properties to easily access and manipulate what the user sees on-screen. The object is accessed just like any other Visual Basic object, such as a Form object or a Control object. Table 5.1 lists the Visual Basic Screen object properties.

TABLE 5.1. VISUAL BASIC Screen OBJECT PROPERTIES.

Property	Function
ActiveControl	Specifies the control with the focus.
ActiveForm	Specifies the form with the focus.
FontCount	Number of fonts available for the current display screen.
Fonts	Specifies the names of the fonts available for the current display screen. This property is in the form of an array, from 0 to FontCount -1.
Height	Height of the screen, always measured in Twips.
MousePointer	Mouse pointer to be used when mouse is positioned over the screen. If the mouse pointer is over a form that specifies a different mouse, the mouse pointer of that form is used.
TwipsPerPixelX	Number of Twips for every horizontal pixel. This is a very useful property so the ScaleMode doesn't have to be changed to do a calculation.
TwipsPerPixelY	Number of Twips for every vertical pixel. This is a very useful property so that the ScaleMode doesn't have to be changed to do a calculation.
Width	Width of the screen, always measured in Twips.

CENTERING A FORM AUTOMATICALLY

You may want to use the Screen object in your applications to automatically center the screen, which gives a much more visually appealing aspect to your programs. As an example, every form in all applications in Part II of this book centers the form automatically upon loading it.

If you don't handle the placement of the form in code, the form appears at the coordinates you left it at design time. The form can appear centered, but if you run your application on a computer with a higher resolution screen, the forms appear in the upper-left corner of the screen.

There is a very simple solution to centering the form automatically in a device independent manner. This means that whatever the resolution, the form appears centered. It can be very useful to have a routine such as the one presented here, `CenterForm()`, that you can call from each form in the `Form_Load()` event. Consider this routine used in all of the applications in this book:

```
Sub CenterForm (F As Form)

    F.Left = (screen.Width - F.Width) / 2
    F.Top = (screen.Height - F.Height) / 2

End Sub
```

The technique is to use the `Screen` object to determine the height and width properties. The form's height and width properties are also used. The routine simply subtracts the form's properties from the screen's properties and divides them by two. If you want to incorporate this from a form's `Form_Load()` event, you call it like this:

```
Private Sub Form_Load()
CenterForm Me
End Sub
```

THE COORDINATE SYSTEM

Visual Basic provides different ways to access the *coordinate system*. The coordinate system allows for a way to access a specific point for drawing. It is designed to let you, the programmer, choose which unit of measure is comfortable to you. The different units of measure ultimately provide the same result, which is to draw graphics at a certain location on a form, picture box, or printer. Table 5.2 shows the different types of units of measure possible in the Visual Basic coordinate system.

TABLE 5.2. VISUAL BASIC COORDINATE SYSTEMS.

Unit	Conversion	ScaleMode *Setting*
Custom	User-defined scale properties	0
Twips	Default unit in Visual Basic—1440 Twips per logical Inch	1
Point	72 points per logical Inch	2
Pixel	Base unit of measure representing the smallest point on a monitor or printer	3
Character	120 Twips horizontally and 240 Twips vertically	4
Inch	Physical Inch	5
Millimeter	Physical Millimeter	6
Centimeter	Physical Centimeter	7

The preceding table demonstrates that if you normally like working with the smallest possible unit for greater resolution control, you probably want to work in Pixels. If you want to work in a more manageable unit, but with less resolution, you probably want to work in Inches.

 Most Windows developers work with Pixels.

To change the unit of measure the coordinate system works with, use the ScaleMode property of the form, picture box, or printer object to set to the desired mode. For example, the following syntax changes the printer coordinate system to respond in Inches:

```
Printer.ScaleMode = 5
```

 There are constants for each of the ScaleMode properties. You can find these constants in the CONSTANT.TXT file, which comes with Visual Basic.

If you want to customize the coordinate system, use the ScaleHeight, ScaleWidth, ScaleLeft, and ScaleTop properties of the form, picture box, or printer object. The ScaleLeft and ScaleTop properties define what the upper-left coordinate will be. The ScaleHeight and ScaleWidth properties define the relative height and width, respectively, of an object. For example, suppose that you want the upper-left coordinate of the printer to be 100,100 instead of 0,0. Then suppose that you want the height and width of the printer to be 200 units each. You set up the properties as follows:

```
Printer.ScaleLeft = 100

Printer.ScaleTop = 100

Printer.ScaleHeight = 200

Printer.ScaleWidth = 200
```

 If you change the Scale properties, the ScaleMode property is set to zero, signifying that you are using user-defined coordinates.

The upper-left coordinate of the page will be 100,100. The lower-right coordinate of the page will be 300,300. This is because the ScaleHeight and ScaleWidth properties specified the height and width, not the absolute coordinate.

STATIC GRAPHICS

Static graphics are basically graphics that are not altered at runtime other than positioning the graphic at a desired location on-screen. For example, a static graphic can be as simple as a line drawn across the screen that is redrawn as the screen is sized.

GRAPHIC HOTSPOTS

A *hotspot* is an area of the screen which, when clicked, produces some desired result. Generally, you don't see the border of the hotspot region. Hotspots are becoming more popular as the information age progresses. Hotspots are incorporated widely in systems that use a touch screen. Many museums use touch screens as a way to convey information interactively. Hotspots can be used in a wide variety of applications such as maps. The program may be able to present statistics of a certain state by touching the area of the screen that represents your state.

You can incorporate hotspots *dynamically*, if necessary. This means that you can allocate or deallocate a hotspot as the program is running. You do not have to predefine all hotspots in advance.

 See Chapter 25, "Dynamic Hotspot Application," for a complete program that illustrates the actual use of dynamic hotspots.

There is no hotspot control in Visual Basic, so you can use the Image control. The reason you need to use a Visual Basic control instead of drawing a rectangle on-screen is that a hotspot needs to independently recognize a mouse click event. If you draw a rectangle on-screen, the mouse events occur on the form, not on the rectangle.

 The reason that the Image control is used instead of the Picture Box control is because of its capability to be transparent. The Image control allows the background to show through the image area when a picture is not displayed. The Picture Box control does not have a `Transparent` property, so all you see is a white rectangular box.

The way to allocate the hotspots dynamically is to use a control array. You use only one Image control and assign it an index of zero. As the user defines a new hotspot, a new Image control is loaded as part of the control array, increasing its index value by one. Following is a code fragment that shows how a control can be loaded dynamically.

```
NextAvailHotspot% = FindNextHotspotIndex()
Load Hotspot(NextAvailHotspot%)
```

In the preceding example, taken from Chapter 25, "Dynamic Hotspot Application," a function is called `FindNextHotspotIndex()`, which determines the next available index to use in the control array. This is necessary because an element in the middle of the control array may have been deleted. This ensures that the next available index is used.

In your application, you need to make sure that the hotspot, which is really just an Image control, has the same coordinates as the position in which the new hotspot is to be located. By default, when Visual Basic loads a new control from a control array, it takes on the same characteristics

53

as the one created at design time. You probably want to incorporate a routine that automatically moves or resizes the hotspot to the desired location.

To do this, you need to know the coordinates of where the hotspot is to be located. It's a good idea to track in a variable where the desired location is. Following is a code fragment taken from Chapter 25 that resizes and moves the dynamic hotspot, where BeginX, BeginY, EndX, and EndY indicate the desired hotspot region:

```
'Modify Vertically
If EndY > BeginY Then
    Hotspot(NextAvailHotspot%).Height = EndY - BeginY + 10
    Hotspot(NextAvailHotspot%).Top = BeginY
Else
    Hotspot(NextAvailHotspot%).Height = BeginY - EndY + 10
    Hotspot(NextAvailHotspot%).Top = EndY
End If

'Modify Horizontally
If EndX > BeginX Then
    Hotspot(NextAvailHotspot%).Width = EndX - BeginX + 10
    Hotspot(NextAvailHotspot%).Left = BeginX
Else
    Hotspot(NextAvailHotspot%).Width = BeginX - EndX + 10
    Hotspot(NextAvailHotspot%).Left = EndX
End If
```

 The constant, 10, is used to verify that the hotspot completely encompasses the desired area. If this isn't done, the hotspot is on the lines of the rectangle drawn. It is simply a matter of personal preference.

The variables used to track coordinates of the desired location are BeginX, BeginY, EndX, and EndY. These variables are assigned after the user draws the area on-screen with the mouse. You don't need to know where the current hotspot is located. You only need to know the index of the hotspot to move. In this case, the hotspot has an index assigned to the variable NextAvailHotspot%.

MANIPULATING PICTURE BOXES AT RUNTIME

An important part of graphics in Visual Basic is the capability to move picture boxes at runtime. This gives the user a more visually appealing application. For example, suppose that you want to display photographs stored in bitmaps on-screen. If you want to display only one, you probably want to center it on-screen. If you display more than one, you want to manipulate the picture boxes containing the photographs into some logical pattern so that they are symmetrical within the screen. You can also use the technique of manipulating a picture box at runtime to load and display icons from the disk.

Your application can manipulate the picture boxes as does the application in Chapter 22, "Icon Printing Application." It allows for the displaying of up to 60 icons in a single screen by using a single picture box control array. All elements of the control array (other than the one created at design time) are allocated dynamically. This means that as the program needs them, they are loaded and positioned. There is no sense in creating 60 picture boxes and wasting valuable system resources if the user never intends to display all of the icons on-screen! The alternative is to have your application load the picture boxes as it needs them.

To manipulate the picture boxes at runtime, you first need to load the next index in the control array. Because element zero is the index created at design time, the next available index is one, and so on. You load a new picture box by using the LOAD command. This loads a new picture box with the next available index number, but it takes on the same characteristics as the picture box created at design time.

After the new control is loaded, you can move it anywhere you want on-screen. You probably want to automatically determine the location. The application in Chapter 22, "Icon Printing Application," assigns a maximum of six rows of picture boxes, each having 10 picture boxes in the row. As a new picture box is created, it is moved to the next position in the row. The next position is determined by the last position plus a predefined border area. If the last position in a row is filled, the application moves the new picture box to the first position in the next row. The next row is determined by the position of the previous row plus a predefined border area. These border areas are stored in constants.

 It's a good idea to use constants so that if you later determine that you need to change the border area, all you have to do is change the value assigned to the constant and not rework your calculations.

These constants, used in Chapter 22, "Icon Printing Application," are defined as

```
Const WIDTHFACTOR = 345     'horizontal space between picture boxes
Const HEIGHTFACTOR = 345    'vertical space between picture boxes
Const BORDERFACTOR = 225    'width of border holding picture boxes
```

The constants are a critical part of making sure the icons line up correctly on the form. Following is a code fragment from Chapter 22, MAIN.FRM, PopulatePicture(), which moves the picture boxes so that they line up with six rows and 10 columns of picture boxes:

```
'0 is already loaded at design time
If IconIndex% <> 0 Then
    Load pictIcon(IconIndex%)
    Load pnlLabel(IconIndex%)
End If
pictIcon(IconIndex%).Visible = True
pnlLabel(IconIndex%).Visible = True

'see if this picture box will fit on this line
If IconIndex% <> 0 Then
    If pictIcon(IconIndex%).Width + pictIcon(IconIndex% - 1).Left + pictIcon(IconIndex% -
    1).Width + WIDTHFACTOR < pnlIconFrame.Width - BORDERFACTOR Then
```

```
      'It WILL fit on the line
      'position picture box
      pictIcon(IconIndex%).Left = pictIcon(IconIndex% - 1).Left + pictIcon(IconIndex% -
      1).Width + WIDTHFACTOR
      pictIcon(IconIndex%).Top = pictIcon(IconIndex% - 1).Top

      'position label box
      pnlLabel(IconIndex%).Left = pictIcon(IconIndex%).Left -
      ((pnlLabel(IconIndex%).Width - pictIcon(IconIndex%).Width) / 2)
      pnlLabel(IconIndex%).Top = pictIcon(IconIndex%).Top - 225
    Else
      'It Won't fit on the line - use next line
      pictIcon(IconIndex%).Left = pictIcon(0).Left
      pictIcon(IconIndex%).Top = pictIcon(IconIndex% - 1).Top + pictIcon(IconIndex% -
      1).Height + HEIGHTFACTOR

      'position label box
      pnlLabel(IconIndex%).Left = pictIcon(IconIndex%).Left -
      ((pnlLabel(IconIndex%).Width - pictIcon(IconIndex%).Width) / 2)
      pnlLabel(IconIndex%).Top = pictIcon(IconIndex%).Top - 225
    End If
End If
```

The preceding code tests to see if the previous picture box plus the WIDTHFACTOR allows for the new picture box to be displayed on the same line without touching the edge. If so, it positions the new picture box in that location. If not, it moves the new picture box to the next line.

It is important not to load index zero. It cannot be loaded or unloaded at runtime because it is the original element in a control array created at design time. That's why the preceding code tests to see if the index value in question is zero.

You can use similar tactics in your application to automatically position picture boxes to suit your needs. The only picture box properties you need to deal with are Left, Top, Width, and Height. From these properties, you can test and manipulate the picture boxes in any fashion that suits your application. If your pictures are different sizes, simply adjust the values of the constants declared earlier.

ANIMATED GRAPHICS

Animated graphics are graphics that are altered in some way on a continuous basis at runtime. For example, an animated graphic can be a bitmap floating across the screen, as in the case of a screen saver.

ANIMATED BOUNDING BOX

When allocating dynamic hotspots, it is a good idea to visually represent on-screen the desired area of the new hotspot. One method you can use is an *animated bounding box* that visually tells the user that an area of the screen is selected for some purpose.

The animated bounding box, or *rubber band*, is a box that looks like it is moving in a rectangular pattern. The animated bounding box is used by many applications that require the selecting of objects. It is used in some programs to represent that a window is selected, or a certain portion of the screen is selected. In Visual Basic, the animated bounding box (from now on referred to as the "rubber band") is used for such a purpose.

There is no simple way to create the rubber band. The rubber band is actually an illusion. It is created by using a Timer control and by actually changing the type of *pen* used in drawing the rectangle. A pen is how Visual Basic refers to a style of drawing. Pen styles can be solid, inverted, dashed, and so on. The illusion is created by drawing a rectangle using a certain pen, using the Timer control to switch the type of pen used at a precise interval, and redrawing the rectangle using the different pen. This is very similar to the way electronic Christmas lights appear to be moving from one end of the strand to another. In reality, all that is happening is that every other light is toggling on and off simultaneously. Table 5.3 lists all of the different types of pens available in Visual Basic. They are also called `DrawMode` settings.

TABLE 5.3. VISUAL BASIC `DrawMode` SETTINGS.

Constant	Mnemonic	Description
1	BLACKNESS	Black pen
2	NOT_MERGE_PEN	Inverse of setting 15 (MERGE_PEN)
3	MASK_NOT_PEN	Combination of common colors in background and inverse of the pen
4	NOT_COPY_PEN	Inverse of setting 13 (COPY_PEN)
5	MASK_PEN_NOT	Combination of common colors in inverse of display and pen
6	INVERT	Inverse of display color
7	XOR_PEN	Combination of colors in pen and display, but not both
8	NOT_MASK_PEN	Inverse of setting 9 (MASK_PEN)
9	MASK_PEN	Combination of colors common to both the pen and display
10	NOT_XOR_PEN	Inverse of setting 7 (XOR_PEN)
11	NOP	Turns off drawing
12	MERGE_NOT_PEN	Combination of display color and inverse of pen color
13	COPY_PEN	Default ForeColor

continues

TABLE 5.3. CONTINUED

Constant	Mnemonic	Description
14	MERGE_PEN_NOT	Combination of the pen and inverse of the display
15	MERGE_PEN	Combination of the pen and display colors
16	WHITENESS	White pen

The first step you take in your application is to draw the rectangle using the INVERSE pen. Make sure that you declare the INVERSE constant in a module with the value of 6, as listed in Table 5.3. Before you draw the rectangle in the desired location, however, remember the DrawMode setting before you draw the rectangle so you can reset it when you're finished. This is exactly the technique used in Chapter 25, "Dynamic Hotspot Application." Following is a function taken from Chapter 25, MAIN.FRM, DrawRubberBand(), which illustrates drawing an animated bounding box:

```
Sub DrawRubberBand (ByVal X1, ByVal Y1, ByVal X2, ByVal Y2 As Single)

    'declare variables
    Dim SaveDrawMode%     'holds previous drawing mode

    'save old drawing mode
    SaveDrawMode% = frmMain.DrawMode

    'invert drawing pen
    frmMain.DrawMode = INVERT

    'actually draw line
    Line (X1, Y1)-(X2, Y2), , B

    'revert to saved mode
    frmMain.DrawMode = SaveDrawMode%

End Sub
```

After you draw the rectangle in the INVERT pen, enable a Timer so that when the Timer event fires, you can redraw the same rectangle using the SOLID pen.

 Using a combination of the SOLID and INVERT pens produces the most visually appealing rubber band. If you use other pens, it can produce adverse effects on-screen.

The action of alternating pens creates the animated look. To draw in SOLID pen is as easy as stated previously, but substitute for each different pen. How you incorporate this technique is up to you. The point is that you simply alternate between the two pens at a certain frequency, dictated by the Timer control. What happens in Chapter 25 when the Timer1_Timer() event fires is as follows:

```
'save old draw style
SaveDrawStyle% = frmMain.DrawStyle

'force new solid drawstyle
frmMain.DrawStyle = SOLID

'draw a rubber band
DrawRubberBand BeginX, BeginY, EndX, EndY

'return to old drawstyle
frmMain.DrawStyle = SaveDrawStyle%
```

You probably want to start this process of displaying the rubber band at an appropriate time. For example, you may want to start the animation as the rubber band is being drawn or only after it is finished being drawn.

If you want the rubber band to be displayed as it is being drawn, this complicates matters. This is because if you draw a rectangle at one location and a split second later your application needs to redraw another rectangle and erase the previous one to reflect the mouse movement, the transition isn't very smooth. For this reason, the application in Chapter 25 uses the Form MouseUp() event procedure.

ANIMATED ICON WHEN MINIMIZED

An animated icon can be useful when an application is minimized. Animated icons are used to represent the fact that some action is taking place in the application, even though it is minimized and "out of sight." This is another way to give the user visual feedback in a graphic way with a touch of flair.

Animated icons are used in many types of applications, such as in a clock, which animates the time while minimized. Other applications can include an animated icon to represent the fact that a process is in progress, or that a CD Player application is playing.

 Refer to the application in Chapter 27, "CD Player Application," for more information.

In any of the preceding examples, the animation is performed using the Timer control, just as with most animation in Visual Basic. The Timer allows for the toggling between predefined icons at a specified interval. You may only need to toggle two icons to create animation, but depending on how much animation is desired, you may toggle more. The animation will appear "smoother" if more icons are used.

To simulate the animation, you must enable the Timer when the form is minimized (WindowState = 1) and disable it when it is not minimized (WindowState = 0 or 3). Disabling the Timer ensures that you do not use too much of the system resources while the application is maximized. This is done because you won't see the icon in this state anyway. Enabling and disabling of the Timer is done in the `Form_Resize()` event procedure. This allows you to query the `Windowstate` property any time the size changes.

Following is the code from the `tmrIcon_Timer()` event procedure used in Chapter 27, "CD Player Application":

```
'toggle icon picture
If frmMain.Icon <> pictIcon(0).Picture Then
    frmMain.Icon = pictIcon(0).Picture
Else
    frmMain.Icon = pictIcon(1).Picture
End If
```

When the Timer event occurs from the `tmrIcon` Timer control, it assigns the icon from one of two static picture boxes containing the icons used in the animation. For example, in the application presented in Chapter 27, there are two static picture boxes that contain the icons. If your application uses three icons for the animation, you need to have three picture boxes that are assigned at the appropriate time by the `tmrIcon` Timer control when the Timer event occurs.

For more information on creating and using resource files, see Chapter 19, "Writing DLLs and VBXs."

In the preceding example, the code is simple to toggle between two icons. This is because no matter which icon is displayed, you simply load the other one. This can be done by using only one `If/Then/Else` statement. If you want to toggle between three icons, for example, you can use code such as this:

```
'toggle icon picture
    If frmMain.Icon = pictIcon(0).Picture Then
        frmMain.Icon = pictIcon(1).Picture
    ElseIf frmMain.Icon = pictIcon(1).Picture Then
        frmMain.Icon = pictIcon(2).Picture
    Else
        frmMain.Icon = pictIcon(0).Picture
    End If
```

This code has an `If/Then/Else` statement with a branch for each of the possible icons. If it finds a match, the code loads the icon with the next highest index number. If it finds no match, the code loads the first index. You can use this technique for any number of icons.

LED SEVEN-SEGMENT DISPLAY GRAPHICS

If you've ever wanted to display graphics that look like a seven-segment LED (Light Emitting Diode) display (like a digital clock or like the example presented in Figure 5.1), you probably have found that Visual Basic comes up a little bit short! Well, that's part of the extensibility of

Visual Basic, which is one of its strongest assets. One reason it is extensible is because you can create a resource DLL file using Microsoft's Visual C++ and call the DLL from Visual Basic.

FIGURE 5.1.
A screen that uses seven-segment LEDs.

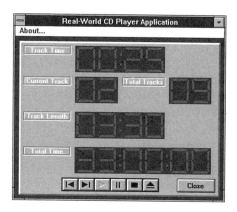

The problem with using this resource DLL from Visual Basic is not its difficulty to distribute or its size, but its speed. One major factor to consider is the speed it takes to load the individual bitmaps inside the DLL resource into Visual Basic versus how fast the display must be updated.

If you are designing a clock interface that only has to be updated every minute or even less frequently, the resource DLL is probably the route to take. This is because it can save on system resources due to the fact that the DLL is dynamically loaded. If you have an application, such as a digital clock that has to update once every second or even faster, you'll find that loading a bitmap from a resource DLL dynamically can be too slow. The consequence of doing this is that it consumes more system resources. The alternative is that you have to have static bitmaps hidden at runtime in your Visual Basic application that can be copied to an appropriate picture box on-screen. This is very similar to the way icons are copied to a picture box in an earlier section, "Animated Icon when Minimized."

It is for this reason that the application in Chapter 27, "CD Player Application," uses seven-segment displays that are statically loaded at design time and copied at runtime when needed. For a seven-segment display to work, each one of the possible "numbers" must be created in the form of a bitmap. Each individual segment inside of each "number" is not isolated separately.

For more information about the CD Player application, refer to Chapter 27, "CD Player Application."

You can incorporate bitmaps representing each of the possible digits that can be displayed. You can create files such as the ones used in Chapter 27 and presented in Figure 5.2.

FIGURE 5.2.
The bitmaps for a seven-segment LED display.

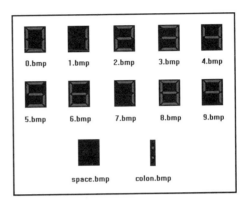

These bitmaps have to be created regardless of whether the pictures are statically loaded at design time and copied into a picture box at runtime, or if you are going to build a resource DLL containing all of the bitmaps. You can include another bitmap that represents the colon separating digits in the display. The COLON.BMP file is used in Chapter 27 to display the colon between sets of numbers (such as between hours and minutes). The BLANK.BMP file is used to simulate clearing the display, effectively displaying only the background with no segments visible.

 For more information about creating resource DLLs, refer to Chapter 19, "Writing DLLs and VBXs."

After you create the bitmaps representing all of the possible digits, you need to create a control array of picture boxes, with one index for each of the ten digits possible (0 through 9) plus the blank and colon. Each of these 12 picture boxes is hidden at runtime, so you don't have to worry too much about placement on the form.

Now that each of the possible digits exists on the form, you can place in every location a different picture box that needs to have a digit displayed at runtime. The way to accomplish this is to copy the appropriate bitmap from the statically loaded hidden picture boxes to the picture boxes your application is to display.

 The 12 static bitmaps placed on the form at design time are compiled by Visual Basic into the executable file. This means that you don't have to actually distribute the bitmap files.

There are pros and cons in using this method of statically linking graphics in your application. Table 5.4 illustrates these pros and cons.

TABLE 5.4. PROS AND CONS OF LOADING PICTURES AT DESIGN TIME VERSUS RUNTIME.

Design Time Loading (Static)	Runtime Loading (Dynamic)
Very fast to copy images	Considerably slower to load images
Don't have to include any resource file(s) with executable upon distribution	Must include resource file or bitmap files for distribution
Uses more memory to store all images	Very memory efficient

You can write a routine to populate the displays the user sees at the appropriate time. The appropriate time can be every second in a digital clock, for example. Consider the application in Chapter 27, "CD Player Application." It updates the displays once every second, but in order to display the statistics of the CD Player such as track time, total disk time, and so on.

Following is a code fragment from Chapter 27, MAIN.FRM, `PopulateDisplay()`:

```
'texttodisplay is previously formatted
temp$ = texttodisplay$

FirstDigit% = Val(Mid$(temp$, 6, 1))
pictTotal(0).Picture = pictSource(FirstDigit%).Picture

SecondDigit% = Val(Mid$(temp$, 5, 1))
pictTotal(1).Picture = pictSource(SecondDigit%).Picture

ThirdDigit% = Val(Mid$(temp$, 4, 1))
pictTotal(2).Picture = pictSource(ThirdDigit%).Picture

FourthDigit% = Val(Mid$(temp$, 3, 1))
pictTotal(3).Picture = pictSource(FourthDigit%).Picture

FifthDigit% = Val(Mid$(temp$, 2, 1))
pictTotal(4).Picture = pictSource(FifthDigit%).Picture

SixthDigit% = Val(Mid$(temp$, 1, 1))
pictTotal(5).Picture = pictSource(SixthDigit%).Picture
```

How the preceding code works is that there is a six-digit display that needs to be updated. The digits are in the form of a Picture Box control array with indexes from 0 to 5. The numbers that need to be displayed are stored as a string in the variable `texttodisplay$`. The object is to convert each character in the `texttodisplay$` string to an integer and copy the static picture box having an index value equal to that integer to the position desired. This is done by using the `Mid$` function and by looking for each character individually in the string, according to the desired position. This character is extracted from the string and then converted into an integer to use as the index value for the `pictSource()` Picture Box control array. `pictSource()` is the static Picture Box control array used as the "source," and `pictTotal()` is the Picture Box control array used as the "target" that will have bitmaps copied into it from the "source."

For example, suppose that the `texttodisplay$` string contains a value of 12534. The first digit, which is the least significant digit, is 4. The second digit is 3, and so on. A 4 has to be displayed for the first position digit, so the `Mid$` extracts the 4 from the first position in the string and converts it to the integer 4. Then the first digit's position, `pictTotal(0)`, has the "source" picture `pictSource(4)` copied into it.

The preceding is an example of how the application in Chapter 27, "CD Player Application," accomplishes the seven-segment display look, but you can adapt this method easily for use in your own applications.

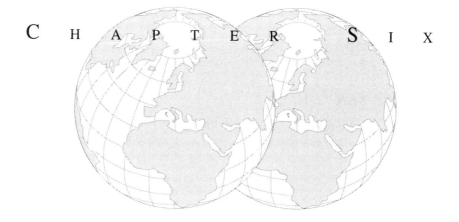

PRINTING

PRINTING PLAYS A VERY IMPOR-TANT ROLE IN VISUAL BASIC. VISUAL BASIC ALLOWS FOR THE PRINTING OF COMPLEX OBJECTS BY USING THE `Printer` OBJECT AND ACCESSING ITS PROPERTIES AND METHODS. NOTE THAT THERE ARE MANY VALUES SHOWN IN THIS CHAPTER FOR WHICH CONSTANTS ARE NOT USED. YOU MAY WANT TO DECLARE CONSTANTS THAT ARE MEANINGFUL TO YOU. FOR EXAMPLE, YOU CAN DECLARE A CONSTANT FOR THE ESCAPE KEY, SUCH AS:

```
Const ESC_KEY = 27
```

THE *PRINTER* OBJECT

The `Printer` object is an object that controls the currently selected printer. The `Printer` object is accessed just as all other Visual Basic objects are accessed, through properties and methods. There can only be one selected (default) printer at a time. Table 6.1 lists the possible `Printer` object properties:

TABLE 6.1. POSSIBLE `Printer` OBJECT PROPERTIES.

Property	Function
CurrentX	Specifies current "X" position using current `ScaleMode`
CurrentY	Specifies current "Y" position using current `ScaleMode`
DrawMode	Specifies appearance of the shape or line control
DrawStyle	Line style for graphics output
DrawWidth	Width of line
FillColor	Color used to fill shapes
FillStyle	Fill style used in filling shapes
FontBold	Boolean (Y/N) for selecting a bold font
FontCount	Number of fonts available for currently selected output device
FontItalic	Boolean (Y/N) for selecting an italic font
FontName	Name of currently used font
Fonts	List of every font name available (from 0 to `FontCount` - 1)
FontSize	Point size of currently selected font
FontStrikethru	Boolean (Y/N) for selecting a strikethru font
FontTransparent	Boolean (Y/N) for selecting a transparent font
FontUnderline	Boolean (Y/N) for selecting an underlined font
ForeColor	Color used in foreground
hDC	Handle to the device context
Height	Height of device in `Twips`
Page	Current page number
ScaleHeight	Number of vertical units for an object to measure its height in current `ScaleMode`
ScaleLeft	Left edge in current `ScaleMode`

Property	Function
ScaleMode	Specifies the unit of measure for coordinates
ScaleTop	Top edge in current ScaleMode
ScaleWidth	Number of horizontal units for an object to measure its width in current ScaleMode
TwipsPerPixelX	Horizontal Twips for every pixel
TwipsPerPixelY	Vertical Twips for every pixel
Width	Width of device in Twips

In addition to the properties listed here, the Printer object has methods that allow certain actions to occur. Table 6.2 lists the possible Printer object methods:

TABLE 6.2. POSSIBLE Printer OBJECT METHODS.

Method	Function
Circle	Draws a circle, ellipse, or arc
EndDoc	Terminates a document and releases the hDC to the Printer object
Line	Draws a line in the current ScaleMode
NewPage	Ends current page, advances to the next page, and resets the coordinates to the top left position
Print	Prints a text string on the default printer in the current color and font
PSet	Prints a graphics point on the default printer in the current color
Scale	Defines a custom coordinate system, or resets to Twips
TextHeight	Height of text as it prints using font properties in Scale coordinates
TextWidth	Width of text as it prints using font properties in Scale coordinates

PRINTING TEXT

It is very simple to print text using the Printer object. To print text to a printer, you only have to set the CurrentX and CurrentY properties (to position the printer "cursor"), use the Print method, and call the EndDoc method to eject the page. As an example, consider the following code fragment:

```
Printer.CurrentX = 1500
Printer.CurrentY = 750
Printer.Print "Real-World Programming With Visual Basic"
Printer.EndDoc
```

The preceding code does not change the `ScaleMode` property. As such, the default unit of measure, `Twips`, is in effect. This code starts by setting the printer coordinates to 1500,750. It then prints the string "Real-World Programming With Visual Basic" at these coordinates. Finally, the `EndDoc` method ejects the page. It's that simple.

Since the unit of measure is `Twips`, the coordinate reference of 1500,750 is a measurement of `Twips`. There are 1440 `Twips` in a logical inch. Therefore, the position of the text is approximately one inch to the right on the X-axis and one-half inch down on the Y-axis. Both of these measurements are from the starting point of 0,0.

 Most printers have a non-printable border of one-half inch around the perimeter of the page. This means that coordinate 0,0 would not be at the top-left corner of the page, but actually one-half inch to the right on the X-axis and one-half inch down on the Y-axis.

If another `Print` method is used directly after the `Print` method in the previous code listing, the printout will be at the beginning of the next line. This is because there are no symbols specified after the print expression in the code. There are two possible symbols that can affect where the next character is printed. The first, ";" (semicolon), instructs the printer to print the next character directly after the text just printed. The second, "," (comma), instructs the printer to print at the next *print zone*. A print zone is the beginning of a set of 14 columns. What determines the width of a column is the average of the width of all characters in a font, considering the current font size. If you do not append the print expression with a symbol, Visual Basic appends a carriage return. This action positions the "cursor" to the beginning of the next line. If you want to print at a different location, you can put the "cursor" anywhere you desire by using the `CurrentX` and `CurrentY` properties.

PRINTING GRAPHICS

Printing graphics is different from printing straight text in Visual Basic. Graphics, however, can spruce up the printouts your applications create. For example, you can add a company logo to the top of the page. There are three methods that allow for printing graphics. They are `Circle`, `Line`, and `PSet`.

THE *CIRCLE* METHOD

The `Circle` method allows for the printing of a circle, ellipse, or arc. It has the following syntax:

```
[object.]Circle[Step](x,y),radius[,[color][,[start][,[end][,aspect]]]]
```

For example, this statement prints a black circle starting in the middle of a form with a radius of 1000 twips, assuming that the `ScaleMode` is set to twips:

```
Me.Circle (Me.Width / 2, Me.Height / 2), 1000    'draw circle
```

The *Line* Method

The `Line` method allows for the printing of a line or rectangle. It has the following syntax:

```
[object.]Line[[Step](x1,y1)]-[Step](x2,y2)[,[color][,B[F]]]
```

 The application in Chapter 20, "MDI File Search Application," uses the `Line` object to print a line under the header of a page to be printed out. It uses the following line of code:

```
Printer.Line (0, Printer.TextHeight(Printer.FontSize))-(Printer.ScaleWidth,
Printer.TextHeight(Printer.FontSize) + 35), , BF
```

The code uses the `Line` method to print a line across the page, starting at the left side of the page, just under the text printed at the top of the page. The line extends across the page and down 35 `Twips`, which creates a box. However, you cannot actually see the area inside the box because the top and bottom of the box are so close together they touch. This, in effect, allows the line to appear thicker. The line can be drawn without using the `BF` option, but then another line of code has to be added to change the `Printer.DrawWidth` property. Instead, you use only one line of code.

You can add a nice touch if you incorporate lines and boxes around headers and other areas of your printed documents. This gives a much more pleasing appearance. By using `ScaleWidth` and `ScaleHeight` properties, you can make this code device-independent, which means that it will work on all printers.

The *PSet* Method

Finally, the `PSet` method allows for the printing of a single point. It has the following syntax:

```
[object.]PSet[Step](x,y)[,color]
```

For example, this statement prints a red point in the middle of a form:

```
Me.PSet (Me.Width / 2, Me.Height / 2), RGB(255, 0, 0)  'draw point
```

Sending Data Directly to the Printer

The concepts presented earlier in the section "The `Printer` Object" send data to the printer via the `Printer` object. Using the `Printer` object is an easy way to efficiently print simple text and graphics. If you want more flexibility in printing, you have to send the data directly to the printer.

This means that the data is sent directly to the printer port (LPT1, LPT2, and so on) which is controlled by the operating system, and not Visual Basic.

There are two ways to send data directly to the printer. The first method is to write the data exactly as you write data to a text file, using the `Print #` method. The second way also writes to the port, but instead of sending text, a special *PCL* language is sent. PCL stands for Printer Control Language. It is a special language that uses escape codes to instruct the printer to do specific things.

 The PCL methods discussed in this chapter only work with printers that support the PCL language, such as the Hewlett Packard LaserJet series II (or compatible) and higher.

To send data directly to the printer, the port must first be opened. You open the port by using the `OPEN` command. The following code opens the printer for writing:

```
Open "LPT1" For Output As #1
```

All data to be sent to `LPT1` is now referenced by `#1`. You can also open `LPT2` or higher, as long as they are supported on your system. The `#1` listed in the preceding code is known as a *file handle*. You can open multiple file handles, each representing a different printer or even a file.

 The number of file handles available to your system is determined by the operating system, not by Visual Basic. In DOS/Windows, the total number of file handles available is dictated by the line in your CONFIG.SYS file as follows:

```
FILES=x
```

where x is the number of total file handles available. Please note that if this number is 20, for example, this does not necessarily mean that you can open 20 files in Visual Basic. Some files may already be open by the environment.

If you want to open a file with another file handle, simply replace `#1` with the appropriate number. If you don't know what number to use, you can use the Visual Basic `FreeFile()` function. The `FreeFile()` function returns an integer representing the next available file handle. You can use it like this:

```
fHandle% = FreeFile()

Open "LPT1" for output as #fHandle%
```

To write data to the port, you use the `PRINT #` command. For example, the following code writes a string directly to the printer port:

```
Print #1, "Real-World Programming..."
```

Consider the following code fragment from Chapter 20, "MDI File Search Application." This code fragment is taken from `cmdPrint_Click()` in MAIN.FRM. It clearly shows how you can incorporate the `PRINT #` command to send text directly to the printer port:

```
'Open Printer Port
Open "LPT1" For Output As #2

'print header
If InStr(comExtensionList.Text, "ALL") > 0 Then
    Print #2, "Search Results of ALL files"
Else
    Print #2, "Search Results of file with extension " + comExtensionList.Text
End If
Print #2, "In the directory: " + Dir1.Path
Print #2,
Print #2, "Files" + String$(2, Chr$(9)) + "Occurrences"
Print #2, "— — — — — — — — — — — —"
Print #2,

'loop through file list
For LoopCount% = 0 To lstFileList.ListCount - 1

    'print file name
    Print #2, RemoveTab((lstFileList.List(LoopCount%)))

Next LoopCount%

'Form Feed Paper
Print #2, Chr$(27) + "&l0H"

'Close Handle
Close #2
```

To see the complete listing used in an application, refer to Chapter 20, "MDI File Search Application."

The problem with not using the `Printer` object in Visual Basic is that you have to handle all printing tasks at a lower programming level. Visual Basic's `Printer` object and its methods are not being used to help out in any way. For example, how do you do something like eject a page? You can't use the `Printer.EndDoc` method because as far as the `Printer` object is concerned, the print job never started. In this case, there is a whole range of functions available for using the escape codes mentioned earlier. These escape codes are so named because before every function, an escape character must be sent to alert the printer that the command will follow.

Notice the line in the previous code fragment that reads

```
Print #2, Chr$(27) + "&l0H"
```

71

It uses this syntax to send an escape code to the printer:

```
Chr$(27)+ command$
```

where `command$` is the code of the function and parameters to send to the printer. The purpose of this line is to eject the page. It is done, not through Visual Basic, but by instructing the printer directly to eject the page. The possible escape codes are listed in Table 6.2. The escape character, `Chr$(27)`, is not shown in Table 6.2 but is necessary to precede each command that will be sent to the printer. The reason it is not shown is for the sake of saving space on every line in the table. Note that anywhere in the table where there is the # symbol, substitute it for the number pertaining to the code. For example, for `&l#X`, use the code substituting the # for the number of copies to print. In this case, to print five copies, send `&l5X`. Also, make sure to use the codes as they're listed because they're case sensitive.

TABLE 6.2. COMMON PCL ESCAPE CODES.

Escape Code	Function
E	Reset Printer
&l#X	Number of Copies
&l0H	Eject Page
&l1H	Feed from tray
&l2H	Manual Feed
&l3H	Manual Envelope Feed
&l1A	Executive Paper Size
&l2A	Letter Paper Size
&l3A	Legal Paper Size
&l26A	A4 Paper Size
&l80A	Monarch Paper Size
&l81A	Commercial 10 Paper Size
&l90A	International DL Paper Size
&l91A	International C5 Paper Size
&l#P	Page Length Number of Lines
&l0O	Portrait Orientation
&l1O	Landscape Orientation
&l#E	Top Margin Number of Lines
&l#E	Text Length Number of Lines
&a#L	Left Margin Number of Lines

Escape Code	Function
&a#M	Right Margin Number of Lines
9	Clear Horizontal Margins
&l0L	Perforation Skip Mode Disabled
&l1L	Perforation Skip Mode Enabled
&k#H	Horizontal Motion Index (1/20-inch increments)
&l#C	Vertical Motion Index (1/48-inch increments)
&l1D	1 line/inch
&l2D	2 lines/inch
&l3D	3 lines/inch
&l4D	4 lines/inch
&l6D	6 lines/inch
&l8D	8 lines/inch
&l12D	12 lines/inch
&l16D	16 lines/inch
&l24D	24 lines/inch
&l48D	48 lines/inch
&a#R	Cursor Positioning-Vertical Row Number
*p#Y	Cursor Positioning-Number of Dots
&a#V	Cursor Positioning-Number of Decipoints
&a#C	Cursor Positioning-Horizontal Row Number
*p#X	Cursor Positioning-Number of Dots
&a#H	Cursor Positioning-Number of Decipoints
=	Half Line Feed
&k0G	CR=CR, LF=LF, FF=FF
&k1G	CR=CR+LF, LF=LF, FF=FF
&k2G	CR=CR, LF=CR+LF, FF=CR+FF
&k3G	CR=CR+LF, LF=CR+LF, FF=CR+FF
&f0S	Cursor Push Position
&f1S	Cursor Pop Position
(0A	HP Math Symbol Set
(0B	HP Line Draw Symbol Set

continues

TABLE 6.2. CONTINUED

Escape Code	Function
(0D	ISO 60 Norwegian Symbol Set
(1D	ISO 61 Norwegian Symbol Set
(0E	HP Roman Symbol Set
(1E	ISO 4 UK Symbol Set
(0F	ISO 25 French Symbol Set
(1F	ISO 69 French Symbol Set
(0G	HP German Symbol Set
(1G	ISO 21 German Symbol Set
(8G	HP Greek Symbol Set
(0I	ISO 15 Italian Symbol Set
(0K	ISO 14 JIS ASCII Symbol Set
(1K	HP Katakana Symbol Set
(2K	ISO 57 Chinese Symbol Set
(0M	HP Math 7 Symbol Set
(1M	Technical Symbol Set
(8M	HP Math 8 Symbol Set
(0N	ISO 100 Latin 1 Symbol Set
(0O	OCR A Symbol Set
(1O	OCR B Symbol Set
(0S	ISO 11 Swedish Symbol Set
(1S	HP Spanish Symbol Set
(2S	ISO 17 Spanish Symbol Set
(3S	ISO 10 Swedish Symbol Set
(4S	ISO 16 Portuguese Symbol Set
(5S	ISO 84 Portuguese Symbol Set
(6S	ISO 85 Spanish Symbol Set
(0U	ISO 6 ASCII Symbol Set
(1U	HP Legal Symbol Set
(2U	ISO 2 IRV Symbol Set
(7U	OEM Symbol Set
(8U	HP Roman 8 Symbol Set

Escape Code	Function
(10U	PC 8 Symbol Set
(11U	PC 8 (D/N) Symbol Set
(15U	HP Pi Symbol Set
(s1P	Proportional Spacing
(s0P	Fixed Spacing
(s#H	Primary Pitch
(s#V	Primary Point Size
(s0S	Primary Upright Style
(s1S	Primary Italic Style
(s0B	Primary Stroke Weight Medium (0)
(s3B	Primary Stroke Weight Bold (3)
(s0T	Line Printer Typeface
(s3T	Courier Typeface
(s4T	Helvetica Typeface
(s5T	Times Roman Typeface
(s6T	Letter Gothic Typeface
(s8T	Prestige Typeface
(s11T	Presentations Typeface
(s17T	Optima Typeface
(s18T	ITC Garamond Typeface
(s19T	Cooper Black Typeface
(s20T	Coronet Bold Typeface
(s21T	Broadway Typeface
(s22T	Black Condensed Typeface
(s23T	Century Schoolbook Typeface
(s24T	University Roman Typeface
(3@	Primary Font Default
)3@	Secondary Font Default
&d0D	Underline Enable Fixed
&d3D	Underline Enable Floating
&d@	Underline Disable

continues

TABLE 6.2. CONTINUED

Escape Code	Function
*c#D	Font ID#
*c0F	Delete All Fonts
*c1F	Delete All Temporary Fonts
*c2F	Delete Last Font ID #
*c4F	Make Font Temporary
*c5F	Make Font Permanent
(#X	Select Primary Font with ID #
)#X	Select Secondary Font with ID #
)s#W[Data]	Create Font Header (# of bytes)
(s#W[Data]	Download Character (# of bytes)
*c#E	Character Code (ASCII Code # in decimal)
*t75R	75 Dots/Inch Printer Resolution
*t100R	100 Dots/Inch Printer Resolution
*t150R	150 Dots/Inch Printer Resolution
*t300R	300 Dots/Inch Printer Resolution
*r0A	Left Graphics Margin
*r1A	Current Cursor Position
*b#W[Data]	Transfer Data (# of rows)
*rB	End Graphics Transfer
*c#A	Rectangle Horizontal # of Dots
*c#H	Rectangle Horizontal # of Decipoints
*c#B	Rectangle Vertical # of Dots
*c#V	Rectangle Vertical # of Decipoints
*c0P	Fill Rectangle Area Rule
*c2P	Fill Rectangle Area Gray Scale
*c3P	Fill Rectangle Area HP Pattern
*c2G	Shape Rectangle 2% Gray
*c10G	Shape Rectangle 10% Gray
*c15G	Shape Rectangle 15% Gray
*c30G	Shape Rectangle 30% Gray
*c45G	Shape Rectangle 45% Gray

Escape Code	Function
*c70G	Shape Rectangle 70% Gray
*c90G	Shape Rectangle 90% Gray
*c100G	Shape Rectangle 100% Gray
*c1G	Pattern 1 Horizontal Line
*c2G	Pattern 2 Vertical Lines
*c3G	Pattern 3 Diagonal Lines
*c4G	Pattern 4 Diagonal Lines
*c5G	Pattern 5 Square Grid
*c6G	Pattern 6 Diagonal Grid

You may want to define constants for the values presented in the Table 6.2. This would make referencing these codes cleaner and easier.

SENDING GRAPHIC DATA DIRECTLY TO THE PRINTER

The previous section covered the basics of sending text data to the printer using the PRINT # command. It also showed how to incorporate PCL escape codes. The PCL codes can be taken one step further to print graphics. Because any pixel on the paper can be printed (as long as it is in the printable area), it is just a question of how to actually access those points. It would take forever to use the Visual Basic PSet method to write to each individual point.

One very reliable way to do this is to send *raster graphics* by using the PCL functions available for this. The term "raster graphics" is defined as images that are composed of groups of dots. A raster graphic is sent to the printer as one bit of data for every dot to be printed.

Applications can use PCL raster graphic methods to send bitmaps. The bitmap could be a logo, a font, or some other graphic. The trick is to break the whole bitmap up into small, manageable pieces. Raster graphics can be used for a variety of purposes, such as printing a logo on the top of every page, or only certain pages. They can also be used to "stamp" graphics across an entire page. This is great for "stamping" the word "Confidential" across a page if it contains certain confidential information. The possibilities are endless because PCL raster graphics allow you to effectively print to any pixel on the printable page.

CREATING A STAMP WITH RASTER GRAPHICS

The term "stamp" is used here to represent what a page would look like if someone took a rubber stamp to a piece of paper. This is useful because it ensures that this is done programmatically instead of relying on someone to physically stamp it. One possible way to create the stamp is to treat each character to be "stamped" as its own bitmap. The bitmap can be stored in a text file. Each line in the text file can represent an individual character to be displayed. On each of the lines, you can determine a scheme for storing the data (what the character looks like) to be sent to the printer.

 This is what happens in the application in Chapter 23, "Raster Graphics Editor Application." The application allows the user to generate the text file suggested earlier to store data about each character.

This section actually shows you how to perform the stamping on a printout. From this point forward, it is assumed that any text needed to be printed on the page has already been printed using the PRINT # command.

Using Table 6.2, you can see the possible PCL escape codes that can be sent to the printer. The codes we are concerned with are the graphics codes.

The first step is to understand how to send the data to the printer. As mentioned earlier, you need to break up the bitmap image into small, manageable pieces. These pieces must be represented in *bytes*. A byte is eight bits of data, which means that eight individual pixels on the paper are represented. The eight pixels are physical printable pixels, regardless of whether they are actually printed or left blank.

For a raster image printed in the Portrait orientation, the image must be broken up into vertical bytes. For a raster image printed in the Landscape orientation, the image must be broken up into horizontal bytes. For example, let's say you have an image that is going to be printed in the Portrait orientation and is 400 pixels wide and 400 pixels high. Since each set of eight pixels is a byte, it is logical to break up the image into 50 bytes, vertically. This means that if you have the image on paper, you can physically draw a vertical line between each set of eight pixels.

After you break up the image into bytes, a decimal value has to be calculated for each byte. If there are 50 bytes in a row to send to the printer, each row has 50 decimals to send to the printer. This is how the printer knows which of the eight bits inside each byte to actually print, and which ones to leave white (unprinted).

The bits are calculated using the standard method of encoding a decimal using the value of one for the least significant bit and 128 for the most significant bit. The maximum possible decimal equivalent value for any byte that has all pixels printed is 255. A value of 255 instructs the printer to print eight pixels in a row. If you send 50 decimal values of 255 to the printer, it prints a line 400 pixels wide. If you send 50 decimal values of 255, 400 times (once per row in a 400-by-400 bitmap), the printer prints a solid square block 400 pixels-by-400 pixels.

Now that you understand conceptually how the data is broken up and sent to the printer, consider the case of the application in Chapter 23, "Raster Graphics Editor Application." Since each character of data is actually its own bitmap, you send the bitmaps to the printer as if they are their own entities, even though the final product *looks* like one "stamp" of all characters. This particular application uses bitmaps that are 32 pixels-by-32 pixels. This means that in the Portrait orientation, 32 rows of four bytes of data are sent to the printer.

To illustrate how these bits and bytes are calculated for a 32 pixel-by-32 pixel bitmap, see Figure 6.1, which shows how the bits are calculated for the Portrait orientation. Refer to Figure 6.2 to see how they are calculated in Landscape orientation. The only difference between Portrait and Landscape is the way the individual bits are calculated. Figure 6.1 shows how the bits are calculated for the Portrait orientation, and Figure 6.2 shows how they are calculated in the Landscape orientation.

FIGURE 6.1
*How to calculate
individual bits
in Portrait
orientation.*

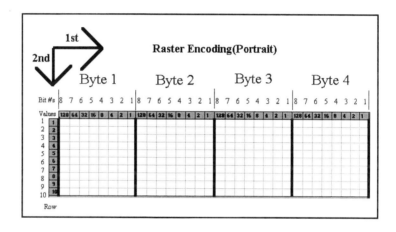

FIGURE 6.2.
*How to calculate
individual bits
in Landscape
orientation.*

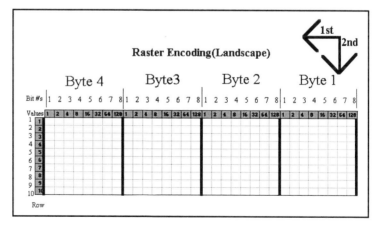

To calculate the decimal equivalent for Portrait orientation, move from left to right, from the top row to the bottom. Note that the rightmost bit is the least significant bit (value 1), and the leftmost bit is the most significant bit (value 128).

To calculate the decimal equivalent for Landscape orientation, move from right to left, from the top row to the bottom. Note that the leftmost bit is the least significant bit (value 1), and the rightmost bit is the most significant bit (value 128).

To actually start sending the data, the first thing you need to do is to tell the printer what orientation to print in (Portrait or Landscape). You can tell the printer to print in the Portrait orientation by sending the following escape code:

```
Print #1, Chr$(27) + "&l0O"
```

The next step is to position the printer cursor. Remember, you are not using Visual Basic methods and properties, so you cannot use the CurrentX and CurrentY properties to position the printer cursor. The cursor can be positioned at any desired location.

Let's say the printer is to start at position 100,100. Again, remember that you are not dealing with Visual Basic properties; you are using the printer's own pixel coordinates, so changing the ScaleMode property has no effect on raster graphics. All of the escape codes used in the following examples are listed in Table 6.2. First instruct the printer to begin printing with the X coordinate at 100 and the Y coordinate at 100:

```
Print #1, Chr$(27) + "*p100X"
Print #1, Chr$(27) + "*p100Y"
```

The next thing you need to do is to set the printer resolution. If you want to set it to 75 dots-per-inch, send the following to the printer:

```
Print #1, Chr$(27) + "*t75R"
```

The reason that a resolution of 75 dots-per-inch is used is because it gives a nice size representation on the page. For a 32 pixel-by-32 pixel bitmap, at this resolution, the image is approximately one-half inch-by-one-half inch.

Now that you have told the printer the position and resolution of the graphic, you must tell the printer to be ready to accept the data. Therefore, you must put it into raster graphics mode by sending the following:

```
Print #1, Chr$(27) + "*r1A"
```

After putting the printer in Raster Graphics mode, the printing will begin at the current position as set with the X and Y coordinates earlier. It does not reset to the top-left corner of the page, which is coordinate location 0,0.

Now graphics mode is set, but the printer needs to know how many bytes per line it will receive. Instruct the printer that it will receive four bytes with the following line:

```
Print #1, Chr$(27) + "*b4W"
```

If you are going to send 50 bytes, you send the following:

```
Print #1, Chr$(27) + "*b50W"
```

The printer needs to know how many bytes to expect to receive so that it can calculate which bits are to be printed correctly. The printer is now ready to accept the actual byte data. To send the byte data, you first calculate the decimal equivalent of each byte to be sent, as shown earlier in figures 6.1 and 6.2. If the printer expects to receive four bytes of data, send the data with this format:

```
Print #1, Chr$(27) + Chr$(decimal)
```

where decimal is the decimal you calculate from the individual bits in the byte. An example of four bytes being sent to the printer is:

```
Print #1, Chr$(27) + Chr$(255)
```

```
Print #1, Chr$(27) + Chr$(105)
```

```
Print #1, Chr$(27) + Chr$(0)
```

```
Print #1, Chr$(27) + Chr$(255)
```

Since four bytes are expected to be received and four bytes are sent, an entire row is printed. It is your choice to send more data or end.

If you are to send more data (more rows), you again tell the printer how many bytes of data to expect and then send the data. The printer is still set in the appropriate resolution and still in Graphics mode. Continue to send the data in this fashion. When you have sent all of the data and are ready to finish, you must tell the printer that you are finished with graphics by using the following line:

```
Print #1, Chr$(27) + "*rB"
```

You can automate the process of calculating the bits and bytes that have to be sent to the printer. As a programmer, you need to keep in mind that whatever scheme you devise to design or display the bitmap, you need to break it up and send it to the printer as described earlier.

 The application in Chapter 23, "Raster Graphics Editor Application," uses a scheme to allow the user to define the bitmap by using the grid control. The grid is setup in a 32-by-32 matrix. Depending on whether the user wants to print in Portrait or Landscape modes depends on how the bytes and bits are calculated. Therefore, the process is automated by cycling through each and every row and column in the grid control and calculating the decimal equivalents. This is performed in the CalculateBits() procedure from CHAP23, MAIN.FRM as follows:

```
'portrait
If WhichMode$ = "PORTRAIT" Then
    'cycle through for portrait from left to right, top to bottom
    For Row% = 1 To Grid1.Rows - 1
        For Col% = 1 To Grid1.Cols - 1
            Grid1.Row = Row%
            Grid2.Row = Row%
            Grid1.Col = Col%

            'move Grid2's col once for every 8 cols in Grid1
            If Grid1.Col >= 1 And Grid1.Col <= 8 Then
                Grid2.Col = 1
            ElseIf Grid1.Col >= 9 And Grid1.Col <= 16 Then
                Grid2.Col = 2
            ElseIf Grid1.Col >= 17 And Grid1.Col <= 24 Then
                Grid2.Col = 3
            ElseIf Grid1.Col >= 25 And Grid1.Col <= 32 Then
                Grid2.Col = 4
            End If

            'assign Grid2 row
            Grid2.Row = Grid1.Row

            'start at row 0 to check text(to see which bit position this is)
            'each row and col has a header at row 0 and col 0 for which bit
            'position this is
            Grid1.Row = 0

            'build bit representation of which bits are printed
            Select Case (Val(Trim$(Grid1.Text)))
                Case 1:
                    Grid1.Row = Row%
                    If Grid1.Picture = Black.Picture Then
                        Grid2.Text = Val(Trim$(Grid2.Text)) + 1
                    End If
                Case 2:
                    Grid1.Row = Row%
                    If Grid1.Picture = Black.Picture Then
                        Grid2.Text = Val(Trim$(Grid2.Text)) + 2
                    End If
                Case 3:
                    Grid1.Row = Row%
                    If Grid1.Picture = Black.Picture Then
                        Grid2.Text = Val(Trim$(Grid2.Text)) + 4
                    End If
                Case 4:
                    Grid1.Row = Row%
                    If Grid1.Picture = Black.Picture Then
                        Grid2.Text = Val(Trim$(Grid2.Text)) + 8
                    End If
                Case 5:
                    Grid1.Row = Row%
                    If Grid1.Picture = Black.Picture Then
                        Grid2.Text = Val(Trim$(Grid2.Text)) + 16
                    End If
                Case 6:
                    Grid1.Row = Row%
```

```
                        If Grid1.Picture = Black.Picture Then
                            Grid2.Text = Val(Trim$(Grid2.Text)) + 32
                        End If
                Case 7:
                    Grid1.Row = Row%
                    If Grid1.Picture = Black.Picture Then
                        Grid2.Text = Val(Trim$(Grid2.Text)) + 64
                    End If
                Case 8:
                    Grid1.Row = Row%
                    If Grid1.Picture = Black.Picture Then
                        Grid2.Text = Val(Trim$(Grid2.Text)) + 128
                    End If
            End Select
        Next Col%
    Next Row%
ElseIf WhichMode$ = "LANDSCAPE" Then
    'cycle through for Landscape bottom to top, left to right
    For Row% = Grid1.Cols - 1 To 1 Step -1
        For Col% = 1 To Grid1.Rows - 1
            Grid1.Col = Row%
            Grid1.Row = Col%
            Select Case (Grid1.Row)
                Case 1 To 8:
                    Grid2.Col = 1
                Case 9 To 16:
                    Grid2.Col = 2
                Case 17 To 24:
                    Grid2.Col = 3
                Case 25 To 32:
                    Grid2.Col = 4
            End Select

            'calculate row
            Grid2.Row = (32 - Grid1.Col) + 1

            'start at col 0 to check text(to see which bit position this is)
            'each row and col has a header at row 0 and col 0 for which bit
            'position this is
            Grid1.Col = 0

            'build bit representation of which bits are printed
            Select Case (Val(Trim$(Grid1.Text)))
                Case 1:
                    Grid1.Col = Row%
                    If Grid1.Picture = Black.Picture Then
                        Grid2.Text = Val(Trim$(Grid2.Text)) + 1
                    End If
                Case 2:
                    Grid1.Col = Row%
                    If Grid1.Picture = Black.Picture Then
                        Grid2.Text = Val(Trim$(Grid2.Text)) + 2
                    End If
                Case 3:
                    Grid1.Col = Row%
```

83

```
            If Grid1.Picture = Black.Picture Then
                Grid2.Text = Val(Trim$(Grid2.Text)) + 4
            End If
        Case 4:
            Grid1.Col = Row%
            If Grid1.Picture = Black.Picture Then
                Grid2.Text = Val(Trim$(Grid2.Text)) + 8
            End If
        Case 5:
            Grid1.Col = Row%
            If Grid1.Picture = Black.Picture Then
                Grid2.Text = Val(Trim$(Grid2.Text)) + 16
            End If
        Case 6:
            Grid1.Col = Row%
            If Grid1.Picture = Black.Picture Then
                Grid2.Text = Val(Trim$(Grid2.Text)) + 32
            End If
        Case 7:
            Grid1.Col = Row%
            If Grid1.Picture = Black.Picture Then
                Grid2.Text = Val(Trim$(Grid2.Text)) + 64
            End If
        Case 8:
            Grid1.Col = Row%
            If Grid1.Picture = Black.Picture Then
                Grid2.Text = Val(Trim$(Grid2.Text)) + 128
            End If
        End Select
    Next Col%
  Next Row%
End If
```

Although this way is not the only way to calculate the decimal equivalents, following is the scheme used in the `CalculateBits()` procedure.

There are two branches of code: one for Portrait and one for Landscape orientations. The basic scheme for either mode is to cycle through each row and column (the order of which depends on which orientation is selected) and for each individual cell location checking the bit value of that particular location. Fortunately, with the grid control, each row and column can be labeled in a fixed row. The application simply relies on these labels (row 0 and column 0) to determine what value to use to calculate the decimal equivalents. If the color of the pixel (cell) is black, then it adds the value of this label to the calculated value of the byte.

That is basically what is happening in the code. It looks more complicated than it really is because of the way the code has to cycle through each cell. Refer to Figures 6.1 and 6.2 to see how the cells must be calculated.

Even though this application uses a 32-by-32 pixel matrix, your application does not have to. It can use any size. You just have to make sure that you manage how you send the data to the printer.

If you want to print multiple bitmaps on the same page, you simply position the cursor to the desired position before printing each bitmap. You can even cycle through bitmaps, automatically incrementing the X or Y coordinates after every bitmap. You can use this method to give a sloping appearance.

Again, as an example, the application in Chapter 23, "Raster Graphics Editor Application," along with the application in Chapter 24, "Raster Printer Application," uses a routine to print all bitmaps and incrementing the x and y coordinates automatically. The following code fragment is taken from the `PrintAllText()` routine that calls the `PrintCharacter()` routine once for every bitmap to be printed:

```
'loop through all characters to be printed
For loopcount% = 1 To (Len(PrintText.Text))
    pnlCurChar.Caption = Mid$(PrintText.Text, loopcount%, 1)

    'increment coordinates
    If PortLandMode% = PORTRAIT Then
        XPValue% = XPValue% + Val(HPOffset.Text)
        YPValue% = YPValue% + Val(VPOffset.Text)
    ElseIf PortLandMode% = LANDSCAPE Then
        XLValue% = XLValue% + Val(HLOffset.Text)
        YLValue% = YLValue% + Val(VLOffset.Text)
    End If
    Call PrintCharacter
Next loopcount%
```

PRINTING A PICTURE BOX BITMAP REPRESENTED ONSCREEN

There is no printer method to print the contents of a picture box. This makes it more difficult to perform some printing. The application in Chapter 22, "Icon Printing Application," gets around this. The same approach used by this application can be used in your applications. The technique is to actually cycle through each bit in the bitmap, determining its color; and if it isn't white, send it to the printer using standard graphics methods.

The first step is to set the scale mode to pixels. This is done with the following line:

```
WhichIcon.ScaleMode = 3
```

Then, you must cycle through all of the coordinates. The specific order (x then y, or y then x) doesn't matter. In this example, the order of the coordinate cycling is first y, then x. The x and y coordinates are assigned based on the screen resolution. This allows for the possibility to print a larger icon than is displayed on-screen.

Note that even though this example uses icons, any bitmapped image will work. Even though the picture box is populated with an icon, it really is just a bitmapped image.

The Screen object is used as the basis of determining the printing resolution. For more information on using the Screen object, refer to Chapter 5, "Graphics."

The screen resolution is defined by using the Screen object. The following code shows how to cycle through each pixel in the picture box and print it if it is not white.

```
'Cycle through y coordinates
For YLoop% = 0 To (WhichIcon.ScaleHeight - 1)
    'assign y coordinate, based on screen resolution
    YAdjust = WhichIcon.Top + (YLoop% * ScrResY)

    'cycle through x coordinates
    For XLoop% = 0 To (WhichIcon.ScaleWidth - 1)
        'assign x coordinate, based on screen resolution
        XAdjust = WhichIcon.Left + OFFSET + (XLoop% * ScrResX)

        'assign particular point to determine color
        XYColor = WhichIcon.Point(XLoop%, YLoop%)

        'for some reason, if the screen repaints(due to moving a window)
        'the color might be -1.
        If XYColor < 0 Then
            XYColor = 7
            m$ = "The window has been moved off the screen." +
            Chr$(13)
            m$ = m$ + "The icons may not print correctly"
            MsgBox m$
            'center form
            CenterForm Me
            'force repaint
            Me.Refresh
        End If
        'if color is not white, print point, using screen resolution
        If XYColor <> QBColor(7) Then
            printer.Line (XAdjust, YAdjust)-Step(ScrResX, ScrResY), XYColor, BF
        End If
    Next XLoop%
    DoEvents
Next YLoop%
```

If the form is moved off screen or if another window is opened on top of the picture box being printed, QBColor will be -1. This is an immediate flag that a window has changed. It affects the printout because you are looking at a certain area of the picture box, which will have changed.

DETERMINING WHICH PRINTER FONTS ARE PRESENT

To determine if a printer has a certain font, use the `FontCount` and `Fonts` properties for the `Printer` object. The `Fonts` property is actually a Visual Basic *collection*. A collection is a way that Visual Basic keeps track of certain objects or properties.

The idea is to cycle through all fonts and test for the possibility you are looking for. You may be looking for a certain font or a particular font size. You loop through `0` to `Printer.FontCount` `-1` to cover all possibilities in the collection. Because there is no collection for the size of the font, there is a work-around. You can assign the size of the font by using the `FontSize` property of the `Printer` object and then test to see if it is selected. If it is not, the size is not possible.

As an example, there is a function in Chapter 22's MAIN.FRM called `FindFont()`. It is used to determine if the printer has a font with a `FontSize` of six. The following code fragment is from that function:

```
'find out which fonts exist for printer, and use first available in size 6
For loopcount% = 0 To printer.FontCount - 1
    'assign to first available font
    printer.FontName = printer.Fonts(loopcount%)

    'assign to size 6
    printer.FontSize = 6

    'test to see if 6 is still assigned, if so, exit loop
    If printer.FontSize = 6 Then

        'set variable flag to print text in print routine
        FontFound% = True

        'exit function
        FindFont = True
        Exit Function
    End If

Next loopcount%
```

The reason for testing the printer for a font size between 5.5 and 6.5 is because if the printer does not have a font size of exactly 6, it may assign a font size close to 6. It is sufficient to check for the point size + or - .5. It is assumed that if a font size is found in this range, then the setting of the font worked.

In your application, you can use the same technique to display a list of all of the possible fonts for a user's selection. You can then list all font sizes available if a user selects one of those fonts.

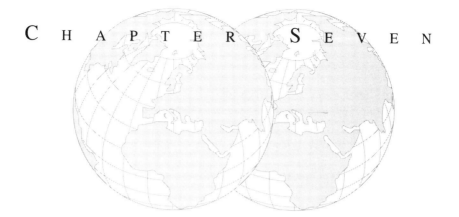

FILE INPUT/OUTPUT (I/O)

FILE INPUT/OUTPUT (I/O) IS VERY EASY IN VISUAL BASIC COMPARED TO ANY OTHER PROGRAMMING LANGUAGE. THIS IS MAINLY BECAUSE YOU DON'T HAVE TO DEAL WITH ANY POINTERS. VISUAL BASIC TAKES CARE OF ALL OF THAT. THERE ARE TWO MAJOR TYPES OF FILES: *text files* AND *binary files*. VISUAL BASIC DEALS WITH BOTH TYPES.

Text files are files that contain ASCII characters only. There are very few special characters for special purposes. Text files are not divided into a series of records, and you can read them with any text file viewer. A text file is useful, for example, when a vendor needs to convey information to the user, such as in a READ.ME file. Text files are also called *sequential access files*.

The application in Chapter 20, "MDI File Search Application," has the capability to view text files.

On the other hand, a binary file can contain any character available in the operating system. These characters can include special characters not recognizable in the English language. They are merely symbols that represent some other value. Binary files are used for most purposes, such as database files, executable files, and many others.

The difference in the types of files really determines only how the format of the file will be interpreted. They all perform the same basic function. However, the different types are designed for the different purposes stated earlier so that they give maximum performance.

OPENING A FILE

Regardless of which type of file you use, you must open the file before it is written to or read from. The syntax to open a file is

```
Open file [For mode] [Access access] [lock] As [#]filenumber [Len=reclen]
```

where:

> `file` is the name of the file to open.
>
> `mode` is the mode to open the file. Possible modes are `Append`, `Binary`, `Input`, `Output`, and `Random`.
>
> `access` is the type of access permitted on the file. Possible access modes are `Read`, `Write`, and `Read Write`.
>
> `lock` is the type of operation permitted by other processes. Possible locks are `Shared`, `Lock Read`, `Lock Write`, and `Lock Read Write`.
>
> `filenumber` is the integer expression of the file number used by Visual Basic. This number is between 1 and 255, inclusive.

To determine the next available file handle, use the `FreeFile()` function. This function returns an integer representing the next available file handle.

Visual Basic has many standard functions and statements available for use with files. These functions and statements are listed in Table 7.1.

TABLE 7.1. STANDARD VISUAL BASIC FILE FUNCTIONS AND STATEMENTS.

Function/Statement	Use	Pertains To
Close	Closes all file handles	Sequential, Random, Binary
Close #	Closes one file handle	Sequential, Random, Binary
Dir	Returns a variant of the directory matching certain file specifications	Sequential, Random, Binary
Dir$	Returns the directory matching certain file specifications	Sequential, Random, Binary
EOF	End of File Marker	Sequential, Random, Binary
FileCopy	Copies a file	Sequential, Random, Binary
FileDateTime	Retrieves the date and time of a file	Sequential, Random, Binary
FileLen	Returns the size of a file in bytes (long)	Sequential, Random, Binary
FreeFile	Returns the next available file handle number	Sequential, Random, Binary
Get	Reads data from a file	Random, Binary
GetAttr	Returns integer of file/directory attributes	Sequential, Random, Binary
Input	Reads data from a file and returns variant	Sequential, Binary
Input #	Reads data from a particular file number	Sequential
Input$	Reads data from a file and returns string	Sequential, Binary
Line Input #	Reads a line from a particular file number	Sequential
Loc	Returns current file position	Random, Binary
LOF	Returns size of open file (bytes)	Sequential, Random, Binary
Open	Opens a file	Sequential, Random, Binary
Print #	Writes data to a file	Sequential

continues

TABLE 7.1. CONTINUED

Function/Statement	Use	Pertains To
Put	Writes data to a file	Random, Binary
Reset	Closes all open files, writing buffer contents to disk first	Sequential, Random, Binary
Seek	Returns the current file position	Sequential, Random, Binary
SetAttr	Sets attributes of a file or directory	Sequential, Random, Binary
Type...End Type	Defines record types	Random
Write #	Writes data to a particular file number	Sequential

These functions and statements deal with directly accessing files. These are some other functions:

FileAttr	Returns the file mode of an open file	Sequential, Random, Binary
Kill	Deletes a file	Sequential, Random, Binary
Name	Renames a file or directory	Sequential, Random, Binary
Lock	Locks a file in a multi-user environment	Sequential, Random, Binary
Unlock	Unlocks a file in a multi-user environment	Sequential, Random, Binary
Dir/Dir$	Returns the name of files that match pattern	Sequential, Random, Binary
ChDir	Changes the current directory	Sequential, Random, Binary
ChDrive	Changes the current drive	Sequential, Random, Binary
MkDir	Creates a new directory	Sequential, Random, Binary
RmDir	Removes a directory	Sequential, Random, Binary
CurDir/CurDir$	Returns current path	Sequential, Random, Binary

A *sequential file* (usually a text file) is simply a list of characters stored in a file. It can be opened for `Input`, `Output`, or `Append`. If the file is open for `Input`, this means that you will be reading data from it. If it is opened for `Output`, you will be writing to the file, and an old file will be overwritten. If it is opened for `Append`, you will be writing to the file, but the data will be appended to the end of the file.

A *random access file* is a file that is stored in records. These records are made up of a certain number of bytes stored as fields. Each and every record in the file must be exactly the same length. This type of file could be used to store database information.

A *binary file* is a file in which any of the bytes in the file can be read or written to in any location. This type of file is probably the most widely used. Executable files are of this type, as well as device drivers, and many other types. The thing to remember about a binary file is that you must know what location in the file to retrieve or store your data. You cannot decipher just by looking at the file where you need to place data or from where you need to retrieve data.

Closing a File

It's a good idea to close the file as soon as you are finished using it. This frees up valuable resources. Don't wait until the user leaves the application or closes Windows. You can close a file by using the following line:

```
Close #filenumber
```

where *filenumber* is the number of the open file. For example, this line closes file number 1:

```
Close #1
```

Working with Text Files

As stated earlier, text files are files that contain only ASCII characters and are often called sequential access files. These files can be opened and/or created by using the `Open` statement. A sequential access file can be opened for `Input`, `Output`, or `Append`. If the file does not exist, the `Open` statement creates the file. A file opened for `Input` reads text from a file. A file opened for `Output` writes text to a file from the beginning of the file, which effectively erases the old file first. A file opened for `Append` appends characters to the end of a file.

INI Files

INI files are text files that have a special meaning in the Windows environment. They are used as *INI*tialization files. Programs can use the information within an INI file to "config" the program. This data can be used for a multitude of tasks, such as giving the application some pertinent data about a configuration, retaining the user's past selections, and more.

Although an INI file can be read or written by using the standard Visual Basic methods for reading or writing a text file (as described in the preceding section), they are usually read and written with Windows API functions. For the rest of this section, the API functions are used when accessing INI files.

 To access these API functions, you must declare the functions first. These declarations are shown in Chapter 3, "Calling Windows APIs and DLLs."

 You generally open an INI file with a Text editor if you need to change data external of the running program. An API call is made if you want to read or write data for the running program itself.

 For more information about Windows API functions, refer to Chapter 3.

There are two types of INI files: *public* and *private*. The public INI file is an alias for the WIN.INI file. The private INI file is an INI file usually used only for one application. Another way to differentiate these two types of INI files is that *usually* a public INI file is used for system information, not application specific information. There are six API functions used in accessing INI files. They are listed in Table 7.2.

TABLE 7.2. STANDARD VISUAL BASIC FILE FUNCTIONS AND STATEMENTS.

API Function	Purpose
GetPrivateProfileString()	Reads a string from a private INI file
GetProfileString()	Reads a string from the WIN.INI file
GetPrivateProfileInt()	Reads an integer from a private INI file
GetProfileInt()	Reads an integer from the WIN.INI file
WritePrivateProfileString()	Writes a string to a private INI file
WriteProfileString()	Writes a string to the WIN.INI file

 The words "public" and "private" are used to describe how the files are used. It does not indicate that these are keywords that should be used in your code.

INI files contain certain parts that need to be accessed. These parts must be specified in the API functions. Following is a sample entry from an INI file:

```
[Section1]
KeyName1=Entry1
```

94

```
KeyName2=Entry2
[Section2]
KeyName1=Entry1
KeyName2=Entry2
```

All of the fields listed here are variables. The entry was set up to show that there can be multiple sections and multiple keynames inside each of the sections. These keynames can be the same inside the different sections. There are two rules to follow when considering the format of the text inside the INI file. They are:

◆ The sections are always enclosed in brackets.

◆ There is no space before or after the "=" (equal) sign.

 The format shown in the preceding entry is needed only if you use a text editor to edit the INI file. If you use the Windows APIs, they handle the formatting of the file automatically. You need not be concerned about spacing or specific characters such as [,] or =.

 As a reference, it may be helpful to know which applications in Part II of this book use INI files. The following is a list of these chapters:

◆ Chapter 20, "MDI File Search Application"

◆ Chapter 23, "Raster Graphics Editor Application"

◆ Chapter 24, "Raster Graphics Printer Application"

◆ Chapter 25, "Dynamic Hotspot Application"

◆ Chapter 28, "MAPI Application"

READING INI FILES

To read an INI file, you need to know whether to read from the WIN.INI file or a private INI file. If you want to read from the WIN.INI file, you use the GetProfileString() API function. It has the general syntax

```
result = GetProfileString(application, keyname, default, return, size)
```

where:

result is the number of characters returned.

application is the name of the section.

keyname is the keyname inside the section.

default is the default string assigned if the requested entry doesn't exist.

return is the string returned—the string must be preallocated by using the Space$() function.

size is the maximum size of the return string.

As an example, if you want to find out what Windows wallpaper is used, you look in the WIN.INI file under the application "Desktop" and keyname "Wallpaper." Doing this returns the string of the bitmap being used. You can find this out by the following lines of code:

```
Temp$ = Space$(128)
result% = GetProfileString("Desktop", "Wallpaper", "", Temp$, 128)
```

result% will be the number of characters returned in Temp$. If the value is 0, the string is not found. If the value is greater than 0, Temp$ will contain the string value from the INI file, but padded with spaces until the total length is 128 or whatever value is declared with the Space$() function. For example, if you are using a wallpaper file called TAZ.BMP, Temp$ will contain the string TAZ.BMP, followed by 121 spaces. The value of Result% will be 7, which is the length of Temp$.

    For more information about how to declare these API functions, refer to Chapter 3.

To retrieve a string from a private INI file, use the GetPrivateProfileString() API function. It takes one argument more than the GetProfileString() API function—the file name. It uses the syntax

```
result = GetPrivateProfileString(application, keyname, default, return, size, filename)
```

where the only difference is the variable *filename*, which is the name of the file to search.

For example, if you want to find out what the Windows startup group is called, use the GetPrivateProfileString() API function like this:

```
Temp$ = Space$(128)
result% = GetPrivateProfileString("Settings", "Startup", "", Temp$, 128, "PROGMAN.INI")
```

The preceding example will return values exactly as with the GetProfileString() API function. The only difference is that you have specified to look for the string in the "PROGMAN.INI" file instead of the "WIN.INI" file.

    The reason that you use the private INI file for this, even though it is a system setting, is because it is not stored in the WIN.INI file. The GetProfileString() API function is only used with the WIN.INI file.

There are many applications in this book that also use INI files. These INI files are very useful for storing configuration information about an application. The application in Chapter 20, "MDI File Search Application," uses these INI files to store information about eight separate sound files. The following code fragment is taken from the application:

```
RetString = Space$(75)
'get Line 1
    res% = GetPrivateProfileString(lpApplicationName$, lpKeyName0$, lpDefault0$,
    RetString, 75, SearchPath$ + lpFileName$)
    SoundFile0$ = Left$(RetString, res%)

    'get Line 2
    res% = GetPrivateProfileString(lpApplicationName$, lpKeyName1$, lpDefault1$,
    RetString, 75, SearchPath$ + lpFileName$)
    SoundFile1$ = Left$(RetString, res%)

    'get Line 3
    res% = GetPrivateProfileString(lpApplicationName$, lpKeyName2$, lpDefault2$,
    RetString, 75, SearchPath$ + lpFileName$)
    SoundFile2$ = Left$(RetString, res%)

    'get Line 4
    res% = GetPrivateProfileString(lpApplicationName$, lpKeyName3$, lpDefault3$,
    RetString, 75, SearchPath$ + lpFileName$)
    SoundFile3$ = Left$(RetString, res%)

    'get Line 5
    res% = GetPrivateProfileString(lpApplicationName$, lpKeyName4$, lpDefault4$,
    RetString, 75, SearchPath$ + lpFileName$)
    SoundFile4$ = Left$(RetString, res%)

    'get Line 6
    res% = GetPrivateProfileString(lpApplicationName$, lpKeyName5$, lpDefault5$,
    RetString, 75, SearchPath$ + lpFileName$)
    SoundFile5$ = Left$(RetString, res%)

    'get Line 7
    res% = GetPrivateProfileString(lpApplicationName$, lpKeyName6$, lpDefault6$,
    RetString, 75, SearchPath$ + lpFileName$)
    SoundFile6$ = Left$(RetString, res%)

    'get Line 8
    res% = GetPrivateProfileString(lpApplicationName$, lpKeyName7$, lpDefault7$,
    RetString, 75, SearchPath$ + lpFileName$)
    SoundFile7$ = Left$(RetString, res%)
```

In the preceding text, the SOUND.INI file contents look like this:

```
[Real-World Sound]
FontChange=FTCHG.WAV
FontCancel=FTCAN.WAV
PrintText=PTTXT.WAV
PrintError=PTERR.WAV
FileSave=FLSAV.WAV
```

```
FileError=FLERR.WAV
CloseViewer=CLVIEW.WAV
CloseSound=CLSND.WAV
```

 You could have used arrays to significantly shorten the amount of code needed to perform the functions listed earlier. However, for the sake of example and clarity, this was not done.

All variables for section names, keynames, and filenames have been declared in a module so that they don't have to be typed in. One more issue that has not been mentioned is how to use the string that is returned. Because the integer returned is the number of bytes returned, simply extract only that number of characters from the returned string by using the LEFT$ command. You need to do this because the string returned has been set to a certain number of spaces by using the SPACE$ command.

WRITING INI FILES

To write an INI file, you need to know whether to write to the WIN.INI file or a private INI file. If you want to write to the WIN.INI file, you use the WriteProfileString() API function. It has the general syntax:

```
result% = WriteProfileString(application, keyname, string)
```

where

>   result% is the status of the success.
>
>   application is the name of the section.
>
>   keyname is the keyname inside the section.
>
>   string is the string to write.

As an example, if you want to change the spacing of the icons on your desktop, you write a value to the WIN.INI file, under the application "Desktop" and keyname "IconSpacing". You can do this with the following line of code:

```
result% = WriteProfileString("Desktop", "IconSpacing", "100")
```

To write a string to a private INI file, use the WritePrivateProfileString() API function. It takes one argument more than the WriteProfileString() API function—the file name. It uses this syntax

```
result% = WriteProfileString(application, keyname, string, filename)
```

where the only difference is the variable filename, which is the name of the file to write to.

If you want to change the name of the Windows startup group, you can use the WritePrivateProfileString() API function like this:

```
result% = WritePrivateProfileString("Settings", "Startup", "Visual Basic 3.0",
"PROGMAN.INI")
```

The preceding example will write (or overwrite) a section that looks like this in the "PROGMAN.INI" file:

```
[Startup]
Settings=Visual Basic 3.0
```

 If you write to an INI file using Windows APIs, the API will create the file, section, or key if it doesn't already exist. If it does exist, it will be overwritten without prompting for confirmation first.

SAVING TEXT FILES

Saving text files is performed by using the Visual Basic sequential file I/O functions. Sequential file I/O means that as each character is written, it is placed at the end of the file. A sequential file is written by using the Print # statement. You can write one or more characters at a time. For example, assuming that the file has been opened, you can write one character to file handle number one with this line:

```
Print #1, "C"
```

You can also write the contents of a Visual Basic text box by using this line:

```
Print #1, Text1.Text
```

 The application in Chapter 20, "MDI File Search Application," uses this technique to print the contents of a text box. The following code fragment is taken from Chapter 20, which shows how to write to the specified file:

```
'open the file
Open frmMDIView.cmDialog.Filename For Output As #1

'write the file
Print #1, Source.Text

'close the file
Close #1
```

The code opens a file named in the common dialog box. (For more information about common dialog boxes, see the later section "Opening Multiple Files with the Common Dialog Control.") Then the code writes the entire contents of the text box passed through the object variable *Source*. Finally, the file is closed after all text has been written.

SEARCHING THROUGH TEXT FILES

It can be very useful to search through a text file and determine how many occurrences of a particular string there are. You can use this technique to search through a file for Search/Replace operations, such as replacing all references of a directory to another directory. To search through a text file for occurrences of a certain string, you must perform the following steps:

◆ Open the file

◆ Find the next occurrence of the specified string

◆ Increment counter to represent number of occurrences

◆ Continue searching until the end of file is reached

◆ Close the file

To open the file, use the Open statement. To find the number of occurrences of a given string, loop through the open file and count the number of times the Instr() Visual Basic function returns a value greater than zero. This indicates that the specified string exists inside the file. The Instr() function allows for the possibility to search for case sensitivity. If the argument of 0 is used, the Instr() function performs a case sensitive search. If 1 is used, or if it is omitted, no case sensitive search is performed.

The application in Chapter 20, "MDI File Search Application," is designed to perform a search such as the one described here. The following code fragment shows how to loop through the file and determine the number of occurrences. Notice that there are two branches. One is for case sensitivity, and one is for no case sensitivity. The only difference in this is the optional argument in the Instr() Visual Basic function.

```
Do While Not EOF(1)

        'Get a line
        Input #1, TheLine$

        'search for string in the line
        If optNotSensitive.Value = True Then
            'NOT case sensitive

            'Test to see if the search string exists in this line
            If InStr(1, TheLine$, Trim$(txtSearchString.Text), 1) <> 0 Then

                'initialize TempPos%
                TempPos% = 1

                'the string exists, test for other occurrences in same line
                Do While TempPos% <= Len(TheLine$)

                    If InStr(1, Mid$(TheLine$, TempPos%, Len(txtSearchString.Text)),
                    txtSearchString.Text, 1) > 0 Then
                    Stringcount% = Stringcount% + 1
                    End If
```

```
                TempPos% = TempPos% + 1
            Loop
        End If
    Else
        'IS case sensitive

        'Test to see if the search string exists in this line
        If InStr(1, TheLine$, Trim$(txtSearchString.Text), 0) <> 0 Then

            'initialize TempPos%
            TempPos% = 1

            'the string exists, test for other occurrences in same line
            Do While TempPos% <= Len(TheLine$)
                If InStr(1, Mid$(TheLine$, TempPos%, Len(txtSearchString.Text)),
                txtSearchString.Text, 1) > 0 Then
                Stringcount% = Stringcount% + 1
                End If
                    TempPos% = TempPos% + 1
            Loop
        End If
    End If

    Loop
```

The technique used in this code is really very simple to follow. The code cycles through every line in the text file, one line at a time. As each line is read, the `Instr()` function is used to determine where the next occurrence is. If there is an occurrence, it is counted, and it searches for the next occurrence of the string in the same line. The looping continues until the end of `TheLine$`. This entire looping process continues until the end of the file is reached.

Your application can incorporate this technique, and even possibly add to it. You can replace a string found with a string defined by the user to affect a Search/Replace function. This technique can be used to make a powerful text editor.

Working with Binary Files

Binary files are files that can contain special characters representing some other purpose besides reading text. A binary file is really just a file that contains a series of symbols. These symbols do not necessarily mean anything to anyone except the programmer. It is up to the programmer to determine what the scheme is behind how the data is stored. Binary files can be opened for Random or Binary access. A random access file is a file for which any record inside the file can be updated randomly because each record has a certain predefined length. When opening the file, you must use the Len argument to tell Visual Basic how long each record is, in bytes. A file opened for Binary is similar to a file opened for Random, except that each record is not necessarily the same size. This means that once again, it is up to the programmer to decide how to incorporate some scheme for accessing the file. It could be as simple as an extra two byte integer before each record to identify how many bytes are in the following record.

FILE COPYING

You can certainly copy a file in Visual Basic without having to know anything about file handling. You can copy a file by using the FileCopy() statement. The problem with using this statement is that it does not provide any feedback to the programmer, such as percentage complete. If you want to use the FileCopy() statement, use the syntax

```
FileCopy srcFile,destFile
```

where the following variables are used:

> srcFile is the complete filespec of the file to copy.

> destFile is the complete filespec of the file's destination.

There is a way around this; however, you have to handle the file I/O yourself, and it is slower than using the FileCopy() statement. The theory behind doing this is to do the following:

◆ Determine the size of the file to be copied

◆ Open the file for Binary

◆ Copy one byte at a time

◆ Keep track of how many bytes have been copied

◆ Calculate the percentage based on the size of the file and the number of bytes copied

◆ Close the file

The application in Chapter 21, "File Copy Application," uses this technique to copy files and provide a percentage status. Your application can apply similar techniques to copy files or simply to read or write a binary file.

For more information about how to copy one byte at a time, refer to Chapter 21, "File Copy Application."

The following code fragment from Chapter 21 performs the necessary steps to copy the file stored in the variable FromFile$ to the location stored in the variable ToFile$:

```
TheLen& = FileLen(FromFile$)
Open FromFile$ For Binary Access Read As #1
Open ToFile$ For Binary Access Write As #2
LoopVar& = 1
Do Until EOF(1)
    TheTemp$ = String$(1, " ")
    Get #1, LoopVar&, TheTemp$
    If EOF(1) Then Exit Do
    Put #2, LoopVar&, TheTemp$
    'update floodpercent, if percentage is different
    'this helps eliminate flicker
    If pnlFloodStatus.FloodPercent <> Int((LoopVar& / TheLen&) * 100) Then
        pnlFloodStatus.FloodPercent = Int((LoopVar& / TheLen&) * 100)
```

```
    End If
    LoopVar& = LoopVar& + 1
Loop
```

What the preceding code demonstrates is that the source file is opened for Read, and the destination file is opened for Write. Then the code loops through the contents of the source file, one byte at a time, and writes the bytes to the destination file. After writing each file, it calculates the percentage of the file that has been copied and then updates a 3-D panel's FloodPercent property with the appropriate percentage. The file is then closed, but not shown in this fragment.

OPENING MULTIPLE FILES WITH THE COMMON DIALOG CONTROL

The Common dialog control is a very simple way to open a file without an additional form or control that the user has to designate just for opening the file. This control does allow for the possibility to open more than one file at one time.

For the control to allow the multiple selection of files, you must set a flag. This flag is set in the Flag property for the Common dialog control. It is set as follows:

```
cmDialog1.Flag = OFN_ALLOWMULTISELECT
```

where OFN_ALLOWMULTISELECT has been declared as the constant &H200&.

If you have ever used the Common dialog control to open files, you know how to retrieve the name of a file from it. The file selected is listed in the FileName property. The only difference between single selection and multiple selection of files is that the control lists all files selected, separated by a space. As a programmer, you simply have to parse the string and determine what the individual files are.

 Even though the control allows you to open multiple files, there is a limit to the number of files you can open at one time. The limit is based on the total size of all characters in each file name to be opened simultaneously. For example, you can't open 100 files, each containing *8.3 filenames*. An 8.3 filename is a file that has eight characters for the name of the file itself, a period, and three characters for the file extension. For example AUTOEXEC.BAT is an 8.3 filename. The size is limited to 255 characters, including spaces, which is approximately 15 files at a time. This limitation is not based on the number of files set in the CONFIG.SYS file, but the limitation of the Common dialog control itself.

 This technique comes from the application in Chapter 22, "Icon Printing Application." It allows the user to select many files to open for viewing in the application at one time.

The following code fragment shows how Chapter 22 parses this string to open each file:

```
'Get file names
FileString$ = cmDialog.Filename

Do While FileString$ <> ""
    pos% = InStr(FileString$, " ")
    If pos% > 0 Then
        'assign file
        TheFile$ = Left$(FileString$, pos% - 1)
    Else
        'assign file
        TheFile$ = FileString$
        FileString$ = ""
    End If

    'assign rest of string to filestring$
    FileString$ = Right$(FileString$, Len(FileString$) - pos%)

    'populate picture box
    Call PopulatePicture(TheDirectory$ + TheFile$)
Loop
```

The preceding code cycles through the string returned from the common dialog box and extracts each file individually. After the file is extracted, it reassigns the FileString$ variable to include the remaining files in the string for the next loop. Then it populates a picture with the corresponding file name. If you try the preceding code, every item in the Visual Basic group will be executed in turn. This may not be what you have intended to do. It is really for informational purposes only.

ERROR HANDLING WITH FILES

It is important to have some type of error handling in your applications that contain File I/O. If no error handling is performed and an error occurs, your application can exit abruptly. This has serious consequences for files because there is data that has not been written, the user lost his changes, and now you have one or more open file handles that are not closed.

It is important to account for all possible file handling errors. Table 7.3 lists the possible errors that relate to files.

TABLE 7.3. VISUAL BASIC FILE RELATED ERRORS.

Error Number	Explanation
52	Bad file name or number
53	File not found
54	Bad file mode
55	File already open

Error Number	Explanation
57	Device I/O error
58	File already exists
59	Bad record length
61	Disk full
62	Input past end of file
63	Bad record number
64	Bad file name
67	Too many files
68	Device unavailable
70	Permission denied
71	Disk not ready
74	Can't rename with different drive
75	Path/File access error
76	Path not found

 For more information on error handling, refer to Chapter 2, "Error Handling."

The exception to the rule of error handling is if you are using API functions for INI files. There is no error handling when dealing with Windows API functions. This is because the most likely errors to occur are General Protection Faults. There is no way to "handle" these, only avoid them.

 For more information on how to avoid errors with Windows API functions, refer to Chapter 3, "Calling Windows APIs and DLLs."

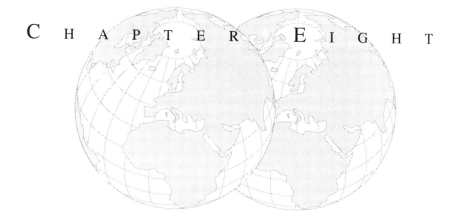

MULTIPLE DOCUMENT INTERFACE (MDI)

MULTIPLE DOCUMENT INTERFACE (MDI) IS A TYPE OF INTERFACE THAT ALLOWS FOR MULTIPLE FORMS TO BE CONTAINED WITHIN ONE HIERARCHICAL FORM, CALLED A *PARENT*. THESE MDI FORMS ARE COMMONLY CALLED *CHILD FORMS*. IN OTHER WORDS, ONE MDI PARENT FORM CAN HAVE ONE OR MORE MDI CHILD FORMS. THERE CAN BE ONLY ONE MDI FORM IN A VISUAL BASIC APPLICATION.

The opposite of an MDI form is an *SDI* form. SDI stands for *Single Document Interface*. Although this is not the topic of this chapter, it is mentioned just as a comparison. An SDI application is basically just one form that contains a text box or some other control to display text and data. There is no way to have multiple instances of that form or to control them in a hierarchical relationship.

A new MDI form is generated from a single template. This template is not taken from the parent form, as you might expect. The template is taken from a regular form that has its MDIChild property set to True. This means that you can load a new instance of a child form by referencing this form. These child forms then become children of the MDI form, not the form that acts as a template.

An MDI child form really acts just like any other form. It can contain multiple controls, has many properties, and can be accessed individually. There is one feature, however, that is handled differently than a Visual Basic form that is not a child form—the menus. The way a menu is handled in an MDI child form is that the parent form shows the menu of the currently active child form. If you click on a different MDI child form, the menu of that form is shown in the parent form. The child form does not show the menu options.

MDI Toolbars

An MDI form can also contain toolbars. An example of this is how Microsoft Word or Excel works. The application itself is the MDI parent window. Each document or spreadsheet that you open is an MDI child form. As each of these forms becomes active, the menus or toolbars become active, based on certain settings in the individual windows. For example, if you make a Microsoft Word document active, the menus (and possibly the toolbars) make certain menu items available based on the contents of the document.

To design a toolbar for use with MDI, you design the toolbar using the PictureBox control or some other control that allows you to display bitmaps representing the tools. The PictureBox control can be either on the MDI parent form or the children. You decide how to negotiate the toolbars (and menus). Negotiation is the process of determining how the toolbars and menus are displayed.

Including MDI in Your Application

To include MDI in your application, first add an MDI form by selecting the File->New MDI Form menu option. This menu option inserts a form that is used as an MDI parent form.

After you have added your MDI parent form, you have to decide what the child forms will look like. Most often, you only have one type of form as the child form, but simply have multiple instances of it. To create the child form, add a regular form to the project, but set the MDIChild

8

property to `True`. This tells Visual Basic that this form (or another instance of it) is to be displayed in the MDI form's window.

CREATING A NEW INSTANCE OF A CHILD FORM

After you have created a form to be used as a child form, you can use it to create new instances of that form. You do so by including a module level declaration with the following syntax:

```
Global newreference([elements]) As New childform
```

where:

`newreference` is the array of form names. This reference is how you refer to each instance in code.

`elements` is an optional parameter that states how many child forms are used. It is not advised to use this parameter. If it is used, the maximum number of child forms will be only the number entered here. If it is left out, you can use the `ReDim` keyword to assign a number at runtime, which is how it is normally done.

`childform` is the name of the form that you set the `MDIChild` property to `True`.

 The application in Chapter 20, "MDI File Search Application," is the only application in Part II of this book that uses MDI. It includes the declaration as follows:

```
Global NewViewer() As New frmViewerForm
```

This means that as a new instance of `frmViewerForm` is wanted, `NewViewer` is loaded. Before loading the new form, however, you must tell Visual Basic how many elements the form array is to have. If you do not declare how many elements there are in the array at design time, you must do it at runtime with the `Redim` statement. Following is an example of how Chapter 20 `Redims` the array based on how many files are needed to be displayed in the child forms; it uses the following statement:

```
ReDim NewViewer(NumberOfSelections%)
```

The new instance is loaded with the `Load` statement or the `Show` statement (which actually loads the form first). Chapter 20 uses it like this:

```
NewViewer(IndexInUse%).Show
```

You can use this same technique in your applications, but substitute the name of the form and index for the ones in your application.

You can even have an application that is a *Compound Document Interface (CPI)*. A CPI application is an application that has MDI child forms that allow multimedia. Because the standard text box does not allow for this, you can use the OLE2 or MCI controls, or even some other custom controls. This works because the MDI child form allows any control on it that a regular form can have.

For more information on OLE and the OLE2 control, refer to Chapter 15, "Object Linking and Embedding (OLE)."

For more information on the MCI control, refer to Chapter 12, "Multimedia."

MDI FILE VIEWER

It is typical to use MDI for file viewer applications. Visual Basic has the capability to make a very powerful MDI text editor. The application in Chapter 20, "MDI File Search Application," is one such viewer, with search capabilities. The individual characteristics of the file viewer can vary. It is the point of this chapter to demonstrate how the MDI part of it works. Previously you saw how to load an MDI form. Following is the listing of the OpenViewer() routine from Chapter 20, which shows how to use MDI in a real-world situation:

```
Sub OpenViewer ()

    'declare variables
    Dim m$                          'Holds message building string
    Dim ControlWithFocus As Control 'Stores control which has the focus
    Dim LoopCount%                  'Looping Variable
    Dim TheFile$                    'holds file name to open(including path)
    Dim TextToHold$                 'holds text to be placed in file viewer
    Dim NextIndex%                  'holds next available index
    Dim NumberOfSelections%         'holds number of selections to redim
                                    ' Viewer
    Dim IndexInUse%                 'holds the index number used in Viewer
                                    ' array
    Dim pos%                        'holds position of tab

    'initialize
    NumberOfSelections% = 0
    IndexInUse% = 0

    'handle errors
    On Error GoTo FError:

    'find out which list box has the focus
    'Viewer will be populated with all selected files from this list
    'Test Proposed List
    For LoopCount% = 0 To lstProposed.ListCount - 1

        'test for lstProposed contents to avoid errors
        If lstProposed.ListCount > 0 Then
            If lstProposed.Selected(LoopCount%) = True Then
```

```
                        'Proposed List has the focus
                        Set ControlWithFocus = lstProposed
                        NumberOfSelections% = NumberOfSelections% + 1
                End If
        End If
Next LoopCount%

'Test File List
For LoopCount% = 0 To lstFileList.ListCount - 1

        'test for lstFileList contents to avoid errors
        If lstFileList.ListCount > 0 Then
                If lstFileList.Selected(LoopCount%) = True Then
                        'File List has the focus
                        Set ControlWithFocus = lstFileList
                        NumberOfSelections% = NumberOfSelections% + 1
                End If
        End If
Next LoopCount%

'redim array to hold all of the selections
ReDim NewViewer(NumberOfSelections%)

For LoopCount% = 0 To ControlWithFocus.ListCount - 1
        'if selected, open file
        If ControlWithFocus.Selected(LoopCount%) = True Then
                'assign file temporary-will reassign below
                TheFile$ = ControlWithFocus.List(LoopCount%)

                'test to see if there is a tab in the format
                pos% = InStr(TheFile$, Chr$(9))'
                If pos% > 0 Then
                        'this contained a tab-remove
                        TheFile$ = Left$(TheFile$, pos% - 1)
                End If

                'assign the file, making sure it's in the proper format
                If Right$(Dir1.Path, 1) = "\" Then
                        TheFile$ = Dir1.Path + TheFile$
                Else
                        TheFile$ = Dir1.Path + "\" + TheFile$
                End If

                'open file
                Open TheFile$ For Input As #1

                'read entire file
                TextToHold$ = Input$(LOF(1), #1)

                'Test to see if entire file was read
                If Len(TextToHold$) <> LOF(1) Then

                        'change cursor
                        Screen.MousePointer = DEFAULT
```

```
                'build message
                m$ = "The complete file cannot be read." + Chr$(13)
                m$ = m$ + "It contains unreadable characters."

                'display message
                MsgBox m$

            Else
                NewViewer(IndexInUse%).Caption = TheFile$

                'flag populating viewer, so viewer change event
                'can be ignored
                PopulatingViewer% = True

                'assign text
                NewViewer(IndexInUse%).txtViewer.Text = TextToHold$

                'show form
                NewViewer(IndexInUse%).Show

                'reset viewer flag
                PopulatingViewer% = False

                'increment IndexInUse for next iteration
                IndexInUse% = IndexInUse% + 1
            End If

            'Close File
            Close #1

            'change cursor
            Screen.MousePointer = DEFAULT

        End If

    Next LoopCount%

    'exit
    Exit Sub

FError:
    'there were errors

    'change cursor
    Screen.MousePointer = DEFAULT

    'build message
    m$ = "Error- Cannot Read This File"

    'display message
    MsgBox m$

    Resume Next


End Sub
```

This application has two file lists that can be used to select files. Because of this, the first two loops in the code test for which list has files selected. After the application identifies which file list has files selected, the application counts the number of text files that need to be displayed in an MDI child form. The reason you need to know how many text files are selected is because you need to Redim the form array with the appropriate number of MDI child forms.

The third loop (the larger loop) is used to cycle through each file selected, to open it, and to populate the contents in its own MDI child form.

This application only reads text files, not binary files. Because of this, the routine tests to see if the number of characters read is the same as the number of characters in the file. You accomplish this by testing for the Length of File (LOF) with the line of code from the previous code listing:

```
If Len(TextToHold$) <> LOF(1) Then
```

If the number of characters read is not the same as the length of the file, the file cannot be read. In this case an appropriate message box is shown.

 For more information on File Input/Output, refer to Chapter 7, "File Input/Output (I/O)."

THE SOURCE OBJECT

MDI child forms are very efficient because they can reuse the same code in procedures. This is because an MDI form is really just a form array with special characteristics. This concept is similar to the fact that a control array can share code, but just passes the index value into a procedure. For an MDI child form, you can use the Source object to differentiate between child forms. An example of how to do this is taken from Chapter 20, "MDI File Search Application," in the CloseRoutine() procedure. This example shows how the code is reusable for each of the MDI child forms:

```
Sub CloseRoutine (Source As Control)

    'declare variables
    Dim res%     'holds msgbox results
    Dim m$       'constructor variable for msgbox

    If Source Is Nothing Then
        'user selected menu option
        'unload current MDI Child Form

        'if change has been made, prompt for save
        If Left$(frmMDIView.ActiveForm.Caption, 1) = "*" Then
            'build message
            m$ = "Close without saving changes?"
            res% = MsgBox(m$, 292, "Warning")
```

```
            If res% = IDNO Then Exit Sub
        End If
        Unload frmMDIView.ActiveForm
    Else
        'user selected drag/drop
        'unload current MDI Child Form

        'if change has been made, prompt for save
        If Left$(Source.Parent.Caption, 1) = "*" Then
            'build message
            m$ = "Close without saving changes?"
            res% = MsgBox(m$, 292, "Warning")
            If res% = IDNO Then Exit Sub
        End If
        Unload Source.Parent
    End If

    'if active form is MDI parent, that means that there
    'are no more children left-unload parent
    If screen.ActiveForm.hWnd = frmMDIView.hWnd Then
        Unload frmMDIView
    End If

End Sub
```

This code presents an important concept: The CloseRoutine() procedure is declared with an argument, Source As Control. The Source can either be a text box (containing the text file on an MDI child form) or set to Nothing. Without getting too much into the nitty-gritty of the application, the Source is set to Nothing if the user selects to close the form from a menu option. The Source is set to a text box if the user uses the Drag/Drop feature. If the Source is set to a text box, after checking if a change has been made, it unloads the Parent. This is important because the Source is a text box. The Parent is the form containing the text box. If the object variable, Source, is set to Nothing, after checking to see if a change has been made, the ActiveForm property is used to unload the active form (the form on which any control has the focus).

CLOSING MDI CHILD FORMS

Having an MDI form with multiple child forms presents some problems when trying to track changes to the child forms for saving purposes. The problems stem from the fact that the MDI form does not keep track of the child form making changes. It is up to the child forms individually.

One possible suggestion for accommodating this is to flag the form's Tag property with some value. When unloading the MDI form, you can cycle through all of the child forms and check the Tag property for some value. This is a very easy method to incorporate.

Another suggestion is to use the method used in Chapter 20, "MDI File Search Application." This method actually removes the system menu (the menu in the upper-left corner). This action prohibits the possibility of closing the MDI form before the child forms. Then each child form can be unloaded individually without problems. This technique is done in Chapter 20 mainly to show how to use API functions for removing the system menu. This technique is more formally known as *destroying* the menu.

For more information about using Windows API functions, refer to Chapter 3, "Calling Windows APIs and DLLs."

You probably wonder why you have to go through the process of removing the system menu. Why not just set the ControlBox property to False? The problem is that there is no ControlBox property on an MDI form—only a regular form. Therefore, the API function is used to destroy the menu.

ARRANGING MDI CHILD FORMS

Arranging MDI child forms is really very simple. Visual Basic takes care of all of it for you. Visual Basic has an Arrange method that handles this. All you do is supply the program a constant representing the style of arrangement. Your code can incorporate the manual or automatic arrangement of the MDI child forms. You can automatically arrange when a new form is created, or upon the Form_Load() or Form_Unload() events.

To declare the constants used with the Arrange method, use the following declarations:

```
Global Const CASCADE = 0
Global Const TILE_HORIZONTAL = 1
Global Const TILE_VERTICAL = 2
Global Const ARRANGE_ICONS = 3
```

To use the Arrange method, supply the constant like this:

```
frmMDIView.Arrange CASCADE
```

As you can see from the contents (and size) of this chapter, there is not much to MDI. The real advantage is that Visual Basic handles all of the functionality for you. This enables you to make more professional-looking applications.

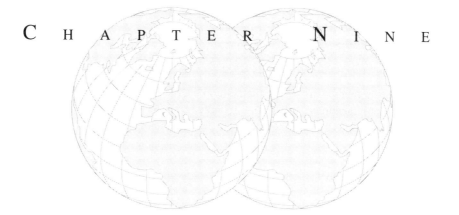

COMMUNICATIONS

THE *COMMUNICATIONS CONTROL* IS SUPPOSED TO BE A CUSTOM CONTROL THAT GREATLY ENHANCES YOUR POSSIBILITIES WITH VISUAL BASIC. UNFORTUNATELY, THERE ARE MANY PROBLEMS WITH IT. IT IS A GREAT IDEA TO INCLUDE SUCH A CONTROL WITH VISUAL BASIC; HOWEVER, IF YOU WANT RELIABLE COMMUNICATIONS, YOU SHOULD EITHER UPGRADE THE CONTROL OR PURCHASE A COMPLETELY DIFFERENT CONTROL. IF YOU WANT TO PERFORM SIMPLE TASKS WITH THE CONTROL, SUCH AS SENDING MESSAGES BETWEEN TWO COMPUTER SCREENS, THIS CONTROL WILL WORK SATISFACTORILY. THIS CHAPTER OUTLINES SOME OF THE WAYS THAT THE COMMUNICATIONS CONTROL WORKS AND SOME POSSIBLE WORK-AROUNDS FOR ITS SHORTCOMINGS. THE CONTROL CAN ALSO BE USED TO COMMUNICATE WITH DEVICES BESIDES MODEMS, SUCH AS SCANNERS AND SERIAL PRINTERS.

I spent many hours with Microsoft on the phone to determine just how to make the Communications control more reliable and to do some of the things it can't do. Following is a list of the things the control cannot do:

◆ Transfer binary files

◆ Reliably hang up the phone

◆ Reliably handshake with another terminal for sending text files.

Microsoft bought the control written by Sheridan, a major player in the third-party custom control market. As such, Sheridan no longer supports the control. However, Microsoft doesn't know as much about the control as Sheridan. The bottom line is that if you need to do any type of reliable communications other than transferring text from one terminal to another, I suggest you purchase an updated control from Sheridan. The updated control allows for different transfer protocols.

 Chapter 26, "Communications Terminal Application," presents an application that allows for communications between two computers.

 The control contained on the CD accompanying this book in the CHAP26 subdirectory, MSCOMM.VBX, is not the version of the control that comes with Visual Basic. It was downloaded from CompuServe from the MSBASIC forum. The application uses this version in the application in Chapter 26. It allows for some minor bug fixes, but it is not greatly enhanced.

UNDERSTANDING THE COMMUNICATIONS CONTROL

The Communications control has only one event—the OnComm event. It is invoked almost continuously based on certain properties. The properties used in the Communications control are listed in Table 9.1.

TABLE 9.1. COMMUNICATION CONTROL PROPERTIES.

Property	DataType	Used For
Break	Boolean	Setting break state
CDHolding	Boolean	High if Carrier Detect is True
CDTimeout	Long	Timeout of Carrier Detect
CommEvent	Integer	Returns the most recent OnComm event

Property	DataType	Used For
CommID	Integer	Handle of Communications device Used for API functions
CommPort	Integer	Communications port (1-4)
CTSHolding	Boolean	High if CTS is True
CTSTimeout	Long	Timeout of CTS Line (Clear to Send)
DSRHolding	Boolean	High if DSR is True
DSRTimeout	Long	Timeout of DSR Line (Data Set Ready)
DTREnable	Boolean	Sets DTR (Data Terminal Ready) line
Handshaking	Integer	Handshaking protocol
InBufferCount	Integer	Number of characters in Receive buffer
InBufferSize	Integer	Size of Return buffer
Input	String	Data in Receive buffer
InputLen	Integer	Number of characters to read from the Receive buffer
Interval	Long	Hardware polling interval
NullDiscard	Integer	True if Null characters are not transferred to the Receive buffer
OutBufferCount	Integer	Number of characters in Transmit buffer
OutBufferSize	Integer	Size of Transmit buffer
Output	String	Data in Transmit buffer
ParityReplace	String	Character used when Parity error occurs
PortOpen	Boolean	Opens or closes the port
RThreshold	Integer	Number of characters to receive before generating the OnComm event
RTSEnable	Boolean	True if RTS (Request To Send) line is High
Settings	String	String of Baud Rate, Parity, Data bit, and Stop bit
SThreshold	Integer	Number of characters to send before generating the OnComm event
OnComm	Integer	Event that ultimately controls the behavior of the com port
ComInput	Integer	Same as Input property
ComOutput	Integer	Same as Output property

Modems are configured and respond based on certain commands sent to the modem. If you write any application using a modem, you must communicate in code with the modem in your program to be able to test your application. This is because the modem must know how to respond to certain events and conditions in your programs. These commands are sent in "Command mode." That is, the modem is not connected to another terminal and responds to commands from your terminal. After the modem is connected, if you are not in Command mode, the modem sends any characters typed on your keyboard to the other terminal. These commands are also known as *AT* commands. This is because all commands to be sent to a modem are prefixed by "AT," which stands for "*AT*tention."

It can be tricky to debug a problem with the communications terminal. This is mainly because you may not be aware that the modem is in a certain mode and that it is not supposed to respond as you think. It is very helpful to refer to the manual that comes with the modem. In case you don't have a manual, Table 9.2 lists some of the more common Hayes compatible "AT" modem commands. If you have a special modem, such as a fax modem, you have additional commands available that are not listed here.

TABLE 9.2. STANDARD MODEM COMMANDS.

Command	Function
+++	Puts modem into Command mode (not followed by CR)
A	Immediately answers call
B0	V22 connection at 1200 baud
B1	Bell 212A connection at 1200 baud
DT	Dials a telephone number using touch tone
DP	Dials a telephone number using pulse
DL	Dials last telephone number
DW	Waits for dial tone
D'	Pauses during dial as specified in register S8
D@	Waits for at least five seconds
D;	Returns to terminal mode after dialing
D!	Goes on hook as specified in the S29 register
E0	Command characters are not echoed to the screen
E1	Command characters are echoed to the screen
H0	Forces modem to hang up (on hook)
H1	Forces modem to pick up line (off hook)
L0	Lowest modem speaker volume

Command	Function
L1	Low modem speaker volume
L2	Medium modem speaker volume
L3	Highest modem speaker volume
M0	Speaker always off
M1	Speaker on until carrier detected
M2	Speaker always on
M3	Speaker on during answering only
O0	Returns to Data mode
O1	Returns to Data mode and initiates equalizer sequence
Q0	Modem sends responses
Q1	Modem does not send responses
S_?	Reads a value from the register, where _ is the register number
S_=n	Sets a value into a register, where _ is the register number, and n is the new value
S0=1	Answers the phone on the first ring
V0	Single digit responses
V1	Word responses
X0	Sends OK, CONNECT, RING, NO CARRIER, ERROR, and NO ANSWER messages
X1	Sends X0 messages and CONNECT speed
X2	Sends X1 messages and NO DIAL TONE
X3	Sends X2 messages and BUSY
X4	Sends all messages
Y0	Modem does not send or respond to break signals
Y1	Modem sends and responds to break signals
Z_	Most modems reset to some stored profile or state, where _ could be the number of the profile. Not all modems support this
&C0	Always keep Carrier Detect (CD) on
&C1	Carrier Detect (CD) on only where carrier present
&D0	Modem ignores Data Terminal Ready (DTR)
&D1	If DTR goes On to Off, the modem returns to Command mode

continues

TABLE 9.2. CONTINUED

Command	Function
&D2	If DTR goes On to Off, the modem returns to Command mode and hangs up the phone
&F	Restores the modem to factory default settings
&G0	Guard tone disabled
&G1	550 Hz guard tone enabled
&G2	1800 Hz guard tone enabled
&J0	Modem will use an RJ11, RJ41S, or RJ45S telephone jack—not all modems support this
&J1	Modem will use an RJ12 or RJ13 telephone jack—not all modems support this
&K0	Disables flow control—not all modems support this
&K3	Enables RTS/CTS flow control—not all modems support this
&K4	Enables XON/XOFF flow control—not all modems support this
&L0	Modem is set up for dialup operation—not all modems support this
&L1	Modem is set for leased-line operation—not all modems support this
&M0	Modem is configured for asynchronous operation—not all modems support this
&M1	Modem enters synchronous mode after dialing asynchronously—not all modems support this
&M2	Synchronous terminal support only—not all modems support this
&M3	Manually originating a synchronous call—not all modems support this
&P0	United States Make/Break dial ratio of 39/61 at 10 pps
&P1	UK and Hong Kong Make/Break dial ratio of 33/67 at 10 pps
&P2	Make/Break dial ratio of 39/61 at 20 pps—not all modems support this
&P3	Make/Break dial ratio of 33/67 at 20 pps—not all modems support this
&T0	For testing purposes only. Ends test in progress.
&T1	For testing purposes only. Starts local analog loopback test.
&T3	For testing purposes only. Starts local digital loopback test.
&T4	For testing purposes only. Responds to remote modem request for digital loopback.
&T5	For testing purposes only. Ignores remote modem request for digital loopback.

Command	Function
&T6	For testing purposes only. Requests remote digital loopback without self-test.
&T7	For testing purposes only. Same as &T6, but with self-test.
&T8	For testing purposes only. Starts local analog loopback with self-test.
&W_	Most modems store profiles or states, where _ can be the number of the profile. Not all modems support this.
&Z	Stores the telephone number in nonvolatile memory

Most of these modem commands work with any modem. There may be some that will not, but they are indicated as appropriate. Any of these commands can be sent to the modem on one line or in single statements, but each command must be preceded by "AT." For example,

```
ATS0=1{Enter}
AT&F{Enter}
```

is the same as

```
ATS0=1&F{Enter}
```

If there is a problem in your program that isn't responding correctly, refer to your modem manual to determine if you are using the correct settings.

 These commands can be sent to the modem programmatically. They do not have to be typed in. It is important to know that when you send the commands to the modem in code, you must mimic the keystrokes, including the "Enter" keystroke. For example, consider the following code taken from Chapter 26, "Communications Terminal Application":

```
mscomm.Output = "ATS0=1" + Chr$(13)
```

The previous line of code, according to Table 9.2, tells the modem to answer the phone line on the first ring. Notice the Chr$(13) in the line. It is used to simulate the "Enter" key being pressed.

AUTOMATICALLY DETECTING A PORT

Automatically detecting a port is really as easy as cycling through each available port and waiting for a response from the modem. You want to automatically check the port in case you are not sure which port the modem is connected to. If the modem responds, then obviously there is a modem connected to the port. If you are going to automatically detect the com port, it is a good idea to test for all possible ports (1-4) and use an error handler routine. This is because even if the computer doesn't have four ports, the code allows for computers that do. If a test is made for a communications port that doesn't exist, the code simply goes through the error handler routine and tries the next port.

 For more information about handling errors, refer to Chapter 2, "Error Handling."

Below is a code fragment from Chapter 26, which loops through all available com ports (1-4) and tests for the presence of a modem:

```
For LoopCount% = 1 To 4
    'assign port
    mscomm.CommPort = LoopCount%

    'assign settings
    mscomm.Settings = BuildSettings()

    'open port
    mscomm.PortOpen = True

    'assign output string
    mscomm.Output = "AT" + Chr$(13)

    'show and unload terminal form only for time to wait for modem
    'doevents doesn't work
    frmTerminal.Show
    Unload frmTerminal
    DoEvents
    DoEvents

    'read input from modem
    If InStr(TempInput$, "OK") > 0 Then
        ModemFound% = mscomm.CommPort

        'exit loop
        Exit For
    End If

    'close port
    mscomm.PortOpen = False

Next LoopCount%
```

Notice that to test for the response from the modem, the following line is sent:

```
mscomm.Output = "AT" + Chr$(13)
```

The AT command by itself simply requests that the modem responds. It does not change any configuration or put the modem into any different mode. If an "OK" is not returned from the modem, this may be because the modem is off, or there is a hardware conflict. To resolve this conflict, refer to your PC manual and modem manual.

THE MYSTERIOUS *OnCOMM* EVENT

The OnComm event is the only event in the Communications control and is used for a couple of purposes. The event can be generated when a character is sent or received to or from the modem. Two properties listed in Table 9.1 control how often the OnComm event is generated: the RThreshold and SThreshold properties.

If the Rthreshold property is set to 0, there is no OnComm event when a character is received in the modem. Therefore, it is difficult to read the characters coming into the port because you won't know when they arrive.

If the Sthreshold property is set to 0, there is no OnComm event when a character is sent to the modem. This does not have as significant an impact because you are controlling when to send the character.

The OnComm event is generated for actions that occur as well as errors that occur. It is really just a question of decoding what happens. There are constants in the Visual Basic CONSTANT.TXT file that are defined for each of these actions and errors.

In your application, you may decide only to receive characters for some purpose. In this case, you can set the SThreshold property to 0. This also makes it easier to handle the OnComm event because you don't have to deal with much code. On the other hand, if you want to send and receive characters to the screen as well as transfer text files between machines, you use quite a bit of code. Transferring text files is exactly what Chapter 26, "Communications Terminal Application," does.

Following is a code fragment from the OnComm event in Chapter 26. The Select Case statement decodes the messages.

```
Select Case mscomm.CommEvent
        '--- Event messages
        Case MSCOMM_EV_RECEIVE

            'assign input to temp variable
            temp$ = mscomm.Input

            'assign TempInput(for port detection) to Temp$
            TempInput$ = temp$

            If InStr(temp$, "CONN") > 0 Then
                'connected
                frmTerminal.Show
                DoEvents

                'send welcome message
                mscomm.Output = "HELLO FROM CHAPTER 26 APPLICATION" + Chr$(13) + Chr$(10)
                DoEvents
                DoEvents
                DoEvents
```

```vb
    ElseIf InStr(temp$, "NO CARR") > 0 Then
        'lost connection
        m$ = "Connection was broken!"
        MsgBox m$
        Unload frmTerminal
    ElseIf InStr(temp$, "FILE SENT") > 0 Then

        'determine position of "File Sent"
        pos% = InStr(temp$, "FILE SENT")
        If pos% <> 0 Then
            temp$ = Left$(temp$, pos% - 2)
        End If
        'write to file
        If Len(temp$) > 0 Then
            Put hSend, , temp$
        End If

        'unflag receiving
        Receiving% = False

        'close all open file handles
        Close

    End If

    'determine special cases
    If Len(temp$) > 0 Then
        Select Case Asc(temp$)
            Case 127:   'Backspace
                Exit Sub
            Case 27:    'arrow keys
                Exit Sub
        End Select
    End If

    Temp1$ = Left$(temp$, Len(temp$))
    If Right$(Temp1$, 1) = Chr$(13) Then
        'last character is a carriage return
        CRsFound% = 1
        'backup until there are no more carriage returns
        For LoopCount% = Len(Temp1$) To 1 Step -1
            If Mid$(Temp1$, LoopCount%, 1) <> Chr$(13) Then
                'append line feed
                Temp1$ = Left$(Temp1$, CRsFound% + 1) + Chr$(13)
                Exit For
            Else
                CRsFound% = CRsFound% + 1
            End If
        Next LoopCount%
        Temp1$ = Temp1$ + Chr$(10)
        temp$ = Temp1$
    End If

    'show receive in client area
    frmTerminal.txtClientArea = frmTerminal.txtClientArea + temp$
```

```
            If Receiving% = True Then
                'write to file
                If Len(temp$) > 0 Then
                    Put hSend, , temp$
                End If
            Else
                'set insertion point to end of text
                frmTerminal.txtClientArea.SelStart = Len(frmTerminal.txtClientArea.Text)
            End If
        Case MSCOMM_EV_SEND
        Case MSCOMM_EV_CTS
            'unflag receiving
            Receiving% = False

            'close file handles
            Close
        Case MSCOMM_EV_DSR
        Case MSCOMM_EV_CD
        Case MSCOMM_EV_RING
            If cbRecMode.Text = "Auto Answer" Then
                'answer
                Call AnswerPhone

            ElseIf cbRecMode.Text = "Conditional" Then
                m$ = "        Phone is ringing!" + Chr$(13)
                m$ = m$ + "Would you like to answer it?"
                res% = MsgBox(m$, 292, "Question")
                If res% = IDYES Then
                    'answer
                    Call AnswerPhone
                End If
            End If
        Case MSCOMM_EV_EOF
        Case MSCOMM_ER_BREAK
        Case MSCOMM_ER_CTSTO
        Case MSCOMM_ER_DSRTO
        Case MSCOMM_ER_FRAME
        Case MSCOMM_ER_OVERRUN
        Case MSCOMM_ER_CDTO
        Case MSCOMM_ER_RXOVER
        Case MSCOMM_ER_RXPARITY
        Case MSCOMM_ER_TXFULL
        Case Else
    End Select
```

REM

Take note in the previous code that there are many cases that have not been handled in the Chapter 26 application. For example, the line

```
Case MSCOMM_ER_TXFULL
```

is left in to show you the different errors and conditions that can be handled, although not every application uses all of them.

127

There is no automatic handling of anything in the Communications control as far as sending and/or receiving data, characters, or files. You need to account for everything and handle it manually. That is the reason why there is code listed here that looks for carriage returns, line feeds, and other parameters.

 It is important to note that because the OnComm event is called so often, you probably don't want to put a DoEvents statement in this event. The event may be called every time a character is received in the input buffer, which will certainly cause a stack overflow error.

SENDING AND RECEIVING TEXT FILES

As noted previously, there is no way to send and receive binary files—that is, unless you devise your own protocol. This situation can be a nightmare! You can, however, send and receive text files. It is just not terribly reliable. The Communications control has problems with RTS/CTS flow control to know when to send the text from one modem to another.

Because there are problems with sending and receiving text files, you have to implement a work-around. You can determine some scheme for handshaking between two terminals, but then you cannot use your application with any other communications application. You are limited to using your application on both ends. This is not the greatest solution, but with this control, there is not much choice. You may find other work-arounds for this problem for your application. If you don't create a work-around solution, when you instruct one terminal (such as Windows Terminal program) to send the text file, it sends it even before the receiving terminal is ready for it. On the other hand, if you send a text file using the Communications control to the Windows Terminal program, the text inside the file appears on-screen and is not written to the file itself.

The application in Chapter 26 gets around this by implementing its own handshaking "protocol." Therefore, if you want to use this application to send text files, you must use it at both ends because it knows the handshaking protocol you have used. If you implement a similar method, again, you must use your application at both ends.

The following describes how the application in Chapter 26 implements this handshaking. Even though you may devise a different method for your application, the best way to show one possible solution is to refer to Chapter 26. It uses code from the listing in the previous section, "The Mysterious OnComm Event."

The receiving of the file is left up to the OnComm event. It is actually quite simple. If the flag, Receiving%, is set to True, every character that would have been displayed on-screen is captured to a file. The way that the program knows when the file is finished is that the sending terminal sends a "FILE SENT" string at the end of the file. The OnComm event looks for this string for two reasons:

- So it knows where the end of the file is
- So it does not save the string "FILE SENT" to the file

The sending of the file simply reads every byte individually and sends it to the modem. Before sending any characters, it flags Receiving% so that the OnComm event can process the data correctly. The reason that the Windows Terminal program won't work is because it doesn't have a flag that works correctly. Following is a code fragment that sends the file one byte at a time.

```
Do Until EOF(hSend)

            'Read a byte of data
            Temp$ = Space$(BSize)
            Get hSend, , Temp$

            'Transmit the byte
            frmMain.msComm.Output = Temp$

    Loop
```

HANGING UP THE MODEM

It seems that hanging up the modem is one of the simplest things for a modem to do. Unfortunately, this is not true with this particular control. The VBTERM program that comes with Visual Basic samples simply toggles DTR to hang up the modem. This is supposed to work (in theory), but it doesn't. The most probable cause is the different types of modems on the market.

A more reliable way to hang up the modem is by using the following code fragment:

```
frmMain.msComm.Output = "+++ATH0"
frmMain.msComm.PortOpen = False
```

The first line puts the modem in Command mode and forces the modem to hang up. The second line closes the port. This method is more reliable than to toggle DTR, but it doesn't work 100 percent of the time.

The bottom line is that the Communications control that comes with Visual Basic version 3.0, Professional Edition, is adequate for some communications, but for a more robust communications control, you may want to consider purchasing an upgrade from Sheridan.

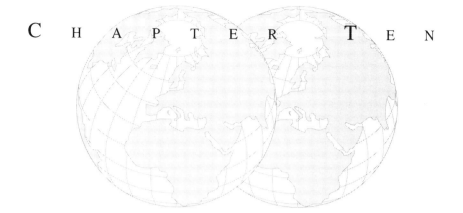

CREATING CONTEXT SENSITIVE HELP

THIS CHAPTER SHOWS HOW TO CREATE AND INCORPORATE CONTEXT SENSITIVE HELP INTO YOUR VISUAL BASIC APPLICATIONS. BY THE END OF THE CHAPTER, YOU WILL BE ABLE TO:

- ◆ PLAN HELP FILES

- ◆ COMPILE HELP FILES

- ◆ INCORPORATE HELP FILES INTO VISUAL BASIC APPLICATIONS

It is important to include context sensitive Help (sometimes called on-line Help) when distributing applications. Users of windows-based programs have come to expect that any topic they need to look up can be searched by using the Help file or files included with the application. A Help file can be created and used without context sensitivity. However, context sensitivity can be easily integrated into the Help file and provides for a much more professional application.

REM

In this intermediate-advanced level book, it is understood that you have at least a basic knowledge of the Visual Basic programming language. This chapter, however, will cover creating context sensitive Help from the beginning. This is because very few programmers actually incorporate Help into their programs. Of the many seasoned Visual Basic programmers I have interviewed, none of them knew how to create or incorporate Help into their applications.

WHAT IS CONTEXT SENSITIVE HELP?

Context sensitivity is a feature that allows users to invoke the Windows Help program (WINHELP.EXE) to display a Help topic based on where the cursor is located in the program. The user does not have to search through the Help system for the topic desired. Invoking Help is as simple as pressing the F1 key. This key is the convention accepted by Microsoft to invoke context sensitive Help from an application.

WINHELP.EXE is the Help engine program supplied by Microsoft and usually installed in the \WINDOWS directory (or whatever the default directory for Windows is) when windows is installed.

There are many aspects of a good Help file. They include:

◆ **Context sensitivity**

◆ **Static graphics**—Graphics such as icons and bitmaps that serve as simple pictures.

◆ **Hypergraphics**—Graphics that contain multiple *hotspots*. A hotspot is an area of text or graphics that is capable of invoking another topic.

◆ **Browsing capabilities**—Navigating through Help in a predefined sequence.

◆ **Glossary**—A summary of terms.

THE TOOLS FOR CREATING HELP FILES

There are two main tools necessary to create a Help file. One is the Help compiler. Microsoft includes a Help compiler, HC31.EXE, with Visual Basic 3.0, professional edition. It is used for creating Help in the Windows 3.1 environment. HC31.EXE is also found on the Microsoft Developer's Network CD.

The other tool necessary is a word processor that can display and save files in the RTF format. *RTF* stands for *Rich Text Format*. It is a format that saves the text along with all of the formatting, including fonts, colors, positions, special characters, and any special formatting such as hidden text. Microsoft Word version 6.0 is probably the best word processor for creating Help. It is also the word processor with which all of the examples in this chapter were created. Some of the screen shots shown in this chapter will look different if you are using a different word processor. You will be able to create the RTF files; however, you may need to refer to the editor's documentation to find out how to invoke certain options.

One other tool that can be useful, but not absolutely necessary, is the hotspot editor (SHED.EXE), which comes with Visual Basic 3.0, professional edition. This tool is very helpful in creating multiple hotspots on a single bitmap image.

Together, these tools can create or generate many files for use in the Help authoring process. Each file has a special file extension that the Help compiler expects. See Table 10.1 for a listing of the extensions to these files.

TABLE 10.1. FILE EXTENSIONS COMPRISING THE HELP AUTHORING PROCESS.

File Extension	Description	Used By
HLP	Compiled Help file	End user to invoke Help
HPJ	Help project file	Compiler as a directive of what to do
RTF	Rich Text Format Topic source file	Compiler to know what to compile
BMP, WMF	Graphics files	Compiler to include graphics
SHG	Hotspot editor file	Compiler to include hotspot graphics
ERR	Error log file	Developer to review errors generated by compiler

CREATING A HELP FILE

It is important to plan the Help file, just as it is important to plan the Visual Basic application. Generally, you don't just sit down and write the application as you go. It takes careful planning to determine your goals, objectives, audience, functions, features, and logic flow. A Help file is no different.

As with any application, a Help file will probably need to be revised or updated at a later point in time. This is not a problem if the Help file is well structured. A well-structured Help file is comprised of established naming conventions for variables, called *context strings*, and consistent logic flow. Functions and features can usually be added or deleted later if structured properly.

REM A context string is the way the Help compiler internally references one topic to another. This is *not* how Visual Basic refers to the topics. Visual Basic refers to the topics by mapping a variable of type long to the context string. For more information on mapping, refer to Step 11, "Linking Visual Basic and Context Sensitivity," later in this chapter.

STEP 1: PLANNING THE HELP FILE

The first step in planning is to develop a top-down design of the flow of your Help system. Top-down design refers to a hierarchical design diagram, beginning with the major components at the top and extending downward to the lower levels to show the different levels of hierarchy, organization, and flow. Figure 10.1 shows a sample top-down diagram of the Help file in Chapter 20. The major component at the top is Contents. The next level has four components, Introduction, Main Search, File Viewer, and Sound Files. It is not important that the wording of these blocks be identical to topics in the Help file itself. This diagram is for conceptual purposes only.

FIGURE 10.1.
Top-down design block diagram of the Help file in Chapter 20.

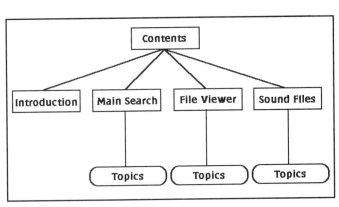

The next level shows the actual topics. Depending on the complexity of the Help file, you may need to break this down further to show the individual topics. In this case, the individual topics will refer to graphic hotspots (hypergraphics) created by SHED.EXE.

STEP 2: CREATING AN EDITOR OUTLINE

The next step is to create an outline using the editor or word processor that has RTF capabilities (see Introduction earlier in this chapter). To perform this step, it is necessary to think in terms of what the compiler expects. Every item you want to list in your Help file, whether it is its own entity or a pop-up definition, is considered to be a topic. Basically, each unique idea to be presented is a topic. You may want to display the name of the topic in uppercase letters, as shown in Figure 10.2.

FIGURE 10.2.
How the word processor looks after listing the initial topics and contents.

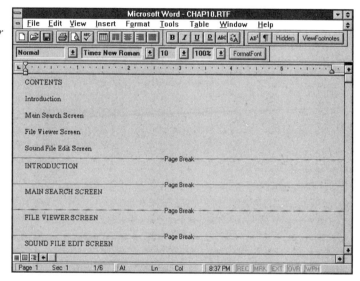

Using your editor or word processing program, preferably Microsoft Word, you can begin by listing the major topics that will be presented in the Help file. Use the top-down design diagram you created in Step 1 as a template. The compiler expects each topic to be separated by a page break. If you are using Microsoft Word, press the Ctrl and Enter keys to insert a page break. Otherwise, refer to your word processor's manual on how to insert a page break. After you list the major topics, make sure to save the file in the RTF format. Refer to Figure 10.2 to see how Microsoft Word looks after listing the major topics, contents. and inserting page breaks.

STEP 3: LISTING MAJOR FUNCTIONS OF TOPICS

Now that we have a base template to work from in the RTF file, it is a good idea to list each major function the topics are to discuss or use. Figure 10.3 is an example of the major functions that each topic can provide.

The reason for listing the major functions is simply to provide a way to make sure that all appropriate links are in place. These functions are not needed or used by the compiler; they are used solely as a means of keeping track of your topics. Figure 10.3 shows the major functions, such as Provide Jump. As you provide the links, remove the listings of the major functions you entered previously. Figure

10.6, presented later in the chapter, shows the major functions removed and replaced with the actual formatting to provide the function listed.

FIGURE 10.3.
Contents and Introduction screen after listing major functions.

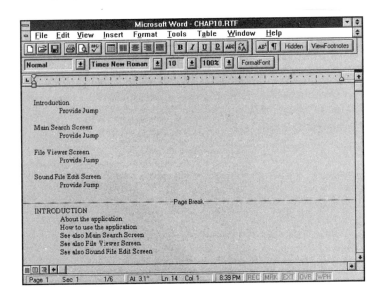

STEP 4: DEFINING CONTEXT STRINGS

A context string is a way for the Help file to reference one topic to another. Each topic must have its own unique context string. Make sure to use appropriate naming conventions for the context strings. This will make it easier to add topics later, if necessary.

The way to tell the compiler that you want to specify a context string (as well as other topic specifiers) is to add a footnote in the text. The footnote to use is based on the actual function desired. To assign a context string to a topic, use the # footnote. Table 10.2 shows the accepted footnotes for creating Help files. For example, if you want to specify that the topic title CONTENTS will have a context string of CONTENTS, you must first position the cursor in front of the word CONTENTS and select the Insert Footnote option on your word processor. Instead of using a standard footnote series of 1, 2, 3, and so on, insert a custom footnote by typing # in the Custom section of the dialog box.

TABLE 10.2. ACCEPTED TOPIC FOOTNOTES AND THEIR FUNCTIONS.

Footnote	Function
#	Assign a context string
$	Assign the name of the topic
K	Assign keywords for searching

Footnote	Function
!	Define a macro to run when entering a topic
+	Assign a browse sequence
*	Specify a build tag (not used often)
@	Author defined comment
Others	Specify alternate keywords

Figure 10.4 shows how you insert the custom footnote # in Microsoft Word version 6.0.

After the # footnote is entered, click the OK button and the footnote section will pop up. Simply type the name of the context string. This context string is now associated with the topic. Repeat this step for all topics. Figure 10.5 shows how the screen looks with the Footnote window open.

REM You may want to verify that each unique topic is separated by a page break.

FIGURE 10.4.
Inserting a footnote in Microsoft Word 6.0.

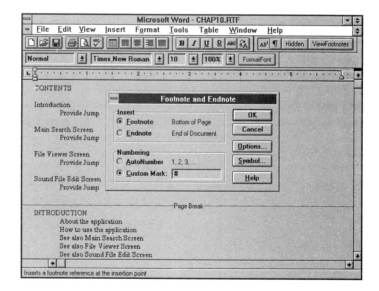

FIGURE 10.5.
Footnote window in
Microsoft Word 6.0.

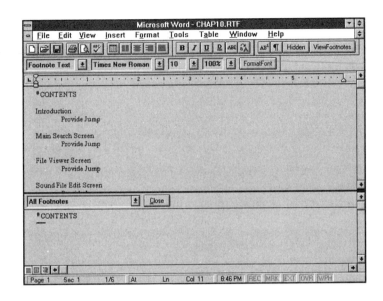

STEP 5: LINKING MAJOR TOPICS

Now that you have actually defined the context strings, the next step is to decide how these context strings will fit together. How can you navigate from one topic to another? There are two major ways of linking topics in a Help file. They are called *jumps* and *pop-ups*. A jump is a link that tells the Help engine to jump immediately from one topic (context string) to another. A jump in Help terms is equivalent to a Visual Basic GOTO statement. It is a method that specifies to go to a specific topic immediately and unconditionally.

The way to specify to the compiler that you want to use functions such as jumps and pop-ups is to format your text using predefined formatting codes. Table 10.3 shows the accepted formatting codes. If you want to indicate that the text Introduction is to jump to the context string INTRODUCTION, for example, this tells the compiler to automatically change the cursor to the hand pointing upward when the cursor is dragged over the text. It also tells the Help compiler to make the text green in color, which is the familiar convention.

TABLE 10.3. ACCEPTED FORMATTING CODES.

Format	Function
Double underline	Jump
Single underline	Pop-up
Hidden text	Specifies where to jump or pop-up

The formatting codes tell the compiler what to do, such as jump or pop-up, but you still need to specify which context string to jump or pop-up to. As mentioned earlier, the Help system navigates by internally using context strings. Because you want to specify that the text Introduction will jump to the context string INTRODUCTION, you must position the cursor after the jump text (with the double underline), and type the context string associated with the jump or pop-up desired.

One final step to associate the jump or pop-up is to actually hide the text. Your RTF word processor has an option to hide the text. In Microsoft Word, you must highlight the text to be hidden, choose Format Character, and select the hidden check box. Once hidden, you will not be able to see your text unless you select the RTF editor's Show/Hide feature. You will notice many special characters after you select the Show option. Hidden text in RTF format is signified by a broken underline. Figure 10.6 shows an example of these special characters. It is important to notice the assigning of the context strings because if you print this file, the strings won't be printed because they are hidden.

FIGURE 10.6.
Displaying hidden text within Microsoft Word 6.0.

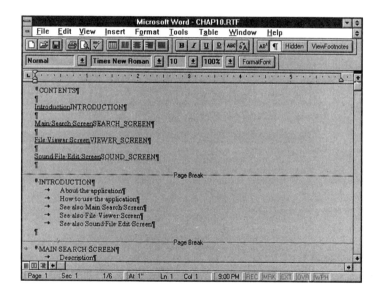

STEP 6: COMPILING THE HELP FILE

If you followed the previous instructions, assigning context strings for all topics, indicating jumps and pop-ups between topics, and associating those jumps or pop-ups with context strings, you are ready to compile the Help file to see if it works so far.

In order to compile, however, you must build a makefile, which tells the compiler actually what to compile. The makefile has the extension of HPJ. The makefile is in a standard text format, not RTF, but saved with the extension HPJ. Inside the makefile, you must instruct the compiler where to find files, options available during the compilation, and many other possibilities. To list these instructions, you choose from certain predefined sections (similar to the Windows WIN.INI file sections). The possible sections are listed in Table 10.4

TABLE 10.4. POSSIBLE SECTIONS IN THE HELP MAKEFILE, *.HPJ.

Section	Description	Required
[Options]	Specifies options used for the compiler. There are many possible options for the compiler. For more information, consult the Help compiler Guide in the Microsoft Visual Basic Professional Features Book 1.	No, but if used, must be first in file
[Files]	Specifies the files to be "included" in the compilation.	Yes
[BuildTags]	Specifies topics to share or exclude when sharing files.	No
[Config]	Specifies menus and buttons that can be included in the Help file.	No
[Bitmaps]	Specifies the bitmaps, metafiles, and hotspot graphics to be used in the Help File. This section is only required if there are files included in the Help file and the path is not specified in the [Options] section.	Only if files are included in [Files] and path not specified in [Options]
[Map]	Specifies the context string to context ID mapping.	Only for context sensitive Help
[Alias]	Specifies multiple context strings for a topic.	No
[Windows]	Specifies the characteristics of the windows used in the Help file.	Only if more than one window is used
[Baggage]	Specifies the files that are used in the Help system with their own file system.	No

Even though there are a lot of options possible with the makefile, you will find that you typically use the same makefiles over and over—just as you probably do for Visual Basic *.MAK files, and slightly modify them for a new project.

 After you create your first makefile, use it as a template for future makefiles. A few modifications to the original should be all that is required.

To compile the Help file so far, you only need to add two lines to the makefile, in this case, called CHAP20.HPJ. Create the makefile with the extension HPJ and add these lines:

```
[Files]
CHAP20.RTF
```

To invoke the Help compiler, it is suggested to create a PIF file, since the HC31.EXE Help compiler is DOS based. Use the PIF file editor, usually located in the accessories group.

You can actually test the Help file if you successfully compiled one. To test it, you can either add an icon to the program manager screen or run it directly by typing `WINHELP` plus the name of your Help file. For example, `WINHELP CHAP20.HPJ`.

STEP 7: ADDING OTHER NECESSARY SPECIFIERS

If you compiled and ran a Help file after only using Steps 1 through 6, you may notice that although the Help file works, the Bookmark function doesn't list topics, and the History function only shows `<< untitled topic >>`.

 The Bookmark and History functions are included automatically. You do not need to specify anything in the makefile or RTF file to include these functions.

These functions don't list topics because although you have specified the context string by using the # footnote, the Help system doesn't know the name of the topic yet. Simply typing text at the top of the screen doesn't specify the name of the topic. To specify the topic name, you must insert the $ footnote, exactly like you did in Step 4. This footnote tells the compiler what the topic name is. If this is done for all topics, the Bookmark function and History function will work.

The Search function also doesn't work yet. To make the Search function work, you need to specify keywords that will be associated to this topic. For example, if you have a topic called `How To Open Files`, you may want to make the keywords `Opening Files`, `Open`, `How To`, and `Files`, `Opening`. You can specify all of these keywords on one line, again by using a footnote. The footnote for keywords is the `K` symbol. You insert the `K` footnote and type the string of keywords, separated by a semicolon. For a listing of all accepted footnotes, refer to Table 10.2.

STEP 8: INCLUDING GRAPHICS

Including graphics is very important to the Help file. Graphics convey a lot of information at a glance. They also give the user a real example of what he/she will be looking at, instead of just text. Graphics can be included in the form of static graphics or hypergraphics. Static graphics are bitmaps which have no hotspot areas. It will not be linked to any other topic. Hypergraphics are bitmaps with one or more hotspots, which are able to link to other topics.

If you wish to include either type of graphic, entering it into the RTF file is done the same way. The only difference is that with a hypergraphic, the hotspot editor, SHED.EXE must be used. If it is used, the graphic included will have a file extension of SHG. Otherwise static graphics can have an extension of BMP or WMF.

The inclusion of either type of file is done by inserting the following syntax in the RTF file, at the location in which the graphic is to be placed:

```
{bmX Graphic}
```

where "X" can be l (left justified), c (centered), or r (right justified), and "Graphic" is the actual name of the graphic, including extension. The first three characters must be in lowercase.

 If you do not specify the path with the bitmap name, you must include the path in the BMROOT variable of the [OPTIONS] section.

For example, if you want to include the file SAMPLE.BMP in the CONTENTS screen and center the graphic, place the word processor's insertion point exactly where the bitmap is to appear and type {bmc SAMPLE.BMP}. Figure 10.7 shows the hypergraphic file SCREEN2.SHG, which is from Chapter 20's MDI file viewer screen. This file is really nothing more than a bitmap that has been encoded by SHED.EXE to include hotspots.

Before you can compile the new file, including hypergraphics, you must make sure that you create the topics that the hypergraphic will reference. If you don't, you will get a compile error.

You can also directly place bitmaps into Help files. To do this, select the Insert Picture option on your word processor. The Help compiler automatically includes the bitmap when compiling. Be aware that the limitation on the size of the bitmap is 64K.

142

FIGURE 10.7.
Creating hypergraphics.

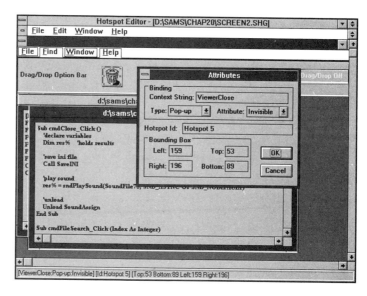

STEP 9: INCLUDING BROWSING

Browsing is the capability to navigate by using the << and >> keys. Browsing simply moves between topics in a specified sequence. There are two steps to include browsing into the Help file. The first step is to specify the sequence in which the browsing will occur. A browsing sequence is specified by using the + footnote (refer to Step 4 to insert a footnote) and using the following syntax:

```
+ [sequence name:]sequence #
```

The sequence name is optional. It allows you to browse through only one or more specified topics. If the sequence name is omitted, browsing will occur in all topics, according to the sequence number specified.

The second step is to tell the compiler to include the Browse button on the Help command line. To instruct the compiler to do this, you need to add a section to the makefile, called [CONFIG], and add the predefined macro BrowseButtons(). Include these lines in the makefile:

```
[CONFIG]
BrowseButtons()
```

STEP 10: INCLUDING A GLOSSARY

Including a glossary is really no different than creating a topic called GLOSSARY and providing pop-up hotspots under the topic. The main difference is how you invoke the glossary.

Since the Help system allows for many standard and custom macros, the addition of this functionality is very easy. All you have to do is add a button on the toolbar labeled Glossary, and provide functionality to jump to the GLOSSARY topic. To do this, add a line in the [CONFIG] section of the HPJ file for this button. Add this line:

```
CreateButton("btn_glossary","&Glossary","JumpId(`',`GLOSSARY')")
```

CreateButton is a standard macro that allows for the addition of a button on the toolbar. It takes three arguments. All three arguments must be in quotations, regardless of whether or not the argument calls another macro or function.

The first argument is the name of the button. The second is the button label. The & symbol specifies that the G in Glossary will be underlined for Alt+G access, just as in Visual Basic. The third argument is the macro to be executed when the button is clicked. The macro you need to execute doesn't exist yet. The functionality you want to invoke is to jump to the context string GLOSSARY. To do this, use the JumpId standard macro.

The JumpId macro accepts two arguments. The first is the Help file to find the context string. The empty quotes signify that you will use the current Help file. The second argument is the actual context string defined in the Help file.

 Because the argument in the CreateButton macro must be in quotes, the JumpId macro must have its arguments in single quotes. The compiler will generate a syntax error if the opening quote is a ' instead of a `.

STEP 11: LINKING VISUAL BASIC AND CONTEXT SENSITIVITY

To link Visual Basic to the Help file, you must map context strings (topic) to context IDs. You don't actually have to map every context string—only the ones that will provide context sensitive Help in Visual Basic.

To tell the compiler how you would like to map the context strings to the context IDs, you need to add a section in the makefile called [MAP]. You then list each context string using the following syntax:

```
Context String [space] Context ID
```

For example, suppose that you want to add context sensitive Help to Visual Basic for the Contents Screen. You can add the following lines of code to your makefile:

```
[MAP]
CONTENTS 1
```

You must supply every control that will be context sensitive to its own representative constant. If the constant is incorrect, the wrong topic could be invoked.

Now that the Help file is structured to react to context sensitive Help, you still need to instruct Visual Basic on how to address these Context IDs. There are two things that need to be done in Visual Basic: identifying the actual Help file and identifying the Context ID.

Identifying the Help file in Visual Basic is simple. You add one line of code to your application, in the `form_load()` event, with the following syntax:

```
App.HelpFile = help file
```

where *help file* is the name of your Help file. For example, for the program in Chapter 20, you add the following:

```
App.HelpFile = "CHAP20.HLP"
```

This assigns the Help file to the `App` object and stays in effect until changed or the application is ended.

To specify the Context ID, simply specify the Context ID value for each context string in the `[MAP]` section of the makefile in the `HelpContextID` property. The following Visual Basic controls accept the `HelpContextID` property:

- Form
- MDI Form
- Check Box
- Combo Box
- Command Button
- Directory List Box
- Drive List Box
- File List Box
- Grid
- Horizontal Scroll Bar
- Vertical Scroll Bar
- List Box
- Menu Items
- OLE Control
- Option Button
- Picture Box
- Text Box

Assuming the `HelpContextID` has been assigned to the Visual Basic controls and the Help file has been specified, the user can invoke the Help file simply by pressing the F1 key. The control that has the focus will send the command to WINHELP.EXE (automatically invoked) and the `HelpContextID` used will be the one for that particular control.

CLOSING REMARKS

Creating Help can be simple or complex. The more complex, the more intuitive. Extremely elaborate Help files can be created using the Help compiler. Very complex Help files are beyond the scope of this book, however. This chapter is designed to present enough information for you to begin with your own Help files.

Help file creation really is its own language. The most comprehensive guide available on creating Help is located on the Microsoft Developer's network CD. Unfortunately, it is not available from Microsoft or the Microsoft Press. It is only available from the CD. It is called the *Microsoft Windows Help Authoring Guide*, and printing it requires approximately 750 pages.

After having gone through the drudgery of creating your own Help file, there is light at the end of the tunnel. There are many commercial and shareware programs available for assisting in creating Help. One of Microsoft's unsupported tools is the Help Author. It is on the Microsoft Developer's Network CD. There are also two shareware programs included on the CD accompanying this book, each in its own subdirectory under the HELP subdirectory. They are Visual Help and VB AHA. Each has its own pros and cons, but are very useful. If nothing else, allow these tools to create a template RTF file for you, and add the functions that may be missing. It saves a lot of time!

You can see a fully implemented Help system with the CHAP20.HLP file contained on the CD accompanying this book in the CHAP20 subdirectory. There are other third-party Help creation tools available, such as RoboHELP. RoboHELP takes the drudgery out of creating a help file from scratch. For more information, call 1-800-677-4946.

AUDIO

THERE ARE REALLY TWO TYPES OF AUDIO THAT CAN BE PLAYED THROUGH THE PC. THEY ARE *SOUND FILES* AND *FREQUENCY GENERATION*. THIS CHAPTER FOCUSES ON FREQUENCY GENERATION, WHICH IS PLAYING A SPECI-FIED SOUND FREQUENCY FOR A SPECIFIED DURATION. THIS TECHNIQUE ALLOWS YOU TO PLAY MUSIC OR TO ALERT THE USER THAT SOME ACTION HAS OC-CURRED THROUGH THE PC SPEAKER.

Sound files are covered in depth in Chapter 12, "Multimedia."

PLAYING SOUNDS AT A CERTAIN FREQUENCY

Playing a sound at a certain frequency is sometimes necessary in Visual Basic. However, Visual Basic does not provide a way to do this. It does provide a way to play a sound file, but not individual frequencies that can be programmed into your code. An example of the necessity to generate a frequency in code is presented in Chapter 25, "Dynamic Hotspot Application." The application plays an increasingly higher note directly proportional with the index of the hotspot clicked. This is also very useful in game programming.

 See Chapter 25, "Dynamic Hotspot Application," for the example mentioned in the previous paragraph.

There is very little information about how to play a specified frequency through the PC in Windows. There are some Windows API functions that can be used to allow for direct support of this. Although the uses of these API functions are shown in some other books, Microsoft says that the API functions are obsolete and to use Multimedia functions instead. These functions are presented in Table 11.1.

 Because Microsoft states that the sound frequency API functions are obsolete, you should not use them. This includes all the functions listed in Table 11.1.

TABLE 11.1. WINDOWS API FUNCTIONS THAT SUPPORT SOUND.

Function	Purpose
SetSoundNoise()	Generates a noise to be played by the speaker
SetVoiceAccent()	Sets the tempo, volume, and pitch for a noise
SetVoiceNote()	Adds a note into the voice queue
SetVoiceQueueSize()	Sets the size of the voice queue
SetVoiceSound()	Adds a sound into the voice queue
SetVoiceThreshold()	Sets the threshold level for the voice queue
StartSound()	Starts playing the voice queue
StopSound()	Stops the voice queue
SyncAllVoices()	Used to sync voices (channels). This function has no effect for the PC speaker
WaitSoundState()	Determines state when control will return to the program after playing a sound

There is virtually nothing in the Windows SDK that shows how to use the multimedia functions that are supposed to replace these obsolete API functions. These API functions serve a great purpose: they allow for the playback of a sound through the PC speaker. The multimedia functions are based on sound being played through a sound card.

Although many people, by now, have a sound card, it is not applicable for some situations. Business environments very rarely have a sound card in their PCs. It is helpful, however, to play a sound through the PC speaker. This presents a problem now that the API functions listed in Table 11.1 are obsolete. If you want to play sound files thorough the PC speaker, there are speaker drivers available that allow you to re-route the sounds meant to be played on a sound card to your PC speaker.

AN ALTERNATIVE TO THE API FUNCTIONS

The API functions listed in Table 11.1 do not always work. Fortunately, there is a DLL on the CD accompanying this book, INOUT.DLL, which plays sound at a specified frequency through the PC speaker. It is in the RESOURCE subdirectory.

 It should be noted that if you do not need to play sounds at specified frequencies but only one frequency, you can use the Visual Basic Beep statement instead.

The file, INOUT.DLL, contains one function and one subroutine. Before you can play a sound using the routines inside the INOUT.DLL file, you must declare the functions in the declarations section of either a form or module. You must declare them like this:

```
Declare Function INP Lib "INOUT.DLL" (ByVal address&) As Integer
Declare Sub OUT Lib "INOUT.DLL" (ByVal address&, ByVal value%)
```

The INP() function is used to return an 8-bit byte from a PC port. Because this function can be used to return a byte from any PC port, we must specify the port of the PC speaker. The syntax for this function is as follows:

```
result% = INP(port)
```

where *port* is the number of the port to retrieve, and *result%* is the result of the function.

The OUT() subroutine is used to send a byte of data to a PC port:

```
OUT(port, data)
```

where *port* is the number of the port to send data to and *data* is the data to send to the port.

The trick to using these two routines inside the INOUT.DLL file is to know what data to send to which port. The steps to take to play a single sound are the following:

- ◆ Calculate the number of clock ticks needed to play a sound at a certain frequency.
- ◆ Send the number of clock ticks to the PC speaker (this is the data to send).

◆ Turn on the speaker.

◆ Loop for a certain duration. The speaker will still be playing at a specified frequency.

◆ Turn off the speaker.

As an example, consider the code from a routine in Chapter 25, "Dynamic Hotspot Application," called MakeSound(), which is responsible for playing a sound through the PC speaker:

REM If a sound card is installed, the sounds will also be played through the sound card as well as the PC speaker.

 The MakeSound() routine is a part of the "Dynamic Hotspot Application" from Chapter 25.

```
1:    Sub MakeSound (Frequency&)
2:
3:    'declare variables
4:    Dim ClockTicks%      'number of clock ticks
5:    Dim loopcount%       'loop counting variable
6:
7:    'calculate clicks -> Clock/sound frequency = clock ticks
8:    ClockTicks% = CInt(1193280 \ Frequency&)
9:
10:   'prepare for data
11:   OUT 67, 182
12:
13:   ' Send data
14:   OUT 66, ClockTicks% And &HFF
15:   OUT 66, ClockTicks% \ 256
16:
17:   'turn speaker on
18:   OUT 97, INP(97) Or &H3
19:
20:   'make sure sound plays for a period of time
21:   For loopcount% = 1 To 200
22:       DoEvents
23:   Next loopcount%
24:
25:   ' Turn speaker off
26:   OUT 97, INP(97) And &HFC
27:   End Sub
```

REM The line numbers on the left of the code are used for instructional purposes. They are not part of the code.

None of the numbers used as parameters in these procedures should be changed. If they are changed, the sound functions won't work. The numbers address specific hardware addresses and are a given. The only two things you should change in your application are the frequency and duration that the frequency plays. The frequency is passed into the MakeSound() function, and the duration is specified by the length of the loop mentioned previously.

The first step, as in line 8, is to calculate the number of clock ticks it takes to play a specified frequency. This is done by taking a constant value, 1193280, and dividing it by the frequency desired. Then it is converted into an integer. This is the number of clock ticks necessary to play the specified frequency.

The next step is to prepare the port to receive data. You do this with line 11. After that, lines 14 and 15 are used to tell the port which frequency to play.

Line 18 turns the speaker on. It plays the specified frequency until you explicitly turn it off with line number 26.

The routine uses preset durations to play the sound by playing a sound during the time it takes to cycle through a loop. This loop is shown in lines 21, 22, and 23. You can alter the value of the loop in your program to adjust the duration to your needs. The preceding example loops from 1 to 200, which is about $1/4$ of a second on a 486 processor machine at a clock speed of 50 Mhz. This number is going to vary, depending on the speed of your machine.

REM A more accurate way to perform the timing duration of a musical note would be to use the Visual Basic Timer control. If your application requires more accurate methods, you may want to consider this.

The frequency you want to play corresponds to a certain musical note. Table 11.2 lists the correlation between musical notes and frequencies.

TABLE 11.2. MUSICAL NOTE TO FREQUENCY CONVERSION.

Note	Octave (Range Hz)	Frequency (Hz)
A	1 (16 to 32)	27.5
B	1 (16 to 32)	30.87
C	2 (33 to 64)	32.70
D	2 (33 to 64)	36.71
E	2 (33 to 64)	41.20

continues

TABLE 11.2. CONTINUED

Note	Octave (Range Hz)	Frequency (Hz)
F	2 (33 to 64)	43.65
G	2 (33 to 64)	49.00
A	2 (33 to 64)	55.00
B	2 (33 to 64)	61.74
C	3 (65 to 128)	65.41
D	3 (65 to 128)	73.42
E	3 (65 to 128)	82.41
F	3 (65 to 128)	87.31
G	3 (65 to 128)	98.00
A	3 (65 to 128)	110.00
B	3 (65 to 128)	123.47
C	4 (129 to 256)	130.81
D	4 (129 to 256)	146.83
E	4 (129 to 256)	164.81
F	4 (129 to 256)	174.61
G	4 (129 to 256)	196.00
A	4 (129 to 256)	220.00
B	4 (129 to 256)	246.94
C	5 (257 to 512)	261.63
D	5 (257 to 512)	293.66
E	5 (257 to 512)	329.63
F	5 (257 to 512)	349.23
G	5 (257 to 512)	392.00
A	5 (257 to 512)	440.00
B	5 (257 to 512)	493.88
MIDDLE C	6 (513 to 1024)	523.25
D	6 (513 to 1024)	587.33
E	6 (513 to 1024)	659.26
F	6 (513 to 1024)	698.46
G	6 (513 to 1024)	783.99

Note	Octave (Range Hz)	Frequency (Hz)
A	6 (513 to 1024)	880.00
B	6 (513 to 1024)	987.77
C	7 (1025 to 2048)	1046.50
D	7 (1025 to 2048)	1174.70
E	7 (1025 to 2048)	1318.50
F	7 (1025 to 2048)	1396.90
G	7 (1025 to 2048)	1568.00
A	7 (1025 to 2048)	1760.00
B	7 (1025 to 2048)	1975.50
C	8 (2049 to 4096)	2023.00
D	8 (2049 to 4096)	2349.30
E	8 (2049 to 4096)	2637.00
F	8 (2049 to 4096)	2973.80
G	8 (2049 to 4096)	3136.00
A	8 (2049 to 4096)	3520.00
B	8 (2049 to 4096)	3951.10
C	9 (4097 to 8192)	4186.00

As an example, here is how you would play an "A" in the fifth octave using the `MakeSound()` routine:

```
Call MakeSound(440)
```

This line of code calls the `MakeSound()` routine and passes it a value of 440. If you look up the value of 440 in Table 11.2, you see that this corresponds to the musical note "A" in the fifth octave. The duration is approximately $1/4$ of a second, due to the loop of 1 to 200. You can change this if you wish, or even change the number of parameters passed into the routine. For example, you may want to declare the routine like this:

```
Sub MakeSound (Frequency&, Duration%)
```

and then pass a value like this:

```
Call MakeSound(440,200)
```

For those who are not musical experts, an *octave* is the interval of eight musical notes between two musical tones.

Playing sound at a specified frequency can be an important way for your applications to give feedback to your users. For example, if you want to write an application that uses sounds you would find in a game program, you can do something like this:

```
MakeSound 440
MakeSound 493.88
MakeSound 523.25
MakeSound 587.33
MakeSound 659.26
MakeSound 698.46
MakeSound 783.99
MakeSound 880
```

This simply plays a series of eight musical notes (octave) between A and A, centered around middle C. The notes are played so quickly that it creates an audio effect similar to those used in games.

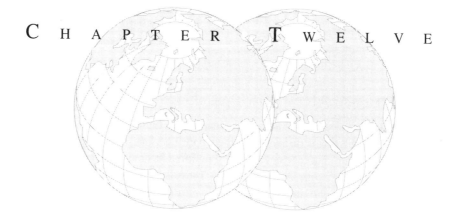

CHAPTER TWELVE

MULTIMEDIA

MULTIMEDIA IS A FAIRLY NEW TECHNOLOGY THAT ALLOWS THE PC TO INTERACT WITH MANY DIFFERENT TYPES OF MEDIA. THIS MEDIA CAN BE A CD-ROM, AUDIO, VIDEO, A COMBINATION OF THESE, OR EVEN SPECIALIZED MEDIA CREATED BY THIRD-PARTY VENDORS. THIS TECHNOLOGY CAN GREATLY ENHANCE AN INDIVIDUAL'S PRODUCTIVITY, ENJOYMENT, AND KNOWLEDGE.

THE KEY TO USING THIS TECHNOLOGY IN WINDOWS IS THROUGH MICROSOFT MULTIMEDIA EXTENSIONS. IT IS AN EXTENSION TO THE OPERATING SYSTEM THAT ALLOWS FOR MULTIMEDIA. IT IS A FILE CALLED MSCDEX.EXE AND MUST BE LOADED IN THE AUTOEXEC.BAT FILE.

MULTIMEDIA AND VISUAL BASIC

With the multimedia extensions loaded, you can access multimedia devices in one of two ways in Visual Basic. The first is through Windows API functions. There are many functions in the Windows API that allow access and control of multimedia devices. The other way is through the *MCI* control that comes with Visual Basic. MCI stands for *Multimedia Control Interface*. This control is really a nice interface to the Windows API functions. You access properties of the control, and the control makes the appropriate Windows API function calls. The MCI control is a very good means to access the API functions, and as such, is the main focus of this chapter.

 If you want to experiment with the API functions, refer to Chapter 3, "Calling Windows APIs and DLLs," for more information.

THE MCI CONTROL

The MCI control enables you to click on the buttons on the control itself (if it is visible and enabled) or to hide the control and access it only in code, allowing you to design a custom interface.

 The applications in Chapter 27, "CD Player Application," and Chapter 32, "Multimedia Player Application," both use the buttons on the control itself.

ABOUT THE MCI CONTROL

The MCI control is used as the interface to the Microsoft Multimedia Extensions (MSCDEX). It has many properties that greatly simplify using multimedia. These properties are listed in Table 12.1.

TABLE 12.1. MCI CONTROL UNIQUE PROPERTIES.

Property	DataType	Use
AutoEnable	Integer(Boolean)	Automatically enabling appropriate buttons when CD or file is ready to play
BackEnabled	Integer(Boolean)	Enabling the appropriate button
EjectEnabled	Integer(Boolean)	Enabling the appropriate button
NextEnabled	Integer(Boolean)	Enabling the appropriate button
PauseEnabled	Integer(Boolean)	Enabling the appropriate button
PlayEnabled	Integer(Boolean)	Enabling the appropriate button

Property	DataType	Use
PrevEnabled	Integer(Boolean)	Enabling the appropriate button
RecordEnabled	Integer(Boolean)	Enabling the appropriate button
StepEnabled	Integer(Boolean)	Enabling the appropriate button
StopEnabled	Integer(Boolean)	Enabling the appropriate button
BackVisible	Integer(Boolean)	Making the appropriate button visible
EjectVisible	Integer(Boolean)	Making the appropriate button visible
NextVisible	Integer(Boolean)	Making the appropriate button visible
PauseVisible	Integer(Boolean)	Making the appropriate button visible
PlayVisible	Integer(Boolean)	Making the appropriate button visible
PrevVisible	Integer(Boolean)	Making the appropriate button visible
RecordVisible	Integer(Boolean)	Making the appropriate button visible
StepVisible	Integer(Boolean)	Making the appropriate button visible
StopVisible	Integer(Boolean)	Making the appropriate button visible
CanEject	Integer(Boolean)	True if Media type can eject
CanPlay	Integer(Boolean)	True if Media type can play
CanRecord	Integer(Boolean)	True if Media type can record
CanStep	Integer(Boolean)	True if Media type can step one frame at a time
Command	String	Specifies which MCI command to execute
DeviceID	Integer	ID of the currently open device
DeviceType	String	Specifies type of media to play
Error	Integer	Last error from MCI control
ErrorMessage	String	Message of last error from MCI control
FileName	String	File Name to play if media is file based
Frames	Long	Number of frames for STEP command to skip
From	Long	Specifies starting point if playing sequence
hWndDisplay	Integer	Handle of display in Visual Basic for Video files
Length	Long	Length of media
Mode	Long	Mode of open MCI device
Notify	Integer(Boolean)	True if MCI uses notification services

continues   157

TABLE 12.1. CONTINUED

Property	DataType	Use
NotifyMessage	String	Message from the Done event if Notify is true
NotifyValue	Integer	Value of result from last MCI command
Orientation	Integer	0 for horizontal, 1 for vertical
Position	Long	Current position of MCI control
RecordMode	Integer	0-Insert, 1-Overwrite
Shareable	Integer(Boolean)	True if another program can share MCI device
Silent	Integer(Boolean)	True if sound is off
Start	Long	Starting position of current media
TimeFormat	Long	Time reporting format
To	Long	Specifies ending point if playing sequence
Track	Long	Track for use with TrackLength and TrackPosition
TrackLength	Long	Length of track in Track property
TrackPosition	Long	Position of track in Track property
Tracks	Long	Number of tracks in media
UpdateInterval	Integer	Number of milliseconds between StatusUpdate events
UsesWindows	Integer(Boolean)	True if media type uses a window for output
Wait	Integer(Boolean)	True if MCI completes command before returning control

One nice thing about the control is that it automatically detects when a CD-ROM is in the drive and enables the appropriate buttons, if the AutoEnable property is set to True. The individual elements of the control (such as play, stop, and so on) are automatically enabled based on additional properties you can set. For example, if you set the PlayEnabled property to False, then even if the CD-ROM is in the drive, the play button is not enabled. You can even hide buttons that you don't ever want to be enabled. For example, the Forward and Back buttons can be hidden, if desired. You do this by setting the appropriate Visible property to False. For example, if you didn't want the Back button to be visible, you can set the property with the code

```
control.BackVisible = False
```

where *control* is the name of your control.

Refer to Table 12.1 for a listing of all of the properties that are unique to the MCI control. It does not list the properties that are common, such as Name, Height, and so on.

The key to effectively using the MCI control is to learn how the StatusUpdate event works. The StatusUpdate event is generated by the control itself. The event is generated at a certain interval that you can set. You set this interval with the UpdateInterval property. As you would with the Visual Basic Timer control, you set the interval for the number of milliseconds before the next event is generated. For example, if you want the event to be generated every second, you set the UpdateInterval property to 1000.

The reason you need to understand the UpdateInterval property is because it is the way you receive information from the control to notify the user of certain things. For example, suppose that you want to provide a visual feedback to the user about how many seconds have passed since a musical CD has been playing. You update the display on your screen by using the StatusUpdate event. If you set the UpdateInterval property to 1000, as long as you put code in the StatusUpdate event to find out what the current playing time is, you know that every second your display will be updated.

 The application in Chapter 27, "CD Player Application," uses the StatusUpdate event to update the display for the user in the manner described in the previous paragraph. Refer to the application in Chapter 27, to see how the StatusUpdate event works.

USING THE MCI CONTROL

After loading the MCI control into your project, you place it on your form and size it according to your needs. Because the MCI control can access many different types of media, you must tell the control which type to use. This is done by accessing the DeviceType property. The DeviceType property accepts a string data type. The possible DeviceTypes are listed in Table 12.2.

TABLE 12.2. POSSIBLE VALUES FOR THE DeviceType PROPERTY.

String	Media Type
"AVIVideo"	Audio Video Interleave (AVI) file
"CDAudio"	CD audio from a musical CD
"DAT"	Digital Audio Tape
"MMMovie"	Multimedia Movie file
"Other"	Undefined type
"Scanner"	Scanner

TABLE 12.2. CONTINUED

String	Media Type
"Sequencer"	Musical Instrument Digital Interface File (MIDI) file
"VCR"	Video Cassette Recorder (VCR)
"VideoDisc"	Video Disc
"WaveAudio"	WAV audio file

To ensure that these device types work, make sure to have them listed in the SYSTEM.INI file under the [MCI] section. Listing them in the SYSTEM.INI file tells the MCI control through MSCDEX which driver to use for the specific media type. Make sure these device types point to a valid driver.

 It is possible for the MCI control not to become enabled, without any error notification, just because of the driver specified being physically deleted from the disk.

Make sure the [MCI] section in the SYSTEM.INI file looks similar to this:

```
[MCI]
CDAUDIO=MCICDA.DRV
SEQUENCER=MCISEQ.DRV
WAVEAUDIO=MCIWAVE.DRV
```

 It is possible to use a media type not listed in Table 12.2 as long as it points to a valid driver in the SYSTEM.INI file.

After you select the DeviceType, you must then open the device. Opening the device is necessary to tell the device to be ready to begin accessing the type of media specified. This is done by using the OPEN command, which has this syntax:

```
control.Command = "Open"
```

where control is the name of your MCI control.

Typically, the OPEN command is used in conjunction with other properties. For example, consider these lines of code, using an MCI control with the Name property set to mmControl:

```
mmControl.Notify = False
mmControl.Wait = True
mmControl.Shareable = False
mmControl.Command = "Open"
```

If the Notify property is set to True, the control generates the Done event after a command is issued. In most applications, the Notify property will not be used, so here it is set to False. The Wait property is used to determine how your program resumes control after accessing the multimedia device. If the Wait property is set to False, the MCI control will *not* wait for the specified media to finish playing before returning control. If the Wait property is set to True, program control will not return to your program until the specified media is finished playing. The Shareable property determines if another program will be allowed to share the MCI device. This property is set to True if it is allowed and False if it is not. The values of these properties may change in your programs, but it is important to know that if you are going to set these values, they must be set before issuing the OPEN command.

The preceding steps are true for all types of media. The next step depends on a specific type of media. It is used to assign the file name. It is dependent because not all media types accept a file name. For example, if you are playing an audio CD, it does not have a file name. If you are playing a WAV audio file, it has a file name. Otherwise, the MCI control will not know which file to play. If you want to set the file name, use the FileName property. You set this property with this syntax:

```
control.FileName = fname
```

where *control* is the name of your MCI control, and *fname* is the string containing the file name to play.

After you set the file name, if appropriate, you are ready to play. You start playing the desired media type by issuing the PLAY command. Use this syntax:

```
control.Command = "Play"
```

where *control* is the name of your MCI control.

From this point, you can issue any other commands at your leisure, such as PAUSE and STOP. To issue these commands, use the syntax listed earlier with the PLAY command. For a listing of possible commands, refer to Table 12.1.

When you are finished playing the desired media type, you must close the device. You close the device for the same reason you must close a Visual Basic file after it is opened—to conserve resources. You can close the device by issuing the CLOSE command by using the preceding syntax for the PLAY command.

AUDIO CDS

Audio CD is probably one of the most common uses of multimedia. It allows you to work on your PC while you listen to music from your CD-ROM. All CD-ROMs have the capability to play music, providing that you have a working audio card in your PC connected to speakers or stereo.

You can write a program to control the audio CD by using Visual Basic and the MCI control. It employs the methods described earlier, but there are some additional concerns when writing with the user interface for your program. If you are only going to allow the user to play, stop, and skip through the tracks, the MCI control does this automatically by issuing the appropriate commands.

Refer to the previous discussion and Table 12.1 for more information about how to do this. However, if you are going to provide any visual feedback to the user (as a good application does), this becomes a little more difficult.

The StatusUpdate event is generated at an interval set with the UpdateInterval property. When this event is generated, you must query the control to find out some information about the position of the CD. For example, you have to find out how far along the CD is inside the current track and how much time has elapsed since the beginning of the disc.

REM The position of the CD refers to the amount of time that has elapsed in the CD. The position is measured with respect to time, not distance; and it is not the physical position of the CD. The position reports time not in a HH:MM:SS format, but in a packed integer format. Refer to following section "Unpacking a Packed Integer," for more information.

You can determine the track time of any track, not necessarily the currently playing track. To do this, you specify which track you want information about by using the Track property. Then you can query the TrackLength property to find out the length of the track. You can query the TrackPosition property to determine what position the CD is currently in.

Unfortunately, the one thing that the MCI control needs help on is calculating the time of the current track. By using the Track and TrackPosition properties, you can find the position of the CD with respect to the total disk time, not the current track only. With the MCI control, there is only one way to do this. If you know which track is playing, you must add up the time of all of the previous tracks and subtract the total from the TrackPosition of the current track to find the actual elapsed time for the current track.

UNPACKING A PACKED INTEGER

The MCI control uses *packed integers* to return data from the control. A packed integer makes the data smaller for the control to handle, but it is a pain for programmers! You must unpack the integer value to separate it into its usable parts. The parts are stored in terms of bytes. Depending on the format set with the TimeFormat property, the value stored in each byte can be different. For example, if the TimeFormat property is set to 2, the value of Byte 1 is minutes, Byte 2 is seconds, Byte 3 is frames, and Byte 4 is unused. If you change the TimeFormat property, the values represented in these bytes will be different.

The technique is to apply bit-wise operators to separate the individual byte values stored in the packed integer. The best way to show how this is done is to use a code fragment from Chapter 27's Unformat() subroutine. It is used to unpack the integer value coming from the MCI control and separate it into separate bytes. See the following:

```
Sub Unformat (CodedValue As Long)

    'decode coded value and separate into byte components
    'Byte 1 is least significant
    'Byte 4 is most significant

    Byte1 = CodedValue And &HFF&
    Byte2 = (CodedValue And &HFF00&) \ &H100
    Byte3 = (CodedValue And &HFF0000) \ &H10000
    Byte4 = (CodedValue And &H7F000000) \ &H1000000
    If (CodedValue And &H80000000) <> 0 Then
        Byte4 = Byte4 + &H80
    End If

End Sub
```

The variable `CodedValue` is the value that comes from the `TrackPosition` property of the MCI control. Byte 1 now is the number of minutes that have elapsed. Byte 2 is the number of seconds. Bytes 3 and 4 are not used. In your application, you may not implement a routine like this one, but you must apply the same hexadecimal values with the bit-wise operators shown earlier to determine which byte holds which value.

CALCULATING ELAPSED TIME OF A CD PLAYER TRACK

To calculate the elapsed time of the currently playing CD track, you must calculate the total time for previous tracks and subtract that number from the current position. For example, suppose the CD is playing track three. If you know that track one has a time of one minute and track two has a time of three minutes, and the `TrackPosition` property reports six minutes, the following can be deduced:

◆ The aggregate time of track one and two is four minutes.

◆ If the aggregate time of track one, two, and three is greater than the current `TrackPosition`, the CD player must still be in track three. You need to check this because the display could show five but actually be playing three. This method forces the display to be correct.

◆ The current `TrackPosition` of six minutes minus the aggregate time of tracks one and two of four minutes means that you *have* to be two minutes into track three.

Following is a code fragment of how the application in Chapter 27, "CD Player Application," calculates the current time within a track. It uses the method described earlier. The only other thing the procedure has to do is to convert all time into seconds before it performs an arithmetic function. Time is converted back into hours, minutes, and seconds after all computations have been performed. That is the easiest way of performing calculations on different units of measure. For more information on converting all bytes to seconds, refer to the following section entitled "Converting into One Unit of Measure."

```
'total all tracks from beginning to previous track
For loopcount% = 0 To mmControl.Track - 1
    TempTotal& = TempTotal& + TrackTime&(loopcount%)
Next loopcount%

'convert from seconds only to minutes and seconds
ConvertToMMSS (ConvertToSeconds(temp&) - ConvertToSeconds(TempTotal&))

'populate display with new byte values(calculated in ConvertToMMSS)
PopulateDisplay PTIME, Format$(Trim$(Str(Byte1)), "00") + Format$(Trim$(Str(Byte2)),
"00") + Format$(Trim$(Str(Byte3)), "00") + Format$(Trim$(Str(Byte4)), "00")
```

Notice that there are four variables: `Byte1`, `Byte2`, `Byte3`, and `Byte4`. These bytes are module level variables, which is why they are not declared here. These bytes are needed because the data that comes from the `TrackPosition` property is in the form of a packed integer. These bytes are as a result of "unpacking" the integer. If the data is not unpacked, there is no way to accurately update the display.

An aggregate time is determined for each of the previous tracks. Then the aggregate time is converted into seconds (with the `ConvertToSeconds()` function) and subtracted from the current position stored in the variable `Temp&`, which is also converted into seconds.

After the arithmetic has been performed, the number of seconds is converted back into the MM:SS format. After the conversion process has taken place, the display is updated to reflect the elapsed time within the current track. This process goes on once every second. Your application can apply this technique in a different way, but the theory behind the conversion process is still the same.

CONVERTING INTO ONE UNIT OF MEASURE

You need to convert into one unit of measure because you cannot perform arithmetic functions on different units of measure. For example, you cannot add one hour, 25 minutes to three hours, 55 minutes without converting to one unit. Your application needs to convert the time into one unit: the smallest unit. In the case of the CD player, all values are converted into seconds with the following function:

```
Function ConvertToSeconds (ConvertWhat&)

    'declare variables
    Dim TheTotal&

    'initialize
    TheTotal& = 0

    Unformat (ConvertWhat&)

    'byte1- minutes
    TheTotal& = TheTotal& + (Byte1 * 60)
```

```
        'byte2- .minutes
        TheTotal& = TheTotal& + (Byte2)

        ConvertToSeconds = TheTotal&
End Function
```

After the values are converted into seconds, the program performs the arithmetic functions and converts back into bytes by using this routine:

```
Sub ConvertToMMSS (ConvertWhat&)

    'ConvertWhat& is in seconds
    'byte1 is minutes
    'byte2 is seconds

    'ConvertWhat& will always be 3 seconds ahead-so adjust
    ConvertWhat& = ConvertWhat& - 3

    Byte1 = Int(ConvertWhat& \ 60)
    Byte2 = ConvertWhat& Mod 60
    Byte3 = Int(ConvertWhat& \ 3600)

End Sub
```

OTHER MEDIA TYPES

Other media types are perhaps easier to deal with than the "CDAudio" media type. This is because you do not have to update the screen on a real-time basis. If you want to play a WAV audio file, simply play it. You do not necessarily have to update a display with the elapsed time. This is why everything but audio CDs are grouped into this "Other Media Types" category.

PLAYING AUDIO FILES

Playing audio files does not require any special techniques as with displaying CD information. You must specify the media type by using the `DeviceType` property, as described earlier. The audio file is selected by using the standard common dialog control. If you want to play a WAV file, the device type is set by using the following code:

```
control.DeviceType = "WaveAudio"
```

If you want to play a MIDI file, the device type is set by using the followingcode:

```
control.DeviceType = "Sequencer"
```

Where in both cases, the `control` is the name of the MCI control in your application.

After the device is opened, you can play your file. For more information about opening the device, see the previous section entitled "Using the MCI Control."

The application in Chapter 32, "Multimedia Player Application," specifies the media type using the `DeviceType` property. It also presents an example of playing audio files.

PLAYING VIDEO FILES

Playing video files is basically the same as playing audio files, with one exception. The video has to be played in some window. The easiest way to play video is to use the standard picture box in Visual Basic. The picture box is well adapted to this, mainly because it handles pictures and provides a handle, which is needed by the MCI control. That's how the MCI control knows where to play the video file.

The handle can be obtained by using the following line:

```
control.hWndDisplay = pictControl.hWnd
```

where *pictControl* is the name of the Visual Basic picture box to use, and *control* is the name of the MCI control in your application.

 You can play the video file on any window that has the capability of playing a video file, as long as you can obtain its handle. You can get the handle of any window by using the Windows API function, `FindWindow()`. Refer to Chapter 3, "Calling Windows APIs and DLLs," for more information on API functions.

AUTOMATICALLY DETERMINING DEVICE TYPE

If you need to account for all types of devices that your application supports, you can do it with a simple select-case statement. This means you can use a common dialog box to select a file name. You can then determine within your programs which `DeviceType` to select based on the extension of the file. For example, if you are trying to play a wave audio file, it always has the file extension WAV. If you need to select the appropriate `DeviceType` based on a file extension, and your application only supports files with the extension WAV, MID, AVI, or MMM, you can incorporate code like this:

```
Select Case UCase$((Right$(cmDialog.FileName, 3)))
    Case "WAV":
        'set device type
        Control.DeviceType = "WaveAudio"

    Case "MID":
        'set device type
        Control.DeviceType = "Sequencer"
```

```
    Case "AVI":
        'set device type
        Control.DeviceType = "AVIVideo"

        'assign handle of window to display video
        Control.hWndDisplay = pictControl.hWnd

    Case "MMM":
        'set device type
        Control.DeviceType = "MMMovie"

        'assign handle of window to display movie
        Control.hWndDisplay = pictControl.hWnd

    Case Else:
        'construct message for bad file type
        m$ = "Cannot recognize file type!" + Chr$(13)
        m$ = m$ + "It must be (*.WAV),(*.MID),(*.AVI),(*.MMM)"
        MsgBox m$
End Select
```

where *cmDialog* is the control name of your common dialog control, and *control* is the name of your MCI control. *pictControl* is the name of your picture box that plays the video file.

The application in Chapter 32, "Multimedia Player Application," uses this technique to select a DeviceType. Refer to this chapter for more information.

MAPI

MAPI STANDS FOR *MESSAGING APPLICATION PROGRAMMING INTERFACE*. IT IS THE BASIS FOR MICROSOFT MAIL AND OTHER MAPI-COMPLIANT SYSTEMS. A MAPI-COMPLIANT SYSTEM IS A MESSAGING SYSTEM THAT COMPLIES WITH ALL OF THE SPECIFICATIONS LAID OUT BY MICROSOFT TO USE THE MESSAGING API. MESSAGING SERVICES ARE TYPICALLY USED IN AN OFFICE ENVIRONMENT TO ENABLE PC USERS TO SEND MESSAGES AND FILES TO EACH OTHER ELECTRONICALLY. THERE HAS TO BE SOME TYPE OF MESSAGING SERVER IN PLACE, SUCH AS MICROSOFT MAIL. THIS SERVER IS WHAT DOES THE ROUTING AND HOLDS THE ADDRESSES FOR EACH OF THE USERS. THE FRONT END CAN BE ANY NUMBER OF SYSTEMS. MICROSOFT MAIL, FOR EXAMPLE, COMES WITH A FRONT END TO ENABLE A USER TO SEND AND RECEIVE MESSAGES AND FILES VIA THE MAIL SERVER. HOWEVER, THIS FRONT END CAN BE LIMITED.

With Visual Basic, you can include the MAPI control into your project and create a customized front end for the MAPI compliant back-end server. This chapter shows you how to do this. The MAPI control only comes with the Professional Edition of Visual Basic, version 3.0.

MAPI SUPPORT WITHIN VISUAL BASIC

The MAPI support in Visual Basic actually consists of two separate controls: *MAPI Session* and *MAPI Message*. The MAPI Session control is used to create the MAPI session, and the MAPI Message control is used to handle all aspects of messaging. Creating the MAPI session consists of logging into the MAPI-compliant system and returning a handle to that session. A session is the connection made by logging into the MAPI-compliant system. The MAPI Message control is used to send and receive messages as well as all message-related functions.

REM
It is important to note that the Microsoft Office Developer's Kit (ODK) that now comes with Visual Basic, Professional Edition, contains the Electronic Forms Designer (E-FORMS). This is very useful if you want to send an actual form through the mail system, not just the text. It is also available separately if you purchased Visual Basic before the ODK was bundled with it. Refer to this kit for more information.

If there is no MAPI-compliant system present on the PC and if you attempt to load or run an application that contains the MAPI controls, you receive an error. This is because the controls themselves look for the MAPI components. If the components are not present, you cannot load or run the application.

There are two types of MAPI functions: *simple* and *extended*. The simple MAPI functions are a set of functions that can handle most of the everyday messaging tasks and are a subset of the extended MAPI functions. Extended MAPI functions are available in Windows, provide extended capabilities, but are not included with this control. The MAPI custom controls use simple MAPI functions only. These functions are accessed by specifying values for properties in the custom controls. Table 13.1 lists the simple MAPI functions and message types found in the Messaging API.

TABLE 13.1. SIMPLE MAPI FUNCTIONS AND MESSAGE TYPES.

Function	Used For
MAPILogon()	Begins a MAPI session
MAPIFindNext()	Returns the ID of the next message of a specified type
MAPIReadMail()	Reads a mail message
MAPISaveMail()	Saves a mail message

Function	Used For
MAPIDeleteMail()	Deletes a mail message
MAPISendMail()	Sends a mail message—allows more flexibility than MAPISendDocuments
MAPISendDocuments()	Sends a mail message, using a dialog box
MAPIAddress()	Address of the mail message
MAPIResolveName()	Resolves incomplete name references
MAPIDetails()	Details dialog box
MAIPLogoff()	Ends a MAPI session
MapiFile()	Message type containing file attachment information
MapiMessage()	Message type containing message information
MapiRecip()	Contains recipient information

These MAPI functions are handled by the Visual Basic custom controls. Table 13.2 lists the MAPI Session control's unique properties. Table 13.3 lists the MAPI Message control's unique properties.

TABLE 13.2. MAPI SESSION CONTROL UNIQUE PROPERTIES.

Property	DataType	Used For
Action	Integer	1-Logon, 2-Logoff
DownloadMail	Integer(Boolean)	Download messages upon logon if True
LogonUI	Integer(Boolean)	Logon Dialog box displayed if True
NewSession	Integer(Boolean)	Specifies a new session if True
Password	String	Password used to login
SessionID	Long	Session handle
UserName	String	User name used to login

TABLE 13.3. MAPI MESSAGE CONTROL UNIQUE PROPERTIES.

Property	DataType	Used For
Action	Integer	Specifies action to take
AddressCaption	String	Caption on address book window
AddressEditFieldCount	Integer	Specifies which controls to place on address book

continues

TABLE 13.3. CONTINUED

Property	DataType	Used For
AddressLabel	String	Specifies appearance of the "To" edit control in address book
AddressModifiable	Integer(Boolean)	True if address book can be modified
AddressResolveUI	Integer(Boolean)	True if address book is to resolve misspelled or incomplete names
AttachmentCount	Long	Number of attachments for particular message index
AttachmentIndex	Long	Currently indexed attachment
AttachmentName	String	Name of currently indexed attachment
AttachmentPathName	String	Full path of currently indexed attachment
AttachmentPosition	Long	Position of currently indexed attachment within body of message
AttachmentType	Integer	Specifies type of attachment
FetchMsgType	String	Type of message to fetch
FetchSorted	Integer(Boolean)	True if messages are to be sorted
FetchUnreadOnly	Integer(Boolean)	True if only to fetch unread messages
MsgConversationID	String	Specifies message set identifier
MsgCount	Long	Number of messages
MsgDateReceived	String	Date that currently indexed message is received
MsgID	String	String identifier of currently indexed message
MsgIndex	Long	Index of currently indexed message
MsgNoteText	String	Specifies the text body of the message
MsgOrigAddress	String	Mail address of message originator
MsgOrigDisplayName	String	Originator's name of currently indexed message

Property	DataType	Used For
MsgRead	Integer(Boolean)	True if currently indexed message has been read
MsgReceiptRequested	Integer(Boolean)	True if return receipt is requested
MsgSent	Integer(Boolean)	True if currently indexed message has been sent
MsgSubject	String	Specifies the message subject for the currently indexed message
MsgType	String	Specifies the type of message
RecipAddress	String	Address of currently indexed recipient
RecipCount	Long	Total number of recipients in currently indexed message
RecipDisplayName	String	Name of currently indexed recipients
RecipIndex	Long	Index for use with recipients
RecipType	Integer	Specifies the type of currently indexed recipient
SessionID	Long	Session ID from MAPI Session control

When using the MAPI controls, you need to invoke error handling routines so that a runtime error doesn't abort the application. Table 13.4 shows the possible errors in using the MAPI control.

 For more information about error handling, refer to Chapter 2, "Error Handling."

TABLE 13.4. POSSIBLE MAPI ERRORS.

Error	Explanation
32000	Success
32001	User Abort
32002	General Failure
32003	Login Failure
32004	Disk Full
32005	Insufficient Memory

continues

TABLE 13.4. CONTINUED

Error	Explanation
32006	Access Denied
32008	Too Many Sessions
32009	Too Many Files
32010	Too Many Recipients
32011	Attachment Not Found
32012	Attachment Open Failure
32013	Attachment Write Failure
32014	Unknown Recipient
32015	Bad Recipient Type
32016	No Messages
32017	Invalid Message
32018	Text Too Large
32019	Invalid Session
32020	Type Not Supported
32021	Ambiguous Recipient
32022	Message in Use
32023	Network Failure
32024	Invalid Edit Fields
32025	Invalid Recipients
32026	Not Supported
32050	Session ID Already Exists
32051	Read-only in Read Buffer
32052	Valid in Compose Buffer Only
32053	No Valid Session ID
32054	Originator Information Not Available
32055	Action Not Valid in Compose Buffer
32056	Control Failure
32057	No Recipients
32058	No Attachments

It is important to note that the errors listed here can occur in a Real-World program. It may be sufficient in your application to invoke an error handling routine to simply tell the user about the error and take no further action. On the other hand, you may want to take action in some cases. For example, if you get the error 32014, which occurs if you try to send a message to a recipient who doesn't exist, you may want to open an address book and allow the user to pick a recipient.

LOGGING IN TO AND OUT OF A MAPI-COMPLIANT SYSTEM

If you intend to write your own MAPI-compliant front end, your user must log in to the system. Logging in registers you as a valid user to the back-end server. To log in to a MAPI-compliant system, use the MAPI Session control. The MAPI Session control is very easy to use. You log in by setting the Action property to 1, or by using the Visual Basic constant SESSION_SIGNON. You can also request that the system search for your messages, if there are any, when you log in. To do this, set the DownloadMail property to True before you log in with the Action property.

As an example, consider how the application in Chapter 28 logs in:

```
If menu_LogonMsg.Checked = True Then
    MAPISession1.DownloadMail = True
Else
    MAPISession1.DownloadMail = False
End If

'handle errors
On Error GoTo LogonError

'logon
If MAPISession1.SessionID = 0 Then
    MAPISession1.Action = SESSION_SIGNON
End If

'assign mapi session id
MAPIMessages1.SessionID = MAPISession1.SessionID
```

The code in your application won't vary much because these properties have to be set to the values indicated to perform the desired log in function. The only real difference is the control names of the MAPI Session and MAPI Message controls. After a session is started, it is important that the SessionID of the MAPI Session control has a handle to it. This handle is an integer value that the MAPI Message control needs. Therefore, you must assign the value after logging in to or out of a MAPI-compliant system. Assigning a value is accomplished in Chapter 28 with the last line shown in the preceding code.

When you want to close the application, you must log off to conserve system resources on the server and clear the user's ID number. To log out of the MAPI-compliant system, simply set the Action property of the MAPI Session control to 2, or use the Visual Basic constant SESSION_SIGNOFF. Logging out of the mail system is done with the following line of code:

```
MAPISession1.Action = SESSION_SIGNOFF
```

Basically, the only difference between the two Chapter 28 functions, login() and logoff(), is the action property. If you do not assign the SessionID of the MAPI Session control to the SessionID of the MAPI Message control, you can't perform any messaging functions.

INVOKING THE MAPI ADDRESS BOOK

A MAPI-compliant application has an address book located on the MAPI-compliant server that can search for recipients to send messages and files to. You invoke the MAPI address book by using the Message control and setting the Action property. The address book would have been created by a system administrator and will appear automatically. It is assumed that you have logged in to the MAPI-compliant system, as stated in the previous section. To invoke the address book, simply set the Action property to 11 or use the MESSAGE_SHOWADBOOK constant in the CONSTANT.TXT file. Before invoking the address book, you can specify the appearance and characteristics the address book will have. For example, you can specify that you want to choose a recipient to receive a carbon copy of the message you send to someone else. This line usually appears in a document as CC: followed by the name of the individual.

To specify how the address book will appear, you can set the AddressEditFieldCount property. The possible options are listed in Table 13.5.

TABLE 13.5. AddressEditFieldCount PROPERTY OPTIONS.

Value	Description
0	No editing controls. Only browsing is allowed.
1	Only the To: edit box is presented
2	The To: and CC: edit boxes are presented
3	The To:, CC:, and BCC: edit boxes are presented
4	All possible edit boxes are presented

You must also set the MsgIndex property to -1 before opening the address book. This ensures that the names selected in the address book are put into the recipient related properties for the MAPI Message control. For example, consider the code from Chapter 28 to show that the address book is invoked. Your application will not be much different. By design, the code has to be used in this way:

```
'enable the To: box to be shown on address book
MAPIMessages1.AddressEditFieldCount = 1

'set index to -1 to enable saving of names chosen(automatically)
MAPIMessages1.MsgIndex = -1

'invoke address book
MAPIMessages1.Action = MESSAGE_SHOWADBOOK
```

After the address book is closed, you need to retrieve the addresses you have selected and return them to the MAPI application. You do this by looping through all of the recipients chosen and processing the names in any way your application is designed to. For example, if you simply want to populate a list box with all of the names chosen from the address book, you can use the following code fragment:

```
'clear list box
lstTo.Clear

'loop through all recipients and populate
For loopcount% = 0 To MAPIMessages1.RecipCount - 1
    'assign index
    MAPIMessages1.RecipIndex = loopcount%

    'add to name
    lstTo.AddItem MAPIMessages1.RecipDisplayName
Next loopcount%
```

SENDING A MESSAGE

To send a message through a MAPI-compliant system by using the MAPI custom controls, you must first log in, construct the message, address it, and then send it. The preceding sections described how to log in and address the message. Constructing the message is an extremely simple task. It is really just one text string that is sent. You can hard-code this string into your application, or you can use a text box, allowing the user to construct a dynamic message.

There are many possibilities in sending a message. For example, you can construct a form in which the user fills in the blanks and sends a formatted text message to recipients. You can also consider the way that the application in Chapter 28 works. It takes some predetermined strings and sends them to the list of recipients in a list box. These predetermined strings are:

◆ Greeting

◆ Body of the message consisting of a list of changes to an executable file and the version of the executable file, as well as the name of the application

◆ Closing

You can use the same theory in your application to create a specific message when some action occurs. You can even have the executable file run automatically when some condition occurs and have the login performed in code. This procedure can completely automate sending a message through a MAPI-compliant system.

To send a message, you must first set the MsgIndex property of the MAPI Message control to -1, which enables the control to compose a message. Then you must tell the control that you want to begin composing the message by, once again, setting the Action property. Setting the Action property to 6 or using the constant MESSAGE_COMPOSE starts this action.

After the composition of the message has begun, you can specify the subject of the message by using the MsgSubject property. You assign the string you send as the message by using the MsgNoteText property. After all the strings have been assigned, you actually send the message by setting the Action property to 3, or by using the constant MESSAGE_SEND.

Following is a code fragment from Chapter 28 that shows how the message string is built and how it sends a message:

```
'set msgindex to enable compose buffer
MAPIMessages1.MsgIndex = -1

'clear compose buffer
MAPIMessages1.Action = MESSAGE_COMPOSE

'assign recipients
Call BuildToList

'allow mail system to resolve bad names
MAPIMessages1.AddressResolveUI = True

'assign subject
MAPIMessages1.MsgSubject = txtSubject.Text

'build message
msg$ = frmRemark.txtGreeting.Text + Chr$(13)
msg$ = msg$ + "APPLICATION:" + Chr$(9) + txtApplication.Text + Chr$(13) + Chr$(13)
msg$ = msg$ + "VERSION:" + Chr$(9) + txtVersion.Text + Chr$(13) + Chr$(13)

If lstChanges.ListCount > 0 Then
    msg$ = msg$ + "CHANGES:" + Chr$(9)
End If

'build list of changes
For loopcount% = 0 To lstChanges.ListCount - 1
    If lstChanges.List(loopcount%) <> "" Then
        msg$ = msg$ + lstChanges.List(loopcount%) + Chr$(13)
        'if this is not the last item in the list, add 2 tabs to line up
        If loopcount% < lstChanges.ListCount - 1 Then
            msg$ = msg$ + Chr$(9) + Chr$(9)
        End If
    End If
Next loopcount%

'add new line before closing remark
msg$ = msg$ + Chr$(13)

'add closing string to message
msg$ = msg$ + frmRemark.txtClosing.Text

'send actual text
MAPIMessages1.MsgNoteText = msg$

'change cursor
screen.MousePointer = HOURGLASS
```

```
'actually send message
MAPIMessages1.Action = MESSAGE_SEND

'change cursor
screen.MousePointer = DEFAULT

'show message
MsgBox "Message Sent!"
```

Even though the preceding code is application specific, many aspects of the code will be the same in your application. The only thing that is really different is the way the message string is built. All of the preceding lines of code that assign text to the string variable msg$ are specific to the application in Chapter 28. Your application will build a string differently, but the concept is the same.

MANUALLY RECEIVING A MESSAGE

To manually receive a message with the MAPI custom controls, you simply use the Action property for the MAPI Message control. You set the Action property to 1 or use the constant MESSAGE_FETCH. Before you set the Action property, if you want to retrieve only unread messages, you can set the FetchUnreadOnly property to True. If there are any messages after setting the Action property, the MsgCount property contains a nonzero value. You can cycle through the messages using the MsgCount property and build a list of subjects by using the MsgSubject property.

For each possible message waiting, there is a MsgIndex property associated with it. For example, if there are two messages, there are indexes 0 and 1, respectively, associated with it. This allows you to access the individual messages. This is very similar to the way you access a control array in Visual Basic.

Consider the way that the application in Chapter 28 allows the user to manually retrieve messages with the following code:

```
'set to fetch all messages
MAPIMessages1.FetchUnreadOnly = False

If MAPISession1.SessionID <> 0 Then
    'fetch messages
    MAPIMessages1.Action = MESSAGE_FETCH

    If MAPIMessages1.MsgCount > 0 Then
        'there are messages waiting-show inbox form
        frmInbox.Show
        DoEvents

        'display number of messages
        frmInbox.pnlNumMsg.Caption = MAPIMessages1.MsgCount

        'clear list box
        frmInbox.lstMessage.Clear
```

```
        'populate messages
        For loopcount% = 0 To MAPIMessages1.MsgCount - 1

             'change index
             MAPIMessages1.MsgIndex = loopcount%

             'get subject
             frmInbox.lstMessage.AddItem MAPIMessages1.MsgSubject
        Next loopcount%
    End If

  End If
```

The preceding code requests the messages for the particular login ID. If there are messages waiting, the INBOX.FRM form is shown. To determine if there are messages waiting, the MsgCount property is used. If this property is greater than 0, there are messages waiting.

The code then cycles through a list of all available messages and populates a list of the subject content. The code accesses individual messages by using the MsgIndex property, and it accesses the individual subjects by using the MsgSubject property.

FINDING ATTACHMENTS FOR A MESSAGE

A message not only contains the text part of the message, but can also contain *attachments*. Attachments are files attached to the messages. For example, if you want to send a Microsoft Word document to a recipient as an attachment and explain what the document is used for, you can do this in the same message.

For each possible message waiting, there is a MsgIndex property associated with it. For example, if there are two messages, there are indexes 0 and 1, respectively, associated with it. This allows you to access the individual messages. This is very similar to the way you access a control array in Visual Basic. However, for each individual MsgIndex, there can be one or more attachments. These attachments are accessed through the AttachmentIndex property. If you want to determine how many attachments there are, you can access the AttachmentCount property.

You can build a list of attachments for each message, which is what the application in Chapter 28 does. When a user clicks on a message, the code cycles through all possible attachments and builds a list of them. The following code determines if there are attachments:

```
'find all attachments and build string
For loopcount% = 0 To frmmain.MapiMessages1.AttachmentCount - 1

     'assign index
     frmmain.MapiMessages1.AttachmentIndex = loopcount%

     'assign name to string
     Attach$ = Attach$ + frmmain.MapiMessages1.AttachmentName
```

```
'append semi-colon if not last item
If loopcount% < frmmain.MapiMessages1.AttachmentCount - 1 Then
    Attach$ = Attach$ + ";"
End If

Next loopcount%
```

The same technique is used for attachments as for messages. In other words, just as you can loop through the total number of messages and index them individually, there is a total number of attachments, each of which can be indexed individually. The total number of attachments is obtained by using the AttachmentCount property. The individual index of any one attachment is found by using the AttachmentIndex property. To find out the attachment filename of the indexed attachment, use the AttachmentName property. Your application must use the same theory to build a list of attachments as presented here, although the specific methods can vary.

DELETING A MESSAGE OR ATTACHMENTS

The MAPI controls also allow for the deletion of messages or attachments. To delete a message, simply use the Action property to delete the currently indexed message. Setting this property to 10 or using the constant MESSAGE_DELETE deletes the message. The MAPI-compliant system gives you no warning. You have to check to make sure the user wants to continue with this action. The following code fragment deletes the currently indexed message and ensures that the item is deleted from the list box where it is listed:

```
'do delete
frmmain.MapiMessages1.Action = MESSAGE_DELETE

'remove item from lstMessage
lstMessage.RemoveItem lstMessage.listindex
```

You can use the same technique to delete attachments. The only difference is that you set the Action property to 15, or use the constant ATTACHMENT_DELETE.

You can delete an attachment with the following line of code:

```
MapiMessages1.Action = ATTACHMENT_DELETE
```

You can even take this one step further and delete all attachments at one time, which is what the application in Chapter 28 does. It does this with the following code:

```
'loop through all attachments and delete
For loopcount% = 0 To frmmain.MapiMessages1.AttachmentCount - 1
    'do delete
    frmmain.MapiMessages1.Action = ATTACHMENT_DELETE
Next loopcount%
```

POLLING FOR NEW MESSAGES

Chances are that you want to be automatically notified when a new message comes in. You do this by setting a *polling frequency*. A polling frequency is a way for your program to check if there are messages at certain intervals. Polling can't be done continuously because that eats up system resources. Therefore, you probably want to set a polling frequency somewhere in the range of 5 to 10 minutes. That means that every 5 to 10 minutes, the application checks for new messages. If any new messages have been received in that time, you need to notify the user in some way. You can put up a message box or even change the icon used if the application is minimized.

Polling presents a unique problem for Visual Basic because you must use a timer control to schedule the polling. The problem is that the timer control can have its Interval property set only to a maximum value of 65535. This is just over one minute. What if you want to poll every five minutes? Well, there is a solution. You use an integer variable in Visual Basic to count the number of minutes that have passed. For example, set the Timer's Interval property to 60000. This generates the Timer event once a minute. In the Timer event code, keep adding one to the counter variable you are using. When this counter variable gets to the polling interval you want, manually check for messages, as described in the previous section, "Manually Receiving a Message." Your code in the Timer event may look like this:

```
CurrentInterval& = CurrentInterval& + 1
```

Consider, as an example, how the application in Chapter 28 performs it's polling:

```
'check to see if polling time has elapsed
If CurrentInterval& = DesiredInterval& Then
    If MAPISession1.SessionID <> 0 Then
        'fetch only new messages
        MAPIMessages1.FetchUnreadOnly = True

        'fetch messages
        MAPIMessages1.Action = MESSAGE_FETCH

        'test for new messages - this insures that the message will only be displayed
        'once, and not once each polling period!
        If MAPIMessages1.MsgCount > 0 And MAPIMessages1.MsgCount > NewMessages% Then

            If frmMain.WindowState = 1 Then
                'form is minimized then assign In icon
                frmMain.Icon = pictMailIn.Picture
            Else
                'advise about new message
                MsgBox "You have new message(s)!"
            End If

            'increment number of new messages
            NewMessages% = NewMessages% + 1
        End If
```

```
        'set back to fetch all messages
        MAPIMessages1.FetchUnreadOnly = False

    End If

    'reset current interval&
    CurrentInterval& = 0
End If
```

If the desired interval equals the current interval, the system only checks for new messages by setting the FetchUnreadOnly property to True. After the new messages are received, the property is set back to False. If there are new messages, the user is notified by either a message box or by changing the icon, depending on the state of the window.

CHAPTER FOURTEEN

DYNAMIC DATA EXCHANGE (DDE)

DYNAMIC DATA EXCHANGE (DDE) IS A WAY FOR TWO WINDOWS APPLICATIONS TO EXCHANGE DATA. WITH DDE, EACH APPLICATION SHARES MEMORY CONTAINING DATA TO TRANSFER BETWEEN THE APPLICATIONS. DYNAMIC DATA EXCHANGE PROGRAMMING AND WINDOWS MAKE SURE THAT THE SHARED MEMORY IS ACCESSED AT THE APPROPRIATE TIMES. DYNAMIC DATA EXCHANGE, FROM NOW ON CALLED DDE, IS INITIATED IN A PROCESS CALLED A CONVERSATION. ONE APPLICATION, CALLED THE SOURCE, IS RESPONSIBLE FOR SENDING THE DATA. THE OTHER APPLICATION, CALLED THE DESTINATION, IS RESPONSIBLE FOR RECEIVING THE DATA SENT BY THE SOURCE APPLICATION. EITHER APPLICATION CAN ACTUALLY INITIATE THE DDE CONVERSATION.

There was a time when DDE was the sole source of interprocess communication with two applications. This chapter shows how to use DDE in depth. However, DDE is vastly dying out and being replaced by *OLE (Object Linking and Embedding)*.

 For more information on OLE, see Chapter 15, "Object Linking and Embedding (OLE)," and the application in Chapter 30, "Object Linking and Embedding (OLE) Application."

In Visual Basic, there are two modes of operation for DDE: *Manual* and *Automatic*. The Automatic mode is supposed to perform all updates automatically, but there is often a problem with timing. The source does not always update the destination as it should. The Automatic mode allows for the destination application in a DDE conversation to be updated automatically by the source application whenever it changes. For example, suppose that a DDE conversation exists between Excel and a Visual Basic application, and Excel is the source and Visual Basic is the destination. Therefore, if the data is changed inside Excel, the change is automatically sent to the destination. This does not necessarily mean that Visual Basic is ready to receive the data.

Therefore, it is recommended to always use the Manual mode for DDE. This mode allows for a Visual Basic application to request the data from the source application. This capability can make a DDE application in Visual Basic more reliable and also saves precious resources. It is a good idea to manually request an update, for example, when the user of a Visual Basic application wants to save or exit. You simply manually request the data in the DDE source application to send the data.

One last option is to use a combination of the Automatic and Manual modes of DDE operation. This use of modes conserves resources and frees up some programming code at the same time.

Visual Basic provides many properties and methods to enable a DDE conversation between two applications. Table 14.1 lists the DDE properties and methods available in Visual Basic.

TABLE 14.1. DDE PROPERTIES AND METHODS.

Property/Method	Description
LinkItem	The item used in the conversation. For an Excel spreadsheet, it is a particular cell. Use the *RxCx* format, where *R* is the row number and *C* is the column number. Do not use the format such as B5.
LinkTopic	Identifies the *topic* of the conversation. The topic is typically the name of the application. For Excel, the LinkTopic is Excel concatenated with the pipe symbol "¦" and finally the name of the spreadsheet, including the path.

Property/Method	Description
LinkMode	Type of DDE conversation.
LinkRequest	Method used to request a link when LinkMode is manual
LinkTimeout	Timeout for waiting for a response from a DDE conversation
LinkPoke	Pokes data into the source application from the destination application
LinkExecute	Used for executing macro commands in the destination application
LinkSend	Sends the contents of a picture control to another application

Although there are few Visual Basic properties and methods available for DDE, it can be difficult to set up a DDE conversation. The reason for this is that the application with which your Visual Basic application will be communicating must be loaded and running. This fact can create some problems. The reason for this is because the application, such as Excel, may already be running. You need to account for the possibility of multiple instances. You also need to account for the possibility that the application may not be found.

The destination application is actually the application that initiates the conversation. The destination application requests that the source application communicates with it and sends its data. The destination application then receives the data. This is the opposite of how you may think it works. You may think that the source actually initiates the sequence. Your Visual Basic applications are probably the destination applications, and other commercial applications, such as Excel, Word, or Access, are the source applications.

RUNNING THE SOURCE APPLICATION

The first step in running an application, such as Microsoft Excel, is to determine if it is already running. To do this, you can use the FindWindow() API function.

 For more information about Windows API functions, refer to Chapter 3, "Calling Windows APIs and DLLs."

You use the FindWindow() API function to determine if a certain window is running. You can use it in one of two ways. You can determine if Excel is running a specific spreadsheet, or if Excel is running—period. If you want to find out if Excel is running a specific spreadsheet, you can use the FindWindow() API function with this syntax:

```
result% = FindWindow(0&, WindowName)
```

where:

> *result%* is the result of the FindWindow() function. If the result is 0, the window is not found. If it is greater than 0, that *result%* is the handle to the window found.
>
> *WindowName* is the title of the window. This name is enclosed in quotation marks. It must be spelled exactly as the window name, including spaces, or the function returns 0.

The other way to use the FindWindow() API function is to determine if a certain class of window is running. To use the function in this way, use this syntax:

```
result% = FindWindow(ClassName, 0&)
```

where:

> *result%* is the result of the FindWindow() function. If the result is 0, the window is not found. If it is greater than 0, that *result%* is the handle to the window found.
>
> *ClassName* is the name of the class of window. For example, the class of the main Excel window is "XLMAIN". If you are looking for this window, use the FindWindow() API function like this:

```
result% = FindWindow("XLMAIN", 0&)
```

The function returns nonzero if Excel is running.

 If you want to determine the name of the class of a certain window, you can use the Microsoft utility program called SPY.EXE. It comes with Microsoft Visual C++ or the Windows SDK. The program is also available elsewhere, such as the Developer's Network CD and/or the Microsoft Download Service.

The application in Chapter 29, "Dynamic Data Exchange (DDE) Application," uses the first FindWindow() option presented earlier. This application determines if Excel is to find out if it's already running with the FINANCE.XLS spreadsheet open. Following is a code fragment from Chapter 29, showing how this is done:

```
If GlobalPassword$ = "" Or GlobalFileName$ = "" Then
    'no password or file name, but is finance running?
    res% = FindWindow(0&, "Microsoft Excel - FINANCE.XLS")
    If res% > 0 Then
        'the window is already open, don't ask for password
        Call OpenExcel
    Else
        frmFile.Show
    End If
Else
    Call OpenExcel
End If
```

If you are going to use Excel, it's a good idea to determine the following:

◆ Is Excel running the specified spreadsheet?

◆ Is Excel running minimized?

◆ Is Excel running maximized or in a normal window?

If the answer to all of these questions is "No," then you must invoke Excel. To determine if Excel is open in a window, once again, you can use the `FindWindow()` API function; however, you must test for different classes of windows. If Excel is running a maximized or normal window, you can test for the class name of `"XLMAIN"`, as stated earlier. However, if you want to test to see if Excel is minimized, you must test for a different class name of `"EXCEL>"`. You can do this with the following line of code:

```
res% = FindWindow("EXCEL>", 0&)
```

If you have determined that Excel is not running on a machine, it's simple enough to invoke Excel. You can do it with the `Shell()` function like this:

```
res% = Shell("d:\msoffice\excel\EXCEL.EXE")
```

where the result of the function is a handle to the instance of the program. All of this code is necessary just to get Excel running. You then have to open the specific spreadsheet that you will have the DDE conversation with and set up the conversation.

Opening the Topic

The *topic* of the conversation is the item of interest that the two applications are talking about. For example, Excel may be the source application, but the topic is the specific spreadsheet that is involved in the DDE conversation. Assuming that the source application, such as Excel, is opened as described in the preceding section, you must open the topic, such as the Excel spreadsheet or Word document.

The properties discussed in this section are properties of Visual Basic controls that are acting as the destination in a DDE conversation. The destination must be a control because if data is sent from the source application, it has to be sent somewhere. Therefore, it can be sent from the source application to a text box, picture box, or label. These three controls are the only controls that come with Visual Basic that can be used in a destination application.

The first thing to do is to set the `LinkMode` property to the constant `None`, or `0`. This is necessary when beginning the process. The `LinkMode` determines what type of link is used. You then assign the topic of conversation with the `LinkTopic` property. It uses this general syntax:

```
LinkTopic = "Application_Name¦Topic"
```

where *Application_Name* is the name of the application, such as "EXCEL" for Microsoft Excel, and *Topic* is the name of the topic, such as the specific spreadsheet in Excel or document in Word. For example, you can use code like this to set the topic of a new Excel 5.0 spreadsheet:

```
frmMain.Text1.LinkTopic = "EXCEL¦Book1"
```

 Even if you plan to open an existing spreadsheet, you must first identify the topic that you initiate the conversation with simply to open the DDE channel. This means that before you can tell Excel to open a spreadsheet, you must establish a DDE link. Therefore, the `LinkTopic` has to exist with the spreadsheet that comes up as default. At that point, you can load an existing spreadsheet.

The next step is to set the item to be discussed in the topic. In the case of Excel, you specify the specific cell location in question. You do this with the `LinkItem` property. The syntax for using this with Excel is

```
LinkItem = "RrowCcolumn"
```

where *row* is the row of the cell, and *column* is the column of the cell to be involved in the topic of conversation. For example, if cell "A1" is to be used in the topic of conversation, this line of code specifies that for the DDE conversation:

```
frmMain.Text1.LinkItem = "R1C1"
```

 Even though you don't actually exchange data with cell "R1C1", Visual Basic requires that there be a `LinkItem` setup. You can set up an arbitrary link such as this one just to satisfy the Visual Basic requirement, but you must reassign the `LinkItem` before you actually exchange data.

After all of this preliminary work is in place, you can activate the link by assigning the `LinkMode` property to the constant `AUTOMATIC` or 1 like this:

```
frmMain.Text1.LinkMode = AUTOMATIC
```

Now that the link is established, you can actually open the spreadsheet you wanted to work with in the first place. To do this, you actually use macro commands available in the source application. Consult your documentation for the specific application you're using as a source application to determine which commands are available. In Microsoft Excel, you use the `OPEN` command to open an existing spreadsheet. This book cannot cover all of the possibilities of how to use the `OPEN` command, but you implement the `OPEN` command by using the `LinkExecute` method, similar to the way that Chapter 29 does it with this code:

```
'build open file string
cmd$ = "[OPEN(" + Chr$(34) + GlobalFileName$ + Chr$(34) + ",0,FALSE,," + Chr$(34) +
```

```
GlobalPassword$ + Chr$(34) + ")]"

    'execute opening file
    frmMain.Text1.LinkExecute cmd$
```

This code builds a string of parameters with the OPEN command that Excel expects. Then the string is sent to the source application with the LinkExecute method. For more information about executing a macro command, see the later section entitled, "Executing a Macro Command in the Source Application."

To conserve system resources, you may want to close the link after you open the new spreadsheet by setting the LinkMode to the constant None, or 0.

It's a good idea to incorporate error handling when using DDE. You probably want to use an On Error Goto statement just before any of the DDE properties or methods are accessed. Sometimes, because DDE is not terribly reliable, an error can occur and the operation may have been performed anyway. Mostly what this error handler does is check to see if the operation is performed anyway.

For more information about handling errors, refer to Chapter 2, "Error Handling."

Sending Data to the Destination Application

Your application will probably want to send data from the source application, such as Excel, to your Visual Basic destination application. This is performed by setting up the LinkTopic, LinkItem, and LinkMode properties. These properties are available only for text boxes, labels, and picture boxes.

One of the things that makes DDE so cumbersome is that if you want to update a Visual Basic grid control with the data from an Excel spreadsheet, you must cycle through each and every cell in the grid, each and every cell in Excel, and send the data cell by cell. There is no provision for any control other than the text box, label, or picture box to take part in a DDE conversation.

That is what the application in Chapter 29, "Dynamic Data Exchange (DDE) Application," does. It updates a Visual Basic grid control from an Excel spreadsheet. This is a perfect example of how difficult it can be to use DDE. Consider the following code taken from Chapter 29:

```
'set topic
frmMain.Text1.LinkTopic = "EXCEL¦FINANCE"

'loop through all cells in each row, starting with row 4
For looprow% = 4 To 20
    For loopcol% = 1 To 14
        'clear text box
        frmMain.Text1.Text = ""
```

191

```
'no link
frmMain.Text1.LinkMode = NONE

'set cell location
frmMain.Text1.LinkItem = "R" + Trim$(Str$(looprow%)) + "C" +
Trim$(Str$(loopcol%))

'set link to automatic
frmMain.Text1.LinkMode = AUTOMATIC

'increment grid1
frmMain.Grid1.Col = loopcol% - 1
frmMain.Grid1.Row = looprow% - 4

'remove formatting
pos% = InStr(frmMain.Text1.Text, "$")
If pos% > 0 Then
    lefttext$ = Left$(frmMain.Text1.Text, pos% - 1)
    righttext$ = Right$(frmMain.Text1.Text, Len(frmMain.Text1.Text) - pos%)
    frmMain.Text1.Text = lefttext$ + righttext$
End If

'assign text
frmMain.Grid1.Text = frmMain.Text1.Text

    Next loopcol%
  Next looprow%
```

The preceding code first sets up the topic of conversation using the LinkTopic property. Then it cycles through a predetermined area of cells in the Visual Basic grid. As it cycles through each cell, it sets the LinkItem property to a corresponding Excel cell location. Before it assigns the new LinkItem, it sets the LinkMode property to None. This allows your program to assign a new LinkItem without error. After the new LinkItem is assigned, the LinkMode is set to AUTOMATIC. Bear in mind that you are dealing with a text box in the DDE destination application. This means that the text box is updated, not the grid. Therefore, the next step is to assign the text in the text box to the cell in the grid, but first remove the formatting that can come from Excel.

EXECUTING A MACRO COMMAND IN THE SOURCE APPLICATION

If you need to perform a function in the source application, you must execute the macro command available in that application. For example, if you want to print an Excel spreadsheet involved as the source application in a DDE conversation, you must use the PRINT macro available in Excel. You must also make sure that you follow the specific format it expects. For a list of macros available and the format required, consult the user's manual or command reference manual that comes with the product used as the source application.

In Excel, the PRINT command executes a macro that performs the printing. Many times, the entire reason for initiating a DDE conversation with Excel is to use its printing capabilities. Suppose that you used a Visual Basic grid control as a spreadsheet. If you want to print the contents of the grid, you have to cycle through each cell and use code to determine how it will be printed. Even if you do this, it takes a tremendous amount of work to incorporate shading and lines between cells, and so on. I have seen this technique used so many times that it's the basis for the application in Chapter 29. It takes advantage of the printing capabilities in Excel.

To execute a macro, use the LinkExecute method. It is available for text boxes, labels, and picture boxes. To illustrate how your application can use the Excel PRINT macro, consider this code from Chapter 29:

```
'no link
text1.LinkMode = NONE

'set topic
text1.LinkTopic = "EXCEL¦FINANCE"

'set arbitrary cell location, because VB needs it
text1.LinkItem = "R1C1"

'set link to automatic
text1.LinkMode = AUTOMATIC

'build print file string
cmd$ = "[PRINT]"

'handle error
On Error GoTo printerror

'execute printing
text1.LinkExecute cmd$

'set mode back to manual
text1.LinkMode = MANUAL
```

The Visual Basic DDE operation requires that there be a LinkItem. An error is generated if there is no link item. Because it isn't actually needed to execute a macro function, an arbitrary cell location, R1C1, is set just to satisfy Visual Basic and avoid errors.

You can use the same macro technique to save an Excel spreadsheet. Again, you can incorporate this into your application much as the Chapter 29 application has, as follows:

```
'no link
text1.LinkMode = NONE

'set topic
text1.LinkTopic = "EXCEL¦FINANCE"

'set arbitrary cell location, because VB needs it
text1.LinkItem = "R1C1"
```

```
'set link to automatic
text1.LinkMode = AUTOMATIC

'build save file string
cmd$ = "[SAVE()]"

'handle error
On Error GoTo saveerror

'execute saving file
text1.LinkExecute cmd$

'set mode back to manual
text1.LinkMode = MANUAL
```

As a further illustration of how your application can use macros in the source application, consider one more example from Chapter 29. This example shows how you can close an Excel spreadsheet by using the QUIT command macro:

```
'no link
text1.LinkMode = NONE

'set topic
text1.LinkTopic = "EXCEL¦FINANCE"

'set arbitrary cell location, because VB needs it
text1.LinkItem = "R1C1"

'handle error
On Error GoTo exiterror

'set link to automatic
text1.LinkMode = AUTOMATIC

'build quit string
cmd$ = "[QUIT()]"

'execute quitting
text1.LinkExecute cmd$

'set mode back to manual
text1.LinkMode = MANUAL
```

OBJECT LINKING AND EMBEDDING (OLE)

OBJECT LINKING AND EMBEDDING (OLE) IS AN EXCITING NEW TECHNOLOGY THAT WILL BE THE BASIS FOR ALL OF MICROSOFT'S PRODUCTS, INCLUDING PROGRAMMING LANGUAGES, OPERATING SYSTEMS, AND APPLICATIONS. I CALL IT A NEW TECHNOLOGY BECAUSE EVEN THOUGH IT HAS BEEN AROUND FOR A COUPLE OF YEARS, IT HAS BEEN RARELY USED. IT IS JUST NOW BECOMING WIDELY ACCEPTED. OLE WAS BASICALLY DESIGNED TO REPLACE DYNAMIC DATA EXCHANGE (DDE).

For more information on DDE, refer to Chapter 14, "Dynamic Data Exchange (DDE)."

OLE enables applications to communicate with each other reliably. OLE is a very powerful means to create a document that has multiple sources of information and data. The types of data can include sound, video, graphics, bitmaps—almost anything. OLE allows for in-place activation. This means, for example, that if an Excel spreadsheet is embedded into a Word document, the user can double-click on the spreadsheet and edit it right inside Word. You do not have to edit the spreadsheet in Excel.

There are three basic types of OLE:

- ◆ Linking
- ◆ Embedding
- ◆ OLE Automation

The first two, *Linking* and *Embedding*, apply to documents, such as in Microsoft Word. Linking means that an object in the container document is only linked to the server document. This is very similar to DDE (except that it's much more reliable). The server document is the document that contains the object to be linked in the container document. Linking conserves memory because there is no copy of the linked object in the container application. The drawback is that it is not portable. In other words, if you have a Word document with a linked spreadsheet, you cannot copy the document to a disk, load it on another machine, and have the spreadsheet visible. If an object is linked, the container document only increases in size by the amount of overhead necessary to link the document. It does not contain the object itself.

On the other hand, Embedding actually makes a copy of the object and embeds it into the container document. It has more overhead, but it provides for faster updates and more portability.

The third type of OLE is *OLE Automation*, which makes it possible to access another application's objects programmatically. For example, from Visual Basic you can access Microsoft Excel's `Print` object programmatically. OLE Automation is going to greatly increase the power and productivity of the Visual Basic programming language.

Because OLE Automation enables an application to have access to another application's objects programmatically, a custom solution can have access to an object that may not be directly available in OLE. An application that makes the objects it contains available to other applications is said to *expose its objects*. An application that exposes its objects is a *server application*. Visual Basic version 3.0, using OLE 2.0, only has the capability to generate OLE container applications; it cannot expose any objects to the outside world.

Eventually, most of the Microsoft applications will be OLE Servers. For now, Microsoft Word 6.0 is a special case. All macros and functions available are accessed through the `WordBasic` object. Word 6.0 does not expose its objects in the typical manner. The macros available in Word 6.0 are too numerous to mention. Table 15.1 lists the macros not available through OLE Automation.

TABLE 15.1. MICROSOFT WORD 6.0 MACROS AND FUNCTIONS THAT ARE NOT AVAILABLE.

Keyword	Description of USE
Close	Closes an active document or dialog box
LineInput	Reads a line from a sequential file
Name	Renames or moves a file
Open	Opens a sequential file for I/O
Print	Prints to a sequential file
Read	Reads from a sequential file
Write	Writes to a sequential file
Call	Calls a subroutine or macro
For...Next	Conditional loop
Goto	Jump to a specific programmatical location
If...Then...Else	Branching conditions
Select Case	Selecting certain values
Stop	Stops a running macro
While...Wend	Conditional loop
Begin Dialog...End Dialog	Beginning a dialog procedure
Declare	Declaring DLL routines
Dim	Declaring variables
Function...End Function	Declaring a user-defined function
Let	Assigns a value to a variable
Redim	Resizes an array
Rem	Remarks
Sub...End Sub	Declaring a user-defined sub-routine
Err	Most recent error code
Error	Most recent error string
On Error	Error handling
Dialog	Displays a dialog box

continues

197

Keyword	Description of USE
Dialog()	Displays a dialog box and returns the value of the button chosen
GetCurValues	Values for a defined dialog box
ToolsGetSpelling	Fills an array with words suggested from the Spell Checker
ToolsGetSpelling()	Fills an array with words suggested from the Spell Checker and returns the number of replacements
ToolsGetSynonyms	Fills an array with synonyms suggested for a word
ToolsGetSynonyms()	Fills an array with synonyms suggested for a word and returns the number of synonyms

Writing a document application in Visual Basic that will be an OLE container application is very simple and, therefore, is not covered in this book. You simply add the MSOLE2 custom control (either VBX or OCX) into your project. It will prompt you for the type of object to link or embed in your application. It is very straightforward.

OLE AUTOMATION

As mentioned earlier, OLE Automation allows for a server application that exposes its objects to be accessed and programmed from Visual Basic. For example, Microsoft Excel version 5.0 can have its objects programmed from Visual Basic. This capability allows for greater flexibility in programming because you can include some of the functionality of Excel into your Visual Basic application without having to buy any special custom controls.

 To determine which objects are exposed on your system, you can use the Object Browser application that comes with the Office Development Kit (ODK). The ODK is now bundled with Visual Basic version 3.0, Professional Edition, but it has not always been offered this way. If you do not own the ODK, you can purchase it separately.

OLE AUTOMATION AND MICROSOFT WORD 6.0

Microsoft Word does not actually expose its objects. It really only exposes one object, called WordBasic. You can access this or any OLE Automation by using either the OLE custom control in Visual Basic, or by accessing the exposed object registered in the registry database programmatically. If you decide to access the object through the Visual Basic OLE custom control, you must include the MSOLE2.VBX custom control in your project.

Because only one object is exposed in Microsoft Word 6.0, there are a few functions or macros that exist but can't be accessed programmatically. Refer to Table 15.1, which lists these functions and macros.

OLE Automation Using the OLE Custom Control

You can access OLE objects programmatically by placing an OLE2 container control object on your Visual Basic form. To do this, you must include the MSOLE2.VBX custom control in your Visual Basic project. After the control is added, choose the Word 6 document as the type of class.

 Windows maintains a registry (database) of the types of OLE classes available. This registry is not editable or viewable from any part of Windows. There is a way to look at it, however. You must run the REGEDIT.EXE program or add it into the program manager. These actions access the registry that contains all OLE classes. You should not change any entries in the registry because this can seriously affect the way OLE works on your machine.

After the type of class is specified in the OLE custom control, you're ready to access the WordBasic object.

The access of a Word macro or function is really a four-step process, as follows:

◆ Create the OLE link

◆ Access the WordBasic object

◆ Perform any functions or run macros desired

◆ Close the link

These methods create a link. It is not necessary to embed any object because you're only temporarily accessing the functions and macros available in Word 6.0. You must create a Visual Basic object variable and assign the WordBasic object to the Visual Basic object through the OLE custom control. As an example, you can use the following line of code:

```
Set wordobj = oleWord.Object.application.wordbasic
```

 The object variable that you create in Visual Basic must be declared as a variable of Type object with this line: DIM wordobj As Object.

OLE Automation Using Exposed Objects

You can also access OLE Automation functions by using exposed objects. This means that any OLE object registered in the Windows registry database can have its methods and properties accessed and programmed.

What this really means is that you do not necessarily have to add the OLE custom control into your project. Assuming that the OLE object is registered in Windows, you can access the `WordBasic` object using the `CreateObject()` function like this:

```
Set wordobj = CreateObject("Word.Basic")
```

The rest of the programming of the object is the same as in the previous section.

INVOKING MICROSOFT WORD 6.0'S SPELL CHECKER

Invoking the Word Spell Checker is as easy as accessing the `ToolsSpelling` function in Word 6.0. Your application can, for example, check the spelling of a Visual Basic text box. This is a great way to avoid having to purchase an expensive custom control just for spell checking.

You could incorporate spell checking in a text box, much the way the application in Chapter 30 does it.

 For more information about how OLE Automation is incorporated into an application, refer to Chapter 30, "Object Linking and Embedding (OLE) Application."

Following is a code fragment from Chapter 30, which invokes the Spell Checker from Word 6.0:

```
'start OLE control
oleWord.Action = OLE_ACTIVATE

'assign wordobj with word basic
Set wordobj = oleWord.Object.application.wordbasic

'initialize flag
Selected% = False

'position to beginning of OLE document
wordobj.startofdocument

'position to end, selecting all in between
wordobj.endofdocument (1)

'clear selection
wordobj.editclear

If txtOLE.SelText <> "" Then
    'flag selected
    Selected% = True

    'insert only selected text
    wordobj.insert txtOLE.SelText
Else
    'insert all text from VB Text box
    wordobj.insert txtOLE.Text
End If

'handle errors
```

```
      On Error GoTo SpellError

      'check spelling
      wordobj.toolsspelling

      'all worked fine
      MsgBox "Finished Spell Checking!"

      'position to beginning
      wordobj.startofdocument

      'position to end, selection all in between
      wordobj.endofdocument (1)

      'cut selection to clipboard
      wordobj.editcut

If Selected% = False Then
    'nothing was selected, replace whole text
    LeftText$ = Left$ (txtOLE.Text, txtOLE.SelStart)
    RightText$ = Right$ (txtOLE.Text, Len(txtOLE) - (txtOLE.SelStart + txtOLE.SelLength))
End If

'close ole object
oleWord.Action = OLE_CLOSE
```

The theory behind what the code is doing here is that after the OLE custom control is activated, one of two things happens. If there is no text selected in the Visual Basic text box, all of the text from the text box is inserted into the Linked OLE control document. Otherwise, if there is text selected in the Visual Basic text box, only the selected text is inserted into the Linked OLE control document. This ensures that only the desired text is spell checked. The standard Microsoft Word dialog box appears if there is an incorrectly spelled word, using the ToolsSpelling Word 6.0 function. (There are some other functions that are used in the preceding code, listed in Table 15.2 for your reference.) Then all of the text in the OLE control document is selected and copied to the clipboard. From the clipboard, the text is placed back into the Visual Basic text box, and the OLE custom control is closed.

TABLE 15.2. MICROSOFT WORD 6.0 FUNCTIONS USED IN SPELL CHECKING.

Keyword	Description of Use
StartOfDocument	Positions the insertion point at the beginning of the document
EndOfDocument	Positions the insertion point at the end of the document, but selects everything in between
EditClear	Deletes the selected text
Insert	Inserts text at the insertion point
ToolsSpelling	Spell checks the selected text
EditCut	Removes the selected text and places it on the clipboard

OLE automation really is very simple, considering all of the functionality you get from it. You can incorporate this into your applications, but the basic code and functions accessed do not change.

INVOKING WORD'S GRAMMAR CHECKER

Invoking Word's Grammar Checker is very similar to the Spell Checker. It may be a good idea for you to incorporate the Grammar Checker with the Spell Checker in your Visual Basic application. This incorporation gives the application more of a professional feel. Invoking the Grammar Checker uses the same methodology as the Spell Checker, but instead of the `ToolsSpelling` function the `ToolsGrammar` function is used. Except for the `ToolsGrammar` function, the functions used in this code are listed in Table 15.2

```
'start OLE control
oleWord.Action = OLE_ACTIVATE

'assign wordobj with word basic
Set wordobj = oleWord.Object.application.wordbasic

'position to beginning of OLE document
wordobj.startofdocument

'position to end, selecting all in between
wordobj.endofdocument (1)

'clear selection
wordobj.editclear

'insert all text from VB Text box
wordobj.insert txtOLE.Text

'handle errors
On Error GoTo GrammarError

'check spelling
wordobj.ToolsGrammar

'all worked fine
MsgBox "Finished Checking Grammar!"

'position to beginning
wordobj.startofdocument

'position to end, selection all in between
wordobj.endofdocument (1)

'cut selection to clipboard
wordobj.editcut

'nothing was selected, replace whole text
```

```
txtOLE.Text = clipboard.GetText(1)

'close ole object
oleWord.Action = OLE_CLOSE
```

INVOKING WORD'S THESAURUS

Invoking Word's Thesaurus is very similar to the Spell Checker and Grammar Checker. It uses the same methodology, but the ToolsThesaurus function is used to invoke the Thesaurus. Except for the ToolsThesaurus function, the functions used in this code are listed in Table 15.2

```
'start OLE control
oleWord.Action = OLE_ACTIVATE

'assign wordobj with word basic
Set wordobj = oleWord.Object.application.wordbasic

'position to beginning of OLE document
wordobj.startofdocument

'position to end, selecting all in between
wordobj.endofdocument (1)

'clear selection
wordobj.editclear

'insert only selected text
wordobj.insert txtOLE.SelText

'handle errors
On Error GoTo ThesaurusError

'check thesaurus
wordobj.toolsthesaurus

'all worked fine
MsgBox "Finished Checking Thesaurus"

'position to beginning
wordobj.startofdocument

'position to end, selection all in between
wordobj.endofdocument (1)

'cut selection to clipboard
wordobj.editcut

'text was selected, replace only selected text
LeftText$ = Left$(txtOLE.Text, txtOLE.SelStart)
RightText$ = Right$(txtOLE.Text, Len(txtOLE) - (txtOLE.SelStart + txtOLE.SelLength))
txtOLE.Text = LeftText$ + clipboard.GetText(1) + RightText$

'close ole object
oleWord.Action = OLE_CLOSE
```

OLE AUTOMATION AND OTHER APPLICATIONS

OLE Automation is currently available in the following Microsoft products:

- Word version 6.0
- Excel version 5.0
- Project version 4.0
- Access 2.0

If you want to access and program exposed objects for one of these applications, use the Office Development Kit (ODK) for information about which objects an application exposes. You can use the Object Browser Application that comes with the ODK to find out which objects are registered on your machine.

You use the techniques described earlier to access these objects. For example, if you want to open and show a new Excel worksheet, you can do it with the following three lines of code:

```
Dim TheObj As Object
Set TheObj = CreateObject("Excel.Application")
TheObj.Visible = True
```

The second line opens Excel (as long as it is registered on your machine). The third line makes the worksheet visible. You can use code similar to this in your applications to access any of the exposed objects for OLE Automation.

You can determine which functions, objects, and methods are available (exposed) in other OLE server applications by using either the documentation for that product or by using a program called the Object Browser, which comes with the ODK.

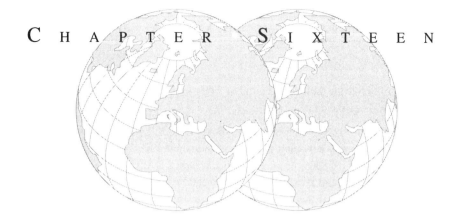

DATA ACCESS

DATA ACCESS WITH VISUAL BASIC CAN BE SIMPLIFIED INTO TWO DIFFERENT CATEGORIES: BY USING THE *DATA ACCESS CONTROL* AND THE *DATA ACCESS OBJECT (DAO)*. THE DATA ACCESS CONTROL IS A CONTROL THAT COMES WITH VISUAL BASIC, PROVIDING A WAY TO CONTROL A TABLE BY ACCESSING THE TABLE DIRECTLY. YOU DO NOT NEED ANY CODE TO EDIT OR ADD TO THE DATABASE BECAUSE THE CONTROL IS BOUND TO A PARTICULAR DATABASE YOU SPECIFY IN A VISUAL BASIC PROPERTY. EACH INDIVIDUAL FIELD CAN BE AC-CESSED BY USING A BOUND CONTROL, SUCH AS A TEXT BOX. THE TEXT BOX IS BOUND TO A PARTICULAR DATABASE CONTROL BY SPECIFYING THE NAME OF THE DATA ACCESS CONTROL, AS WELL AS THE FIELD IT WILL BE BOUND TO. THE `DataSource` PROPERTY IS USED TO SPECIFY THE DATA ACCESS CONTROL USED. THE `DataField` PROPERTY IS USED TO specify the column in the table to be bound to. The use of the data access control allows for code-free manipulation of the data.

The second category is by using the Data Access Object (DAO), a set of objects available in Visual Basic that greatly enhances the data access capabilities by providing a way to construct data queries manually. Code is required if you use DAO. DAO is made possible by using Visual Basic object variables and DAO `Recordset` objects. A `Recordset` object is basically a virtual table containing a view of the data, which you can then manipulate. Table 16.1 lists the Data Access Objects.

TABLE 16.1. DATA ACCESS OBJECTS.

Property	Description of Use
Recordset	A generic term describing all of the fields that make up records, such as a `Dynaset`, `Table`, or `Snapshot`.
Database	Object pointing to a physical database.
Dynaset	View of data containing rows and columns that can update the underlying physical database.
Table	Object pointing to a physical table.
Snapshot	Type of `Recordset` that is a view of data containing rows and columns, but isn't linked to a physical database. It is a copy of the data.
Field	Object pointing to a physical field in a table.
Fields	A collection of all of the fields in a table.
Index	Object pointing to a particular index in a table.
Indexes	A collection of all of the indexes in a table.
TableDef	Object pointing to the structure of a table.
TableDefs	A collection of all of the `TableDefs` in a database.
QueryDef	Definition of a query stored in a database.

To use DAO, you must declare the object variables. After you do this, you can assign the DAO by using the syntaxes listed here.

The syntax for creating a database is as follows:

```
Set database = CreateDatabase(databasename,locale[,options])
```

The syntax for creating a dynaset is as follows:

```
Set dynaset = CreateDynaset(source[,options])
```

The syntax for creating a `querydef` is as follows:

```
Set querydef = CreateQueryDef(name[,sqltext])
```

The syntax for creating a `Snapshot` is as follows:

```
Set snapshot = CreateSnapshot(source[,options])
```

THE DATA ACCESS CONTROL

The *Data Access control* allows for code-free manipulation of a database or table. However, you may want to add code to enhance the way the Data Access control is used to achieve greater functionality. Use of the Data Access control is very simple, so there is only one example here.

DYNAMICALLY BINDING CONTROLS TO TABLES

As stated earlier, to use the Data Access control, you must assign the database to be used, the table, and the column in the table that the control represents. There are many times you may want to assign either the table name or column name in code. This makes it so that you can use one Visual Basic form for many different purposes. You do not have to use one form for every possible table or column name.

An easy way to accomplish this is to have an array of text boxes that is bound to a database by using the Data Access control. The only difference is that these text boxes have the `DataSource` and `DataField` properties assigned dynamically at runtime.

For example, consider the application in Chapter 31, "Data Access Application," which does just this. The text boxes in the application in Chapter 31 are part of a control array. There are routines that populate and assign the text boxes based on the table that is currently being accessed. Based on a menu selection, the text boxes populate the fields based on dynamically selecting the table and assigning the fields. Following is a code fragment from Chapter 31 that is used to populate the controls based on using the "INVENTORY" table:

```
'assign table
Data1.RecordSource = "INVENTORY"

'assign captions
pnlFieldLabel(0).Caption = "Product ID"
pnlFieldLabel(1).Caption = "Description"
pnlFieldLabel(2).Caption = "Supplier ID"
pnlFieldLabel(3).Caption = "Quantity"

'enable text boxes
txtField(0).Enabled = True
txtField(1).Enabled = True
txtField(2).Enabled = True
txtField(3).Enabled = True
```

```
'assign fields to text boxes
txtField(0).DataField = "product_id"
txtField(1).DataField = "description"
txtField(2).DataField = "supplier_id"
txtField(3).DataField = "quantity"

'refresh so new parameters will take effect
Data1.Refresh
```

In the preceding code, first the `RecordSource` property of the Data Access control is set to the table name to be accessed (which is the basis of all of the data in each of the text boxes). Next an appropriate label is shown so that the user knows which column a text box is bound to. Then all text boxes are enabled so that errors don't occur. An error would occur if the text box is disabled when you set the `DataField` property. Then each text box in the control array has its `DataField` property set to a column in the table. To make this change take effect, the Data Access control calls a method, `Refresh`. That's really all there is to it. If you use this technique in your application, the table names change as do the column names, but the concept is identical.

THE DATA ACCESS OBJECT (DAO)

The *Data Access Object* allows for the manipulation of data by using a Visual Basic object. Using DAO is more work because it is more code, but you can achieve more functionality than you can by simply using the Data Access control.

ADDING A NEW RECORD

If you have a table that you are adding a record to, it's a good idea to check to make sure that the record being added is not already in the table. This step prevents duplicates.

 If you add a record that is a duplicate, you will receive an error, providing that an index has been defined to disallow duplicates. The topic presented here is a general way to avoid this error and to provide useful feedback to the user.

As an example, consider the following code fragment from Chapter 31, "Data Access Application," which adds a new record to an Inventory table:

```
Case "INVENTORY":
        'ensure entity integrity by checking primary key of table
        cmd$ = "SELECT * FROM INVENTORY "
        cmd$ = cmd$ + "WHERE product_id = '" + txtField(0).Text + "' "
        Set DS = DB.CreateDynaset(cmd$)

        If DS.RecordCount > 0 Then
            'build message
            m$ = "Product ID " + txtField(0).Text + " already exists"
            MsgBox m$
```

```
        'exit
        Exit Sub
    End If

    'find out if this supplier exists
    cmd$ = "SELECT * FROM SUPPLIER "
    cmd$ = cmd$ + "WHERE supplier_id = '" + txtField(2).Text + "' "
    Set DS = DB.CreateDynaset(cmd$)
    If DS.RecordCount = 0 Then
        'this supplier doesn't exist in the database
        m$ = "Supplier ID " + txtField(2).Text + " doesn't exist in the supplier
        table"
        MsgBox m$
        Exit Sub
    End If

    'create dynaset for new record
    Set DS = DB.CreateDynaset("SELECT * FROM INVENTORY")

    'tell the dynaset to add a new record
    DS.AddNew

    'add individual fields
    DS("product_id") = txtField(0).Text
    DS("description") = txtField(1).Text
    DS("supplier_id") = txtField(2).Text
    DS("quantity") = txtField(3).Text

    'update dynaset
    DS.Update

    'unflag changes made
    ChangeMade% = False

    'repopulate
    Call menu_inventory_Click
```

 Notice that in the first couple of lines in the preceding code that there is SQL (Structured Query Language) code. For more information about SQL, refer to Chapter 18, "Structured Query Language (SQL)."

The technique is to create a dynaset using the `CreateDynaset` function to determine if the primary key exists in a table. The primary key is used to determine how to access a unique row in the table.

If the primary key does not exist, another dynaset is created based on the entire table. Then the `AddNew` method is used to tell the dynaset to make room for a new record. Each of the individual fields in the dynaset is updated with the following format:

```
DS("product_id") = txtField(0).Text
```

where `DS` is the dynaset object, and `"product id"` is the field inside the dynaset. Your application can use this technique to check the primary key of a table or any other field to let the user know if the data has already been added and, therefore, notify the user appropriately.

UPDATING A RECORD

If you are going to update a record with code by using the DAO and you want to update a record, you must find out which fields have changed and, therefore, need to be updated. The reason you need to find this out is because if the field updated is a primary key field, you must make sure that the new value does not exist. This procedure maintains integrity within the table.

It's a good idea if you're going to handle the updating in code (that is, without the Data Access control) to store the old values in a variable before the user changes them. You do this for two reasons:

◆ To perform an update, you must have a way to identify the row in the table

◆ To allow for the possibility to undo all changes

Consider how the application in Chapter 31 updates the Inventory table:

```
'only check if this is the field being updated
If Text1$ <> txtField(0).Text Then
    'ensure entity integrity by checking primary key of table
    cmd$ = "SELECT * FROM INVENTORY "
    cmd$ = cmd$ + "WHERE product_id = '" + txtField(0).Text + "' "
    Set DS = DB.CreateDynaset(cmd$)

    If DS.RecordCount > 0 Then
        'build message
        m$ = "Product ID " + txtField(0).Text + " already exists"
        MsgBox m$

        'exit
        Exit Sub
    End If
End If

'only check if this is the field being updated
If Text3$ <> txtField(2).Text Then
    'find out if this supplier exists
    cmd$ = "SELECT * FROM SUPPLIER "
    cmd$ = cmd$ + "WHERE supplier_id = '" + txtField(2).Text + "' "
    Set DS = DB.CreateDynaset(cmd$)
    If DS.RecordCount = 0 Then
        'this supplier doesn't exist in the database
        m$ = "Supplier ID " + txtField(2).Text + " doesn't exist in the
        supplier table"
        MsgBox m$
        Exit Sub
    End If
End If

'create dynaset from old data
cmd$ = "SELECT * FROM INVENTORY "
cmd$ = cmd$ + "WHERE product_id = '" + Text1$ + "' "
```

```
cmd$ = cmd$ + "AND description = '" + Text2$ + "' "
cmd$ = cmd$ + "AND supplier_id = '" + Text3$ + "' "
cmd$ = cmd$ + "AND quantity = " + Text4$ + " "
Set DS = DB.CreateDynaset(cmd$)

'edit the dynaset
DS.Edit

'add individual fields
DS("product_id") = txtField(0).Text
DS("description") = txtField(1).Text
DS("supplier_id") = txtField(2).Text
DS("quantity") = txtField(3).Text

'update dynaset
DS.Update

'unflag changes made
ChangeMade% = False

'repopulate
Call menu_inventory_Click
```

The technique is to create a `Dynaset` using the `CreateDynaset` function to determine if the primary key exists in a table. If the primary key does not exist, you can edit the record with the `Edit` method.

DELETING A RECORD

You delete a record by using the `Delete` method, which is simple to use. You simply create a `Dynaset` of the data you are going to delete and then delete it. The following code fragment deletes a record from the Inventory table in Chapter 31:

```
Case "INVENTORY":
    'create dynaset before deleting record
    Set DS = DB.CreateDynaset("SELECT * FROM INVENTORY")

    'tell the dynaset to delete current
    DS.Delete

    'unflag changes made
    ChangeMade% = False

    'repopulate
    Call menu_inventory_Click
```

Your application can use the same technique to delete data from a `Recordset` or even prompt the user for confirmation before deleting.

REPORTING ON THE DATA

After all of the tables have been filled with the desired data, it doesn't do much good if you can't report on them. *Crystal Reports* is a reporting system that comes with Visual Basic, Professional Edition. It is the reporting tool used with the application in Chapter 31, but is covered in detail in Chapter 17.

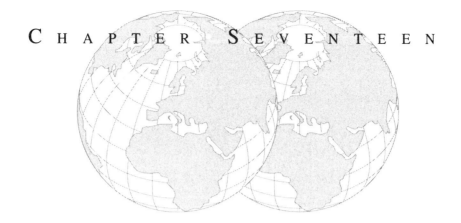

CHAPTER SEVENTEEN

CRYSTAL REPORTS

CRYSTAL REPORTS IS AN EASY-TO-USE REPORT WRITER THAT COMES WITH THE PROFESSIONAL EDITION OF VISUAL BASIC. IF YOU OWN THE STANDARD VERSION, YOU CAN PURCHASE CRYSTAL REPORTS FROM CRYSTAL SERVICES. THE TOPICS DISCUSSED IN THIS CHAPTER APPLY TO CRYSTAL REPORTS VERSION 2.0, THE VERSION THAT COMES WITH VISUAL BASIC VERSION 3.0, PROFESSIONAL EDITION. MANY OF THE TOPICS AND CONCEPTS APPLY TO LATER VERSIONS OF CRYSTAL REPORTS, WHICH ARE AVAILABLE AT AN ADDITIONAL COST.

REM You can order Crystal Reports from Crystal Services by calling (604) 681-3435.

THE DEVELOPMENT CYCLE OF CRYSTAL REPORTS

It's important to understand the development cycle of a Crystal Report. It is designed in two steps:

1. Design the report layout in the Crystal Reports design environment.
2. Write code in your Visual Basic application that runs the report designed in the previous step.

To access the design environment, from now on called the IDE (Integrated Design Environment), simply run the program in the Visual Basic directory named CRW.EXE. There is an icon for this file in your Visual Basic Program Manager group. Also, follow the steps listed in the rest of this chapter. Figure 17.1 shows what the Crystal Reports design environment looks like after double-clicking on the icon. Each of the Crystal Reports icons is listed in the figure.

FIGURE 17.1.
Crystal Reports design environment and its icons.

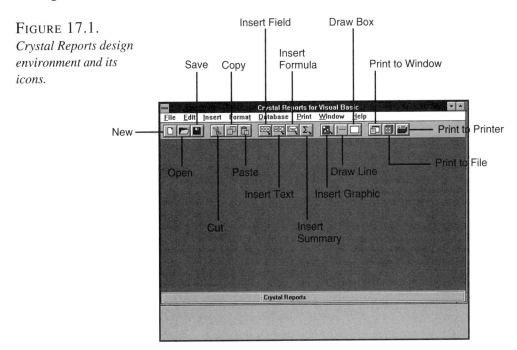

If you have run the JET 2.0 compatibility layer, you will not be able to run the Crystal Reports version that ships with Visual Basic version 3.0, Professional Edition, until you bring Crystal reports up to the JET 2.0 standard. The JET 2.0 compatibility layer allows you to write Access programs that will communicate with JET 2.0. JET 2.0 is the database engine used with Access 2.0.

To bring Crystal Reports up to the JET 2.0 standard, you must run the CRWACC20.EXE program. This program can be found on the Office Development Kit (ODK) CD that is sometimes (but not always) shipped with the Professional Edition of Visual Basic 3.0. You install it from SETUP.EXE in the COMLAYER subdirectory on the ODK CD itself. You can also find it on the CD accompanying this book in the UPDATE subdirectory. Running this program updates the following files:

- PDBJET.DLL
- PDCTJET.DLL
- PDIRJET.DLL
- MSAJT112.DLL

For this update to work, you must have all four DLLs listed here in the same directory as the CRWACC20.EXE program. Use the following syntax:

```
CRWACC20.EXE path
```

where *path* is the name of the path in which your CRW.EXE Crystal Reports executable file is located. If the CRW.EXE is in the same directory in which the five files listed here are, you can omit the *path* variable.

The new files are updated only if the date of each of the DLL files to be replaced is earlier than the date of the files that need to be used instead. Therefore, if you know you need to replace the files anyway, you can simply copy the four DLLs to the \WINDOWS\SYSTEM directory. You will know that this is the case if you attempt to perform this update, and you get an application error Call To Undefined Dynalink when you run a Crystal Report.

THE CONCEPT OF A REPORT WRITER

A Report Writer is designed to make the report designing process greatly simplified. The concept of a report writer is, among other things, to:

- Design how the report is to look.
- Add groupings that break every time the data in this group is changed.
- Add subtotals based on these groupings, if desired.

For example, if you want to show a list of sales and you don't add a grouping, you see a list of *all* sales. You see one line of "Details" for every sale, but you cannot give a subtotal, for example, for all regions. If you want to see a report based on each region individually, you must group by the field "Region."

If in each region you want to see a detailed list of sales of each product in each region, you need to add a second "level" of groupings. This grouping is based on the "Product" field.

The preceding is basically the concept of how you define your report. You cannot dynamically add a grouping from Visual Basic. Therefore, if you want to show a report grouped by region and sometimes by region and product, you have to create two separate reports. Crystal Reports refers to these groupings as *group sections*.

After you define the report, make sure it works correctly in the IDE. The next step is to save the file. Save the file with a *.RPT file extension. Finally, in Visual Basic you must include the CRYSTAL.VBX custom control into your project. This enables you to access its properties that directly use the Crystal Reports Print Engine. This print engine defines how Crystal Reports works and is in a file called CRPE.DLL. You access properties of this VBX to control certain parameters of your report, one of which is the actual report to run. Programming the Visual Basic code is covered later in this chapter.

 A possibly confusing term that Crystal Reports uses is *printing*. Whether a report goes to the printer, screen, or to a file, it is referred to as "printing" a report. It can be confusing if you think of "printing" to a screen. You tend to think of only a BASIC language printing to a screen, not a commercial product.

CREATING A NEW REPORT

To create a new report, select the File->New Report menu option, or click the New Report icon on the toolbar (refer to Figure 17.1).

 You can also create a new Mailing Labels report, but the concepts discussed here apply to both reports and mailing labels.

You are prompted to select the database file that is to be the basis of the report. By default, the Microsoft Access (MDB) database files are presented. If you want to choose a SQL database, choose the SQL Database command button. Figure 17.2 shows what this screen looks like.

After opening a new report, you see a blank screen with the possible fields in the database in a window. The report itself has only three sections to start with: The first section is a Page Header; the second is Details; and the third is a Page Footer. The report is waiting for you to add fields from the database on the report or to modify the report in some way. Figure 17.3 shows the screen waiting for some action to occur after you create a new report.

FIGURE 17.2.
Creating a new report.

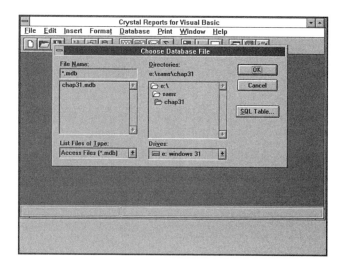

FIGURE 17.3.
Crystal Reports after creating a new report.

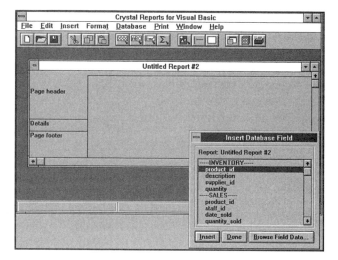

ADDING GROUP SECTIONS

The next step is to add the group sections of your report. It's a good idea to perform this step now because you cannot add a field to a section that doesn't exist yet. To add a group section, select the Insert->Group Section menu option. This action invokes a dialog box prompting you to select a field that the group section is to be based on.

Add sections by planning carefully how you want your report to look. Use the scenario suggested in the "Concept of a Report Writer" section earlier in this chapter for clarification. Figure 17.4 shows the dialog box presented after selecting Insert->Group Section option.

FIGURE 17.4.
*Crystal Reports Insert
Group Section dialog
box.*

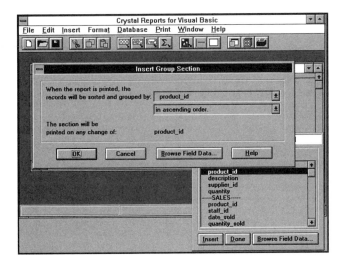

Group sections are used to determine which fields the report breaks on, but they do not have to be shown when the report prints. This effectively lets you sort the report in any way you want. For example, using the previous scenario, if you want to display a tabular format report (all fields, each on every line), you can add Region and Product in the "Details" section, along with the Sale Price. However, to ensure that the report is sorted based first on Region and then on Product, you must still have these two groupings in this order, but you must hide them. This ensures that the report is sorted correctly, but only the desired fields are displayed.

To hide a section, click on the right mouse button while the mouse cursor is in the left margin of the section. If the section is currently hidden, the option available is Show. If the section is shown, the option available is Hide. Simply click on the option to perform the desired function.

 Every section except the Details section actually hides (by collapsing in size) in the Crystal Reports IDE. This is a design time visual representation that the section will not be printed. Any fields placed in the Details section are grayed and do not actually collapse.

ADDING FIELDS TO A NEW REPORT

You can add four different types of fields to a report. They are

◆ Database fields
◆ Text fields
◆ Formula fields
◆ Special fields

A *Database field* is a field that prints data that is retrieved directly from a database.

A *Text field* is used simply as a label. It can identify a field, region of the report, title, or anything else. It is necessary because for these purposes you would not use a database field and, most likely, not a formula field.

A *Formula field* inserts the results of a formula into a report. A formula can be virtually anything: A formula can be a constant value, such as "WELCOME," which is effectively the same as a text field; it can be a static formula, such as "5 * 10"; it can be a date or time; it can be a Database field name. You can combine any of the above. For example, you can multiply a sale price Database field by a sales tax rate to determine sales tax. The possibilities for a Formula field are endless.

A *Special field* is a field that cannot be defined by the user. These fields are predefined in Crystal Reports. They are

- ◆ Print Date field
- ◆ Page Number field
- ◆ Record Number field
- ◆ Group Number field

The meanings of these fields are self-explanatory; their names explain what each field does.

DATABASE FIELDS

To add a new database field to the report, you need to make sure that the Insert Database Field dialog box is open. If it is not, you can invoke it either by clicking the icon on the toolbar or by selecting the Insert->Database Field menu option. After the dialog box appears, you can simply double-click on the field desired. You will see that the icon has changed, indicating that you have selected a certain field. You can then drag and drop the field wherever you want it to appear on the report.

You must keep in mind how the report is going to work. If you put the field in the Header section, the field prints at the top of the page every time a new page prints. Similarly, if you place the field in the Footer section, it prints at the bottom of the page every time a new page prints.

Therefore, using the scenario described earlier in the "Concept of a Report Writer" section, if the field you're trying to place on the report is the Region, you want it to be in the first section called Region. If the first section doesn't exist, you must add it. Refer to the section "Adding Group Sections" earlier in the chapter. If you put the field in the Details section, the field prints every time a new line of detail is encountered. You don't necessarily need to see the region for every line of sales. It's generally sufficient to see a heading, such as Region, at the top of the section.

If you are trying to place a field such as Sale Price on your report, you have to place it in the Details section because it's what you're trying to see at a detail level.

TEXT FIELDS

To insert a text field, select the Insert Text icon on the toolbar or the Insert->Text Field menu option (refer to Figure 17.1 for icon names). You are prompted for the text of the field to place on the report.

FORMULA FIELDS

To insert a Formula field, select the icon on the toolbar or the Insert->Formula Field menu option. You are prompted for the name of the formula. Every formula has to have a name. Choose something that is germane to its usage. After you choose a name and click on the OK button, an Edit Formula dialog box appears. Figure 17.5 shows what this dialog box looks like.

FIGURE 17.5.
*Crystal reports Edit
Formula dialog box.*

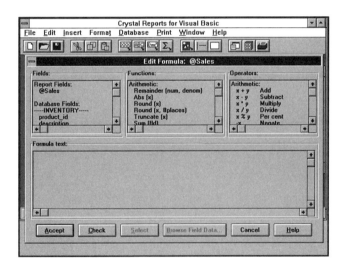

This dialog box is really a "Formula Wizard" because it allows you to point and click fields, functions, and operators to build your formula for you. You can, however, enter the formula text yourself. For example, if you want to use this Formula field as a Text field displaying the text "WELCOME", simply type `"WELCOME"` in quotes because it is a string literal.

This chapter cannot cover all of the possible functions and operators, but the basic rule of thumb is to double-click on the field, function, and operator you want to use. If a function requires three arguments, for example, it leaves commas showing that it expects three arguments in the formula text area. You can then place the cursor where the argument is expected and double-click again on any field, function, or operator to fill the argument required.

Use the Check command button to check the syntax of your formula. You receive an error if there are any problems. For example, if you're trying to compare or assign a string field to an integer, you receive an error. As with any programming language, if you want to compare or assign different data types, they must be converted first. There are some converting functions in the Functions section of the Edit Formula dialog box.

Clicking on the Accept command button is just like clicking on an OK button. This action closes the dialog box but first performs the same function as clicking the Check command button.

MODIFYING OR DELETING FIELDS ON A REPORT

To modify many fields and areas on the report, you can click on the field or area with the right mouse button. This action invokes a pop-up menu showing options you can select. Notice that for a Database field, one of the options is *not* changing the field in a table this is pointing to. To do this, you must actually delete the field and insert a new one, using the desired Database field.

To delete a field or area on the report, you can use the right mouse button to click on the field or area and select the Delete option. You can also choose the Edit->Clear menu option or press the Delete key.

LIMITING RECORDS

You do not have to have the report display all data items in a database. Using the scenario presented earlier, suppose that you want to see only the records dealing with the Northeast region. You can limit the display by selecting the Print->Edit Record Selection Formula menu option. This action invokes a dialog box very similar to the Edit Formula dialog box. To limit the records to the Northeast, you simply select the Region field and type = `'NE'`. Notice that NE is in single quotations. This is for clarification purposes only. Crystal Reports can also use double quotations.

Another way to edit the selection criteria is to click on the field to be limited with the right mouse button. This action invokes a pop-up menu. Select the Select Records menu option, which invokes a dialog box different from the one presented so far. It achieves the same effect as the previous paragraph, but it's a little easier to use. Figure 17.6 shows the Select Records dialog box.

ESTABLISHING LINKS

Very often, it's not sufficient to have the data you need in one table. You need to look up data in one table based on a field in another table. This is called a *join* or *link*. You can set up a link with a table in the database that is already being used (because it was selected when creating the report) or another database. If you want to link to a field in another database, you must add it to the report first. To do this, select the Database->Add File to Report menu option. Select the database file you want to add. If the table is in the same database, you don't need to add the same database file again.

FIGURE 17.6.
*Crystal Reports Select
Records dialog box.*

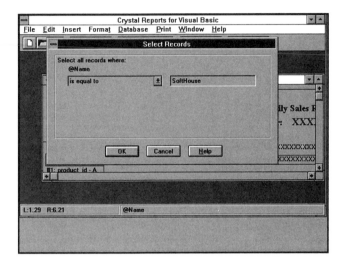

If you want to view which links are present, select the Database->File Links menu option. If you want to add a new link, click the New command button. Figure 17.7 shows the File Links dialog box.

FIGURE 17.7.
*Crystal Reports File
Links dialog box.*

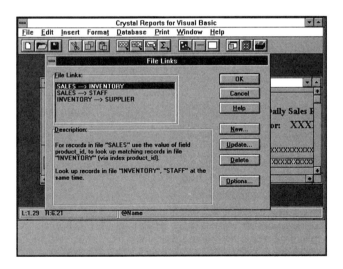

After selecting the New command button, you are presented with yet another dialog box. It is used to select the fields in the tables located in databases that were previously added to the report. Simply click on the table on the left side of the screen that will be linked to the table on the right side of the screen. Then select the appropriate fields to be linked. Figure 17.8 shows the Define Link dialog box.

FIGURE 17.8.
Crystal Reports Define Link dialog box.

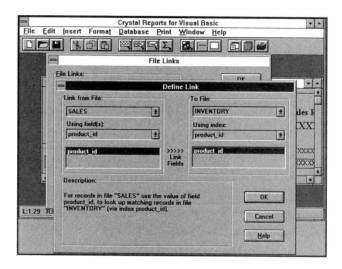

For example, if you have a table of customers and a table of orders, you should have a field that is common to both, probably called CUSTNUM for customer number. This is a much more efficient way to store the data than to have everything repeated in one table.

FILE LOCATIONS AND ALIASES

When you add a database file to the report, you select the location of the file, which is stored internally with the report. What if you move the location of the database? There is a menu option called Database->File Location that allows you to reassign where the database is located. A dialog box appears so you can select the appropriate location.

An alias is necessary if you have two tables you need to add to a report but use the same name. For example, if you need to link two tables called CUSTOMER, you can alias one table as NEWCUSTOMER. An alias is almost never needed because most databases are designed so that this is not necessary. There are times, however, when situations arise that you didn't anticipate, and you find yourself needing an alias for a table. If you alias a table, the name of the table inside Crystal Reports will be that alias, not the original table name.

To assign an alias, select the Database->File Alias menu option. The File Alias dialog box appears for you to enter the name of the alias.

MISCELLANEOUS TOPICS

The following miscellaneous topics are not significant enough to be listed under their own headings but are featured in Crystal Reports.

You can use graphics in Crystal Reports very easily. You can insert a graphic, a line, or a box.

You can format fields just as you do in most other programs, such as font, size, color, and so on. You can click on the field with the right mouse button and select the Change Font, Change Format, or Change Border and Colors menu options. For a Text field, you have an additional option to change the text of the field. For a Formula field, you have an additional option to change the formula in the field. You may also select any of these options under the Format menu option.

It's important that you test the report before you write your Visual Basic code. You can test the report by printing it to the screen, printer, or file. To use any of these options, you can click the appropriate icon on the toolbar or select the menu option under the Print menu.

THE VISUAL BASIC INTERFACE

All topics previously discussed cover creating the report in the Crystal Reports IDE environment. What about how to use the report that was created externally, inside Visual Basic?

The answer to this is that you must add to your Visual Basic project the CRYSTAL.VBX custom control that comes with Crystal Reports. Then add the control to your form. You access properties of the VBX to control the parameters of the report. For example, this is where you enter the name of the report file you've just created. You can also specify many different parameters not available in the Crystal Reports IDE. Table 17.1 lists the properties available in the CRYSTAL.VBX custom control.

TABLE 17.1. CRYSTAL.VBX PROPERTIES.

Property	Purpose
Action	Prints a specified report if set to 1
Connect	Connects string for an ODBC database
CopiesToPrinter	Specifies number of copies to print
DataFiles	Indexed property that sets a new location of a database
Destination	Specifies where to print the report (0-Screen, 1-Printer, 2-File)
Formulas	Indexed property that sets values of formulas
GroupSelectionFormula	Specifies the formula for group selection
GroupSortFields	Indexed property that specifies how fields are sorted
LastErrorNumber	Specifies the last error number
LastErrorString	Specifies the error string of the last error number
Left	Specifies the left coordinate of the CRYSTAL.VBX control
Name	Specifies the name of the CRYSTAL.VBX control
Password	Sets the password of a non-ODBC database

PrintFileName	When Destination is set to 2 (File), the file name is specified here
PrintFileType	When Destination is set to 2 (File), the type of the file is specified here. (0-Record, 1-Tab Separated, 2-Text, 3-DIF, 4-CSV, 5-Reserved, 6-Tab Separated Text)
ReportFileName	Specifies the name of the report created earlier in this chapter
SelectionFormula	Specifies the formula to limit the records returned
SessionHandle	Specifies the session handle for this Crystal Reports session
SortFields	Indexed property that specifies how to sort data
Top	Specifies the top coordinate of the CRYSTAL.VBX control
UserName	Specifies user name for non-ODBC databases
WindowBorderStyle	Specifies the type of border the Print window will have (0-None, 1-Fixed Single, 2-Sizable, 3-Fixed Double)
WindowControlBox	Boolean property specifying if a control box (system menu) will be present on the Print window
WindowHeight	Specifies the height of the Print window
WindowLeft	Specifies the left coordinate of the Print window
WindowMaxButton	Boolean property specifying if a maximize button will be present on the Print window
WindowMinButton	Boolean property specifying if a minimize button will be present on the Print window
WindowParentHandle	Specifies the handle of the form to which the Print window is to be a child of
WindowTitle	Specifies the title of the Print window
WindowTop	Specifies the top coordinate of the Print window
WindowWidth	Specifies the width of the Print window

For the properties listed here that are indexed, you can pass multiple values (arrays) to the Crystal Reports Print Engine (CRPE) through the control. For example, if you want to pass five formulas to the CRPE, you don't have five Formulas properties. You specify the five formulas with five different indexes for the Formulas property, starting with zero.

To see how to use the CRYSTAL.VBX custom control, consider the application in Chapter 31, "Data Access Application." It uses the CRYSTAL.VBX custom control to run one of three reports designed in the Crystal Reports IDE.

For more information about how the Crystal Report is defined, open any of the reports in the CHAP31 directory using the Crystal Reports IDE.

You typically won't use many of the properties in the CRYSTAL.VBX custom control. Consider this code from Chapter 31:

```
'determine which report to print
If optStaff.Value = True Then
    rptCrystal.ReportFileName = "STAFF.RPT"
ElseIf optSales.Value = True Then
    rptCrystal.ReportFileName = "SALES.RPT"
    'also send date to filter output of report
    If optToday.Value = True Then
        rptCrystal.Formulas(0) = "PrintDate = '" + Format$(Now, "MM/DD/YY") + "'"
    Else
        rptCrystal.Formulas(0) = "PrintDate = '" + txtOther.Text + "'"
    End If
ElseIf optInventory.Value = True Then
    rptCrystal.ReportFileName = "INVENT.RPT"
End If
```

The preceding code selects one of three reports previously defined, based on which option button is selected. There is one other condition if the Sales report is desired. If the Sales report is selected, either all sales or only today's sales appear on the report.

You do this by sending a formula. You can test the formula in the Crystal Reports IDE. After you know the formula works, you can paste it into your Visual Basic code. If you want to send another formula, you give it an index of 1, and so on.

 After you try your formulas in the Crystal IDE design environment, make sure that you remove the formulas before trying the Visual Basic code. This is because if you have an option that sends no formulas to the CRYSTAL.VBX custom control, the number of records in the report are still limited because your formula is still compiled in the report.

The only things you *have* to do when using the CRYSTAL.VBX custom control are

◆ Set the name of the report using the ReportFileName property.

◆ Set the destination using the Destination property.

◆ If the database is protected, set the UserName and Password properties for a non-ODBC database and the Connect property for an ODBC database.

◆ If the print window is set to 2 (File), set the PrintFileName property.

◆ Run the report by setting the Action property to 1.

It is very common to have three option buttons on your Visual Basic form to give the user the option of printing to the screen, printer, or a file. This option is invoked when you press a command button to start the action. Another way to do this is to have three separate command buttons, instead of three option buttons and a command button. Each command button in this case causes the Crystal Report to print to the screen, printer, or a file. If you are going to include a file option, you need to provide a way for the user to enter a file name. You can use a common dialog box to handle this—it is just additional code—as in Chapter 31. Following is a code fragment taken from Chapter 31 that handles the option of printing to the screen, printer, or file.

```
'determine where to print report
If optScreen.Value = True Then
    rptCrystal.Destination = 0
ElseIf optPrinter.Value = True Then
    rptCrystal.Destination = 1
ElseIf optFile.Value = True Then
    rptCrystal.Destination = 2

    'file was selected-get file name
    TempFileName$ = GetcmDialogFile()

    'assign file name to crystal
    If TempFileName$ <> "" Then
        rptCrystal.PrintFileName = TempFileName$
    Else
        'build message
        m$ = "No Valid File Name" + Chr$(13)
        m$ = m$ + "Operation Cancelled!"
        MsgBox m$

        'exit
        Exit Sub
    End If
End If
```

Before running a Crystal Report, it is a good idea to test to see if the report exists. This test avoids unexpected runtime errors.

     For more information about error handling, refer to Chapter 2, "Error Handling."

To test to see if the file exists, you can simply test for the length of the file. If it returns a length, run the report by setting the Action property to 1. If it produces an error, this file does not exist. You can then notify the user and exit. Chapter 31 uses this technique as follows:

```
'handle errors
On Error GoTo FileError:

'test for report file name to see if it exists
TempFileLen& = FileLen(rptCrystal.ReportFileName)

'start report
rptCrystal.Action = 1

'exit
Exit Sub
```

```
FileError:
    Select Case (Err)
        Case 53:    'file not found
            'build message
            m$ = "File " + rptCrystal.ReportFileName + " doesn't exist!"
            MsgBox m$
        Case Else
            MsgBox Error$
    End Select

    'exit
    Exit Sub

    'avoid errors
    Resume

End Sub
```

 You can use techniques such as these in your applications to achieve the desired result. Refer to the examples in Chapter 31 because all possibilities could not be covered in this chapter.

STRUCTURED QUERY LANGUAGE (SQL)

STRUCTURED QUERY LANGUAGE (FROM NOW ON REFERRED TO AS *SQL*) HAS QUICKLY BECOME THE STANDARD RELATIONAL DATABASE LANGUAGE. SQL PROVIDES FOR A WAY TO IMPOSE STANDARDS WHEN USING A RELATIONAL DATABASE. THERE ARE STILL SOME RELATIONAL DATABASES THAT DO NOT SUPPORT SQL, BUT THE VAST MAJORITY OF THEM DO. SOME OF THE RELATIONAL DATABASES THAT SUPPORT SQL ARE

- ◆ SQL SERVER
- ◆ ACCESS
- ◆ SYBASE
- ◆ ORACLE
- ◆ INFORMIX
- ◆ SQLBASE
- ◆ INGRES

It is very important to note that this chapter covers some of the basics of the SQL language, but it is the *ANSI (American National Standards Institute)* SQL language. It is *not* database specific. This means that certain database engines may have a slightly different syntax. This also means that some of the code presented *may* not work correctly for a given database engine. You must consult the documentation for your specific database engine to be sure.

This SQL standard can be used by either a client-server environment or a stand-alone environment. Either way, SQL is the language used to query the *database engine*. A database engine is the heart of the database. It is how the database vendor decides the database will operate and function, such as how data is stored, how syntax is used, and how processing occurs.

You can actually use SQL to do more than construct queries. A query implies that you will be querying the database and returning data from it. In fact, there is much more to it than this. SQL is used to insert new data, update existing data, and even control the parameters of the database engine.

SQL can be sent to a database engine by many means. The database engine comes with some sort of interactive tool for sending SQL statements to get some result. This is sometimes referred to as *ISQL (Interactive Structured Query Language)*.

This chapter deals with SQL as a whole. The subject of SQL can be, and has been, the subject of entire books. This one chapter cannot cover every aspect of SQL, but it covers the basics. It also does not get into specific database engines. There are certain things common in all SQL databases. These commonalities are the subject of the rest of this chapter. However, to provide examples, the application in Chapter 31, "Data Access Application," is used as the basis. The data in the tables for the database in this chapter, CHAP31.MDB, are shown in Figures 18.1 through 18.4.

FIGURE 18.1.

CHAP31.MDB,

INVENTORY table.

FIGURE 18.2.
CHAP31.MDB,
SALES table.

FIGURE 18.3.
CHAP31.MDB,
STAFF table.

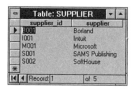

FIGURE 18.4.
CHAP31.MDB,
SUPPLIER table.

The tables from Chapter 31 are shown to give an idea of the structure of a database and how the fields relate to each other. Designing databases is not the topic of this chapter; however, it is important to see how the data relates so that the examples presented later make sense.

Using Figures 18.1 through 18.4, the INVENTORY table contains a list of all of the items a company can stock. The table also contains a field for the quantity in stock and a product id used to identify when a sale is made in the SALES table. It is inefficient to list the description of the product every time a sale occurs. There is also a supplier id field that identifies the company who supplies the product from the SUPPLIER table.

The SALES table relates to the tables discussed in the preceding paragraph, but the SALES table also has a field for the staff id, the person selling the item. The table looks up the name of the person selling the item in the STAFF table, based on the staff id.

That is how the four tables relate to each other. Each of the tables contains *very* simple data. However, if the database is designed correctly, it makes no difference how much data is in the tables.

RETRIEVING DATA

By far the most common SQL statement is the SELECT statement. This statement is used to retrieve rows of data from a table and for many other purposes, presented in the rest of this chapter. To use this statement, you must know the names of the columns in the table you are trying to receive. The statement has the following general syntax:

```
SELECT [ALL¦DISTINCT] select_list
FROM table_names
[WHERE {search_criteria¦join_criteria}
[{AND¦OR search_criteria}]]
[GROUP BY [ALL]aggregate_free_expression [,aggregate_free_expression...]]
[HAVING search_conditions]
[ORDER BY {field_list} [ASC¦DESC]]
```

where

◆ ALL specifies that every row is returned, including duplicates. This is the default and need not be used.

◆ DISTINCT specifies that only non-duplicate rows are to be returned.

◆ *select_list* is the list of column names in the table(s) to return, separated by commas.

◆ *table_names* is the list of the table(s) that return data.

◆ *search_criteria* is the list of column names in the table(s) to return.

◆ *join_criteria* is the list of column names in one table that joins to other column names in a different table.

◆ *aggregate_free_expression* is an expression that does not include an aggregate. Refer to Table 18.2 for a list of aggregate functions that cannot be included in this expression.

◆ *field_list* is a list of the columns the data is sorted on.

◆ ASC specifies that the sort order is ascending. This is the default and need not be used.

◆ DESC specifies that the sort order is descending.

If you are not familiar with SQL, the preceding can seem pretty confusing. Let me simplify it by providing examples from the tables used in the Chapter 31 application. Refer to the Figures 18.1 through 18.4.

SIMPLE *SELECT*

A simple SELECT is a SELECT statement with very few of the optional parameters listed earlier.

 The keywords throughout this chapter, such as SELECT, FROM, and so on, are not case sensitive. They are listed here in uppercase to set them apart from the regular text, but you can type them in lowercase.

The SELECT statement requires that you know what you want to select and from what. This means that you need to know the column names and the table names you are trying to select. For example, if you want to select all values from the supplier column in the SUPPLIER table, you use this statement:

```
SELECT supplier
FROM SUPPLIER
```

REM Even though the keywords are not case sensitive, the column names and table names are. For this example, the table names have been designed in uppercase, while the column names have been designed in lowercase. Columns are sometimes referred to as *fields* and column names as *field names*. They are synonymous.

REM A SQL statement may consist of many lines of text, but it is actually one statement. As a general rule, to help understand this concept, a statement will consist of all lines of SQL text between two SELECT keywords.

Also, even though these SQL text lines are shown on separate lines, they can actually be put on one line. They are generally constructed on multiple lines because they are easier to read. The SQL standard calls for the database engine (whichever one is used) to ignore the carriage return between SQL keywords in the statement.

The preceding SQL statement produces a complete list of the suppliers in the SUPPLIER table, but the order returned is the order in which they are entered into the table. If you want to sort the list alphabetically, you can use this statement:

```
SELECT supplier
FROM SUPPLIER
ORDER BY supplier
```

The ORDER BY keyword (sometimes referred to as the ORDER BY *clause*) needs a column name to know which column to sort on. This ensures that the data is ordered by supplier column. By default, the data is ordered in ascending order. To sort in descending order, this statement is used:

```
SELECT supplier
FROM SUPPLIER
ORDER BY supplier DESC
```

If you want to select multiple columns, use the following statement:

```
SELECT supplier,supplier_id
FROM SUPPLIER
ORDER BY supplier
```

The preceding statement selects the supplier column first, followed by the supplier_id column. All values in the table are returned because you did not limit the search. Two columns are selected in the preceding statement which, coincidentally, is the total number of columns in the SUPPLIER table. However, if you have a table with 100 columns and you want to select all of the columns, you don't have to type in the names of all 100 columns. You can select all columns in a table with a statement like this:

```
SELECT *
FROM SUPPLIER
ORDER BY supplier
```

The asterisk indicates that all columns are selected from the SUPPLIER table. The table is still sorted by the supplier column in ascending order.

LIMITING THE SELECTION

You do not have to return all data from a table. You can limit the number of rows returned by using the WHERE keyword. Suppose that you want to find out what the supplier_id is for SoftHouse. You want to limit the number of rows in the SUPPLIER table to all rows where the supplier is equal to "SoftHouse". You can do this with the following code:

```
SELECT *
FROM SUPPLIER
WHERE supplier = "SoftHouse"
ORDER BY supplier
```

The data returned is only the data that matches the WHERE keyword, or referred to as the WHERE clause. If there is no supplier named "SoftHouse", then no rows are returned.

 The string literal in the WHERE clause is case sensitive. Therefore, "SoftHouse" is not the same as "SOFTHOUSE".

The ORDER BY clause is not necessary in the preceding statement, but it doesn't hurt it either. This is because by design, each supplier appears in the SUPPLIER table only once. Because you are only looking for one supplier, the order is irrelevant. You can look for more than one supplier, and it does become relevant. For example, suppose that you are looking for "SoftHouse" or "Microsoft". Use this SQL statement:

```
SELECT *
FROM SUPPLIER
WHERE supplier = "SoftHouse" OR supplier = "Microsoft"
ORDER BY supplier
```

In this case, two rows are returned: first the "Microsoft" row and then the "SoftHouse" row. This is because of the ORDER BY clause.

Another way to write the preceding statement is to use the IN keyword. The IN keyword allows you to list a range of values to test for. The values are separated by a comma. The preceding statement is rewritten as:

```
SELECT *
FROM SUPPLIER
WHERE supplier IN ("SoftHouse","Microsoft")
ORDER BY supplier
```

Using the IN keyword can generally save a lot of typing because the column name does not have to be repeated. Additional keywords that can be used in the WHERE clause are listed in Table 18.1.

TABLE 18.1 KEYWORDS THAT CAN BE USED IN A WHERE CLAUSE.

Keywords	Purpose
IN	Tests for values in a range
NOT IN	Tests for values not in a range
LIKE	Tests for values that are like a value
NOT LIKE	Tests for values that are not like a value
IS NULL	Tests for values that are null
IS NOT NULL	Tests for values that are not null
AND	Tests for multiple conditions
OR	Tests for either of conditions
BETWEEN	Tests for values between a set of values
NOT BETWEEN	Tests for values not between a set of values
EXISTS	Tests for values that exist
NOT EXISTS	Tests for values that do not exist
ANY	Tests for any values
ALL	Tests for all values

A very common necessity is to return values that, for example, start with a certain letter, such as "S." You can do this by using the LIKE keyword.

If you want to return all rows from the SUPPLIER table for the supplier starting with an "S," use this statement:

```
SELECT *
FROM SUPPLIER
WHERE supplier LIKE "S%"
ORDER BY supplier
```

This statement returns rows containing the suppliers "SAMS Publishing" and "SoftHouse". The syntax for using the LIKE keyword is

```
LIKE "[%]constant[%]"
```

where you may have a percent sign either before the *constant*, after the *constant*, or both. The *constant* is the value that you are testing for. The percent signs are wild card symbols, as are asterisks in DOS. If you are looking for any supplier that has an "S" in its name, use this statement:

```
SELECT *
FROM SUPPLIER
WHERE supplier LIKE "%S%"
ORDER BY supplier
```

 You must use at least one percent sign in a LIKE clause. If you don't, no rows are returned.

Because the SELECT keyword is used to return values, you can even go so far as to return a value that is not even part of the database. This is referred to as a *calculated column*. For example, you can return a percentage of the quantity in the INVENTORY table. Instead of this SQL statement that returns the quantity that is actually in the database,

```
SELECT quantity
FROM INVENTORY
```

you can use this SQL statement to return 10 percent of the quantities:

```
SELECT quantity * .10
FROM INVENTORY
```

This only works for a numeric data type. You certainly cannot do this if quantity is a string.

JOINS

A *join* is a way to return some data from one table and some data from another table. The key to doing this is that you must "join" or "link" the column(s) of data between the two tables so the database engine knows how to look it up. The join is done in the WHERE clause. If you want to select all items in the INVENTORY table but also with the company that supplied the item, you have to do a join between the INVENTORY table and the SUPPLIER table. This is because there is a column (supplier_id) that is common to both tables and is what the join is based on. This is also called a *common key*. A *key* is a "key" field that is used as a join. For the SUPPLIER table, it is the primary key. That means that this is the column that is used to access a row in the table. It is not the primary key in the INVENTORY table. It is not used to access a row in this table. The product_id column is the primary key in that table. Again, how to determine primary keys and database design is not the purpose of this chapter.

To perform the join mentioned earlier, use this code:

```
SELECT supplier, description, quantity
FROM SUPPLIER s, INVENTORY i
WHERE i.supplier_id = s.supplier_id
ORDER BY supplier
```

This statement selects the `supplier`, `description`, and `quantity` columns from the `SUPPLIER` and `INVENTORY` tables. For every occurrence of a `supplier_id` in the `INVENTORY` table, the supplier is looked up using the same `supplier_id` column and assigning the values to be equal.

The individual letters "s" and "i" you see in the preceding code are *aliases*. You use these to identify a column in a table that has the same name in another table you are trying to access. If you do not specify this alias, you receive an error telling you that the column name is ambiguous. This alias gives the database engine a way to decipher which column you are referring to. The alias name goes after the table names in the `FROM` clause. The alias name can be any unique value (treated as a string without quotes) as long as it is not the name of a table you are trying to access.

After the alias is established in the `FROM` clause, you can reference it by using this format:

`alias.column`

where `alias` is the name of the alias defined and `column` is the name of the column in the table that is aliased. For example, consider the `WHERE` clause in the previous statement:

```
WHERE i.supplier_id = s.supplier_id
```

It follows the syntax of `alias.column` on each side of the = sign. After the alias is established, you can use it in any of the SQL clauses that are part of that same statement.

If you are trying to select (return) columns in different tables, you must also reference the alias to avoid any ambiguity. Even if you are not selecting columns with the same name, you may still use the alias. For example, the following is not incorrect:

```
SELECT s.supplier, i.description, i.quantity
FROM SUPPLIER s, INVENTORY i
WHERE i.supplier_id = s.supplier_id
ORDER BY s.supplier
```

It performs the same function. It does, however, introduce a possible element of error. If you change the last line to

```
ORDER BY i.supplier
```

you receive an error because the `supplier` column does not exist in the `INVENTORY` table.

You can even create more complex joins. Suppose that you want to select the supplier, product description, and quantity, but return only the rows in the `INVENTORY` table where the supplier is `"Microsoft"`. You have to do a join again to the `SUPPLIER` table because the only reference to supplier in the `INVENTORY` table is an ID, `supplier_id`, which is used as a lookup key in the `SUPPLIER` table. You can do the join with this statement:

```
SELECT s.supplier, i.description, i.quantity
FROM SUPPLIER s, INVENTORY i
WHERE i.supplier_id = s.supplier_id
AND s.supplier = "Microsoft"
ORDER BY s.supplier
```

Again, the ORDER BY clause is not absolutely necessary because there can only be one row in the SUPPLIER table with the name "Microsoft".

You can use the techniques and topics discussed here to join many multiple tables in your application. However, remember that the more joins you do, the longer it takes the database engine to come back with the results.

AGGREGATES

An *aggregate* is a mathematical SQL function. Table 18.2 lists the types of SQL aggregates that are available.

TABLE 18.2. SQL AGGREGATES.

Aggregate	Purpose
COUNT()	Counts the number of rows returned
SUM()	Sums the number of rows returned
AVG()	Averages the number of rows returned
MAX()	Finds the maximum value in the rows returned
MIN()	Finds the minimum value in the rows returned

In each of the aggregates listed here, an expression (typically a column name) is expected in the parentheses. However, the expression can be any valid SQL expression.

If you want to find out how many rows are returned from this statement:

```
SELECT s.supplier, i.description, i.quantity
FROM SUPPLIER s, INVENTORY i
WHERE i.supplier_id = s.supplier_id
ORDER BY s.supplier
```

you can use this statement instead:

```
SELECT COUNT(*), s.supplier, i.description, i.quantity
FROM SUPPLIER s, INVENTORY i
WHERE i.supplier_id = s.supplier_id
ORDER BY s.supplier
```

This statement returns four columns: the count of the number of rows returned, the supplier, the description, and the quantity. The joins in the statement are discussed earlier in the "Joins" section.

When using an aggregate function, you can use a GROUP BY clause to tell the database engine how to do the calculation. For example, if you want to sum the number of items stocked for each supplier, you have to use a GROUP BY clause. If you don't, how does the database engine know how to return the sum? Refer to Figure 18.1 to follow this example. Would the database engine sum the quantities for each `product_id`, `description`, `supplier_id`, or a combination of the three? That's where the `GROUP BY` clause comes in. In the scenario presented at the beginning of this paragraph, you can perform the necessary function by using this statement:

```
SELECT SUM(quantity)
FROM SUPPLIER s, INVENTORY i
WHERE i.supplier_id = s.supplier_id
GROUP BY s.supplier
ORDER BY s.supplier
```

This means that for every new supplier, the quantity is summed. If the `GROUP BY` clause is omitted, only one row is returned, and it is the sum of all quantities.

INSERTS

Inserting rows (or records) into a table requires an `INSERT` statement. The syntax of the `INSERT` statement is

```
INSERT [INTO] table[(column_list)]
VALUES{(insert_values)}¦sql_select_statement
```

where

♦ *table* is the name of the table to insert into.

♦ *column_list* is a listing of columns that have data inserted, separated by commas.

♦ *insert_values* is the list of values to be inserted into the columns in *column_list*. There must be the same number of values in the *insert_values* list as in the *column_list* list.

♦ *sql_select_statement* is an alternate way to insert values into a table. You can select values of another table to the inserting. In this case, you do not use the `VALUES` keyword. You must make sure that the number of columns you are returning in your SQL statement is the same number as in the *column_list* list.

To use the `INSERT` statement to insert a new supplier into the `SUPPLIER` table, you can use this statement:

```
INSERT SUPPLIER(supplier_id,supplier)
VALUES ("C001","Crystal Services")
```

The row is simply inserted into the table. Here are some considerations, however:

♦ Does the primary key field already exist?

♦ Are you concerned about case sensitivity?

♦ Are you inserting values using the correct data type?

These questions are very important. Except for the case sensitivity question, the questions presented here can result in error if not addressed properly.

239

For example, the following will result in error:

```
INSERT SUPPLIER(supplier_id,supplier)
VALUES (1,"Crystal Services")
```

because the `supplier_id` column does not expect a numeric data type; it expects a string data type. If you are not going to include any characters, you must construct the SQL statement this way:

```
INSERT SUPPLIER(supplier_id,supplier)
VALUES ("1","Crystal Services")
```

Instead of inserting into a table by hard coding the values, you can also insert by selecting the values from another table. Suppose that you have a table, MASTER, which also has `supplier_id` and `supplier` columns that you are going to select values from. You can insert all items from the MASTER table like this:

```
INSERT SUPPLIER(supplier_id,supplier)
SELECT supplier_id,supplier
FROM MASTER
```

On the other hand, if you only wanted to insert based on a certain value from the MASTER table, you could construct your SQL SELECT statement based on any valid SQL rule. You could do this:

```
INSERT SUPPLIER(supplier_id,supplier)
SELECT supplier_id,supplier
FROM MASTER
WHERE supplier="Crystal Services"
```

As presented in the "Retrieving Data" section earlier in the chapter, the WHERE clause limits the number of rows returned.

DELETES

Deleting rows (or records) from a table requires a DELETE statement. The syntax of the DELETE statement is

```
DELETE FROM table
[WHERE search_conditions]
```

where

- ◆ `table` is the name of the table to delete from.
- ◆ `search_conditions` are any valid SQL expression to limit the number of rows deleted.

The DELETE statement deletes an entire row or rows in the database. You cannot delete only one column.

You can use the DELETE statement to delete all rows in the SUPPLIER table by using this statement:

```
DELETE FROM SUPPLIER
```

There is no confirmation when using the DELETE statement. If the statement is executed, the rows are deleted. It's that simple. Be very careful when using the DELETE statement.

If you want to delete the rows only where the supplier is a certain value, you do it like this:

```
DELETE FROM SUPPLIER
WHERE supplier = "Borland"
```

This statement deletes all values in the SUPPLIER table where the supplier is "Borland".

 You have to be careful when you delete a row in a table in case a value relates to a value in another table. If it does, it's possible that you "orphaned" a row in another table. This means that the value related to data in the table that you deleted from and now has no way to be referenced. This means that the row in this second table is just taking up space.

There are ways around this that are not in the scope of this chapter, as stated earlier. When designing the database, a trigger can be placed on the column so that this doesn't happen inadvertently.

UPDATES

Updating rows (or records) in a table requires an UPDATE statement. The syntax of the UPDATE statement is

```
UPDATE table
SET assignment_list
[WHERE search_conditions]
```

where

◆ table is the name of the table to insert into.

◆ assignment_list is a listing of all updates that will take place.

◆ search_conditions are any valid SQL expression to limit the number of rows updated.

If you want to update the supplier_id column of the SUPPLIER table, you can use the UPDATE statement:

```
UPDATE SUPPLIER
SET supplier_id="XXX"
```

All rows in the `supplier_id` column are updated to `"XXX"`. To prevent this from happening, you need to limit the search by using a WHERE clause with any valid SQL expression. You can limit the updating as described earlier to only where the supplier is equal to `"Borland"`. You do this as follows:

```
UPDATE SUPPLIER
SET supplier_id="XXX"
WHERE supplier = "Borland"
```

 There is no confirmation when using the UPDATE statement. If the statement is executed, the rows are updated. It's that simple. Be very careful when using the UPDATE statement.

 You have to be careful when you update a row in a table in case the old value relates to a value in another table. If it does, it's possible that you "orphaned" a row in another table. This means that the value related to data in the table that you updated and now has no way to be referenced. This means that the row in this second table is just taking up space.

There are ways around this that are not the scope of this chapter, as stated earlier. When designing the database, a trigger can be placed on the column so that this doesn't happen inadvertently.

On the other hand, if you only want to update based on a certain value from another table, you can use any valid SQL SELECT statement in place of the *assignment_list* in the syntax presented earlier. Suppose that you have a table, MASTER, that also has `supplier_id` and `supplier` columns that you are going to select values out of. You can insert an item from the MASTER table to update a record in the SUPPLIER table like this:

```
UPDATE SUPPLIER
SET supplier_id = (SELECT supplier_id
FROM MASTER
WHERE supplier = "SoftHouse")
WHERE supplier = "SoftHouse"
```

The last two lines of the preceding statement look like they are repeated. In actuality, they are not. Notice the parentheses around the statement between the second and fourth lines. This is actually a query within a query. The inner query selects from the MASTER table the `supplier_id` where the `supplier` is `"SoftHouse"`.

The outer query, which is the UPDATE statement, updates the `supplier_id` to the value returned from the inner query, but limits the rows for which this applies to where the supplier is equal to `"SoftHouse"`. If the last line is not present, all rows in the `supplier_id` column are updated.

The query within a query concept (called *nested queries*) opens the possibilities for the SQL language. As you develop more advanced applications that retrieve data, you will find that understanding SQL is vital.

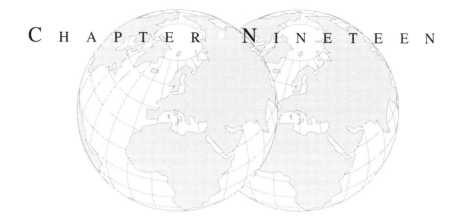

WRITING DLLS AND VBXS

DLLS (DYNAMIC LINK LIBRARIES) AND VBXS (VISUAL BASIC EXTENSION CONTROLS) ALLOW YOU TO EXTEND VISUAL BASIC TO PERFORM FUNCTIONS THAT ARE NOT BUILT INTO ITS ORIGINAL DESIGN. MANY THIRD-PARTY VENDORS ARE TAKING ADVANTAGE OF THIS BY WRITING DLLS AND VBXS TO ALLOW YOU TO PERFORM AMAZING FEATS. FOR EXAMPLE, MY COMPANY, SOFTHOUSE, MARKETS AND SELLS A CUSTOM CONTROL USED FOR HOME AUTOMATION. THIS ALLOWS YOU TO BUILD A CUSTOM FRONT END TO A HOME AUTOMATION APPLICATION, WHICH ALLOWS YOU TO CONTROL LIGHTS, APPLIANCES, AND OTHER DEVICES AROUND YOUR HOME OR OFFICE. THIS IS ALL DONE BY ADDING A CUSTOM VBX INTO YOUR PROJECT.

For more information about the SoftHouse VBX-10 home automation custom control, see the advertisement in the back of this book.

There is not much difference between a DLL and a VBX. The only real difference is that a VBX is a DLL that contains a Visual Basic *wrapper*. This wrapper enables you to pass parameters to the DLL by changing properties and methods instead of having to pass parameters programmatically to a DLL.

Writing either a DLL or VBX requires a C or C++ compiler and knowledge of C or C++. This chapter assumes that you have both the compiler and knowledge. It makes no attempt to teach the C language.

All examples and screen shots in this chapter use Microsoft Visual C++ version 1.5. Although any C or C++ compiler capable of compiling Windows applications will work, the screens will look different.

If you want to learn C, there is an excellent book by Sams Publishing, written by Peter Aitken and Bradley Jones, called *Teach Yourself C in 21 Days*. The order form at the back of this book includes information on ordering this and other Sams Publishing books.

The advantage of writing a DLL or VBX is that Visual Basic does not have the capability to do everything. For example, you may want to write a DLL that performs graphics functions. Because C or C++ is a lower-level language than Visual Basic, the graphics functions are faster. On the other hand, it can be complicated to write a DLL or VBX. If you do not want to write a VBX from scratch, there is a program available from AJS publishing called VBXPress, which can help you. It will generate custom VBXs from properties and options that you select. ADJ's telephone number is (800) 992-3383.

DLLs

There are basically two types of DLLs. The first is a *resource DLL*. This DLL allows you to compile many different resources, such as bitmaps, cursors, and icons in one file. These files can then be loaded dynamically in Visual Basic. A good example of this is one of those programs on the market that contains more than 500 icons you can use. These icons all reside in the same file.

Although a DLL usually has the extension of *.DLL, it can be in the form of an executable file, which is how the icon programs listed earlier work.

The second type of DLL is a *functional DLL*. This is the type of DLL that performs some type of function. It can be either a subroutine, which doesn't return a value, or a function, which does return a value. For example, you can use a DLL to return the data present at a serial port.

RESOURCE DLLs

To create a resource DLL, the compiler expects files with certain file extensions. Table 19.1 shows which of these files are needed to create a resource DLL.

TABLE 19.1. MINIMUM FILES NEEDED TO CREATE A RESOURCE DLL.

File Extension	Purpose
*.RC	File containing resources
*.C	File containing the Windows entry and exit code
*.DEF	File used to handle Windows parameters and exports
*.MAK	File that tells the compiler how to make the DLL file. This file is created by the compiler when creating the project.

THE "RC" FILE

The first step in creating a resource DLL is to create the individual resources. To create a resource, open the App Studio by selecting the Tools->App Studio menu option in the Visual C++ application. This action invokes the Microsoft App Studio application, which is part of Visual C++. Figure 19.1 shows the App Studio with no resources.

FIGURE 19.1.
App Studio with
no resources.

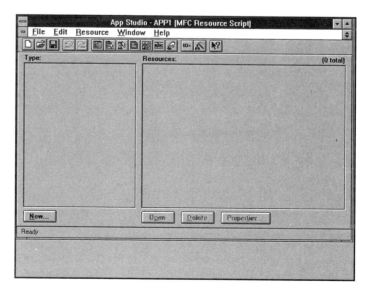

To create a new resource, such as a bitmap, select the Resource->New menu option. Pick the type of resource you want to create. If you want to add a bitmap resource, select Bitmap. This invokes an editor that allows you to edit the bitmap.

Use the toolbox to select colors and tools to create the bitmap. After the bitmap is created, you must name it as you call it from Visual Basic. For example, if you create a bitmap of the outside of a house, you might call it "HOUSE_EXTERNAL." To assign the name of the bitmap, select the Resource->Properties menu option. Change the name of the bitmap from whatever the default is to the name that you will refer to from Visual Basic.

 To use the API functions listed in this chapter, you must make sure that you put the name of your resource in quotes.

After you name the bitmap, you can close it by double-clicking the system menu for the bitmap. Of the two system menus in the upper-left corner, it is the lower one. You see a list of the different resources in your resource file.

Continue creating bitmaps, icons, cursors, and so on, as described earlier. After all desired resources are created, save the file by using the File->Save menu option. This saves a resource file with an RC file extension. This resource file will be used by the compiler to create the resource DLL.

A great example of how useful a resource DLL is in Chapter 27, "CD Player Application." The CD Player uses resources in a DLL named RWPROGVB.DLL to emulate a digital display.

 The source files for the RWPROGVB.DLL dynamic link library are contained on the CD accompanying this book in the \RESOURCE\RWPROGVB subdirectory.

Figure 19.2 lists what the App Studio looks like after these resources have been created. Note that there is also a custom cursor resource in the file. It is used by the application in Chapter 25, "Dynamic Hotspot Application," to display a cursor that does not exist in Visual Basic. It is created exactly the same way a bitmap is created, but saved as a cursor resource instead of a bitmap resource.

THE "C" SOURCE FILE

After the resource file is created with an RC file extension, you must have a C source file that contains functions so that windows knows how to enter into and exit from the DLL. Even though your individual resources will be different, the following code in the C source file will not. Enter this code:

```
#include <windows.h>

int _far _pascal LibMain (HANDLE hInstance,
                WORD wDataSeg,
                WORD cbHeapSize,
                LPSTR lpszCmdLine)
{
    return(1);
}

int _far _pascal WEP (int nParameter)
{
    return(1);
}
```

FIGURE 19.2.
App Studio with resources from RWPROGVB.RC.

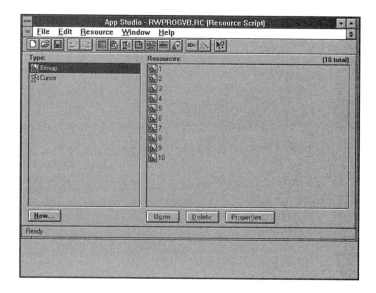

This code includes a LibMain() function, which is the entry point into the DLL and a WEP() function, which is the exit point from the function. The value being returned, 1, is a value only to avoid warnings from the compiler. There is no actual functionality in these functions.

THE "DEF" FILE

You must create a definition file (*.DEF). This tells the compiler how to compile the file. Enter this code and save it as a *.DEF file:

```
LIBRARY RWPROGVB
DESCRIPTION 'RWPROGVB DLL'
EXETYPE WINDOWS
```

```
STUB 'WINSTUB.EXE'
CODE MOVEABLE DISCARDABLE
DATA MOVEABLE SINGLE
HEAPSIZE 0
EXPORTS
    WEP @1  RESIDENTNAME
```

The only thing that will change in your *.DEF file is the LIBRARY and the DESCRIPTION. Because this is not a lesson on how to write Windows applications, each element of the *.DEF file is not explained.

The last thing you must do before compiling your file is to create the project. You do this by selecting the Project->New menu option. The New Project dialog box appears, as in Figure 19.3.

FIGURE 19.3.

New Project dialog box.

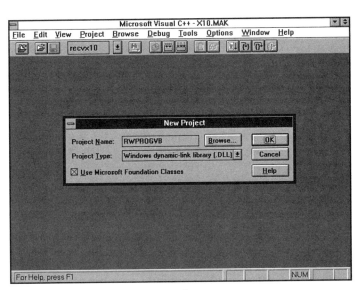

Type in the name of your new project. The name can only be eight characters because this will become the base name of the target files as well. Also, select from the pick list the type of file you are trying to create. Select Windows dynamic-link Library(.DLL) and click the OK button. This opens another dialog box. You need to add all three files you have just created into your project file. These three files have the extensions RC, C, and DEF. Although the order does not matter, they are listed here in the order in which they were created earlier.

You are now ready to compile the DLL. To do this, simply select the Project->Build menu option. When finished, you will have a DLL file that you can use in your Visual Basic projects.

Depending on how you have the Visual C++ options set up, you may receive a warning when compiling/linking regarding the segments being set to PRELOAD. This is not a problem. The DLL will be generated anyway.

IMPLEMENTING THE DLL IN VISUAL BASIC

Now that you have a compiled resource DLL file, you must implement code in Visual Basic to use the resources. To use this file from Visual Basic, you must load the resource dynamically. How you do this depends on which type of resources are compiled into the DLL. For example, if you are trying to retrieve a bitmap, you use the LoadResource() API function. If you are trying to load a cursor, you use the LoadCusor() API function. An example of how to incorporate this is taken from the application in Chapter 25, "Dynamic Hotspot Application." It uses a custom cursor that is compiled inside of the RWPROGVB.DLL resource DLL.

Your Visual Basic code to load a custom cursor requires the use of some Windows APIs.

 For more information about calling Windows APIs, refer to Chapter 3, "Calling Windows APIs and DLLs."

The required API declarations are as follows:

```
Declare Function LoadCursorByString Lib "User" Alias "LoadCursor" (ByVal hInstance As
Integer, ByVal lpCursorName As String) As Integer
Declare Function LoadLibrary Lib "Kernel" (ByVal lpLibFileName As String) As Integer
Declare Function SetClassWord Lib "User" (ByVal hWnd As Integer, ByVal nIndex As Integer,
ByVal wNewWord As Integer) As Integer
Integer)
Declare Function GetModuleUsage Lib "Kernel" (ByVal hModule As Integer) As Integer
Declare Function DestroyCursor Lib "User" (ByVal hCursor As Integer) As Integer
```

Then declare the constant representing that you want to retrieve a handle to the cursor as follows:

```
Const GCW_HCURSOR = (1-12)
```

To use the new cursor, you must first load the library. You do that with this code:

```
LibInst% = LoadLibrary("RWPROGVB.DLL")
```

You can substitute "RWPROGVB.DLL" for the name of your DLL. The next step is to load the specific cursor inside the resource DLL. You do that with this line:

```
cHandle% = LoadCursorByString(LibInst%, "HandCursor")
```

Substitute "HandCursor" for the name of your cursor resource. The final step is to assign the cursor to the handle of the form. You do that with this code:

```
hSystemCursor% = SetClassWord(frmMain.hWnd, GCW_HCURSOR, cHandle%)
```

You simply substitute the name of the form (which is the first argument) with the name of your form. If you want to free the cursor resource after using it, you do it with this code:

```
res% = DestroyCursor(cHandle%)
```

Make sure that the handle to destroy is the correct handle; otherwise, you can destroy another resource. The one last thing to do is to free the library that was loaded earlier. You free the library with this line:

```
FreeLibrary (LibInst%)
```

That's all there is to creating a resource DLL.

If you have loaded the library more than once, you need to free the library more than once. To determine how many times the library has been loaded, you can use the GetModuleUsage API function. To see how this is done, refer to the code in Chapter 25, "Dynamic Hotspot Application," frmMain.Form_Unload() event procedure.

FUNCTIONAL DLLS

Creating a functional DLL is somewhat easier than creating a resource DLL. This is because you do not have to create as many files as you do with a resource DLL. You do not have to create the individual resources. Also, there is no RC file because there are no resources to compile.

The example listed in this section is an example of how you can call a function in a DLL, written in C, and return the amount of time that has elapsed. This can be very useful because you can time different processes. You can call this function before the process and then call the function after the process. By subtracting the two times, you can determine the elapsed time of the process. By using the syntax and technique listed in this section, you can adapt this code to your applications.

As an example of how to create a functional DLL to perform the functions listed earlier, create a DLL called TIME.DLL.

The TIME.DLL dynamic link library and its associated files are contained on the CD accompanying this book in the \RESOURCE\TIME subdirectory.

To create TIME.DLL, the compiler expects files with certain file extensions. Table 19.2 shows which of these files are needed to create a functional DLL.

TABLE 19.2. MINIMUM FILES NEEDED TO CREATE A FUNCTIONAL DLL.

File Extension	Purpose
*.C	Source file for DLL
*.DEF	File used to handle Windows parameters and exports
*.MAK	File that tells the compiler how to make the DLL file. This file is created by the compiler when creating the project.

THE "C" SOURCE FILE

The "C" source file is the file that contains the code for the actual functions or subroutines that your DLL is to contain. If the functions or subroutines that your DLL contains are to be exported (available in Visual Basic), then these functions must be declared as _export.

 Notice that the export keyword is preceded by an underscore character. This is necessary for the function or subroutine to work.

The "C" source code for the TIME.DLL file is listed here:

```
#include <windows.h>
#include <time.h>

//--------------------------------------------------------------------------
// Variables
//--------------------------------------------------------------------------
time_t TimeStruct;

//--------------------------------------------------------------------------
// Local Prototypes
//--------------------------------------------------------------------------
double _export PASCAL FindElapsed(void);

//--------------------------------------------------------------------------
// Actual Function
//--------------------------------------------------------------------------
double _export PASCAL FindElapsed(void)
{
    return time(&TimeStruct);
}

//--------------------------------------------------------------------------
// Initialize library. This routine is called when the first client loads
// the DLL.
//--------------------------------------------------------------------------
int FAR PASCAL LibMain
(
    HANDLE hModule,
    WORD   wDataSeg,
```

```
    WORD    cbHeapSize,
    LPSTR   lpszCmdLine
)
{
    // Avoid warnings on unused (but required) formal parameters
    wDataSeg    = wDataSeg;
    cbHeapSize  = cbHeapSize;
    lpszCmdLine = lpszCmdLine;

    return 1;
}


int FAR PASCAL WEP
(
    int fSystemExit
)
{
    // Avoid warnings on unused (but required) formal parameters
    fSystemExit = fSystemExit;

    return 1;
}
```

Notice that in all of the code listed here, there are only a couple of lines that are used to actually create the function you will export. This function name is FindElapsed(). The code in this function simply returns the time elapsed since midnight. Therefore, this timing process only works within a single day. It is preceded by _export PASCAL. Your C source file contains the same syntax.

THE "DEF" FILE

The DEF file is used to tell the compiler about the Windows parameters used in the DLL file, as well as the name of the functions and subroutines to export. The DEF code for the TIME.DLL file is as follows:

```
LIBRARY    TIME
EXETYPE    WINDOWS
CODE       PRELOAD MOVEABLE DISCARDABLE
DATA       PRELOAD MOVEABLE SINGLE
HEAPSIZE   1024
EXPORTS
    WEP    @1    RESIDENTNAME
```

Notice on the last line that the constant RESIDENTNAME is used to export the functions previously declared as _export.

Once the C source and DEF files are created, you can create a new project by selecting the Project->New menu option. Select the Dynamic Link Library (DLL) menu option for the project type. After the wizard is shown to create the new DLL, add the C source and DEF files into the project. Closing this screen creates the project file with the MAK file.

You are now ready to compile the DLL. To do this, select the Project->Build menu option. The DLL is created.

IMPLEMENTING THE DLL IN VISUAL BASIC

After the DLL is created, you are ready to use it in your Visual Basic project. The first step in doing this is to declare it as you do any other API or DLL. In the case of the `FindElapsed()` function in the TIME.DLL file, you declare it like this:

```
Declare Function FindElapsed Lib "time.dll" () As Double
```

This declaration allows you to use the function `FindElapsed()` in your Visual Basic code. You use the same technique presented in this section to write your own functional DLL. This declaration could be used to show the time elapsed since midnight with this line:

```
MsgBox FindElapsed()
```

VBXs

A VBX is basically a DLL, with a special hook for Visual Basic (or any other environment that supports VBXs) called a *wrapper*. This is because this hook wraps all of the functionality into an easy-to-use interface through the accessing of the VBXs properties. A VBX is considerably more difficult to write, however. You must include all of the functionality as you do in a DLL, but also write the wrapper to control how the user interacts with the VBX. When writing a VBX, the compiler expects files with certain file extensions. Table 19.3 shows which of these files are needed to create a VBX.

TABLE 19.3. MINIMUM FILES NEEDED TO CREATE A VBX.

File Extension	Purpose
*.RC	File containing resources.
VBAPI.H	VBX header file that comes from Microsoft. It is in the CDK subdirectory under Visual Basic, Professional Edition.
*.H	Header file containing structure of VBX.
*.C	File containing the Windows entry and exit code as well as your functions and subroutines.
*.DEF	File used to handle Windows parameters and exports.
*.MAK	File that tells the compiler how to make the VBX file. This file is created by the compiler when creating the project.

It is impossible to cover all possible ways to create a custom control. Therefore, it is the purpose of this section to give an overall view of what the structure of the VBX is and how to create it.

 The source files for the ELAPSED.VBX custom control are contained on the CD accompanying this book in the \RESOURCE\ELAPSED subdirectory.

The "RC" File

The first step in creating a VBX is to create the bitmaps that will be used in the Visual Basic toolbox. You need to create at least two bitmaps: one for the Up position and one for the Down position. You may possibly have one for an EGA screen and one for a monochrome screen. However, this example only has two. Each bitmap has to be a certain size. It *must* be 28 pixels-by-28 pixels.

To create the bitmaps for the toolbox, open the App Studio as described earlier and create your bitmaps. As an example, Figure 19.4 shows the App Studio with the Up position bitmap from ELAPSED.RC.

FIGURE 19.4.
ELAPSED.RC, Up position bitmap.

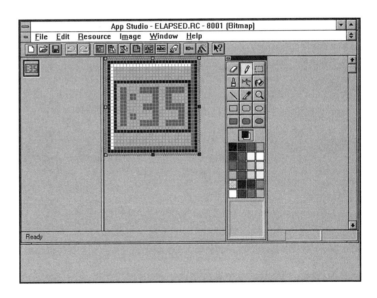

Create all of your bitmaps for the toolbox the same way. When you name them controls, use consecutive numbers because that is how you refer to them in code. When you are finished creating the bitmaps, save the file. It is saved with an RC file extension.

THE HEADER FILE

The next step is to create the header file that contains the structure of the VBX control. This file, with an H file extension, is used to determine which properties and events the control will have, along with many other parameters.

You cannot specify custom methods when writing a VBX, although you can specify custom events.

To create a header file, select the File->New menu option, which brings up an editor screen. After you write your header file, you must save it with an H file extension. It is not done automatically. Because there are so many topics and theories that cannot be covered in the context of this chapter regarding writing VBXs, the following code is shown so that you get an idea of the elements that go into a VBX header file. The listing is taken from the ELAPSED.H file. It is as follows:

```
 1:   //-----------------------------------------------------------------
 2:   // Toolbox bitmap resource IDs numbers.
 3:   //-----------------------------------------------------------------
 4:   #define IDBMP_ELAPSEDUP         8001
 5:   #define IDBMP_ELAPSEDDOWN       8002
 6:
 7:   //-----------------------------------------------------------------
 8:   // Change these for each new VBX file
 9:   //-----------------------------------------------------------------
10:   #define VBX_FILEDESCRIPTION     "Elapsed Time Control\0"
11:   #define VBX_INTERNALNAME        "Elapsed\0"
12:   #define VBX_ORIGINALFILENAME    "ELAPSED.VBX\0"
13:   #define VBX_PRODUCTNAME         "Elapsed Time Control\256\0"
14:
15:   //-----------------------------------------------------------------
16:   // Update these fields for each build.
17:   //-----------------------------------------------------------------
18:   #define VBX_VERSION      1,00,0,00
19:   #define VBX_VERSION_STR  "1.00.000\0"
20:
21:   #ifndef RC_INVOKED
22:   //-----------------------------------------------------------------
23:   // Macro for referencing member of structure
24:   //-----------------------------------------------------------------
25:   #define OFFSETIN(struc,field)  ((USHORT)&(((struc *)0)->field))
26:
27:   //-----------------------------------------------------------------
28:   // Function Prototypes
29:   //-----------------------------------------------------------------
30:   LONG FAR PASCAL _export ElapsedCtlProc(HCTL, HWND, USHORT, USHORT, LONG);
31:
32:   //-----------------------------------------------------------------
33:   // Elapsed control data and structs
```

```
34:  //-----------------------------------------------------------
35:  typedef struct tagElapsedSTRUCT
36:     {
37:      ENUM Action;
38:      ENUM DisplayResults;
39:      short Hours;
40:      short Minutes;
41:      short Seconds;
42:     } ElapsedSTRUCT;
43:
44:  typedef ElapsedSTRUCT FAR * LPElapsedSTRUCT;
45:
46:  #define LpElapsedSTRUCTDEREF(hctl) ((LPElapsedSTRUCT)VBDerefControl(hctl))
47:
48:  CHAR szActionTypes[] =      "0 - Stop\0"\
49:                              "1 - Start\0"\
50:                              "";
51:  CHAR szDisplayResultsTypes[] =  "False\0"\
52:                                  "True\0"\
53:                                  "";
54:
55:  //-----------------------------------------------------------
56:  // Property info
57:  //-----------------------------------------------------------
58:
59:  PROPINFO Property_Action =
60:    {
61:     "Action",
62:     DT_ENUM  |  PF_fSetMsg | PF_fGetData | PF_fSetData | PF_fSaveData,
63:     OFFSETIN(ElapsedSTRUCT,Action),
64:     0,
65:     0,
66:     szActionTypes,
67:     3
68:    };
69:
70:  PROPINFO Property_DisplayResults =
71:    {
72:     "DisplayResults",
73:     DT_ENUM  |  PF_fSetMsg | PF_fGetData | PF_fSetData | PF_fSaveData,
74:     OFFSETIN(ElapsedSTRUCT,DisplayResults),
75:     0,
76:     0,
77:     szDisplayResultsTypes,
78:     3
79:    };
80:
81:  PROPINFO Property_Hours =
82:    {
83:     "Hours",
84:     DT_SHORT | PF_fGetData | PF_fSetData | PF_fSaveData,
85:     OFFSETIN(ElapsedSTRUCT, Hours),
86:     0,
87:     0,
88:     NULL,
89:     0
```

```
 90:   };
 91:
 92:   PROPINFO Property_Minutes =
 93:   {
 94:     "Minutes",
 95:     DT_SHORT | PF_fGetData | PF_fSetData | PF_fSaveData,
 96:     OFFSETIN(ElapsedSTRUCT, Minutes),
 97:     0,
 98:     0,
 99:     NULL,
100:     0
101:   };
102:
103:   PROPINFO Property_Seconds =
104:   {
105:     "Seconds",
106:     DT_SHORT | PF_fGetData | PF_fSetData | PF_fSaveData,
107:     OFFSETIN(ElapsedSTRUCT, Seconds),
108:     0,
109:     0,
110:     NULL,
111:     0
112:   };
113:
114:   //-------------------------------------------------------------------
115:   // Define the consecutive indices for the properties
116:   //-------------------------------------------------------------------
117:   #define IPROP_CTLNAME                 0
118:   #define IPROP_INDEX                   1
119:   #define IPROP_ACTION                  2
120:   #define IPROP_DISPLAYRESULTS          3
121:   #define IPROP_HOURS                   4
122:   #define IPROP_MINUTES                 5
123:   #define IPROP_SECONDS                 6
124:
125:   //-------------------------------------------------------------------
126:   // Property list
127:   //-------------------------------------------------------------------
128:   PPROPINFO Elapsed_Properties[] =
129:     {
130:     PPROPINFO_STD_CTLNAME,      // Always First
131:     PPROPINFO_STD_INDEX,        // Always Second
132:     &Property_Action,           // Start Custom Properties
133:     &Property_DisplayResults,
134:     &Property_Hours,
135:     &Property_Minutes,
136:     &Property_Seconds,
137:     PPROPINFO_STD_LEFT,         // Start Standard Properties
138:     PPROPINFO_STD_TOP,
139:     NULL
140:     };
141:
142:   PEVENTINFO Elapsed_Events[] = //No Events
143:     {
144:       NULL
145:     };
```

257

```
146:
147:   //-----------------------------------------------------------------
148:   // Model struct
149:   //-----------------------------------------------------------------
150:   // Define the control model (using the event and property structures).
151:   //-----------------------------------------------------------------
152:   MODEL modelElapsed =
153:       {
154:       VB_VERSION,                        // VB version being used
155:       MODEL_fLoadMsg|MODEL_fInitMsg,     // Model Flags
156:       (PCTLPROC)ElapsedCtlProc,          // Control procedure
157:       CS_VREDRAW | CS_HREDRAW,           // Class style
158:       0L,                                // Default Windows style
159:       sizeof(ElapsedSTRUCT),             // Size of Elapsed structure
160:       IDBMP_ELAPSEDUP,                   // Palette bitmap ID
161:       "Elapsed",                         // Default control name
162:       "ELAPSED",                         // Visual Basic class name
163:       NULL,                              // Parent class name
164:       Elapsed_Properties,                // Property information table
165:       Elapsed_Events,                    // Event information table
166:       IPROP_ACTION,                      // Default property
167:       NULL,                              // Default event
168:       NULL                               // Property representing value of ctl
169:       };
170:
171:   #endif    // RC_INVOKED
```

REM The line numbers shown at the left of the lines in the preceding listing are for informational purposes only. They are not actually listed in the code.

Here's what's happening in the preceding code. Lines 4 and 5 define a constant that refers to the bitmaps created earlier. Make sure that the ID numbers used in the App Studio are numbers.

Lines 10–13 and 18–19 are used for versioning and description information. They are self explanatory.

Line 25 is necessary to reference the VBX structure in code. The name of your structure will be different, but the idea is the same.

Line 30 lists that you will export the VBX control procedure. This control procedure is the procedure that controls every aspect of the control.

Lines 35–42 define a structure containing user-defined properties. These properties are referenced in your code. The code does not actually set up the properties inside the structure. That comes later. The code just defines what the properties are. This is only for determining which property is changed in your code. It's a good idea to keep these in alphabetical order.

Line 44 defines a structure as a far pointer to the structure defined in lines 35–42.

Line 46 is used to set up how you will de-reference the control in your code.

Lines 48–53 are used to set up enumerated properties. These are very common types of properties to use in a VBX. They allow a user to select from a predefined list of values.

Lines 59–112 set up how the properties behave and their default values. Each of the properties uses flags that are defined in the VBAPI.H file. The basic setup of the properties is as follows:

```
PROPINFO Property =
    {
    "name",
    flags
    OFFSETIN(structure,whichindex),
    infodata,
    default,
    enumlist,
    maxenum
    };
```

where:

> *name* is the name of the property as it appears in the Properties window.

> *flags* are the flags that determine the behavior of the control.

> *structure* is the name of your structure. Refer to line 48 for the name of the structure.

> *whichindex* is the item in the structure that refers to the property. Refer to lines 43–47.

> *infodata* is only used for a bitfield. Normally this value is 0.

> *default* is also only used for a bitfield. Normally this value is also 0.

> *enumlist* is only used for an enumerated list. If this is what you are using, specify the name of the list that you defined earlier. One was defined in lines 54–56.

> *maxenum* is only used for an enumerated list. It is the maximum legal value for the enumerated list.

The flags that are possible to use are listed in Table 19.4. If you want to use more than one flag, separate it by using the pipe "¦" symbol. For these flags to work, you must include the header file, VBAPI.H, which comes with Visual Basic. It is in the CDK subdirectory under the Visual Basic directory.

 In most applications, the Action property is not shown in the Property window. If you want to incorporate this feature with your applications, you can specify the PF_NoShow flag.

TABLE 19.4. VBX FLAGS THAT CAN BE USED.

Flag	Purpose
DT_HSZ	Data type is a string
DT_SHORT	Data type is a short
DT_LONG	Data type is a long
DT_BOOL	Data type is a boolean
DT_COLOR	Data type is a color value
DT_ENUM	Data type is an enumerated property
DT_REAL	Data type is a real
DT_XPOS	Data type is an X-coordinate in twips
DT_XSIZE	Data type is an X-size in twips
DT_YPOS	Data type is a Y-coordinate in twips
DT_YSIZE	Data type is a Y-size in twips
DT_PICTURE	Data type is a picture
PF_fPropArray	Flag specifying that property is an array
PF_fSetData	Flag specifying that property sets data in a programmer-defined data structure
PF_fSetMsg	Flag specifying that property will generate VBM_SETPROPERTY message
PF_fNoShow	Flag specifying that property is not to be shown at runtim
PF_fNoRuntimeW	Flag specifying that property is read only at runtime
PF_fGetData	Flag specifying that property will get property value from programmer-supplied data
PF_fGetMsg	Flag specifying that property will generate VBM_GETPROPERTY message
PF_fSetCheck	Flag specifying that VBM_SETPROPERTY message is sent before the property value is saved
PF_fSaveData	Flag specifying that property setting is saved along with the form when file is saved to disk
PF_fSaveMsg	Flag specifying that the VBM_SAVEPROPERTY/VBM_LOADPROPERTY message is sent when property value is saved or loaded to or from a file
PF_fGetHszMsg	Flag specifying that the VBM_GETPROPERTYHSZ message is sent when property value is displayed in the properties bar

Flag	Purpose
PF_fUpdateOnEdit	Flag specifying that property is updated as characters are typed on-screen
PF_fEditable	Flag specifying that programmer can edit text in settings box
PF_fPreHwnd	Flag specifying that the property is loaded before the control's window struct is created
PF_fDefVal	Flag specifying that property is not saved if it is equal to the default value
PF_fNoInitDef	Flag specifying that property does not load default data in PROPINFO when loading the control

Lines 117–123 assign constant values to each one of the properties.

Lines 128–140 set up which properties are used in the control. Prior to this point, you define how the properties behave, but they are not added into the control. These lines do this. Notice that there are some standard properties used that are not defined earlier. These properties, such as control name, can be added automatically by simply including them.

 Before you add your own custom properties, you must have the following standard properties listed first:

```
PPROPINFO_STD_CTLNAME,
PPROPINFO_STD_INDEX,
```

The control may not work correctly if they are in any other order. After these two properties, add your custom properties that are defined earlier.

The property listing must end in NULL. This specifies the end of the list. Lines 142–145 are used to specify which events are used by the control. The ELAPSED.VBX control has no events. It also ends in NULL.

Lines 152–169 define the properties and behavior of the control itself. These lines have comments to the right of them that show which element of the control is addressed.

The "C" Source File

The next step is to create the C source file, which contains your actual code. This C source file contains all functionality for how the control reacts. It determines how the control reacts in Design mode or Run mode. It also contains the processing for when the user clicks, selects, or changes a property. Because there are so many topics and theories that cannot be covered in the context of this chapter regarding writing VBXs, the following code is shown so you get an idea of the elements that go into a C source file. The listing is taken from the ELAPSED.C file. It is as follows:

```
 1:   //-----------------------------------------------------------------
 2:   // Contains control procedure for Elapsed control
 3:   //-----------------------------------------------------------------
 4:
 5:   #include <windows.h>
 6:   #include <time.h>
 7:   #include <stdio.h>
 8:   #include <string.h>
 9:   #include "vbapi.h"
10:   #include "ELAPSED.h"
11:
12:   //-----------------------------------------------------------------
13:   // Global Variables
14:   //-----------------------------------------------------------------
15:   HANDLE hmodDLL;
16:   HANDLE HBitmap;
17:   BITMAP bmp;
18:   HINSTANCE hInst;
19:   HANDLE hndle;
20:   HWND    Window;
21:
22:   int bmpWidth;
23:   int bmpHeight;
24:   int nResult;
25:   char buffer[3];
26:   time_t TimeStart;
27:   time_t TimeFinish;
28:   double dElapsedTime;
29:   int far nFactor;
30:   int far nTimeLeft;
31:   int far nVBMode;
32:   short far TempDeref;
33:   char far MsgConstructor[9];
34:
35:   //-----------------------------------------------------------------
36:   // Local Prototypes
37:   //-----------------------------------------------------------------
38:   VOID PASCAL PaintControl(HWND hwnd);
39:
40:   //-----------------------------------------------------------------
41:   // Constants
42:   //-----------------------------------------------------------------
43:   const NUMBER = 1;
44:   const LETTER = 2;
45:   const CONTROLHEIGHT = 27;
46:   const CONTROLWIDTH = 27;
47:
48:   //-----------------------------------------------------------------
49:   // Elapsed Control Procedure
50:   //-----------------------------------------------------------------
```

```
51:   LONG FAR PASCAL _export ElapsedCtlProc
52:   (
53:       HCTL   hctl,
54:       HWND   hwnd,
55:       USHORT msg,
56:       USHORT wp,
57:       LONG   lp
58:   )
59:   {
60:
61:       LPElapsedSTRUCT lpElapsedSTRUCT = LpElapsedSTRUCTDEREF(hctl);
62:       switch (msg)
63:       {
64:       case WM_NCCREATE:
65:           break;
66:        case WM_RBUTTONDOWN:
67:           break;
68:        case WM_LBUTTONDBLCLK:
69:           break;
70:        case WM_LBUTTONUP:
71:           break;
72:        case WM_PAINT:
73:           PaintControl(hwnd);
74:           break;
75:        case WM_SIZE:
76:           // set size of control for design time
77:       SetWindowPos(hwnd,NULL,0,0,CONTROLWIDTH,CONTROLHEIGHT,SWP_NOMOVE¦SWP_NOZORDER);
78:           break;
79:        case VBM_SETPROPERTY:
80:          switch (wp)
81:             {
82:             case IPROP_ACTION:
83:                 // stop
84:                 if ((lpElapsedSTRUCT->Action) == 0)
85:                 {
86:                    if (nVBMode == MODE_DESIGN)
87:                    return 0L;
88:
89:                 time(&TimeFinish);
90:                 dElapsedTime = difftime(TimeFinish,TimeStart);
91:
92:                    // initialize all values
93:                    lpElapsedSTRUCT->Hours = 0;
94:                    lpElapsedSTRUCT->Minutes = 0;
95:                    lpElapsedSTRUCT->Seconds = 0;
96:
97:                    nTimeLeft = dElapsedTime;
98:
99:                    // handle hours
100:                   if (nTimeLeft >= 3600)
101:                   {
102:                   nFactor = nTimeLeft/3600;
103:                   lpElapsedSTRUCT->Hours = nFactor;
104:                   nTimeLeft = nTimeLeft - (nFactor * 3600);
105:                   }
106:
```

263

```
107:                    // handle minutes
108:                    if (nTimeLeft >= 60)
109:                    {
110:                        nFactor = nTimeLeft/60;
111:                        lpElapsedSTRUCT->Minutes = nFactor;
112:                        nTimeLeft = nTimeLeft - (nFactor * 60);
113:                    }
114:
115:                    //everything left is seconds
116:                    lpElapsedSTRUCT->Seconds = nTimeLeft;
117:
118:
119:                    // display dialog if Flag is set
120:                    if ((lpElapsedSTRUCT->DisplayResults) == 1)
121:                 {
122:                  // initialize strings
123:                  strcpy(MsgConstructor,"\0\0\0\0\0\0\0\0\0");
124:                  strcpy(buffer,"\0\0\0");
125:
126:                  // add hours to string
127:                  TempDeref = (lpElapsedSTRUCT->Hours);
128:                  nResult = sprintf(buffer," %-00i ",TempDeref);
129:                  strcat(MsgConstructor,buffer);
130:                  strcat(MsgConstructor,":");
131:
132:                  // initialize buffer
133:                     strcpy(buffer,"\0\0\0");
134:
135:                  // add minutes to string
136:                  TempDeref = (lpElapsedSTRUCT->Minutes);
137:                  nResult = sprintf(buffer," %-00i ",TempDeref);
138:                  strcat(MsgConstructor,buffer);
139:                     strcat(MsgConstructor,":");
140:
141:                  // initialize buffer
142:                     strcpy(buffer,"\0\0\0");
143:
144:                  // add seconds to string
145:                  TempDeref = (lpElapsedSTRUCT->Seconds);
146:                  nResult = sprintf(buffer," %-00i ",TempDeref);
147:                  strcat(MsgConstructor,buffer);
148:                  strcat(MsgConstructor,"\n");
149:
150:                  nResult = MessageBox(NULL,MsgConstructor,"Elapsed",0x0000);
151:                 }
152:
153:                 return 0;
154:             }
155:          else
156:           // start
157:           if ((lpElapsedSTRUCT->Action) == 1)
158:             {
159:                 // initialize all values
160:                 lpElapsedSTRUCT->Hours = 0;
161:                 lpElapsedSTRUCT->Minutes = 0;
162:                 lpElapsedSTRUCT->Seconds = 0;
```

```
163:
164:                    time(&TimeStart);
165:                    return 0;
166:
167:                }
168:
169:          }
170:       break;
171:    case VBM_INITPROPPOPUP:
172:          break;
173:     case VBM_CREATED:
174:        nVBMode = VBGetMode();
175:        if(nVBMode != MODE_DESIGN)
176:        return 0L;
177:        break;
178:     case VBM_INITIALIZE:
179:        // make resource of up toolbox bitmap so that it can be redrawn in
180:        // on the form
181:        nVBMode = VBGetMode();
182:        if(nVBMode !=MODE_DESIGN)
183:        return 0L;
184:
185:        if (HBitmap == (HANDLE)NULL)
186:        {
187:            HBitmap = LoadBitmap(hmodDLL,MAKEINTRESOURCE(IDBMP_ELAPSEDUP));
188:
189:            if (HBitmap == (HANDLE)NULL)
190:                return 0L;
191:
192:            GetObject(HBitmap,sizeof(BITMAP),(LPSTR)&bmp);
193:            bmpWidth=(USHORT)bmp.bmWidth;
194:            bmpHeight=(USHORT)bmp.bmHeight;
195:        }
196:        break;
197:
198:  }
199:
200:
201:     return VBDefControlProc(hctl, hwnd, msg, wp, lp);
202: }
203:
204: VOID PASCAL PaintControl(HWND hwnd)
205: {
206: //paint bitmap of hidden control(mirror up control)
207: BITMAP bmp;
208: HDC hdcMem;
209: PAINTSTRUCT ps;
210:
211:
212: if (HBitmap == NULL)
213:      return;
214:
215: BeginPaint(hwnd, &ps);
216: GetObject(HBitmap, sizeof(BITMAP), (LPSTR)&bmp);
217: hdcMem = CreateCompatibleDC(ps.hdc);
218: SelectObject(hdcMem, HBitmap);
```

```
219:
220:    BitBlt(ps.hdc,0,0,bmp.bmWidth,bmp.bmHeight,hdcMem, 0,0,SRCCOPY);
221:
222:    DeleteDC(hdcMem);
223:    EndPaint(hwnd,&ps);
224: }
225:
226: //----------------------------------------------------------------
227: // Initialize library. This routine is called when the first client
228: // loads the DLL.
229: //----------------------------------------------------------------
230: int FAR PASCAL LibMain
231: (
232:    HANDLE hModule,
233:    WORD   wDataSeg,
234:    WORD   cbHeapSize,
235:    LPSTR  lpszCmdLine
236: )
237: {
238:    // Avoid warnings on unused (but required) formal parameters
239:    wDataSeg     = wDataSeg;
240:    cbHeapSize   = cbHeapSize;
241:    lpszCmdLine  = lpszCmdLine;
242:
243:    hmodDLL = hModule;
244:
245:  return 1;
246: }
247:
248: //----------------------------------------------------------------
249: // Register custom control.  This routine is called by VB when the
250: // custom control DLL is loaded for use.
251: //----------------------------------------------------------------
252: BOOL FAR PASCAL _export VBINITCC
253: (
254:    USHORT usVersion,
255:    BOOL   fRuntime
256: )
257: {
258:    // Avoid warnings on unused (but required) formal parameters
259:    fRuntime = fRuntime;
260:    usVersion = usVersion;
261:
262:    // Register control(s)
263:    return VBRegisterModel(hmodDLL, &modelElapsed);
264: }
265:
266: #if (_MSC_VER < 610)
267:
268: int FAR PASCAL WEP(int fSystemExit);
269:
270: #pragma alloc_text(WEP_TEXT,WEP)
271: int FAR PASCAL WEP
```

```
272: (
273:    int fSystemExit
274: )
275: {
276:    // Avoid warnings on unused (but required) formal parameters
277:    fSystemExit = fSystemExit;
278:
279:    return 1;
280: }
281:
282: #endif
```

 The line numbers shown at the left of the lines in the preceding listing are for informational purposes only. They are not actually listed in the code.

Here's what's happening in the preceding code. Lines 5–10 list the header files to include in the compilation. Notice that on line 10, the ELAPSED.H file created in the previous step is included here.

Lines 15–33 list the variables used in the ELAPSED.C file.

Line 38 is a prototype for the `PaintControl()` function.

Lines 43–46 are used to declare constant values.

Lines 51–202 define the control procedure mentioned earlier. It really is a procedure that encompasses the entire control as a whole. It is what Windows and Visual Basic messages are passed to. Windows and Visual Basic messages really are just constants that the VBX passes into the control procedure. Notice that not all Windows messages are used, but the most common ones to use in a VBX are listed. Some of them are left for explanation purposes even though there is no code behind them. Examples of the messages left in code but not used are the `WM_NCCREATE` and the `WM_RBUTTONDOWN` messages.

Table 19.5 lists the most commonly used messages in a VBX control.

TABLE 19.5. COMMON VBX MESSAGES.

Message	Purpose
WM_PAINT	Message when control is to be painted on-screen.
WM_SIZE	Message when the control is sized.
VBM_SETPROPERTY	Message when the user changes a property setting. This property is used in conjunction with the `PF_fSetData` and `PF_fSaveData` flags in the H header file.
VBM_INITIALIZE	Message when control is first initialized.

For more information about the possible Windows messages, refer to the WIN31WH.HLP help file located in the WINAPI subdirectory under the Visual Basic directory.

For more information about the possible Visual Basic messages, refer to the VBAPI.HLP help file located in the CDK subdirectory under the Visual Basic directory.

Lines 204–224 handle the automatic sizing of the control. This means that no matter how the user sizes the control, it returns to the size of the toolbox bitmap. It is called by the branch of code in the control procedure listed previously when the WM_PAINT message is sent.

Lines 230–246 are the VBX (or DLL, for that matter) entry point. Your code will not change. You need to use this code as it is.

Lines 252–264 register the control with Visual Basic. The only code you change is in line 263. Include the name of your control structure.

Lines 266–282 are the Windows exit point. Your code will not be different in this function.

After you use the code listed earlier as a template for your C source file, save it with a C file extension.

THE "DEF" FILE

The DEF file is used to tell the compiler about the Windows parameters used in the VBX file, as well as the name of the functions and subroutines to export. The DEF code for the ELAPSED.VBX file is as follows:

```
LIBRARY      ELAPSED
EXETYPE      WINDOWS
DESCRIPTION  'Elapsed Time Control'
CODE         MOVEABLE PRELOAD
DATA         MOVEABLE SINGLE PRELOAD
HEAPSIZE     2048
EXPORTS
    WEP   @1   RESIDENTNAME
SEGMENTS
    WEP_TEXT FIXED
```

Notice on the second-to-last line that the constant RESIDENTNAME is used to export the functions previously declared as _export.

After the RC, C, and DEF files are created, you can create a new project by selecting the Project>New menu option. Select the Visual Basic Custom Control (VBX) menu option for the project type. After the wizard is shown to create the new DLL, add the C source and DEF files into the project. Closing this screen creates the project file with the MAK file.

You are now ready to compile the DLL. To do this, select the Project->Build menu option. The DLL is created.

 It is important for you to add the VBAPI library that comes with Visual Basic in the CDK subdirectory to the libraries your project will use. After you create your project, select the Options->Project menu option. This invokes the Project Options dialog box. You see three command buttons: Compiler, Linker, and Resources. Select the Linker command button. This invokes the Linker Options dialog box. You must add "VBAPI" to the libraries line. Figure 19.5 shows what this screen looks like.

If you do not add this file, you receive the following errors when you compile:

```
error L2029: 'VBREGISTERMODEL' : unresolved external

error L2029: 'VBGETMODE' : unresolved external

error L2029: 'VBDEFCONTROLPROC' : unresolved external

error L2029: 'VBDEREFCONTROL' : unresolved external
```

FIGURE 19.5.
Visual C++ Linker options.

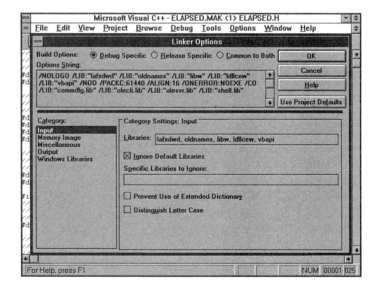

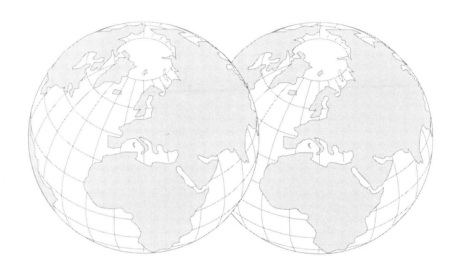

APPLICATIONS
FOR THE REAL WORLD

MDI File Search
Application

The MDI File Search application allows the user to
search a directory of files for
the number of occurrences of
a certain string. The application then builds a list of the
files that contain the search string. The user can view any
or all of these files (as long
as they are text files) in the
MDI File Viewer part of the
application. Figure 20.1 shows
the main screen (MAIN.FRM)
at runtime.

FIGURE 20.1.
MDI File Search
application MAIN.FRM
at runtime.

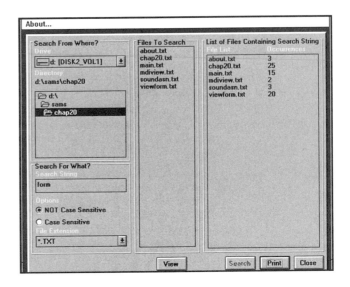

Once the file viewer MDI form is displayed, certain options become available if the right mouse button is pressed. Figure 20.2 shows the MDIVIEW screen at runtime. Each MDI form can have the following attributes changed or accessed separately, if the right mouse button is pressed:

◆ Toggle Drag/Drop

◆ Save As

◆ Font

◆ Print

◆ Sound

◆ Help Contents

◆ About

If Drag/Drop is off (denoted by the label on the icon bar), the form can't be dragged. This is because there are times when you need to scroll up and down the text box, which is not possible if the Drag/Drop is on. If Drag/Drop is turned on, you can drag each text box individually to the icons on the icon bar, which represent some of the items listed earlier. These items include printing files, changing sound options, changing fonts, or saving the file.

The Help Contents option invokes the Help file included in this application. For more information about creating the Help file, refer to Chapter 10, "Creating Context Sensitive Help." The About option invokes the About box, just as in the MAIN.FRM form.

The application allows for certain sounds to be played at certain times in the application. This gives an example of how to incorporate audio into an application. For more information on

Audio, refer to Chapter 11. Figure 20.3 shows the SOUNDASN.FRM form that allows for the assigning of sound files to certain events. Table 20.1 lists the events that cause a sound file and the default file to be played, unless changed.

FIGURE 20.2.
MDI File Search application MDIVIEW.FRM at runtime with multiple VIEWFORM.FRM files.

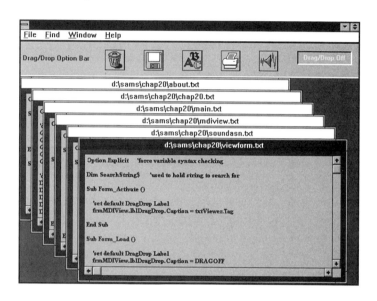

FIGURE 20.3.
MDI File Search application SOUNDASN.FRM at runtime.

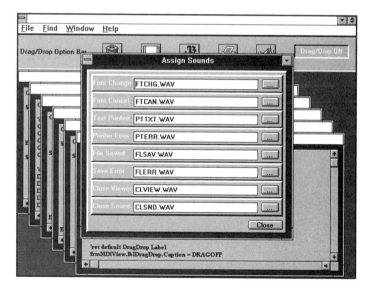

TABLE 20.1. EVENTS THAT CAUSE SOUND FILES TO BE PLAYED, WITH THE DEFAULT FILE NAME.

Event	Default File
Font is changed	FTCHG.WAV
Font change is cancelled	FTCAN.WAV
Text file printed	PTTXT.WAV
Error printing text file	PTERR.WAV
Text file saved	FLSAV.WAV
Error saving text file	FLERR.WAV
Closing file viewer screen	CLVIEW.WAV
Closing change sound screen	CLSND.WAV

To use the application, enter a string to search for in the Search String (txtStringSearch) text box. Select the option for case sensitivity or not. Select the appropriate drive and directory to search. Limit the search by selecting an appropriate file extension. Click on the Search command button.

The lstFileList listbox contains the results of the search. You can then select files in either listbox. Once selected, click the View command button to invoke the MDI file viewer. With an MDI form active, press F7 to find the next occurrence of the search string inside the file. Press F8 to find the next occurrence of a specified string inside the file. This option invokes an Inputbox() to input the string to search for.

To change any of the options, you can either press the right mouse button and select the option or if the Drag/Drop mode is ON, you can drag the text box to the appropriate icon.

For more information, see the following chapters:

"The Mouse," Chapter 4

"Printing," Chapter 6

"File Input/Output (I/O)," Chapter 7

"Multiple Document Interface (MDI)," Chapter 8

"Creating Context Sensitive Help," Chapter 10

"Audio," Chapter 11

CODE LISTINGS

The MDI File Search application contains the following files and listings:

- CHAP20.MAK
- MAIN.FRM
- MDIVIEW.FRM
- VIEWFORM.FRM
- SOUNDASN.FRM
- ABOUT.FRM
- CHAP20.BAS
- SOUND.INI
- CHAP20.ICO
- DRAGFLDR.ICO
- CLOSE.BMP
- SAVE.BMP
- PRINTER.BMP
- FONT.BMP
- SOUND.BMP
- FTCHG.WAV
- FTCAN.WAV
- PTTXT.WAV
- PTERR.WAV
- FLSAV.WAV
- FLERR.WAV
- CLVIEW.WAV
- CLSND.WAV
- CHAP20.HLP
- CHAP20.RTF
- CHAP20.HPJ
- SCREEN1.SHG
- SCREEN2.SHG
- SCREEN3.SHG
- CHAP20.EXE

THE CHAP20.MAK FILE

CHAP20.MAK is the project file for the MDI File Search application, CHAP20.EXE. It contains a listing of all the files necessary to load the project into Visual Basic. The CHAP20.MAK file is contained on the CD accompanying this book in the CHAP20 subdirectory. The file listing is:

LISTING 20.1. CHAP20.MAK.

```
MAIN.FRM
VIEWFORM.FRM
MDIVIEW.FRM
SOUNDASN.FRM
ABOUT.FRM
CHAP20.BAS
THREED.VBX
CMDIALOG.VBX
ProjWinSize=150,414,248,205
ProjWinShow=2
IconForm="frmMain"
Title="SEARCH"
ExeName="CHAP20.EXE"
```

THE MAIN.FRM FILE

MAIN.FRM is one of five forms in this application. It is the startup form for the application, as well as the form used to search for the number of occurrences of a particular string inside a directory of files. Figure 20.4 shows the form as it appears at design time. Table 20.2 lists all the relevant properties of each control on the form that have been changed from their standard default values. The MAIN.FRM file is contained on the CD accompanying this book in the CHAP20 subdirectory.

FIGURE 20.4.
MDI File Search application MAIN.FRM at design time.

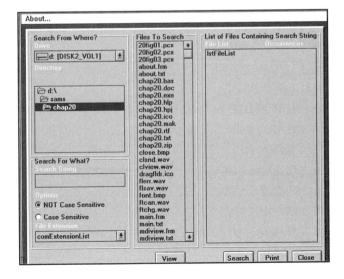

TABLE 20.2. PROPERTIES OF EACH CONTROL ON MAIN.FRM.

Object	Control Type	Property	Value
frmMain	Form	BackColor	&H00404000&
		Caption	"Real-World MDI File Search Application"
		Height	7320
		HelpContextID	3
		Icon	"CHAP20.ICO"
		Left	705
		MaxButton	False
		Top	195
		Width	8715
Panel3D1	SSPanel	BackColor	&H00C0C0C0&
		BevelWidth	3
		FloodColor	&H00C0C000&
		Font3D	None
		ForeColor	&H00C0C0C0&
		Height	6615
		Left	120
		RoundedCorners	False
		ShadowColor	Black
		Top	120
		Width	8415
cmdView	CommandButton	Caption	"View"
		Height	375
		HelpContextID	22
		Left	3960
		Top	6120
		Width	855
cmdClose	CommandButton	Caption	"Close"
		Height	375
		HelpContextID	25
		Left	7440

continues

TABLE 20.2. CONTINUED

Object	Control Type	Property	Value
		Top	6120
		Width	855
cmdPrint	CommandButton	Caption	"Print"
		Height	375
		HelpContextID	24
		Left	6480
		Top	6120
		Width	855
cmdSearch	CommandButton	Caption	"Search"
		Height	375
		HelpContextID	23
		Left	5520
		Top	6120
		Width	855
Frame3D4	SSFrame	Caption	"Files To Search"
		Font3D	None
		ForeColor	&H00000000&
		Height	5895
		Left	3000
		ShadowStyle	Raised
		Top	120
		Width	1815
Frame3D1	SSFrame	Caption	"Search From Where?"
		Font3D	None
		ForeColor	&H00000000&
		Height	3375
		Left	120
		ShadowStyle	Raised
		Top	120
		Width	2775
Frame3D2	SSFrame	Caption	"Search For What?"

Object	Control Type	Property	Value
		Font3D	None
		ForeColor	&H00000000&
		Height	2535
		Left	120
		ShadowStyle	Raised
		Top	3480
		Width	2775
Frame3D3	SSFrame	Caption	"List Of Files Containing Search String"
		Font3D	None
		ForeColor	&H00000000&
		Height	5895
		Left	4920
		ShadowStyle	Raised
		Top	120
		Width	3775
lstProposed	FileListBox	Height	5490
		HelpContextID	27
		Left	120
		MultiSelect	Extended
		Top	240
		Width	1575
lstFileList	ListBox	Height	5295
		HelpContextID	26
		Left	120
		MultiSelect	Extended
		Top	480
		Width	3135
Drive1	DriveListBox	Height	315
		HelpContextID	17
		Left	120
		Top	480

continues

TABLE 20.2. CONTINUED

Object	Control Type	Property	Value
		Width	2535
Dir1	DirListBox	Height	1830
		HelpContextID	18
		Left	120
		Top	1430
		Width	2535
Label1	Label	BackColor	&H00C0C0C0&
		Caption	"Directory"
		ForeColor	&H0000FFFF&
		Height	255
		Left	120
		Top	840
		Width	1095
Label2	Label	BackColor	&H00C0C0C0&
		Caption	"Drive"
		ForeColor	&H0000FFFF&
		Height	255
		Left	120
		Top	240
		Width	1095
Label4	Label	BackColor	&H00C0C0C0&
		Caption	"Search String"
		ForeColor	&H0000FFFF&
		Height	255
		Left	120
		Top	240
		Width	1335
Label5	Label	BackColor	&H00C0C0C0&
		Caption	"Options"
		ForeColor	&H0000FFFF&

Object	Control Type	Property	Value
		Height	255
		Left	120
		Top	960
		Width	1095
Label6	Label	BackColor	&H00C0C0C0&
		Caption	"File Extension"
		ForeColor	&H0000FFFF&
		Height	255
		Left	120
		Top	1800
		Width	1455
Label7	Label	BackColor	&H00C0C0C0&
		Caption	"Occurrences"
		ForeColor	&H0000FFFF&
		Height	255
		Left	1800
		Top	240
		Width	1205
Label3	Label	BackColor	&H00C0C0C0&
		Caption	"File List"
		ForeColor	&H0000FFFF&
		Height	255
		Left	120
		Top	240
		Width	1575
DisplayDir	Label	BackColor	&H00C0C0C0&
		Height	255
		Left	120
		Top	1080
		Width	2535
optSensitive	SSOption	Caption	"Case Sensitive"

continues

TABLE 20.2. CONTINUED

Object	Control Type	Property	Value
		Font3D	None
		Height	195
		HelpContextID	20
		Left	120
		Top	1560
		Width	2415
optNotSensitive	SSOption	Caption	"NOT Case Sensitive"
		Font3D	None
		Height	255
		HelpContextID	20
		Left	120
		Top	1200
		Value	True
		Width	2535
txtSearchString	TextBox	Height	375
		HelpContextID	19
		Left	120
		Top	480
		Width	2535
comExtensionList	ComboBox	Height	300
		HelpContextID	20
		Left	120
		Style	Dropdown List
		Top	2040
		Width	2535
menu_about	Menu	Caption	"&About..."

FUNCTION, SUBROUTINE, AND EVENT PROCEDURES

There are several procedures of code for each object(control) that comprise this form. Each is listed in the following sections.

THE *(GENERAL)* OBJECT

The (general) object contains declarations and procedures at the form level. The procedures for the (general) object are

- ◆ (declarations)
- ◆ CheckPermission()
- ◆ ExtractFileOnly()
- ◆ OpenViewer()
- ◆ RemoveTab()
- ◆ SearchFile()

THE *(DECLARATIONS)* PROCEDURE

The (declarations) procedure contains only one line of code. All variable declarations are in CHAP20.BAS. Following is a listing of the (declarations) procedure:

LISTING 20.2. MAIN.FRM, (general)(declarations).

```
Option Explicit
```

THE *CHECKPERMISSION()* PROCEDURE

The CheckPermission() procedure checks to see if the Search command button can be enabled. Following is a listing of the CheckPermission procedure:

LISTING 20.3. MAIN.FRM, CheckPermission().

```
Sub CheckPermission ()

    'if there are files proposed and a search string, enable Search Button
    If lstProposed.ListCount > 0 And Len(Trim$(txtSearchString)) > 0 Then
    cmdSearch.Enabled = True
    Else
    cmdSearch.Enabled = False
    End If

End Sub
```

THE *EXTRACTFILEONLY()* PROCEDURE

The ExtractFileOnly() procedure extracts the file from the string containing the drive and directory. The ExtractFileOnly() procedure accepts one argument, TheFile, which is the complete filespec of the file. The procedure is also a function that returns the name of the file.

Following is a listing of the `ExtractFileOnly()` procedure:

LISTING 20.4. MAIN.FRM, `ExtractFileOnly()`.

```
Function ExtractFileOnly (TheFile As String) As String

    'declare variables
    Dim IndexPos%

    'initialize
    IndexPos% = Len(TheFile)

    'determine what the filename is without directory

    'search for the backslash character(indicates directory)
    Do While Mid$(TheFile, IndexPos%, 1) <> "\"
    IndexPos% = IndexPos% - 1
    Loop

    ExtractFileOnly = Right$(TheFile, Len(TheFile) - IndexPos%)

End Function
```

THE *OPENVIEWER()* PROCEDURE

The `OpenViewer()` procedure opens the MDI File Search and populates an MDI form for each file that can be read in its entirety. Following is a listing of the `OpenViewer()` procedure:

LISTING 20.5. MAIN.FRM, `OpenViewer()`.

```
Sub OpenViewer ()

    'declare variables
    Dim m$                           'Holds message building string
    Dim ControlWithFocus As Control  'Stores control which has the focus
    Dim LoopCount%                   'Looping Variable
    Dim TheFile$                     'holds file name to open(including path)
    Dim TextToHold$                  'holds text to be placed in file viewer
    Dim NextIndex%                   'holds next available index
    Dim NumberOfSelections%          'holds number of selections to redim Viewer
    Dim IndexInUse%                  'holds the index number used in Viewer array
    Dim pos%                         'holds position of tab

    'initialize
    NumberOfSelections% = 0
    IndexInUse% = 0

    'handle errors
    On Error GoTo FError:

    'find out which list box has the focus
    'Viewer will be populated with all selected files from this list
```

```
'Test Proposed List
For LoopCount% = 0 To lstProposed.ListCount - 1

'test for lstProposed contents to avoid errors
If lstProposed.ListCount > 0 Then
    If lstProposed.Selected(LoopCount%) = True Then
    'Proposed List has the focus
    Set ControlWithFocus = lstProposed
    NumberOfSelections% = NumberOfSelections% + 1
    End If
End If
Next LoopCount%

'Test File List
For LoopCount% = 0 To lstFileList.ListCount - 1

'test for lstFileList contents to avoid errors
If lstFileList.ListCount > 0 Then
    If lstFileList.Selected(LoopCount%) = True Then
    'File List has the focus
    Set ControlWithFocus = lstFileList
    NumberOfSelections% = NumberOfSelections% + 1
    End If
End If
Next LoopCount%

'redim array to hold all of the selections
ReDim NewViewer(NumberOfSelections%)

For LoopCount% = 0 To ControlWithFocus.ListCount - 1
'if selected, open file
If ControlWithFocus.Selected(LoopCount%) = True Then
    'assign file temporary-will reassign below
    TheFile$ = ControlWithFocus.List(LoopCount%)

    'test to see if there is a tab in the format
    pos% = InStr(TheFile$, Chr$(9))'
    If pos% > 0 Then
    'this contained a tab-remove
    TheFile$ = Left$(TheFile$, pos% - 1)
    End If

    'assign the file, making sure it's in the proper format
    If Right$(Dir1.Path, 1) = "\" Then
    TheFile$ = Dir1.Path + TheFile$
    Else
    TheFile$ = Dir1.Path + "\" + TheFile$
    End If

    'open file
    Open TheFile$ For Input As #1

    'read entire file
    TextToHold$ = Input$(LOF(1), #1)

    'Test to see if entire file was read
```

continues

LISTING 20.5. CONTINUED

```vb
        If Len(TextToHold$) <> LOF(1) Then

            'change cursor
            Screen.MousePointer = DEFAULT

            'build message
            m$ = "The complete file cannot be read." + Chr$(13)
            m$ = m$ + "It contains unreadable characters."

            'display message
            MsgBox m$

        Else
            NewViewer(IndexInUse%).Caption = TheFile$

            'flag populating viewer, so viewer change event
            'can be ignored
            PopulatingViewer% = True

            'assign text
            NewViewer(IndexInUse%).txtViewer.Text = TextToHold$

            'show form
            NewViewer(IndexInUse%).Show

            'reset viewer flag
            PopulatingViewer% = False

            'increment IndexInUse for next iteration
            IndexInUse% = IndexInUse% + 1
        End If

            'Close File
            Close #1

            'change cursor
            Screen.MousePointer = DEFAULT

    End If

    Next LoopCount%

    'exit
    Exit Sub

FError:
    'there were errors

    'change cursor
    Screen.MousePointer = DEFAULT

    'build message
    m$ = "Error- Cannot Read This File"

    'display message
```

```
        MsgBox m$

        Resume Next

End Sub
```

THE *REMOVETAB( )* PROCEDURE

The RemoveTab() procedure removes tabs from the name of the file stored in a listbox. The reason that tabs are in the file in the first place is for formatting purposes only. The tabs are used to separate the filename from the number of occurrences of a string inside a file. The RemoveTab() procedure accepts one argument, TheFile, which is the listbox element containing a tab. It is also a function that returns the filename without the tab. Following is a listing of the RemoveTab() procedure:

LISTING 20.6. MAIN.FRM, RemoveTab( ).

```
Function RemoveTab (TheFile As String) As String

    'declare variables
    Dim IndexPos1% 'position of 1st tab
    Dim IndexPos2% 'position of 2nd tab

    'find position of 1st tab
    IndexPos1% = InStr(TheFile, Chr$(9))

    If IndexPos1% > 0 Then
    'At least one tab, test for another
    IndexPos2% = InStr(Mid$(TheFile, IndexPos1% + 1, Len(TheFile) - IndexPos1%), Chr$(9))
    If IndexPos2% > 0 Then
        'There were 2 tabs

        'remove tab and return
        RemoveTab = Left$(TheFile, IndexPos1% - 1) + Right$(TheFile, Len(TheFile)
        -IndexPos1%)
    Else
        'only 1 tab - return file
        RemoveTab = TheFile
    End If
    Else
    'No tabs-return file
    RemoveTab = TheFile
    End If

End Function
```

THE *SEARCHFILE( )* PROCEDURE

The SearchFile() procedure is the procedure that does the main portion of work in the application. It searches for the number of occurrences of a string within all files in a directory.

It accepts one argument, `FileName$`, that is the name of the file to search for the string. It is also a function that returns the number of occurrences of the string. Following is a listing of the `SearchFile()` procedure:

LISTING 20.7. MAIN.FRM, `SearchFile()`.

```
Function SearchFile (FileName$) As Integer

    'declare variables
    Dim TheLine$        'gets line of text
    Dim Stringcount%    'number of occurrences
    Dim TempPos%        'temporary position of instr

    'initialize
    Stringcount% = 0
    TempPos% = 0

    'Handle Errors
    On Error GoTo FileError

    'open file
    Open FileName$ For Input As #1

    'Loop through file, while it doesn't find an End Of File marker
    Do While Not EOF(1)

    'Get a line
    Input #1, TheLine$

    'search for string in the line
    If optNotSensitive.Value = True Then
        'NOT case sensitive

        'Test to see if the search string exists in this line
        If InStr(1, TheLine$, Trim$(txtSearchString.Text), 1) <> 0 Then

        'initialize TempPos%
        TempPos% = 1

        'the string exists, test for other occurrences in same line
        Do While TempPos% <= Len(TheLine$)

            If InStr(1, Mid$(TheLine$, TempPos%, Len(txtSearchString.Text)), _
            txtSearchString.Text, 1) > 0 Then
            Stringcount% = Stringcount% + 1
            End If
            TempPos% = TempPos% + 1
        Loop
        End If
    Else
        'IS case sensitive

        'Test to see if the search string exists in this line
        If InStr(1, TheLine$, Trim$(txtSearchString.Text), 0) <> 0 Then
```

```
            'initialize TempPos%
            TempPos% = 1

            'the string exists, test for other occurrences in same line
            Do While TempPos% <= Len(TheLine$)
                If InStr(1, Mid$(TheLine$, TempPos%, Len(txtSearchString.Text)),
                txtSearchString.Text, 1) > 0 Then
                Stringcount% = Stringcount% + 1
                End If
                TempPos% = TempPos% + 1
            Loop
            End If
    End If

    Loop

    'Close Handle
    Close #1

    'Return the number of occurrences
    SearchFile = Stringcount%

    'Exit
    Exit Function
'error occurred
FileError:
    'Close Handle
    Close #1

    'Return error code
    SearchFile = -1

    'Exit
    Exit Function

    'resume to avoid errors
    Resume

End Function
```

 For more information on File I/O, refer to Chapter 7, "File Input/Output (I/O)."

THE *cmdCLOSE* CONTROL

cmdClose is the name of the command button control that, when clicked, invokes closing the application by unloading the form. The cmdClose control has code in only one event procedure. It is

◆ cmdClose_Click()

THE *CMDCLOSE_CLICK( )* EVENT PROCEDURE

Listing 20.8 is the cmdClose_Click() event procedure, which unloads the main form, frmMain:

LISTING 20.8. MAIN.FRM, cmdClose_Click().

```
Sub cmdClose_Click ()

    'close
    Unload frmMain

End Sub
```

THE *CMDPRINT* CONTROL

cmdPrint is the name of the command button control that, when clicked, prints the results of the search, not each individual file. See MDIVIEW.FRM and CHAP20.BAS for more details on printing an individual file. The cmdPrint control has code in only one event procedure. It is

◆ cmdPrint_Click()

THE *CMDPRINT_CLICK( )* EVENT PROCEDURE

The cmdPrint_Click() event procedure initiates the printing sequence. Listing 20.9 contains cmdPrint_Click() event procedure:

LISTING 20.9. MAIN.FRM, cmdPrint_Click().

```
Sub cmdPrint_Click ()

    'declare variables
    Dim LoopCount%          'loopcount variable
    Dim m$                  'message box variable

    'Define Error Handling
    On Error GoTo PrintError

    'Change Cursor
    Screen.MousePointer = HOURGLASS

    'Open Printer Port
    Open "LPT1" For Output As #2

    'print header
    If InStr(comExtensionList.Text, "ALL") > 0 Then
    Print #2, "Search Results of ALL files"
    Else
    Print #2, "Search Results of file with extension " + comExtensionList.Text
    End If
    Print #2, "In the directory: " + Dir1.Path
```

```
        Print #2,
        Print #2, "Files" + String$(2, Chr$(9)) + "Occurrences"
        Print #2, "------------------------"
        Print #2,

        'loop through file list
        For LoopCount% = 0 To lstFileList.ListCount - 1

        'print file name
        Print #2, RemoveTab((lstFileList.List(LoopCount%)))

        Next LoopCount%

        'Form Feed Paper
        Print #2, Chr$(27) + "&l0H"

        'Close Handle
        Close #2

        'Change Cursor
        Screen.MousePointer = DEFAULT

        'send message of completion
        m$ = "Results were sent to the printer"
        MsgBox m$

        'Exit
        Exit Sub

'There was an error
PrintError:
        'Change Cursor
        Screen.MousePointer = DEFAULT

        'Build message
        m$ = "There is a problem with the printer!"

        'display message
        MsgBox m$

        'Close Handle
        Close #2

        'Exit
        Exit Sub

        'resume to avoid errors
        Resume

End Sub
```

For more information about printing, refer to Chapter 6, "Printing."

THE *cmdSearch* CONTROL

cmdSearch is the name of the command button control that, when clicked, performs the searching of each file in the file listbox, lstProposed. The cmdSearch control has code only in one event procedure. It is

◆ cmdSearch_Click()

THE *cmdSearch_Click()* EVENT PROCEDURE

The cmdSearch Click() event procedure initiates the file searching. Following is a listing of the cmdSearch_Click() event procedure:

LISTING 20.10. MAIN.FRM, cmdSearch_Click().

```
Sub cmdSearch_Click ()

    'declare variables
    Dim LoopCount%        'loop counting variable
    Dim FileName$         'holds name of file
    Dim Res%              'holds number of occurrences in file
    Dim m$                'message constructor

    'test to see if there are files to search on
    If lstProposed.ListCount = 0 Then
    'build message
    m$ = "There are no files to search on!"

    'display message
    MsgBox m$

    'Exit
    Exit Sub
    End If

    'change cursor
    Screen.MousePointer = HOURGLASS

    'clear lstFileList listbox
    lstFileList.Clear

    'cycle through file list
    For LoopCount% = 0 To lstProposed.ListCount - 1

    'Open files in lstProposed listbox

    'make sure file has proper format
    If Right$(Dir1.Path, 1) <> "\" Then
        FileName$ = Dir1.Path + "\" + lstProposed.List(LoopCount%)
    Else
        FileName$ = Dir1.Path + lstProposed.List(LoopCount%)
    End If
```

```
    'call search function
    Res% = SearchFile(FileName$)
    If Res% = -1 Then
        'there was an error

        'build message
        m$ = "There was an error opening file:" + Chr$(13)
        m$ = m$ + FileName$

        'Change Cursor
        Screen.MousePointer = DEFAULT

        'Display Message
        MsgBox m$

        'Change Cursor
        Screen.MousePointer = HOURGLASS

    ElseIf Res% > 0 Then
        'there were no errors

        'the string was found, add to lstFileList listbox

        'for aesthetic purposes, if the file is less than
        '10 characters, we need to add 2 tabs
        If TextWidth(ExtractFileOnly(FileName$)) < 800 Then
        lstFileList.AddItem ExtractFileOnly(FileName$) + String$(2, Chr$(9)) +
        Trim$(Str$(Res%))
        Else
        lstFileList.AddItem ExtractFileOnly(FileName$) + Chr$(9) + Trim$(Str$(Res%))
        End If
        DoEvents

        'enable print button
        cmdPrint.Enabled = True
    End If
    Next LoopCount%

    'Change Cursor
    Screen.MousePointer = DEFAULT

    'disable search button
    cmdSearch.Enabled = False

    'if print button is not enabled, then there were no results
    If cmdPrint.Enabled = False Then
    'build message
    m$ = "There were no results found!"

    'display message
    MsgBox m$
    End If

End Sub
```

THE *CMDVIEW* CONTROL

cmdView is the name of the command button control that, when clicked, invokes the file viewer based on the file selected in either the lstProposed file listbox or the lstFileList listbox. The cmdView control has code only in one event procedure. It is

◆ cmdView_Click()

THE *CMDVIEW_CLICK()* EVENT PROCEDURE

The cmdView_Click() event procedure invokes the MDI file viewer(s). Following is a listing of the cmdView_Click() event procedure:

LISTING 20.11. MAIN.FRM, cmdView_Click().

```
Sub cmdView_Click ()

    'declare variables
    Dim SelectionFound% 'holds boolean for selection found
    Dim LoopCount%        'holds loop counting

    'initialize
    SelectionFound% = False

    'test to see if anything is selected
    For LoopCount% = 0 To lstProposed.ListCount - 1
    If lstProposed.Selected(LoopCount%) = True Then
        SelectionFound% = True
        Exit For
    End If
    Next LoopCount%
    For LoopCount% = 0 To lstFileList.ListCount - 1
    If lstFileList.Selected(LoopCount%) = True Then
        SelectionFound% = True
        Exit For
    End If
    Next LoopCount%

    'exit if there was no selection
    If SelectionFound% = False Then
    MsgBox "You must select files to view first!"
    Exit Sub
    End If

    'initialize
    Screen.MousePointer = HOURGLASS

    'initialize Change Flag
    ViewerChange% = False

    'Show MDI Form
    frmMDIView.lblDragDrop.Caption = DRAGOFF
    frmMDIView.Show
```

```
            'Maximize
            frmMDIView.WindowState = 2

            'Invoke Viewer
            Call OpenViewer

End Sub
```

THE *comExtensionList* CONTROL

comExtensionList is the name of the combo box control that allows the user to select files with a different file extension to be populated in the lstProposed file listbox. The comExtensionList control has code in only one event procedure. It is

◆ comExtensionList_Click()

THE *comExtensionList_Click()* EVENT PROCEDURE

Following is a listing of the comExtensionList_Click() event procedure:

LISTING 20.12. MAIN.FRM, comExtensionList_Click().

```
Sub comExtensionList_Click ()

    'Determine File Pattern
    If InStr(comExtensionList.Text, "ALL") > 0 Then
    lstProposed.Pattern = "*.*"
    Else
    lstProposed.Pattern = comExtensionList.Text
    End If

    'Clear lstFileList listbox
    lstFileList.Clear

    'Disable Print Button
    cmdPrint.Enabled = False

    'enable buttons
    Call CheckPermission

End Sub
```

THE *Dir1* CONTROL

Dir1 is the name of the dir listbox control that provides the name of the directory to search. The Dir1 control has code in only one event procedure. It is

◆ Dir1_Change()

THE *Dir1_Change()* EVENT PROCEDURE

The Dir1_Change() event procedure is the procedure that handles the processing necessary when the user changes the desired directory. Following is a listing of the Dir1_Change() event procedure:

LISTING 20.13. MAIN.FRM, Dir1_Change().

```
Sub Dir1_Change ()

    'Update all File controls for new path
    lstProposed.Path = Dir1.Path
    DisplayDir.Caption = Dir1.Path

    'Clear lstFileList listbox
    lstFileList.Clear

    'Disable Print Button
    cmdPrint.Enabled = False

    'enable buttons
    Call CheckPermission

End Sub
```

THE *Drive1* CONTROL

Drive1 is the name of the drive listbox control that provides the name of the drive to search. The Drive1 control has code in only one event procedure. It is

◆ Drive1_Change()

THE *Drive1_Change()* EVENT PROCEDURE

The Drive1_Change() event procedure is the procedure that handles the processing necessary when the user changes the drive. Following is a listing of the Drive1_Change() event procedure:

LISTING 20.14. MAIN.FRM, Drive1_Change().

```
Sub Drive1_Change ()

    'Update all File controls for new path
    Dir1.Path = Drive1.Drive
    DisplayDir.Caption = Dir1.Path

    'Clear lstFileList listbox
    lstFileList.Clear

    'Disable Print Button
    cmdPrint.Enabled = False
```

```
'enable buttons
Call CheckPermission

End Sub
```

The *Form* Object

The Form object has code in two event procedures. They are

◆ Form_Load()

◆ Form_Unload()

The *Form_Load()* Event Procedure

The Form_Load() event procedure initializes, loads defaults from SOUND.INI, and loads the main form. Following is a listing of the Form_Load() event procedure:

Listing 20.15. MAIN.FRM, Form_Load().

```
Sub Form_Load ()

    'define help file
    App.HelpFile = "CHAP20.HLP"

    'center the form
    Call centerform(Me)

    'populate extension box
    comExtensionList.AddItem "*.TXT"
    comExtensionList.AddItem "*.DOC"
    comExtensionList.AddItem "*.SQL"
    comExtensionList.AddItem "*.PRC"
    comExtensionList.AddItem "*.MAK"
    comExtensionList.AddItem "*.BAS"
    comExtensionList.AddItem "*.QRY"
    comExtensionList.AddItem "*.INI"
    comExtensionList.AddItem "ALL FILES"

    'set default file extension
    comExtensionList.ListIndex = comExtensionList.ListCount - 1

    'set defaults on Command Buttons
    cmdSearch.Enabled = False
    cmdPrint.Enabled = False

    'update label with current path
    DisplayDir.Caption = Dir1.Path

    'assign path
    SearchPath$ = CurDir
```

```
'check format
If Right$(SearchPath$, 1) <> "\" Then
SearchPath$ = SearchPath$ + "\"
End If

'populate INI variables
Call GetINI

End Sub
```

THE *FORM_UNLOAD()* EVENT PROCEDURE

The Form_Unload() event procedure prompts the user to confirm ending the program. Following is a listing of the Form_Unload() event procedure:

LISTING 20.16. MAIN.FRM, Form_Unload().

```
Sub Form_Unload (Cancel As Integer)

    'declare variables
    Dim m$       'Message constructor
    Dim Res%     'holds Results

    'Build Message
    m$ = "Are you sure you want to close?"

    'Prompt for input
    Res% = MsgBox(m$, 292, "Search Application")

    'if user doesn't want to exit, then exit sub
    If Res% = IDNO Then
    'cancel
    Cancel = True

    'exit
    Exit Sub
    End If

End Sub
```

THE *LSTFILELIST* CONTROL

lstFileList is the name of the listbox control that lists all the results of the search. The lstFileList control has code in only one event procedure. It is

◆ lstFileList_MouseDown()

THE *LSTFILELIST_MOUSEDOWN()* EVENT PROCEDURE

The lstFileList_MouseDown() event procedure makes sure the lstProposed list has no selected items. Following is a listing of the lstFileList_MouseDown() event procedure:

LISTING 20.17. MAIN.FRM, lstFileList_MouseDown().

```
Sub lstFileList_MouseDown (Button As Integer, Shift As Integer, X As Single, Y As Single)

    'declare variables
    Dim LoopCount%   'holds loop counting

    'mouse is on file list, unselect all Proposed List
    For LoopCount% = 0 To lstProposed.ListCount - 1
    lstProposed.Selected(LoopCount%) = False
    Next LoopCount%

End Sub
```

THE *LSTPROPOSED* CONTROL

lstProposed is the name of the file listbox control that lists all the files to search. The lstProposed control has code in three event procedures. They are

- ◆ lstProposed_MouseDown()
- ◆ lstProposed_PathChange()
- ◆ lstProposed_PatternChange()

THE *LSTPROPOSED_MOUSEDOWN()* EVENT PROCEDURE

The lstProposed_MouseDown() event procedure makes sure the lstFileList list has no selected items. Following is a listing of the lstProposed_MouseDown() event procedure:

LISTING 20.18. MAIN.FRM, lstProposed_MouseDown().

```
Sub lstProposed_MouseDown (Button As Integer, Shift As Integer, X As Single, Y As Single)

    'declare variables
    Dim LoopCount%   'holds loop counting

    'mouse is on file list, unselect all File List
    For LoopCount% = 0 To lstFileList.ListCount - 1
    lstFileList.Selected(LoopCount%) = False
    Next LoopCount%

End Sub
```

THE *LSTPROPOSED_PATHCHANGE()* EVENT PROCEDURE

The lstProposed_PathChange() event procedure checks if it is acceptable to enable the View command button. Following is a listing of the lstProposed_PathChange() event procedure:

LISTING 20.19. MAIN.FRM, lstProposed_PathChange().

```
Sub lstProposed_PathChange ()

    'disable View Button if there is nothing to view
    If lstProposed.ListCount > 0 Or lstFileList.ListCount > 0 Then
    cmdView.Enabled = True
    Else
    cmdView.Enabled = False
    End If

End Sub
```

THE *LSTPROPOSED_PATTERNCHANGE()* EVENT PROCEDURE

The lstProposed_PatternChange() event procedure checks if it is acceptable to enable the View command button. Following is a listing of the lstProposed_PatternChange() event procedure:

LISTING 20.20. MAIN.FRM, lstProposed_PatternChange().

```
Sub lstProposed_PatternChange ()

    'disable View Button if there is nothing to view
    If lstProposed.ListCount > 0 Or lstFileList.ListCount > 0 Then
    cmdView.Enabled = True
    Else
    cmdView.Enabled = False
    End If

End Sub
```

THE *MENU* OBJECT

The menu object was created by using Visual Basic's built-in menu editor. It has code associated with only one click() event procedure. It is

◆ menu_about()

THE *MENU_ABOUT_CLICK( )* PROCEDURE

The menu_about_Click() procedure simply shows the about form for program information. Following is a listing of the menu_about_Click() procedure:

LISTING 20.20. MAIN.FRM, `menu_about_Click()`.

```
Sub menu_about_Click ()

    'show about form
    frmAbout.Show MODAL frmAbout.Show MODAL

End Sub
```

THE *optNotSensitive* CONTROL

optNotSensitive is the name of the radio button control that is responsible for selecting not to be case sensitive. The optNotSensitive control has code in only one event procedure. It is

◆ optNotSensitive_Click()

THE *optNotSensitive_Click()* EVENT PROCEDURE

The optNotSensitive_Click() event procedure simply clears the lstFileList listbox and disables the Print command button. Following is a listing of the optNotSensitive_Click() event procedure:

LISTING 20.22. MAIN.FRM, `optNotSensitive_Click()`.

```
Sub optNotSensitive_Click (Value As Integer)

    'Clear lstFileList listbox
    lstFileList.Clear

    'Disable Print Button
    cmdPrint.Enabled = False

    'enable buttons
    Call CheckPermission

End Sub
```

THE *optSensitive* CONTROL

optSensitive is the name of the radio button control that is responsible for selecting to be case sensitive. The optSensitive control has code in only one event procedure. It is

◆ optSensitive_Click()

THE *optSensitive_Click( )* EVENT PROCEDURE

The optSensitive_Click() event procedure simply clears the lstFileList listbox and disables the Print command button. Following is a listing of the optSensitive_Click() event procedure:

LISTING 20.23. MAIN.FRM, optSensitive_Click().

```
Sub optSensitive_Click (Value As Integer)

    'Clear lstFileList listbox
    lstFileList.Clear

    'Disable Print Button
    cmdPrint.Enabled = False

    'enable buttons
    Call CheckPermission

End Sub
```

THE *txtSearchString* CONTROL

txtSearchString is the name of the text box control that contains the text to search for in the files contained in the lstFileList file listbox control. The txtSearchString control has code in only one event procedure. It is

◆   txtSearchString_Change()

THE *txtSearchString_Change( )* EVENT PROCEDURE

The txtSearchString_Change() event procedure simply clears the lstFileList listbox and disables the Print command button. Following is a listing of the txtSearchString_Change() event procedure:

LISTING 20.24. MAIN.FRM, txtSearchString_Change().

```
Sub txtSearchString_Change ()

    'clear the list of returned files
    lstFileList.Clear

    'Disable Print Button
    cmdPrint.Enabled = False

    'enable buttons
    Call CheckPermission

End Sub
```

THE MDIVIEW.FRM FILE

MDIVIEW.FRM is one of five forms in this application. It is the form that is the MDI form containing the child forms of the individual files to view. Figure 20.2 presents this form as it appears at runtime. Figure 20.5 shows the form as it appears at design time. Table 20.3 lists all the relevant properties of each control on the form, which have been changed from their standard default values. The MDIVIEW.FRM file is contained on the CD accompanying this book in the CHAP20 subdirectory.

FIGURE 20.5.
MDI File Search application MDIVIEW.FRM at design time.

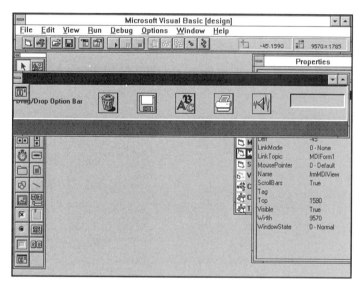

TABLE 20.3. PROPERTIES OF EACH CONTROL ON MDIVIEW.FRM.

Object	Control Type	Property	Value
frmMDIView	MDIForm	Height	1785
		HelpContextID	4
		Left	1035
		Top	1035
		Width	5910
pnlStatus	SSPanel	Align	Align Top
		Alignment	Left Justify - MIDDLE
		BackColor	&H00C0C0C0&
		BevelOuter	Inset
		BevelWidth	2

continues

TABLE 20.3. CONTINUED

Object	Control Type	Property	Value
		BorderWidth	2
		Font3D	None
		ForeColor	&H00000080&
		Height	975
		Left	0
		RoundedCorners	False
		ShadowColor	Black
		Top	0
		Width	5790
cmDIalog	CommonDialog	CancelError	True
		Flags	256
		Left	0
		Top	0
pictSave	PictureBox	AutoSize	True
		Height	555
		HelpContextID	6
		Left	3480
		Picture	"SAVE.BMP"
		Top	240
		Width	555
pictClose	PictureBox	AutoSize	True
		Height	555
		HelpContextID	5
		Left	2400
		Picture	"CLOSE.BMP"
		Top	240
		Width	555
pictSound	PictureBox	AutoSize	True
		Height	555
		HelpContextID	11

Object	Control Type	Property	Value
		Left	6720
		Picture	"SOUND.BMP"
		Top	240
		Width	555
pictFont	PictureBox	AutoSize	True
		Height	555
		HelpContextID	7
		Left	4560
		Picture	"FONT.BMP"
		Top	240
		Width	555
pictPrinter	PictureBox	AutoSize	True
		Height	555
		HelpContextID	8
		Left	5640
		Picture	"PRINTER.BMP"
		Top	240
		Width	555
lblDragDrop	SSPanel	BackColor	&H00C0C0C0&
		BevelOuter	Inset
		BorderWidth	2
		Font3D	None
		ForeColor	&H0000FFFF&
		Height	375
		HelpContextID	12
		Left	7800
		RoundedCorners	False
		ShadowColor	Black
		Top	240
		Width	1575

FUNCTION, SUBROUTINE, AND EVENT PROCEDURES

There are several procedures of code for each object(control) that comprise this form. Each is listed in the following sections.

THE (GENERAL) OBJECT

The (general) object contains form level declarations and no form level procedures. The procedure for the (general) object is

◆ (declarations)

THE (DECLARATIONS) PROCEDURE

The (declarations) procedure contains only one line of declarations used in the form, MDIVIEW.FRM. All declarations are in the CHAP20.BAS file. It is only to allow for variable syntax checking and forcing the declaration of variables in each procedure. Following is a listing of the (declarations) procedure:

LISTING 20.25. MDIVIEW.FRM, (general)(declarations).

```
Option Explicit
```

THE MDIFORM OBJECT

The MDIForm object has code in two event procedures. They are

◆ MDIForm_Activate()
◆ MDIForm_Unload()

THE MDIFORM_ACTIVATE() EVENT PROCEDURE

The MDIForm_Activate() event deletes all menu items in the system menu. It needs to do this to prevent the form (as a whole) to unload itself. If it didn't do this, it would be extremely difficult to track the activity of each MDI child form for changes. There is no ControlBox property in an MDI form to set to false, so you must destroy the menu. Following is a listing of the MDIForm_Activate() event procedure:

LISTING 20.26. MDIVIEW.FRM, MDIForm_Activate().

```
Sub MDIForm_Activate ()

    'declare variables
    Dim hSysMenu%    'holds handle of sysmenu
    Dim res%         'holds results of destroying sys menu

    'get system menu
    hSysMenu% = GetSystemMenu(hWnd, 0&)
```

```
    'destroy system menu
    res = DestroyMenu(hSysMenu)

End Sub
```

 For more information about MDI, refer to Chapter 8, "Multiple Document Interface (MDI)."

THE *MDIFORM_UNLOAD()* EVENT PROCEDURE

The MDIForm_Unload() event simply plays the sound file indicating that the form is being closed. It will only be closed when all MDI child forms are closed. Following is a listing of the MDIForm_Unload() event procedure:

LISTING 20.27. MDIVIEW.FRM, MDIForm_Unload().

```
Sub MDIForm_Unload (Cancel As Integer)

    'declare variables
    Dim res%      'holds results

    'play sound
    res% = sndPlaySound(SoundFile6$, SND_ASYNC Or SND_NODEFAULT)

End Sub
```

THE *PICTCLOSE* CONTROL

pictClose is the name of the picture box control that represents the same function as the Close Menu option. The pictClose control has code in only one event procedure. It is

◆ pictClose_DragDrop()

THE *PICTCLOSE_DRAGDROP()* EVENT PROCEDURE

The pictClose_DragDrop() event procedure initiates the Drag/Drop closing routine. Following is a listing of the pictClose_DragDrop() event procedure:

LISTING 20.28. MDIVIEW.FRM, pictClose_DragDrop().

```
Sub pictClose_DragDrop (Source As Control, X As Single, Y As Single)

    'call routine to invoke font dialog
    Call CloseRoutine(Source)

End Sub
```

THE *PICTFONT* CONTROL

`pictFont` is the name of the picture box control that represents the same function as the Font menu option. The `pictFont` control has code in only one event procedure. It is

◆ `pictFont_DragDrop()`

THE *PICTFONT_DRAGDROP()* EVENT PROCEDURE

The `pictFont_DragDrop()` event procedure initiates the Drag/Drop font assigning routine. Following is a listing of the `pictFont_DragDrop()` event procedure:

LISTING 20.29. MDIVIEW.FRM, `pictFont_DragDrop()`.

```
Sub pictFont_DragDrop (Source As Control, X As Single, Y As Single)

    'call routine to invoke font dialog
    Call FontRoutine(Source)

End Sub
```

THE *PICTPRINTER* CONTROL

`pictPrinter` is the name of the picture box control that represents the same function as the Print menu option. The `pictPrinter` control has code in only one event procedure. It is

◆ `pictPrinter_DragDrop()`

THE *PICTPRINTER_DRAGDROP( )* EVENT PROCEDURE

The `pictPrinter_DragDrop()` event procedure initiates the Drag/Drop printing routine. Following is a listing of the `pictPrinter_DragDrop()` event procedure:

LISTING 20.30. MDIVIEW.FRM, `pictPrinter_DragDrop()`.

```
Sub pictPrinter_DragDrop (Source As Control, X As Single, Y As Single)

    'call printer routine
    Call PrintRoutine(Source)

End Sub
```

THE *PICTSAVE* CONTROL

`pictSave` is the name of the picture box control that represents the same function as the Save menu option. The `pictSave` control has code in only one event procedure. It is

◆ `pictSave_DragDrop()`

THE *pictSave_DragDrop()* EVENT PROCEDURE

The `pictSave_DragDrop()` event procedure initiates the saving Drag/Drop routine. Following is a listing of the `pictSave_DragDrop()` event procedure:

LISTING 20.31. MDIVIEW.FRM, `pictSave_DragDrop()`.

```
Sub pictSave_DragDrop (Source As Control, X As Single, Y As Single)

    'call routine to invoke save dialog
    Call SaveRoutine(Source)

End Sub
```

THE *pictSOUND* CONTROL

`pictSound` is the name of the picture box control that represents the same function as the Sound menu option. The `pictSound` control has code in only one event procedure. It is

♦ `pictSound_DragDrop()`

THE *pictSOUND_DragDrop()* EVENT PROCEDURE

The `pictSound_DragDrop()` event procedure initiates the sound assigning Drag/Drop routine. Following is a listing of the `pictSound_DragDrop()` event procedure:

LISTING 20.32. MDIVIEW.FRM, `pictSound_DragDrop()`.

```
Sub pictSound_DragDrop (Source As Control, X As Single, Y As Single)

    'invoke sound options-ignore Source in this case
    Call SoundRoutine

End Sub
```

THE VIEWFORM.FRM FILE

VIEWFORM.FRM is one of five forms in this application. It is used as an MDI child form, one for each text file to display. Figure 20.2 presents this form (along with the MDIVIEW.FRM form) as it appears at runtime. Figure 20.6 shows the form as it appears at design time. Table 20.4 lists all the relevant properties of each control on the form, which have been changed from their standard default values. The VIEWFORM.FRM file is contained on the CD accompanying this book in the CHAP20 subdirectory.

FIGURE 20.6.
*MDI File Search
application
VIEWFORM.FRM at
design time.*

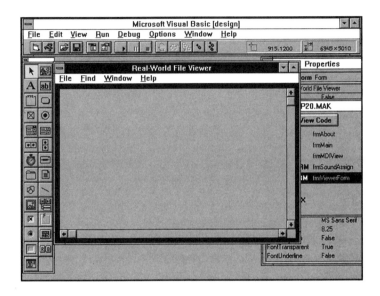

TABLE 20.4. PROPERTIES OF EACH CONTROL ON **VIEWFORM.FRM.**

Object	Control Type	Property	Value
frmViewerForm	Form	BackColor	&H00404000&
		Caption	"Real-World File Viewer"
		Height	5010
		Left	390
		MaxButton	False
		MDIChild	True
		MinButton	False
		Top	1740
		Width	6945
txtViewer	TextBox	DragIcon	"DRAGFLDR.ICO"
		FontBold	True
		FontItalic	False
		FontName	"Times New Roman"
		FontSize	8.25
		FontStrikethru	False
		FontUnderline	False

Object	Control Type	Property	Value
		Height	4095
		HelpContextID	10
		Left	120
		MultiLine	True
		ScrollBars	3—Both
		Top	120
		Width	6615
menu_file	Menu	Caption	"&File"
		HelpContextID	13
menu_close	Menu	Caption	"&Close"
menu_separator1	Menu	Caption	"-"
menu_exit	Menu	Caption	"&Exit"
menu_find	Menu	Caption	"&Find"
		HelpContextID	14
menu_findsearch	Menu	Caption	"Find Search String"
		Shortcut	{F7}
menu_another	Menu	Caption	"Find Another String"
		Shortcut	{F8}
menu_window	Menu	Caption	"&Window"
		HelpContextID	15
		WindowList	True
menu_cascade	Menu	Caption	"&Cascade"
menu_Tile	Menu	Caption	"&Tile"
menu_TileHorizontal	Menu	Caption	"&Horizontally"
menu_TileVertically	Menu	Caption	"&Vertically"
menu_help	Menu	Caption	"&Help"
		HelpContextID	16
menu_invoke	Menu	Caption	"&Contents"
		HelpContextID	1
menu_about	Menu	Caption	"&About"
menu_popup	Menu	Caption	"Popup Options"
		Visible	False

continues

TABLE 20.4. CONTINUED

Object	Control Type	Property	Value
menu_popup_dragdrop	Menu	Caption	"&Toggle Drag/Drop"
		HelpContextID	40
menu_separator2	Menu	Caption	"-"
menu_popup_saveas	Menu	Caption	"Save &As"
		HelpContextID	41
menu_popup_font	Menu	Caption	"&Font"
		HelpContextID	42
menu_popup_print	Menu	Caption	"&Print"
		HelpContextID	43
menu_popup_sound	Menu	Caption	"&Sound"
		HelpContextID	44
menu_popup_Help	Menu	Caption	"&Help Contents"
		HelpContextID	45
menu_popup_about	Menu	Caption	"&About"
		HelpContextID	46

FUNCTION, SUBROUTINE, AND EVENT PROCEDURES

There are several procedures of code for each object(control) that comprise this form. Each is listed in the following sections.

THE (GENERAL) OBJECT

The (general) object contains only one form level declaration and no form level procedures. The procedure for the (general) object is

◆ (declarations)

THE (DECLARATIONS) PROCEDURE

The (declarations) procedure contains only two lines of declarations used in the form, VIEWFORM.FRM. One is only to allow for variable syntax checking and forcing the declaration of variables in each procedure. The other is only one form level declaration. Following is a listing of the (declarations) procedure:

LISTING 20.33. VIEWFORM.FRM, (general)(declarations).

```
Option Explicit       'force variable syntax checking

Dim SearchString$     'used to hold string to search for
```

THE *FORM* OBJECT

The Form object has code in two event procedures. They are

- ◆ Form_Activate()
- ◆ Form_Unload()

THE *FORM_ACTIVATE()* EVENT PROCEDURE

The Form_Activate() event procedure simply makes sure that the DragDrop label is current with the active form. Following is a listing of the Form_Activate() event procedure:

LISTING 20.34. VIEWFORM.FRM, Form_Activate().

```
Sub Form_Activate ()

    'set default DragDrop Label
    frmMDIView.lblDragDrop.Caption = txtViewer.Tag

End Sub
```

THE *FORM_LOAD()* EVENT PROCEDURE

The Form_Load() event procedure simply makes sure that the DragDrop label is current with the active form and makes the active form Drag/Drop off, by default. Following is a listing of the Form_Load() event procedure:

LISTING 20.35. VIEWFORM.FRM, Form_Load().

```
Sub Form_Load ()

    'set default DragDrop Label
    frmMDIView.lblDragDrop.Caption = DRAGOFF
    txtViewer.Tag = DRAGOFF

End Sub
```

 For more information about Drag/Drop, refer to Chapter 4, "The Mouse."

THE *FORM_MOUSEDOWN()* EVENT PROCEDURE

The Form_MouseDown() event procedure performs the same as the Form_Activate() event procedure as a catch-all. Following is a listing of the Form_MouseDown() event procedure:

LISTING 20.36. VIEWFORM.FRM, Form_MouseDown().

```
Sub Form_MouseDown (Button As Integer, Shift As Integer, X As Single, Y As Single)

    'set default DragDrop Label
    frmMDIView.lblDragDrop.Caption = txtViewer.Tag

End Sub
```

THE *FORM_RESIZE()* EVENT PROCEDURE

The Form_Resize() event procedure makes sure that the text box holding the text of the file is resized along with the form. Following is a listing of the Form_Resize() event procedure:

LISTING 20.37. VIEWFORM.FRM, Form_Resize().

```
Sub Form_Resize ()

    'make sure text box is sized accordingly
    'make sure run time error doesn't occur by having
    'negative Height Or Width
    If ScaleHeight > SCROLLBARWIDTH Then
        txtViewer.Height = ScaleHeight - SCROLLBARWIDTH
    Else
        txtViewer.Height = ScaleHeight
    End If

    If ScaleWidth > SCROLLBARWIDTH Then
        txtViewer.Width = ScaleWidth - SCROLLBARWIDTH
    Else
        txtViewer.Width = ScaleWidth
    End If

End Sub
```

THE *MENU* OBJECT

The menu object was created by using Visual Basic's built-in menu editor. All of the objects with the word popup in them are used as a popup menu, only when the right mouse button is clicked in the text box holding a text file. The menu object has code associated with 16 click() event procedures. They are

- ◆ menu_about()
- ◆ menu_another()
- ◆ menu_cascade()
- ◆ menu_close()
- ◆ menu_exit()
- ◆ menu_filesearch()
- ◆ menu_invoke()
- ◆ menu_popup_about()
- ◆ menu_popup_dragdrop()
- ◆ menu_popup_font()
- ◆ menu_popup_Help()
- ◆ menu_popup_print()
- ◆ menu_popup_saveas()
- ◆ menu_popup_sound()
- ◆ menu_popup_TileHorizontally()
- ◆ menu_popup_TileVertically()

THE *MENU_ABOUT_CLICK()* PROCEDURE

The menu_about_Click() procedure simply shows the about form for program information. Following is a listing of the menu_about_Click() procedure:

LISTING 20.38. VIEWFORM.FRM, menu_about_Click().

```
Sub menu_about_Click ()

    'show about box
    frmAbout.Show

End Sub
```

THE *MENU_ANOTHER_CLICK()* PROCEDURE

The menu_another_Click() procedure finds the next occurrence of a string specified by the results of an Inputbox() statement. Following is a listing of the menu_another_Click() procedure:

LISTING 20.39. VIEWFORM.FRM, menu_another_Click().

```
Sub menu_another_Click ()

    'declare variables
    Dim CurrentPos%        'holds current position in string
    Dim Pos%               'holds temporary position in string

    'prompt for string to search for
    SearchString$ = InputBox("Enter the string to search for", , SearchString$)

    'assign current variable
    CurrentPos% = frmMDIView.ActiveForm.txtViewer.SelStart
    If CurrentPos% = 0 Then
        CurrentPos% = 1 + frmMDIView.ActiveForm.txtViewer.SelLength
    Else
        CurrentPos% = CurrentPos% + Len(SearchString$) + 1
    End If

    'do search, not case sensitive
    Pos% = InStr(CurrentPos%, frmMDIView.ActiveForm.txtViewer.Text, SearchString$, 1)

    'test to see if the string exists from current point forward
    If Pos% = 0 Then
        MsgBox "'" + SearchString$ + "' not found!"
    Else
        frmMDIView.ActiveForm.txtViewer.SelStart = Pos% - 1
        frmMDIView.ActiveForm.txtViewer.SelLength = Len(SearchString$)
    End If

End Sub
```

THE *MENU_CASCADE_CLICK()* PROCEDURE

The menu_cascade_Click() procedure arranges all the MDI child windows in a cascaded fashion, based on the submenu, horizontally or vertically. Following is a listing of the menu_cascade_Click() procedure:

LISTING 20.40. VIEWFORM.FRM, menu_cascade_Click().

```
Sub menu_cascade_Click ()

    'cascade windows
    frmMDIView.Arrange CASCADE

End Sub
```

THE *MENU_CLOSE_CLICK()* PROCEDURE

The menu_close_Click() procedure closes the active MDI child window by calling the CloseRoutine() procedure, located in the CHAP20.BAS file. Following is a listing of the menu_close_Click() procedure:

LISTING 20.41. VIEWFORM.FRM, `menu_close_Click()`.

```
Sub menu_close_Click ()

    'declare variables
    Dim Source As control

    'assign control to nothing to avoid errors
    Set Source = Nothing

    'call routine to close form
    Call CloseRoutine(Source)

End Sub
```

THE *MENU_EXIT_CLICK()* PROCEDURE

The `menu_exit_Click()` procedure closes the VIEWFORM.FRM form, prompting for confirmation first. Following is a listing of the `menu_exit_Click()` procedure:

LISTING 20.42. VIEWFORM.FRM, `menu_exit_Click()`.

```
Sub menu_exit_Click ()

    'declare variables
    Dim LoopCount%  'loop counting variable
    Dim m$          'message constructing variable
    Dim res%        'holds result of msgbox

    If ViewerChange% = True Then
        'build message
        m$ = "Exit without saving changes?"
        res% = MsgBox(m$, 292, "Warning")
        If res% = IDNO Then Exit Sub
    End If

    'Unload each individual MDI Child Form
    For LoopCount% = 0 To frmMDIView.Controls.Count - 1
        If TypeOf Controls(LoopCount%) Is frmViewerForm Then
            If Controls(LoopCount%).Enabled = True Then
                Unload Controls(LoopCount%)
            End If
        End If
    Next LoopCount%

    'Unload This Form
    Unload frmMDIView

End Sub
```

THE *MENU_FINDSEARCH_CLICK( )* PROCEDURE

The `menu_findsearch_Click()` procedure finds the next occurrence of the search string. Following is a listing of the `menu_findsearch_Click()` procedure:

LISTING 20.43. VIEWFORM.FRM, `menu_findsearch_Click()`.

```
Sub menu_findsearch_Click ()

    'declare variables
    Dim CurrentPos%       'holds current position in string
    Dim Pos%              'holds temporary position in string
    Dim m$                'message box constructor

    'if there is no search string, exit
    If frmMain.txtSearchString.Text = "" Then
        m$ = "There is no search string!"
        MsgBox m$
        Exit Sub
    End If

    'assign current position
    CurrentPos% = frmMDIView.ActiveForm.txtViewer.SelStart
    If frmMDIView.ActiveForm.txtViewer.SelLength = 0 Then
        CurrentPos% = 1
    Else
        CurrentPos% = CurrentPos% + Len(frmMain.txtSearchString.Text) + 1
    End If

    If frmMain.optNotSensitive.Value = True Then
        'NOT case sensitive
        Pos% = InStr(CurrentPos%, frmMDIView.ActiveForm.txtViewer.Text,
        frmMain.txtSearchString.Text, 1)
    Else
        'case sensitive
        Pos% = InStr(CurrentPos%, frmMDIView.ActiveForm.txtViewer.Text,
        frmMain.txtSearchString.Text, 0)
    End If

    'test to see if the string exists from current point forward
    If Pos% = 0 Then
        MsgBox "'" + frmMain.txtSearchString.Text + "' not found!"
    Else
        frmMDIView.ActiveForm.txtViewer.SelStart = Pos% - 1
        frmMDIView.ActiveForm.txtViewer.SelLength = Len(frmMain.txtSearchString.Text)
    End If

End Sub
```

THE *MENU_INVOKE_CLICK( )* PROCEDURE

The `menu_invoke_Click()` procedure invokes the help file, CHAP20.HLP, at the contents page. Following is a listing of the `menu_invoke_Click()` procedure:

LISTING 20.44. VIEWFORM.FRM, `menu_invoke_Click()`.

```
Sub menu_invoke_Click ()

    'invoke help system
    frmMDIView.cmDIalog.HelpCommand = HELP_CONTEXT
    frmMDIView.cmDIalog.HelpFile = "CHAP20.HLP"
    frmMDIView.cmDIalog.HelpContext = 1
    frmMDIView.cmDIalog.Action = DLG_HELP

End Sub
```

THE *MENU_POPUP_ABOUT_CLICK()* PROCEDURE

The `menu_popup_about_Click()` procedure simply shows the about form for program information. Following is a listing of the `menu_popup_about_Click()` procedure:

LISTING 20.45. VIEWFORM.FRM, `menu_popup_about_Click()`.

```
Sub menu_popup_about_Click ()

    'show about box
    frmAbout.Show

End Sub
```

THE *MENU_POPUP_DRAGDROP_CLICK()* PROCEDURE

The `menu_popup_dragdrop_Click()` procedure toggles the drag/drop mode of the active form from ON to OFF, and vice versa. If drag/drop is on, you can drag the form to an icon to perform an action. If drag/drop is off, you can scroll through the data in the text box. Following is a listing of the `menu_popup_dragdrop_Click()` procedure:

LISTING 20.46. VIEWFORM.FRM, `menu_popup_dragdrop_Click()`.

```
Sub menu_popup_dragdrop_Click ()

    'user selected drag/drop on popup menu

    'toggle DragDrop caption
    If frmMDIView.lblDragDrop.Caption = DRAGON Then
        frmMDIView.lblDragDrop.Caption = DRAGOFF
        txtViewer.DragMode = MANUAL
        txtViewer.Tag = DRAGOFF
    Else
        frmMDIView.lblDragDrop.Caption = DRAGON
        txtViewer.DragMode = AUTOMATIC
        txtViewer.Tag = DRAGON
    End If

End Sub
```

THE *MENU_POPUP_FONT_CLICK()* PROCEDURE

The menu_popup_font_Click() procedure allows you to change the active MDI child form's font by calling the FontRoutine, located in the CHAP20.BAS file. Following is a listing of the menu_popup_font_Click() procedure:

LISTING 20.47. VIEWFORM.FRM, menu_popup_font_Click().

```
Sub menu_popup_font_Click ()

    'declare variables
    Dim Source As control

    'assign control to nothing to avoid errors
    Set Source = Nothing

    'call routine to invoke font dialog
    Call FontRoutine(Source)

End Sub
```

THE *MENU_POPUP_HELP_CLICK()* PROCEDURE

The menu_popup_Help_Click() procedure invokes the Help file, CHAP20.HLP, at the contents page. Following is a listing of the menu_popup_Help_Click() procedure:

LISTING 20.48. VIEWFORM.FRM, menu_popup_Help_Click().

```
Sub menu_popup_Help_Click ()

    'invoke help system
    frmMDIView.cmDIalog.HelpCommand = HELP_CONTEXT
    frmMDIView.cmDIalog.HelpFile = "CHAP20.HLP"
    frmMDIView.cmDIalog.HelpContext = 1
    frmMDIView.cmDIalog.Action = DLG_HELP

End Sub
```

THE *MENU_POPUP_PRINT_CLICK()* PROCEDURE

The menu_popup_print_Click() procedure prints the active MDI child form's text by invoking the Print_Routine() procedure, located in the CHAP20.BAS file. Following is a listing of the menu_popup_print_Click() procedure:

LISTING 20.49. VIEWFORM.FRM, `menu_popup_print_Click()`.

```
Sub menu_popup_print_Click ()

    'declare variables
    Dim Source As control

    'assign control to nothing to avoid errors
    Set Source = Nothing

    'call routine to invoke printing
    Call PrintRoutine(Source)

End Sub
```

THE *MENU_POPUP_SAVEAS_CLICK()* PROCEDURE

The menu_popup_saveas_Click() procedure saves the active MDI child form's text by invoking the Save_Routine() procedure, located in the CHAP20.BAS file. Following is a listing of the menu_popup_saveas_Click() procedure:

LISTING 20.50. VIEWFORM.FRM, `menu_popup_saveas_Click()`.

```
Sub menu_popup_saveas_Click ()

    'declare variables
    Dim Source As control

    'assign control to nothing to avoid errors
    Set Source = Nothing

    'call routine to invoke save dialog
    Call SaveRoutine(Source)

End Sub
```

THE *MENU_POPUP_SOUND_CLICK()* PROCEDURE

The menu_popup_sound_Click() procedure saves the active MDI child form's text by invoking the Sound_Routine() procedure, located in the CHAP20.BAS file. Following is a listing of the menu_popup_sound_Click() procedure:

LISTING 20.51. VIEWFORM.FRM, `menu_popup_sound_Click()`.

```
Sub menu_popup_sound_Click ()

    'invoke sound options
    Call SoundRoutine

End Sub
```

THE *MENU_TILEHORIZONTALLY_CLICK()* PROCEDURE

The `menu_TileHorizontally_Click()` procedure arranges all the MDI child windows in a cascaded horizontal fashion. Following is a listing of the `menu_TileHorizontally_Click()` procedure:

LISTING 20.52. VIEWFORM.FRM, `menu_TileHorizontally_Click()`.

```
Sub menu_TileHorizontal_Click ()

    'tile windows
    frmMDIView.Arrange TILE_HORIZONTAL

End Sub
```

THE *MENU_TILEVERTICALLY_CLICK()* PROCEDURE

The `menu_TileVertically_Click()` procedure arranges all the MDI child windows in a cascaded vertical fashion. Following is a listing of the `menu_TileVertically_Click()` procedure:

LISTING 20.53. VIEWFORM.FRM, `menu_TileVertically_Click()`.

```
Sub menu_TileVertically_Click ()

    'tile windows
    frmMDIView.Arrange TILE_VERTICAL

End Sub
```

THE *TXTVIEWER* CONTROL

`txtViewer` is the name of the text box control that contains the text file. The `txtViewer` control has code in two event procedures. They are

- ◆ `txtViewer_Change()`
- ◆ `txtViewer_MouseDown()`

THE *TXTVIEWER_CHANGE()* EVENT PROCEDURE

The `txtViewer_Change()` event is used to flag to the system that a change has taken place. Following is a listing of the `txtViewer_Change()` event procedure:

324

Listing 20.54. VIEWFORM.FRM, `txtViewer_Change()`.

```
Sub txtViewer_Change ()

    'if populating viewer-exit.  This is not a valid change
    If PopulatingViewer% = True Then Exit Sub

    'if text has changed, indicate by preceding file name with "*"
    If txtViewer.Text <> "" Then
        If Left$(txtViewer.Parent.Caption, 1) <> "*" Then
            txtViewer.Parent.Caption = "*" + txtViewer.Parent.Caption
        End If
    End If

    'flag viewer change
    ViewerChange% = True

End Sub
```

The *txtViewer_MouseDown()* Event Procedure

The `txtViewer_MouseDown()` event is used to invoke the right mouse button popup menu. Following is a listing of the `txtViewer_MouseDown()` event procedure:

Listing 20.55. VIEWFORM.FRM, `txtViewer_MouseDown()`.

```
Sub txtViewer_MouseDown (Button As Integer, Shift As Integer, X As Single, Y As Single)

    'set default DragDrop Label
    frmMDIView.lblDragDrop.Caption = txtViewer.Tag

    'if user presses the right mouse button, display popup
    If Button = RIGHT_BUTTON Then
        'make sure form has focus
        Me.SetFocus

        'invoke popup menu
        Me.PopupMenu menu_popup
    End If

End Sub
```

The SOUNDASN.FRM File

SOUNDASN.FRM is one of five forms in this application. It is used to assign the name of the sound file (*.WAV) to certain events that happen in the application. The events are application induced, not Visual Basic events. Table 20.1 lists these events and the default sound files. Figure 20.3 presents this form as it appears at runtime. It is fundamentally no different at design time, so it is not shown again. Table 20.5 lists all the relevant properties of each control on the form that have been changed from their standard default values. The SOUNDASN.FRM file is contained on the CD accompanying this book in the CHAP20 subdirectory, along with the default sound files listed in Table 20.1.

TABLE 20.5. PROPERTIES OF EACH CONTROL ON SOUNDASN.FRM.

Object	Control Type	Property	Value
frmSoundAssign	Form	BackColor	&H00404000&
		Caption	"Assign Sounds"
		Height	5085
		HelpContextID	28
		Left	1035
		MaxButton	False
		Top	1140
		Width	6015
cmFileDialog	CommonDialog	Left	0
		Top	0
Panel3D1	SSPanel	BackColor	&H00C0C0C0&
		BevelWidth	3
		Font3D	None
		ForeColor	&H0000FFFF&
		Height	4455
		Left	120
		RoundedCorners	False
		ShadowColor	Black
		Top	120
		Width	5655
pnlSoundPanel	SSPanel	Alignment	Left Justify - MIDDLE
		BackColor	&H00C0C0C0&
		BevelWidth	3
		Caption	"Font Change", "Font Cancel", "Text Printed", "Printer Error", "File Saved", "Save Error", "Close Viewer", "Close Sound"*

Object	Control Type	Property	Value
		Font3D	None
		ForeColor	&H0000FFFF&
		Height	495
		Index	0,1,2,3,4,5,6,7*
		Left	120
		RoundedCorners	False
		ShadowColor	Black
		Top	120,600,1080,1560, 2040,2520,3000,3480*
		Width	495
cmdFileSearch	CommandButton	Caption	"..."
		Height	255
		Index	0,1,2,3,4,5,6,7*
		Left	4800
		Top	120
		Width	495
txtINI	TextBox	BackColor	&H00FFFFFF&
		Height	285
		HelpContextID	29,30,31,32,33,34,35,36*
		Index	0,1,2,3,4,5,6,7*
		Left	1200
		Top	120
		Width	3495
cmdClose	CommandButton	Caption	"Close"
		Height	255
		HelpContextID	38
		Left	4560
		Top	4080
		Width	975

*This control is a control array, and these are the only properties that vary within the control. To save space, they were not listed separately.

FUNCTION, SUBROUTINE, AND EVENT PROCEDURES

There are several procedures of code for each object(control) that comprise this form. Each is listed in the following sections.

THE *(GENERAL)* OBJECT

The (general) object contains only one form level declaration and two form level procedures. The procedures for the (general) object are

◆ (declarations)

◆ LoadINI()

◆ SaveINI()

THE *(DECLARATIONS)* PROCEDURE

The (declarations) procedure contains only one line of declarations used in the form SOUNDASN.FRM. It is only to allow for variable syntax checking and forcing the declaration of variables in each procedure. Following is a listing of the (declarations) procedure:

LISTING 20.56. SOUNDASN.FRM, (general)(declarations).

```
Option Explicit
```

THE *LoadINI* PROCEDURE

The LoadINI() procedure loads the text box array with the values of the global sound variables. Following is a listing of the LoadINI() procedure:

LISTING 20.57. SOUNDASN.FRM, LoadINI().

```
Sub LoadINI ()

    'get each of the eight sounds and put them into the text boxes

    'get Line 1
    txtINI(0).Text = SoundFile0$
    'get Line 2
    txtINI(1).Text = SoundFile1$
    'get Line 3
    txtINI(2).Text = SoundFile2$
    'get Line 4
    txtINI(3).Text = SoundFile3$
    'get Line 5
    txtINI(4).Text = SoundFile4$
    'get Line 6
    txtINI(5).Text = SoundFile5$
    'get Line 7
```

```
txtINI(6).Text = SoundFile6$
'get Line 8
txtINI(7).Text = SoundFile7$

End Sub
```

THE *SaveINI()* PROCEDURE

The SaveINI() procedure writes the values of the text box array to an INI file and assigns it to the global sound variables so that it takes effect immediately. Following is a listing of the SaveINI() procedure:

LISTING 20.58. SOUNDASN.FRM, SaveINI().

```
Sub SaveINI ()

    'declare variables
    Dim res%        'holds results of APIs

    'assign text boxes to global variables
    SoundFile0$ = txtINI(0).Text
    SoundFile1$ = txtINI(1).Text
    SoundFile2$ = txtINI(2).Text
    SoundFile3$ = txtINI(3).Text
    SoundFile4$ = txtINI(4).Text
    SoundFile5$ = txtINI(5).Text
    SoundFile6$ = txtINI(6).Text
    SoundFile7$ = txtINI(7).Text

    'write new variables
    res% = WritePrivateProfileString(lpApplicationName$, lpKeyName0$, SoundFile0$,
    SearchPath$ + lpFileName$)
    res% = WritePrivateProfileString(lpApplicationName$, lpKeyName1$, SoundFile1$,
    SearchPath$ + lpFileName$)
    res% = WritePrivateProfileString(lpApplicationName$, lpKeyName2$, SoundFile2$,
    SearchPath$ + lpFileName$)
    res% = WritePrivateProfileString(lpApplicationName$, lpKeyName3$, SoundFile3$,
    SearchPath$ + lpFileName$)
    res% = WritePrivateProfileString(lpApplicationName$, lpKeyName4$, SoundFile4$,
    SearchPath$ + lpFileName$)
    res% = WritePrivateProfileString(lpApplicationName$, lpKeyName5$, SoundFile5$,
    SearchPath$ + lpFileName$)
    res% = WritePrivateProfileString(lpApplicationName$, lpKeyName6$, SoundFile6$,
    SearchPath$ + lpFileName$)
    res% = WritePrivateProfileString(lpApplicationName$, lpKeyName7$, SoundFile7$,
    SearchPath$ + lpFileName$)

End Sub
```

 For more information about the WritePrivateProfileString API, refer to Chapter 3, "Calling Windows APIs and DLLs."

THE *CMDCLOSE* CONTROL

cmdClose is the name of the command button control that, when clicked, saves the INI file automatically. The cmdClose control has code in only one event procedure. It is

◆ cmdClose_Click()

THE *CMDCLOSE_CLICK()* EVENT PROCEDURE

The cmdClose_Click() event procedure simply closes the sound assign form and saves the changes to the INI file. Following is a listing of the cmdClose_Click() event procedure:

LISTING 20.59. SOUNDASN.FRM, cmdClose_Click().

```
Sub cmdClose_Click ()

    'declare variables
    Dim res%    'holds results

    'save ini file
    Call SaveINI

    'play sound
    res% = sndPlaySound(SoundFile7$, SND_ASYNC Or SND_NODEFAULT)

    'unload
    Unload frmSoundAssign

End Sub
```

THE *CMDFILESEARCH* CONTROL

cmdFileSearch is the name of the command button control that, when clicked, opens the common Open File dialog box to pick a new WAV file to assign. The cmdFileSearch control has code in only one event procedure. It is

◆ cmdFileSearch_Click()

THE *CMDFILESEARCH_CLICK()* EVENT PROCEDURE

The cmdFileSearch_Click() event procedure allows the user to search for a sound file. Following is a listing of the cmdFileSearch_Click() event procedure:

LISTING 20.60. SOUNDASN.FRM, cmdFileSearch_Click().

```
Sub cmdFileSearch_Click (Index As Integer)

    'declare variables
    Dim OldText$    'holds original text before change
```

```
    'assign old text
    OldText$ = txtINI(Index).Text

    'handle error
    On Error GoTo OpenError

    'set properties
    cmFileDialog.Filter = "*.WAV¦*.WAV"
    cmFileDialog.FilterIndex = 0
    cmFileDialog.DialogTitle = "Open File"
    'cmFileDialog.Flags = OFN_CREATEPROMPT Or OFN_OVERWRITEPROMPT

    'invoke common dialog
    cmFileDialog.Action = DLG_FILE_OPEN

    'save file
    If cmFileDialog.Filename <> "" Then
        txtINI(Index).Text = cmFileDialog.Filename
    Else
        MsgBox "Cannot Open, No File Name Specified"
        txtINI(Index) = OldText$
    End If

    Exit Sub

OpenError:

    Select Case (Err)
        Case 32755:
            'cancel-
            Exit Sub
        Case Else:
            MsgBox "There was an Open Dialog Error!"
            Exit Sub
    End Select

    'resume to avoid errors
    Resume

End Sub
```

 For more information about using the common dialog box, refer to Chapter 7, "File Input/Output (I/O)."

THE *FORM* OBJECT

The Form object has code in only one event procedure. It is

◆ Form_Load()

THE *FORM_LOAD()* EVENT PROCEDURE

The Form_Load() event procedure populates the text box array and centers the form. Following is a listing of the Form_Load() event procedure:

LISTING 20.61. SOUNDASN.FRM, Form_Load().

```
Sub Form_Load ()

    'center form
    centerform Me

    'load INI data
    Call LoadINI

End Sub
```

THE ABOUT.FRM FILE

ABOUT.FRM is one of five forms in this application. It shows information about the application. Figure 20.7 presents the form as it appears at runtime. Fundamentally, there is no difference in the form at design time, so it is not presented. Table 20.6 lists all the relevant properties of each control on the form that have been changed from their standard default values. The ABOUT.FRM file is contained on the CD accompanying this book in the CHAP20 subdirectory.

FIGURE 20.7.
MDI File Search application About Form at runtime.

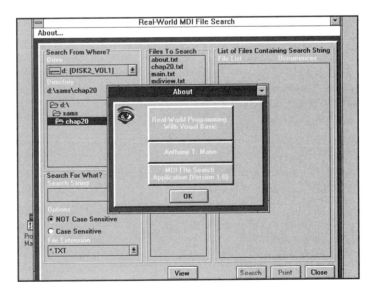

TABLE 20.6. PROPERTIES OF EACH CONTROL ON **ABOUT.FRM**.

Object	Control Type	Property	Value
frmAbout	Form	BackColor	&H00404000&
		Caption	"About"
		Height	3525
		Left	1035
		MaxButton	False
		MinButton	False
		Top	1140
		Width	4545
pnlMain	SSPanel	BackColor	&H00C0C0C0&
		BevelWidth	3
		Caption	""
		Font3D	None
		ForeColor	&H00C0C0C0&
		Height	2095
		Left	120
		RoundedCorners	False
		ShadowColor	Black
		Top	120
		Width	4205
pnl1	SSPanel	BackColor	&H00C0C0C0&
		BevelWidth	3
		Caption	"Real-World Programming With Visual Basic"
		Font3D	None
		ForeColor	&H0000FFFF&
		Height	975
		Left	960
		RoundedCorners	False

continues

TABLE 20.6. CONTINUED

Object	Control Type	Property	Value
		ShadowColor	Black
		Top	120
		Width	2415
pnl2	SSPanel	BackColor	&H00C0C0C0&
		BevelWidth	3
		Caption	"Anthony T. Mann"
		Font3D	None
		ForeColor	&H0000FFFF&
		Height	615
		Left	960
		RoundedCorners	False
		ShadowColor	Black
		Top	1080
		Width	2415
pnl3	SSPanel	BackColor	&H00C0C0C0&
		BevelWidth	3
		Caption	"MDI file search Application (Version 1.0)"
		Font3D	None
		ForeColor	&H0000FFFF&
		Height	615
		Left	960
		RoundedCorners	False
		ShadowColor	Black
		Top	1680
		Width	2415
cmdOK	CommandButton	Caption	"OK"
		Height	375
		Left	1680
		Top	2400
		Width	1095

Object	Control Type	Property	Value
pictAbout	PictureBox	Autosize	True
		BackColor	&H00C0C0C0&
		BorderStyle	None
		Height	615
		Left	120
		Top	120
		Width	735

FUNCTION, SUBROUTINE, AND EVENT PROCEDURES

There are several procedures of code for each object(control) that comprise this form. Each is listed in the following sections.

The (general) object contains only one form level declaration and no form level procedures. The procedures for the (general) object are

◆ (declarations)

THE (DECLARATIONS) PROCEDURE

The (declarations) procedure contains only one line of declarations used in the form ABOUT.FRM. It is only to allow for variable syntax checking and forcing the declaration of variables in each procedure. Following is a listing of the (declarations) procedure:

LISTING 20.62. ABOUT.FRM, (general)(declarations).

```
Option Explicit
```

THE CMDOK CONTROL

cmdOK is the name of the command button control that, when clicked, closes the frmAbout form. The cmdOK control has code only in one event procedure. It is

◆ cmdOK_Click()

THE CMDOK_CLICK() EVENT PROCEDURE

The cmdOK_Click() event procedure simply unloads the form. Following is a listing of the cmdOK_Click() event procedure:

LISTING 20.63. ABOUT.FRM, cmdOK_Click().

```
Sub cmdOK_Click ()

    'unload
    Unload frmAbout

End Sub
```

THE *FORM* OBJECT

The Form object has code in only one event procedure. It is

◆ Form_Load()

THE *FORM_LOAD()* EVENT PROCEDURE

The Form_Load() event procedure centers the form and assigns an icon to the pictAbout control. Following is a listing of the Form_Load() event procedure:

LISTING 20.64. ABOUT.FRM, Form_Load().

```
Sub Form_Load ()

    'center form
    CenterForm Me

    'load icon
    pictAbout.Picture = frmMain.Icon

End Sub
```

THE CHAP20.BAS FILE

CHAP20.BAS is the module that contains application level variables and procedures. The CHAP20.BAS file is contained on the CD accompanying this book in the CHAP20 subdirectory.

FUNCTION, SUBROUTINE, AND EVENT PROCEDURES

There are several procedures of code for each object(control) that comprises this module. Each is listed in the following sections.

The (general) object contains application level variables and procedures. The procedures for the (general) object are

◆ (declarations)

◆ CenterForm()

- ◆ CloseRoutine()
- ◆ FindNextIndex()
- ◆ FontRoutine()
- ◆ GetINI()
- ◆ PrintRoutine()
- ◆ SaveRoutine()
- ◆ SoundRoutine()

THE (DECLARATIONS) PROCEDURE

The (declarations) procedure contains variables and API declarations used in the application. Following is a listing of the (declarations) procedure:

LISTING 20.65. CHAP20.BAS, (GENERAL) (DECLARATIONS).

```
Option Explicit

'declare globals
Global Const SCROLLBARWIDTH = 240
Global PopulatingViewer%
Global NewViewer() As New frmViewerForm
Global Const DRAGOFF = "Drag/Drop Off"
Global Const DRAGON = "Drag/Drop On"
Global Const MODAL = 1

'declare API's
Declare Function sndPlaySound Lib "MMSYSTEM.DLL" (ByVal lpszSoundName$, ByVal wFlags%) As
Integer
Declare Function GetPrivateProfileString Lib "Kernel" (ByVal lpApp$, ByVal lpKey$, ByVal
lpDef$, ByVal lpReturn$, ByVal nSize%, ByVal lpFile$) As Integer
Declare Function WritePrivateProfileString Lib "Kernel" (ByVal lpApp$, ByVal lpKey$,
ByVal lpStr$, ByVal lplFile$) As Integer
Declare Function GetSystemMenu Lib "User" (ByVal hWnd%, ByVal bRevert%) As Integer
Declare Function DestroyMenu Lib "User" (ByVal hMenu As Integer) As Integer

'sound file constants
Global Const SND_ASYNC = &H1
Global Const SND_NODEFAULT = &H2

'message box constants
Global Const IDNO = 7
Global Const IDYES = 6

'mousepointers
Global Const HOURGLASS = 11
Global Const DEFAULT = 0

' arrange methods for MDI Forms
Global Const CASCADE = 0
Global Const TILE_HORIZONTAL = 1
```

continues

LISTING 20.65. CONTINUED

```
Global Const TILE_VERTICAL = 2
Global Const ARRANGE_ICONS = 3

' DragMode
Global Const MANUAL = 0      ' 0 - Manual
Global Const AUTOMATIC = 1 ' 1 - Automatic

' Button parameter masks
Global Const LEFT_BUTTON = 1
Global Const RIGHT_BUTTON = 2

'Help Constants
Global Const HELP_CONTEXT = &H1

'Viewer Variable to denote change made
Global ViewerChange%

'"SOUND.INI" constants
Global Const lpApplicationName$ = "Real-World Sound"
Global Const lpKeyName0$ = "FontChange"
Global Const lpKeyName1$ = "FontCancel"
Global Const lpKeyName2$ = "PrintText"
Global Const lpKeyName3$ = "PrintError"
Global Const lpKeyName4$ = "FileSave"
Global Const lpKeyName5$ = "FileError"
Global Const lpKeyName6$ = "CloseViewer"
Global Const lpKeyName7$ = "CloseSound"
Global Const lpFileName$ = "SOUND.INI"

'defaults
Global Const lpDefault0$ = "FTCHG.WAV"
Global Const lpDefault1$ = "FTCAN.WAV"
Global Const lpDefault2$ = "PTTXT.WAV"
Global Const lpDefault3$ = "PTERR.WAV"
Global Const lpDefault4$ = "FLSAV.WAV"
Global Const lpDefault5$ = "FLERR.WAV"
Global Const lpDefault6$ = "CLVIEW.WAV"
Global Const lpDefault7$ = "CLSND.WAV"

'global sound file names(number will represent index)
Global SoundFile0$
Global SoundFile1$
Global SoundFile2$
Global SoundFile3$
Global SoundFile4$
Global SoundFile5$
Global SoundFile6$
Global SoundFile7$

'stores path program was run from
Global SearchPath$

'File Open/Save Dialog Flags
Global Const OFN_OVERWRITEPROMPT = &H2&
```

```
Global Const OFN_CREATEPROMPT = &H2000&
'Common Dialog Control
Global Const DLG_FILE_OPEN = 1
Global Const DLG_FILE_SAVE = 2
Global Const DLG_FONT = 4
Global Const DLG_HELP = 6
```

THE *CenterForm( )* Procedure

The CenterForm( ) procedure simply centers the form in the client area upon form loading. The CenterForm( ) procedure accepts one argument, F. It is the actual form to be centered. Following is a listing of the CenterForm( ) procedure:

LISTING 20.66. CHAP20.BAS, CenterForm( ).

```
Sub CenterForm (F As Form)

    'center the form
    F.Left = (screen.Width - F.Width) / 2
    F.Top = (screen.Height - F.Height) / 2

End Sub
```

For more information on manipulating graphics and forms, refer to Chapter 5, "Graphics."

THE *CloseRoutine( )* Procedure

The CloseRoutine( ) procedure is the name of the procedure that closes an MDI child form, but prompts to save the file first. The procedure accepts one argument, Source, which is the control to close. The control will be a text box. Following is a listing of the CloseRoutine( ) procedure:

LISTING 20.67. CHAP20.BAS, CloseRoutine( ).

```
Sub CloseRoutine (Source As Control)

    'declare variables
    Dim res%    'holds msgbox results
    Dim m$      'constructor variable for msgbox

    If Source Is Nothing Then
        'user selected menu option
        'unload current MDI Child Form

        'if change has been made, prompt for save
        If Left$(frmMDIView.ActiveForm.Caption, 1) = "*" Then
```

continues

339

LISTING 20.67. CONTINUED

```
                'build message
                m$ = "Close without saving changes?"
                res% = MsgBox(m$, 292, "Warning")
                If res% = IDNO Then Exit Sub
            End If
            Unload frmMDIView.ActiveForm
        Else
            'user selected drag/drop
            'unload current MDI Child Form

            'if change has been made, prompt for save
            If Left$(Source.Parent.Caption, 1) = "*" Then
                'build message
                m$ = "Close without saving changes?"
                res% = MsgBox(m$, 292, "Warning")
                If res% = IDNO Then Exit Sub
            End If
            Unload Source.Parent
        End If

        'if active form is MDI parent, that means that there
        'are no more children left-unload parent
        If screen.ActiveForm.hWnd = frmMDIView.hWnd Then
            Unload frmMDIView
        End If

End Sub
```

THE *FindNextIndex()* PROCEDURE

The FindNextIndex() procedure finds the next available index for a new MDI child form. The procedure is also a function that returns the integer of the next available index. Following is a listing of the FindNextIndex() procedure:

LISTING 20.68. CHAP20.BAS, FindNextIndex().

```
Function FindNextIndex () As Integer

    'finds next available index for NewViewer Array
    FindNextIndex = UBound(NewViewer)

End Function
```

THE *FontRoutine()* PROCEDURE

The FontRoutine() procedure is the name of the procedure that changes the font on an MDI child form. The procedure accepts one argument, Source, which is the control that will have the font changed. The control will be a text box. Following is a listing of the FontRoutine() procedure:

LISTING 20.69. CHAP20.BAS, FontRoutine().

```
Sub FontRoutine (Source As Control)

    'declare variables
    Dim res%     'holds results

    'make sure flags are set properly to handle fonts
    frmMDIView.cmDIalog.Flags = &H2&

    'handle error
    On Error GoTo FontError

    'invoke common dialog for fonts
    frmMDIView.cmDIalog.Action = 4

    'assign properties from common dialog
    If Source Is Nothing Then
        'user selected font popup
        screen.ActiveForm.txtViewer.FontBold = frmMDIView.cmDIalog.FontBold
        screen.ActiveForm.txtViewer.FontItalic = frmMDIView.cmDIalog.FontItalic
        screen.ActiveForm.txtViewer.FontStrikeThru = frmMDIView.cmDIalog.FontStrikeThru
        screen.ActiveForm.txtViewer.FontUnderLine = frmMDIView.cmDIalog.FontUnderLine
        screen.ActiveForm.txtViewer.FontName = frmMDIView.cmDIalog.FontName
        screen.ActiveForm.txtViewer.FontSize = frmMDIView.cmDIalog.FontSize
    Else
        'user selected drag drop
        Source.FontBold = frmMDIView.cmDIalog.FontBold
        Source.FontItalic = frmMDIView.cmDIalog.FontItalic
        Source.FontStrikeThru = frmMDIView.cmDIalog.FontStrikeThru
        Source.FontUnderLine = frmMDIView.cmDIalog.FontUnderLine
        Source.FontName = frmMDIView.cmDIalog.FontName
        Source.FontSize = frmMDIView.cmDIalog.FontSize
    End If

    res% = sndPlaySound(SoundFile0$, SND_ASYNC Or SND_NODEFAULT)

    Exit Sub

FontError:

    Select Case (Err)
        Case 32755:
            'cancel-do nothing
        Case Else:
            MsgBox "There was a Font Dialog Error!"
    End Select
    res% = sndPlaySound(SoundFile1$, SND_ASYNC Or SND_NODEFAULT)
    Exit Sub

    'resume to avoid errors
    Resume

End Sub
```

THE *GetINI()* PROCEDURE

The GetINI() procedure retrieves the configuration of the sound files and assigns them to global variables. Following is a listing of the GetINI() procedure:

LISTING 20.70. CHAP20.BAS, GETINI().

```
Sub GetINI ()

    'declare variables
    Dim res%      'holds results

    'get each of the eight sounds and put them into variables

    'declare specific size to avoid GPF's
    Dim RetString As String
    RetString = Space$(75)

    'get Line 1
    res% = GetPrivateProfileString(lpApplicationName$, lpKeyName0$, lpDefault0$,
    RetString, 75, SearchPath$ + lpFileName$)
    SoundFile0$ = Left$(RetString, res%)

    'get Line 2
    res% = GetPrivateProfileString(lpApplicationName$, lpKeyName1$, lpDefault1$,
    RetString, 75, SearchPath$ + lpFileName$)
    SoundFile1$ = RetString

    'get Line 3
    res% = GetPrivateProfileString(lpApplicationName$, lpKeyName2$, lpDefault2$,
    RetString, 75, SearchPath$ + lpFileName$)
    SoundFile2$ = RetString

    'get Line 4
    res% = GetPrivateProfileString(lpApplicationName$, lpKeyName3$, lpDefault3$,
    RetString, 75, SearchPath$ + lpFileName$)
    SoundFile3$ = RetString

    'get Line 5
    res% = GetPrivateProfileString(lpApplicationName$, lpKeyName4$, lpDefault4$,
    RetString, 75, SearchPath$ + lpFileName$)
    SoundFile4$ = RetString

    'get Line 6
    res% = GetPrivateProfileString(lpApplicationName$, lpKeyName5$, lpDefault5$,
    RetString, 75, SearchPath$ + lpFileName$)
    SoundFile5$ = RetString

    'get Line 7
    res% = GetPrivateProfileString(lpApplicationName$, lpKeyName6$, lpDefault6$,
    RetString, 75, SearchPath$ + lpFileName$)
    SoundFile6$ = RetString

    'get Line 8
```

```
res% = GetPrivateProfileString(lpApplicationName$, lpKeyName7$, lpDefault7$,
RetString, 75, SearchPath$ + lpFileName$)
SoundFile7$ = RetString

End Sub
```

For more information about the `GetPrivateProfileString()` API, refer to Chapter 3, "Calling Windows APIs and DLLs."

THE *PRINTROUTINE( )* PROCEDURE

The `PrintRoutine()` procedure is the name of the procedure that prints the text file on a MDI child form. The procedure accepts one argument, `Source`, which is the control which will be printed. The control will be a text box. Following is a listing of the `PrintRoutine()` procedure:

LISTING 20.71. CHAP20.BAS, `PrintRoutine()`.

```
Sub PrintRoutine (Source As Control)

    'declare variables
    Dim LoopCount%        'loopcount variable
    Dim m$                'message box variable
    Dim res%              'holds results

    'Define Error Handling
    On Error GoTo PrintError

    'Change Cursor
    screen.MousePointer = HOURGLASS

    'assign properties
    If Source Is Nothing Then
        'user selected font popup
        Printer.FontBold = screen.ActiveControl.FontBold
        Printer.FontItalic = screen.ActiveControl.FontItalic
        Printer.FontStrikethru = screen.ActiveControl.FontStrikeThru
        Printer.FontUnderline = screen.ActiveControl.FontUnderLine
        Printer.FontName = screen.ActiveControl.FontName
        Printer.FontSize = screen.ActiveControl.FontSize

        'perform printing
        Printer.Print "File Name: " + screen.ActiveForm.Caption
        Printer.Line (0, Printer.TextHeight(Printer.FontSize))-(Printer.ScaleWidth,
        Printer.TextHeight(Printer.FontSize) + 35), , BF
        Printer.Print screen.ActiveControl.Text
        Printer.EndDoc
    Else
        'user selected drag drop
        Printer.FontBold = Source.FontBold
        Printer.FontItalic = Source.FontItalic
```

continues

343

LISTING 20.71. CONTINUED

```
        Printer.FontStrikethru = Source.FontStrikeThru
        Printer.FontUnderline = Source.FontUnderLine
        Printer.FontName = Source.FontName
        Printer.FontSize = Source.FontSize

        'perform printing
        Printer.Print "File Name: " + Source.Parent.Caption
        Printer.Line (0, Printer.TextHeight(Printer.FontSize))-(Printer.ScaleWidth,
        Printer.TextHeight(Printer.FontSize) + 35), , BF
        Printer.Print Source.Text
        Printer.EndDoc
    End If

    'Change Cursor
    screen.MousePointer = DEFAULT

    'play sound
    res% = sndPlaySound(SoundFile2$, SND_ASYNC Or SND_NODEFAULT)

    'send message of completion
    m$ = "Text was sent to the printer"
    MsgBox m$

    'Exit
    Exit Sub

    'There was an error
PrintError:
    'Change Cursor
    screen.MousePointer = DEFAULT

    'Build message
    Select Case (Err)
        Case 380:
            m$ = "Printer cannot print using these properties!"
        Case Else:
            m$ = "There is a problem with the printer!"
    End Select

    'display message
    MsgBox m$

    'play sound
    res% = sndPlaySound(SoundFile3$, SND_ASYNC Or SND_NODEFAULT)

    'Exit
    Exit Sub

    'resume to avoid errors
    Resume

End Sub
```

THE *SAVEROUTINE( )* PROCEDURE

The SaveRoutine( ) procedure is the name of the procedure that saves the text file on an MDI child form. The procedure accepts one argument, Source, which is the control that will be printed. The control will be a text box. Following is a listing of the SaveRoutine( ) procedure:

LISTING 20.72. CHAP20.BAS, SaveRoutine( ).

```
Sub SaveRoutine (Source As Control)

    'declare variables
    Dim res%    'holds results

    'handle error
    On Error GoTo SaveError

    'set properties
    frmMDIView.cmDIalog.Filter = "*.TXT¦*.TXT¦*.DOC¦*.DOC¦*.INI¦*.INI"
    frmMDIView.cmDIalog.FilterIndex = 0
    frmMDIView.cmDIalog.DialogTitle = "Save As"
    frmMDIView.cmDIalog.Flags = OFN_CREATEPROMPT Or OFN_OVERWRITEPROMPT

    'invoke common dialog for saving
    frmMDIView.cmDIalog.Action = DLG_FILE_SAVE

    'save file
    If frmMDIView.cmDIalog.Filename <> "" Then
        Open frmMDIView.cmDIalog.Filename For Output As #1
        If Source Is Nothing Then
            'user selected save popup
            Print #1, screen.ActiveControl.Text
        Else
            'user selected drag/drop
            Print #1, Source.Text
        End If
        Close #1

        'play sound
        res% = sndPlaySound(SoundFile4$, SND_ASYNC Or SND_NODEFAULT)

        'confirm with message
        MsgBox frmMDIView.cmDIalog.Filename + " Saved!"

    Else
        MsgBox "Cannot Save, No File Name Specified"

        'play sound
        res% = sndPlaySound(SoundFile5$, SND_ASYNC Or SND_NODEFAULT)
    End If


    Exit Sub
```

LISTING 20.72. CONTINUED

```
SaveError:

    Select Case (Err)
        Case 32755:
            'cancel-do nothing
        Case Else:
            MsgBox "There was a Save Dialog Error!"
    End Select

    'play sound
    res% = sndPlaySound(SoundFile5$, SND_ASYNC Or SND_NODEFAULT)

    'exit
    Exit Sub

    'resume to avoid errors
    Resume

End Sub
```

THE *SoundRoutine()* PROCEDURE

The SoundRoutine() procedure is the name of the procedure that opens the SOUNDASN.FRM form. Following is a listing of the SoundRoutine() procedure:

LISTING 20.73. CHAP20.BAS, SoundRoutine().

```
Sub SoundRoutine ()

    'load assign sound form
    frmSoundAssign.Show

End Sub
```

THE SOUND.INI FILE

This file contains the configuration of the sound files that will be played when certain events occur in the application. The SOUND.INI file is contained on the CD accompanying this book in the CHAP20 subdirectory. Following is a listing of the SOUND.INI file:

LISTING 20.74. SOUND.INI.

```
[Real-World Sound]
FontChange=FTCHG.WAV
FontCancel=FTCAN.WAV
PrintText=PTTXT.WAV
```

```
PrintError=PTERR.WAV
FileSave=FLSAV.WAV
FileError=FLERR.WAV
CloseViewer=CLVIEW.WAV
CloseSound=CLSND.WAV
```

 For more information about working with INI files, refer to Chapter 7, "File Input/ Output (I/O)."

THE CHAP20.ICO FILE

This file contains the icon that has been attached to the form at design time. The CHAP20.ICO file is contained on the CD accompanying this book in the CHAP20 subdirectory.

FIGURE 20.8.
*MDI File Search
Application Form icon.*

THE DRAGFLDR.ICO FILE

This file contains the icon that is used when a drag/drop operation occurs. The DRAGFLDR.ICO file is contained on the CD accompanying this book in the CHAP20 subdirectory.

FIGURE 20.9.
*MDI File Search
Application Drag icon.*

THE CLOSE.BMP FILE

This file contains the bitmap used in the picture box to which an MDI child text box can be dragged to close the file. The CLOSE.BMP file is contained on the CD accompanying this book in the CHAP20 subdirectory.

FIGURE 20.10.
*MDI File Search
Application Close
Bitmap icon.*

THE SAVE.BMP FILE

This file contains the bitmap used in the picture box to which an MDI child text box can be dragged to save the file. The SAVE.BMP file is contained on the CD accompanying this book in the CHAP20 subdirectory.

FIGURE 20.11.
MDI File Search
Application Save
Bitmap icon.

THE PRINTER.BMP FILE

This file contains the bitmap used in the picture box to which an MDI Child text box can be dragged to print the file. The PRINTER.BMP file is contained on the CD accompanying this book in the CHAP20 subdirectory.

FIGURE 20.12.
MDI File Search
Application Print
Bitmap icon.

THE FONT.BMP FILE

This file contains the bitmap used in the picture box to which an MDI Child text box can be dragged to change the font. The FONT.BMP file is contained on the CD accompanying this book in the CHAP20 subdirectory.

FIGURE 20.13.
MDI File Search
Application Font
Bitmap icon.

THE SOUND.BMP FILE

This file contains the bitmap used in the picture box to which an MDI child text box can be dragged to change the global sound files. The SOUND.BMP file is contained on the CD accompanying this book in the CHAP20 subdirectory.

FIGURE 20.14.
*MDI File Search
Application Sound
Bitmap icon.*

THE *.WAV FILES

These are the default sound files to be played when certain events occur in the application. There are a total of eight sound files. They are listed in Table 20.1.

THE CHAP20.HLP FILE

This is the file that is compiled in the Windows 3.1 Help file format. It is the file that is invoked when choosing any Help option in the application. To create this Help file, refer to the following file listings as well as Chapter 10, "Creating Context Sensitive Help."

THE CHAP20.RTF FILE

This is the file that is the main source of the CHAP20.HLP file. This file is contained on the CD accompanying this book in the CHAP20 subdirectory. It was created using Microsoft Word version 6.0. It is important to note that in the following listing, the words {page break} indicate that {page break} should be entered. Listing 20.75 shows a listing of the main body of the CHAP20.RTF file. Listing 20.76 shows a listing of the footnotes of the CHAP20.RTF file.

LISTING 20.75. CHAP20.RTF, MAIN BODY.

```
Contents
Introduction


Main Search Screen

File Viewer Screen

Sound File Edit Screen

{page break}
Introduction
```

This Real-World File Search with Viewer is a useful utility that allows you to do the following:

Search in a directory of files, containing a certain file extension (*.TXT) or all (*.*), for the number of occurrences of a string within those files.

View either the proposed file(s) or returned file(s) in an MDI file viewer screen.

continues

LISTING 20.75. CONTINUED

Edit and save any or all of the file(s) shown in the MDI file viewer.

The application also demonstrates how to incorporate drag/drop operations and play sound files.

```
{page break}
Main File Search Screen
{bml SCREEN1.SHG}
{page break}
File Viewer Screen
{bml SCREEN2.SHG}
{page break}
Close Icon
```

Closes a file and MDI form when the form is DRAGGED to this icon.

The Toggle Drag/Drop right mouse menu option must be set to Drag/Drop ON for an MDI form to have the capability to be DRAGGED.

Closing can also be performed directly through the right mouse button option.

```
{page break}
Save Icon
```

Saves a file on an MDI form when the form is DRAGGED to this icon.

The Toggle Drag/Drop right mouse menu option must be set to Drag/Drop ON for an MDI form to have the capability to be DRAGGED.

File saving can also be performed directly through the right mouse button option.

```
{page break}
Font Icon
```

Changes a font on an MDI form when the form is DRAGGED to this icon.

The Toggle Drag/Drop right mouse menu option must be set to Drag/Drop ON for an MDI form to have the capability to be DRAGGED.

Font changing can also be performed directly through the right mouse button option.

```
{page break}
Print Icon
```

Prints a file on an MDI form when the form is DRAGGED to this icon.

The Toggle Drag/Drop right mouse menu option must be set to Drag/Drop ON for an MDI form to have the capability to be DRAGGED.

File printing can also be performed directly through the right mouse button option.

```
{page break}
Background MDI Form
This MDI form is in the background.
```

```
{page break}
Foreground MDI Form
This MDI form is in the foreground.
{page break}
Sound Icon
```

Shows the change sound form to change global sounds. It is NOT `MDI` form specific.

The Toggle Drag/Drop right mouse menu option must be set to `Drag/Drop ON` for an `MDI` form to have the capability to be `DRAGGED`.

Global sound changing can also be performed directly through the right mouse button option.

```
{page break}
Drag/Drop Label
```

Indicates that an `MDI` form has the capability to be `DRAGGED` to any of the icons at the top of the screen.

The label can have one of two states:

> `Drag/Drop ON`, the `MDI` form has this capability.

> `Drag/Drop OFF`, the `MDI` form does not have this capability.

To toggle between `ON` and `OFF`, simply press the right mouse button while located over any `MDI` form. Select the first option, `Toggle Drag/Drop`.

```
{page break}
File Menu Option
```

The File menu has these options:

> Close—Closes currently selected `MDI` form.

> Exit—Exits viewer form and returns to search screen.

```
{page break}
Find Menu Option
```

The Find menu has these options:

> Find Search String (F7)   Finds next occurrence of the search string within file.

> Find Another String (F8)   Finds next occurrence of another string within the file, prompting for the string to search on.

```
{page break}
Window Menu Option
```

The Window menu has these options:

> Cascade—   Cascades all open windows.
> Tile (Horizontally)— Horizontally tiles all open windows.
> Tile (Vertically)—   Vertically tiles all open windows.

continues

351

LISTING 20.75. CONTINUED

MDI File List— Lists all open MDI files, to activate them directly.

```
{page break}
Help Menu Option
```

The Help menu has these options:

Contents—	Invokes Help file.
About—	Displays about box for application information.

```
{page break}
Drive Box
```

Visual Basic Drive Box, used to select the drive that files will be searched from.

```
{page break}
Directory Box
```

Visual Basic Directory Listbox, used to select the directory which files will be searched from.

```
{page break}
Search String
```

The string that will be searched for in the Proposed List of files.

```
{page break}
Option Buttons
```

Selects either case sensitivity or not for the search.

```
{page break}
File Extension
```

Selects the extension of the file that will be used to filter the Visual Basic File List Control.

```
{page break}
View Button
```

Invokes the File Viewer, adding a new MDI form for each file selected in either the Proposed List or the Result File List.

Only one of these lists can have items selected at a time.

```
{page break}
Search Button
```

Starts the file searching of the Search String within the file list.

```
{page break}
Print Button
```

Prints a list of the RESULT files and the number of occurrences.

```
{page break}
Close Button
```

Button to close application.

```
{page break}
Result File List
```

The result list of the files returned from the search.

```
{page break}
Proposed List
```

Visual Basic File List that will be searched when the Search button is clicked.

```
{page break}
Edit Sound Files Screen
{bml SCREEN3.SHG}
{page break}
Change Font Sound
```

Sound file played when changing a font in the file viewer.

```
{page break}
Cancel Font Sound
```

Sound file played when cancelling a font change or when there is a font error in the file viewer.

```
{page break}
Print Text Sound
```

Sound file played when the text is finished being printed by the file viewer.

```
{page break}
Print Error Sound
```

Sound file played when the file viewer cannot print a file due to an error.

```
{page break}
Save File Sound
```

Sound file played when the file viewer finishes saving a file.

```
{page break}
Save Error Sound
```

Sound file played when the file viewer cannot save a file due to an error.

```
{page break}
Close Viewer Sound
```

Sound file played when closing the file viewer.

```
{page break}
Close Sound
```

Sound file played when closing the sound change form.

```
{page break}
Find Sound File Button
```

Pops up the common dialog box and allows selection of a sound file.

continues

LISTING 20.75. CONTINUED

```
{page break}
Close Button
```

Closes the Changing Sound form.

```
{page break}
MDI
```

Multiple Document Interface.

Used for multiple compound documents. These are based on a single template and contained within one form.

```
{page break}
Popup - Toggle Drag/Drop
```

This option toggles the Drag/Drop operation between Drag/Drop ON and Drag/Drop OFF for each MDI form independently.

The Drag/Drop label displays the Drag/Drop status for the currently selected MDI form.

```
{page break}
Popup - Save As
```

This option can be used to save the file in the currently selected MDI form.

This option is available regardless of the Drag/Drop status.

```
{page break}
Popup - Font
```

This option can be used to change the font in the currently selected MDI form.

This option is available regardless of the Drag/Drop status.

```
{page break}
Popup - Print
```

This option can be used to print the file in the currently selected MDI form.

This option is available regardless of the Drag/Drop status.

```
{page break}
Popup - Sound
```

This option can be used to change the global sounds. These sounds are not specific to any one MDI form.

This option is available regardless of the Drag/Drop status.

```
{page break}
Popup - Help Contents
```

This option can be used to display the contents of the Help file.

This option is available regardless of the Drag/Drop status.

```
{page break}
Popup - About
```

This option can be used to display information in the Visual Basic About form.

This option is available regardless of the Drag/Drop status.

```
{page break}
```

LISTING 20.76. CHAP20.RTF, FOOTNOTES.

```
Contents
Contents
Introduction;Search Screen;Main Screen;File Viewer Screen;Viewer;Sound File Screen;
Introduction
Introduction
00001:002
Introduction;
MainScreen
Main File Search Screen
00001:003
Main Screen;Search Screen;
FileViewerScreen
File Viewer Screen
00001:004
Close;Saving Files;Font Changing;Printing;MDI;Changing Sounds;Drag/Drop;
ViewerClose
Close Icon
File Viewer;Viewing Files;Drag/Drop File Closing;Closing File Viewer;
ViewerSave
Save Icon
File Viewer;Viewing Files;DragDrop Saving;Saving Files;Saving;
ViewerFont
Font Icon
File Viewer;Viewing Files;Drag/Drop Font Changing;Changing Fonts;
ViewerPrint
Print Icon
File Viewer;Viewing Files;DragDrop Printing;Printing;
ViewerMDI1
Background MDI Form
File Viewer;Viewing Files;MDI;
ViewerMDI2
Foreground MDI Form
File Viewer;Viewing Files;MDI;
ViewerSound
Sound Icon
File Viewer;Viewing Files;DragDrop Sound Changing;Changing Sounds;
ViewerDragDrop
Drag/Drop Icon
File Viewer;Viewing Files;Drag/Drop;
ViewerMenuFile
File Menu Option
```

continues

LISTING 20.76. CONTINUED

```
File Viewer;Viewing Files;File Menu Options;
ViewerMenuFind
Find Menu Option
File Viewer;Viewing Files;Find Menu Options;
ViewerMenuWindow
Window Menu Option
File Viewer;Viewing Files;Window Menu Options;
ViewerMenuHelp
Help Menu Option
File Viewer;Viewing Files;Help Menu Options;Invoking Help;
MainDrive
Drive Box
Main Screen;Search Screen;Drive Selection;
MainDirectory
Directory Box
Main Screen;Search Screen;Directory Selection;
MainSearchString
Search String
Main Screen;Search Screen;Search String;Search;
MainOptions
Option Buttons
Main Screen;Search Screen;Options;Case Sensitivity;
MainExtension
File Extension
Main Screen;Search Screen;File Extension;Extension;
MainView
View Button
Main Screen;Search Screen;View;Invoking Viewer;
MainSearch
Search Button
Search;
MainPrint
Print Button
Main Screen;Search Screen;Printing;
MainClose
Close Button
Main Screen;Search Screen;Close;
MainFileList
Result File List
Main Screen;Search Screen;File List;Returned List;
MainProposedList
Proposed List
Main Screen;Search Screen;Proposed List;Returned List;
SoundFileEditScreen
Edit Sound Files
00001:005
Sound Screen;Changing Sounds;
SoundFontChg
Change Font Sound
Sound Screen;Changing Sounds;Changing Font Change Sound;
SoundFontCancel
Cancel Font Sound
Sound Screen;Changing Sounds;Changing Font Cancel Sound;
SoundPrintText
```

```
Print Text Sound
Sound Screen;Changing Sounds;Changing Print Finished Sound;
SoundPrintError
Print Error Sound
Sound Screen;Changing Sounds;Changing Print Error Sound;
SoundSaveFile
Save File Sound
Sound Screen;Changing Sounds;Changing Save Finished Sound;
SoundSaveError
Save Error Sound
Sound Screen;Changing Sounds;Changing Save Error Sound;
SoundCloseViewer
Close Viewer Sound
Sound Screen;Changing Sounds;Changing Close Viewer Sound;
SoundCloseSound
Close Sound
Sound Screen;Changing Sounds;Changing Close Dialog Sound;
SoundCmDialog
Find Sound File Button
Sound Screen;Changing Sounds;Changing Sound Files;
SoundCloseButton
Close Button
Sound Screen;Changing Sounds;Close;
MDI
MDI
MDI;
PopupToggle
Popup Menu
Popup;Toggle Drag/Drop;
PopupSaveAs
Popup Menu
Popup;Saving Files;SaveAs;
PopupFont
Popup Menu
Popup;Changing Fonts;
PopupPrint
Popup Menu
Popup;Printing;
PopupSound
Popup Menu
Popup;Changing Sounds;
PopupHelpContents
Popup Menu
Popup;Help;Contents;
PopupAbout
Popup Menu
Popup;About;
```

THE SCREEN1.SHG FILE

This is the file that is the project file needed to generate the CHAP20.HLP file. It is conceptually the same as the *.MAK file in Visual Basic. Below is a listing of the CHAP20.HPJ file:

LISTING 20.77. CHAP20.HPJ.

```
[Options]
Compress=High
Contents=Contents
OldKeyPhrase=No
Warning=2

[Files]
chap20.rtf

[BuildTags]

[Config]
BrowseButtons()

[Bitmaps]
SCREEN1.SHG
SCREEN2.SHG
SCREEN3.SHG


[Map]
Contents 1
Introduction 2
MainScreen 3
FileViewerScreen 4
ViewerClose 5
ViewerSave 6
ViewerFont 7
ViewerPrint 8
ViewerMDI1 9
ViewerMDI2 10
ViewerSound 11
ViewerDragDrop 12
ViewerMenuFile 13
ViewerMenuFind 14
ViewerMenuWindow 15
ViewerMenuHelp 16
MainDrive 17
MainDirectory 18
MainSearchString 19
MainOptions 20
MainExtension 21
MainView 22
MainSearch 23
MainPrint 24
MainClose 25
MainFileList 26
MainProposedList 27
SoundFileEditScreen 28
SoundFontChg 29
SoundFontCancel 30
```

```
SoundPrintText 31
SoundPrintError 32
SoundSaveFile 33
SoundSaveError 34
SoundCloseViewer 35
SoundCloseSound 36
SoundCmDialog 37
SoundCloseButton 38
MDI 39
PopupToggle 40
PopupSaveAs 41
PopupFont 42
PopupPrint 43
PopupSound 44
PopupHelpContents 45
PopupAbout 46

[Alias]

[Windows]
ZZZZZZZZ="",(0,0,350,623),0,(255,255,255),(192,192,192), 0

[Baggage]
```

This file contains the hotspots defined by using the SHED.EXE Hotspot editor, which comes with Visual Basic, Professional Edition. Figure 20.15 shows the SCREEN1.SHG file as it appears in the SHED.EXE program. The SCREEN1.SHG file is contained on the CD accompanying this book in the CHAP20 subdirectory.

FIGURE 20.15.
SCREEN1 hotspot, as it appears in SHED.EXE.

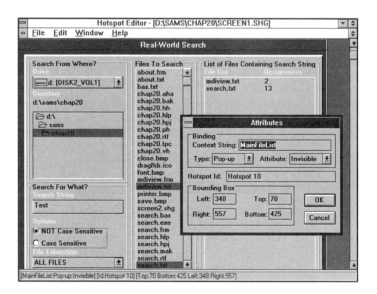

THE SCREEN2.SHG FILE

This file contains the hotspots defined by using the SHED.EXE Hotspot editor, which comes with Visual Basic, Professional Edition. Figure 20.16 shows the SCREEN2.SHG file as it appears in the SHED.EXE program. The SCREEN2.SHG file is contained on the CD accompanying this book in the CHAP20 subdirectory.

FIGURE 20.16.
SCREEN2 hotspot, as it appears in SHED.EXE.

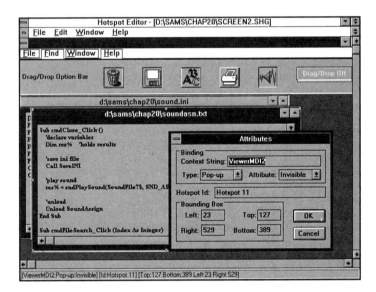

THE SCREEN3.SHG FILE

This file contains the hotspots defined by using the SHED.EXE Hotspot editor, which comes with Visual Basic, Professional Edition. Figure 20.17 shows the SCREEN3.SHG file as it appears in the SHED.EXE program. The SCREEN3.SHG file is contained on the CD accompanying this book in the CHAP20 subdirectory.

FIGURE 20.17.
SCREEN3 hotspot, as it appears in SHED.EXE.

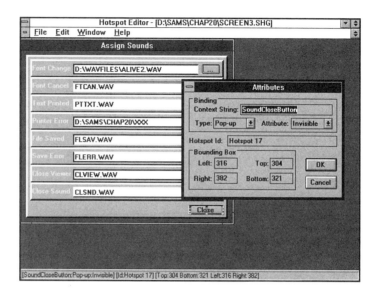

THE CHAP20.EXE FILE

This is the executable file that is distributable. If you distribute this application, you must include the following files:

- ◆ CHAP20.EXE
- ◆ CMDIALOG.VBX
- ◆ COMMDLG.DLL
- ◆ VBRUN300.DLL
- ◆ THREED.VBX

The CHAP20.EXE file and source files are contained on the CD accompanying this book in the CHAP20 subdirectory, while all DLLs and VBXs are in the RESOURCE subdirectory.

RELATING THE MDI FILE SEARCH APPLICATION TO YOUR APPLICATION

The MDI File Search application shows how to do many things. It demonstrates the use of help files, MDI child forms, opening files, printing, special uses of the mouse (right mouse button), and audio.

You can use any of these techniques to enhance your applications—especially, the Help file. There are very few resources available that will show how to build a Help file from start to finish.

Refer to Chapter 10, "Creating Context Sensitive Help," to see how to create the help file.

FINAL NOTES

This application was created on a standard VGA display using 16 colors. Your particular hardware could have adverse effects on the code the way it is written. You may need to modify it slightly.

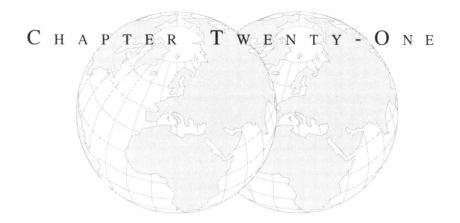

FILE COPY APPLICATION

THE FILE COPY application is a good demonstration of how to use some specialized methods of Visual Basic programming. It allows you to copy, move, or delete a file. This is not the most terrific feat of programming ever devised; however, what's special about this application is the way it does it! You certainly can copy a file from one location to another by using Visual Basic's FileCopy function. However, this does not provide feedback as to the progress of the copy. To show the progress of the copy process, you must open the file and copy one byte at a time. This allows for the monitoring of the process, but it is considerably slower. As such, a Slow Mode command button and a Fast Mode command button are provided. The Fast mode allows for the

`FileCopy` function to be used. The application is also unique in that it shows you how to drag and drop files from a listbox. Normally, in a drag/drop operation with a list box, you don't know which index in the list box the mouse is currently over. This application shows how to do that. Figure 21.1 shows the main screen (MAIN.FRM) at runtime.

FIGURE 21.1

File Copy application MAIN.FRM at runtime.

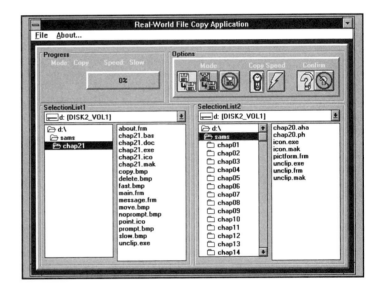

To use the application, select directories of files by standard selection methods on either list box. Either box can be a "source" or "target." Select the mode desired, Copy or Move. Then select the files desired in one list box, which will now become the source. Press the right mouse button to start the dragging. Move the cursor to the desired directory in the opposite, "target," directory. If the Confirmation command button is selected, you will be prompted to perform the desired operation. If the No-Confirmation command button is selected, the process will start immediately. The time it takes to complete the operation will depend on the mode selected, Fast or Slow. By default, the Slow mode is chosen.

While copying, deleting, or moving is taking place, the MESSAGE.FRM form is shown. This form is used to display the status of the copy or move operation, as well as to limit the area where the cursor can travel. This prevents any outside influences from aborting or corrupting the process. Figure 21.2 shows the MESSAGE.FRM form at runtime.

If you want to delete files, select them first and then click on the Delete command button.

 The File Copy application demonstrates using "The Mouse," Chapter 4, and "File Input/Output (I/O)," Chapter 7.

FIGURE 21.2.
File Copy application
MESSAGE.FRM at
runtime.

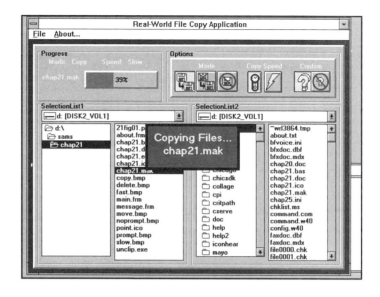

REM If the application crashes, run the program UNCLIP.EXE from the Program Manager by using the keyboard. This program is located in the CHAP21 subdirectory on the CD accompanying this book. The program will restore the cursor to the full screen.

CODE LISTINGS

The File Copy application contains the following files and listings:

- ◆ CHAP21.MAK
- ◆ MAIN.FRM
- ◆ MESSAGE.FRM
- ◆ ABOUT.FRM
- ◆ CHAP21.BAS
- ◆ CHAP21.ICO
- ◆ POINT.ICO
- ◆ PROMPT.BMP
- ◆ NOPROMPT.BMP
- ◆ MOVE.BMP

- ◆ COPY.BMP
- ◆ DELETE.BMP
- ◆ FAST.BMP
- ◆ SLOW.BMP
- ◆ CHAP21.EXE
- ◆ UNCLIP.EXE

THE CHAP21.MAK FILE

CHAP21.MAK is the project file for the File Copy application, CHAP21.EXE. It contains a listing of all the files necessary to load the project into Visual Basic. The CHAP21.MAK file is contained on the CD accompanying this book in the CHAP21 subdirectory. The file listing is:

LISTING 21.1. CHAP21.MAK.

```
MAIN.FRM
CHAP21.BAS
GAUGE.VBX
THREED.VBX
MESSAGE.FRM
ABOUT.FRM
ProjWinSize=152,402,248,215
ProjWinShow=2
IconForm="frmMain"
Title="File Copy"
ExeName="CHAP21.EXE"
```

THE MAIN.FRM FILE

MAIN.FRM is one of three forms in this application. It is the startup form for the application as well as the form used to copy, move, and delete files. Figure 21.1 shows the form as it appears at runtime. Figure 21.3 shows the form as it appears at design time. Table 21.1 lists all the relevant properties of each control on the form that have been changed from their standard default values. The MAIN.FRM file is contained on the CD accompanying this book in the CHAP21 subdirectory.

FIGURE 21.3.
File Copy application MAIN.FRM at design time.

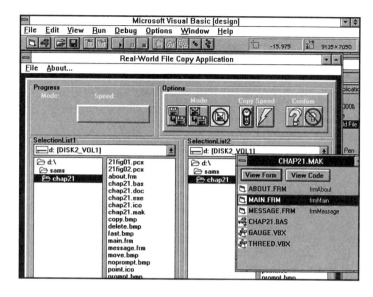

TABLE 21.1. PROPERTIES OF EACH CONTROL ON MAIN.FRM.

Object	Control Type	Property	Value
frmMain	Form	BackColor	&H00404000&
		Caption	"Real-World File Copy Application"
		Height	7050
		Icon	"CHAP21.ICO"
		Left	270
		MaxButton	False
		Top	345
		Width	9135
Panel3D1	SSPanel	BackColor	&H00C0C0C0&
		BevelWidth	3
		Font3D	None
		Height	6135
		Left	120
		Top	120
		Width	8775
Frame3D1	SSFrame	Caption	"Progress"

TABLE 21.1. CONTINUED

Object	Control Type	Property	Value
		Font3D	None
		Height	1455
		Left	120
		Top	120
		Width	3495
Frame3D2	SSFrame	Caption	"Options"
		Font3D	None
		Height	1455
		Left	3720
		Top	120
		Width	4935
Panel3D2	SSPanel	BackColor	&H00C0C0C0&
		BevelWidth	3
		FloodColor	&H00808080&
		Font3D	None
		Height	1095
		Left	120
		Top	240
		Width	4695
Panel3D7	SSPanel	Alignment	Center - TOP
		BackColor	&H00C0C0C0&
		BevelOuter	None
		BevelWidth	3
		Caption	"Confirm"
		Font3D	None
		ForeColor	&H0000FFFF&
		Height	855
		Left	3360
		Top	120
		Width	1215

Object	Control Type	Property	Value
Panel3D4	SSPanel	Alignment	Center - TOP
		BackColor	&H00C0C0C0&
		BevelOuter	None
		BevelWidth	3
		Caption	"Copy Speed"
		Font3D	None
		ForeColor	&H0000FFFF&
		Height	855
		Left	2040
		Top	120
		Width	1215
Panel3D3	SSPanel	Alignment	Center - TOP
		BackColor	&H00C0C0C0&
		BevelOuter	None
		BevelWidth	3
		Caption	"Mode"
		Font3D	None
		ForeColor	&H0000FFFF&
		Height	855
		Left	120
		Top	120
		Width	1815
pnlSpeed	SSPanel	Alignment	Left Justify - MIDDLE
		BackColor	&H00C0C0C0&
		BevelOuter	None
		BevelWidth	3
		Font3D	None
		ForeColor	&H0000FFFF&
		Height	255
		Left	2520
		Top	240

continues

Table 21.1. continued

Object	Control Type	Property	Value
		Width	735
Panel3D6	SSPanel	Alignment	Right Justify - MIDDLE
		BackColor	&H00C0C0C0&
		BevelOuter	None
		BevelWidth	3
		Caption	"Speed:"
		Font3D	None
		ForeColor	&H0000FFFF&
		Height	255
		Left	1680
		Top	240
		Width	735
Panel3D5	SSPanel	Alignment	Right Justify - MIDDLE
		BackColor	&H00C0C0C0&
		BevelOuter	None
		BevelWidth	3
		Caption	"Mode:"
		Font3D	None
		ForeColor	&H0000FFFF&
		Height	255
		Left	120
		Top	240
		Width	735
pnlMode	SSPanel	Alignment	Left Justify - MIDDLE
		BackColor	&H00C0C0C0&
		BevelOuter	None
		BevelWidth	3
		Font3D	None
		ForeColor	&H0000FFFF&
		Height	255

Object	Control Type	Property	Value
		Left	960
		Top	240
		Width	735
pnlFileName	SSPanel	BackColor	&H00C0C0C0&
		BevelOuter	None
		BevelWidth	3
		Font3D	None
		ForeColor	&H0000FFFF&
		Height	375
		Left	120
		Top	600
		Width	1095
pnlFloodStatus	SSPanel	BackColor	&H00C0C0C0&
		BevelWidth	3
		FloodColor	&H00808080&
		FloodType	Left To Right
		Font3D	None
		Height	495
		Left	1320
		Top	600
		Width	2055
cmdNoPrompt	SSRibbon	BackColor	&H00C0C0C0&
		GroupAllowAllUp	False
		GroupNumber	3
		Height	570
		Left	600
		PictureDisabled	None
		PictureDn	None
		PictureDnChange	1
		PictureUp	"NOPROMPT.BMP"
		Top	240

continues

TABLE 21.1. CONTINUED

Object	Control Type	Property	Value
		Width	570
cmdPrompt	SSRibbon	BackColor	&H00C0C0C0&
		GroupAllowAllUp	False
		GroupNumber	3
		Height	570
		Left	120
		PictureDisabled	None
		PictureDn	None
		PictureDnChange	1
		PictureUp	"PROMPT.BMP"
		Top	240
		Width	570
cmdSlow	SSRibbon	BackColor	&H00C0C0C0&
		GroupAllowAllUp	False
		GroupNumber	2
		Height	600
		Left	120
		PictureDisabled	None
		PictureDn	None
		PictureDnChange	1
		PictureUp	"SLOW.BMP"
		Top	240
		Width	405
cmdFast	SSRibbon	BackColor	&H00C0C0C0&
		GroupAllowAllUp	False
		GroupNumber	2
		Height	585
		Left	600
		PictureDisabled	None
		PictureDn	None

Object	Control Type	Property	Value
		PictureDnChange	1
		PictureUp	"FAST.BMP"
		Top	240
		Width	510
cmdCopy	SSRibbon	BackColor	&H00C0C0C0&
		GroupAllowAllUp	False
		Height	570
		Left	0
		PictureDisabled	None
		PictureDn	None
		PictureDnChange	1
		PictureUp	"COPY.BMP"
		Top	240
		Width	570
cmdMove	SSRibbon	BackColor	&H00C0C0C0&
		GroupAllowAllUp	False
		Height	570
		Left	600
		PictureDisabled	None
		PictureDn	None
		PictureDnChange	1
		PictureUp	"MOVE.BMP"
		Top	240
		Width	570
cmdDelete	SSRibbon	BackColor	&H00C0C0C0&
		GroupAllowAllUp	False
		Height	570
		Left	1200
		PictureDisabled	None
		PictureDn	None
		PictureDnChange	1

continues

TABLE 21.1. CONTINUED

Object	Control Type	Property	Value
		PictureUp	"DELETE.BMP"
		Top	240
		Value	True
		Width	570
SelectionFrame	SSFRame	Caption	"SelectionList1", "SelectionList2"*
		Font3D	None
		Height	4455
		Index	0,1,*
		Left	120,4440*
		Top	1560
		Width	4215
lbFile	FileListBox	BackColor	&H00FFFFFF&
		DragIcon	"POINT.ICO"
		Height	3735
		Index	0,1*
		Left	2160
		MultiSelect	Extended
		Top	600
		Width	1935
lbDirectory	DirListBox	BackColor	&H00FFFFFF&
		DragIcon	"POINT.ICO"
		Height	3630
		Index	0,1*
		Left	120
		Top	600
		Width	1935
Drive1	DriveListBox	BackColor	&H00FFFFFF&
		Height	315
		Index	0,1*

Object	Control Type	Property	Value
		Left	120
		Top	240
		Width	3975
menu_about	Menu	Caption	"&About..."
menu_file	Menu	Caption	"&File"
menu_File_Exit	Menu	Caption	"&Exit"

*This control is a control array and these are the only properties that vary within the control. To save space, they were not listed separately.

FUNCTION, SUBROUTINE, AND EVENT PROCEDURES

There are several procedures of code for each object(control) that comprise this form. Each is listed in the following sections.

THE (GENERAL) OBJECT

The general object contains declarations and procedures at the form level. The procedures for the (general) object are

- ◆ (declarations)
- ◆ DecodeRow()
- ◆ DoDelete()
- ◆ DoFastCopy()
- ◆ DoFastMove()
- ◆ DoSlowCopy()
- ◆ DoSlowMove()
- ◆ Refreshall()

THE (DECLARATIONS) PROCEDURE

The (declarations) procedure contains only two lines of code. All other variable declarations are in CHAP21.BAS. Following is a listing of the (declarations) procedure:

LISTING 21.2. MAIN.FRM, (general)(declarations).

```
Option Explicit

'declare form level variables
Dim FromDirectory$
```

THE *DecodeRow( )* PROCEDURE

The DecodeRow( ) procedure decodes which row the user is trying to drop an object into. This is necessary because none of the listbox type controls provide the listindex of where the dragdrop event occurs. They do provide the coordinates of where the mouse is. This function decodes which row the cursor is on. The procedure accepts two arguments. The first, Index, specifies which list box you're dealing with. The second, y, specifies the y coordinate of the mouse position. The procedure is also a function that returns the corresponding row. Following is a listing of the DecodeRow( ) procedure:

LISTING 21.3. MAIN.FRM, DecodeRow( ).

```
Function DecodeRow (Index As Integer, y As Single) As Single

    'declare variables
    Dim m$                 'message constructor
    Dim TheHeight%         'height of listbox
    Dim ProposedIndex%     'current index

    'force positive values
    If y < 0 Then y = 0

    'determine the height of each item in list
    TheHeight% = TextHeight(lbDirectory(Index).List(0))

    '25 allows for the area above and below the actual text, but still
    'in the index area
    ProposedIndex% = (Int(y / (TheHeight% + 25))) - 3


    'since directory list box can have - listindexes
    'test to see if this particular index, shows the root.  If not
    'add 2 to it-this allows the selected text to be in line with the icon
    If lbDirectory(Index).List(-2) = "" Then
    ProposedIndex% = ProposedIndex% + 2
    End If

    DecodeRow = ProposedIndex%

End Function
```

THE *DoDelete( )* PROCEDURE

The DoDelete( ) procedure is the procedure that actually deletes the file, if selected. The procedure accepts one argument, FromIndex%, which is the index of the list box that contains files to delete. Following is a listing of the DoDelete( ) procedure:

LISTING 21.4. MAIN.FRM, DoDelete().

```
Sub DoDelete (FromIndex%)

    'declare variables
    Dim res%          'holds results
    Dim loopcount%    'loop counting variable
    Dim FileName$     'name of file only
    Dim FromFile$     'name of file filespec
    Dim m$            'message constructor


    'this function performs the actual deletion, confirmation has already
    'been obtained

    'change cursor
    screen.MousePointer = HOURGLASS

    'ensure the screen is redrawn
    DoEvents
    DoEvents
    DoEvents

    If cmdDelete.Value = True Then
    frmmessage.lblMode.Caption = "Deleting Files..."
    frmmessage.Show
    res% = ShowCursor%(True)
    DoEvents
    End If

    For loopcount% = 0 To lbFile(FromIndex%).ListCount - 1
    If lbFile(FromIndex%).Selected(loopcount%) = True Then
        'blank out labels
        pnlFileName.Caption = ""
        frmmessage.lblFile.Caption = FileName$
        DoEvents

        'assign file name
        FileName$ = lbFile(FromIndex%).List(loopcount%)

        'make sure directory is in the correct format
        If Right$(FromDirectory$, 1) <> "\" Then
        FromFile$ = FromDirectory$ + "\" + FileName$
        Else
        FromFile$ = FromDirectory$ + FileName$
        End If

        'show which file is being deleted, if not already done
        If pnlFileName.Caption = "" Then
        frmmessage.lblFile.Caption = FileName$
        pnlFileName.Caption = FileName$
        'doevents to make sure it gets updated in a timely manner
        'and all screen redraws are done
        DoEvents
        End If
```

continues

377

LISTING 21.4. CONTINUED

```
        If cmdPrompt.Value = True And cmdDelete.Value = True Then
        'Prompt for individual files

        m$ = "Delete file " + FileName$ + " ?"
        screen.MousePointer = DEFAULT
        res% = MsgBox(m$, 292, "Warning")
        screen.MousePointer = HOURGLASS
        If res% = IDYES Then
            'actually delete file
            Kill FromFile$
        End If
        Else
        'Don't prompt for individual files

        'actually delete file
        Kill FromFile$
        End If

    End If

    Next loopcount%

    If cmdDelete.Value = True Then
    m$ = "Deletion Complete!"
    MsgBox m$
    End If

    'remove cursor restriction
    CursorClip False, frmmessage
    Unload frmmessage

    'cleanup
    pnlFileName.Caption = ""
    pnlFloodStatus.FloodPercent = 0
    Call Refreshall

    'unselect delete option
    cmdCopy.Value = True

    'reset mouse
    screen.MousePointer = DEFAULT

End Sub
```

THE *DoFastCopy()* PROCEDURE

The DoFastCopy() procedure is the procedure that actually performs the file copying functions. It performs in the Fast Copy mode, which uses the Visual Basic FileCopy function, but doesn't update the progress bar display. The procedure accepts two arguments. The first, ToDirectory$, is the directory to copy to. The second, FromIndex%, is the index of the file list box containing files to copy. Following is a listing of the DoFastCopy() procedure:

LISTING 21.5. MAIN.FRM, DoFastCopy().

```
Sub DoFastCopy (ToDirectory$, FromIndex%)

    'this function performs the actual copy, confirmation has already been
    'obtained

    'declare variables
    Dim FromFile$          'from file with filespec
    Dim ToFile$            'to file with filespec
    Dim FileName$          'filename only
    Dim m$                 'message constructor
    Dim res%               'holds results
    Dim loopcount%         'loop counting variable

    'change cursor
    screen.MousePointer = HOURGLASS

    'ensure the screen is redrawn
    DoEvents
    DoEvents
    DoEvents

    If cmdCopy.Value = True Then
    frmmessage.lblMode.Caption = "Copying Files..."
    ElseIf cmdMove.Value = True Then
    frmmessage.lblMode.Caption = "Moving Files..."
    End If
    frmmessage.Show
    res% = ShowCursor%(True)
    DoEvents

    'loop through each file
    For loopcount% = 0 To lbFile(FromIndex%).ListCount - 1
    If lbFile(FromIndex%).Selected(loopcount%) = True Then
        'blank out labels
        pnlFileName.Caption = ""
        frmmessage.lblFile.Caption = FileName$
        DoEvents

        'assign file name
        FileName$ = lbFile(FromIndex%).List(loopcount%)

        'make sure directory is in the correct format
        If Right$(FromDirectory$, 1) <> "\" Then
        FromFile$ = FromDirectory$ + "\" + FileName$
        Else
        FromFile$ = FromDirectory$ + FileName$
        End If

        If Right$(ToDirectory$, 1) <> "\" Then
        ToFile$ = ToDirectory$ + "\" + FileName$
        Else
        ToFile$ = ToDirectory$ + FileName$
        End If
```

continues

379

LISTING 21.5. CONTINUED

```
        'handle error
        On Error GoTo FastFileError

        If cmdPrompt.Value = True Then
        'Prompt for individual files

        If cmdCopy.Value = True Then
            m$ = "Copy file " + FileName$ + " ?"
        ElseIf cmdMove.Value = True Then
            m$ = "Move file " + FileName$ + " ?"
        End If
        screen.MousePointer = DEFAULT
        res% = MsgBox(m$, 292, "Warning")
        screen.MousePointer = HOURGLASS
        If res% = IDYES Then
            'show which file is being copied, if not already done
            If pnlFileName.Caption = "" Then
            frmmessage.lblFile.Caption = FileName$
            pnlFileName.Caption = FileName$
            'doevents to make sure it gets updated in a timely manner
            'and all screen redraws are done
            DoEvents
            End If


            'perform copy
            FileCopy FromFile$, ToFile$
        End If
        Else
        'Don't prompt for individual files

        'show which file is being copied, if not already done
        If pnlFileName.Caption = "" Then
            frmmessage.lblFile.Caption = FileName$
            pnlFileName.Caption = FileName$
            'doevents to make sure it gets updated in a timely manner
            'and all screen redraws are done
            DoEvents
        End If

        'perform copy
        FileCopy FromFile$, ToFile$

        End If
    FastFileError:
        If Err <> 0 Then
        'an error occurred
        m$ = "Cannot copy file" + Chr$(13)
        m$ = m$ + "Error " + Error$
        MsgBox m$
        End If

    End If
    Next loopcount%
```

```
    'reset cursor
    screen.MousePointer = DEFAULT

    If cmdCopy.Value = True Then
    m$ = "Copying Complete!"
    ElseIf cmdMove.Value = True Then
    m$ = "Moving Complete!"
    End If
    MsgBox m$

    'remove cursor restriction
    CursorClip False, frmmessage
    Unload frmmessage

    pnlFileName.Caption = ""

End Sub
```

THE *DoFastMove()* PROCEDURE

The DoFastMove() procedure is the procedure that actually performs the file moving functions. It performs in the Fast Move mode. It simply calls the Copy function, then the Delete function. Moving can also be performed by using the Visual Basic Name function. It is not used here to save the space of writing a separate procedure. The procedure accepts two arguments. The first, ToDirectory$, is the directory to move to. The second, FromIndex%, is the index of the file list box containing files to move. Following is a listing of the DoFastMove() procedure:

LISTING 21.6. MAIN.FRM, DoFastMove().

```
Sub DoFastMove (ToDirectory$, FromIndex%)

    'moving is simply copying then deleting

    Call DoFastCopy(ToDirectory$, FromIndex%)
    Call DoDelete(FromIndex%)

End Sub
```

THE *DoSlowCopy()* PROCEDURE

The DoSlowCopy() procedure is the procedure that actually performs the file copying functions. It performs in the Slow Copy mode, which opens the file and copies it byte-by-byte. It updates the progress display bar, but can take quite a lot of time to copy, especially with large files. The procedure accepts two arguments. The first, ToDirectory$, is the directory to copy to. The second, FromIndex%, is the index of the file list box containing files to copy. Following is a listing of the DoSlowCopy() procedure:

381

LISTING 21.7. MAIN.FRM, DoSlowCopy().

```
Sub DoSlowCopy (ToDirectory$, FromIndex%)

    'this function performs the actual copy, confirmation has already been
    'obtained

    'declare variables
    Dim FromFile$           'from file name with filespec
    Dim ToFile$             'to file name with filespec
    Dim FileName$           'file name only
    Dim LoopVar&            'loop counting variable
    Dim TheTemp$            'temporary string
    Dim TheLen&             'length variable
    Dim m$                  'message constructor
    Dim loopcount%          'loop counting variable
    Dim res%                'holds results

    'change cursor
    screen.MousePointer = HOURGLASS

    'ensure the screen is redrawn
    DoEvents
    DoEvents
    DoEvents

    If cmdCopy.Value = True Then
    frmmessage.lblMode.Caption = "Copying Files..."
    ElseIf cmdMove.Value = True Then
    frmmessage.lblMode.Caption = "Moving Files..."
    End If
    frmmessage.Show
    res% = ShowCursor%(True)
    DoEvents

    'loop through files
    For loopcount% = 0 To lbFile(FromIndex%).ListCount - 1
    If lbFile(FromIndex%).Selected(loopcount%) = True Then
        'blank out labels
        pnlFileName.Caption = ""
        frmmessage.lblFile.Caption = FileName$
        DoEvents

        'assign file name
        FileName$ = lbFile(FromIndex%).List(loopcount%)

        'make sure directory is in the correct format
        If Right$(FromDirectory$, 1) <> "\" Then
        FromFile$ = FromDirectory$ + "\" + FileName$
        Else
        FromFile$ = FromDirectory$ + FileName$
        End If

        If Right$(ToDirectory$, 1) <> "\" Then
        ToFile$ = ToDirectory$ + "\" + FileName$
        Else
```

```
ToFile$ = ToDirectory$ + FileName$
End If

'handle error
On Error GoTo SlowFileError

If cmdPrompt.Value = True Then
'Prompt for individual files

If cmdCopy.Value = True Then
    m$ = "Copy file " + FileName$ + " ?"
ElseIf cmdMove.Value = True Then
    m$ = "Move file " + FileName$ + " ?"
End If
screen.MousePointer = DEFAULT
res% = MsgBox(m$, 292, "Warning")
screen.MousePointer = HOURGLASS
If res% = IDYES Then

    TheLen& = FileLen(FromFile$)
    Open FromFile$ For Binary Access Read As #1
    Open ToFile$ For Binary Access Write As #2

    'show which file is being copied, if not already done
    If pnlFileName.Caption = "" Then
    frmmessage.lblFile.Caption = FileName$
    pnlFileName.Caption = FileName$
    'doevents to make sure it gets updated in a timely manner
    'and all screen redraws are done
    DoEvents
    End If

    LoopVar& = 1
    Do Until EOF(1)
    TheTemp$ = String$(1, " ")
    Get #1, LoopVar&, TheTemp$
    If EOF(1) Then Exit Do
    Put #2, LoopVar&, TheTemp$
    'update floodpercent, if percentage is different
    'this helps eliminate flicker
    If pnlFloodStatus.FloodPercent <> Int((LoopVar& / TheLen&) * 100) Then
        pnlFloodStatus.FloodPercent = Int((LoopVar& / TheLen&) * 100)
    End If
    LoopVar& = LoopVar& + 1
    Loop
End If
Else
'Don't prompt for individual files

TheLen& = FileLen(FromFile$)
Open FromFile$ For Binary Access Read As #1
Open ToFile$ For Binary Access Write As #2

'show which file is being copied, if not already done
If pnlFileName.Caption = "" Then
    frmmessage.lblFile.Caption = FileName$
```

continues

383

LISTING 21.7. CONTINUED

```
            pnlFileName.Caption = FileName$
            'doevents to make sure it gets updated in a timely manner
            'and all screen redraws are done
            DoEvents
        End If

        LoopVar& = 1
        Do Until EOF(1)
            TheTemp$ = String$(1, " ")
            Get #1, LoopVar&, TheTemp$
            If EOF(1) Then Exit Do
            Put #2, LoopVar&, TheTemp$
            'update floodpercent, if percentage is different
            'this helps elimate flicker
            If pnlFloodStatus.FloodPercent <> Int((LoopVar& / TheLen&) * 100) Then
                pnlFloodStatus.FloodPercent = Int((LoopVar& / TheLen&) * 100)
            End If
            LoopVar& = LoopVar& + 1
        Loop
        End If
SlowFileError:
        If Err <> 0 Then
        'an error occurred
        m$ = "Cannot copy file" + Chr$(13)
        m$ = m$ + "Error " + Error$
        MsgBox m$
        End If
        Close #1
        Close #2

    End If
    Next loopcount%

    'reset cursor
    screen.MousePointer = DEFAULT

    If cmdCopy.Value = True Then
    m$ = "Copying Complete!"
    ElseIf cmdMove.Value = True Then
    m$ = "Moving Complete!"
    End If
    MsgBox m$

    'remove cursor restriction
    CursorClip False, frmmessage
    Unload frmmessage

    pnlFileName.Caption = ""
    pnlFloodStatus.FloodPercent = 0

End Sub
```

THE *DoSLOWMOVE()* PROCEDURE

The DoSlowMove() procedure is the procedure that actually performs the file moving functions. It performs in the Slow Move mode. It simply calls the Copy function, and then the Delete. Moving can also be performed by using the Visual Basic Name function. It is not used here to save the space of writing a separate procedure. The procedure accepts two arguments. The first, ToDirectory$, is the directory to move to. The second, FromIndex%, is the index of the file list box containing files to move. Following is a listing of the DoSlowMove() procedure:

LISTING 21.8. MAIN.FRM, DoSlowMove().

```
Sub DoSlowMove (ToDirectory$, FromIndex%)

    'moving is simply copying then deleting

    Call DoSlowCopy(ToDirectory$, FromIndex%)
    Call DoDelete(FromIndex%)

    Call Refreshall

End Sub
```

THE *REFRESHALL()* PROCEDURE

The Refreshall() procedure refreshes all file controls to make sure the displays reflects the most recent activity. Following is a listing of the Refreshall() procedure:

LISTING 21.9. MAIN.FRM, Refreshall().

```
Sub Refreshall ()

    'this sub refreshes all file and directory lists

    lbDirectory(0).Refresh
    lbDirectory(1).Refresh
    lbFile(0).Refresh
    lbFile(1).Refresh

End Sub
```

THE *CMDCOPY* CONTROL

cmdCopy is the name of the command button control that, when clicked, tells the program to use the Copy mode. The cmdCopy control has code in only one event procedure. It is

- ◆ cmdCopy_Click()

THE *CMDCOPY_CLICK( )* EVENT PROCEDURE

The cmdCopy_Click() event procedure simply assigns a label to pnlMode. Following is a listing of the cmdCopy_Click() event procedure:

LISTING 21.10. MAIN.FRM, cmdCopy_Click().

```
Sub cmdCopy_Click (Value As Integer)

    If Value = True Then
    'assign label
    pnlMode.Caption = "Copy"
    End If

End Sub
```

THE *CMDDELETE* CONTROL

cmdDelete is the name of the command button control that, when clicked, starts the delete action. The cmdDelete control has code only in one event procedure. It is

◆ cmdDelete_Click()

THE *CMDDELETE_CLICK( )* EVENT PROCEDURE

The cmdDelete_Click() event procedure invokes the Delete routine. Following is a listing of the cmdDelete_Click() event procedure:

LISTING 21.11. MAIN.FRM, cmdDelete_Click().

```
Sub cmdDelete_Click (Value As Integer)

    If Value = False Then Exit Sub

    'assign label
    pnlMode.Caption = "Delete"

    'declare variables
    Dim loopcount%  'loop counting variables
    Dim NumFound%   'number of selections found
    Dim m$          'message constructor
    Dim res%        'holds results
    Dim FromIndex%  'from index

    'find out how many items were selected to be deleted
    NumFound% = 0
    For loopcount% = 0 To lbFile(0).ListCount - 1
    If lbFile(0).Selected(loopcount%) = True Then
        NumFound% = NumFound% + 1
        FromIndex% = 0
    End If
```

```
    Next loopcount%

    'if NumFound% is 0, this may not be the list selected, try the other
    'since there can only be one file list selected at a time
    If NumFound% = 0 Then
    For loopcount% = 0 To lbFile(1).ListCount - 1
        If lbFile(1).Selected(loopcount%) = True Then
        NumFound% = NumFound% + 1
        FromIndex% = 1
        End If
    Next loopcount%
    End If

    'see if there are any items selected
    If NumFound% = 0 Then
    m$ = "There are no items selected to DELETE"
    MsgBox m$

    'unselect delete option
    cmdCopy.Value = True
    Exit Sub
    End If

    'verify delete
    m$ = "Are you sure you would like to DELETE" + Chr$(13)

    'appropriately handle plurals(nice touch)
    If NumFound% = 1 Then
    m$ = m$ + Chr$(9) + Trim$(Str$(NumFound%)) + " file" + Chr$(13) + Chr$(13)
    Else
    m$ = m$ + Chr$(9) + Trim$(Str$(NumFound%)) + " files" + Chr$(13) + Chr$(13)
    End If

    m$ = m$ + "FROM " + Chr$(9) + FromDirectory$ + " ?"
    res% = MsgBox(m$, 292, "Warning")
    If res% = IDNO Then
    'unselect delete option
    cmdCopy.Value = True
    Exit Sub
    End If

    Call DoDelete(FromIndex%)

End Sub
```

THE *CMDFAST* CONTROL

cmdFast is the name of the command button control that, when clicked, tells the program to use the Fast mode. The cmdFast control has code only in one event procedure. It is

◆ cmdFast_Click()

THE *CMDFAST_CLICK( )* EVENT PROCEDURE

The cmdFast_Click() event procedure simply assigns a label to pnlSpeed and enables the Status indicator. Following is a listing of the cmdFast_Click() event procedure:

LISTING 21.12. MAIN.FRM, cmdFast_Click().

```
Sub cmdFast_Click (Value As Integer)

    If Value = True Then
    'assign label
    pnlSpeed.Caption = "Fast"

    'disable progress graph
    pnlFloodStatus.Visible = False
    End If

End Sub
```

THE *CMDMOVE* CONTROL

cmdMove is the name of the command button control that, when clicked, tells the program to use the Move mode. The cmdMove control has code only in one event procedure. It is

◆   cmdMove_Click()

THE *CMDMOVE_CLICK( )* EVENT PROCEDURE

The cmdMove_Click() event procedure simply assigns a label to pnlMode. Following is a listing of the cmdMove_Click() event procedure:

LISTING 21.13. MAIN.FRM, cmdMove_Click().

```
Sub cmdMove_Click (Value As Integer)

    If Value = True Then
    'assign label
    pnlMode.Caption = "Move"
    End If

End Sub
```

THE *CMDSLOW* CONTROL

cmdSlow is the name of the command button control that, when clicked, tells the program to use the Slow mode. The cmdSlow control has code only in one event procedure. It is

◆   cmdSlow_Click()

THE *CMDSLOW_CLICK()* EVENT PROCEDURE

The cmdSlow_Click() event procedure simply assigns a label to pnlSpeed and enables the Status indicator. Following is a listing of the cmdSlow_Click() event procedure:

LISTING 21.14. MAIN.FRM, cmdSlow_Click().

```
Sub cmdSlow_Click (Value As Integer)

    If Value = True Then
    'assign label
    pnlSpeed.Caption = "Slow"

    'enable progress graph
    pnlFloodStatus.Visible = True
    End If

End Sub
```

THE *DRIVE1* CONTROL

Drive1 is the name of the drive control array that is only used to populate the directory and file list boxes. The Drive1 control has code only in one event procedure. It is

◆ Drive1_Change()

THE *DRIVE1_CHANGE()* EVENT PROCEDURE

The Drive1_Change() event procedure handles the directory assignment when the drive changes. Following is a listing of the Drive1_Change() event procedure:

LISTING 21.15. MAIN.FRM, Drive1_Change().

```
Sub Drive1_Change (Index As Integer)

    lbDirectory(Index).Path = Drive1(Index).Drive

End Sub
```

THE *FORM* OBJECT

The Form object has code in two event procedures. They are

◆ Form_Load()
◆ Form_Unload()

THE *FORM_LOAD()* EVENT PROCEDURE

The Form_Load() event procedure simply centers the form and sets defaults. Following is a listing of the Form_Load() event procedure:

LISTING 21.16. MAIN.FRM, Form_Load().

```
Sub Form_Load ()

    'center the form
    centerform Me

    'set default options
    cmdCopy.Value = True
    cmdSlow.Value = True
    cmdPrompt.Value = True

End Sub
```

THE *FORM_UNLOAD()* EVENT PROCEDURE

The Form_Unload() event procedure prompts the user to confirm ending the program. Following is a listing of the Form_Unload() event procedure:

LISTING 21.17. MAIN.FRM, Form_Unload().

```
Sub Form_Unload (cancel As Integer)

    'declare variables
    Dim m$
    Dim res%

    m$ = "Are you sure you want to close?"
    res% = MsgBox(m$, 292, "Warning?")
    If res% = IDNO Then
    'cancel
    cancel = True

    'exit
    Exit Sub
    End If

    End

End Sub
```

THE *lbDIRECTORY* CONTROL

lbDirectory is the name of the directory list box control (Dirlistbox) array that lists directories based on the Drive1 Drive control array. The lbDirectory control has code in four event procedures. They are

- ◆ lbDirectory_Change()
- ◆ lbDirectory_DragDrop()
- ◆ lbDirectory_DragOver()
- ◆ lbDirectory_MouseDown()

THE *lbDirectory_Change()* EVENT PROCEDURE

The lbDirectory_Change() event procedure is used to populate the lbFile control array. Following is a listing of the lbDirectory_Change() event procedure:

LISTING 21.18. MAIN.FRM, lbDirectory_Change().

```
Sub lbDirectory_Change (Index As Integer)

    'assign path to file box
    lbFile(Index).Path = lbDirectory(Index).Path

    'assign variable to note where files came from
    FromDirectory$ = lbDirectory(Index).List(lbDirectory(Index).ListIndex)

End Sub
```

THE *lbDirectory_DragDrop()* EVENT PROCEDURE

The lbDirectory_DragDrop() event procedure is the procedure that starts the process (Move or Copy) based on the command buttons selected. Following is a listing of the lbDirectory_DragDrop() event procedure:

LISTING 21.19. MAIN.FRM, lbDirectory_DragDrop().

```
Sub lbDirectory_DragDrop (Index As Integer, Source As Control, X As Single, y As Single)

    'declare variables
    Dim DecodedIndex%       'decoded listindex
    Dim ToDirectory$        'to directory
    Dim loopcount%          'loop counting variable
    Dim NumFound%           'number found
    Dim m$                  'message constructor
    Dim res%                'results
    Dim FromIndex%          'from index

    'drag/drop is invalid for DELETION
    If cmdDelete.Value = True Then Exit Sub

    'find out which index this coordinate equates to
    DecodedIndex% = DecodeRow(Index, y)

    'assign messagebox variables for confirmation
    ToDirectory$ = lbDirectory(Index).List(DecodedIndex%)
```

continues

391

LISTING 21.19. CONTINUED

```
'find out how many items were selected to be moved
NumFound% = 0
For loopcount% = 0 To lbFile(0).ListCount - 1
If lbFile(0).Selected(loopcount%) = True Then
    NumFound% = NumFound% + 1
    FromIndex% = 0
End If
Next loopcount%

'if NumFound% is 0, this may not be the list selected, try the other
'since there can only be one file list selected at a time
If NumFound% = 0 Then
For loopcount% = 0 To lbFile(1).ListCount - 1
    If lbFile(1).Selected(loopcount%) = True Then
    NumFound% = NumFound% + 1
    FromIndex% = 1
    End If
Next loopcount%
End If

'see if there are any items selected
If NumFound% = 0 Then
If cmdCopy.Value = True Then
    m$ = "There are no items selected for COPY"
ElseIf cmdMove.Value = True Then
    m$ = "There are no items selected for MOVE"
End If
MsgBox m$
Exit Sub
End If

'verify copy or move
If cmdCopy.Value = True Then
m$ = "Are you sure you would like to COPY" + Chr$(13)
ElseIf cmdMove.Value = True Then
m$ = "Are you sure you would like to MOVE" + Chr$(13)
End If

'appropriately handle plurals(nice touch)
If NumFound% = 1 Then
m$ = m$ + Chr$(9) + Trim$(Str$(NumFound%)) + " file" + Chr$(13) + Chr$(13)
Else
m$ = m$ + Chr$(9) + Trim$(Str$(NumFound%)) + " files" + Chr$(13) + Chr$(13)
End If

m$ = m$ + "FROM " + Chr$(9) + FromDirectory$ + Chr$(13)
m$ = m$ + "TO " + Chr$(9) + ToDirectory$ + " ?" + Chr$(13)

If FromDirectory$ = ToDirectory$ Then
m$ = "You cannot copy files to the same directory!"
MsgBox m$
Exit Sub
Else
res% = MsgBox(m$, 292, "Warning")
If res% = IDNO Then Exit Sub
```

```
End If

    'determine which modes to use
    If cmdSlow.Value = True Then
    If cmdCopy.Value = True Then
        Call DoSlowCopy(ToDirectory$, FromIndex%)
    ElseIf cmdMove.Value = True Then
        Call DoSlowMove(ToDirectory$, FromIndex%)
    End If
    ElseIf cmdFast.Value = True Then
    If cmdCopy.Value = True Then
        Call DoFastCopy(ToDirectory$, FromIndex%)
    ElseIf cmdMove.Value = True Then
        Call DoFastMove(ToDirectory$, FromIndex%)
    End If
    End If

    Call Refreshall

End Sub
```

 For more information about handling files, refer to Chapter 7, "File Input/Output (I/O)."

THE *lbDirectory_DragOver()* EVENT PROCEDURE

The lbDirectory_DragOver() event procedure is used to determine where the mouse pointer is in the list box. Following is a listing of the lbDirectory_DragOver() event procedure:

LISTING 21.20. MAIN.FRM, lbDirectory_DragOver().

```
Sub lbDirectory_DragOver (Index As Integer, Source As Control, X As Single, y As Single,
State As Integer)

    'declare variables
    Dim TheIndex%          'current index

    TheIndex% = DecodeRow(Index, y)
    On Error GoTo indexerror
    If TheIndex% < lbDirectory(Index).ListCount Then
    lbDirectory(Index).ListIndex = TheIndex%
    End If

    'exit
    Exit Sub

indexerror:
    TheIndex% = TheIndex% + 1
    Resume

End Sub
```

THE *lbDirectory_MouseDown()* EVENT PROCEDURE

The lbDirectory_MouseDown() event procedure is one of the procedures used to start the dragging operation, if the right mouse button is clicked. The other is lbFile_MouseDown(). Following is a listing of the lbDirectory_MouseDown() event procedure:

LISTING 21.21. MAIN.FRM, lbDirectory_MouseDown().

```
Sub lbDirectory_MouseDown (Index As Integer, Button As Integer, Shift As Integer, X As
Single, y As Single)

    'declare variables
    Dim loopcount%        'loop counting variable

    If Button = RIGHT_BUTTON Then
    'start drag/drop
    lbDirectory(Index).Drag
    End If

    'unselect opposite lists
    If Index = 0 Then
    'unselect each file item
    For loopcount% = 0 To lbFile(1).ListCount - 1
        lbFile(1).Selected(loopcount%) = False
    Next loopcount%

    Else
    'unselect each file item
    For loopcount% = 0 To lbFile(0).ListCount - 1
        lbFile(0).Selected(loopcount%) = False
    Next loopcount%
    End If

End Sub
```

THE *lbFile* CONTROL

lbFile is the name of the file list box control array that lists files in the directory specified. The lbFile control has code only in one event procedure. It is

◆ lbFile_MouseDown()

THE *lbFile_MouseDown()* EVENT PROCEDURE

The lbFile_MouseDown() event procedure is one of two procedures used to start the dragging operation, if the right mouse button is clicked. The other is lbDirectory_MouseDown(). Following is a listing of the lbFile_MouseDown() event procedure:

LISTING 21.22. MAIN.FRM, `lbFile_MouseDown()`.

```
Sub lbFile_MouseDown (Index As Integer, Button As Integer, Shift As Integer, X As Single,
y As Single)

    'declare variables
    Dim loopcount%  'loop counting variable

    If Button = RIGHT_BUTTON Then
    lbFile(Index).Drag

    'assign variable to note where files came from
    FromDirectory$ = lbDirectory(Index).List(lbDirectory(Index).ListIndex)
    End If

    'unselect opposite lists
    If Index = 0 Then
    'unselect each file item
    For loopcount% = 0 To lbFile(1).ListCount - 1
        lbFile(1).Selected(loopcount%) = False
    Next loopcount%
    Else
    'unselect each file item
    For loopcount% = 0 To lbFile(0).ListCount - 1
        lbFile(0).Selected(loopcount%) = False
    Next loopcount%
    End If

End Sub
```

THE *MENU* OBJECT

The menu object was created using Visual Basic's built-in Menu editor. It has code associated with two Click() event procedures. They are

◆ menu_about()

◆ menu_exit()

THE *MENU_ABOUT_CLICK()* PROCEDURE

The menu_about_click() procedure simply shows the about form for program information. Following is a listing of the menu_about_Click() procedure:

LISTING 21.23. MAIN.FRM, `menu_about_Click()`.

```
Sub menu_about_Click ()

    'show about form
    frmAbout.Show MODAL

End Sub
```

THE *MENU_EXIT_CLICK( )* PROCEDURE

The menu_exit_click() procedure ends the application by unloading the form. Following is a listing of the menu_exit_click() procedure:

LISTING 21.24. MAIN.FRM, menu_exit_Click().

```
Sub menu_exit_Click ()

    'close application
    Unload frmMain

End Sub
```

THE MESSAGE.FRM FILE

MESSAGE.FRM is one of three forms in this application. It is the form that is used to display a message as to the status of the copy or move operation. Figure 21.2 presents this form as it appears at runtime. It is fundamentally no different at design time, so it is not shown. Table 21.2 lists all the relevant properties of each control on the form that have been changed from their standard default values. The MESSAGE.FRM file is contained on the CD accompanying this book in the CHAP21 subdirectory.

TABLE 21.2. PROPERTIES OF EACH CONTROL ON MESSAGE.FRM.

Object	Control Type	Property	Value
frmMessage	Form	BackColor	&H00808000&
		BorderStyle	FixedDouble
		Height	1530
		Left	1140
		MaxButton	False
		MinButton	False
		Top	4650
		Width	2625
lblFile	Label	Alignment	Center
		BackColor	&H00808000&
		FontBold	True
		FontItalic	False
		FontName	"MS Sans Serif"

Object	Control Type	Property	Value
		FontSize	13.5
		ForeColor	&H0000C0C0&
		Height	375
		Left	120
		Top	480
		Width	2295
lblMode	Label	Alignment	Center
		BackColor	&H00808000&
		FontBold	True
		FontItalic	False
		FontName	"MS Sans Serif"
		FontSize	13.5
		ForeColor	&H0000C0C0&
		Height	375
		Left	120
		Top	120
		Width	2295

FUNCTION, SUBROUTINE, AND EVENT PROCEDURES

There are several procedures of code for each object(control) that comprise this form. Each is listed in the following sections.

THE *(GENERAL)* OBJECT

The (general) object contains form level declarations and no form level procedures. The procedure for the (general) object is

◆ (declarations)

THE *(DECLARATIONS)* PROCEDURE

The (declarations) procedure contains only one line of declarations used in the form, MESSAGE.FRM. It is only to allow for variable syntax checking and forcing the declaration of variables in each procedure. All declarations are in the CHAP21.BAS file. Following is a listing of the (declarations) procedure:

397

LISTING 21.25. MESSAGE.FRM, (general) (declarations).

```
Option Explicit
```

THE *FORM* OBJECT

The Form object has code in two event procedures. They are

◆ Form_Activate()

◆ Form_Load()

THE *FORM_ACTIVATE()* EVENT PROCEDURE

The Form_Activate() event is used to restrict the cursor movement because the form is not unloaded each time. Following is a listing of the Form_Activate() event procedure:

LISTING 21.26. MESSAGE.FRM, Form_Activate().

```
Sub Form_Activate ()

    'clip cursor
    CursorClip True, Me

End Sub
```

THE *FORM_LOAD()* EVENT PROCEDURE

The Form_Load() event is used to center the form and restrict the cursor movement. Following is a listing of the Form_Load() event procedure:

LISTING 21.27. MESSAGE.FRM, Form_Load().

```
Sub Form_Load ()

    'center form
    centerform Me

    'clip cursor
    CursorClip True, Me

End Sub
```

THE ABOUT.FRM FILE

ABOUT.FRM is one of three forms in this application. It shows information about the application. Figure 21.4 presents the form as it appears at runtime. Fundamentally, there is no difference in the form at design time, so it is not presented. Table 21.3 lists all the relevant properties of each control on the form that have been changed from their standard default values. The ABOUT.FRM file is contained on the CD accompanying this book in the CHAP21 subdirectory.

FIGURE 21.4.

File Copy application About Form at runtime.

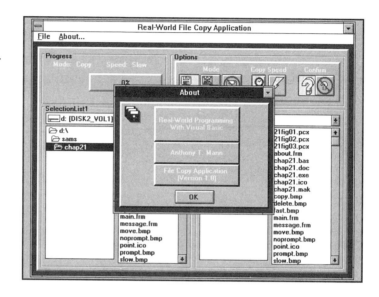

TABLE 21.3. PROPERTIES OF EACH CONTROL ON ABOUT.FRM.

Object	Control Type	Property	Value
frmAbout	Form	BackColor	&H00404000&
		Caption	"About"
		Height	3525
		Left	1035
		MaxButton	False
		MinButton	False
		Top	1140
		Width	4545
pnlMain	SSPanel	BackColor	&H00C0C0C0&
		BevelWidth	3
		Caption	""
		Font3D	None

continues

TABLE 21.3. CONTINUED

Object	Control Type	Property	Value
		ForeColor	&H00C0C0C0&
		Height	2195
		Left	121
		RoundedCorners	False
		ShadowColor	Black
		Top	121
		Width	4215
pnl1	SSPanel	BackColor	&H00C0C0C0&
		BevelWidth	3
		Caption	"Real-World Programming With Visual Basic"
		Font3D	None
		ForeColor	&H0000FFFF&
		Height	975
		Left	960
		RoundedCorners	False
		ShadowColor	Black
		Top	121
		Width	2415
pnl2	SSPanel	BackColor	&H00C0C0C0&
		BevelWidth	3
		Caption	"Anthony T. Mann"
		Font3D	None
		ForeColor	&H0000FFFF&
		Height	615
		Left	960
		RoundedCorners	False
		ShadowColor	Black
		Top	1080
		Width	2415
pnl3	SSPanel	BackColor	&H00C0C0C0&

Object	Control Type	Property	Value
		BevelWidth	3
		Caption	"File Copy Application (Version 1.0)"
		Font3D	None
		ForeColor	&H0000FFFF&
		Height	615
		Left	960
		RoundedCorners	False
		ShadowColor	Black
		Top	1680
		Width	2415
cmdOK	CommandButton	Caption	"OK"
		Height	375
		Left	1680
		Top	2400
		Width	1095
pictAbout	PictureBox	Autosize	True
		BackColor	&H00C0C0C0&
		BorderStyle	None
		Height	615
		Left	121
		Top	121
		Width	735

FUNCTION, SUBROUTINE, AND EVENT PROCEDURES

There are several procedures of code for each object(control) that comprise this form. Each is listed in the following sections.

The (general) object contains only one form level declaration and no form level procedures. The procedures for the (general) object is

◆ (declarations)

401

THE *(DECLARATIONS)* PROCEDURE

The (declarations) procedure contains only one line of declarations used in the form, ABOUT.FRM. It is only to allow for variable syntax checking and forcing the declaration of variables in each procedure. Following is a listing of the (declarations) procedure:

LISTING 21.28. ABOUT.FRM, (general)(declarations).

```
Option Explicit
```

THE *CMDOK* CONTROL

cmdOK is the name of the command button control that, when clicked, closes the frmAbout form. The cmdOK control has code only in one event procedure. It is

◆ cmdOK_Click()

THE *CMDOK_CLICK()* EVENT PROCEDURE

The cmdOK_Click() event procedure simply unloads the form. Following is a listing of the cmdOK_Click() event procedure:

LISTING 21.29. ABOUT.FRM, cmdOK_Click().

```
Sub cmdOK_Click ()

        'unload
        Unload frmAbout

End Sub
```

THE *FORM* OBJECT

The Form object has code in only one event procedure. It is

◆ Form_Load()

THE *FORM_LOAD()* EVENT PROCEDURE

The Form_Load() event procedure centers the form and assigns an icon to the pictAbout control. Following is a listing of the Form_Load() event procedure:

LISTING 21.30. ABOUT.FRM, Form_Load().

```
Sub Form_Load ()

        'center form
```

```
    CenterForm Me

    'load icon
    pictAbout.Picture = frmMain.Icon

End Sub
```

THE CHAP21.BAS FILE

CHAP21.BAS is the module that contains application level variables and procedures. The CHAP21.BAS file is contained on the CD accompanying this book in the CHAP21 subdirectory.

FUNCTION, SUBROUTINE, AND EVENT PROCEDURES

There are several procedures of code for each object(control) that comprise this module. Each is listed in the following sections.

The (general) object contains application level variables and procedures. The procedures for the (general) object are:

- ◆ (declarations)
- ◆ CenterForm()
- ◆ CursorClip()

THE *(DECLARATIONS)* PROCEDURE

The (declarations) procedure contains variables and API declarations used in the application. Following is a listing of the (declarations) procedure:

LISTING 21.31. CHAP21.BAS, (general)(declarations).

```
Option Explicit

'declare rectangle
Type RECT
    Left As Integer
    Top As Integer
    Right As Integer
    Bottom As Integer
End Type

'windows API's
Declare Function ShowCursor% Lib "User" (ByVal bShow%)

'For CursorClip
Declare Sub ClipCursorRect Lib "User" Alias "ClipCursor" (lpRect As RECT)
Declare Sub ClipCursorClear Lib "User" Alias "ClipCursor" (ByVal lpRect&)
Declare Sub SetCursorPos Lib "User" (ByVal x%, ByVal y%)
```

continues

LISTING 21.31. CONTINUED

```
Declare Sub GetWindowRect Lib "User" (ByVal hWnd As Integer, lpRect As RECT)

' Button parameter masks
Global Const LEFT_BUTTON = 1
Global Const RIGHT_BUTTON = 2
Global Const MIDDLE_BUTTON = 4

' MsgBox return values
Global Const IDYES = 6                     ' Yes button pressed
Global Const IDNO = 7                      ' No button pressed

'cursor values
Global Const HOURGLASS = 11                'hourglass cursor
Global Const DEFAULT = 0                    'default cursor

Global Const MODAL = 1
```

For more information about Windows APIs, see Chapter 3, "Calling Windows APIs and DLLs."

THE *CenterForm()* PROCEDURE

The CenterForm() procedure simply centers the form in the client area upon form loading. The CenterForm() procedure accepts one argument, F. It is the actual form to be centered. Following is a listing of the CenterForm() procedure:

LISTING 21.32. CHAP21.BAS, CenterForm().

```
Sub CenterForm (f As Form)

    f.Move (screen.Width - f.Width) / 2, (screen.Height - f.Height) / 2

End Sub
```

For more information on manipulating graphics and forms, refer to Chapter 5, "Graphics."

THE *CursorClip()* PROCEDURE

The CursorClip() procedure is the name of the procedure that actually limits the cursor to an area of the perimeter of a form. The procedure accepts two arguments. The first, Value, is a boolean expression: True to Clip, False to Unclip. The second, f, is the form object that the cursor should be limited to. Following is a listing of the CursorClip() procedure:

A boolean expression is one that evaluates to either True or False.

LISTING 21.33. CHAP21.BAS, CursorClip().

```
Sub CursorClip (Value As Integer, f As Form)

    'declare variables
    Dim CopyRect As RECT      'declare rectangle
    Const Cl& = 0             'declare clear constant

    'turns the clip cursor on
    If Value = True Then
    'Get current window position (in pixels) and compute width & height
    GetWindowRect f.hWnd, CopyRect
    'clip the cursor
    ClipCursorRect CopyRect
    'move cursor to center of form
    SetCursorPos ((CopyRect.Right - CopyRect.Left) / 2) + CopyRect.Left,
    ((CopyRect.Bottom - CopyRect.Top) / 2) + CopyRect.Top
    'turns the clip cursor off
    Else
    ClipCursorClear Cl&
    End If

End Sub
```

THE CHAP21.ICO FILE

This file contains the icon that has been attached to the form at design time. The CHAP21.ICO file is contained on the CD accompanying this book in the CHAP21 subdirectory.

FIGURE 21.5.
*File Copy application
Form icon.*

THE POINT.ICO FILE

This file contains the icon that is used when a drag/drop operation occurs. The POINT.ICO file is contained on the CD accompanying this book in the CHAP21 subdirectory.

FIGURE 21.6.
*File Copy application
Drag icon.*

THE PROMPT.BMP FILE

This file contains the bitmap used to represent that the user wants to be prompted for each file. The PROMPT.BMP file is contained on the CD accompanying this book in the CHAP21 subdirectory.

FIGURE 21.7.
File Copy application
Prompt Bitmap.

THE NOPROMPT.BMP FILE

This file contains the bitmap used to represent that the user does NOT want to be prompted for each file. The NOPROMPT.BMP file is contained on the CD accompanying this book in the CHAP21 subdirectory.

FIGURE 21.8.
File Copy application
No Prompt Bitmap.

THE MOVE.BMP FILE

This file contains the bitmap used to represent that the user wants to select the Move mode. The MOVE.BMP file is contained on the CD accompanying this book in the CHAP21 subdirectory.

FIGURE 21.9.
File Copy application
Move Bitmap.

THE COPY.BMP FILE

This file contains the bitmap used to represent that the user wants to select the Copy mode. The COPY.BMP file is contained on the CD accompanying this book in the CHAP21 subdirectory.

FIGURE 21.10.
File Copy application
Copy Bitmap.

THE DELETE.BMP FILE

This file contains the bitmap used to represent that the user wants to select the Delete mode. The DELETE.BMP file is contained on the CD accompanying this book in the CHAP21 subdirectory.

FIGURE 21.11.
File Copy application
Delete Bitmap.

THE FAST.BMP FILE

This file contains the bitmap used to represent that the user wants to select the Fast mode. The FAST.BMP file is contained on the CD accompanying this book in the CHAP21 subdirectory.

FIGURE 21.12.
File Copy application
Fast Bitmap.

THE SLOW.BMP FILE

This file contains the bitmap used to represent that the user wants to select the Slow mode. The SLOW.BMP file is contained on the CD accompanying this book in the CHAP21 subdirectory.

FIGURE 21.13.
File Copy application
Slow Bitmap.

THE CHAP21.EXE FILE

This is the executable file that is distributable. If you distribute this application, you must include the following files:

◆ CHAP21.EXE
◆ VBRUN300.DLL
◆ THREED.VBX
◆ GAUGE.VBX

The CHAP21.EXE file and source files are contained on the CD accompanying this book in the CHAP21 subdirectory, while all DLLs and VBXs are in the RESOURCE subdirectory.

THE UNCLIP.EXE FILE

This is the executable file that restores the cursor to its original size (full screen) if the application crashes. If this happens, it has to be run from the Program Manager by using the keyboard.

The source files for the program are not shown separately in this chapter. The routine used to create the UNCLIP.EXE program is the `CursorClip` routine in the CHAP21.BAS file. The only difference is that the program uses the branch as if the boolean passed in were `f`. The UNCLIP.EXE program is contained on the CD accompanying this book.

RELATING THE FILE COPY APPLICATION TO YOUR APPLICATION

The File Copy application shows how to do many things. Among these, it demonstrates the use of opening files and special uses of the mouse (right mouse button).

You can use the techniques in this application to visually enhance your applications. Enhancing can be as simple as providing bitmaps on a ribbon button or preventing events from happening by limiting the cursor. If the cursor is limited, however, you must remember that the cursor is limited system-wide. It is not only for this application. If for any reason the application crashes, the cursor will be stuck in the rectangle with no way to get out. That's why the program UNCLIP.EXE is provided on the CD in the CHAP21 directory. You can run it from the Program Manager by using the keyboard, and the mouse will be restored.

 For more information on restricting mouse movement, refer to Chapter 4, "The Mouse."

FINAL NOTES

This application was created on a standard VGA display using 16 colors. Your particular hardware could have adverse effects on the code the way it is written. You may need to modify it slightly.

ICON PRINTING

APPLICATION

THE ICON PRINTING APPLICATION IS AN EXAMPLE OF USING GRAPHICS AND PRINTING. THE APPLICATION ALLOWS YOU TO VIEW AND PRINT UP TO 60 ICONS AT A TIME. FIGURE 22.1 SHOWS THE MAIN SCREEN (MAIN.FRM) AT RUNTIME.

FIGURE 22.1.
Icon Printing applica-
tion MAIN.FRM at
runtime.

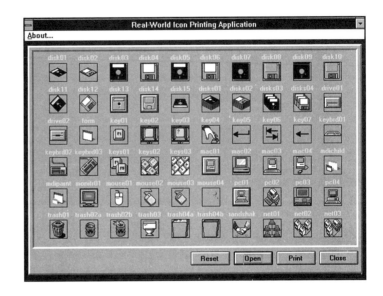

To use the application, select the Open command button. This invokes the common dialog box to multiselect icon files. The common dialog box returns a string of files that must be parsed and opened individually. The string returned has a limit of 256 characters. For example, you cannot open 100 files at once, unless the sum of the length of each file is 256 characters or less. As an average, you can open 15 files at once. You can reopen the common dialog box to populate up to the rest of the 60 files.

By default, the maximum number of characters that can be returned in a common dialog box string is 256, as stated earlier. However, you can change the common dialog box property, MaxFileSize, to allow for more characters, up to a maximum of 2048.

CODE LISTINGS

The Icon Printing application contains the following files and listings:

◆ CHAP22.MAK
◆ MAIN.FRM
◆ ABOUT.FRM
◆ CHAP22.ICO
◆ CHAP22.EXE

THE CHAP22.MAK FILE

CHAP22.MAK is the project file for the Icon Printing application, CHAP22.EXE. It contains a listing of all the files necessary to load the project into Visual Basic. The CHAP22.MAK file is contained on the CD accompanying this book in the CHAP22 subdirectory. The file listing is

LISTING 22.1. CHAP22.MAK.

```
MAIN.FRM
THREED.VBX
CMDIALOG.VBX
ABOUT.FRM
ProjWinSize=146,403,248,215
ProjWinShow=2
IconForm="frmMain"
Title="Icon Print"
ExeName="CHAP22.EXE"
```

THE MAIN.FRM FILE

MAIN.FRM is one of two forms in this application. It is the startup form for the application as well as the form used to display and print the icons. Figure 22.1 shows the form as it appears at runtime. Figure 22.2 shows the form as it appears at design time. Table 22.1 lists all the relevant properties of each control on the form that have been changed from their standard default values. The MAIN.FRM file is contained on the CD accompanying this book in the CHAP22 subdirectory.

FIGURE 22.2.
Icon Printing application MAIN.FRM at design time.

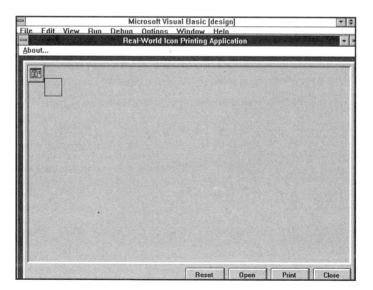

TABLE 22.1. PROPERTIES OF EACH CONTROL ON MAIN.FRM.

Object	Control Type	Property	Value
frmMain	Form	BackColor	&H00404000&
		Caption	"Real-World Icon Printing Application"
		Height	7185
		Icon	"CHAP22.ICO"
		Left	300
		MaxButton	False
		Top	315
		Width	9650
Panel3D1	SSPanel	BackColor	&H00C0C0C0&
		BevelWidth	3
		Font3D	None
		Height	6255
		Left	120
		Top	120
		Width	9375
pnlPrintingLabel	SSPanel	BackColor	&H00C0C0C0&
		BevelOuter	None
		BevelWidth	0
		BorderWidth	0
		Font3D	None
		FontBold	True
		FontItalic	False
		FontName	"MS Sans Serif"
		FontSize	12
		ForeColor	&H0000FFFF&
		Height	375
		Left	120
		Top	5640
		Width	4215
pnlIconFrame	SSPanel	BackColor	&H00C0C0C0&
		BevelOuter	Inset

Object	Control Type	Property	Value
		BevelWidth	3
		Font3D	None
		Height	5415
		Left	120
		Top	120
		Width	9135
pnlLabel	SSPanel	BackColor	&H00C0C0C0&
		BevelOuter	None
		BevelWidth	0
		BorderWidth	0
		Font3D	None
		Height	195
		Index	0
		Left	360
		Top	120
		Width	735
pictIcon	PictureBox	AutoSize	True
		BackColor	&H00C0C0C0&
		Height	495
		Index	0
		Left	480
		Top	360
		Width	495
cmdReset	CommandButton	Caption	"Reset"
		Height	375
		Left	4560
		Top	5640
		Width	1095
cmdPrint	CommandButton	Caption	"Print"
		Height	375
		Left	6960
		Top	5640

continues   413

TABLE 22.1. CONTINUED

Object	Control Type	Property	Value
		Width	1095
cmdOpen	CommandButton	Caption	"Open"
		Height	375
		Left	5760
		Top	5640
		Width	1095
cmdClose	CommandButton	Caption	"Close"
		Height	375
		Left	8160
		Top	5640
		Width	1095
cmFileDialog	CommonDialog	Left	0
		Top	0
menu_about	Menu	Caption	"&About..."

FUNCTION, SUBROUTINE, AND EVENT PROCEDURES

There are several procedures of code for each object(control) that comprise this form. Each is listed in the following sections.

THE (GENERAL) OBJECT

The general object contains declarations and procedures at the form level. The procedures for the (general) object are

- ◆ (declarations)
- ◆ CenterForm()
- ◆ FindFont()
- ◆ PopulatePicture()
- ◆ PrintIcon()

THE (DECLARATIONS) PROCEDURE

The (declarations) procedure contains form level declarations. Following is a listing of the (declarations) procedure:

LISTING 22.2. MAIN.FRM, (General)(Declarations).

```
Option Explicit

Dim IconIndex%    'holds number of picture icon control array indexes
Dim FontFound%    'if true, then printer font,size 6 was found
Dim Printing%     'flag if currently printing

Const WIDTHFACTOR = 345      'horizontal space between picture boxes
Const HEIGHTFACTOR = 345     'vertical space between picture boxes
Const BORDERFACTOR = 225     'width of border holding picture boxes
Const MODAL = 1

' MsgBox return values
Const IDYES = 6                  ' Yes button pressed
Const IDNO = 7                   ' No button pressed

'cursor values
Const HOURGLASS = 11             'hourglass cursor
Const DEFAULT = 0               'default cursor

'common dialog constants
Const OFN_ALLOWMULTISELECT = &H200&
Const OFN_PATHMUSTEXIST = &H800&
Const OFN_FILEMUSTEXIST = &H1000&
Const DLG_FILE_OPEN = 1
```

THE *CENTERFORM()* PROCEDURE

The CenterForm() procedure simply centers the form in the client area. This procedure also exists in the ABOUT.FRM. This is because it is not worth the overhead of having a separate BAS file for only this one procedure. Following is a listing of the CenterForm() procedure:

LISTING 22.3. MAIN.FRM, CenterForm().

```
Sub CenterForm (f As Form)

    'center the form
    f.Move (screen.Width - f.Width) / 2, (screen.Height - f.Height) / 2

End Sub
```

THE *FINDFONT()* PROCEDURE

The FindFont() procedure tests to see if the font is actually found on the printer. The procedure is also a function that returns a boolean (true or false), indicating if the font was found on the printer (true) or not (false). Following is a listing of the FindFont() procedure:

415

LISTING 22.4. MAIN.FRM, FindFont().

```
Function FindFont () As Integer

    'declare variables
    Dim loopcount%         'looping variable

    'there could be a printer font error
    On Error GoTo fonterror

    'find out which fonts exist for printer, and use first available in size 6
    For loopcount% = 0 To printer.FontCount - 1
        'assign to first available font
        printer.FontName = printer.Fonts(loopcount%)

        'assign to size 6
        printer.FontSize = 6

        'test to see if 6 is still assigned, if so, exit loop
        If printer.FontSize = 6 Then

            'set variable flag to print text in print routine
            FontFound% = True

            'exit function
            FindFont = True
            Exit Function
        End If

    Next loopcount%

    'font was not found
    FindFont = False
    Exit Function

fonterror:
    'an error occurred
    Resume Next

End Function
```

THE *POPULATEPICTURE()* PROCEDURE

The PopulatePicture() procedure loads a picture file in a picture box and positions the picture box in the proper location based on the last picture box position. The procedure accepts one argument, WhichFile$, which is the name of the icon to populate. Following is a listing of the PopulatePicture() procedure:

LISTING 22.5. MAIN.FRM, PopulatePicture().

```
Sub PopulatePicture (ByVal WhichFile$)

    'declare variables
    Dim pos%                'holds position
    Dim TempString$         'holds temporary string

    'only display 60 list boxes·due to memory constraints
    If IconIndex% = 59 Then
        MsgBox "Only 60 Icons can be displayed"
        Exit Sub
    End If

    'increment to next icon index
    IconIndex% = IconIndex% + 1

'FORMAT PICTURE AND LABEL
    '0 is already loaded at design time
    If IconIndex% <> 0 Then
        Load pictIcon(IconIndex%)
        Load pnlLabel(IconIndex%)
    End If
    pictIcon(IconIndex%).Visible = True
    pnlLabel(IconIndex%).Visible = True

    'see if this picture box will fit on this line
    If IconIndex% <> 0 Then
        If pictIcon(IconIndex%).Width + pictIcon(IconIndex% - 1).Left +
pictIcon(IconIndex% - 1).Width + WIDTHFACTOR < pnlIconFrame.Width - BORDERFACTOR Then

            'It WILL fit on the line
            'position picture box
            pictIcon(IconIndex%).Left = pictIcon(IconIndex% - 1).Left +
pictIcon(IconIndex% - 1).Width + WIDTHFACTOR
            pictIcon(IconIndex%).Top = pictIcon(IconIndex% - 1).Top

        Else
            'It Won't fit on the line - use next line
            pictIcon(IconIndex%).Left = pictIcon(0).Left
            pictIcon(IconIndex%).Top = pictIcon(IconIndex% - 1).Top + pictIcon(IconIndex%
- 1).Height + HEIGHTFACTOR
        End If

            'position label box
            pnlLabel(IconIndex%).Left = pictIcon(IconIndex%).Left -
((pnlLabel(IconIndex%).Width - pictIcon(IconIndex%).Width) / 2)
            pnlLabel(IconIndex%).Top = pictIcon(IconIndex%).Top - BORDERFACTOR
    End If

'POPULATE PICTURE AND LABEL WITH PICTURE AND TEXT
    pictIcon(IconIndex%).Picture = LoadPicture(WhichFile$)
```

continues

417

LISTING 22.5. CONTINUED

```
'find position of "."
pos% = InStr(WhichFile$, ".")
TempString$ = LCase$(Left$(WhichFile$, pos% - 1))

'cycle through string to remove "\"'s to list file name above picture
Do While InStr(TempString$, "\") <> 0
    pos% = InStr(TempString$, "\")
    TempString$ = Right$(TempString$, Len(TempString$) - pos%)
Loop

'assign label with parsed string
pnlLabel(IconIndex%).Caption = TempString$

End Sub
```

THE *PRINTICON()* PROCEDURE

The PrintIcon() procedure actually prints the icon. The procedure accepts two arguments. The first, WhichIcon, is the picturebox that has the icon loaded into it. The second, Index%, is the index of the picturebox. Following is a listing of the PrintIcon() procedure:

LISTING 22.6. MAIN.FRM, PrintIcon().

```
Sub PrintIcon (WhichIcon As PictureBox, ByVal Index%)

    'declare variables
    Dim ScrResX       'x - screen resolution
    Dim ScrResY       'y - screen resolution
    Dim XLoop%        'x looping variable
    Dim YLoop%        'y looping variable
    Dim XYColor       'color of individual point
    Dim XAdjust       'x position accounting for screen resolution
    Dim YAdjust       'y position accounting for screen resolution
    Dim m$            'message constructor

    'set constant
    Const OFFSET = 1000

    'set current coordinates
    printer.CurrentX = 0
    printer.CurrentY = 0

    'determine screen resolution
    ScrResX = screen.TwipsPerPixelX
    ScrResY = screen.TwipsPerPixelY

    'set mode to pixels
    WhichIcon.ScaleMode = 3

    'set printing caption
```

```
    pnlPrintingLabel.Caption = "Printing " + UCase$(pnlLabel(Index%)) + "..."

    'Cycle through y coordinates
    For YLoop% = 0 To (WhichIcon.ScaleHeight - 1)
        'assign y coordinate, based on screen resolution
        YAdjust = WhichIcon.Top + (YLoop% * ScrResY)

        'cycle through x coordinates
        For XLoop% = 0 To (WhichIcon.ScaleWidth - 1)
            'assign x coordinate, based on screen resolution
            XAdjust = WhichIcon.Left + OFFSET + (XLoop% * ScrResX)

            'assign particular point to determine color
            XYColor = WhichIcon.Point(XLoop%, YLoop%)

            check to see if window moved
            If XYColor < 0 Then
                XYColor = 7
                m$ = "The window has been moved off the screen." + Chr$(13)
                m$ = m$ + "The icons may not print correctly"
                MsgBox m$
                'center form
                CenterForm Me
                'force repaint
                Me.Refresh
            End If
            'if color is not white, print point, using screen resolution
            If XYColor <> QBColor(7) Then
                printer.Line (XAdjust, YAdjust)-Step(ScrResX, ScrResY), XYColor, BF
            End If
        Next XLoop%
        DoEvents
    Next YLoop%

    'print font, if font was found
    If FontFound% = True Then
        'print the icon title
        If WhichIcon.Width > printer.TextWidth(pnlLabel(Index%)) Then
            'icon size is greater than text size
            printer.CurrentX = WhichIcon.Left + OFFSET + ((WhichIcon.Width -
printer.TextWidth(pnlLabel(Index%))) / 2)
        ElseIf WhichIcon.Width <= printer.TextWidth(pnlLabel(Index%)) Then
            'icon size is less than or equal to text size
            printer.CurrentX = WhichIcon.Left + OFFSET -
((printer.TextWidth(pnlLabel(Index%)) - WhichIcon.Width) / 2)
        End If

        printer.CurrentY = WhichIcon.Top + WhichIcon.Height + 100
        printer.Print pnlLabel(Index%)
    End If

    'reset printing caption
    pnlPrintingLabel.Caption = ""

End Sub
```

The reason for the preceding code to check for the XYColor being less than 0 is necessary because if the window is moved or another window is on top of the icon form, the icon won't be printed correctly. It is for this reason that a DoEvents statement is not used. It prevents the user from interacting with the icon form while it is being printed.

THE *CMDCLOSE* CONTROL

cmdClose is the name of the command button control that, when clicked, closes the application by calling the form_unload() event. The cmdClose control has code only in one event procedure. It is

◆ cmdClose_Click()

THE *CMDCLOSE_CLICK()* EVENT PROCEDURE

Following is a listing of the cmdClose_Click() event procedure:

LISTING 22.7. MAIN.FRM, cmdClose_Click().

```
Sub cmdClose_Click ()

    'close application
    Unload frmMain

End Sub
```

THE *CMDOPEN* CONTROL

cmdOpen is the name of the command button control that, when clicked, invokes the common dialog box to open the icon files. The cmdOpen control has code only in one event procedure. It is

◆ cmdOpen_Click()

THE *CMDOPEN_CLICK()* EVENT PROCEDURE

Following is a listing of the cmdOpen_Click() event procedure:

LISTING 22.8. MAIN.FRM, cmdOpen_Click().

```
Sub cmdOpen_Click ()

    'declare variables
    Dim pos%              'holds string position
    Dim TheDirectory$     'holds current directory
    Dim FileString$       'holds string of files to load
```

```
Dim TheFile$          'holds individual file

'handle error
On Error GoTo OpenError

'set properties
cmFileDialog.Filter = "Icon Files|*.ICO"
cmFileDialog.FilterIndex = 0
cmFileDialog.DialogTitle = "Open Icon File"
cmFileDialog.Flags = OFN_ALLOWMULTISELECT Or OFN_FILEMUSTEXIST Or OFN_PATHMUSTEXIST

cmFileDialog.Filename = ""

'invoke common dialog
cmFileDialog.Action = DLG_FILE_OPEN

'open file
If cmFileDialog.Filename <> "" Then

    'find out if there is a space in the returned file name
    'if there is, then there were multiple files selected
    pos% = InStr(cmFileDialog.Filename, " ")
    If pos% = 0 Then
        'there were no spaces, only one file was selected

        'populate picture box
        Call PopulatePicture(cmFileDialog.Filename)

    Else
        'there were spaces - multiple files were selected
        TheDirectory$ = Left$(cmFileDialog.Filename, pos% - 1)
        'make sure directory is in proper format
        If Right$(TheDirectory$, 1) <> "\" Then
            TheDirectory$ = TheDirectory$ + "\"
        End If
        FileString$ = Right$(cmFileDialog.Filename, Len(cmFileDialog.Filename) -
        pos%)

        'loop through string, parsing for file names and fill picture boxes
        Do While FileString$ <> ""
            pos% = InStr(FileString$, " ")
            If pos% > 0 Then
                'assign file
                TheFile$ = Left$(FileString$, pos% - 1)
            Else
                'assign file
                TheFile$ = FileString$
                FileString$ = ""
            End If

            'assign rest of string to filestring$
            FileString$ = Right$(FileString$, Len(FileString$) - pos%)

            'populate picture box
            Call PopulatePicture(TheDirectory$ + TheFile$)
```

continues

421

LISTING 22.8. CONTINUED

```
            Loop
        End If
    Else
        MsgBox "Cannot Open, No File Name Specified"
    End If

    Exit Sub

OpenError:
    Select Case (Err)
        Case 32755: 'cancel selected
            Exit Sub
        Case 20476: 'buffer too small
            MsgBox "Too many files were selected"
        Case Else:
            MsgBox "There was an Open Dialog Error!"
            Err = 0
            Exit Sub
    End Select

    'resume to avoid errors
    Resume

End Sub
```

THE *CMDPRINT( )* CONTROL

cmdPrint() is the name of the command button control that, when clicked, prints the icons. The cmdPrint() control has code in only one event procedure. It is

◆ cmdPrint_Click()

THE *CMDPRINT_CLICK( )* EVENT PROCEDURE

 For more information about printing, refer to Chapter 6, "Printing."

Following is a listing of the cmdPrint_Click() event procedure:

LISTING 22.9. MAIN.FRM, cmdPrint_Click().

```
Sub CmdPrint_Click ()

    'declare variables
    Dim m$                          'message constructor
    Dim oldfontsize As Single       'float holding old font size
    Dim oldfontname As String       'string holding old font name
    Dim Heading$                    'heading for top of printout
    Dim loopcount%                  'looping variable

    'check to see if there is something to print
```

```
    If IconIndex% = -1 Then
        m$ = "There is nothing to print!"
        MsgBox m$
        Exit Sub
    End If

    'initialize
    FontFound% = False
    Heading$ = "Real-World Icon Printing Application"

    'change cursor
    screen.MousePointer = HOURGLASS

    'flag printing
    Printing% = True

    'print heading
    printer.CurrentX = (printer.ScaleWidth - printer.TextWidth(Heading$)) / 2
    printer.CurrentY = 0
    printer.Print Heading$

    'print line under heading
    printer.CurrentX = 0
    printer.CurrentY = printer.TextHeight(Heading$) + 50
    printer.Line Step(CurrentX, CurrentY)-Step(printer.ScaleWidth, CurrentY), , BF

    'remember old font size
    oldfontsize = printer.FontSize
    oldfontname = printer.FontName

    'assign font of size 6, if available
    If FindFont() = False Then
        'font not found
        m$ = "Appropriate font was not found" + Chr$(13)
        m$ = m$ + "on your printer.  Text Disabled!"
        MsgBox m$
    End If

    'loop through icons, printall
    For loopcount% = 0 To IconIndex%
        Call PrintIcon(pictIcon(loopcount%), loopcount%)
    Next loopcount%

    'eject page
    printer.EndDoc

    'unflag printing
    Printing% = False

    'reset to old font size
    printer.FontSize = oldfontsize
    printer.FontName = oldfontname

    'reset cursor
    screen.MousePointer = DEFAULT

End Sub
```

The *cmdReset( )* Control

cmdReset() is the name of the command button control that, when clicked, resets the display by unloading all picture boxes. The cmdReset() control has code only in one event procedure. It is

◆ cmdReset_Click()

The *cmdReset_Click( )* Event Procedure

Following is a listing of the cmdReset_Click() event procedure:

Listing 22.10. MAIN.FRM, cmdReset_Click().

```
Sub cmdReset_Click ()

    'declare variables
    Dim loopcount%          'looping variable

    'change cursor
    screen.MousePointer = HOURGLASS

    'hide design-time picture box
    pictIcon(0).Visible = False
    pnlLabel(0).Visible = False

    'unload all run-time added picture boxes
    For loopcount% = 1 To IconIndex%
        Unload pictIcon(loopcount%)
        Unload pnlLabel(loopcount%)
    Next loopcount%

    'reset IconIndex
    IconIndex% = -1

    'reset cursor
    screen.MousePointer = DEFAULT

End Sub
```

The *Form* Object

The Form object has code in three event procedures. They are:

◆ Form_Load()

◆ Form_Paint()

◆ Form_Unload()

The *Form_Load( )* Event Procedure

The Form_Load() event procedure simply centers the form and sets defaults. Following is a listing of the Form_Load() event procedure

424

LISTING 22.11. MAIN.FRM, Form_Load().

```
Sub Form_Load ()

    'center the form
    CenterForm Me

    'set defaults
    pictIcon(0).Visible = False

    'initialize
    IconIndex% = -1
    Printing% = False

End Sub
```

THE *FORM_PAINT()* EVENT PROCEDURE

The Form_Paint() event procedure occurs when the form is repainted. This happens when the form is moved. If the event occurs, the form is re-centered. Following is a listing of the Form_Paint() event procedure:

LISTING 22.12. MAIN.FRM, Form_Paint().

```
Sub Form_Paint ()

    'if form has been moved off the screen, the icon will
    'no longer be visible. center the form back.
    CenterForm Me

End Sub
```

The reason that the form has to be centered after it is moved is because if the form is moved while printing icons, any icon moved off the screen is not printed correctly. This is because the color of the individual pixels is checked to determine if it should be printed. If it is off the screen, the color cannot be determined. Therefore, the form is automatically centered after it is moved.

THE *FORM_UNLOAD()* EVENT PROCEDURE

The Form_Unload() event procedure prompts the user to confirm ending the program. Following is a listing of the Form_Unload() event procedure:

LISTING 22.13. MAIN.FRM, Form_Unload().

```
Sub Form_Unload (cancel As Integer)

    'declare variables
    Dim m$       'message constructor
    Dim res%     'holds results

    If Printing% = True Then
        m$ = "You cannot close while printing!"
        MsgBox m$
        'Cancel
        cancel = True

        'exit
        Exit Sub
    End If
    m$ = "Are you sure you want to close?"
    res% = MsgBox(m$, 292, "Warning?")
    If res% = IDNO Then
        'cancel
        cancel = True

        'exit
        Exit Sub
    End If

    End

End Sub
```

THE *MENU* OBJECT

The menu object was created by using Visual Basic's built-in menu editor. It has code associated with only one click() event procedure. It is

◆ menu_about()

THE *MENU_ABOUT_CLICK()* PROCEDURE

The menu_about_click() procedure simply shows the about form for program information. Following is a listing of the menu_about_click() procedure:

LISTING 22.14. MAIN.FRM, menu_about_click().

```
Sub menu_about_Click ()

    'show about form
    frmAbout.Show MODAL

End Sub
```

THE ABOUT.FRM FILE

ABOUT.FRM is one of two forms in this application. It shows information about the application. Figure 22.3 presents the form as it appears at runtime. Fundamentally, there is no difference in the form at design time, so it is not presented. Table 22.2 lists all the relevant properties of each control on the form that have been changed from their standard default values. The ABOUT.FRM file is contained on the CD accompanying this book in the CHAP22 subdirectory.

FIGURE 22.3.

Icon Printing application About Form at runtime.

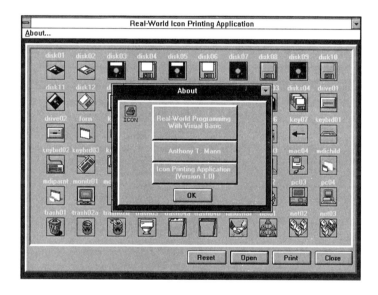

TABLE 22.2. PROPERTIES OF EACH CONTROL ON ABOUT.FRM.

Object	Control Type	Property	Value
frmAbout	Form	BackColor	&H00404000&
		Caption	"About"
		Height	3525
		Left	1035
		MaxButton	False
		MinButton	False
		Top	1140
		Width	4545
pnlMain	SSPanel	BackColor	&H00C0C0C0&
		BevelWidth	3

continues

427

TABLE 22.2. CONTINUED

Object	Control Type	Property	Value
		Caption	""
		Font3D	None
		ForeColor	&H00C0C0C0&
		Height	2895
		Left	122
		RoundedCorners	False
		ShadowColor	Black
		Top	122
		Width	4225
pnl1	SSPanel	BackColor	&H00C0C0C0&
		BevelWidth	3
		Caption	"Real-World Programming With Visual Basic"
		Font3D	None
		ForeColor	&H0000FFFF&
		Height	975
		Left	960
		RoundedCorners	False
		ShadowColor	Black
		Top	122
		Width	2415
pnl2	SSPanel	BackColor	&H00C0C0C0&
		BevelWidth	3
		Caption	"Anthony T. Mann"
		Font3D	None
		ForeColor	&H0000FFFF&
		Height	615
		Left	960
		RoundedCorners	False
		ShadowColor	Black

Object	Control Type	Property	Value
		Top	1080
		Width	2415
pnl3	SSPanel	BackColor	&H00C0C0C0&
		BevelWidth	3
		Caption	"Icon Printing Application (Version 1.0)"
		Font3D	None
		ForeColor	&H0000FFFF&
		Height	615
		Left	960
		RoundedCorners	False
		ShadowColor	Black
		Top	1680
		Width	2415
cmdOK	Command Button	Caption	"OK"
		Height	375
		Left	1680
		Top	2400
		Width	1095
pictAbout	Picture Box	Autosize	True
		BackColor	&H00C0C0C0&
		BorderStyle	None
		Height	615
		Left	122
		Top	122
		Width	735

Function, Subroutine, and Event Procedures

There are several procedures of code for each object(control) that comprise this form. Each is listed in the following sections.

The (general) object contains only one form level declaration and one form level procedure. The procedures for the (general) object are

◆ (declarations)

◆ CenterForm()

THE *(DECLARATIONS)* PROCEDURE

The (declarations) procedure contains only one line of declarations used in the form, ABOUT.FRM. It is only to allow for variable syntax checking and forcing the declaration of variables in each procedure. Following is a listing of the (declarations) procedure:

LISTING 22.15. ABOUT.FRM, (General)(Declarations).

```
Option Explicit
```

THE *CENTERFORM()* PROCEDURE

The CenterForm() procedure simply centers the form in the client area. This procedure also exists in the MAIN.FRM. This is because it is not worth the overhead of having a separate BAS file only for this one procedure. Following is a listing of the CenterForm() procedure:

LISTING 22.16. ABOUT.FRM, CenterForm().

```
Sub CenterForm (f As Form)

    f.Move (screen.Width - f.Width) / 2, (screen.Height - f.Height) / 2

End Sub
```

THE *CMDOK* CONTROL

cmdOK is the name of the command button control that, when clicked, closes the frmAbout form. The cmdOK control has code only in one event procedure. It is

◆ cmdOK_Click()

THE *CMDOK_CLICK()* EVENT PROCEDURE

The cmdOK_Click() event procedure simply unloads the form. Following is a listing of the cmdOK_Click() event procedure:

LISTING 22.17. ABOUT.FRM, cmdOK_Click().

```
Sub cmdOK_Click ()

    'unload
    Unload frmAbout

End Sub
```

THE *FORM* OBJECT

The Form object has code in only one event procedure. It is

◆ Form_Load()

THE *FORM_LOAD()* EVENT PROCEDURE

The Form_Load() event procedure centers the form and assigns an icon to the pictAbout control. Following is a listing of the Form_Load() event procedure:

LISTING 22.18. ABOUT.FRM, FORM_LOAD().

```
Sub Form_Load ()

    'center form
    CenterForm Me

    'load icon
    pictAbout.Picture = frmMain.Icon

End Sub
```

THE CHAP22.ICO FILE

This file contains the icon that has been attached to the form at design time. The CHAP22.ICO file is contained on the CD accompanying this book in the CHAP22 subdirectory.

FIGURE 22.4.
Icon Printing appli-
cation Form icon.

THE CHAP22.EXE FILE

This is the executable file that is distributable. If you distribute this application, you must include the following files:

◆ CHAP22.EXE

◆ THREED.VBX

◆ CMDIALOG.VBX

◆ COMMDLG.DLL

◆ VBRUN300.DLL

The CHAP22.EXE file and source files are contained on the CD accompanying this book in the CHAP22 subdirectory, while all DLLs and VBXs are in the RESOURCE subdirectory.

RELATING THE ICON PRINTING APPLICATION TO YOUR APPLICATION

The Icon Printing application shows how to print icons. You can expand this to print any type of graphic file. Visual Basic, however, has limited capabilities in this area. The Visual Basic picture box can only accept bitmaps, icons, and metafiles. Therefore, you have to use some other means if you want to display GIF files, for example. If you want to print bitmaps or metafiles, change the calculations that position the picture boxes. Use the same code to cycle through each bit in the picture box to actually perform the printing.

FINAL NOTES

This application was created on a standard VGA display, 16 colors. Your particular hardware could have adverse effects on the code the way it is written. You may need to modify it slightly.

CHAPTER TWENTY-THREE

RASTER GRAPHICS EDITOR APPLICATION

THE RASTER GRAPHICS EDITOR APPLICATION IS AN IMPORTANT APPLICATION THAT SHOWS HOW TO SEND BITMAPPED GRAPHICS TO A HEWLETT PACKARD COMPATIBLE LASER PRINTER. THIS TYPE OF GRAPHICS IS CALLED *RASTER GRAPHICS*. IT IS SENDING A PARTICULAR NUMBER OF BYTES TO THE PRINTER IN A SPECIFIC BITMAP PATTERN. IT IS AN ADVANCED TOPIC THAT REQUIRES CAREFUL READING.

This application allows the user to actually edit a bitmap pattern for each printable character, and store the raster codes in an INI configuration file. Really, the sole purpose of this application is to code the INI file. The file can then be distributed with your applications along with the minimum code needed to read and print the file. Chapter 24, "Raster Graphics Printer Application," is an example of the minimum code needed and a sample of how this would be done.

The importance of this application is that a predetermined bitmap (stored in the INI file) can be printed on top of text that was already sent to the printer. For example, if you have text that was sent to the printer, you can overlay the word CONFIDENTIAL across the entire page. Figure 23.1 shows the main screen (MAIN.FRM) at runtime.

FIGURE 23.1.
Raster Graphics Editor application at runtime.

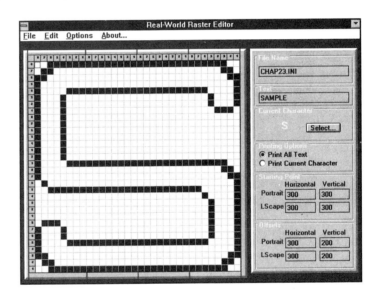

To use the application, run the CHAP23.EXE file. You will see a grid presented in a 32-by-32 matrix. This matrix constitutes one character. Note that the file name to use is by default CHAP23.INI. Change it if you wish. Select a character to edit by clicking on the Select... command button. This invokes the CHARSEL.FRM form. This form presents an array of command buttons that have the caption of all possible characters that can be edited and stored. Figure 23.2 shows the CHARSEL.FRM form at runtime.

FIGURE 23.2.
*Raster Graphics Editor
CHARSEL.FRM at
runtime.*

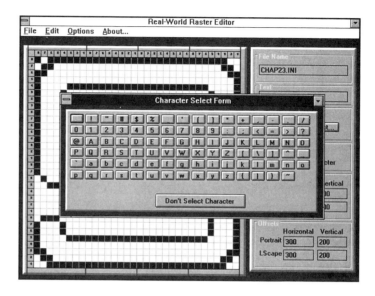

To select a character to edit, simply click on it. The CHARSEL.FRM form will close. To exit without selecting, click the corresponding command button.

After a character is selected, you can begin outlining the bitmap. To toggle an individual dot (*pixel*) on and off, click it. To turn a range of pixels on or off, select the range and then the option desired from the Edit menu.

Continue for each character until you have edited all desired characters. Note that although you can edit bitmaps for each character selected in the CHARSEL form, only the characters listed in the Text text box are actually printed. This allows you to design an entire font if you wish, but display different parts for different computers. You will be prompted to save each character before continuing to the next.

At any time, you can test print either the current character or the entire text message. To print, select the File->Print menu option and choose from Portrait or Landscape. To print the current character, select the Print Current Character radio button. To print the entire text message, select the Print All Text radio button.

It is important to note the starting point and offsets frames at the lower right corner of the screen. These coordinates determine where each character will be printed in relation to each other. This will take some practice to see where the characters will be printed. These coordinates will actually determine the slope, if any, that the characters will be printed with. Note that there are separate coordinates for Landscape and Portrait. If you don't intend to print in one or the other, you need not enter that one.

What is happening with all of this is that each row and column of 32 bits (pixels) is being encoded into 4, 8-bit bytes for the printer to understand. Separate arrays of bytes are needed for Portrait orientation as for Landscape. To view the actual codes that are sent to the printer in 4-byte rows, select the Show/Hide Codes option under the options menu. This will bring up a frame that shows these bytes. It is important to note that the codes being shown are only the Portrait orientation codes. They are shown for illustration purposes. Unfortunately, the font to show these codes is extremely small (3.75 points). It is difficult to view; however, it is the only font that will fit in the given space. Figure 23.3 shows the main screen again, but this time with the code frame shown.

 To learn more about raster graphics and the bytes that are sent to the printer, refer to Chapter 6, "Printing."

FIGURE 23.3.
Raster Graphics Editor MAIN.FRM with raster codes at runtime.

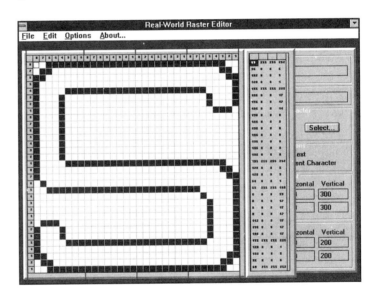

CODE LISTINGS

The Raster Graphics Editor application contains the following files and listings:

- ◆ CHAP23.MAK
- ◆ MAIN.FRM
- ◆ CHARSEL.FRM
- ◆ MESSAGE.FRM
- ◆ ABOUT.FRM
- ◆ CHAP23.BAS

- ◆ CHAP23.INI
- ◆ CHAP23.ICO
- ◆ BLACK.BMP
- ◆ CHAP23.EXE

THE CHAP23.MAK FILE

CHAP23.MAK is the project file for the Raster Graphics Editor application, CHAP23.EXE. It contains a listing of all the files necessary to load the project into Visual Basic. The CHAP23.MAK file is contained on the CD accompanying this book in the CHAP23 subdirectory. The file listing is

LISTING 23.1. CHAP23.MAK.

```
MAIN.FRM
CHARSEL.FRM
MESSAGE.FRM
ABOUT.FRM
CHAP23.BAS
THREED.VBX
GRID.VBX
ProjWinSize=152,436,203,215
ProjWinShow=2
IconForm="frmMain"
Title="Raster Editor"
ExeName="CHAP23.EXE"
```

THE MAIN.FRM FILE

MAIN.FRM is one of four forms in this application. It is the startup form for the application as well as the form used for bitmap editing. Figure 23.1 shows the MAIN.FRM form at runtime. It is fundamentally no different at design time, so it is not presented. Table 23.1 lists all the relevant properties of each control on the form that have been changed from their standard default values. The MAIN.FRM file is contained on the CD accompanying this book in the CHAP23 subdirectory.

TABLE 23.1. PROPERTIES OF EACH CONTROL ON MAIN.FRM.

Object	Control Type	Property	Value
frmMain	Form	BackColor	&H00404000&
		Caption	"Real-World Raster Editor"

continues

437

TABLE 23.1. CONTINUED

Object	Control Type	Property	Value
		Height	5655
		Icon	"CHAP23.ICO"
		Left	1215
		MaxButton	False
		Top	1125
		Width	8250
		WindowState	Maximized
BinaryFrame	SSPanel	BackColor	&H00C0C0C0&
		BevelInner	Raised
		BevelWidth	2
		BorderWidth	0
		Font3D	None
		Height	6255
		Left	5160
		Top	240
		Visible	False
		Width	1575
Grid1	Grid	BackColor	&H00FFFFFF&
		Cols	33
		FontBold	True
		FontItalic	False
		FontName	"Small Fonts"
		FontSize	3.75
		Height	5950
		Left	120
		Rows	33
		ScrollBars	None
		Top	120
		Width	5950

Object	Control Type	Property	Value
Grid2	Grid	Cols	5
		FontBold	True
		FontItalic	False
		FontName	"Small Fonts"
		FontSize	3.75
		Height	5950
		Left	120
		Rows	33
		ScrollBars	None
		Top	120
		Width	1575
Panel3D1	SSPanel	BackColor	&H00C0C0C0&
		BevelInner	Raised
		BevelWidth	2
		BorderWidth	0
		Font3D	None
		Height	6135
		Left	6480
		Top	240
		Width	3015
pnlCurChar	SSPanel	BackColor	&H00C0C0C0&
		BevelInner	Raised
		BevelOuter	None
		BevelWidth	0
		BorderWidth	0
		Font3D	None
		FontBold	True
		FontName	"MS Sans Serif"
		FontSize	13.5
		ForeColor	&H0000FFFF&
		Height	390

continues

TABLE 23.1. CONTINUED

Object	Control Type	Property	Value
		Left	600
		Top	360
		Width	495
BoxFrame	SSPanel	BackColor	&H00C0C0C0&
		BevelInner	Raised
		BevelOuter	None
		BevelWidth	2
		BorderWidth	0
		Font3D	None
		Height	6255
		Left	120
		Top	240
		Visible	False
		Width	6255
StartingPoint	SSFrame	Caption	"Starting Point"
		Font3D	None
		ForeColor	&H0000FFFF&
		Height	1335
		Left	120
		Top	3360
		Width	2775
Frame3D6	SSFrame	Caption	"Printing Options"
		Font3D	None
		ForeColor	&H0000FFFF&
		Height	855
		Left	120
		Top	2520
		Width	2775
Offsets	SSFrame	Caption	"Offsets"
		Font3D	None
		ForeColor	&H0000FFFF&

Object	Control Type	Property	Value
		Height	1335
		Left	120
		Top	4650
		Width	2775
Frame3D5	SSFrame	Caption	"FileName"
		Font3D	None
		ForeColor	&H0000FFFF&
		Height	855
		Left	120
		Top	120
		Width	2775
Frame3D3	SSFrame	Caption	"Text"
		Font3D	None
		ForeColor	&H0000FFFF&
		Height	615
		Left	120
		Top	960
		Width	2775
Frame3D4	SSFrame	Caption	"Current Character"
		Font3D	None
		ForeColor	&H0000FFFF&
		Height	975
		Left	120
		Top	1560
		Width	2775
VLStart	TextBox	Alignment	Center
		BackColor	&H00C0C0C0&
		Height	285
		Left	1800
		Top	840
		Width	855

continues

441

TABLE 23.1. CONTINUED

Object	Control Type	Property	Value
HLStart	TextBox	Alignment	Center
		BackColor	&H00C0C0C0&
		Height	285
		Left	840
		Top	840
		Width	855
HPStart	TextBox	Alignment	Center
		BackColor	&H00C0C0C0&
		Height	285
		Left	840
		Top	480
		Width	855
VPStart	TextBox	Alignment	Center
		BackColor	&H00C0C0C0&
		Height	285
		Left	840
		Top	480
		Width	855
HLOffset	TextBox	Alignment	Center
		BackColor	&H00C0C0C0&
		Height	285
		Left	840
		Top	840
		Width	855
VLOffset	TextBox	Alignment	Center
		BackColor	&H00C0C0C0&
		Height	285
		Left	1800
		Top	840
		Width	855

Object	Control Type	Property	Value
VPOffset	TextBox	Alignment	Center
		BackColor	&H00C0C0C0&
		Height	285
		Left	1800
		Top	480
		Width	855
HPOffset	TextBox	Alignment	Center
		BackColor	&H00C0C0C0&
		Height	285
		Left	840
		Top	480
		Width	855
FileName	TextBox	Alignment	Center
		BackColor	&H00C0C0C0&
		Height	285
		Left	120
		Text	"CHAP23.INI"
		Top	360
		Width	2535
PrintText	TextBox	Alignment	Center
		BackColor	&H00C0C0C0&
		Height	285
		Left	120
		Top	240
		Width	2535
Label5	Label	Alignment	Center
		BackColor	&H00C0C0C0&
		Caption	"LScape"
		ForeColor	&H00000080&
		Height	255
		Left	120

continues

TABLE 23.1. CONTINUED

Object	Control Type	Property	Value
		Top	840
		Width	735
Label2	Label	Alignment	Center
		BackColor	&H00C0C0C0&
		Caption	"Portrait"
		ForeColor	&H00000080&
		Height	255
		Left	120
		Top	480
		Width	735
Label4	Label	Alignment	Center
		BackColor	&H00C0C0C0&
		Caption	"Horizontal"
		ForeColor	&H00000080&
		Height	255
		Left	840
		Top	240
		Width	855
Label3	Label	Alignment	Center
		BackColor	&H00C0C0C0&
		Caption	"Vertical"
		ForeColor	&H00000080&
		Height	255
		Left	1800
		Top	240
		Width	855
Label7	Label	Alignment	Center
		BackColor	&H00C0C0C0&
		Caption	"LScape"
		ForeColor	&H00000080&

Object	Control Type	Property	Value
		Height	255
		Left	120
		Top	840
		Width	735
Label6	Label	Alignment	Center
		BackColor	&H00C0C0C0&
		Caption	"Portrait"
		ForeColor	&H00000080&
		Height	255
		Left	120
		Top	480
		Width	735
Label	Label	Alignment	Center
		BackColor	&H00C0C0C0&
		Caption	"Vertical"
		ForeColor	&H00000080&
		Height	255
		Left	1800
		Top	240
		Width	855
Label1	Label	Alignment	Center
		BackColor	&H00C0C0C0&
		Caption	"Horizontal"
		ForeColor	&H00000080&
		Height	255
		Left	840
		Top	240
		Width	855
PrintCharOption	SSOption	Caption	"Print Current Character"
		Font3D	None

continues

TABLE 23.1. CONTINUED

Object	Control Type	Property	Value
		Height	255
		Left	120
		Top	480
		Width	2535
PrintTextOption	SSOption	Caption	"Print All Text"
		Font3D	None
		Height	255
		Left	120
		Top	240
		Value	True
		Width	2535
cmdSelect	SSCommand	Caption	"Select..."
		Font3D	None
		Height	255
		Left	1440
		Picture	(none)
		Top	480
		Width	975
Blank	SSCommand	Font3D	None
		Height	255
		Left	240
		Picture	(none)
		Top	0
		Visible	False
		Width	255
Black	SSCommand	Font3D	None
		Height	255
		Left	0
		Picture	"BLACK.BMP"
		Top	0

Object	Control Type	Property	Value
		Visible	False
		Width	255
Line1	Line	BorderColor	&H000000C0&
		BorderWidth	2
		X1	1750
		Y1	1750
		Y1	0
		Y2	6720
Line2	Line	BorderColor	&H000000C0&
		BorderWidth	2
		X1	3190
		Y1	3190
		Y1	0
		Y2	6720
Line3	Line	BorderColor	&H000000C0&
		BorderWidth	2
		X1	4630
		Y1	4630
		Y1	0
		Y2	6720
Line4	Line	BorderColor	&H000000C0&
		BorderWidth	2
		X1	6070
		Y1	6070
		Y1	0
		Y2	6720
Line5	Line	BorderColor	&H000000C0&
		BorderWidth	2
		X1	120
		Y1	120
		Y1	0

continues

TABLE 23.1. CONTINUED

Object	Control Type	Property	Value
		Y2	6720
menu_file	Menu	Caption	"&File"
menu_save	Menu	Caption	"&Save"
menu_print	Menu	Caption	"&Print"
menu_portrait	Menu	Caption	"&Portrait"
menu_landscape	Menu	Caption	"&Landscape"
menu_separator	Menu	Caption	"-"
menu_exit	Menu	Caption	"&Exit"
menu_edit	Menu	Caption	"&Edit"
menu_black	Menu	Caption	"&Black"
menu_white	Menu	Caption	"&White"
menu_options	Menu	Caption	"&Options"
menu_show	Menu	Caption	"&Show/Hide Codes"
menu_reset	Menu	Caption	"&Reset"
menu_about	Menu	Caption	"&About..."

REM The reason that SSCommand buttons are used to store the white and black bitmaps is to show how you can overlay a picture onto a command button, not only a picture box. Also, the difference between Grid1 and Grid2 is that Grid1 shows how the bitmap will look. Grid2 contains codes that will be sent to the printer and, therefore, are hidden.

FUNCTION, SUBROUTINE, AND EVENT PROCEDURES

There are several procedures of code for each object(control) that comprise this form. Each is listed in the following sections.

THE (GENERAL) OBJECT

The (general) object contains declarations and procedures at the form level. The procedures for the (general) object are

◆ (declarations)

◆ CalculateBits()

◆ PrintAllText()

◆ PrintCharacter()

THE *(DECLARATIONS)* PROCEDURE

The (general) object contains variables declarations and procedures at the form level. Following is a listing of the (declarations) procedure:

LISTING 23.2. MAIN.FRM, (general)(declarations).

```
Option Explicit

'declare variables
Dim XPValue% '- current x printing coordinate(Portrait)
Dim YPValue% '- current y printing coordinate(Portrait)
Dim XLValue% '- current x printing coordinate(Landscape)
Dim YLValue% '- current y printing coordinate(landscape)
```

THE *CALCULATEBITS()* PROCEDURE

The CalculateBits() procedure calculates the bits to be sent to the printer from the pixels turned on (black) in grid1. The first thing that happens is that Grid2 is cleared. Grid2 is the grid that contains the values to be sent to the printer. Depending on which mode (Portrait or Landscape) is selected, the bits are calculated differently. Either way, the code cycles through each bit in Grid1 and fills the value of the 8-bit byte to be printed in the corresponding area in Grid2. Following is a listing of the CalculateBits() procedure:

LISTING 23.3. MAIN.FRM, CalculateBits().

```
Sub CalculateBits (WhichMode$)

    'declare variables
    Dim Row%        'loop counting variable for row
    Dim Col%        'loop counting variable for col


    'first clear 2nd grid
    For Row% = 1 To Grid2.Rows - 1
        For Col% = 1 To Grid2.Cols - 1
            Grid2.Row = Row%
            Grid2.Col = Col%
            Grid2.Text = ""
        Next Col%
    Next Row%

    'portrait
    If WhichMode$ = "PORTRAIT" Then
        'cycle through for portrait from left to right, top to bottom
        For Row% = 1 To Grid1.Rows - 1
            For Col% = 1 To Grid1.Cols - 1
                Grid1.Row = Row%
```

continues

LISTING 23.3. CONTINUED

```
Grid2.Row = Row%
Grid1.Col = Col%

'move Grid2's col once for every 8 cols in Grid1
If Grid1.Col >= 1 And Grid1.Col <= 8 Then
    Grid2.Col = 1
ElseIf Grid1.Col >= 9 And Grid1.Col <= 16 Then
    Grid2.Col = 2
ElseIf Grid1.Col >= 17 And Grid1.Col <= 24 Then
    Grid2.Col = 3
ElseIf Grid1.Col >= 25 And Grid1.Col <= 32 Then
    Grid2.Col = 4
End If

'assign Grid2 row
Grid2.Row = Grid1.Row

'start at row 0 to check text(to see which bit position this is)
'each row and col has a header at row 0 and col 0 for which bit
'position this is
Grid1.Row = 0

'build bit representation of which bits are printed
Select Case (Val(Trim$(Grid1.Text)))
    Case 1:
        Grid1.Row = Row%
        If Grid1.Picture = Black.Picture Then
            Grid2.Text = Val(Trim$(Grid2.Text)) + 1
        End If
    Case 2:
        Grid1.Row = Row%
        If Grid1.Picture = Black.Picture Then
            Grid2.Text = Val(Trim$(Grid2.Text)) + 2
        End If
    Case 3:
        Grid1.Row = Row%
        If Grid1.Picture = Black.Picture Then
            Grid2.Text = Val(Trim$(Grid2.Text)) + 4
        End If
    Case 4:
        Grid1.Row = Row%
        If Grid1.Picture = Black.Picture Then
            Grid2.Text = Val(Trim$(Grid2.Text)) + 8
        End If
    Case 5:
        Grid1.Row = Row%
        If Grid1.Picture = Black.Picture Then
            Grid2.Text = Val(Trim$(Grid2.Text)) + 16
        End If
    Case 6:
        Grid1.Row = Row%
        If Grid1.Picture = Black.Picture Then
            Grid2.Text = Val(Trim$(Grid2.Text)) + 32
        End If
    Case 7:
        Grid1.Row = Row%
```

```
                    If Grid1.Picture = Black.Picture Then
                        Grid2.Text = Val(Trim$(Grid2.Text)) + 64
                    End If
                Case 8:
                    Grid1.Row = Row%
                    If Grid1.Picture = Black.Picture Then
                        Grid2.Text = Val(Trim$(Grid2.Text)) + 128
                    End If
            End Select
        Next Col%
    Next Row%
ElseIf WhichMode$ = "LANDSCAPE" Then
    'cycle through for Landscape bottom to top, left to right
    For Row% = Grid1.Cols - 1 To 1 Step -1
        For Col% = 1 To Grid1.Rows - 1
            Grid1.Col = Row%
            Grid1.Row = Col%
            Select Case (Grid1.Row)
                Case 1 To 8:
                    Grid2.Col = 1
                Case 9 To 16:
                    Grid2.Col = 2
                Case 17 To 24:
                    Grid2.Col = 3
                Case 25 To 32:
                    Grid2.Col = 4
            End Select

            'calculate row
            Grid2.Row = (32 - Grid1.Col) + 1

            'start at col 0 to check text(to see which bit position this is)
            'each row and col has a header at row 0 and col 0 for which bit
            'position this is
            Grid1.Col = 0

            'build bit representation of which bits are printed
            Select Case (Val(Trim$(Grid1.Text)))
                Case 1:
                    Grid1.Col = Row%
                    If Grid1.Picture = Black.Picture Then
                        Grid2.Text = Val(Trim$(Grid2.Text)) + 1
                    End If
                Case 2:
                    Grid1.Col = Row%
                    If Grid1.Picture = Black.Picture Then
                        Grid2.Text = Val(Trim$(Grid2.Text)) + 2
                    End If
                Case 3:
                    Grid1.Col = Row%
                    If Grid1.Picture = Black.Picture Then
                        Grid2.Text = Val(Trim$(Grid2.Text)) + 4
                    End If
                Case 4:
                    Grid1.Col = Row%
                    If Grid1.Picture = Black.Picture Then
                        Grid2.Text = Val(Trim$(Grid2.Text)) + 8
```

continues

451

LISTING 23.3. CONTINUED

```
                            End If
                    Case 5:
                        Grid1.Col = Row%
                        If Grid1.Picture = Black.Picture Then
                            Grid2.Text = Val(Trim$(Grid2.Text)) + 16
                        End If
                    Case 6:
                        Grid1.Col = Row%
                        If Grid1.Picture = Black.Picture Then
                            Grid2.Text = Val(Trim$(Grid2.Text)) + 32
                        End If
                    Case 7:
                        Grid1.Col = Row%
                        If Grid1.Picture = Black.Picture Then
                            Grid2.Text = Val(Trim$(Grid2.Text)) + 64
                        End If
                    Case 8:
                        Grid1.Col = Row%
                        If Grid1.Picture = Black.Picture Then
                            Grid2.Text = Val(Trim$(Grid2.Text)) + 128
                        End If
                End Select
            Next Col%
        Next Row%
    End If

End Sub
```

THE *PRINTALLTEXT( )* PROCEDURE

The PrintAllText() procedure prints all graphic characters in the PrintText text box by using raster graphics methods. It does this by reading the INI file to determine how to print the character and then increments the x and y coordinates for the next characters by the value specified in the offset text boxes. Following is a listing of the PrintAllText() procedure:

LISTING 23.4. MAIN.FRM, PrintAllText( ).

```
Sub PrintAllText ()

    'declare variables
    Dim loopcount%   'loop counting variable

    'change cursor
    screen.MousePointer = HOURGLASS

    'open port
    Open "LPT1" For Output As #1

    'initialize printer
    Print #1, Chr$(27) + "E"         'reset printer
    Print #1, Chr$(27) + "&l2A"      'letter size
    Print #1, Chr$(27) + "(s0P"      'fixed spacing
```

```
Print #1, Chr$(27) + "(8U" + Chr$(27) + "(s0p12h10v0s0b3T"  'courier 12 pitch, 10
point,regular
If PortLandMode% = PORTRAIT Then
    'set portrait orientation
    Print #1, Chr$(27) + "&l0O"
    'read from file to populate coordinates
    Call ReadFromFile
    'set default coordinates
    XPValue% = Val(HPStart.Text) - Val(HPOffset.Text)
    YPValue% = Val(VPStart.Text) - Val(VPOffset.Text)

ElseIf PortLandMode% = LANDSCAPE Then
    'set landscape orientation
    Print #1, Chr$(27) + "&l1O"
    'read from file to populate coordinates
    Call ReadFromFile
    'set default coordinates
    XLValue% = Val(HLStart.Text) - Val(HLOffset.Text)
    YLValue% = Val(VLStart.Text) - Val(VLOffset.Text)

End If

'loop through all characters to be printed
For loopcount% = 1 To (Len(PrintText.Text))
    pnlCurChar.Caption = Mid$(PrintText.Text, loopcount%, 1)

    'increment coordinates
    If PortLandMode% = PORTRAIT Then
        XPValue% = XPValue% + Val(HPOffset.Text)
        YPValue% = YPValue% + Val(VPOffset.Text)
    ElseIf PortLandMode% = LANDSCAPE Then
        XLValue% = XLValue% + Val(HLOffset.Text)
        YLValue% = YLValue% + Val(VLOffset.Text)
    End If
    Call PrintCharacter
Next loopcount%

'reset grid
Call menu_reset_click

Print #1, Chr$(27) + "&l0H" 'form feed
Close #1

'change cursor
screen.MousePointer = DEFAULT

End Sub
```

THE *PRINTCHARACTER( )* PROCEDURE

The PrintCharacter() procedure prints only the graphic character shown in the Current Character Frame using raster graphics methods. Following is a listing of the PrintCharacter() procedure:

LISTING 23.5. MAIN.FRM, PrintCharacter().

```
Sub PrintCharacter ()

    'declare variables
    Dim pr$          'holds string to send to printer
    Dim Outerloop%   'loop counting variable
    Dim Innerloop%   'loop counting variable
    Dim m$           'message constructor

    'handle errors
    On Error GoTo charerror


    If PrintCharOption.Value = True Then
        If pnlCurChar.Caption = "" Then
            m$ = "There is no character to print!"
            MsgBox m$
            Exit Sub
        End If
    End If

    'change cursor
    screen.MousePointer = HOURGLASS

    'read data from file
    Call ReadFromFile

    If PrintCharOption.Value = True Then
        Open "LPT1" For Output As #1
        pr$ = Chr$(27) + "E"            'reset printer
        pr$ = pr$ + Chr$(27) + "&l2A"      'letter size
        pr$ = pr$ + Chr$(27) + "(s0P"      'fixed spacing
        pr$ = pr$ + Chr$(27) + "(8U" + Chr$(27) + "(s0p12h10v0s0b3T" 'courier 12 pitch,
        10 point,regular
        If PortLandMode% = PORTRAIT Then
            pr$ = pr$ + Chr$(27) + "&l0O"        'portrait

            'set default coordinates
            XPValue% = Val(HPStart.Text) - Val(HPOffset.Text)
            YPValue% = Val(VPStart.Text) - Val(VPOffset.Text)

        ElseIf PortLandMode% = LANDSCAPE Then
            pr$ = pr$ + Chr$(27) + "&l1O"        'landscape

            'set default coordinates
            XLValue% = Val(HLStart.Text) - Val(HLOffset.Text)
            YLValue% = Val(VLStart.Text) - Val(VLOffset.Text)
        End If
    Else
        pr$ = ""
    End If
    If PortLandMode% = PORTRAIT Then
        'set horizontal position(row)
        pr$ = pr$ + Chr$(27) + "*p" + Trim$(Str$(XPValue%)) + "X"
```

```
                'set vertical position(row)
            pr$ = pr$ + Chr$(27) + "*p" + Trim$(Str$(YPValue%)) + "Y"
        ElseIf PortLandMode% = LANDSCAPE Then
                'set horizontal position(row)
            pr$ = pr$ + Chr$(27) + "*p" + Trim$(Str$(XLValue%)) + "X"

                'set vertical position(row)
            pr$ = pr$ + Chr$(27) + "*p" + Trim$(Str$(YLValue%)) + "Y"
        End If
            'set resolution
            pr$ = pr$ + Chr$(27) + "*t75R"

            'begin raster data entry
            pr$ = pr$ + Chr$(27) + "*r1A"

            'cycle through grid2 and send data
            For Outerloop% = 1 To Grid2.Rows - 1
                pr$ = pr$ + Chr$(27) + "*b4W"
                For Innerloop% = 1 To 4
                    Grid2.Row = Outerloop%
                    Grid2.Col = Innerloop%
                    If Trim$(Grid2.Text) <> "" Then
                        pr$ = pr$ + Chr$(Val(Trim$(Grid2.Text)))
                    Else
                        pr$ = pr$ + Chr$(0)
                    End If
                Next Innerloop%
            Next Outerloop%

            'end with graphics
            pr$ = pr$ + Chr$(27) + "*rB"

            If PrintCharOption.Value = True Then
                pr$ = pr$ + Chr$(27) + "&l0H" 'form feed
                Print #1, pr$
                Close #1
            ElseIf PrintTextOption.Value = True Then
                Print #1, pr$
            End If

        'change cursor
        screen.MousePointer = DEFAULT

    Exit Sub

charerror:
    m$ = "Printer error!"
    MsgBox m$
    Exit Sub

    'avoid errors
    Return

End Sub
```

THE *CMDSELECT* CONTROL

cmdSelect is the name of the command button control that, when clicked, invokes the CHARSEL form to select a character to edit. The cmdSelect control has code only in one event procedure. It is

♦ cmdSelect_Click()

THE *CMDSELECT_CLICK()* EVENT PROCEDURE

The cmdSelectClick() event procedure involves the CHARSEL form. Following is a listing of the cmdSelect_Click() event procedure:

LISTING 23.6. MAIN.FRM, cmdSelect_Click().

```
Sub cmdSelect_Click ()

    'declare variables
    Dim m$        'message constructor
    Dim res%      'holds results

    If SaveNeeded% = True Then
        m$ = "Continue without saving" + Chr$(13)
        m$ = m$ + "current character or text change?"
        res% = MsgBox(m$, 292, "Warning")
        If res% = IDNO Then Exit Sub
    End If

    'reset save flag
    SaveNeeded% = False
    frmCharSelect.Show

End Sub
```

THE *FORM* OBJECT

The Form object has code in two event procedures. They are

♦ Form_Load()
♦ Form_Unload()

THE *FORM_LOAD()* EVENT PROCEDURE

The Form_Load() event procedure initializes, centers, and loads the main form. Following is a listing of the Form_Load() event procedure:

LISTING 23.7. MAIN.FRM, Form_Load().

```
Sub Form_Load ()

    'declare variables
```

```
Dim Factor%      'holds row height
Dim Row%         'loop counting variable for row
Dim Col%         'loop counting variable for col
Dim Cnt%         'holds count for labeling columns "1"-"8"

'change cursor
screen.MousePointer = HOURGLASS

'center the form
CenterForm Me

'flag that form is loading
FormLoading% = True

Factor% = 172

'Setup Grid 1
For Col% = 0 To Grid1.Cols - 1
    For Row% = 0 To Grid1.Rows - 1
        Grid1.RowHeight(Row%) = Factor%
    Next Row%
    Grid1.ColWidth(Col%) = Factor%
Next Col%

'Setup Grid 2
For Col% = 0 To Grid2.Cols - 1
    For Row% = 0 To Grid2.Rows - 1
        Grid2.RowHeight(Row%) = Factor%
    Next Row%
    Grid2.ColWidth(Col%) = 240
Next Col%

'Initialize
Grid1.Width = 5950
Grid1.Height = 5950
Grid2.ColWidth(0) = 1
Grid2.Width = 1125
Grid2.Height = 5950
BinaryFrame.Width = 1425
BoxFrame.Visible = True
BinaryFrame.Left = 6360
BinaryFrame.Top = BoxFrame.Top
SaveNeeded% = False
PortLandMode% = PORTRAIT

'setup grid1.captions
'column headings
Grid1.Row = 0
Cnt% = 8
For Col% = 1 To Grid1.Cols - 1
    Grid1.FixedAlignment(Col%) = 0
    Grid1.ColAlignment(Col%) = 0
    Grid1.Col = Col%
    Grid1.Text = Str$(Cnt%)
    Cnt% = Cnt% - 1
    If Cnt% = 0 Then Cnt% = 8
Next Col%
```

continues

457

LISTING 23.7. CONTINUED

```
    'row headings
    Grid1.Col = 0
    Cnt% = 8
    For Col% = 1 To Grid1.Rows - 1
        Grid1.FixedAlignment(Col%) = 0
        Grid1.ColAlignment(Col%) = 0
        Grid1.Row = Col%
        Grid1.Text = Str$(Cnt%)
        Cnt% = Cnt% - 1
        If Cnt% = 0 Then Cnt% = 8
    Next Col%

    DoEvents

    'read data from file
    Call ReadFromFile

    'unflag form load
    FormLoading% = False

    'hide message form
    Unload frmMessage

    'change cursor
    screen.MousePointer = DEFAULT

End Sub
```

THE *FORM_UNLOAD( )* EVENT PROCEDURE

The Form_Unload( ) event procedure prompts the user to confirm ending the program. Following is a listing of the Form_Unload( ) event procedure:

LISTING 23.8. MAIN.FRM, Form_Unload( ).

```
Sub Form_Unload (cancel As Integer)

    'declare variables
    Dim m$      'message constructor
    Dim res%    'holds results

    If SaveNeeded% = True Then
        m$ = "Exit without saving?"
        res% = MsgBox(m$, 292)
        If res% = IDNO Then
            'cancel
            cancel = True

            'exit
            Exit Sub
        End If
    End If
```

```
        'exit
        End

End Sub
```

THE *GRID1* CONTROL

Grid1 is the name of the grid control that, when clicked, toggles the bitmap to black or white. The Grid1 control has code in only one event procedure. It is

◆ Grid1_Click()

REM   When toggling the bitmap, black is considered to be on and white is considered to be off.

THE *GRID1_CLICK()* EVENT PROCEDURE

The Grid1_Click() event procedure handles the toggling of the bitmap. Following is a listing of the Grid1_Click() event procedure:

LISTING 23.9. MAIN.FRM, Grid1_Click().

```
Sub Grid1_Click ()

    'declare variables
    Dim Row%        'loop counting variable for row
    Dim Col%        'loop counting variable for col
    Dim m$          'message constructor

    'check to see if this bitmap is assigned to a character
    If pnlCurChar.Caption = "" Then
        m$ = "You must assign this bitmap to a letter!"
        MsgBox m$
    End If

    'initialize
    SaveNeeded% = True

    'Do if rows and cols are not selected
    If Not (Grid1.SelStartCol = 1 And Grid1.SelEndCol = Grid1.Cols - 1) Then
        If Not (Grid1.SelStartRow = 1 And Grid1.SelEndRow = Grid1.Rows - 1) Then
            If Grid1.Picture = Black.Picture Then
                Grid1.Picture = Blank.Picture
            Else
                Grid1.Picture = Black.Picture
            End If
        End If
    End If

End Sub
```

THE *HLOFFSET* CONTROL

HLOffset is the name of the text box control where the horizontal Landscape offset is entered. The offset is the value that determines the spacing between characters on the page. The HLOffset control has code in only one event procedure. It is

◆ HLOffset_Change()

THE *HLOFFSET_CHANGE()* EVENT PROCEDURE

The HLOffset_Change() event procedure simply flags that a save is needed. Following is a listing of the HLOffset_Change() event procedure:

LISTING 23.10. MAIN.FRM, HLOffset_Change().

```
Sub HLOffset_Change ()

    'if form is loading, enabling save flag is invalid
    If FormLoading% = True Then Exit Sub

    'flag save
    SaveNeeded% = True

End Sub
```

THE *HPOFFSET* CONTROL

HPOffset is the name of the text box control where the horizontal Portrait offset is entered. The offset is the value that determines the spacing between characters on the page. The HPOffset control has code in only one event procedure. It is

◆ HPOffset_Change()

THE *HPOFFSET_CHANGE()* EVENT PROCEDURE

The HPOffset_Change() event procedure simply flags that a save is needed. Following is a listing of the HPOffset_Change() event procedure:

LISTING 23.11. MAIN.FRM, HPOffset_Change().

```
Sub HPOffset_Change ()

    'if form is loading, enabling save flag is invalid
    If FormLoading% = True Then Exit Sub

    'flag save
    SaveNeeded% = True

End Sub
```

THE *MENU* OBJECT

The menu object was created by using Visual Basic's built-in menu editor. It has code associated with nine Click event procedures. They are

- ◆ `menu_about()`
- ◆ `menu_black()`
- ◆ `menu_exit()`
- ◆ `menu_landscape()`
- ◆ `menu_portrait()`
- ◆ `menu_reset()`
- ◆ `menu_save()`
- ◆ `menu_show()`
- ◆ `menu_white()`

THE *MENU_ABOUT_CLICK()* EVENT PROCEDURE

The `menu_about_Click()` event procedure simply shows the about form for program information. Following is a listing of the `menu_about_Click()` event procedure:

LISTING 23.12. MAIN.FRM, `menu_about_Click()`.

```
Sub menu_about_Click ()

    'show about form
    frmAbout.Show MODAL

End Sub
```

THE *MENU_BLACK_CLICK()* EVENT PROCEDURE

The `menu_black_Click()` event procedure turns the currently selected cells in `Grid1` to black. Following is a listing of the `menu_black_Click()` event procedure:

LISTING 23.13. MAIN.FRM, `menu_black_Click()`.

```
Sub menu_black_Click ()

    'declare variables
    Dim Row%        'loop counting variable for row
    Dim Col%        'loop counting variable for col


    'turn all selected cells black
    For Col% = Grid1.SelStartCol To Grid1.SelEndCol
        For Row% = Grid1.SelStartRow To Grid1.SelEndRow
```

continues

LISTING 23.13. CONTINUED

```
            Grid1.Row = Row%
            Grid1.Col = Col%
            Grid1.Picture = Black.Picture
        Next Row%
    Next Col%

End Sub
```

THE *MENU_EXIT_CLICK( )* EVENT PROCEDURE

The menu_exit_Click() event procedure starts the program exit procedure, invoked in the Form_Unload() event. Following is a listing of the menu_exit_Click() event procedure:

LISTING 23.14. MAIN.FRM, menu_exit_Click().

```
Sub menu_exit_Click ()

    'exit
    Unload frmMain

End Sub
```

THE *MENU_LANDSCAPE_CLICK( )* EVENT PROCEDURE

The menu_landscape_Click() event procedure prints raster graphics by using the specified offsets in the Landscape orientation. Following is a listing of the menu_landscape_Click() event procedure:

LISTING 23.15. MAIN.FRM, menu_landscape_Click().

```
Sub menu_landscape_Click ()

    'declare variables
    Dim m$        'message constructor

    If SaveNeeded% = True Then
        m$ = "You must save changes first!"
        MsgBox m$, 16
        Exit Sub
    End If

    'change cursor
    screen.MousePointer = HOURGLASS

    'calculate bits to send to printer
    Call CalculateBits("LANDSCAPE")
    PortLandMode% = LANDSCAPE

    If PrintTextOption.Value = True Then
            Call PrintAllText
```

```
    ElseIf PrintCharOption.Value = True Then
        If pnlCurChar.Caption = "" Then
            screen.MousePointer = DEFAULT
            m$ = "There is no character to print!"
            MsgBox m$, 16
            Exit Sub
        Else
            Call PrintCharacter
        End If
    End If

    'change cursor
    screen.MousePointer = DEFAULT

End Sub
```

THE *MENU_PORTRAIT_CLICK( )* EVENT PROCEDURE

The menu_portrait_Click() event procedure prints raster graphics by using the specified offsets in the Portrait orientation. Following is a listing of the menu_portrait_Click() event procedure:

LISTING 23.16. MAIN.FRM, menu_portrait_Click().

```
Sub menu_portrait_Click ()

    'declare variables
    Dim m$          'message constructor

    If SaveNeeded% = True Then
        m$ = "You must save changes first!"
        MsgBox m$, 16
        Exit Sub
    End If

    'change cursor
    screen.MousePointer = HOURGLASS

    'calculate bits to send to printer
    Call CalculateBits("PORTRAIT")
    PortLandMode% = PORTRAIT

    If PrintTextOption.Value = True Then
            Call PrintAllText
    ElseIf PrintCharOption.Value = True Then
        If pnlCurChar.Caption = "" Then
            screen.MousePointer = DEFAULT
            m$ = "There is no character to print!"
            MsgBox m$, 16
            Exit Sub
        Else
            Call PrintCharacter
        End If
    End If
```

continues

463

LISTING 23.16. CONTINUED

```
        'change cursor
        screen.MousePointer = DEFAULT

End Sub
```

THE *MENU_RESET_CLICK()* EVENT PROCEDURE

The menu_reset_Click() event procedure resets the grid so that all cells in the grid are turned off (white). Following is a listing of the menu_reset_Click() event procedure:

LISTING 23.17. MAIN.FRM, menu_reset_Click().

```
Sub menu_reset_click ()

    'declare variables
    Dim m$        'message constructor
    Dim res%      'holds results
    Dim Row%      'loop counting variable for row
    Dim Col%      'loop counting variable for col


    If SaveNeeded% = True Then
        m$ = "Reset without saving?"
        res% = MsgBox(m$, 292)
        If res% = IDNO Then Exit Sub
    End If

    'change cursor
    screen.MousePointer = HOURGLASS

    'set every element of Grid 1 to white (effectively clear)
    For Row% = 1 To Grid1.Rows - 1
        For Col% = 1 To Grid1.Cols - 1
            Grid1.Row = Row%
            Grid1.Col = Col%
            Grid1.Picture = Blank.Picture
        Next Col%
    Next Row%

    'move position
    Grid1.Col = 1
    Grid1.Row = 1

    'initialize
    pnlCurChar = ""
    SaveNeeded% = False
    screen.MousePointer = DEFAULT

End Sub
```

THE *MENU_SAVE_CLICK( )* EVENT PROCEDURE

The menu_save_Click() event procedure saves the current character in both Landscape and Portrait orientations to the INI file as well as all offset information. Following is a listing of the menu_save_Click() event procedure:

LISTING 23.18. MAIN.FRM, menu_save_Click( ).

```
Sub menu_save_Click ()

    'declare variables
    Dim lpFileName$  'holds name of file for INI file
    Dim res          'holds results of INI file
    Dim loopcount%   'loop counting variable
    Dim lpAppName$   'holds name of application ([]) for INI file
    Dim TheLetter$   'temporary letter for saving
    Dim GridText$    'temporary variable for storing text of grid
    Dim Row%         'loop counting variable for row
    Dim Col%         'loop counting variable for col

    'change cursor
    screen.MousePointer = HOURGLASS

    'save configuration to file
    lpFileName$ = UCase$(FileName.Text)

    'save text information
    If PrintText.Text <> "" Then
        res = WritePrivateProfileString("TEXT", "Line1", Trim$(PrintText.Text),
        lpFileName$)
    End If

    'save coordinate information
        'PORTRAIT
        If HPStart.Text <> "" Then
            res = WritePrivateProfileString("COORDINATES", "Portrait1StartX",
            Trim$(HPStart.Text), lpFileName$)
        End If
        If VPStart.Text <> "" Then
            res = WritePrivateProfileString("COORDINATES", "Portrait1StartY",
            Trim$(VPStart.Text), lpFileName$)
        End If
        If HPOffset.Text <> "" Then
            res = WritePrivateProfileString("COORDINATES", "PortraitIncrementX",
            Trim$(HPOffset.Text), lpFileName$)
        End If
        If VPOffset.Text <> "" Then
            res = WritePrivateProfileString("COORDINATES", "PortraitIncrementY",
            Trim$(VPOffset.Text), lpFileName$)
        End If

        'LANDSCAPE
        If HLStart.Text <> "" Then
            res = WritePrivateProfileString("COORDINATES", "Landscape1StartX",
            Trim$(HLStart.Text), lpFileName$)
```

continues

LISTING 23.18. CONTINUED

```
        End If
        If VLStart.Text <> "" Then
            res = WritePrivateProfileString("COORDINATES", "Landscape1StartY",
            Trim$(VLStart.Text), lpFileName$)
        End If
        If HLOffset.Text <> "" Then
            res = WritePrivateProfileString("COORDINATES", "LandscapeIncrementX",
            Trim$(HLOffset.Text), lpFileName$)
        End If
        If VLOffset.Text <> "" Then
            res = WritePrivateProfileString("COORDINATES", "LandscapeIncrementY",
            Trim$(VLOffset.Text), lpFileName$)
        End If

    'save data
    If pnlCurChar.Caption <> "" Then

        'cycle through both portrait and landscape
        For loopcount% = 1 To 2
            If loopcount% = 1 Then
                lpAppName$ = "PORTRAIT"
                PortLandMode% = PORTRAIT
                Call CalculateBits("PORTRAIT")
                frmMessage.pnlMessage.Caption = "Please Wait..." + Chr$(13) + "Saving
                Portrait"
                frmMessage.Show
                DoEvents
            ElseIf loopcount% = 2 Then
                lpAppName$ = "LANDSCAPE"
                PortLandMode% = LANDSCAPE
                Call CalculateBits("LANDSCAPE")
                frmMessage.pnlMessage.Caption = "Please Wait..." + Chr$(13) + "Saving
                Landscape"
                DoEvents
            End If

            'assign the letter
            TheLetter$ = pnlCurChar.Caption
            'cycle through each row in grid
            GridText$ = ""
            For Row% = 1 To Grid2.Rows - 1
                'cycle through each column in grid2
                For Col% = 1 To 4
                    Grid2.Row = Row%
                    Grid2.Col = Col%
                    If Trim$(Grid2.Text) <> "" Then
                        GridText$ = GridText$ + Trim$(Grid2.Text)
                    Else
                        GridText$ = GridText$ + "0"
                    End If
                    GridText$ = GridText$ + ","
                Next Col%
            Next Row%
```

```
                    'remove last ','
                    GridText$ = Left$(GridText$, Len(GridText$) - 1)

                    'test for case
                    If Asc(TheLetter$) > 96 And Asc(TheLetter$) < 123 Then
                        'lower case
                        res = WritePrivateProfileString(lpAppName$, "LC" + TheLetter$, GridText$,
                        lpFileName$)
                    Else
                        'all others(uppercase and numbers, etc...)
                        res = WritePrivateProfileString(lpAppName$, TheLetter$, GridText$,
                        lpFileName$)
                    End If

            Next loopcount%

        End If

        'initialize
        SaveNeeded% = False

        Unload frmMessage
        DoEvents

        'change cursor
        screen.MousePointer = DEFAULT

End Sub
```

For more information about the `WritePrivateProfileString` API function, refer to Chapter 3, "Calling Windows APIs and DLLs."

THE *menu_show_Click()* EVENT PROCEDURE

The `menu_show_Click()` event procedure shows the frame that lists all of the codes that will be sent to the printer in Portrait orientation. If selected again, the procedure will also hide the frame if it is shown. Following is a listing of the `menu_show_Click()` event procedure:

LISTING 23.19. MAIN.FRM, `menu_show_Click()`.

```
Sub menu_show_Click ()

    'toggle binary frame (bit representation)
    If BinaryFrame.Visible = True Then
        BinaryFrame.Visible = False
    Else
        BinaryFrame.Visible = True
    End If

End Sub
```

THE *menu_white_Click()* EVENT PROCEDURE

The menu_white_Click() event procedure turns the currently selected cells in Grid1 to white (off). Following is a listing of the menu_white_Click() event procedure:

LISTING 23.20. MAIN.FRM, menu_white_Click().

```
Sub menu_white_Click ()

    'declare variables
    Dim Row%            'loop counting variable for row
    Dim Col%            'loop counting variable for col

    'turn all selected cells white
    For Col% = Grid1.SelStartCol To Grid1.SelEndCol
        For Row% = Grid1.SelStartRow To Grid1.SelEndRow
            Grid1.Row = Row%
            Grid1.Col = Col%
            Grid1.Picture = Blank.Picture
        Next Row%
    Next Col%

End Sub
```

THE *PrintText* CONTROL

PrintText is the name of the textbox control that indicates the characters that print from the INI file. The PrintText control has code in one event procedures. It is

◆   PrintText_Change()

THE *PrintText_Change()* EVENT PROCEDURE

The PrintText_Change() event procedure simply flags that a save is needed. Following is a listing of the PrintText_Change() event procedure:

LISTING 23.21. MAIN.FRM, PrintText_Change().

```
Sub PrintText_Change ()

    'if form is loading, enabling save flag is invalid
    If FormLoading% = True Then Exit Sub

    'flag save
    SaveNeeded% = True

End Sub
```

THE *VLOFFSET* CONTROL

VLOffset is the name of the text box control where the vertical Landscape offset is entered. The offset is the value that determines the spacing between characters on the page. The VLOffset control has code in only one event procedure. It is

◆ VLOffset_Change()

THE *VLOFFSET_CHANGE()* EVENT PROCEDURE

The VLOffset_Change() event procedure simply flags that a save is needed. Following is a listing of the VLOffset_Change() event procedure:

LISTING 23.22. MAIN.FRM, VLOffset_Change().

```
Sub VLOffset_Change ()

    'if form is loading, enabling save flag is invalid
    If FormLoading% = True Then Exit Sub

    'flag save
    SaveNeeded% = True

End Sub
```

THE *VPOFFSET* CONTROL

VPOffset is the name of the text box control where the vertical Portrait offset is entered. The offset is the value that determines the spacing between characters on the page. The VPOffset control has code in only one event procedure. It is

◆ VPOffset_Change()

THE *VPOFFSET_CHANGE()* EVENT PROCEDURE

The VPOffset_Change() event procedure simply flags that a save is needed. Following is a listing of the VPOffset_Change() event procedure:

LISTING 23.23. MAIN.FRM, VPOffset_Change().

```
Sub VPOffset_Change ()

    'if form is loading, enabling save flag is invalid
    If FormLoading% = True Then Exit Sub

    'flag save
    SaveNeeded% = True

End Sub
```

THE CHARSEL.FRM FILE

CHARSEL.FRM is one of four forms in this application. It is used to select the characters that can be edited and saved in the INI file. Figure 23.2 presented this form as it appears at runtime. Figure 23.4 shows the form as it appears at design time. Only one command button is shown because it is a control array that loads the controls at runtime. Table 23.2 lists all the relevant properties of each control on the form that have been changed from their standard default values. The CHARSEL.FRM file is contained on the CD accompanying this book in the CHAP23 subdirectory.

FIGURE 23.4.
Raster Graphics Editor application CHARSEL.FRM at design time.

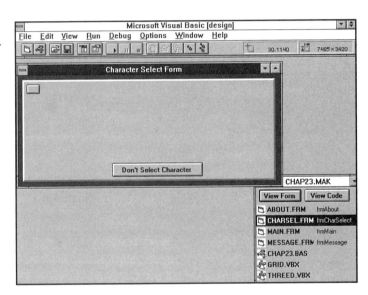

TABLE 23.2. PROPERTIES OF EACH CONTROL ON CHARSEL.FRM.

Object	Control Type	Property	Value
frmCharsel	Form	BackColor	&H00404000&
		Caption	"Character Select Form"
		Height	3420
		Left	1035
		MaxButton	False
		Top	1140
		Width	7485
Panel3D1	SSPanel	BackColor	&H00C0C0C0&
		BevelWidth	3
		Font3D	None

Object	Control Type	Property	Value
		ForeColor	&H0000FFFF&
		Height	2775
		Left	120
		Top	120
		Width	7095
cmdNoSelect	CommandButton	Caption	"Don't Select Character"
		Height	375
		Left	2520
		Top	2280
		Width	2535
cmdChar	CommandButton	Height	255
		Index	0
		Left	120
		Top	120
		Width	375

FUNCTION, SUBROUTINE, AND EVENT PROCEDURES

There are several procedures of code for each object(control) that comprise this form. Each is listed in the following sections.

THE *(GENERAL)* OBJECT

The (general) object contains form level declarations and no form level procedures. The procedure for the (general) object is

◆ (declarations)

THE *(DECLARATIONS)* PROCEDURE

The (declarations) procedure contains only one line of declarations used in the form, CHARSEL.FRM. It is only to allow for variable syntax checking and forcing the declaration of variables in each procedure. Following is a listing of the (declarations) procedure:

LISTING 23.24. CHARSEL.FRM, (general)(declarations).

```
Option Explicit
```

THE *CMDCHAR* CONTROL

cmdChar is the name of the command button control that, when clicked, selects the character represented on the caption of the command button and closes the form. The cmdChar control has code in only one event procedure. It is

◆ cmdChar_Click()

THE *CMDCHAR_CLICK()* EVENT PROCEDURE

The cmdChar_Click() event procedure selects a character and unloads the form. Following is a listing of the cmdChar_Click() event procedure:

LISTING 23.25. CHARSEL.FRM, cmdChar_Click().

```
Sub cmdChar_Click (Index As Integer)

    'change caption to letter selected
    frmMain.pnlCurChar.Caption = cmdChar(Index).Caption
    DoEvents

    'unload form, yield to processor with doevents
    Unload frmCharSelect
    DoEvents
    DoEvents
    DoEvents

    'flag character as changing so that the new char
    'can be populated
    Call CharacterChange

End Sub
```

THE *CMDNOSELECT* CONTROL

cmdNoSelect is the name of the command button control that, when clicked, closes the form without selection. The cmdNoSelect control has code in only one event procedure. It is

◆ cmdNoSelect_Click()

THE *CMDNOSELECT_CLICK()* EVENT PROCEDURE

The cmdNoSelect_Click() event procedure simply unloads the form. Following is a listing of the cmdNoSelect_Click() event procedure:

LISTING 23.26. CHARSEL.FRM, cmdNoSelect_Click().

```
Sub cmdNoSelect_Click ()

    'unload
```

```
        Unload frmCharSelect

End Sub
```

THE *FORM* OBJECT

The Form object has code in only one event procedure. It is

◆ Form_Load()

THE *FORM_LOAD()* EVENT PROCEDURE

The Form_Load() event simply calls the routine to center the form and to load and position the control array of command buttons to select. Following is a listing of the Form_Load() event procedure:

LISTING 23.27. CHARSEL.FRM, Form_Load().

```
Sub Form_Load ()

    'declare variables
    Dim loopcount%   'loop counting variable
    Dim ThisIndex%   'index of current control array
    Dim PrevIndex%   'index of previous control array

    'change cursor
    screen.MousePointer = HOURGLASS

    'center the form
    CenterForm Me

    'loop through all printable ansi values
    For loopcount% = 33 To 126

        ThisIndex% = loopcount% - 32
        PrevIndex% = loopcount% - 33

        Load cmdChar(ThisIndex%)
        cmdChar(ThisIndex%).Caption = Chr$(loopcount%)
        cmdChar(ThisIndex%).Visible = True


        'reset if line is filled up
        If (ThisIndex%) Mod 16 = 0 Then
            'filled up, restart
            cmdChar(ThisIndex%).Left = cmdChar(0).Left
            cmdChar(ThisIndex%).Top = cmdChar(ThisIndex% - 16).Top + cmdChar(ThisIndex% -
            16).Height + 50
        Else
            'position the button
            cmdChar(ThisIndex%).Left = cmdChar(PrevIndex%).Left +
            cmdChar(PrevIndex%).Width + 50
```

continues

473

LISTING 23.27. CONTINUED

```
                cmdChar(ThisIndex%).Top = cmdChar(PrevIndex%).Top
        End If
    Next loopcount%

    'reset cursor
    screen.MousePointer = DEFAULT

End Sub
```

THE MESSAGE.FRM FILE

MESSAGE.FRM is one of four forms in this application. It is used to display the status of the state the application is in, such as `Populating` or `Saving Landscape`. Figure 23.5 shows the MESSAGE.FRM at runtime. It is not significant enough to show it at design time. Table 23.3 lists all the relevant properties of each control on the form that have been changed from their standard default values. The MESSAGE.FRM file is contained on the CD accompanying this book in the CHAP23 subdirectory.

FIGURE 23.5.
*Raster Graphics
Editor application
MESSAGE.FRM at
runtime.*

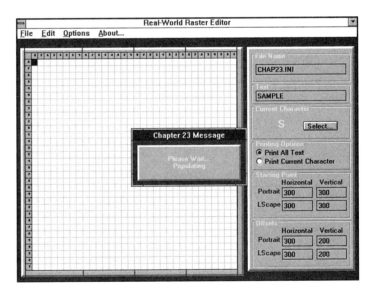

TABLE 23.3. PROPERTIES OF EACH CONTROL ON MESSAGE.FRM.

Object	Control Type	Property	Value
frmMessage	Form	BackColor	&H00404000&
		Caption	"Chapter 23 Message"

Object	Control Type	Property	Value
		Height	1590
		Left	3165
		MaxButton	False
		MinButton	False
		Top	2970
		Width	3255
pnlMessage	SSPanel	BackColor	&H00C0C0C0&
		BevelWidth	3
		Font3D	None
		ForeColor	&H0000FFFF&
		Height	975
		Left	120
		Top	120
		Width	2895

FUNCTION, SUBROUTINE, AND EVENT PROCEDURES

There are several procedures of code for each object(control) that comprise this form. Each is listed in the following sections.

THE (GENERAL) OBJECT

The (general) object contains only one form level declaration and no form level procedures. The procedure for the (general) object is

- ◆ (declarations)

THE (DECLARATIONS) PROCEDURE

The (declarations) procedure contains only one line of declarations used in the form, MESSAGE.FRM. It is only to allow for variable syntax checking and forcing the declaration of variables in each procedure. Following is a listing of the (declarations) procedure:

LISTING 23.28. MESSAGE.FRM, (general)(declarations).

```
Option Explicit
```

THE *FORM* OBJECT

The Form object has code in only one event procedure. It is

◆ Form_Load()

THE *FORM_LOAD()* EVENT PROCEDURE

The Form_Load() event procedure simply centers the form. Following is a listing of the Form_Load() event procedure:

LISTING 23.29. MESSAGE.FRM, Form_Load().

```
Sub Form_Load ()

    'center the form
    CenterForm Me

End Sub
```

THE ABOUT.FRM FILE

ABOUT.FRM is one of four forms in this application. It shows information about the application. Figure 23.6 presents the form as it appears at runtime. Fundamentally, there is no difference in the form at design time, so it is not presented. Table 23.4 lists all the relevant properties of each control on the form that have been changed from their standard default values. The ABOUT.FRM file is contained on the CD accompanying this book in the CHAP23 subdirectory.

FIGURE 23.6.
Raster Graphics Editor application About form at runtime.

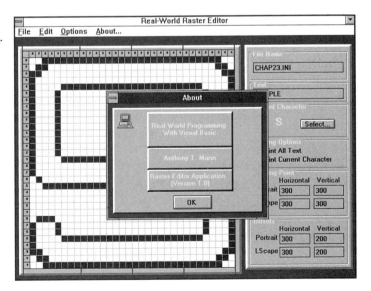

TABLE 23.4. PROPERTIES OF EACH CONTROL ON **ABOUT.FRM.**

Object	Control Type	Property	Value
frmAbout	Form	BackColor	&H00404000&
		Caption	"About"
		Height	3525
		Left	1035
		MaxButton	False
		MinButton	False
		Top	1140
		Width	4545
pnlMain	SSPanel	BackColor	&H00C0C0C0&
		BevelWidth	3
		Caption	" "
		Font3D	None
		ForeColor	&H00C0C0C0&
		Height	2395
		Left	120
		RoundedCorners	False
		ShadowColor	Black
		Top	120
		Width	4215
pnl1	SSPanel	BackColor	&H00C0C0C0&
		BevelWidth	3
		Caption	"Real-World Programming With Visual Basic"
		Font3D	None
		ForeColor	&H0000FFFF&
		Height	975
		Left	960
		RoundedCorners	False
		ShadowColor	Black
		Top	120
		Width	2415

continues

TABLE 23.4. CONTINUED

Object	Control Type	Property	Value
pnl2	SSPanel	BackColor	&H00C0C0C0&
		BevelWidth	3
		Caption	"Anthony T. Mann"
		Font3D	None
		ForeColor	&H0000FFFF&
		Height	615
		Left	960
		RoundedCorners	False
		ShadowColor	Black
		Top	1080
		Width	2415
pnl3	SSPanel	BackColor	&H00C0C0C0&
		BevelWidth	3
		Caption	"Raster Editor Application (Version 1.0)"
		Font3D	None
		ForeColor	&H0000FFFF&
		Height	615
		Left	960
		RoundedCorners	False
		ShadowColor	Black
		Top	1680
		Width	2415
cmdOK	CommandButton	Caption	"OK"
		Height	375
		Left	1680
		Top	2400
		Width	1095
pictAbout	PictureBox	Autosize	True
		BackColor	&H00C0C0C0&

Object	Control Type	Property	Value
		BorderStyle	None
		Height	615
		Left	120
		Top	120
		Width	735

FUNCTION, SUBROUTINE, AND EVENT PROCEDURES

There are several procedures of code for each object(control) that comprise this form. Each is listed in the following sections.

THE *(DECLARATIONS)* PROCEDURE

The (declarations) procedure contains only one line of declarations used in the form, ABOUT.FRM. It is only to allow for variable syntax checking and forcing the declaration of variables in each procedure. Following is a listing of the (declarations) procedure:

LISTING 23.30. ABOUT.FRM, (general)(declarations).

```
Option Explicit
```

THE *CMDOK* CONTROL

cmdOK is the name of the command button control that, when clicked, closes the frmAbout form. The cmdOK control has code in only one event procedure. It is

◆ cmdOK_Click()

THE *CMDOK_CLICK()* EVENT PROCEDURE

The cmdOK_Click() event procedure simply unloads the form. Following is a listing of the cmdOK_Click() event procedure:

LISTING 23.31. ABOUT.FRM, cmdOK_Click().

```
Sub cmdOK_Click ()

    'unload
    Unload frmAbout

End Sub
```

479

THE *FORM* OBJECT

The Form object itself has code in only one event procedure. It is

◆ Form_Load()

THE *FORM_LOAD()* EVENT PROCEDURE

The Form_Load() event procedure centers the form and assigns an icon to the pictAbout control. Following is a listing of the Form_Load() event procedure:

LISTING 23.32. ABOUT.FRM, Form_Load().

```
Sub Form_Load ()

    'center form
    CenterForm Me

    'load icon
    pictAbout.Picture = frmMain.Icon

End Sub
```

THE CHAP23.BAS FILE

CHAP23.BAS is the module that contains application level variables and procedures. The CHAP23.BAS file is contained on the CD accompanying this book in the CHAP23 subdirectory.

FUNCTION, SUBROUTINE, AND EVENT PROCEDURES

There are several procedures of code for each object(control) that comprise this module. Each is listed in the following sections.

The (general) object contains application level variables and procedures. The procedures for the (general) object are

◆ (declarations)
◆ CenterForm()
◆ CharacterChange()
◆ FillDots()
◆ ReadFromFile()

THE *(DECLARATIONS)* PROCEDURE

The (declarations) procedure contains variable declarations used in the application. Following is a listing of the (declarations) procedure:

LISTING 23.33. CHAP23.BAS, (general)(declarations).

```
Option Explicit

'declare variables
Global PortLandMode%      'holds current view (PORTRAIT or LANDSCAPE)
Global FormLoading%       'flag for form loading
Global SaveNeeded%        'flag for saving needing to be performed

'API declarations
Declare Function GetPrivateProfileString Lib "Kernel" (ByVal lpAppName
 As String, ByVal lpKeyName As String, ByVal lpDefault As String,
 ByVal lpReturnedString As String, ByVal nSize As Integer, ByVal
 lpFileName As String) As Integer
Declare Function WritePrivateProfileString Lib "Kernel" (ByVal lpApplicationName As
String, ByVal lpKeyName As String, ByVal lpString
 As String, ByVal lpFileName As String) As Integer

'Printing Mode values
Global Const PORTRAIT = 1
Global Const LANDSCAPE = 2

' MsgBox return values
Global Const IDYES = 6              ' Yes button pressed
Global Const IDNO = 7               ' No button pressed

' Cursor values
Global Const HOURGLASS = 11         ' Hourglass
Global Const DEFAULT = 0            ' Arrow
Global Const MODAL = 1
```

THE *CENTERFORM()* PROCEDURE

The CenterForm() procedure simply centers the form in the client area. Following is a listing of the CenterForm() procedure:

LISTING 23.34. CHAP23.BAS, CenterForm().

```
Sub CenterForm (F As Form)

    'center the form
    F.Move (Screen.Width - F.ScaleWidth) / 2, (Screen.Height -F.ScaleHeight) / 2

End Sub
```

THE *CHARACTERCHANGE()* PROCEDURE

The CharacterChange() procedure populates the grid with data for the new character selected. Following is a listing of the CharacterChange() procedure:

481

LISTING 23.35. CHAP23.BAS, `CharacterChange()`.

```
Sub CharacterChange ()

    'change cursor
    Screen.MousePointer = HOURGLASS

    If frmMain.pnlCurChar.Caption <> "" Then
    'read data from ini file
    Call ReadFromFile
    End If

    'fill grid with bitmap
    Call FillDots

    'change cursor
    Screen.MousePointer = DEFAULT

End Sub
```

THE *FILLDOTS()* PROCEDURE

The `FillDots()` procedure fills each pixel in `Grid1` with the data read from the INI file. The `FillDots()` procedure is doing quite a log. It has to determine which orientation is desired and cycle through each grid and populate it. `Grid1` contains the on/off bitmaps that the user sees, and `Grid2` contains the integer representation of the corresponding bit codes.

 For more information about how this process works, refer to Chapter 6, "Printing."

Following is a listing of the `FillDots()` procedure:

LISTING 23.36. CHAP23.BAS, `FillDots()`.

```
Sub FillDots ()

    'declare variables
    Dim loopcount%   'loopcounting variable
    Dim InnerLoop%   'loop counting variable
    Dim Temp%        'temporary variable
    Dim NewTemp%     'temporary variable


    'show user message
    frmMessage.pnlMessage.Caption = "Please Wait..." + Chr$(13) + "Populating"
    frmMessage.Show
    DoEvents

    'clear grid1
    For loopcount% = 1 To frmMain.Grid1.Rows - 1
    For InnerLoop% = 1 To frmMain.Grid1.Cols - 1
        frmMain.Grid1.Row = loopcount%
        frmMain.Grid1.Col = InnerLoop%
        frmMain.Grid1.Picture = frmMain.Blank.Picture
```

```
Next InnerLoop%
Next loopcount%
DoEvents

'portrait
If PortLandMode% = PORTRAIT Then
For loopcount% = 1 To frmMain.Grid1.Rows - 1
    For InnerLoop% = 1 To frmMain.Grid1.Cols - 1
    frmMain.Grid1.Row = loopcount%
    frmMain.Grid2.Row = loopcount%
    frmMain.Grid1.Col = InnerLoop%

    If frmMain.Grid1.Col >= 1 And frmMain.Grid1.Col <= 8 Then
        frmMain.Grid2.Col = 1
    ElseIf frmMain.Grid1.Col >= 9 And frmMain.Grid1.Col <= 16 Then
        frmMain.Grid2.Col = 2
    ElseIf frmMain.Grid1.Col >= 17 And frmMain.Grid1.Col <= 24 Then
        frmMain.Grid2.Col = 3
    ElseIf frmMain.Grid1.Col >= 25 And frmMain.Grid1.Col <= 32 Then
        frmMain.Grid2.Col = 4
    End If

    frmMain.Grid2.Row = frmMain.Grid1.Row
    frmMain.Grid1.Row = 0
    Temp% = Val(Trim$(frmMain.Grid1.Text))
        frmMain.Grid1.Row = loopcount%
        Select Case (Temp%)
            Case 8:
            NewTemp% = 128
            Case 7:
            NewTemp% = 64
            Case 6:
            NewTemp% = 32
            Case 5:
            NewTemp% = 16
            Case 4:
            NewTemp% = 8
            Case 3:
            NewTemp% = 4
            Case 2:
            NewTemp% = 2
            Case 1:
            NewTemp% = 1
        End Select
        If (Val(Trim$(frmMain.Grid2.Text)) And (NewTemp%)) > 0 Then
            frmMain.Grid1.Picture = frmMain.Black.Picture
        End If
    Next InnerLoop%
Next loopcount%
ElseIf PortLandMode% = LANDSCAPE Then
For loopcount% = frmMain.Grid1.Cols - 1 To 1 Step -1
    For InnerLoop% = 1 To frmMain.Grid1.Rows - 1
    frmMain.Grid1.Col = loopcount%
    frmMain.Grid1.Row = InnerLoop%
    Select Case (frmMain.Grid1.Row)
        Case 1 To 8:
        frmMain.Grid2.Col = 1
```

LISTING 23.36. CONTINUED

```
            Case 9 To 16:
            frmMain.Grid2.Col = 2
            Case 17 To 24:
            frmMain.Grid2.Col = 3
            Case 25 To 32:
            frmMain.Grid2.Col = 4
        End Select


        frmMain.Grid2.Row = (32 - frmMain.Grid1.Col) + 1
        frmMain.Grid1.Col = 0
        Temp% = (Val(Trim$(frmMain.Grid1.Text)))
            frmMain.Grid1.Row = InnerLoop%
            frmMain.Grid1.Col = loopcount%
            Select Case (Temp%)
                Case 8:
                NewTemp% = 128
                Case 7:
                NewTemp% = 64
                Case 6:
                NewTemp% = 32
                Case 5:
                NewTemp% = 16
                Case 4:
                NewTemp% = 8
                Case 3:
                NewTemp% = 4
                Case 2:
                NewTemp% = 2
                Case 1:
                NewTemp% = 1
            End Select
            If (Val(Trim$(frmMain.Grid2.Text)) And (NewTemp%)) > 0 Then
                frmMain.Grid1.Picture = frmMain.Black.Picture
            End If

        Next InnerLoop%
    Next loopcount%
    End If
    DoEvents


    'hide user message
    Unload frmMessage
    DoEvents

End Sub
```

THE *READFROMFILE( )* PROCEDURE

The ReadFromFile() procedure reads all data from the INI file and places the dots into the appropriate controls on the form, frmMain. Following is a listing of the ReadFromFile() procedure:

LISTING 23.37. CHAP23.BAS, ReadFromFile().

```
Sub ReadFromFile ()

    'declare variables
    Dim TextInfo$    'holds text from INI file
    Dim res          'holds results
    Dim Coord$       'holds coordinate results from INI file
    Dim lpAppName$   'holds name of application ([]) in INI file
    Dim String1$     'holds return data from INI file
    Dim loopcount%   'loop counting variable
    Dim InnerLoop%   'loop counting variable
    Dim Row%         'loop counting variable for row
    Dim Col%         'loop counting variable for col
    Dim pos%         'holds position of character

    'change cursor
    Screen.MousePointer = HOURGLASS

    'show user message
    frmMessage.pnlMessage.Caption = "Please Wait..." + Chr$(13) + "Reading File"
    frmMessage.Show
    DoEvents

    'read text info
    TextInfo$ = Space(100)
    res = GetPrivateProfileString("TEXT", "Line1", "", TextInfo$, 100,
    CurDir$ + "\" + frmMain.FileName.Text)
    frmMain.PrintText.Text = Left$(TextInfo$, res)

    'read coordinate info
    'PORTRAIT
    Coord$ = Space(10)
    res = GetPrivateProfileString("COORDINATES", "Portrait1StartX",
    "", Coord$, 10,. CurDir$ + "\" + frmMain.FileName.Text)
    frmMain.HPStart.Text = Left$(Coord$, res)

    res = GetPrivateProfileString("COORDINATES", "Portrait1StartY",
    "", Coord$, 10, CurDir$ + "\" + frmMain.FileName.Text)
    frmMain.VPStart.Text = Left$(Coord$, res)

    res = GetPrivateProfileString("COORDINATES", "PortraitIncrementX",
    "", Coord$, 10, CurDir$ + "\" + frmMain.FileName.Text)
    frmMain.HPOffset.Text = Left$(Coord$, res)

    res = GetPrivateProfileString("COORDINATES", "PortraitIncrementY",
    "", Coord$, 10, CurDir$ + "\" + frmMain.FileName.Text)
    frmMain.VPOffset.Text = Left$(Coord$, res)

    'LANDSCAPE
    Coord$ = Space(10)
    res = GetPrivateProfileString("COORDINATES", "Landscape1StartX",
    "", Coord$, 10, CurDir$ + "\" + frmMain.FileName.Text)
    frmMain.HLStart.Text = Left$(Coord$, res)

    res = GetPrivateProfileString("COORDINATES", "Landscape1StartY",
    "", Coord$, 10, CurDir$ + "\" + frmMain.FileName.Text)
```

continues

LISTING 23.37. CONTINUED

```
frmMain.VLStart.Text = Left$(Coord$, res)
res = GetPrivateProfileString("COORDINATES", "LandscapeIncrementX",
"", Coord$, 10, CurDir$ + "\" + frmMain.FileName.Text)
frmMain.HLOffset.Text = Left$(Coord$, res)

res = GetPrivateProfileString("COORDINATES", "LandscapeIncrementY",
"", Coord$, 10, CurDir$ + "\" + frmMain.FileName.Text)
frmMain.VLOffset.Text = Left$(Coord$, res)

'don't read actual characters on form load
If FormLoading% = True Then Exit Sub

'read data
If PortLandMode% = PORTRAIT Then
lpAppName$ = "PORTRAIT"
ElseIf PortLandMode% = LANDSCAPE Then
lpAppName$ = "LANDSCAPE"
End If

String1$ = Space$(4096)
If frmMain.pnlCurChar.Caption <> "" Then
If Asc(frmMain.pnlCurChar.Caption) > 96 And Asc(frmMain.pnlCurChar.Caption) < 123
Then
    'lower case
    res = GetPrivateProfileString(lpAppName$, "LC" + frmMain.pnlCurChar.Caption, "",
    String1$, 4096, CurDir$ + "\" + frmMain.FileName.Text)
Else
    'all others (uppercase and numbers)
    res = GetPrivateProfileString(lpAppName$, frmMain.pnlCurChar.Caption,
    "", String1$, 4096, CurDir$ + "\" + frmMain.FileName.Text)
End If
Else
res = GetPrivateProfileString(lpAppName$, frmMain.pnlCurChar.Caption,
"", String1$, 4096, CurDir$ + "\" + frmMain.FileName.Text)
End If
'String1$ = Trim$(String1$)
String1$ = Left$(String1$, res)

'first clear 2nd grid
For loopcount% = 1 To frmMain.Grid2.Rows - 1
For InnerLoop% = 1 To frmMain.Grid2.Cols - 1
    frmMain.Grid2.Row = loopcount%
    frmMain.Grid2.Col = InnerLoop%
    frmMain.Grid2.Text = ""
Next InnerLoop%
Next loopcount%

'input data into 2nd grid
For Row% = 1 To frmMain.Grid2.Rows - 1
For Col% = 1 To 4
    frmMain.Grid2.Row = Row%
    frmMain.Grid2.Col = Col%
    pos% = InStr(String1$, ",")
    If pos% <> 0 Then
    frmMain.Grid2.Text = Left$(String1$, pos% - 1)
    String1$ = Right$(String1$, Len(String1$) - pos%)
```

```
        Else
            frmMain.Grid2.Text = String1$
        End If
    Next Col%
    Next Row%

    'hide user message
    Unload frmMessage
    DoEvents

    'change cursor
    Screen.MousePointer = DEFAULT

End Sub
```

For more information about the GetPrivateProfileString() API function, refer to Chapter 3, "Calling Windows APIs and DLLs."

THE CHAP23.INI FILE

This is the file that will be read from the CD. It contains all of the information needed to load and print the raster data. The following lists the contents of the CHAP23.INI file as it appears on the CD in the CHAP23 subdirectory.

LISTING 23.38. CHAP23.INI FILE.

```
[TEXT]
Line1=SAMPLE

[PORTRAIT]
S=63,255,255,252,96,0,0,6,192,0,0,3,128,0,0,1,135,255,255,225,136,0,0,
17,136,0,0,17,136,0,0,14,136,0,0,0,136,0,0,0,136,0,0,0,136,0,0,0,136,
0,0,0,136,0,0,0,136,0,0,0,135,255,255,252,128,0,0,6,128,0,0,3,64,0,0,
1,63,255,255,193,0,0,0,33,0,0,0,17,0,0,0,17,0,0,0,17,112,0,0,17,136,0,
0,17,136,0,0,17,135,255,255,225,128,0,0,1,192,0,0,3,96,0,0,6,63,255,255,
252
A=127,255,255,254,128,0,0,1,128,0,0,1,128,0,0,1,135,255,255,225,136,0,
0,17,136,0,0,17,136,0,0,17,136,0,0,17,136,0,0,17,136,0,0,17,136,0,0,17,
136,0,0,17,136,0,0,17,136,0,0,17,135,255,255,225,128,0,0,1,128,0,0,1,128,
0,0,1,135,255,255,225,136,0,0,17,136,0,0,17,136,0,0,17,136,0,0,17,136,0,
0,17,136,0,0,17,136,0,0,17,136,0,0,17,136,0,0,17,136,0,0,17,136,0,0,17,
112,0,0,14
M=127,255,255,254,128,0,0,1,128,0,0,1,128,0,0,1,135,248,63,225,136,4,64,
17,136,4,64,17,136,4,64,17,136,4,64,17,136,4,64,17,136,4,64,17,136,4,64,
17,136,4,64,17,136,4,64,17,136,4,64,17,136,4,64,17,136,4,64,17,136,4,64,
17,136,4,64,17,136,3,128,17,136,0,0,17,136,0,0,17,136,0,0,17,136,0,0,17,
136,0,0,17,136,0,0,17,136,0,0,17,136,0,0,17,136,0,0,17,136,0,0,17,136,0,
0,17,112,0,0,14
P=127,255,255,254,128,0,0,1,128,0,0,1,128,0,0,1,135,255,255,225,136,0,0,
17,136,0,0,17,136,0,0,17,136,0,0,17,136,0,0,17,136,0,0,17,136,0,0,17,136,
```

continues

Listing 23.38. continued

```
0,0,17,136,0,0,17,135,255,255,225,128,0,0,1,128,0,0,1,128,0,0,1,135,255,
255,254,136,0,0,0,136,0,0,0,136,0,0,0,136,0,0,0,136,0,0,0,136,0,0,0,136,
0,0,0,136,0,0,0,136,0,0,0,136,0,0,0,136,0,0,0,136,0,0,0,112,0,0,0
L=112,0,0,0,136,0,0,0,136,0,0,0,136,0,0,0,136,0,0,0,136,0,0,0,136,0,0,0,
136,0,0,0,136,0,0,0,136,0,0,0,136,0,0,0,136,0,0,0,136,0,0,0,136,0,0,0,
136,0,0,0,136,0,0,0,136,0,0,0,136,0,0,0,136,0,0,0,136,0,0,0,136,0,0,0,
136,0,0,0,136,0,0,0,136,0,0,0,136,0,0,0,136,0,0,0,136,0,0,0,135,255,255,
240,128,0,0,8,128,0,0,8,128,0,0,8,127,255,255,240
E=255,255,255,254,128,0,0,1,128,0,0,1,128,0,0,1,135,255,255,254,136,0,0,
0,136,0,0,0,136,0,0,0,136,0,0,0,136,0,0,0,136,0,0,0,136,0,0,0,136,0,0,0,
136,0,0,0,135,255,224,0,128,0,16,0,128,0,16,0,128,0,16,0,135,255,224,0,
136,0,0,0,136,0,0,0,136,0,0,0,136,0,0,0,136,0,0,0,136,0,0,0,136,0,0,0,
136,0,0,0,135,255,255,254,128,0,0,1,128,0,0,1,128,0,0,1,255,255,255,254

[LANDSCAPE]
S=62,0,127,252,97,0,192,6,193,1,128,3,129,1,0,1,134,1,7,225,136,1,8,17,
136,1,16,17,136,1,16,17,136,1,16,17,136,1,16,17,136,1,16,17,136,1,16,17,
136,1,16,17,136,1,16,17,136,1,16,17,136,1,16,17,136,1,16,17,136,1,16,17,
136,1,16,17,136,1,16,17,136,1,16,17,136,1,16,17,136,1,16,17,136,1,16,17,
136,1,16,17,136,1,16,17,136,1,16,17,135,254,16,97,128,0,16,129,192,0,16,
131,96,0,32,134,63,255,192,124
A=127,255,255,254,128,0,0,1,128,0,0,1,128,0,0,1,135,254,15,254,136,1,16,
0,136,1,16,0,136,1,16,0,136,1,16,0,136,1,16,0,136,1,16,0,136,1,16,0,136,
1,16,0,136,1,16,0,136,1,16,0,136,1,16,0,136,1,16,0,136,1,16,0,136,1,16,0,
136,1,16,0,136,1,16,0,136,1,16,0,136,1,16,0,136,1,16,0,136,1,16,0,136,1,
16,0,136,1,16,0,135,254,15,254,128,0,0,1,128,0,0,1,128,0,0,1,127,255,255,
254
M=127,255,255,254,128,0,0,1,128,0,0,1,128,0,0,1,135,255,255,254,136,0,0,
0,136,0,0,0,136,0,0,0,136,0,0,0,136,0,0,0,136,0,0,0,136,0,0,0,136,0,0,0,
136,0,0,0,135,255,224,0,128,0,16,0,128,0,16,0,128,0,16,0,135,255,224,0,
136,0,0,0,136,0,0,0,136,0,0,0,136,0,0,0,136,0,0,0,136,0,0,0,136,0,0,0,
136,0,0,0,135,255,255,254,128,0,0,1,128,0,0,1,128,0,0,1,127,255,255,
254
P=127,255,192,0,128,0,32,0,128,0,32,0,128,0,32,0,135,252,32,0,136,2,32,0,
136,2,32,0,136,2,32,0,136,2,32,0,136,2,32,0,136,2,32,0,136,2,32,0,136,2,
32,0,136,2,32,0,136,2,32,0,136,2,32,0,136,2,32,0,136,2,32,0,136,2,32,0,
136,2,32,0,136,2,32,0,136,2,32,0,136,2,32,0,136,2,32,0,136,2,32,0,136,2,
32,0,136,2,32,0,135,252,31,254,128,0,0,1,128,0,0,1,128,0,0,1,127,255,255,
254
L=0,0,0,0,0,0,0,0,0,0,0,0,0,0,0,0,14,0,0,0,17,0,0,0,17,0,0,0,17,0,0,0,17,0,
0,0,17,0,0,0,17,0,0,0,17,0,0,0,17,0,0,0,17,0,0,0,17,0,0,0,17,0,0,0,17,0,
0,0,17,0,0,0,17,0,0,0,17,0,0,0,17,0,0,0,17,0,0,0,17,0,0,0,17,0,0,0,17,0,
0,0,17,0,0,0,17,0,0,0,17,127,255,255,225,128,0,0,1,128,0,0,1,128,0,0,1,
127,255,255,254
E=112,0,0,14,136,0,0,17,136,0,0,17,136,0,0,17,136,0,0,17,136,0,0,17,136,
0,0,17,136,0,0,17,136,0,0,17,136,0,0,17,136,0,0,17,136,1,192,
17,136,2,32,17,136,2,32,17,136,2,32,17,136,2,32,17,136,2,32,17,136,2,32,
17,136,2,32,17,136,2,32,17,136,2,32,17,136,2,32,17,136,2,32,17,136,2,32,
17,136,2,32,17,136,2,32,17,135,252,31,225,128,0,0,1,128,0,0,1,128,0,0,1,
255,255,255,255

[COORDINATES]
Portrait1StartX=300
```

```
Portrait1StartY=300
PortraitIncrementX=300
PortraitIncrementY=200
Landscape1StartX=300
Landscape1StartY=300
LandscapeIncrementX=300
LandscapeIncrementY=200
```

 For more information on deciphering these codes, refer to Chapter 6, "Printing."

THE CHAP23.ICO FILE

This file contains the icon that has been attached to the form at design time. The CHAP23.ICO file is contained on the CD accompanying this book in the CHAP23 subdirectory.

FIGURE 23.7.
Raster Editor
application
CHAP23 Icon.

THE BLACK.BMP FILE

This file simply contains simply a completely black bitmap to copy the picture when the user clicks on the grid. The BLACK.BMP file is contained on the CD accompanying this book in the CHAP23 subdirectory.

THE CHAP23.EXE FILE

This is the executable file that is distributable. If you distribute this application, you must include the following files:

- ◆ CHAP23.EXE
- ◆ CHAP23.INI
- ◆ THREED.VBX
- ◆ GRID.VBX
- ◆ VBRUN300.DLL

The CHAP23.EXE file and source files are contained on the CD accompanying this book in the CHAP23 subdirectory, while all DLLs and VBXs are in the RESOURCE subdirectory.

RELATING THE RASTER GRAPHICS EDITOR APPLICATION TO YOUR APPLICATION

The Raster Graphics Editor application shows how to create raster graphics. You can use this example to make a raster-graphic "Stamp" of some bitmapped graphic over the entire form or even as a heading. You can use this heading to imprint a company's logo, for example. If you do this, you use most of the code from this chapter.

FINAL NOTES

This application was created on a standard VGA display using 16 colors. Your particular hardware could have adverse effects on the code the way it is written. You may need to modify it slightly.

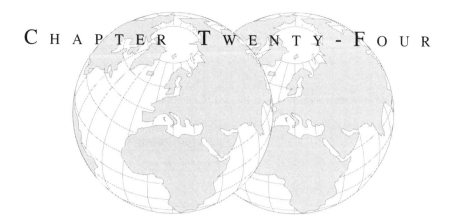

CHAPTER TWENTY-FOUR

RASTER GRAPHICS
PRINTER APPLICATION

THE RASTER PRINTER APPLICATION IS THE APPLICATION THAT IS THE COUNTERPART TO THE APPLICATION IN CHAPTER 23, "RASTER GRAPHICS EDITOR APPLICATION." THE DIFFERENCE BETWEEN THE APPLICATIONS IS THAT THE EDITOR APPLICATION (CHAPTER 23) ALLOWS FOR THE DESIGNING OF INDIVIDUAL RASTER GRAPHIC BITMAPS WHILE THE PRINTER APPLICATION (THIS CHAPTER) SHOWS HOW TO INCORPORATE ONLY THE MINIMUM CODE NECESSARY FOR AN APPLICATION IN THE REAL WORLD. THE TEXT COULD BE ANY TEXT FILE. FIGURE 24.1 SHOWS THE MAIN SCREEN (MAIN.FRM) AT RUNTIME.

REM This program assumes that you have a printer connected to "LPT1."

FIGURE 24.1.
*Raster Printer appli-
cation at runtime.*

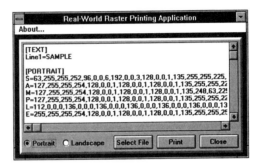

The application uses the INI file generated in the Editor application and prints in either the portrait or landscape orientation. It simply superimposes the graphic over the printed text selected from a file. The majority of the work has already been performed by the Editor application.

To use the application, run the CHAP24.EXE file. Open the text file to print by clicking the Select File command button. This will invoke the common dialog control.

Once the file is opened and populated in the text box, the Print button will become enabled. To print both the text and the raster graphics defined in the INI file, first select the desired orientation using the radio buttons, and then click on the Print command. For more information on raster graphic bitmaps, refer to Chapter 6, "Printing."

CODE LISTINGS

The Raster Printer application contains the following files and listings:

- ◆ CHAP24.MAK
- ◆ MAIN.FRM
- ◆ ABOUT.FRM
- ◆ CHAP24.BAS
- ◆ CHAP24.INI
- ◆ CHAP24.ICO
- ◆ CHAP24.EXE

THE CHAP24.MAK FILE

CHAP24.MAK is the project file for the Raster Printer application, CHAP24.EXE. It contains a listing of all the files necessary to load the project into Visual Basic. The CHAP24.MAK file is contained on the CD accompanying this book in the CHAP24 subdirectory. The file listing is

LISTING 24.1. CHAP24.MAK.

```
MAIN.FRM
ABOUT.FRM
CHAP24.BAS
THREED.VBX
CMDIALOG.VBX
ProjWinSize=70,436,203,215
ProjWinShow=2
IconForm="frmMain"
Title="Raster Printer"
ExeName="CHAP24.EXE"
```

THE MAIN.FRM FILE

MAIN.FRM is one of two forms in this application. It is the startup form for the application as well as the form used for selecting or entering text in the text box and to select the Printing option. Figure 24.1 presents the MAIN.FRM at runtime. It is fundamentally no different than the runtime form, so it is not shown. Table 24.1 lists all the relevant properties of each control on the form that have been changed from their standard default values. The MAIN.FRM file is contained on the CD accompanying this book in the CHAP24 subdirectory.

TABLE 24.1. PROPERTIES OF EACH CONTROL ON MAIN.FRM.

Object	Control Type	Property	Value
frmMain	Form	BackColor	&H00404000&
		Caption	"Real-World Raster Printer"
		Height	4035
		Icon	"CHAP24.ICO"
		Left	2250
		MaxButton	False
		Top	2670
		Width	6600
frText	SSPanel	BackColor	&H00C0C0C0&
		BevelInner	Raised
		BevelWidth	2
		BorderWidth	0
		Font3D	None
		Height	3135
		Left	120

continues

493

TABLE 24.1. CONTINUED

Object	Control Type	Property	Value
		Top	120
		Width	6255
cmDialog	CommonDialog	CancelError	True
		Left	0
		Top	0
txtPrintText	TextBox	BackColor	&H00FFFFFF&
		Height	2415
		Left	120
		MultiLine	True
		ScrollBars	Both
		Top	120
		Width	6015
optLandscape	SSOption	Caption	"Landscape"
		Font3D	None
		Height	375
		Left	1200
		Top	2640
		Width	1215
optPortrait	SSOption	Caption	"Portrait"
		Font3D	None
		Height	375
		Left	120
		Top	2640
		Value	True
		Width	975
cmdClose	CommandButton	Caption	"Close"
		Height	375
		Left	5040
		Top	2640
		Width	1095
cmdSelect	CommandButton	Caption	"Select File"
		Height	375

Object	Control Type	Property	Value
		Left	2640
		Top	2640
		Width	1095
cmdPrint	CommandButton	Caption	"Print"
		Height	375
		Left	3840
		Top	2640
		Width	1095
menu_about	Menu	Caption	"&About..."

FUNCTION, SUBROUTINE, AND EVENT PROCEDURES

There are several procedures of code for each object(control) that comprise this form. Each is listed in the following sections.

THE (GENERAL) OBJECT

The (general) object contains declarations and procedures at the form level. The procedures for the (general) object are

- ◆ (declarations)
- ◆ PrintRaster()

THE (DECLARATIONS) PROCEDURE

The (general) object contains variables, declarations, and procedures at the form level. Following is a listing of the (declarations) procedure:

LISTING 24.2. MAIN.FRM, (general)(declarations).

```
Option Explicit

'declare variables
Dim XValue%      'x coordinate
Dim YValue%      'y coordinate
```

THE PRINTRASTER() PROCEDURE

The PrintRaster() procedure prints the raster graphic bitmap in the orientation specified by the radio buttons. Following is a listing of the PrintRaster() procedure:

LISTING 24.3. CONTINUED

```
Sub PrintRaster ()

    'declare variables
    Dim pr$              'holds string of graphics to send to printer
    Dim TempData1$       'holds temporary equiv. of Totalstring$ for processing
    Dim TempData2$       'holds temporary equiv. of each character for processing
    Dim m$               'message constructor
    Dim pos%             'holds position of comma
    Dim loopcount%       'loop counting variable

    'change cursor
    screen.MousePointer = HOURGLASS

    'handle errors
    On Error GoTo printererror

    'open port
    Open "LPT1" For Output As #1

    'initialize printer
    pr$ = ""
    pr$ = pr$ + Chr$(27) + "E"              'reset printer
    pr$ = pr$ + Chr$(27) + "&l2A"           'letter size
    pr$ = pr$ + Chr$(27) + "(s0P"           'fixed spacing
    pr$ = pr$ + Chr$(27) + "(8U" + Chr$(27) + "(s0p12h10v0s0b3T"'courier 12 pitch, 10
    point,regular

    If optPortrait = True Then
        'set portrait orientation
        pr$ = pr$ + Chr$(27) + "&l0O"
    ElseIf optLandscape = True Then
        'set landscape orientation
        pr$ = pr$ + Chr$(27) + "&l1O"
    End If

    'first, send text in TextBox
    pr$ = pr$ + txtPrintText.Text

    'read from file to populate coordinates
    Call ReadINIFile_Data

    'assign temp data
    TempData1$ = TotalString$

    'set default coordinates
    XValue% = HStart% - HOffset%
    YValue% = VStart% - VOffset%

    'loop through all characters to be printed
    Do While TempData1$ <> ""

        'increment coordinates
        XValue% = XValue% + HOffset%
        YValue% = YValue% + VOffset%

        'set horizontal position(row)
```

```
    pr$ = pr$ + Chr$(27) + "*p" + Trim$(Str$(XValue%)) + "X"

    'set vertical position(row)
    pr$ = pr$ + Chr$(27) + "*p" + Trim$(Str$(YValue%)) + "Y"

    'set resolution
    pr$ = pr$ + Chr$(27) + "*t75R"

    'begin raster data entry
    pr$ = pr$ + Chr$(27) + "*r1A"

    'find character separator "\"
    pos% = InStr(TempData1$, "\")
    TempData2$ = Left$(TempData1$, pos% - 1)
    Do While InStr(TempData2$, ",") <> 0
        pr$ = pr$ + Chr$(27) + "*b4W"
        'cycle through 4 sets of bits
        For loopcount% = 1 To 4
            pos% = InStr(TempData2$, ",")
            If pos% > 0 Then
                'assign bit values for each parsed comma
                pr$ = pr$ + Chr$(Val(Left$(TempData2$, pos% - 1)))

                'reassign TempData2$
                TempData2$ = Right$(TempData2$, Len(TempData2$) - pos%)
            Else
                'this is the end of the string

                'assign bit values for each parsed comma
                pr$ = pr$ + Chr$(Val(TempData2$))

                'reassign TempData2$-so that this is the end of the loop
                TempData2$ = ""
            End If
        Next loopcount%

    Loop

    'reassign TempData1$
    TempData1$ = Right$(TempData1$, Len(TempData1$) - InStr(TempData1$, "\"))

Loop

'end with graphics
pr$ = pr$ + Chr$(27) + "*rB"

'form feed
pr$ = pr$ + Chr$(27) + "&l0H"

'send string to printer
Print #1, pr$

'close port
Close #1

'change cursor
screen.MousePointer = DEFAULT
```

continues

LISTING 24.3. CONTINUED

```
        Exit Sub

printererror:
        m$ = "Printer Error!"
        MsgBox m$

        'Close
        Close #1

        'exit
        Exit Sub

        'avoid errors
        Resume

End Sub
```

For more information about raster printing and raster codes, refer to Chapter 6, "Printing."

THE *CMD CLOSE* CONTROL

cmdClose is the name of the command button control that, when clicked, invokes the form_unload() event. The cmdClose control has code in only one event procedure. It is

◆ cmdClose_Click()

THE *CMD CLOSE_CLICK( )* EVENT PROCEDURE

The cmdClose_Click() event procedure simply ends the program. Following is a listing of the cmdClose_Click() event procedure:

LISTING 24.4. MAIN.FRM, cmdClose_Click().

```
Sub cmdClose_Click ()

        'exit
        Unload frmMain

        End

End Sub
```

THE *CMD PRINT* CONTROL

cmdPrint is the name of the command button control that, when clicked, starts the printing process, printing the text from the text box and then the raster graphic bitmap. The cmdPrint control has code in only one event procedure. It is

◆ cmdPrint_Click()

THE *CMDPRINT_CLICK( )* EVENT PROCEDURE

The cmdPrint_Click() event procedure prints the raster graphic by calling the PrintRaster() routine. Following is a listing of the cmdPrint_Click() event procedure:

LISTING 24.5. MAIN.FRM, cmdPrint_Click().

```
Sub cmdPrint_Click ()

    'get general parameters, offsets, coordinates, etc...
    Call ReadINIFile_General

    'do printing
    Call PrintRaster

End Sub
```

THE *CMDSELECT* CONTROL

cmdSelect is the name of the command button control that, when clicked, invokes the common dialog box to open a text file. The cmdSelect control has code in only one event procedure. It is

◆ cmdSelect_Click()

THE *CMDSELECT_CLICK( )* EVENT PROCEDURE

The cmdSelect_Click() event procedure selects the INI file containing the raster graphic data. Following is a listing of the cmdSelect_Click() event procedure:

LISTING 24.6. MAIN.FRM, cmdSelect_Click().

```
Sub cmdSelect_Click ()

    'declare variables
    Dim m$    'message constructor

    'handle errors
    On Error GoTo fileerror

    'set common dialog filter
    cmDialog.Filter = "INI Files¦*.INI¦Text Files¦*.txt¦All Files¦*.*"

    'set default to all files
    cmDialog.FilterIndex = 3

    'invoke open option
    cmDialog.Action = DLG_FILE_OPEN

    'test to see if there is a name
```

continues   499

LISTING 24.6. CONTINUED

```
    If cmDialog.Filename <> "" Then

        'test for existence of file
        If FileLen(cmDialog.Filename) > 0 Then
            'file exists

            'enable print button
            cmdPrint.Enabled = True

            'assign file
            Filename$ = cmDialog.Filename

            'handle errors
            On Error GoTo SelectError

            'open file
            Open Filename$ For Input As #1

            'read entire file-assign text
            txtPrintText.Text = Input$(LOF(1), #1)

            'close file
            Close #1

        Else
            'file doesn't exist
            m$ = cmDialog.Filename + Chr$(13)
            m$ = m$ + "does not exist!"
            MsgBox m$
        End If

    End If

    'exit
    Exit Sub

fileerror:
    Select Case (Err)
        Case 53:
            'file doesn't exist
            m$ = cmDialog.Filename + Chr$(13)
            m$ = m$ + "does not exist!"
            MsgBox m$
            Exit Sub
            Resume
        Case 32755: 'cancel selected
            'resume next for cancelling
            Resume Next
        Case Else:
            'exit
            Exit Sub

            'avoid errors
            Resume
```

```
        End Select

SelectError:
    'error opening file

    'close file
    Close #1

    'exit
    Exit Sub

    'avoid errors
    Resume

End Sub
```

THE *FORM* OBJECT

The Form object has code in two event procedures. They are

- ◆ Form_Load()
- ◆ Form_Unload()

THE *FORM_LOAD()* EVENT PROCEDURE

The Form_Load() event procedure initializes, centers, and loads the main form. Following is a listing of the Form_Load() event procedure:

LISTING 24.7. MAIN.FRM, Form_Load().

```
Sub Form_Load ()

    'center the form
    CenterForm Me

    'initialize
    cmdPrint.Enabled = False

    'assign INI file
    INIFileName$ = "CHAP24.INI"

End Sub
```

THE *FORM_UNLOAD()* EVENT PROCEDURE

The Form_Unload() event procedure prompts the user to confirm ending the program. Following is a listing of the Form_Unload() event procedure:

LISTING 24.8. MAIN.FRM, Form_Unload().

```
Sub Form_Unload (cancel As Integer)

    'declare variables
    Dim m$        'message constructor
    Dim res%      'holds results

    m$ = "Are you sure you want to exit?"
    res% = MsgBox(m$, 292, "Warning")
    If res% = IDNO Then
        'cancel
        cancel = True

        'exit
        Exit Sub

    End If

    End

End Sub
```

THE *MENU* OBJECT

The menu object was created by using Visual Basic's built-in menu printer. It has code associated with only one click() event procedure. It is

◆ menu_about()

THE *MENU_ABOUT_CLICK( )* PROCEDURE

The menu_about_Click() procedure simply shows the about form for program information. Following is a listing of the menu_about_Click() procedure:

LISTING 24.9. MAIN.FRM, menu_about_Click().

```
Sub menu_about_Click ()

    'show about form
    frmAbout.Show MODAL

End Sub
```

THE *TXTPRINTTEXT* CONTROL

txtPrintText is the name of the text box control that holds the text that will be superimposed by the raster graphic. This text is populated by keyboard entry or by a text file from the common dialog control. The txtPrintText control has code in one event procedure. It is:

◆ txtPrintText_Change(

THE *TXTPRINTTEXT_CHANGE( )* EVENT PROCEDURE

The `txtPrintText_Change()` event procedure enables the `txtPrintText` text box. Following is a listing of the `txtPrintText_Change()` event procedure:

LISTING 24.10. MAIN.FRM, `txtPrintText_Change()`.

```
Sub txtPrintText_Change ()

    'check length
    If Len(txtPrintText.Text) > 0 Then
        cmdPrint.Enabled = True
    Else
        cmdPrint.Enabled = False
    End If

End Sub
```

THE ABOUT.FRM FILE

ABOUT.FRM is one of two forms in this application. It shows information about the application. Figure 24.2 presents the form as it appears at runtime. Fundamentally, there is no difference in the form at design time, so it is not presented. Table 24.2 lists all the relevant properties of each control on the form that have been changed from their standard default values. The ABOUT.FRM file is contained on the CD accompanying this book in the CHAP24 subdirectory.

FIGURE 24.2.
Raster Printer application About form at runtime.

TABLE 24.2. PROPERTIES OF EACH CONTROL ON ABOUT.FRM.

Object	Control Type	Property	Value
frmAbout	Form	BackColor	&H00404000&
		Caption	"About"
		Height	3525
		Left	1035

continues

TABLE 24.2. CONTINUED

Object	Control Type	Property	Value
		MaxButton	False
		MinButton	False
		Top	1140
		Width	4545
pnlMain	SSPanel	BackColor	&H00C0C0C0&
		BevelWidth	3
		Caption	" "
		Font3D	None
		ForeColor	&H00C0C0C0&
		Height	2495
		Left	120
		RoundedCorners	False
		ShadowColor	Black
		Top	120
		Width	4215
pnl1	SSPanel	BackColor	&H00C0C0C0&
		BevelWidth	3
		Caption	"Real-World Programming With Visual Basic"
		Font3D	None
		ForeColor	&H0000FFFF&
		Height	975
		Left	960
		RoundedCorners	False
		ShadowColor	Black
		Top	120
		Width	2415
pnl2	SSPanel	BackColor	&H00C0C0C0&
		BevelWidth	3
		Caption	"Anthony T. Mann"

Object	Control Type	Property	Value
		Font3D	None
		ForeColor	&H0000FFFF&
		Height	615
		Left	960
		RoundedCorners	False
		ShadowColor	Black
		Top	1080
		Width	2415
pnl3	SSPanel	BackColor	&H00C0C0C0&
		BevelWidth	3
		Caption	"Raster Printer Application (Version 1.0)"
		Font3D	None
		ForeColor	&H0000FFFF&
		Height	615
		Left	960
		RoundedCorners	False
		ShadowColor	Black
		Top	1680
		Width	2415
cmdOK	CommandButton	Caption	"OK"
		Height	375
		Left	1680
		Top	2400
		Width	1095
pictAbout	PictureBox	Autosize	True
		BackColor	&H00C0C0C0&
		BorderStyle	None
		Height	615
		Left	120
		Top	120
		Width	735

FUNCTION, SUBROUTINE, AND EVENT PROCEDURES

There are several procedures of code for each object(control) that comprise this form. Each is listed in the following sections.

THE *(DECLARATIONS)* PROCEDURE

The (declarations) procedure contains only one line of declarations used in the form, ABOUT.FRM. It is only to allow for variable syntax checking and forcing the declaration of variables in each procedure. Following is a listing of the (declarations) procedure:

LISTING 24.11. ABOUT.FRM, (general)(declarations).

```
Option Explicit
```

THE *CMDOK* CONTROL

cmdOK is the name of the command button control that, when clicked, closes the frmAbout form. The cmdOK control has code in only one event procedure. It is

◆ cmdOK_Click()

THE *CMDOK_CLICK()* EVENT PROCEDURE

The cmdOK_Click() event procedure simply unloads the form. Following is a listing of the cmdOK_Click() event procedure:

LISTING 24.12. ABOUT.FRM, cmdOK_Click().

```
Sub cmdOK_Click ()

    'unload
    Unload frmAbout

End Sub
```

THE *FORM* OBJECT

The Form object has code in only one event procedure. It is

◆ Form_Load()

THE *FORM_LOAD()* EVENT PROCEDURE

The Form_Load() event procedure centers the form and assigns an icon to the pictAbout control. Following is a listing of the Form_Load() event procedure:

LISTING 24.13. ABOUT.FRM, Form_Load().

```
Sub Form_Load ()

    'center form
    CenterForm Me

    'load icon
    pictAbout.Picture = frmMain.Icon

End Sub
```

THE CHAP24.BAS FILE

CHAP24.BAS is the module that contains application level variables and procedures. The CHAP24.BAS file is contained on the CD accompanying this book in the CHAP24 subdirectory.

FUNCTION, SUBROUTINE, AND EVENT PROCEDURES

There are several procedures of code for each object(control) that comprise this module. Each is listed in the following sections.

The (general) object contains application level variables and procedures. The procedures for the (general) object are

◆ (declarations)

◆ CenterForm()

◆ ReadINIFile_Data()

◆ ReadINIFile_General()

THE (DECLARATIONS) PROCEDURE

The (declarations) procedure contains variable declarations used in the application. Following is a listing of the (declarations) procedure:

LISTING 24.14. CHAP24.BAS, (general)(declarations).

```
Option Explicit

'declare variables
Global HStart%           'Horizontal starting coordinate
Global VStart%           'Vertical starting coordinate
Global HOffset%          'Horizontal offset value
Global VOffset%          'Vertical offset value
Global PrintText$        'holds text to be printed
Global FileName$         'file name from common dialog
Global INIFileName$      'file name for INI file
Global TotalString$      'holds total bits for all letters to be printed
```

continues   507

LISTING 24.14. CONTINUED

```
'API declarations
Declare Function GetPrivateProfileString Lib "Kernel" (ByVal lpAppName
 As String, ByVal lpKeyName As String, ByVal lpDefault As String, ByVal lpReturnedString
As String, ByVal nSize As Integer, ByVal lpFileName
 As String) As Integer

'Printing Mode values
Global Const PORTRAIT = 1
Global Const LANDSCAPE = 2

' MsgBox return values
Global Const IDYES = 6                    ' Yes button pressed
Global Const IDNO = 7                     ' No button pressed

' Cursor values
Global Const HOURGLASS = 11               ' Hourglass
Global Const DEFAULT = 0                  ' Arrow

Common Dialog
Global Const DLG_FILE_OPEN = 1

Global Const MODAL = 1
```

THE *CENTERFORM( )* PROCEDURE

The CenterForm( ) procedure simply centers the form in the client area. Following is a listing of the CenterForm( ) procedure:

LISTING 24.15. CHAP24.BAS, CenterForm( ).

```
Sub CenterForm (F As Form)

    'center the form
    F.Move (Screen.Width - F.ScaleWidth) / 2, (Screen.Height - F.ScaleHeight) / 2

End Sub
```

THE *READINIFILE_DATA( )* PROCEDURE

The ReadINIFile_Data( ) procedure reads the data for the actual raster graphics from the INI file. Following is a listing of the ReadINIFile_Data( ) procedure:

LISTING 24.16. CHAP24.BAS, ReadINIFile_Data( ).

```
Sub ReadINIFile_Data ()

    'declare variables
    Dim CurrentChar$        'holds current character while cycling through
```

```
string
    Dim loopcount%         'loop counting variable
    Dim lpAppName$         'portrait/landscape
    Dim Temp$              'temporary string
    Dim res%               'holds results

    'initialize
    Temp$ = Space$(1000)
    TotalString$ = ""

    'determine portrait or landscape
    If frmMain.optPortrait.Value = True Then
    lpAppName$ = "PORTRAIT"
    ElseIf frmMain.optLandscape.Value = True Then
    lpAppName$ = "LANDSCAPE"
    End If

    'loop through all text to print
    For loopcount% = 1 To Len(PrintText$)
    'assign current character
    CurrentChar$ = Mid$(PrintText$, loopcount%, 1)
    'determine case to look up
    If Asc(CurrentChar$) > 96 And Asc(CurrentChar$) < 123 Then
        'lower case
        res% = GetPrivateProfileString(lpAppName$, "LC" + CurrentChar$,
  "", Temp$, 1000, CurDir$ + "\" + INIFileName$)
    Else
        'all others (uppercase and numbers)
        res% = GetPrivateProfileString(lpAppName$, CurrentChar$, "",
  Temp$, 1000, CurDir$ + "\" + INIFileName$)
    End If

    'concatenate total string
    TotalString$ = TotalString$ + Left$(Temp$, res%)

    'append "\" to the end of string for next character
    TotalString$ = TotalString$ + "\"
    Next loopcount%

End Sub
```

THE *READINIFILE_GENERAL( )* PROCEDURE

The ReadINIFile_General() procedure reads general data from the INI file, such as the coordinates for offsets and starting points. Following is a listing of the ReadINIFile_General() procedure:

LISTING 24.17. CHAP24.BAS, ReadINIFile_General().

```
Sub ReadINIFile_General ()

    'declare variables
    Dim TextInfo$    'holds text from INI file
```

continues

LISTING 24.17. CONTINUED

```
Dim res          'holds results
Dim Coord$       'holds coordinate results from INI file
Dim lpAppName$   'holds name of application ([]) in INI file
Dim String1$     'holds return data from INI file
Dim loopcount%   'loop counting variable
Dim InnerLoop%   'loop counting variable
Dim Row%         'loop counting variable for row
Dim Col%         'loop counting variable for col
Dim pos%         'holds position of character

'change cursor
Screen.MousePointer = HOURGLASS

'read text info
TextInfo$ = Space(100)
res = GetPrivateProfileString("TEXT", "Line1", "", TextInfo$, 100,
CurDir$ + "\" + INIFileName$)
PrintText$ = Left$(TextInfo$, res)

'read coordinate info
If frmMain.optPortrait.Value = True Then
'PORTRAIT
Coord$ = Space(10)
res = GetPrivateProfileString("COORDINATES", "Portrait1StartX", "",
Coord$, 10, CurDir$ + "\" + INIFileName$)
HStart% = Val(Left$(Coord$, res))

res = GetPrivateProfileString("COORDINATES", "Portrait1StartY", "",
Coord$, 10, CurDir$ + "\" + INIFileName$)
VStart% = Val(Left$(Coord$, res))

res = GetPrivateProfileString("COORDINATES", "PortraitIncrementX",
"", Coord$, 10, CurDir$ + "\" + INIFileName$)
HOffset% = Val(Left$(Coord$, res))

res = GetPrivateProfileString("COORDINATES", "PortraitIncrementY",
"", Coord$, 10, CurDir$ + "\" + INIFileName$)
VOffset% = Val(Left$(Coord$, res))
ElseIf frmMain.optLandscape.Value = True Then
'LANDSCAPE
Coord$ = Space(10)
res = GetPrivateProfileString("COORDINATES", "Landscape1StartX",
"", Coord$, 10, CurDir$ + "\" + INIFileName$)
HStart% = Val(Left$(Coord$, res))

res = GetPrivateProfileString("COORDINATES", "Landscape1StartY",
"", Coord$, 10, CurDir$ + "\" + INIFileName$)
VStart% = Val(Left$(Coord$, res))

res = GetPrivateProfileString("COORDINATES", "LandscapeIncrementX",
"", Coord$, 10, CurDir$ + "\" + INIFileName$)
HOffset% = Val(Left$(Coord$, res))

res = GetPrivateProfileString("COORDINATES", "LandscapeIncrementY",
"", Coord$, 10, CurDir$ + "\" + INIFileName$)
```

```
        VOffset% = Val(Left$(Coord$, res))

        End If

        'change cursor
        Screen.MousePointer = DEFAULT

End Sub
```

THE CHAP24.INI FILE

This is the file that will be read from the CD. It contains all of the information needed to load and print the raster data. The following lists the contents of the CHAP24.INI file as it appears on the CD in the CHAP24 subdirectory:

LISTING 24.18. CHAP24.INI FILE.

```
[TEXT]
Line1=SAMPLE

[PORTRAIT]
S=63,255,255,252,96,0,0,6,192,0,0,3,128,0,0,1,135,255,255,225,136,0,0,
17,136,0,0,17,136,0,0,14,136,0,0,0,136,0,0,0,136,0,0,0,136,0,0,0,136,0,
0,0,136,0,0,0,136,0,0,0,135,255,255,252,128,0,0,6,128,0,0,3,64,0,0,1,63,
255,255,193,0,0,0,33,0,0,0,17,0,0,0,17,0,0,0,17,112,0,0,17,136,0,0,17,
136,0,0,17,135,255,255,225,128,0,0,1,192,0,0,3,96,0,0,6,63,255,255,252
A=127,255,255,254,128,0,0,1,128,0,0,1,128,0,0,1,135,255,255,225,136,0,0,
17,136,0,0,17,136,0,0,17,136,0,0,17,136,0,0,17,136,0,0,17,136,0,0,17,136,
0,0,17,136,0,0,17,136,0,0,17,135,255,255,225,128,0,0,1,128,0,0,1,128,0,0,
1,135,255,255,225,136,0,0,17,136,0,0,17,136,0,0,17,136,0,0,17,136,0,0,17,
136,0,0,17,136,0,0,17,136,0,0,17,136,0,0,17,136,0,0,17,136,0,0,17,112,0,
0,14
M=127,255,255,254,128,0,0,1,128,0,0,1,128,0,0,1,135,248,63,225,136,4,64,
17,136,4,64,17,136,4,64,17,136,4,64,17,136,4,64,17,136,4,64,17,136,4,64,
17,136,4,64,17,136,4,64,17,136,4,64,17,136,4,64,17,136,4,64,17,136,4,64,
17,136,4,64,17,136,3,128,17,136,0,0,17,136,0,0,17,136,0,0,17,136,0,0,17,
136,0,0,17,136,0,0,17,136,0,0,17,136,0,0,17,136,0,0,17,136,0,0,17,136,0,
0,17,112,0,0,14
P=127,255,255,254,128,0,0,1,128,0,0,1,128,0,0,1,135,255,255,225,136,0,0,
17,136,0,0,17,136,0,0,17,136,0,0,17,136,0,0,17,136,0,0,17,136,0,0,17,136,
0,0,17,136,0,0,17,135,255,255,225,128,0,0,1,128,0,0,1,128,0,0,1,135,255,
255,254,136,0,0,0,136,0,0,0,136,0,0,0,136,0,0,0,136,0,0,0,136,0,0,0,136,
0,0,0,136,0,0,0,136,0,0,0,136,0,0,0,136,0,0,0,112,0,0,0
L=112,0,0,0,136,0,0,0,136,0,0,0,136,0,0,0,136,0,0,0,136,0,0,0,136,0,0,0,
136,0,0,0,136,0,0,0,136,0,0,0,136,0,0,0,136,0,0,0,136,0,0,0,136,0,0,0,
136,0,0,0,136,0,0,0,136,0,0,0,136,0,0,0,136,0,0,0,136,0,0,0,136,0,0,0,
136,0,0,0,136,0,0,0,136,0,0,0,136,0,0,0,136,0,0,0,136,0,0,0,135,255,255,
240,128,0,0,8,128,0,0,8,128,0,0,8,127,255,255,240
E=255,255,255,254,128,0,0,1,128,0,0,1,128,0,0,1,135,255,255,254,136,0,0,
0,136,0,0,0,136,0,0,0,136,0,0,0,136,0,0,0,136,0,0,0,136,0,0,0,
136,0,0,0,135,255,224,0,128,0,16,0,128,0,16,0,128,0,16,0,135,255,224,0,
136,0,0,0,136,0,0,0,136,0,0,0,136,0,0,0,136,0,0,0,136,0,0,0,136,0,0,0,
136,0,0,0,135,255,255,254,128,0,0,1,128,0,0,1,128,0,0,1,255,255,255,254
```

continues

LISTING 24.18. CONTINUED

```
[LANDSCAPE]
S=62,0,127,252,97,0,192,6,193,1,128,3,129,1,0,1,134,1,7,225,136,1,8,17,
136,1,16,17,136,1,16,17,136,1,16,17,136,1,16,17,136,1,16,17,136,1,16,17,
136,1,16,17,136,1,16,17,136,1,16,17,136,1,16,17,136,1,16,17,136,1,16,17,
136,1,16,17,136,1,16,17,136,1,16,17,136,1,16,17,136,1,16,17,136,1,16,17,
136,1,16,17,136,1,16,17,136,1,16,17,135,254,16,97,128,0,16,129,192,0,16,
131,96,0,32,134,63,255,192,124
A=127,255,255,254,128,0,0,1,128,0,0,1,128,0,0,1,135,254,15,254,136,1,16,
0,136,1,16,0,136,1,16,0,136,1,16,0,136,1,16,0,136,1,16,0,136,1,16,0,136,
1,16,0,136,1,16,0,136,1,16,0,136,1,16,0,136,1,16,0,136,1,16,0,136,1,16,0,
136,1,16,0,136,1,16,0,136,1,16,0,136,1,16,0,136,1,16,0,136,1,16,0,136,1,
16,0,136,1,16,0,135,254,15,254,128,0,0,1,128,0,0,1,128,0,0,1,127,255,255,
254
M=127,255,255,254,128,0,0,1,128,0,0,1,128,0,0,1,135,255,255,254,136,0,0,
0,136,0,0,0,136,0,0,0,136,0,0,0,136,0,0,0,136,0,0,0,136,0,0,0,136,0,0,0,
136,0,0,0,135,255,224,0,128,0,16,0,128,0,16,0,128,0,16,0,135,255,224,0,
136,0,0,0,136,0,0,0,136,0,0,0,136,0,0,0,136,0,0,0,136,0,0,0,136,0,0,0,
136,0,0,0,135,255,255,254,128,0,0,1,128,0,0,1,127,255,255,254
P=127,255,192,0,128,0,32,0,128,0,32,0,128,0,32,0,135,252,32,0,136,2,32,0,
136,2,32,0,136,2,32,0,136,2,32,0,136,2,32,0,136,2,32,0,136,2,32,0,136,2,
32,0,136,2,32,0,136,2,32,0,136,2,32,0,136,2,32,0,136,2,32,0,136,2,32,0,
136,2,32,0,136,2,32,0,136,2,32,0,136,2,32,0,136,2,32,0,136,2,32,0,136,2,
32,0,136,2,32,0,135,252,31,254,128,0,0,1,128,0,0,1,128,0,0,1,127,255,255,
254
L=0,0,0,0,0,0,0,0,0,0,0,0,0,0,0,14,0,0,0,17,0,0,0,17,0,0,0,17,0,0,0,17,0,
0,0,17,0,0,0,17,0,0,0,17,0,0,0,17,0,0,0,17,0,0,0,17,0,0,0,17,0,0,0,17,0,
0,0,17,0,0,0,17,0,0,0,17,0,0,0,17,0,0,0,17,0,0,0,17,0,0,0,17,0,0,0,17,0,
0,0,17,0,0,0,17,0,0,0,17,127,255,255,225,128,0,0,1,128,0,0,1,128,0,0,1,
127,255,255,254
E=112,0,0,14,136,0,0,17,136,0,0,17,136,0,0,17,136,0,0,17,136,0,0,17,136,
0,0,17,136,0,0,17,136,0,0,17,136,0,0,17,136,0,0,17,136,0,0,17,136,1,192,
17,136,2,32,17,136,2,32,17,136,2,32,17,136,2,32,17,136,2,32,17,136,2,32,
17,136,2,32,17,136,2,32,17,136,2,32,17,136,2,32,17,136,2,32,17,136,2,32,
17,136,2,32,17,136,2,32,17,135,252,31,225,128,0,0,1,128,0,0,1,128,0,0,1,
255,255,255,255

[COORDINATES]
Portrait1StartX=300
Portrait1StartY=300
PortraitIncrementX=300
PortraitIncrementY=200
Landscape1StartX=300
Landscape1StartY=300
LandscapeIncrementX=300
LandscapeIncrementY=200
```

 For more information on deciphering these codes, refer to Chapter 6, "Printing."

THE CHAP24.ICO FILE

This file contains the icon that has been attached to the form at design time. The CHAP24.ICO file is contained on the CD accompanying this book in the CHAP24 subdirectory.

FIGURE 24.3.
Raster Printer appli-
cation CHAP24 icon.

THE CHAP24.EXE FILE

This is the executable file that is distributable. If you distribute this application, you must include the following files:

- CHAP24.EXE
- CHAP24.INI
- CMDIALOG.VBX
- THREED.VBX
- VBRUN300.DLL
- COMMDLG.DLL

The CHAP24.EXE file and source files are contained on the CD accompanying this book in the CHAP24 subdirectory, while all DLLs and VBXs are in the RESOURCE subdirectory.

RELATING THE RASTER PRINTER APPLICATION TO YOUR APPLICATION

The Raster Printer application shows how to print raster graphics from an existing INI file. You can use this example to make a raster graphic "Stamp" of some bitmapped graphic over the entire form, or even as a heading. You can use this heading to imprint a company's logo, for example.

FINAL NOTES

This application was created on a standard VGA display, 16 colors. Your particular hardware could have adverse effects on the code the way it is written. You may need to modify it slightly.

DYNAMIC HOTSPOT APPLICATION

THE *DYNAMIC HOTSPOT APPLICATION* IS A VERY UNIQUE APPLICATION THAT SHOWS HOW TO INCORPORATE USER ACTION WITH GRAPHICS. THE APPLICATION ALLOWS YOU TO LOAD A BITMAP FILE ONTO THE DESKTOP. FROM THE BITMAP, YOU CAN CREATE MULTIPLE HOTSPOTS IN DESIGN MODE. ONCE THE HOTSPOTS ARE CREATED, HIDE THEM AND THE APPLICATION IS IN RUN MODE, ALLOWING YOU TO CLICK ON THE HOTSPOTS. WHILE NOTHING SIGNIFICANT HAPPENS WHEN THE HOTSPOTS ARE CLICKED, IT SHOWS A GREAT EXAMPLE OF HOW THIS TYPE OF INTERACTION CAN BE ACCOMPLISHED. WHEN THE HOTSPOT IS CLICKED, HOWEVER, YOU DO HEAR A TONE FROM THE PC'S SPEAKER. FIGURE 25.1 SHOWS THE MAIN SCREEN (MAIN.FRM) AT RUNTIME.

Although this application by itself would not be used in the Real World, it does contain components and techniques that you can apply to your Real-World applications, which can incorporate hotspots.

FIGURE 25.1.

Dynamic Hotspot application MAIN.FRM at runtime.

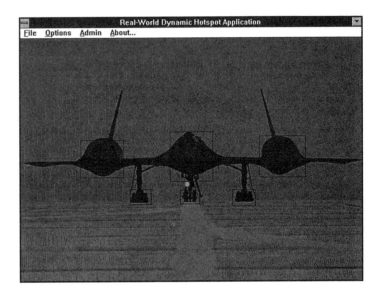

To use the application, you do not have to have a bitmap in the background. It will function on the completely white screen. If you do want to add a bitmap background, select the Admin->Load Bitmap menu option. This will invoke a common dialog box. Select the desired bitmap. To clear a bitmap, type in the word **none** for a file name.

To add a new hotspot, select the Options->Show menu option. This will put the application in Design mode. Click and drag on the actual form. You will see a rubber-band type bounding box signifying that this is where the hotspot will be placed. The hotspot can be any height or width. When finished, release the mouse button. If this is the location desired, select the Options->New menu option. A new hotspot will be drawn in the specified location. If this is not the location desired, you can simply draw another bounding box in the desired location.

Add as many hotspots as desired. If you want to move a hotspot, draw a bounding box (as described earlier) *completely* around the hotspot. You will see the hotspot selected. If the bounding box is not completely around the hotspot, the application assumes you are trying to design a new hotspot. After the hotspot is selected, you can drag/drop the hotspot to any location desired on the screen. It is possible for hotspots to overlap each other.

For more information on hotspots, see Chapter 5, "Graphics."

REM
If you attempt to drag/drop the hotspot while the actual mouse pointer is inside another hotspot, the `DragDrop()` event will never occur.

To delete a hotspot, select it by using the method described earlier. Select the Options->Delete menu option. The application will prompt for confirmation first.

Once the desktop is designed the way you want it to look, you can test it by selecting the Options->Hide menu option. This will hide all hotspots and put the application in Run mode. This allows you to use the hotspots. Notice that the cursor changes when the mouse is positioned over the hotspot. The application is loading a custom cursor, stored in the RWPROGVB.DLL file contained on the CD accompanying this book, in the RESOURCE subdirectory. Also, when the mouse pointer is positioned over a hotspot in Run mode, the upper-left corner label identifies the index of the hotspot.

For more information about the `ImageBox` control array used as hotspots, refer to Chapter 5, "Graphics."

Once the application operates the way you want it to, you can save the entire application—up to 100 hotspot locations—and the bitmap used in the background. These elements are called the *desktop*. To save the desktop, select the Admin->Save Desktop menu option. The application generates an INI file called CHAP25.INI in the current directory.

REM
There is a constant, 10, used throughout this application to verify that the hotspot completely encompasses the desired area. If this isn't done, the hotspot will be on the lines of the rectangle drawn. It is simply a matter of personal preference. You can change this number to suit your needs.

CODE LISTINGS

The Dynamic Hotspot application contains the following files and listings:

- ◆ CHAP25.MAK
- ◆ MAIN.FRM
- ◆ ABOUT.FRM
- ◆ CHAP25.ICO
- ◆ CHAP25.EXE
- ◆ RWPROGVB.DLL
- ◆ CHAP25.INI

THE CHAP25.MAK FILE

CHAP25.MAK is the project file for the Dynamic Hotspot application, CHAP25.EXE. It contains a listing of all the files necessary to load the project into Visual Basic. The CHAP25.MAK file is contained on the CD accompanying this book in the CHAP25 subdirectory. The file listing is

LISTING 25.1. CHAP25.MAK.

```
MAIN.FRM
ABOUT.FRM
THREED.VBX
CMDIALOG.VBX
ProjWinSize=74,390,248,215
ProjWinShow=2
IconForm="frmMain"
Title="Dynamic Hotspot"
ExeName="CHAP25.EXE"
```

THE MAIN.FRM FILE

MAIN.FRM is one of two forms in this application. It is the startup form for the application as well as the form used for creating and using the hotspots. Figure 25.1 shows the form as it appears at runtime. Figure 25.2 shows the form as it appears at design time. Table 25.1 lists all the relevant properties of each control on the form that have been changed from their standard default values. The MAIN.FRM file is contained on the CD accompanying this book in the CHAP25 subdirectory.

FIGURE 25.2.
DYNAMIC HOTSPOT application MAIN.FRM at design time.

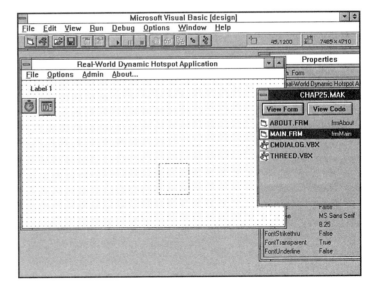

TABLE 25.1. PROPERTIES OF EACH CONTROL ON **MAIN.FRM**.

Object	Control Type	Property	Value
frmMain	Form	BackColor	&H00FFFFFF&
		Caption	"Real-World Dynamic Hotspot Application"
		Height	4710
		Icon	"CHAP25.ICO"
		Left	1935
		MaxButton	False
		Top	1155
		Width	7485
cmDialog	CommonDialog	CancelError	True
		Filter	"Bitmaps|*.BMP"
		Left	480
		Top	480
Timer1	Timer	Interval	100
		Left	0
		Top	480
lblDisplayIndex	Label	BackStyle	Transparent
		Caption	""
		Height	375
		Left	240
		Top	120
		Width	1815
Image1	Image	Height	1455
		Left	0
		Top	5160
		Width	15
Hotspot	Image	Height	855
		Index	0
		Left	3840
		Top	2280
		Width	855

continues

TABLE 25.1. CONTINUED

Object	Control Type	Property	Value
menu_file	Menu	Caption	"&File"
menu_exit	Menu	Caption	"&Exit"
menu_options	Menu	Caption	"&Options"
menu_show	Menu	Caption	"&Show"
menu_hide	Menu	Caption	"&Hide"
menu_new	Menu	Caption	"&New"
menu_delete	Menu	Caption	"&Delete"
menu_admin	Menu	Caption	"&Admin"
menu_admin_save	Menu	Caption	"&Save Desktop"
menu_admin_load	Menu	Caption	"&Load Bitmap"
menu_about	Menu	Caption	"&About..."

FUNCTION, SUBROUTINE, AND EVENT PROCEDURES

There are several procedures of code for each object(control) that comprise this form. Each is listed in the following sections.

THE (GENERAL) OBJECT

The (general) object contains declarations and procedures at the form level. The procedures for the (general) object are

◆ (declarations)

◆ ClearOldImage()

◆ DrawRubberBand()

◆ FindNextHotspotIndex()

◆ GetINI()

◆ HotspotInside()

◆ MakeSound()

◆ SaveINI()

The *(declarations)* Procedure

The (declarations) procedure contains form level declarations. Following is a listing of the (declarations) procedure:

Listing 25.2. MAIN.FRM, (general)(declarations).

```
Option Explicit

' MsgBox return values
Const IDYES = 6                   ' Yes button pressed
Const IDNO = 7                    ' No button pressed

'cursor values
Const HOURGLASS = 11              'hourglass cursor
Const DEFAULT = 0                 'default cursor

' DrawStyle
Const SOLID = 0          ' 0 - Solid
Const DASH = 1           ' 1 - Dash
Const DOT = 2            ' 2 - Dot
Const DASH_DOT = 3       ' 3 - Dash-Dot
Const DASH_DOT_DOT = 4   ' 4 - Dash-Dot-Dot
Const INVISIBLE = 5      ' 5 - Invisible
Const INSIDE_SOLID = 6   ' 6 - Inside Solid

' Button parameter mask
Const LEFT_BUTTON = 1

'constants
Const INVERT = 6
Const GCW_HModule = (-16)
Const GCW_HCURSOR = (-12)
Const INILENGTH = 50
Const MODAL = 1
Const DLG_FILE_OPEN = 1

'variables
Dim HotspotIndex%       'holds highest possible control array index
Dim DeleteIndex%        'holds index of selection for possible deletion
Dim MousePosX As Single 'holds relative x position of mouse within hotspot
Dim MousePosY As Single 'holds relative y position of mouse within hotspot
Dim BeginX, BeginY As Single    'holds x,y coords. for starting rubber band
Dim EndX, EndY As Single        'holds x,y coords. for ending rubber band
Dim PictureLoaded$      'holds name of picture loaded into desktop
Dim Changed%            'flag for change made to prompt for saving
Dim hSystemCursor%      'handle to the system cursor-for changing back
Dim cHandle%            'handle to the 'hand' cursor
Dim LibInst%            'library instance
Dim Global LibInst%     'Global library instance-for releasing library
Dim DefaultDirectory$   'default directory when program was run
```

continues

LISTING 25.2. CONTINUED

```
'API's for changing of cursor to hand
Declare Function LoadCursorByString Lib "User" Alias "LoadCursor" (ByVal hInstance As
Integer, ByVal lpCursorName As String) As Integer
Declare Function LoadLibrary Lib "Kernel" (ByVal lpLibFileName As String) As Integer
Declare Function SetClassWord Lib "User" (ByVal hWnd As Integer, ByVal nIndex As Integer,
ByVal wNewWord As Integer) As Integer
Declare Function DestroyCursor Lib "User" (ByVal hCursor As Integer) As Integer
Declare Sub FreeLibrary Lib "Kernel" (ByVal hLibModule As Integer)
Declare Function GetModuleUsage Lib "Kernel" (ByVal hModule As Integer) As Integer

'API's for INI files
Declare Function GetPrivateProfileString Lib "Kernel" (ByVal lpAppName As String, ByVal
lpKeyName As String, ByVal lpDefault As String, ByVal lpReturnedString As String, ByVal
nSize As Integer, ByVal lpFileName As String) As Integer
Declare Function WritePrivateProfileString Lib "Kernel" (ByVal lpApplicationName As
String, ByVal lpKeyName As String, ByVal lpString As String, ByVal lpFileName As String)
As Integer

'CUSTOM DLL Functions
Declare Function INP Lib "INOUT.DLL" (ByVal address&) As Integer
Declare Sub OUT Lib "INOUT.DLL" (ByVal address&, ByVal value%)

'constants for initialization file
Const TheFile$ = "\CHAP25.INI"
Const lpAppName$ = "Initialization"
Const lpKeyName1$ = "Bitmap"
Const lpKeyName2$ = "MaxHotspot"
Const Prefix$ = "Hotspot"
Const Suffix1$ = "X1"
Const Suffix2$ = "Y1"
Const Suffix3$ = "X2"
Const Suffix4$ = "Y2"
```

THE *ClearOldImage()* PROCEDURE

The ClearOldImage() procedure clears the old image boundaries. Following is a listing of the ClearOldImage() procedure:

LISTING 25.3. MAIN.FRM, ClearOldImage().

```
Sub ClearOldImage ()

    'clear old box
    If EndX > BeginX Then
        Image1.Left = BeginX
        Image1.Width = EndX + 10
    Else
        Image1.Left = EndX
        Image1.Width = BeginX + 10
    End If
    If EndY > BeginY Then
```

```
        Image1.Top = BeginY
        Image1.Height = EndY + 10
    Else
        Image1.Top = EndY
        Image1.Height = BeginY + 10
    End If

    'move image control to upper left hand corner and resize
    'so that it is not clicked
    Image1.Width = 1
    Image1.Height = 1
    Image1.Left = 1
    Image1.Top = 1

    'stop timer
    Timer1.Enabled = False

End Sub
```

The reason the image is moved to the upper left after sizing it is because the act of sizing the image alone to the area of an old hotspot with the INVERT pen will effectively clear the old image. Then the image is moved out of the way to the upper left corner.

THE *DRAWRUBBERBAND()* PROCEDURE

The DrawRubberBand() procedure draws a "rubber band" like bounding box to indicate where the hotspot will be drawn. Following is a listing of the DrawRubberBand() procedure:

LISTING 25.4. MAIN.FRM, DrawRubberBand().

```
Sub DrawRubberBand (ByVal X1 As Single, ByVal Y1 As Single, ByVal X2 As Single, ByVal Y2
As Single)

    'declare variables
    Dim SaveDrawMode%    'holds previous drawing mode

    'save old drawing mode
    SaveDrawMode% = frmMain.DrawMode

    'invert drawing pen
    frmMain.DrawMode = INVERT

    'actually draw line
    Line (X1, Y1)-(X2, Y2), , B

    'revert to saved mode
    frmMain.DrawMode = SaveDrawMode%

End Sub
```

523

THE *FindNextHotspotIndex( )* PROCEDURE

The `FindNextHotspotIndex()` procedure finds the next available index for a new hotspot to be created. This must be done because there could have been an index in the middle of the range of indexes that was deleted. The procedure is also a function that returns the integer of the next available hotspot index. Following is a listing of the `FindNextHotspotIndex()` procedure:

LISTING 25.5. MAIN.FRM, `FindNextHotspotIndex()`.

```
Function FindNextHotspotIndex () As Integer

    'declare variables
    Dim loopcount%  'loop counting variable

    'handle errors
    On Error GoTo ThisIsTheIndex

    'loop just to test index
    For loopcount% = 0 To HotspotIndex%
        'this is just a dummy condition to find out if the index exists
        If Hotspot(loopcount%).Visible = False Then
        End If
    Next loopcount%

    'if it got to this point, then all indexes are used-allocate one more
    HotspotIndex% = HotspotIndex% + 1
    FindNextHotspotIndex = HotspotIndex%

    Exit Function

ThisIsTheIndex:
    FindNextHotspotIndex = loopcount%
    'avoid errors
    Exit Function

End Function
```

The reason for the dummy condition loop in the preceding code listing is because the code needs to find the next available index. If the `Visible` property is tested for an index that doesn't exist, it will generate a runtime error, which is trapped by the error handler labeled `ThisIsTheIndex`. If all available `Visible` properties are tested and don't produce any errors, then the next available index is the maximum plus 1.

THE *GetINI( )* PROCEDURE

The `GetINI()` procedure gets the configuration information from the CHAP25.INI file and places all hotspots in the appropriate area of the client area. Following is a listing of the `GetINI()` procedure:

LISTING 25.6. MAIN.FRM, GetINI().

```
Sub GetINI ()

    'declare variables
    Dim res          'holds results of getting INI file
    Dim String1$     'holds temporary string
    Dim Temp$        'holds temporary string
    Dim X1           'first x coordinate
    Dim Y1           'first y coordinate
    Dim X2           'second x coordinate
    Dim Y2           'second y coordinate
    Dim loopcount%   'loop counting variable

    'change cursor
    screen.MousePointer = HOURGLASS

    'Bitmap
    String1$ = Space$(INILENGTH)
    res = GetPrivateProfileString(lpAppName$, lpKeyName1$, "", String1$, INILENGTH,
    CurDir$ + TheFile$)

    'trim off last character (return)
    Temp$ = Left$(String1$, res)
    frmMain.Picture = LoadPicture(Temp$)
    PictureLoaded$ = Temp$

    'maximum Hotspot
    String1$ = Space$(INILENGTH)
    res = GetPrivateProfileString(lpAppName$, lpKeyName2$, "", String1$, INILENGTH,
    CurDir$ + TheFile$)

    'trim off last character (return)
    Temp$ = Left$(String1$, res)
    HotspotIndex% = Val(Temp$)

    'cycle through each indexed hotspot and populate- max 99
    For loopcount% = 0 To HotspotIndex%
        'get 1st X coord
        String1$ = Space$(INILENGTH)
        res = GetPrivateProfileString(lpAppName$, Prefix$ + Trim$(Str$(loopcount%)) +
        Suffix1$, "", String1$, INILENGTH, CurDir$ + TheFile$)

        'trim off last character (return)
        Temp$ = Left$(String1$, res)
        X1 = Val(Temp$)

        'get 1st Y coord
        String1$ = Space$(INILENGTH)
        res = GetPrivateProfileString(lpAppName$, Prefix$ + Trim$(Str$(loopcount%)) +
        Suffix2$, "", String1$, INILENGTH, CurDir$ + TheFile$)

        'trim off last character (return)
        Temp$ = Left$(String1$, res)
        Y1 = Val(Temp$)
```

continues

LISTING 25.6. CONTINUED

```
'get 2nd X coord
String1$ = Space$(INILENGTH)
res = GetPrivateProfileString(lpAppName$, Prefix$ + Trim$(Str$(loopcount%)) +
Suffix3$, "", String1$, INILENGTH, CurDir$ + TheFile$)

'trim off last character (return)
Temp$ = Left$(String1$, res)
X2 = Val(Temp$)

'get 2nd Y coord
String1$ = Space$(INILENGTH)
res = GetPrivateProfileString(lpAppName$, Prefix$ + Trim$(Str$(loopcount%)) +
Suffix4$, "", String1$, INILENGTH, CurDir$ + TheFile$)

'trim off last character (return)
Temp$ = Left$(String1$, res)
Y2 = Val(Temp$)

If loopcount% = 0 Then
    'zero can't be loaded, already loaded at design time
    Hotspot(loopcount%).Move X1, Y1, X2 - X1, Y2 - Y1
    Hotspot(loopcount%).Visible = True
Else
    If X1 <> 0 And Y1 <> 0 And X2 <> 0 And Y2 <> 0 Then
        'load this control array, it existed in INI
        Load Hotspot(loopcount%)
        Hotspot(loopcount%).Visible = True
        Hotspot(loopcount%).Move X1, Y1, X2 - X1, Y2 - Y1
    End If
End If

Next loopcount%

'change cursor
screen.MousePointer = DEFAULT

End Sub
```

THE *HotspotInside( )* PROCEDURE

The HotspotInside( ) procedure tests to see if the bounding box drawn by the user completely contains a hotspot. The procedure is also a function that provides the index of the hotspot inside the bounding box. If there is no hotspot contained in the bounding box, the function returns –1. Following is a listing of the HotspotInside( ) procedure:

LISTING 25.7. MAIN.FRM, HotspotInside( ).

```
Function HotspotInside () As Integer

    'declare variables
```

```
    Dim FoundInside%        'flag if hotspot was found inside rubber band
    Dim loopcount%          'loop counting variable

    'handle errors
    'an error will occur if an index in the middle of range is missing
    On Error GoTo IndexMissing
    For loopcount% = 0 To HotspotIndex%
        If Hotspot(loopcount%).Left >= BeginX Then
            'left side is within rubber band-test right
            If (Hotspot(loopcount%).Width + Hotspot(loopcount%).Left) <= EndX Then
                'right side is within rubber band-test top
                If Hotspot(loopcount%).Top >= BeginY Then
                    'top is within rubber band-test bottom
                    If (Hotspot(loopcount%).Height + Hotspot(loopcount%).Top) <= EndY
                    Then
                        'bottom is within rubber band
                        HotspotInside = loopcount%

                        'flag that item is within range
                        FoundInside% = True

                        'assign form level variable for delete menu
                        DeleteIndex% = loopcount%
                        Exit For
                    End If
                End If
            End If
        End If

    Next loopcount%

If FoundInside% = False Then

    'flag as not found
    HotspotInside = -1
End If

    Exit Function

IndexMissing:
    'resume to the next index-ignore this one
    loopcount% = loopcount% + 1

    'it is possible that the loopcount will be greater than the hotspotindex
    If loopcount% > HotspotIndex% Then
        HotspotInside = -1
        Exit Function
    End If

    'avoid errors
    Resume

End Function
```

THE *MAKESOUND()* PROCEDURE

The MakeSound() procedure is used to create a sound when a hotspot is clicked. The MakeSound() procedure uses functions inside the INOUT.DLL. It accepts one argument, Frequency&, which is the sound frequency to play.

 For more information concerning this DLL and audio, refer to Chapter 11, "Audio."

Following is a listing of the MakeSound() procedure:

LISTING 25.8. MAIN.FRM, MakeSound().

```
Sub MakeSound (Frequency&)

    'declare variables
    Dim ClockTicks%        'number of clock ticks
    Dim loopcount%         'loop counting variable

    'calculate clicks -> Clock/sound frequency = clock ticks
    ClockTicks% = CInt(1193280 \ Frequency&)

    'prepare for data
    OUT 67, 182

    ' Send data
    OUT 66, ClockTicks% And &HFF
    OUT 66, ClockTicks% \ 256

    'turn speaker on
    OUT 97, INP(97) Or &H3

    'make sure sound plays for a period of time
    For loopcount% = 1 To 200
        DoEvents
    Next loopcount%

    ' Turn speaker off
    OUT 97, INP(97) And &HFC

End Sub
```

 For more information about the MakeSound() subroutine, refer to Chapter 11, "Audio."

THE *SAVEINI()* PROCEDURE

The SaveINI() procedure saves the current desktop configuration to the CHAP25.INI file. Following is a listing of the SaveINI() procedure:

Listing 25.9. MAIN.FRM, SaveINI().

```
Sub SaveINI ()

    'declare variables
    Dim res%        'holds results of getting INI file
    Dim lpString$   'holds temporary string
    Dim Temp$       'holds temporary string
    Dim X1%         'first x coordinate
    Dim Y1%         'first y coordinate
    Dim X2%         'second x coordinate
    Dim Y2%         'second y coordinate
    Dim loopcount%  'loop counting variable

    'change cursor
    screen.MousePointer = HOURGLASS

    'Bitmap
    lpString$ = PictureLoaded$
    res% = WritePrivateProfileString%(lpAppName$, lpKeyName1$, lpString$, CurDir$ +
    TheFile$)

    'maximum Hotspot
    lpString$ = Trim$(Str$(HotspotIndex%))
    res% = WritePrivateProfileString%(lpAppName$, lpKeyName2$, lpString$, CurDir$ +
    TheFile$)

    'cycle through each indexed hotspot and populate(from 0 to 99)
    'handle error
    On Error GoTo SaveError
    For loopcount% = 0 To HotspotIndex%
        'assign coordinates
        X1% = Hotspot(loopcount%).Left
        Y1% = Hotspot(loopcount%).Top
        X2% = Hotspot(loopcount%).Width + Hotspot(loopcount%).Left
        Y2% = Hotspot(loopcount%).Height + Hotspot(loopcount%).Top

        'save 1st X coord
        lpString$ = Trim$(Str$(X1%))
        res% = WritePrivateProfileString%(lpAppName$, Prefix$ + Trim$(Str$(loopcount%)) +
        Suffix1$, lpString$, CurDir$ + TheFile$)

        'save 1st Y coord
        lpString$ = Trim$(Str$(Y1%))
        res% = WritePrivateProfileString%(lpAppName$, Prefix$ + Trim$(Str$(loopcount%)) +
        Suffix2$, lpString$, CurDir$ + TheFile$)

        'save 2nd X coord
        lpString$ = Trim$(Str$(X2%))
        res% = WritePrivateProfileString%(lpAppName$, Prefix$ + Trim$(Str$(loopcount%)) +
        Suffix3$, lpString$, CurDir$ + TheFile$)

        'save 2nd Y coord
        lpString$ = Trim$(Str$(Y2%))
        res% = WritePrivateProfileString%(lpAppName$, Prefix$ + Trim$(Str$(loopcount%)) +
        Suffix4$, lpString$, CurDir$ + TheFile$)
```

continues

529

LISTING 25.9. CONTINUED

```
    Next loopcount%

    'change cursor
    screen.MousePointer = DEFAULT

    'flag no change
    Changed% = False

    Exit Sub

SaveError:
    'this index doesn't exist
    'make sure to save 0's for coordinates

        'save 1st X coord
        res% = WritePrivateProfileString%(lpAppName$, Prefix$ + Trim$(Str$(loopcount%)) +
        Suffix1$, "0", CurDir$ + TheFile$)

        'save 1st Y coord
        res% = WritePrivateProfileString%(lpAppName$, Prefix$ + Trim$(Str$(loopcount%)) +
        Suffix2$, "0", CurDir$ + TheFile$)

        'save 2nd X coord
        res% = WritePrivateProfileString%(lpAppName$, Prefix$ + Trim$(Str$(loopcount%)) +
        Suffix3$, "0", CurDir$ + TheFile$)

        'save 2nd Y coord
        res% = WritePrivateProfileString%(lpAppName$, Prefix$ + Trim$(Str$(loopcount%)) +
        Suffix4$, "0", CurDir$ + TheFile$)

    'increment loopcount%
    loopcount% = loopcount% + 1

    'if loopcount gets to be greater than max allowed, then exit
    If loopcount% > 99 Then
        screen.MousePointer = DEFAULT
        'flag no change
        Changed% = False
        Exit Sub
    End If

    'avoid errors
    Resume

End Sub
```

For more information about INI files, refer to Chapter 7, "File Input/Output (I/O)."

The *Form* Object

The Form object has code in six event procedures. They are

- ◆ Form_DragDrop()
- ◆ Form_Load()
- ◆ Form_MouseDown()
- ◆ Form_MouseMove()
- ◆ Form_MouseUp()
- ◆ Form_Unload()

The *Form_DragDrop()* Event Procedure

The Form_DragDrop() event procedure is used to move a hotspot to a new location. Following is a listing of the Form_DragDrop() event procedure:

Listing 25.10. MAIN.FRM, Form_DragDrop().

```
Sub Form_DragDrop (Source As Control, X As Single, Y As Single)

    'move hotspot on form
    Source.Left = X - MousePosX
    Source.Top = Y - MousePosY

    'flag changed
    Changed% = True

End Sub
```

The *Form_Load()* Event Procedure

The Form_Load() event procedure sets defaults and loads the configuration from the CHAP25.INI file, if it exists. Following is a listing of the Form_Load() event procedure:

Listing 25.11. MAIN.FRM, Form_Load().

```
Sub Form_Load ()

    'initialize
    frmMain.DrawStyle = DOT
    Changed% = False

    'initialize menus
    menu_show.Enabled = True
    menu_hide.Enabled = False
    menu_new.Enabled = False
    menu_delete.Enabled = False
```

continues

531

LISTING 25.11. CONTINUED

```
        'read ini file
        Call GetINI

        'remember default directory
        DefaultDirectory$ = CurDir$

End Sub
```

THE *FORM_MOUSEDOWN( )* EVENT PROCEDURE

The Form_Down() event procedure is used to clear the old image. This is because there can't be more than one bounding box at one time. Following is a listing of the Form_Down() event procedure:

LISTING 25.12. MAIN.FRM, Form_Down( ).

```
Sub Form_MouseDown (Button As Integer, Shift As Integer, X As Single, Y As Single)

        If Hotspot(0).BorderStyle = 0 Then Exit Sub

        Timer1.Enabled = False
        menu_new.Enabled = False
        menu_delete.Enabled = False

        'remove old rubber band
        Call ClearOldImage

        'Assign new coordinates
        BeginX = X
        BeginY = Y
        EndX = BeginX
        EndY = BeginY

End Sub
```

THE *FORM_MOUSEMOVE( )* EVENT PROCEDURE

The Form_Move() event procedure resets the cursor back to the default cursor and, if the left mouse button is pressed, will draw the rubber-band bounding box. Following is a listing of the Form_Move() event procedure:

LISTING 25.13. MAIN.FRM, Form_Move( ).

```
Sub Form_MouseMove (Button As Integer, Shift As Integer, X As Single, Y As Single)

        'declare variables
        Dim res%        'holds results
```

```
'reset cursor to original
res% = SetClassWord(frmMain.hWnd, GCW_HCURSOR, hSystemCursor%)

'destroy hand cursor
res% = DestroyCursor(cHandle%)

'initialize LibInst%
LibInst% = 0

'clear display index label
lblDisplayIndex.Caption = ""

'if borderstyle is none then rest is invalid - exit
If Hotspot(0).BorderStyle = 0 Then Exit Sub

'if left button is pressed the draw rubber band
If Button = LEFT_BUTTON Then

    Call DrawRubberBand(BeginX, BeginY, EndX, EndY)
    Call DrawRubberBand(BeginX, BeginY, X, Y)
    EndX = X
    EndY = Y

End If

End Sub
```

THE *FORM_MOUSEUP()* EVENT PROCEDURE

The Form_Up() event procedure is used to test if the bounding box was drawn around a hotspot, and then will make the bounding box appear animated. Following is a listing of the Form_Up() event procedure:

LISTING 25.14. MAIN.FRM, Form_Up().

```
Sub Form_MouseUp (Button As Integer, Shift As Integer, X As Single, Y As Single)

    'if there is no border style, then rest of sub is invalid, so exit
    If Hotspot(0).BorderStyle = 0 Then Exit Sub

    'declare variables
    Dim res%     'holds results

    res% = HotspotInside()
    If res% <> -1 Then
        'rubber band box was drawn around hotspot

        'remove old rubber band
        Call ClearOldImage
```

continues

LISTING 25.14. CONTINUED

```
            'adjust size of rubber band box to size of hotspot
            BeginX = Hotspot(res%).Left
            BeginY = Hotspot(res%).Top
            EndX = Hotspot(res%).Left + Hotspot(res%).Width - 10
            EndY = Hotspot(res%).Top + Hotspot(res%).Height - 10

            'actually draw the line
            Call DrawRubberBand(BeginX, BeginY, EndX, EndY)
            menu_delete.Enabled = True

        Else
            'rubber band box was NOT around hotspot
            menu_new.Enabled = True
        End If

        'enable timer to start animated look
        Timer1.Enabled = True

    End Sub
```

THE *FORM_UNLOAD()* EVENT PROCEDURE

The Form_Unload() event procedure prompts the user to confirm ending the program. Following is a listing of the Form_Unload() event procedure:

LISTING 25.15. MAIN.FRM, Form_Unload().

```
Sub Form_Unload (cancel As Integer)

    'declare variables
    Dim m$        'message contructor
    Dim res%      'holds results

    If Changed% = True Then
        m$ = "Changes made, close anyway?"
        res% = MsgBox(m$, 292, "Warning")
        If res% = IDNO Then
            'cancel
            cancel = True

            'exit
            Exit Sub
        End If
    End If

    'reset cursor to original
    res% = SetClassWord(frmMain.hWnd, GCW_HCURSOR, hSystemCursor%)
```

```
'destroy hand cursor
res% = DestroyCursor(cHandle%)

'free library-once for each time it was loaded
Do While GetModuleUsage (GlobalLibInst%) <> 0
   FreeLibrary (GlobalLibInst%)
Loop

End

End Sub
```

THE *HOTSPOT* CONTROL

Hotspot is the name of the image control array that is actually the hotspot. The Hotspot control
has code in three event procedures. They are

- ◆ Hotspot_Click()
- ◆ Hotspot_MouseDown()
- ◆ Hotspot_MouseMove()

THE *HOTSPOT_CLICK()* EVENT PROCEDURE

The Hotspot_Click() event procedure simply plays a sound through the PC speaker, indicating
that the hotspot was clicked. Following is a listing of the Hotspot_Click() event procedure:

LISTING 25.16. MAIN.FRM, Hotspot_Click().

```
Sub Hotspot_Click (Index As Integer)

    'acknowledge clicking of spot, if borderstyle is 0
    If Hotspot(Index).BorderStyle = 0 Then
        'make a sound
        MakeSound 523# + (Index * 64)
    End If

End Sub
```

 For more information about the MakeSound() subroutine, refer to Chapter 11,
"Audio."

THE *HOTSPOT_MOUSEDOWN()* EVENT PROCEDURE

The Hotspot_MouseDown() event procedure is used to start the drag operation to move the
hotspot. Following is a listing of the Hotspot_MouseDown() event procedure:

LISTING 25.17. MAIN.FRM, `Hotspot_MouseDown()`.

```
Sub Hotspot_MouseDown (Index As Integer, Button As Integer, Shift As Integer, X As
Single, Y As Single)

    'start dragging if border is visible
    If Hotspot(Index).BorderStyle = 1 Then
        MousePosX = X
        MousePosY = Y
        Hotspot(Index).Drag
    End If

End Sub
```

THE *HOTSPOT_MOUSEMOVE()* EVENT PROCEDURE

The `Hotspot_MouseMove()` event procedure loads a custom cursor "hand" for indicating that the mouse is over the hotspot. Following is a listing of the `Hotspot_MouseMove()` event procedure:

LISTING 25.18. MAIN.FRM, `Hotspot_MouseMove()`.

```
Sub Hotspot_MouseMove (Index As Integer, Button As Integer, Shift As Integer, X As
Single, Y As Single)

    'if borderstyle is shown, then can't change cursor-only change if hidden
    If Hotspot(Index).BorderStyle = 1 Then Exit Sub

    'declare variables
    Dim res%      'holds results

    'load different cursor
    If LibInst% = 0 Then
        'load library first
        LibInst% = LoadLibrary("RWPROGVB.DLL")

        'assign Global Instance
        GlobalLibInst% = LibInst%

        'load specific cursor inside library
        cHandle% = LoadCursorByString(LibInst%, "HandCursor")

        'assign cursor to handle of form
        hSystemCursor% = SetClassWord(frmMain.hWnd, GCW_HCURSOR, cHandle%)

        'display index label
        lblDisplayIndex.Caption = "Index: " + Trim$(Str$(Index))

    End If

End Sub
```

THE *MENU* OBJECT

The menu object was created using Visual Basic's built-in Menu editor. It has code associated with eight Click() event procedures. They are

- menu_about()
- menu_admin_load()
- menu_admin_save()
- menu_delete()
- menu_exit()
- menu_hide()
- menu_new()
- menu_show()

THE *MENU_ABOUT_CLICK( )* EVENT PROCEDURE

The menu_about_Click() event procedure simply shows the about form for program information. Following is a listing of the menu_about_Click() event procedure:

LISTING 25.19. MAIN.FRM, menu_about_Click( ).

```
Sub menu_about_Click ()

    'show about form
    frmAbout.Show MODAL

End Sub
```

THE *MENU_ADMIN_LOAD_CLICK( )* EVENT PROCEDURE

The menu_admin_load_Click() event procedure invokes the common dialog box to load a bitmap onto the desktop. Following is a listing of the menu_admin_load_Click() enent procedure:

LISTING 25.20. MAIN.FRM, menu_admin_load_Click( ).

```
Sub menu_admin_load_Click ()

    'declare variables
    Dim loopcount%  'looping variable
    Dim m$          'message contructor

    'handle error if file doesn't exist or cancel selected
    On Error GoTo fileerror
```

continues

537

LISTING 25.20. CONTINUED

```
    'load bitmap
    cmdialog.Action = DLG_FILE_OPEN

    'load new bitmap
    If cmdialog.Filename <> "" Then
        If UCase$(Right$(cmdialog.Filename, 4)) = "NONE" Then
            frmMain.Picture = LoadPicture("")
            PictureLoaded$ = ""
        Else

            frmMain.Picture = LoadPicture(cmdialog.Filename)
            PictureLoaded$ = cmdialog.Filename
        End If
    End If

fileerror:

    'change back to default directory
    ChDrive DefaultDirectory$
    ChDir DefaultDirectory$

    Select Case (Err)
        Case 53:
            m$ = "There is no file named:" + Chr$(13)
            m$ = m$ + cmdialog.Filename
            MsgBox m$

    End Select

    'exit
    Exit Sub

    ' avoid errors
    Resume

End Sub
```

THE *menu_admin_save_Click( )* EVENT PROCEDURE

The menu_admin_save_Click() event procedure saves the current desktop configuration to the CHAP25.INI file. Following is a listing of the menu_admin_admin_save_Click() event procedure:

LISTING 25.21. MAIN.FRM, menu_admin_save_Click().

```
Sub menu_admin_save_Click ()

    'save desktop
    Call SaveINI

End Sub
```

The *menu_delete_Click( )* Event Procedure

The menu_delete_Click() event procedure deletes the currently selected hotspot. To delete a hotspot, the application must be in Design mode (when all the hotspots are visible), and you must select the hotspot by drawing a rubber band around it. Then the Delete menu option will be available.

Following is a listing of the menu_delete_Click() event procedure:

Listing 25.22. MAIN.FRM, menu_delete_Click( ).

```
Sub menu_delete_Click ()

    'declare variables
    Dim m$          'message contructor
    Dim res%        'holds results

    m$ = "Are you sure you want to delete this hotspot?"
    res% = MsgBox(m$, 292, "Warning")
    If res% = IDNO Then Exit Sub

    If DeleteIndex% <> 0 Then
        Unload Hotspot(DeleteIndex%)

        'remove old rubber band
        Call ClearOldImage
    Else
        'can't delete this one, it is the design time control array
        m$ = "You cannot delete this hotspot!"
        MsgBox m$
    End If

    'flag changed
    Changed% = True

End Sub
```

The *menu_exit_Click( )* Event Procedure

The menu_exit_Click() event procedure exits the application by calling the form_unload event. Following is a listing of the menu_exit_Click() event procedure:

Listing 25.23. MAIN.FRM, menu_exit_Click( ).

```
Sub menu_exit_Click ()

    'exit
    Unload frmMain

End Sub
```

THE *MENU_HIDE_CLICK( )* EVENT PROCEDURE

The menu_hide_Click() event procedure hides all hotspots to put the application in Run mode.
Following is a listing of the menu_hide_Click() event procedure:

LISTING 25.24. MAIN.FRM, menu_hide_Click().

```
Sub menu_hide_Click ()

     'declare variables
     Dim loopcount%         'loop counting variable
     Dim m$                 'message constructor
     Dim res%               'holds results


     'test to see if user has not added new hotspot
     If menu_new.Enabled = True Then
         'user has not added hotspot
         m$ = "You have not added a hotspot" + Chr$(13)
         m$ = m$ + "to the desired location!" + Chr$(13) + Chr$(13)
         m$ = m$ + "            Continue?"
         res% = MsgBox(m$, 292, "Warning")
         If res% = IDNO Then Exit Sub
     End If

     'disable loading of bitmap because it causes redraw problems
     menu_admin_load.Enabled = True

     'handle errors
     On Error GoTo HideError

     'loop through hotspots and set borderstyle to 0
     For loopcount% = 0 To HotspotIndex%
         Hotspot(loopcount%).BorderStyle = 0
     Next loopcount%

     'enable menus
     menu_hide.Enabled = False
     menu_show.Enabled = True
     menu_new.Enabled = False

     'remove old rubber band
     Call ClearOldImage

     Exit Sub

HideError:
     'this index did not exist
     Resume Next

End Sub
```

THE *MENU_NEW_CLICK()* EVENT PROCEDURE

The menu_new_Click() event procedure creates a new hotspot in the location specified by the bounding box. Following is a listing of the menu_new_Click() event procedure:

LISTING 25.25. MAIN.FRM, menu_new_Click().

```
Sub menu_new_Click ()

    'if borderstyle is none then rest of sub is invalid-so exit
    If Hotspot(0).BorderStyle = 0 Then Exit Sub

    'declare variables
    Dim NextAvailHotspot%   'holds temporary next available hotspot index

    NextAvailHotspot% = FindNextHotspotIndex()
    Load Hotspot(NextAvailHotspot%)


    If EndY > BeginY Then
        Hotspot(NextAvailHotspot%).Height = EndY - BeginY + 10
        Hotspot(NextAvailHotspot%).Top = BeginY
    Else
        Hotspot(NextAvailHotspot%).Height = BeginY - EndY + 10
        Hotspot(NextAvailHotspot%).Top = EndY
    End If
    If EndX > BeginX Then
        Hotspot(NextAvailHotspot%).Width = EndX - BeginX + 10
        Hotspot(NextAvailHotspot%).Left = BeginX
    Else
        Hotspot(NextAvailHotspot%).Width = BeginX - EndX + 10
        Hotspot(NextAvailHotspot%).Left = EndX
    End If
    Hotspot(NextAvailHotspot%).Visible = True
    Timer1.Enabled = False
    menu_new.Enabled = False

    'flag changed
    Changed% = True

End Sub
```

THE *MENU_SHOW_CLICK()* EVENT PROCEDURE

The menu_show_Click() event procedure shows all hotspots and puts the application in Design mode. Following is a listing of the menu_show_Click() event procedure:

LISTING 25.26. MAIN.FRM, menu_show_Click().

```
Sub menu_show_Click ()
```

continues

LISTING 25.26. CONTINUED

```
    'declare variables
    Dim loopcount%  'loop counting variable

    'disable loading of bitmap because it causes redraw problems
    menu_admin_load.Enabled = False

    'handle errors
    On Error GoTo ShowError

    For loopcount% = 0 To HotspotIndex%
        Hotspot(loopcount%).BorderStyle = 1
    Next loopcount%

    'enable menus
    menu_hide.Enabled = True
    menu_show.Enabled = False

    Exit Sub

ShowError:
    'this index did not exist
    Resume Next

End Sub
```

THE *TIMER1* CONTROL

Timer1 is the name of the timer control that is the control used to make the bounding box appear animated. The Timer1 control has code in only one event procedure. It is

◆ Timer1_Timer()

THE *TIMER1_TIMER()* EVENT PROCEDURE

The Timer1_Timer() event procedure occurs every 1/10th of a second. It toggles the drawing pen to make the illusion of movement in the bounding box. Following is a listing of the Timer1_Timer() event procedure:

LISTING 25.27. MAIN.FRM, Timer1_Timer().

```
Sub Timer1_Timer ()

    'declare variables
    Dim SaveDrawStyle%    'holds previous drawing style

    'save old draw style
    SaveDrawStyle% = frmMain.DrawStyle

    'force new solid drawstyle
```

```
    frmMain.DrawStyle = SOLID

    'draw a rubber band
    DrawRubberBand BeginX, BeginY, EndX, EndY

    'return to old drawstyle
    frmMain.DrawStyle = SaveDrawStyle%

End Sub
```

THE ABOUT.FRM FILE

ABOUT.FRM is one of two forms in this application. It shows information about the application. Figure 25.3 presents the form as it appears at runtime. Fundamentally, there is no difference in the form at design time, so it is not presented. Table 25.2 lists all the relevant properties of each control on the form that have been changed from their standard default values. The ABOUT.FRM file is contained on the CD accompanying this book in the CHAP25 subdirectory.

FIGURE 25.3.
Dynamic Hotspot application About form at runtime.

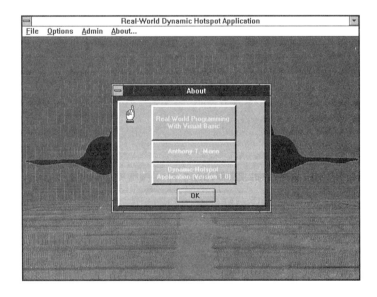

TABLE 25.2. PROPERTIES OF EACH CONTROL ON ABOUT.FRM.

Object	Control Type	Property	Value
frmAbout	Form	BackColor	&H00404000&
		Caption	"About"
		Height	3525

continues

TABLE 25.2. CONTINUED

Object	Control Type	Property	Value
		Left	1035
		MaxButton	False
		MinButton	False
		Top	1140
		Width	4545
pnlMain	SSPanel	BackColor	&H00C0C0C0&
		BevelWidth	3
		Caption	""
		Font3D	None
		ForeColor	&H00C0C0C0&
		Height	2895
		Left	125
		RoundedCorners	False
		ShadowColor	Black
		Top	125
		Width	4255
pnl1	SSPanel	BackColor	&H00C0C0C0&
		BevelWidth	3
		Caption	"Real-World Programming With Visual Basic"
		Font3D	None
		ForeColor	&H0000FFFF&
		Height	975
		Left	960
		RoundedCorners	False
		ShadowColor	Black
		Top	125
		Width	2415
pnl2	SSPanel	BackColor	&H00C0C0C0&
		BevelWidth	3
		Caption	"Anthony T. Mann"

Object	Control Type	Property	Value
		Font3D	None
		ForeColor	&H0000FFFF&
		Height	615
		Left	960
		RoundedCorners	False
		ShadowColor	Black
		Top	1080
		Width	2415
pnl3	SSPanel	BackColor	&H00C0C0C0&
		BevelWidth	3
		Caption	"Dynamic Hotspot Application (Version 1.0)"
		Font3D	None
		ForeColor	&H0000FFFF&
		Height	615
		Left	960
		RoundedCorners	False
		ShadowColor	Black
		Top	1680
		Width	2415
cmdOK	Command Button	Caption	"OK"
		Height	375
		Left	1680
		Top	2400
		Width	1095
pictAbout	Picture Box	Autosize	True
		BackColor	&H00C0C0C0&
		BorderStyle	None
		Height	615
		Left	125
		Top	125
		Width	735

FUNCTION, SUBROUTINE, AND EVENT PROCEDURES

There are several procedures of code for each object(control) that comprise this form. Each is listed in the following sections.

The (general) object contains only one form level declaration and no form level procedures. The procedures for the (general) object are

- ◆ (declarations)
- ◆ CenterForm()

THE *(DECLARATIONS)* PROCEDURE

The (declarations) procedure contains only one line of declarations used in the form, ABOUT.FRM. It is only to allow for variable syntax checking and forcing the declaration of variables in each procedure. Following is a listing of the (declarations) procedure:

LISTING 25.28. ABOUT.FRM, (general)(declarations).

```
Option Explicit
```

THE *CENTERFORM()* PROCEDURE

The CenterForm() procedure simply centers the form in the client area. Following is a listing of the CenterForm() procedure:

LISTING 25.29. ABOUT.FRM, CenterForm().

```
Sub CenterForm (f As Form)

    f.Move (screen.Width - f.Width) / 2, (screen.Height - f.Height) / 2

End Sub
```

THE *CMDOK* CONTROL

cmdOK is the name of the Command button control that, when clicked, will close the frmAbout form. The cmdOK control has code only in one event procedure. It is

- ◆ cmdOK_Click()

THE *cmdOK_Click()* EVENT PROCEDURE

The cmdOK_Click() event procedure simply unloads the form. Following is a listing of the cmdOK_Click() event procedure:

LISTING 25.30. ABOUT.FRM, cmdOK_Click().

```
Sub cmdOK_Click ()

    'unload
    Unload frmAbout

End Sub
```

THE *FORM* OBJECT

The Form object itself has code in only one event procedure. It is

◆ Form_Load()

THE *FORM_LOAD()* EVENT PROCEDURE

The Form_Load() event procedure centers the form and assigns an icon to the pictAbout control. Following is a listing of the Form_Load() event procedure:

LISTING 25.31. ABOUT.FRM, Form_Load().

```
Sub Form_Load ()

    'center form
    CenterForm Me

    'load icon
    pictAbout.Picture = frmMain.Icon

End Sub
```

THE CHAP25.ICO FILE

This file contains the icon that has been attached to the form at design time. The CHAP25.ICO file is contained on the CD accompanying this book in the CHAP25 subdirectory.

FIGURE 25.4.
Dynamic Hotspot
application Form icon.

THE CHAP25.EXE FILE

This is the executable file that is distributable. If you distribute this application, you must include the following files:

- CHAP25.EXE
- THREED.VBX
- CMDIALOG.VBX
- COMMDLG.DLL
- VBRUN300.DLL

The CHAP25.EXE file and source files are contained on the CD accompanying this book in the CHAP25 subdirectory, while all DLLs and VBXs are in the RESOURCE subdirectory.

THE RWPROGVB.DLL FILE

This is the resource file that contains the custom cursor that looks like a hand pointing upward. It is contained on the CD accompanying this book in the RESOURCE subdirectory.

THE CHAP25.INI FILE

This is the configuration file used in loading the desktop. Following is a listing of a sample CHAP25.INI file created by the program. It does not list all the possible keys. If all 100 hotspots existed, the file would have over 400 lines of code in it.

LISTING 25.32. CHAP25.INI CONTAINING TWO HOTSPOTS.

```
[Initialization]
Bitmap=D:\WINDOWS\SAMPLE.BMP
MaxHotspot=2
Hotspot0X1=0
Hotspot0Y1=0
Hotspot0X2=15
Hotspot0Y2=15
Hotspot1X1=3345
Hotspot1Y1=2130
Hotspot1X2=5845
Hotspot1Y2=4450
Hotspot2X1=1095
Hotspot2Y1=1530
Hotspot2X2=1945
Hotspot2Y2=5590
```

If you want to customize this file, you can do so with any text editor, such as the Windows notepad. You can change the bitmap or any of the coordinates of the hotspots. You can even add hotspots by providing the four coordinates of the hotspot area.

Relating the Dynamic Hotspot Application to Your Application

The Dynamic Hotspot application shows how to manipulate graphics to provide user interaction on a static bitmap graphic. The possibilities for this are virtually unlimited. These techniques can be used in game programming as well.

Many applications today use hotspots. These include games, touch screen directories, and many other types of applications. Using a hotspot is a great way to have the user interactively input or request information from the computer. Using the techniques described in this chapter allows you to use Visual Basic controls without having to purchase expensive third-party controls.

Final Notes

This application was created on a standard VGA display using 16 colors. Your particular hardware could have adverse effects on the code the way it is written. You may need to modify it slightly.

549

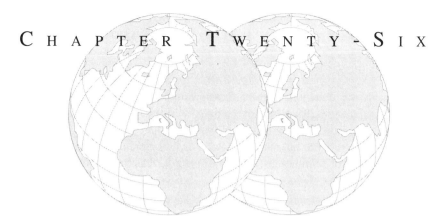

COMMUNICATIONS TERMINAL APPLICATION

THE COMMUNICATIONS TERMINAL APPLICATION ALLOWS THE USER TO SEND TEXT OR TEXT FILES TO ANOTHER COMMUNICATIONS TERMINAL. THE COMMUNICATIONS TERMINAL CAN ALSO BE USED TO TEST A MODEM BY SENDING COMMANDS TO IT AND DETECTING A RESPONSE.

REM   Due to the limitations of the Communications control, this application has some
special features that allow for the transfer of text files. Therefore, you need to use
this application on *both* ends to transfer text files. The application can, for example,
connect to a BBS, but not download files. For more information on the Communications control's limitations, refer to Chapter 9, "Communcations."

Figure 26.1 shows the main screen (MAIN.FRM) at runtime.

FIGURE 26.1.
*Communications
Terminal application
MAIN.FRM at runtime.*

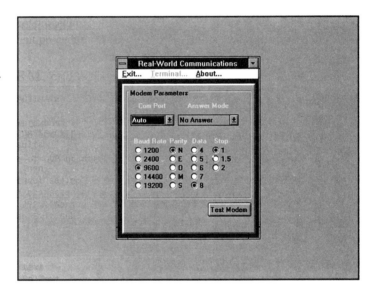

After you use the main form to select the communications parameters, you can transfer text
files or enter modem commands via the TERMINAL.FRM form. Figure 26.2 shows the
TERMINAL.FRM form at runtime.

To use the application, select a com port by using the combo box labeled Com Port. The choices
are Com1 through Com4 and Auto. Auto automatically detects which com port the modem is
connected to when you click on the Test command button. The test cycles through all available
ports and tests the modem. It stops on the first modem encountered and asks if you want to use
this modem. If you do, the test selects the modem automatically. Next, select the appropriate
communications parameters. These are only affected if you want to send or receive files. If you
are only going to test the modem, the communications parameters are not necessary.

To enter the terminal screen, choose the Terminal... menu option. This option brings up the
terminal screen. You can simply enter commands into the modem and wait for a response. This
is also the screen from which you can send or receive files. These options are selected from the
menu. Each option prompts for a filename from the common dialog box.

FIGURE 26.2.
*Communications
Terminal application
TERMINAL.FRM at
runtime.*

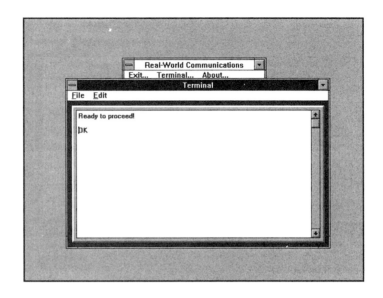

From the TERMINAL.FRM form, you can also dial a telephone number. The Edit->Dial menu option invokes a Visual Basic InputBox() function to prompt for the number to dial.

The Communications Terminal application demonstrates using "File Input/Output I/O," in Chapter 7, and "Communications," in Chapter 9. For more information, refer to these chapters.

CODE LISTINGS

The Communications Terminal application contains the following files and listings:

◆ CHAP26.MAK

◆ MAIN.FRM

◆ TERMINAL.FRM

◆ ABOUT.FRM

◆ CHAP26.BAS

◆ CHAP26.ICO

◆ CHAP26.EXE

THE CHAP26.MAK FILE

CHAP26.MAK is the project file for the Communications Terminal application, CHAP26.EXE. It contains a listing of all the files necessary to load the project into Visual Basic. The

CHAP26.MAK file is contained on the CD accompanying this book in the CHAP26 subdirectory. The file listing is presented in listing 26.1.

LISTING 26.1. CHAP26.MAK.

```
MAIN.FRM
TERMINAL.FRM
ABOUT.FRM
CHAP26.BAS
THREED.VBX
MSCOMM.VBX
CMDIALOG.VBX
ProjWinSize=152,402,248,215
ProjWinShow=2
IconForm="frmMain"
Title="Communications"
ExeName="CHAP26.EXE"
```

THE MAIN.FRM FILE

MAIN.FRM is one of three forms in this application. It is the startup form for the application as well as the form used to enter the communications parameters and assign the modem port. Figure 26.1 presents this form as it appears at runtime. Figure 26.3 shows the form as it appears at design time. Table 26.1 lists all the relevant properties of each control on the form, which have been changed from their standard default values. The MAIN.FRM file is contained on the CD accompanying this book in the CHAP26 subdirectory.

FIGURE 26.3.
Communications Terminal application MAIN.FRM at design time.

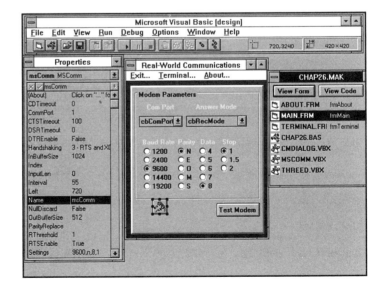

TABLE 26.1. PROPERTIES OF EACH CONTROL ON MAIN.FRM.

Object	Control Type	Property	Value
frmMain	Form	BackColor	&H00404000&
		Caption	"Real-World Communications"
		Height	4995
		Icon	"CHAP26.ICO"
		Left	1575
		MaxButton	False
		Top	1140
		Width	4050
Panel3D1	SSPanel	BackColor	&H00C0C0C0&
		BevelWidth	3
		Font3D	None
		Height	4095
		Left	120
		Top	120
		Width	3735
Panel3D11	SSPanel	BackColor	&H00C0C0C0&
		BevelOuter	None
		BevelWidth	3
		Font3D	None
		ForeColor	&H0000FFFF&
		Height	855
		Left	2400
		Top	1560
		Width	615
Panel3D10	SSPanel	BackColor	&H00C0C0C0&
		BevelOuter	None
		BevelWidth	3
		Caption	"Stop"
		Font3D	None
		ForeColor	&H0000FFFF&
		Height	255
		Left	2400
		Top	1320

continues

TABLE 26.1. CONTINUED

Object	Control Type	Property	Value
		Width	495
Panel3D19	SSPanel	BackColor	&H00C0C0C0&
		BevelOuter	None
		BevelWidth	3
		Font3D	None
		ForeColor	&H0000FFFF&
		Height	1335
		Left	1800
		Top	1560
		Width	495
Panel3D8	SSPanel	BackColor	&H00C0C0C0&
		BevelOuter	None
		BevelWidth	3
		Font3D	None
		ForeColor	&H0000FFFF&
		Height	1335
		Left	1080
		Top	1560
		Width	735
Panel3D7	SSPanel	BackColor	&H00C0C0C0&
		BevelOuter	None
		BevelWidth	3
		Font3D	None
		ForeColor	&H0000FFFF&
		Height	1335
		Left	240
		Top	1560
		Width	855
Panel3D6	SSPanel	BackColor	&H00C0C0C0&
		BevelOuter	None
		BevelWidth	3
		Caption	"Data"
		Font3D	None
		ForeColor	&H0000FFFF&

Object	Control Type	Property	Value
		Height	255
		Left	1800
		Top	1320
		Width	495
Panel3D5	SSPanel	BackColor	&H00C0C0C0&
		BevelOuter	None
		BevelWidth	3
		Caption	"Parity"
		Font3D	None
		ForeColor	&H0000FFFF&
		Height	255
		Left	1200
		Top	1320
		Width	495
Panel3D4	SSPanel	BackColor	&H00C0C0C0&
		BevelOuter	None
		BevelWidth	3
		Caption	"Baud Rate"
		Font3D	None
		ForeColor	&H0000FFFF&
		Height	255
		Left	120
		Top	1320
		Width	1095
Panel3D2	SSPanel	BackColor	&H00C0C0C0&
		BevelOuter	None
		BevelWidth	3
		Caption	"Com Port"
		Font3D	None
		ForeColor	&H0000FFFF&
		Height	255
		Left	120
		Top	360
		Width	1215

continues

TABLE 26.1. CONTINUED

Object	Control Type	Property	Value
Panel3D3	SSPanel	BackColor	&H00C0C0C0&
		BevelOuter	None
		BevelWidth	3
		Caption	"Answer Mode"
		Font3D	None
		ForeColor	&H0000FFFF&
		Height	255
		Left	1440
		Top	360
		Width	1695
cmdTest	CommandButton	Caption	"Test Modem"
		Height	375
		Left	2400
		Top	3240
		Width	1215
msComm	MSComm	CTSTimeout	100
		DTREnable	False
		Handshaking	RTS and XON/XOFF
		Interval	55
		Left	720
		Rthreshold	1
		RTSEnable	True
		SThreshold	1
		Top	3240
Frame3D1	SSFrame	Caption	"Modem Parameters"
		Font3D	None
		Height	3015
		Left	120
		Top	120
		Width	3495
optStop	SSOption	Caption	"1", "1.5", "2"*
		Font3D	None
		Height	255
		Index	0, 1, 2*

Object	Control Type	Property	Value
		Left	0
		TabStop	False
		Top	0, 240, 480*
		Value	True
		Width	495
optData	SSOption	Caption	"4","5","6","7","8"*
		Font3D	None
		Height	255
		Index	0,1,2,3,4
		Left	0
		TabStop	False
		Top	0,240,480,720,960*
		Width	495
optParity	SSOption	Caption	"N","E","O","M","S"*
		Font3D	None
		Height	255
		Index	0,1,2,3,4
		Left	120
		TabStop	False
		Top	0,240,480,720,960*
		Width	495
optBaudRate	SSOption	Caption	"1200","2400","9600", "14400","19200"*
		Font3D	None
		Height	255
		Index	0,1,2,3,4
		Left	0
		TabStop	False
		Top	0,240,480,720,960*
		Width	855
cbComPort	ComboBox	BackColor	&H00C0C0C0&
		Height	300
		Left	120
		Style	Dropdown List
		Top	720

continues

TABLE 26.1. CONTINUED

Object	Control Type	Property	Value
		Width	1215
cbRecMode	ComboBox	BackColor	&H00C0C0C0&
		Height	300
		Left	1440
		Style	Dropdown List
		Top	720
		Width	1695
menu_exit	Menu	Caption	"&Exit..."
menu_terminal	Menu	Caption	"&Terminal..."
menu_about	Menu	Caption	"&About..."

*This control is a control array, and these are the only properties that vary within the control. To save space, they are not listed separately.

FUNCTION, SUBROUTINE, AND EVENT PROCEDURES

There are several procedures of code for each object(control) that comprise this form. Each is listed in the following sections.

THE *(GENERAL)* OBJECT

The (general) object contains declarations and procedures at the form level. The procedures for the (general) object are

◆ (declarations)

◆ AnswerPhone()

◆ BuildSetting()

THE *(DECLARATIONS)* PROCEDURE

The (declarations) procedure contains form level declarations. Following is a listing of the (declarations) procedure:

LISTING 26.2. MAIN.FRM, (general)(declarations).

```
Option Explicit

'declare variables
Dim TempInput$      'string which holds input from comm control,
                    'allowing for input buffer to be cleared
Dim AutoPort%       'holds port where modem was automatically detected
```

THE *ANSWERPHONE( )* PROCEDURE

The AnswerPhone( ) procedure sends commands to the modem to answer the phone. Following is a listing of the AnswerPhone( ) procedure:

LISTING 26.3. MAIN.FRM, AnswerPhone( ).

```
Sub AnswerPhone ()

    'declare variables
    Dim DoEventsLoop%   'loop counting variable

    'answer line
    mscomm.Output = "ATA" + Chr$(13)
    mscomm.Output = "ATH1" + Chr$(13)

    'allow enough doevents to wait for modem
    For DoEventsLoop% = 1 To 100
        DoEvents
    Next DoEventsLoop%

    'send greeting
    mscomm.Output = "Welcome to Real-World Programming with Visual Basic!" + Chr$(13) +
    Chr$(10)

End Sub
```

THE *BUILDSETTINGS( )* PROCEDURE

The BuildSettings( ) procedure builds a string of modem parameters to send to the modem. The procedure is also a function that returns the string. Following is a listing of the BuildSettings( ) procedure:

LISTING 26.4. MAIN.FRM, BuildSettings( ).

```
Function BuildSettings ()

    'declare variables
    Dim BRate$      'holds baud rate
    Dim Parity$     'holds parity choice
    Dim DataBit$    'holds Data bit choice
    Dim StopBit$    'holds stop bit choice
    Dim LoopCount%  'loop counting variable

    'baudrate
    For LoopCount% = 0 To 4
        If optBaudRate(LoopCount%).Value = True Then
            BRate$ = optBaudRate(LoopCount%).Caption
        End If
    Next LoopCount%

    'parity
    For LoopCount% = 0 To 4
```

LISTING 26.4. CONTINUED

```
        If optParity(LoopCount%).Value = True Then
            Parity$ = optParity(LoopCount%).Caption
        End If
    Next LoopCount%

    'data bits
    For LoopCount% = 0 To 4
        If optData(LoopCount%).Value = True Then
            DataBit$ = optData(LoopCount%).Caption
        End If
    Next LoopCount%

    'stop bits
    For LoopCount% = 0 To 2
        If optStop(LoopCount%).Value = True Then
            StopBit$ = optStop(LoopCount%).Caption
        End If
    Next LoopCount%

    BuildSettings = BRate$ + "," + Parity$ + "," + DataBit$ + "," + StopBit$

End Function
```

The `BuildSettings` string contains a listing of the baud rate, parity number of data bits, and number of stop bits, all separated by commas.

THE *cbComPort* CONTROL

cbComPort is the name of the combo box button control that lists all of the possible com ports (1-4). The cbComPort control has code in only one event procedure. It is

◆ cbPort_Click()

THE *cbPort_Click()* EVENT PROCEDURE

The cbPort_Click() event procedure handles what happens when the user clicks a new com port setting. Following is a listing of the cbPort_Click() event procedure:

LISTING 26.5. MAIN.FRM, cbPort_Click().

```
Sub cbComPort_Click ()

    'declare variables
    Dim m$        'message constructor

    'this routine is only valid if auto is selected
    If InStr(cbComPort.Text, "Auto") > 0 Then
        'enable test button
        cmdTest.Enabled = True

        'turn auto answer off-can't auto detect ringing on all ports at once
```

```
        cbRecMode.ListIndex = 1

        Exit Sub
    End If

    'handle errors
    On Error GoTo porterrorclose

    'test to see if there is a selection
    If cbComPort.ListIndex = -1 Then Exit Sub

    'first close port
    mscomm.PortOpen = False

    'handle error
    On Error GoTo porterroropen

    'assign port
    mscomm.CommPort = Val(Right$(cbComPort.List(cbComPort.ListIndex), 1))

    'open port if NOT set to "No Answer"
    If cbRecMode.Text <> "No Answer" Then
        If Not (mscomm.PortOpen = True) Then
            'open port
            mscomm.PortOpen = True

            'enable test button
            cmdTest.Enabled = True

            'configure to answer on first ring
            SendToModem ("ATS0=1" + Chr$(13))

            'enable menus
            menu_terminal.Enabled = True
        End If
    End If

    'exit
    Exit Sub

porterrorclose:
    Resume Next

porterroropen:
    'build message
    m$ = "Can't open port!"
    MsgBox m$

    'disable test button
    cmdTest.Enabled = False

    'disable menu options
    menu_terminal.Enabled = False

    'blank com port display
    cbComPort.ListIndex = -1
```

continues

LISTING 26.5. CONTINUED

```
        Exit Sub
        'avoid errors
        Resume

    End Sub
```

THE *cbRecMode* CONTROL

cbRecMode is the name of the combo box control that lists all of the possible answer modes. The cbRecMode control has code in only one event procedure. It is

◆ cbRecMode_Click()

THE *cbRecMode_Click()* EVENT PROCEDURE

The cbRecMode_Click() event procedure handles dialing Answer mode if user selects Auto for the com port. Following is a listing of the cbRecMode_Click() event procedure:

LISTING 26.6. MAIN.FRM, cbRecMode_Click().

```
Sub cbRecMode_Click ()

    'autoport can only be no answer
    If InStr(cbComPort.Text, "Auto") > 0 Then
        cbRecMode.ListIndex = 1
    End If

End Sub
```

THE *cmdTest* CONTROL

cmdTest is the name of the command button control that, when clicked, tests to see if there is a modem response from the specified com port. If cbComPort is set to Auto, it tests all ports for the response of a modem and stops at the first one found. The cmdTest control has code in only one event procedure. It is

◆ cmdTest_Click()

THE *cmdTest_Click()* EVENT PROCEDURE

The cmdText_Click() event procedure handles the testing of the modem. Following is a listing of the cmdTest_Click() event procedure:

LISTING 26.7. MAIN.FRM, cmdTest_Click().

```
Sub cmdTest_Click ()

        'declare variables
```

```
Dim m$              'message constructor
Dim LoopCount%      'loop counting variable
Dim DoEventsLoop%   'loop counting variable
Dim ModemFound%     'holds port modem found in
Dim res%            'holds results

'exit if no com port is selected
If cbComPort.ListIndex < 0 Then
    m$ = "You must select a com port!"
    MsgBox m$
    Exit Sub
End If

'change cursor
screen.MousePointer = HOURGLASS

'initialize
ModemFound% = -1

'handle error
On Error GoTo TestError

'close port
mscomm.PortOpen = False

If InStr(cbComPort.Text, "Auto") > 0 Then
    'AUTO DETECTION OF PORT REQUESTED

    For LoopCount% = 1 To 4
        'assign port
        mscomm.CommPort = LoopCount%

        'assign settings
        mscomm.Settings = BuildSettings()

        'open port
        mscomm.PortOpen = True

        'assign output string
        mscomm.Output = "AT" + Chr$(13)

        'show and unload terminal form only for time to wait for modem
        'doevents doesn't work
        frmTerminal.Show
        Unload frmTerminal
        DoEvents
        DoEvents

        'read input from modem
        If InStr(TempInput$, "OK") > 0 Then
            ModemFound% = mscomm.CommPort

            'exit loop
            Exit For
        End If

        'close port
```

continues 565

LISTING 26.7. CONTINUED

```
            mscomm.PortOpen = False

    Next LoopCount%

    'change cursor
    screen.MousePointer = DEFAULT

    'display results
    If ModemFound% > 0 Then
        'modem found
        m$ = "Modem Found On Com " + Trim$(Str$(ModemFound%)) + Chr$(13)
        m$ = m$ + "Use port now?"
        res% = MsgBox(m$, 292, "Question")
        If res% = IDNO Then
            'don't use port now
            AutoPort% = ModemFound%
        Else
            'use port now

            'select which modem - cbComPort_Click will be generated
            cbComPort.ListIndex = ModemFound%

            'assign auto answer mode
            cbRecMode.ListIndex = 0

            'open port
            mscomm.PortOpen = True

            'assign which port was opened automatically
            AutoPort% = ModemFound%
        End If
    Else
        'modem not found
        MsgBox "No Modem Found!"
        AutoPort% = -1
    End If

    'exit
    Exit Sub
Else
    'SPECIFIC PORT REQUESTED
    'assign port
    mscomm.CommPort = Val(Right$(cbComPort.List(cbComPort.ListIndex), 1))

    'assign settings
    mscomm.Settings = BuildSettings()

    'open port
    mscomm.PortOpen = True

    'assign output string
    mscomm.Output = "AT" + Chr$(13)

    'show and unload terminal form only for time to wait for modem
    'doevents doesn't work
```

```
        frmTerminal.Show
        Unload frmTerminal
        DoEvents
        DoEvents

        'change cursor
        screen.MousePointer = DEFAULT

        If InStr(TempInput$, "OK") > 0 Then
            MsgBox "Modem OK On Com " + Trim$(Str$(mscomm.CommPort))
        Else
            MsgBox "Modem Doesn't Respond On Com " + Trim$(Str$(mscomm.CommPort))
        End If

        'exit
        Exit Sub
    End If

TestError:
    'error occurred

    Select Case (Err)
        Case 68: '(device unavail)
            Resume Next
            m$ = cbComPort.List(cbComPort.ListIndex) + " is invalid." + Chr$(13)
            m$ = m$ + "It could be the mouse port."

            'change cursor
            screen.MousePointer = DEFAULT

            'show message
            MsgBox m$

            'exit
            Exit Sub

            'avoid errors
            Resume
        Case Else:
            Resume Next
    End Select
End Sub
```

The preceding code first determines if a specific com port is selected or if Auto is selected. If a specific com port is selected, an AT command is sent to the modem to test if it responds on that com port. If Auto is selected, the code tests all four com ports by using the same method.

The *Form* Object

The Form object has code in two event procedures. They are

◆ Form_Load()

◆ Form_Unload()

567

THE *FORM_LOAD()* EVENT PROCEDURE

The Form_Load() event procedure initializes, assigns defaults, and loads the main form. Following is a listing of the Form_Load() event procedure:

LISTING 26.8. MAIN.FRM, Form_Load().

```
Sub Form_Load ()

    'center the form
    CenterForm Me

    'populate com ports
    cbComPort.AddItem "Auto"
    cbComPort.AddItem "Com 1"
    cbComPort.AddItem "Com 2"
    cbComPort.AddItem "Com 3"
    cbComPort.AddItem "Com 4"

    'populate Modes
    cbRecMode.AddItem "Auto Answer"
    cbRecMode.AddItem "No Answer"
    cbRecMode.AddItem "Conditional"

    'set defaults
    cbRecMode.ListIndex = 0

    'diable test button
    cmdTest.Enabled = False

    'disable menu options
    menu_terminal.Enabled = False

End Sub
```

THE *FORM_UNLOAD()* EVENT PROCEDURE

The Form_Unload() event procedure prompts the user to confirm ending the program. Following is a listing of the Form_Unload() event procedure:

LISTING 26.9. MAIN.FRM, Form_Unload().

```
Sub Form_Unload (cancel As Integer)

    'declare variables
    Dim m$       'message constructor
    Dim res%     'holds results

    'build message
    m$ = "Are you sure you want to exit?"
    res% = MsgBox(m$, 292, "Warning")
    If res% = IDNO Then
```

```
            'cancel
            cancel = True

            'exit
            Exit Sub
      End If

      'handle error
      On Error GoTo exiterror

      'hang up
      mscomm.Output = "+++ATH0" + Chr$(13) '+ Chr$(10)

      'toggle DTR twice
      mscomm.DTREnable = True
      mscomm.DTREnable = False
      mscomm.DTREnable = True
      mscomm.DTREnable = False

      'close port
      mscomm.PortOpen = False

exiterror:
      'exit
      End

End Sub
```

The *menu* Object

The menu object is created by using Visual Basic's built-in menu editor. It has code associated with three Click() event procedures. They are

- ◆ menu_about()
- ◆ menu_exit()
- ◆ menu_terminal()

The *menu_about_Click()* Procedure

The menu_about_Click() procedure simply shows the about form for program information. Following is a listing of the menu_about_Click() procedure:

Listing 26.10. MAIN.FRM, menu_about_Click().

```
Sub menu_about_Click ()

      'show about form
      frmAbout.Show MODAL

End Sub
```

569

THE *MENU_EXIT_CLICK()* PROCEDURE

The menu_exit_Click() ends the program by calling the form_unload event. Following is a listing of the menu_exit_Click() procedure:

LISTING 26.11. MAIN.FRM, menu_exit_Click().

```
Sub menu_exit_Click ()

    'close application
    Unload frmMain

End Sub
```

THE *MENU_TERMINAL_CLICK()* PROCEDURE

The menu_terminal_Click() invokes the TERMINAL.FRM form, which is used to manually send commands to the modem and to start transferring text files. Following is a listing of the menu_terminal_Click() procedure:

LISTING 26.12. MAIN.FRM, menu_terminal_Click().

```
Sub menu_terminal_Click ()

    'show terminal form
    frmTerminal.Show

End Sub
```

THE *MSCOMM* CONTROL

msComm is the name of the Communications control that is responsible for controlling all aspects of the modem. The msComm control has code in only one event procedure. It is

◆ msComm_OnComm()

THE *MSCOMM_ONCOMM()* EVENT PROCEDURE

The msComm_OnComm() event procedure has many uses. The control invokes this event depending on certain parameters set. Many error codes are not used but are left in so that it is easier to modify the code, if you wish. Notice that the subroutine is declared as static. This is so that all values are preserved throughout the program. Following is a listing of the msComm_OnComm() event procedure:

Listing 26.13. MAIN.FRM, msComm_OnComm().

```
Static Sub msComm_OnComm ()

    'declare variables
    Dim m$          'message constructor
    Dim res%        'holds results
    Dim temp$       'temporary working string
    Dim Temp1$      'temporary working string
    Dim LoopCount%  'loop counting variable
    Dim CRsFound%   'number of carriage returns found in return string
    Dim pos%        'holds position of instr

     'handle errors
     On Error GoTo comerror:

    'handle specific cases
    Select Case mscomm.CommEvent
        '--- Event messages
        Case MSCOMM_EV_RECEIVE

            'assign input to temp variable
            temp$ = mscomm.Input

            'assign TempInput(for port detection) to Temp$
            TempInput$ = temp$

            If InStr(temp$, "CONN") > 0 Then
                'connected
                frmTerminal.Show
                DoEvents

                'send welcome message
                mscomm.Output = "HELLO FROM CHAPTER 26 APPLICATION" + Chr$(13) + Chr$(10)
                DoEvents
                DoEvents
                DoEvents
            ElseIf InStr(temp$, "NO CARR") > 0 Then
                'lost connection
                m$ = "Connection was broken!"
                MsgBox m$
                Unload frmTerminal
            ElseIf InStr(temp$, "FILE SENT") > 0 Then

                'determine position of "File Sent"
                pos% = InStr(temp$, "FILE SENT")
                If pos% <> 0 Then
                    temp$ = Left$(temp$, pos% - 2)
                End If
                'write to file
                If Len(temp$) > 0 Then
                    Put hSend, , temp$
                End If

                'unflag receiving
```

continues

LISTING 26.13. CONTINUED

```
            Receiving% = False

            'close all open file handles
            Close

        End If

        'determine special cases
        If Len(temp$) > 0 Then
            Select Case Asc(temp$)
                Case 127:    'Backspace
                    Exit Sub
                Case 27:     'arrow keys
                    Exit Sub
            End Select
        End If

        Temp1$ = Left$(temp$, Len(temp$))
        If Right$(Temp1$, 1) = Chr$(13) Then
            'last character is a carraige return
            CRsFound% = 1
            'backup until there are no more carriage returns
            For LoopCount% = Len(Temp1$) To 1 Step -1
                If Mid$(Temp1$, LoopCount%, 1) <> Chr$(13) Then
                    'append line feed
                    Temp1$ = Left$(Temp1$, CRsFound% + 1) + Chr$(13)
                    Exit For
                Else
                    CRsFound% = CRsFound% + 1
                End If
            Next LoopCount%
            Temp1$ = Temp1$ + Chr$(10)
            temp$ = Temp1$
        End If

        'show receive in client area
        frmTerminal.txtClientArea = frmTerminal.txtClientArea + temp$
        If Receiving% = True Then
            'write to file
            If Len(temp$) > 0 Then
                Put hSend, , temp$
            End If
        Else
            'set insertion point to end of text
            frmTerminal.txtClientArea.SelStart = Len(frmTerminal.txtClientArea.Text)
        End If
    Case MSCOMM_EV_SEND
    Case MSCOMM_EV_CTS
        'unflag receiving
        Receiving% = False

        'close file handles
        Close
    Case MSCOMM_EV_DSR
```

```
    Case MSCOMM_EV_CD
    Case MSCOMM_EV_RING
        If cbRecMode.Text = "Auto Answer" Then
            'answer
            Call AnswerPhone

        ElseIf cbRecMode.Text = "Conditional" Then
            m$ = "     Phone is ringing!" + Chr$(13)
            m$ = m$ + "Would you like to answer it?"
            res% = MsgBox(m$, 292, "Question")
            If res% = IDYES Then
                'answer
                Call AnswerPhone
            End If
        End If
    Case MSCOMM_EV_EOF
    Case MSCOMM_ER_BREAK
    Case MSCOMM_ER_CTSTO
    Case MSCOMM_ER_DSRTO
    Case MSCOMM_ER_FRAME
    Case MSCOMM_ER_OVERRUN
    Case MSCOMM_ER_CDTO
    Case MSCOMM_ER_RXOVER
    Case MSCOMM_ER_RXPARITY
    Case MSCOMM_ER_TXFULL
    Case Else
    End Select

    'exit
    Exit Sub

comerror:
    Select Case Err
        Case 53:      'File not found
            'ignore
        Case Else:
            'an error occurred
            MsgBox Error$
    End Select

    Resume Next

End Sub
```

 For more information on this event, refer to Chapter 9, "Communications."

THE TERMINAL.FRM FILE

TERMINAL.FRM is one of three forms in this application. It is the form that allows you to enter commands to send to the modem and invoke text file transfer or receive. Figure 26.2 presents this form as it appears at runtime. Figure 26.4 shows the form as it appears at design time. Table 26.2 lists all the relevant properties of each control on the form, which have been changed from their standard default values. The TERMINAL.FRM file is contained on the CD accompanying this book in the CHAP26 subdirectory.

FIGURE 26.4.
*Communications
Terminal application
TERMINAL.FRM at
design time.*

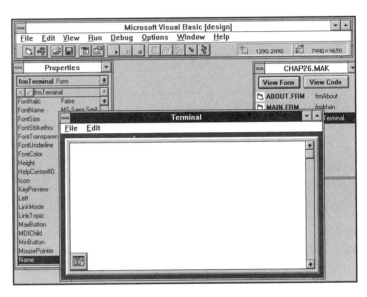

TABLE 26.2. PROPERTIES OF EACH CONTROL ON TERMINAL.FRM.

Object	Control Type	Property	Value
frmTerminal	Form	BackColor	&H00404000&
		Caption	"Terminal"
		Height	4650
		KeyPreview	True
		Left	1935
		MaxButton	False
		Top	1650
		Width	7440
Panel3D1	SSPanel	BackColor	&H00C0C0C0&
		BevelWidth	3
		Font3D	None
		Height	3735
		Left	120

Object	Control Type	Property	Value
		Top	120
		Width	7095
cmDialog	CommonDialog	CancelError	True
		Left	120
		Top	3120
txtClientArea	TextBox	BackColor	&H00FFFFFF&
		Height	3495
		Left	120
		MultiLine	True
		ScrollBars	Vertical
		Top	120
		Width	6855
menu_file	Menu	Caption	"&File"
menu_transmit	Menu	Caption	"&Transmit"
menu_receive	Menu	Caption	"&Receive"
menu_close	Menu	Caption	"&Close"
menu_edit	Menu	Caption	"&Edit"
menu_clear	Menu	Caption	"&Clear Client"
menu_dial	Menu	Caption	"&Dial"
menu_hangup	Menu	Caption	"&Hangup"

FUNCTION, SUBROUTINE, AND EVENT PROCEDURES

There are several procedures of code for each object(control) that comprise this form. Each is listed in the following sections.

THE (GENERAL) OBJECT

The (general) object contains form level declarations and no form level procedures. The procedures for the (general) object is

◆ (declarations)

THE (DECLARATIONS) PROCEDURE

The (declarations) procedure contains form level declarations. Following is a listing of the (declarations) procedure:

LISTING 26.14. TERMINAL.FRM, (general)(declarations).

```
Option Explicit

'declare variables
Dim OutputString$        'holds string to send to control
```

THE *FORM* OBJECT

The Form object has code in two event procedures. They are

- ◆ Form_Load()
- ◆ Form_Unload()

THE *FORM_LOAD()* EVENT PROCEDURE

The Form_Load() event procedure initializes, assigns defaults, and loads the main form. Following is a listing of the Form_Load() event procedure:

LISTING 26.15. TERMINAL.FRM, Form_Load().

```
Sub Form_Load ()

    'handle errors
    On Error GoTo LoadError

    If frmMain.msComm.PortOpen = True Then
        'send default message
        txtClientArea.Text = "Ready to proceed!" + Chr$(13) + Chr$(10)

        'don't echo characters
        frmMain.msComm.Output = "ATE0" + Chr$(13) + Chr$(10)

        'put cursor at end of text
        If txtClientArea.Visible = True Then
            txtClientArea.SetFocus
        End If
        txtClientArea.SelStart = Len(txtClientArea)

    End If
        'exit
        Exit Sub

LoadError:
    MsgBox Error$

    'exit
    Exit Sub

    'avoid errors
    Resume

End Sub
```

The *Form_Unload()* Event Procedure

The Form_Unload() event procedure closes the TERMINAL.FRM form. Following is a listing of the Form_Unload() event procedure:

Listing 26.16. TERMINAL.FRM, Form_Unload().

```
Sub Form_Unload (cancel As Integer)

    'close all files
    Close

End Sub
```

The *menu* Object

The menu object is created by using Visual Basic's built-in menu editor. It has code associated with six Click() event procedures. They are

- ◆ menu_clear()
- ◆ menu_close()
- ◆ menu_dial()
- ◆ menu_hangup()
- ◆ menu_receive()
- ◆ menu_transmit()

The *menu_clear_Click()* Procedure

The menu_clear_Click() procedure simply clears the text box of all text. Following is a listing of the menu_clear_Click() procedure:

Listing 26.17. TERMINAL.FRM, menu_clear_Click().

```
Sub menu_clear_Click ()

    'clear client area and output
    txtClientArea.Text = ""
    OutputString$ = ""
    txtClientArea.SetFocus

End Sub
```

The *menu_close_Click()* Procedure

The menu_close_Click() procedure simply unloads the form. Following is a listing of the menu_close_Click() procedure:

LISTING 26.18. TERMINAL.FRM, menu_close_Click().

```
Sub menu_close_Click ()

    'close
    Unload frmTerminal

End Sub
```

THE *MENU_DIAL_CLICK* ( ) PROCEDURE

The menu_dial_Click() procedure dials a number using the InputBox() Visual Basic function. Following is a listing of the menu_dial_Click() procedure:

LISTING 26.19. TERMINAL.FRM, menu_dial_Click().

```
Sub menu_dial_Click ()

    'declare variables
    Dim PhoneNo$

    PhoneNo$ = InputBox$("Enter the phone number")

    frmMain.msComm.Output = "+++ATDT" + PhoneNo$ + Chr$(13)

End Sub
```

THE *MENU_HANGUP_CLICK()* PROCEDURE

The menu_hangup_Click() procedure hangs up the phone line (on hook). Following is a listing of the menu_hangup_Click() procedure:

LISTING 26.20. TERMINAL.FRM, menu_hangup_Click().

```
Sub menu_hangup_Click ()

    'declare variables
    Dim m$       'message constructor
    Dim res%     'holds results

    m$ = "Are you sure you want to hang up?"
    res% = MsgBox(m$, 292, "Warning")
    If res% = IDNO Then Exit Sub

    'go ahead and hangup
    frmMain.msComm.Output = "+++ATH0"
    frmMain.msComm.PortOpen = False

    'unload the form-it can't be used with no active port
    Unload frmTerminal

End Sub
```

REM Because toggling DTR is not always reliable when hanging up the modem, this routine uses the command string "+++ATH0", which puts the terminal into Command mode and hangs up the modem.

THE *MENU_RECEIVE_CLICK( )* PROCEDURE

The menu_receive_Click() procedure prepares the terminal to receive a text file. Following is a listing of the menu_receive_Click() procedure:

LISTING 26.21. TERMINAL.FRM, menu_receive_Click().

```
Sub menu_receive_Click ()

    'flag receiving
    Receiving% = True

    'handle errors
    On Error GoTo receiveerror

    'invoke common dialog
    cmDialog.Filter = "Text Files¦*.txt"
    cmDialog.FilterIndex = 1
    cmDialog.Action = DLG_FILE_SAVE

    If cmDialog.Filename <> "" Then

        'assign next file handle
        hSend = FreeFile

        'delete file if it exists
        If FileLen(cmDialog.Filename) > 0 Then
            Kill cmDialog.Filename
        End If

        'open file
        Open cmDialog.Filename For Binary Access Write As hSend

    End If

    'exit
    Exit Sub

receiveerror:

    'exit
    Exit Sub

    'avoid errors
    Resume

End Sub
```

THE *MENU_TRANSMIT_CLICK()* PROCEDURE

The menu_transmit_Click() procedure transmits a text file. Following is a listing of the menu_transmit_Click() procedure:

LISTING 26.22. TERMINAL.FRM, menu_transmit_Click().

```
Sub menu_transmit_Click ()

    'handle errors
    On Error Resume Next

    'declare variables
    Dim BSize    'size of block
    Dim Temp$    'temporary string

    'assign to next available file handle
    hSend = FreeFile

    cmDialog.Filter = "Text Files¦*.TXT"
    cmDialog.FilterIndex = DLG_FILE_OPEN
    cmDialog.Action = 1

    If cmDialog.Filename <> "" Then
        Open cmDialog.Filename For Binary Access Read As hSend

        MsgBox "Prepare terminal for receive and press enter"

        'assign block size of 1 byte
        BSize = 1

        Do Until EOF(hSend)

            'Read a byte of data
            Temp$ = Space$(BSize)
            Get hSend, , Temp$

            'Transmit the byte
            frmMain.msComm.Output = Temp$

        Loop
    End If

    Close

    'unflag Receiving
    Receiving% = False

    'finished-send carriage return
    SendToModem ("FILE SENT" + Chr$(13))

End Sub
```

THE *TXTCLIENTAREA* CONTROL

txtClientArea is the name of the TextBox control that is used to enter or receive data to/from the modem. The txtClientArea control has code in only one event procedure. It is

◆ txtClientArea_KeyPress()

THE *TXTCLIENTAREA_KEYPRESS()* EVENT PROCEDURE

The txtClientArea_KeyPress() event procedure handles what happens when a key is pressed while the txtClientArea control has the focus. Following is a listing of the txtClientArea_KeyPress() event procedure:

LISTING 26.23. TERMINAL.FRM, txtClientArea_KeyPress().

```
Sub txtClientArea_KeyPress (KeyAscii As Integer)

    'declare variables
    Dim m$          'message constructor

    'handle errors
    On Error GoTo clienterror

    'handle specific cases
    Select Case (KeyAscii)
        Case KEY_BACK:
        Case KEY_RETURN:
            OutputString$ = OutputString$ + Chr$(13) + Chr$(10)
            'return was pressed-send string
            SendToModem Trim$(OutputString$)

            'reinitialize output string
            OutputString$ = ""
        Case KEY_DELETE:
            'don't display on screen
            KeyAscii = 0
        Case Else:
            OutputString$ = OutputString$ + Chr$(KeyAscii)
    End Select

    'exit
    Exit Sub

clienterror:

    'error
    m$ = "Could not send command!"
    MsgBox m$

    'exit
    Exit Sub

    'avoid errors
```

continues

581

LISTING 26.23. CONTINUED

```
    Resume

End Sub
```

THE ABOUT.FRM FILE

ABOUT.FRM is one of three forms in this application. It shows information about the application. Figure 26.5 presents the form as it appears at runtime. Fundamentally, there is no difference in the form at design time, so it is not presented. Table 26.3 lists all the relevant properties of each control on the form, which have been changed from their standard default values. The ABOUT.FRM file is contained on the CD accompanying this book in the CHAP26 subdirectory.

FIGURE 26.5.
*Communications
Terminal application
ABOUT.FRM at
runtime.*

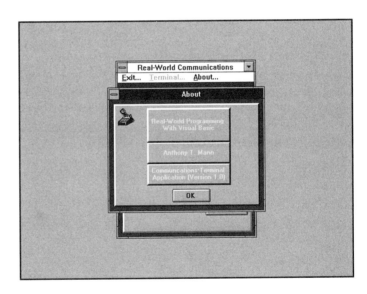

TABLE 26.3. PROPERTIES OF EACH CONTROL ON **ABOUT.FRM.**

Object	Control Type	Property	Value
frmAbout	Form	BackColor	&H00404000&
		Caption	"About"
		Height	3525
		Left	1035
		MaxButton	False
		MinButton	False

Object	Control Type	Property	Value
		Top	1140
		Width	4545
pnlMain	SSPanel	BackColor	&H00C0C0C0&
		BevelWidth	3
		Caption	" "
		Font3D	None
		ForeColor	&H00C0C0C0&
		Height	2695
		Left	126
		RoundedCorners	False
		ShadowColor	Black
		Top	126
		Width	4265
pnl1	SSPanel	BackColor	&H00C0C0C0&
		BevelWidth	3
		Caption	"Real-World Programming With Visual Basic"
		Font3D	None
		ForeColor	&H0000FFFF&
		Height	975
		Left	960
		RoundedCorners	False
		ShadowColor	Black
		Top	126
		Width	2415
pnl2	SSPanel	BackColor	&H00C0C0C0&
		BevelWidth	3
		Caption	"Anthony T. Mann"
		Font3D	None
		ForeColor	&H0000FFFF&
		Height	615
		Left	960
		RoundedCorners	False
		ShadowColor	Black

continues

TABLE 26.3. CONTINUED

Object	Control Type	Property	Value
		Top	1080
		Width	2415
pnl3	SSPanel	BackColor	&H00C0C0C0&
		BevelWidth	3
		Caption	"Communications Terminal Application (Version 1.0)"
		Font3D	None
		ForeColor	&H0000FFFF&
		Height	615
		Left	960
		RoundedCorners	False
		ShadowColor	Black
		Top	1680
		Width	2415
cmdOK	CommandButton	Caption	"OK"
		Height	375
		Left	1680
		Top	2400
		Width	1095
pictAbout	PictureBox	Autosize	True
		BackColor	&H00C0C0C0&
		BorderStyle	None
		Height	615
		Left	126
		Top	126
		Width	735

FUNCTION, SUBROUTINE, AND EVENT PROCEDURES

There are several procedures of code for each object(control) that comprise this form. Each is listed in the following sections.

The (general) object contains only one form level declaration and no form level procedures. The procedure for the (general) object is

◆ (declarations)

THE *(DECLARATIONS)* PROCEDURE

The (declarations) procedure contains only one line of declarations used in the form, ABOUT.FRM. It is only to allow for variable syntax checking and forcing the declaration of variables in each procedure. Following is a listing of the (declarations) procedure:

LISTING 26.24. ABOUT.FRM, (general)(declarations).

```
Option Explicit
```

THE *CMDOK* CONTROL

cmdOK is the name of the command button control that, when clicked, closes the frmAbout form. The cmdOK control has code in only one event procedure. It is

◆ cmdOK_Click()

THE *CMDOK_CLICK()* EVENT PROCEDURE

The cmdOK_Click() event procedure simply unloads the form. Following is a listing of the cmdOK_Click() event procedure:

LISTING 26.25. ABOUT.FRM, cmdOK_Click().

```
Sub cmdOK_Click ()

    'unload
    Unload frmAbout

End Sub
```

THE *FORM* OBJECT

The Form object has code in only one event procedure. It is

◆ Form_Load()

THE *FORM_LOAD()* EVENT PROCEDURE

The Form_Load() event procedure centers the form and assigns an icon to the pictAbout control. Following is a listing of the Form_Load() event procedure:

LISTING 26.26. ABOUT.FRM, `Form_Load()`.

```
Sub Form_Load ()

    'center form
    CenterForm Me

    'load icon
    pictAbout.Picture = frmMain.Icon

End Sub
```

THE CHAP26.BAS FILE

CHAP26.BAS is the module that contains application level variables and procedures. The CHAP26.BAS file is contained on the CD accompanying this book in the CHAP26 subdirectory.

FUNCTION, SUBROUTINE, AND EVENT PROCEDURES

There are several procedures of code for each object(control) that comprise this module. Each is listed in the following sections.

The (general) object contains application level variables and procedures. The procedures for the (general) object are

- ◆ (declarations)
- ◆ CenterForm()
- ◆ SendToModem()

THE (DECLARATIONS) PROCEDURE

The (declarations) procedure contains variable and constant declarations used in the application. Following is a listing of the (declarations) procedure:

LISTING 26.27. CHAP26.BAS, (general)(declarations).

```
Option Explicit

'declare variables
Global Receiving%        'flag for receiving file
Global hSend             'global file handle

' MsgBox return values
Global Const IDYES = 6            ' Yes button pressed
Global Const IDNO = 7            ' No button pressed

' Cursor values
```

```
Global Const HOURGLASS = 11              ' Hourglass
Global Const DEFAULT = 0                 ' Arrow

'MSCOMM constants
Global Const MSCOMM_EV_SEND = 1
Global Const MSCOMM_EV_RECEIVE = 2
Global Const MSCOMM_EV_CTS = 3
Global Const MSCOMM_EV_DSR = 4
Global Const MSCOMM_EV_CD = 5
Global Const MSCOMM_EV_RING = 6
Global Const MSCOMM_EV_EOF = 7

'Error code constants
Global Const MSCOMM_ER_BREAK = 1001
Global Const MSCOMM_ER_CTSTO = 1002
Global Const MSCOMM_ER_DSRTO = 1003
Global Const MSCOMM_ER_FRAME = 1004
Global Const MSCOMM_ER_OVERRUN = 1006
Global Const MSCOMM_ER_CDTO = 1007
Global Const MSCOMM_ER_RXOVER = 1008
Global Const MSCOMM_ER_RXPARITY = 1009
Global Const MSCOMM_ER_TXFULL = 1010
Global Const KEY_BACK = &H8
Global Const KEY_RETURN = &HD
Global Const KEY_SHIFT = &H10
Global Const KEY_CONTROL = &H11
Global Const KEY_ESCAPE = &H1B
Global Const KEY_END = &H23
Global Const KEY_HOME = &H24
Global Const KEY_LEFT = &H25
Global Const KEY_UP = &H26
Global Const KEY_RIGHT = &H27
Global Const KEY_DOWN = &H28
Global Const KEY_INSERT = &H2D
Global Const KEY_DELETE = &H2E

'Common Dialog
Global Const DLG_FILE_OPEN = 1
Global Const DLG_FILE_SAVE = 2

Global Const MODAL = 1
```

THE *CENTERFORM* PROCEDURE

The CenterForm() simply centers the form in the client area on form loading. The CenterForm() procedure accepts one argument, F. It is the actual form to be centered. Following is a listing of the CenterForm() procedure:

See Chapter 5, "Graphics," for more on manipulating graphics and forms.

LISTING 26.28. CHAP26.BAS, CenterForm().

```
Sub CenterForm (F As Form)

    'center the form
    F.Move (Screen.Width - F.Width) / 2, (Screen.Height - F.Height) / 2

End Sub
```

THE *SENDTOMODEM* PROCEDURE

The SendToModem() procedure is the name of the procedure that handles sending data to the modem. The procedure accepts one argument, SendWhat$, which is the text to send to the modem. Following is a listing of the SendToModem() procedure:

LISTING 26.29. CHAP26.BAS, SendToModem().

```
Sub SendToModem (SendWhat$)

    'declare variables
    Dim DoEventsLoop%          'loop counting variable
    Dim m$                     'message constructor

    'handle errors
    On Error GoTo senderror

    'set thresholds to 0-comm event won't be generated
    frmMain.msComm.RThreshold = 0
    frmMain.msComm.SThreshold = 0

    'send command to modem, wait for response
    'send individual strokes
    frmMain.msComm.Output = SendWhat$

    'allow enough doevents to wait for modem
    For DoEventsLoop% = 1 To 100
     DoEvents
    Next DoEventsLoop%

    'reset thresholds
    frmMain.msComm.RThreshold = 1
    frmMain.msComm.SThreshold = 1

    'exit
    Exit Sub

senderror:
    m$ = "Could not send command!"
    MsgBox m$

    'exit
```

```
      Exit Sub

      'avoid errors
      Resume

   End Sub
```

THE CHAP26.ICO FILE

This file contains the icon that has been attached to the form at design time. The CHAP26.ICO file is contained on the CD accompanying this book in the CHAP26 subdirectory.

FIGURE 26.6.
*Communications
Terminal application
Form icon.*

THE CHAP26.EXE FILE

This is the executable file that is distributable. If you distribute this application, you must include the following files:

- ◆ CHAP26.EXE
- ◆ CMDIALOG.VBX
- ◆ THREED.VBX
- ◆ MSCOMM.VBX
- ◆ COMMDLG.DLL
- ◆ VBRUN300.DLL

The CHAP26.EXE file and source files are contained on the CD accompanying this book in the CHAP26 subdirectory, while all DLLs and VBXs are in the RESOURCE subdirectory.

RELATING THE COMMUNICATIONS TERMINAL APPLICATION TO YOUR APPLICATION

The Communications Terminal application shows how to do many things with the communications control. It has some definite limitations, however. There are no file protocols, the handshaking is not successfully implemented, and hanging up the modem is unreliable. The list goes on and on. This application is fairly reliable, but for more stable communications, I suggest you upgrade to Sheridan's updated version of the MSCOMM.VBX custom control.

You can enhance this application by showing a gauge of the progress of the file transfer. This is very difficult given that the handshaking does not successfully implement. Another suggestion is to add a telephone database of frequently called numbers so that you don't have to enter the number to dial every time.

 Refer to Chapter 9, "Communications," for more information.

FINAL NOTES

This application was created on a standard VGA display using 16 colors. Your particular hardware could have adverse effects on the code the way it is written. You may need to modify it slightly. Also, it was created using an upgraded version of the MSCOMM.VBX control, not the standard MSCOMM.VBX that comes with Visual Basic. This file is contained on the CD accompanying this book in the RESOURCE subdirectory.

CD PLAYER
APPLICATION

THE CD PLAYER APPLICATION ALLOWS YOU TO PLAY MUSIC COMPACT DISCS. IT KEEPS TRACK OF THE NUMBER OF TRACKS, CURRENT TRACK, TRACK TIME, AND TOTAL TIME. THIS IS MADE POSSIBLE BY THE MCI.VBX CONTROL THAT COMES WITH THE PROFESSIONAL EDITION OF VISUAL BASIC VERSION 3.0. USING THIS CONTROL WITH AN AUDIO CD CAN BE DIFFICULT BECAUSE YOU MUST CALCULATE VALUES TO DETERMINE CERTAIN INFORMATION ABOUT THE CD YOU ARE PLAYING. THE REST OF THE CHAPTER SHOWS YOU HOW TO DO THIS IN DETAIL. THE KEY BEHIND HOW THE MCI CONTROL REPORTS TIME IS BASED ON THE TimeFormat PROPERTY. FOR THIS APPLICATION, THE TimeFormat PROPERTY IS SET TO 2. THIS SPECIFIES THAT THE LEAST SIGNIFICANT BYTE IS MINUTES, THE SECOND IS SECONDS, AND THE THIRD IS FRAMES. THE FOURTH IS NOT USED.

Figure 27.1 shows the main screen (MAIN.FRM) at runtime.

FIGURE 27.1.
CD Player at runtime.

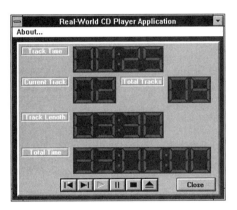

To use the application, click on the VCR-like command buttons. All displays will be updated automatically. If the time displays are blank and the multimedia control is disabled, the control has not registered the disc, or a disc is not in the drive. Try the following:

1. Eject the disc.
2. Close the program, CHAP27.EXE.
3. Insert the disc, making sure it is an AUDIO disc.
4. Run the program, CHAP27.EXE

 The CD Player application demonstrates using "Graphics," in Chapter 5, and "Multimedia," in Chapter 12.

CODE LISTINGS

The CD Player application contains the following files and listings:

- ◆ CHAP27.MAK
- ◆ MAIN.FRM
- ◆ ABOUT.FRM
- ◆ CHAP27.ICO
- ◆ CD1.ICO
- ◆ CD2.ICO

- ◆ 0.BMP
- ◆ 1.BMP
- ◆ 2.BMP
- ◆ 3.BMP
- ◆ 4.BMP
- ◆ 5.BMP
- ◆ 6.BMP
- ◆ 7.BMP
- ◆ 8.BMP
- ◆ 9.BMP
- ◆ BLANK.BMP
- ◆ COLON.BMP
- ◆ CHAP27.EXE

The CHAP27.MAK File

CHAP27.MAK is the project file for the CD Player application, CHAP27.EXE. It contains a listing of all the files necessary to load the project into Visual Basic. The CHAP27.MAK file is contained on the CD accompanying this book in the CHAP27 subdirectory. The file listing is:

Listing 27.1. CHAP27.MAK.

```
MAIN.FRM
ABOUT.FRM
MCI.VBX
CMDIALOG.VBX
THREED.VBX
ProjWinSize=347,72,248,136
ProjWinShow=0
IconForm="frmMain"
Title="CD Player"
ExeName="CHAP27.EXE"
```

The MAIN.FRM File

MAIN.FRM is one of two forms in this application. Figure 27.1 presents the form as it appears at runtime. Figure 27.2 presents the form at design time.

FIGURE 27.2.
*CD Player at
design time.*

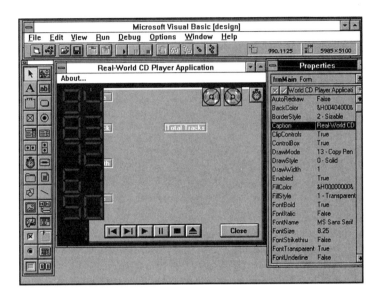

FIGURE 27.2.
*CD Player at
design time.*

Table 27.1 lists all the relevant properties of each control on the form that have been changed from their standard default values. The MAIN.FRM file is contained on the CD accompanying this book in the CHAP27 subdirectory.

TABLE 27.1. PROPERTIES OF EACH CONTROL ON **MAIN.FRM.**

Object	Control Type	Property	Value
frmMain	Form	BackColor	&H00404000&
		Caption	"Real-World CD Player Application"
		Height	4815
		Icon	"CHAP27.ICO"
		Left	990
		MaxButton	False
		Top	1125
		Width	5985
pictSource	PictureBox	AutoSize	True
		Height	720
		Index	0,1,2,3,4,5,6,7,8,9*
		Left	600,600,600,600, 600,0,0,0,0,0*

Object	Control Type	Property	Value
		Picture	"0.BMP", "1.BMP", "2.BMP", "3.BMP", "4.BMP", "5.BMP", "6.BMP", "7.BMP", "8.BMP", "9.BMP"*
		Top	2880,2160,1440,720, 0,2880,2160,1440,720,0*
		Visible	False
		Width	600
pictIcon	PictureBox	AutoSize	True
		Height	510
		Index	0,1*
		Left	3960,4560*
		Picture	"CD1.BMP","CD2.BMP"*
		Top	0
		Visible	False
		Width	510
tmrIcon	Timer	Enabled	False
		Interval	1000
		Left	5280
		Top	0
pictSourceBlank	PictureBox	AutoSize	True
		Height	750
		Left	0
		Picture	"BLANK.BMP"
		Top	3600
		Visible	False
		Width	630
pictSourceColon	PictureBox	AutoSize	True
		Height	750
		Left	600
		Picture	"COLON.BMP"
		Top	3600

continues

TABLE 27.1. CONTINUED

Object	Control Type	Property	Value
		Visible	False
		Width	180
pictTime	PictureBox	AutoSize	True
		BackColor	&H00C0C0C0&
		BorderStyle	None
		Height	750
		Index	0,1,2,3*
		Left	1560,2160,2880,3480*
		Top	120
		Width	630
pictColon	PictureBox	AutoSize	True
		BackColor	&H00C0C0C0&
		BorderStyle	None
		Height	750
		Index	0,1,2,3*
		Left	2760,2760,4080,2760*
		Top	1920,2880,2880,120*
		Width	150
pictLength	Picture Box	AutoSize	True
		BackColor	&H00C0C0C0&
		BorderStyle	None
		Height	750
		Index	0,1,2,3*
		Left	3480,2880,2160,1560*
		Top	1920
		Width	630
pictTotal	PictureBox	AutoSize	True
		BackColor	&H00C0C0C0&
		BorderStyle	None
		Height	750
		Index	0,1,2,3,4,5*

Object	Control Type	Property	Value
		Left	
			4800,4200,3480,2880,2160,1560*
		Top	2880
		Width	630
pictTotalTrack	PictureBox	AutoSize	True
		BackColor	&H00C0C0C0&
		BorderStyle	None
		Height	750
		Index	0,1*
		Left	4800,4200*
		Top	960
		Width	630
pictTrack	PictureBox	AutoSize	True
		BackColor	&H00C0C0C0&
		BorderStyle	None
		Height	750
		Index	0,1*
		Left	2160,1560*
		Top	960
		Width	630
mmControl	MMControl	BackVisible	False
		DeviceType	"CDAUDIO"
		EjectEnabled	True
		Height	370
		Left	1200
		NextEnabled	True
		PauseEnabled	True
		PlayEnabled	True
		PrevEnabled	True
		RecordVisible	False
		StepVisible	False

continues

TABLE 27.1. CONTINUED

Object	Control Type	Property	Value
		StopEnabled	True
		Top	3720
		Width	2730
cmdClose	CommandButton	Caption	"Close"
		Height	375
		Left	4440
		Top	3720
		Width	1095
Panel3D1	SSPanel	BevelWidth	3
		Height	4215
		Left	120
		Top	120
		Width	5655
Panel3D2	SSPanel	BevelInner	2
		BevelOuter	1
		BorderWidth	1
		Caption	"Track Time"
		ForeColor	&H0000FFFF&
		Height	255
		Left	120
		Top	120
		Width	1335
Panel3D3	SSPanel	BevelInner	2
		BevelOuter	1
		BorderWidth	1
		Caption	"Current Track"
		ForeColor	&H0000FFFF&
		Height	255
		Left	120
		Top	960

Object	Control Type	Property	Value
		Width	1335
Panel3D4	SSPanel	BevelInner	2
		BevelOuter	1
		BorderWidth	1
		Caption	"Total Tracks"
		ForeColor	&H0000FFFF&
		Height	255
		Left	2880
		Top	960
		Width	630
Panel3D5	SSPanel	BevelInner	2
		BevelOuter	.1
		BorderWidth	1
		Caption	"Track Length"
		ForeColor	&H0000FFFF&
		Height	255
		Left	120
		Top	1920
		Width	1335
Panel3D6	SSPanel	BevelInner	2
		BevelOuter	1
		BorderWidth	1
		Caption	"Total Time"
		ForeColor	&H0000FFFF&
		Height	255
		Left	120
		Top	2880
		Width	1335
menu_about	Menu	Caption	"About..."

*This control is a control array, and these are the only properties that vary within the control. To save space, they were not listed separately.

599

FUNCTION, SUBROUTINE, AND EVENT PROCEDURES

There are several procedures of code for each object(control) that comprise this form. Each is listed in the following sections.

THE (GENERAL) OBJECT

The (general) object contains declarations and procedures at the form level. You may notice that the ABOUT.FRM file also has a CenterForm() procedure. This is because it is not advantageous to create a separate *.BAS file for this one procedure only. If this procedure has to be used by many files, that is a different story. The procedures for the (general) object are:

- ◆ (declarations)
- ◆ CalculateTrack()
- ◆ CenterForm()
- ◆ ClearAll()
- ◆ ConvertToMMSS()
- ◆ ConvertToSeconds()
- ◆ PopulateDisplay()
- ◆ PopulateStaticDisplays()
- ◆ Unformat()

THE (DECLARATIONS) PROCEDURE

The (declarations) procedure contains variable declarations used in the form, MAIN.FRM. Following is a listing of the (declarations) procedure:

LISTING 27.2. MAIN.FRM, (general) (declarations).

```
Option Explicit

'mousepointers
Const HOURGLASS = 11
Const DEFAULT = 0

'messageboxes
Const IDNO = 7

'MCI constants
Const MCI_MODE_PLAY = 526
Const MCI_MODE_READY = 530
Const MCI_MODE_STOP = 525

'user defined constants
Const PTIME = 1            'indicates which function to perform in populate display
```

```
Const PTRACK = 2          'indicates which function to perform in populate display
Const PTOTALTRACK = 3     'indicates which function to perform in populate display
Const PTRACKLENGTH = 4    'indicates which function to perform in populate display
Const PTOTALLENGTH = 5    'indicates which function to perform in populate display

Dim Byte1 As Integer      'holds integer converted from packed integer format
Dim Byte2 As Integer      'holds integer converted from packed integer format
Dim Byte3 As Integer      'holds integer converted from packed integer format
Dim Byte4 As Integer      'holds integer converted from packed integer format
Dim TotalTime&            'holds sum of all track times
Dim TrackTime&()          'array of individual track times

Const MODAL = 1
```

 For more information about how these byte values are used, refer to Chapter 5, "Graphics."

THE *CALCULATETRACK( )* PROCEDURE

The CalculateTrack() procedure is used to calculate which track is currently playing. The only way to determine which track is playing is if the current time from the beginning of the CD is greater than the sum of track times up to the current track—then the current track must actually be the next track. This is necessary because the MCI control will not automatically update the current track. The CalculateTrack() procedure accepts two arguments: the current position, PositionNow%, and the length of the current track, TrackLen%. Following is a listing of the CaluclateTrack() procedure:

LISTING 27.3. MAIN.FRM, CalculateTrack().

```
Sub CalculateTrack (PositionNow%, TrackLen%)

    'if position is greater than track, must be on next track
    'this is because there is no "Current Track" property with the MCI control
    If PositionNow% > TrackLen% Then
        mmControl.Track = mmControl.Track + 1
    End If

End Sub
```

THE *CENTERFORM( )* PROCEDURE

The CenterForm() procedure simply centers the form in the client area upon form loading. The CenterForm() procedure accepts one argument, F. It is the actual form to be centered. For more information on manipulating graphics and forms, refer to Chapter 5, "Graphics." Following is a listing of the CenterForm() procedure:

LISTING 27.4. MAIN.FRM, CenterForm().

```
Sub CenterForm (F As Form)

    'center the form
    F.Move (Screen.Width - F.Width) / 2, (Screen.Height - F.Height) / 2

End Sub
```

THE *CLEARALL()* PROCEDURE

The ClearAll() procedure clears all displays when the disc is ejected. This ensures that erroneous numbers won't be displayed. Clearing is performed by assigning the picture pictBlank.picture to each of the displays. Following is a listing of the ClearAll() procedure:

LISTING 27.5. MAIN.FRM, ClearAll().

```
Sub ClearAll ()

        'declare variables
        Dim loopcount%  'loop counting variable

        'clear current track time
        For loopcount% = 0 To 3
            pictTime(loopcount%).Picture = pictSourceBlank.Picture
        Next loopcount%

        'clear current track
        For loopcount% = 0 To 1
            pictTrack(loopcount%).Picture = pictSourceBlank.Picture
        Next loopcount%

        'clear total tracks
        For loopcount% = 0 To 1
            pictTotalTrack(loopcount%).Picture = pictSourceBlank.Picture
        Next loopcount%

        'clear track length
        For loopcount% = 0 To 3
            pictLength(loopcount%).Picture = pictSourceBlank.Picture
        Next loopcount%

        'clear total
        For loopcount% = 0 To 5
            pictTotal(loopcount%).Picture = pictSourceBlank.Picture
        Next loopcount%

End Sub
```

THE *CONVERTTOMMSS()* PROCEDURE

The `ConvertToMMSS()` procedure converts the current time into a MM:SS format. The `ConvertToMMSS()` procedure accepts one argument, ConvertWhat&. It is the number of seconds to convert into the MM:SS format. Following is a listing of the `ConvertToMMSS()` procedure:

LISTING 27.5. MAIN.FRM,`ConvertToMMSS()`.

```
Sub ConvertToMMSS (ConvertWhat&)

    'ConvertWhat& is in seconds
    'byte1 is minutes
    'byte2 is seconds

    'ConvertWhat& will always be 3 seconds ahead-so adjust
    ConvertWhat& = ConvertWhat& - 3

    Byte1 = Int(ConvertWhat& \ 60)
    Byte2 = ConvertWhat& Mod 60
    Byte3 = Int(ConvertWhat& \ 3600)

End Sub
```

THE *CONVERTTOSECONDS()* PROCEDURE

The `ConvertToSeconds()` function converts the time to display into seconds. This conversion needs to be done so that the necessary arithmetic can be performed between two track times. The variables, byte1 and byte2, are form level variables. The `ConvertToSeconds()` procedure accepts one argument, ConvertWhat&. It is the number to be converted into seconds. The procedure is also a function that returns the number of seconds after conversion. Following is a listing of the `ConvertToSeconds()` procedure:

LISTING 27.6. MAIN.FRM,`ConvertToSeconds()`.

```
Function ConvertToSeconds (ConvertWhat&)

    'declare variables
    Dim TheTotal&

    'initialize
    TheTotal& = 0

    Unformat (ConvertWhat&)

    'byte1- seconds
    TheTotal& = TheTotal& + (Byte1 * 60)
```

continues

603

LISTING 27.6. CONTINUED

```
    'byte2- minutes
    TheTotal& = TheTotal& + (Byte2)

    ConvertToSeconds = TheTotal&
End Function
```

THE *POPULATEDISPLAY()* PROCEDURE

The PopulateDisplay() procedure is used to populate the different areas of the display, such as track time and current track to visually represent CD activity. Population is performed by assigning appropriate picture bitmaps (already placed on the form at design time) that represent all possible numbers. The PopulateDisplay() procedure accepts two arguments that display for updating: WhichArray and the actual text to display, texttodisplay$. Following is a listing of the PopulateDisplay() procedure:

LISTING 27.7. MAIN.FRM,PopulateDisplay().

```
Sub PopulateDisplay (WhichArray As Integer, texttodisplay$)

    'declare variables
    Dim temp$     'temporary working string
    Dim FirstDigit%      'first integer converted from packed integer(LSB)
    Dim SecondDigit%     'second integer converted from packed integer
    Dim ThirdDigit%      'third integer converted from packed integer
    Dim FourthDigit%     'fourth integer converted from packed integer
    Dim FifthDigit%      'fifth integer converted from packed integer
    Dim SixthDigit%      'sixth integer converted from packed integer(MSB)

    If mmControl.CanPlay = False Then
        Call ClearAll
        Exit Sub
    End If

    If mmControl.Mode = MCI_MODE_READY Then
        'not actively playing-or stopped, but only ready
        Exit Sub
    End If

'CURRENT RUNNING TIME
    If WhichArray = PTIME Then
        'assign eight character format
        temp$ = Format$(texttodisplay$, "00000000")

        FirstDigit% = Val(Mid$(temp$, 4, 1))
        pictTime(0).Picture = pictSource(FirstDigit%).Picture

        SecondDigit% = Val(Mid$(temp$, 3, 1))
        pictTime(1).Picture = pictSource(SecondDigit%).Picture
```

```
            ThirdDigit% = Val(Mid$(temp$, 2, 1))
            pictTime(2).Picture = pictSource(ThirdDigit%).Picture

            FourthDigit% = Val(Mid$(temp$, 1, 1))
            pictTime(3).Picture = pictSource(FourthDigit%).Picture

        ElseIf WhichArray = PTRACK Then
'CURRENT TRACK
            'assign two character format
            temp$ = Format$(texttodisplay$, "00")

            FirstDigit% = Val(Mid$(temp$, 2, 1))
            pictTrack(0).Picture = pictSource(FirstDigit%).Picture

            SecondDigit% = Val(Mid$(temp$, 1, 1))
            pictTrack(1).Picture = pictSource(SecondDigit%).Picture
        ElseIf WhichArray = PTOTALTRACK Then
'TOTAL TRACKS
            'assign two character format
            temp$ = Format$(texttodisplay$, "00")

            FirstDigit% = Val(Mid$(temp$, 2, 1))
            pictTotalTrack(0).Picture = pictSource(FirstDigit%).Picture

            SecondDigit% = Val(Mid$(temp$, 1, 1))
            pictTotalTrack(1).Picture = pictSource(SecondDigit%).Picture

        ElseIf WhichArray = PTRACKLENGTH Then
'TRACK LENGTH

            'assign eight character format

            temp$ = Format$(texttodisplay$, "00000000")

            FirstDigit% = Val(Mid$(temp$, 6, 1))
            pictLength(0).Picture = pictSource(FirstDigit%).Picture

            SecondDigit% = Val(Mid$(temp$, 5, 1))
            pictLength(1).Picture = pictSource(SecondDigit%).Picture

            ThirdDigit% = Val(Mid$(temp$, 4, 1))
            pictLength(2).Picture = pictSource(ThirdDigit%).Picture

            FourthDigit% = Val(Mid$(temp$, 3, 1))
            pictLength(3).Picture = pictSource(FourthDigit%).Picture

        ElseIf WhichArray = PTOTALLENGTH Then
'TOTAL LENGTH OF ALL TRACKS
            'texttodisplay is previously formatted
            temp$ = texttodisplay$

            FirstDigit% = Val(Mid$(temp$, 6, 1))
            pictTotal(0).Picture = pictSource(FirstDigit%).Picture
```

continues

LISTING 27.7. CONTINUED

```
        SecondDigit% = Val(Mid$(temp$, 5, 1))
        pictTotal(1).Picture = pictSource(SecondDigit%).Picture

        ThirdDigit% = Val(Mid$(temp$, 4, 1))
        pictTotal(2).Picture = pictSource(ThirdDigit%).Picture

        FourthDigit% = Val(Mid$(temp$, 3, 1))
        pictTotal(3).Picture = pictSource(FourthDigit%).Picture

        FifthDigit% = Val(Mid$(temp$, 2, 1))
        pictTotal(4).Picture = pictSource(FifthDigit%).Picture

        SixthDigit% = Val(Mid$(temp$, 1, 1))
        pictTotal(5).Picture = pictSource(SixthDigit%).Picture
    End If

End Sub
```

For the preceding code, the `FirstDigit%` is the rightmost digit and `SixthDigit%` is the leftmost. From this, the time is separated into as many picture boxes as those shown. For example, if there are four text boxes, the format is "MM:SS". If there are six text boxes, the format is "HH:MM:SS".

The reason that the `PTOTALLENGTH` branch does not have to be formatted is because the formatting is performed in the calling event procedure for this condition. It is called by `PopulateStaticDisplay`.

THE *POPULATESTATICDISPLAYS* PROCEDURE

The `PopulateStaticDisplays` procedure is used to populate the static areas of the display, such as total disc time and total number of tracks. This information is not changed unless the CD is changed, so there's no sense in updating it continuously. Population is performed by assigning appropriate picture bitmaps (already placed on the form at design time) that represent all possible numbers. Following is a listing of the `PopulateStaticDisplays` procedure:

LISTING 27.8. MAIN.FRM, `PopulateStaticDisplays()`.

```
Sub PopulateStaticDisplays ()

    'declare variables
    Dim loopcount%

    'populate total number of tracks
    PopulateDisplay PTOTALTRACK, Str(mmControl.Tracks)

    'fill array of track times
    ReDim TrackTime&(mmControl.Tracks)
    TotalTime& = 0
```

```
For loopcount% = 1 To mmControl.Tracks
    'assign track(doesn't actually change track)
    mmControl.Track = loopcount%

    'store time of this track
    TrackTime(loopcount%) = mmControl.TrackLength

    'increment total time of all tracks
    TotalTime& = TotalTime& + mmControl.TrackLength
Next loopcount%

'Total track length(for all tracks)
ConvertToMMSS (ConvertToSeconds(TotalTime&))

PopulateDisplay PTOTALLENGTH, Format$(Trim$(Str(Byte3)), "00") +
Format$(Trim$(Str(Byte1)), "00") + Format$(Trim$(Str(Byte2)), "00")
DoEvents

End Sub
```

THE *UNFORMAT( )* PROCEDURE

The Unformat() procedure is used to take the packed integer data coming from the MCI control and separate it into its four-byte equivalent parts. These bytes are form level variables, so the different procedures that need them don't have to have the values passed in as arguments. The Unformat() procedure accepts one argument: the value to be separated into bytes, CodedValue. Following is a listing of the Unformat() procedure:

LISTING 27.9. MAIN.FRM,Unformat( ).

```
Sub Unformat (CodedValue As Long)

    'decode coded value and separate into byte components
    'Byte 1 is least significant
    'Byte 4 is most significant

    Byte1 = CodedValue And &HFF&
    Byte2 = (CodedValue And &HFF00&) \ &H100
    Byte3 = (CodedValue And &HFF0000) \ &H10000
    Byte4 = (CodedValue And &H7F000000) \ &H1000000
    If (CodedValue And &H80000000) <> 0 Then
        Byte4 = Byte4 + &H80
    End If

End Sub
```

 For more information on packed integers, refer to Chapter 12, "Multimedia."

THE *cmdCLOSE* CONTROL

cmdClose is the name of the command button control that, when clicked, closes the application. The cmdClose control has code in only one event procedure. It is

◆ cmdClose_Click()

THE *cmdCLOSE_CLICK()* EVENT PROCEDURE

The cmdClose_Click() event procedure unloads the form, invoking the Form_Unload() event. Following is a listing of the cmdClose_Click() event procedure:

LISTING 27.10. MAIN.FRM, cmdClose_Click().

```
Sub cmdClose_Click ()
    Unload frmMain
End Sub
```

THE *FORM* OBJECT

The Form object has code in three event procedures. They are:

◆ Form_Load()
◆ Form_Resize()
◆ Form_Unload()

THE *FORM_LOAD()* EVENT PROCEDURE

The Form_Load() event procedure opens the CD player, initializes controls, and loads the form. Following is a listing of the Form_Load() event procedure:

LISTING 27.11. MAIN.FRM, Form_Load().

```
Sub Form_Load ()

    'declare variables
    Dim loopcount%   'loop counting variable

    'handle errors
    On Error GoTo loaderror

    'change cursor
    Screen.MousePointer = HOURGLASS

    'center the form
    CenterForm Me
```

```
    'open the device
    mmControl.Notify = False
    mmControl.Wait = True
    mmControl.Shareable = False
    mmControl.DeviceType = "CDAudio"
    mmControl.Command = "Open"

    'assign default colon bitmaps to different locations on screen
    For loopcount% = 0 To 3
        pictColon(loopcount%).Picture = PictSourceColon.Picture
    Next loopcount%

    If mmControl.CanPlay = True Then
        'can play

        Call ClearAll

        'populate all displays which only change with disc
        Call PopulateStaticDisplays

        'if currently playing, update status
        If mmControl.Mode = MCI_MODE_PLAY Then

            'pause so that when the user presses play,
            'status updating will occur.
            mmControl.Command = "Pause"
        End If
    Else
        'can't play-disc not in drive?
        Call ClearAll
    End If

    'assign new icon to form
    frmMain.Icon = pictIcon(0).Picture

    'change cursor
    Screen.MousePointer = DEFAULT

    'exit
    Exit Sub

loaderror:
    Resume Next
End Sub
```

THE *FORM_RESIZE()* EVENT PROCEDURE

The Form_Resize() event procedure simply starts the timer to animate the icons if the form is minimized. Following is a listing of the Form_Resize() event procedure:

LISTING 27.12. MAIN.FRM, `Form_Resize()`.

```
Sub Form_Resize ()
    'if form is minimized-start timer,otherwise stop timer
    If frmMain.WindowState = 1 Then
        tmrIcon.Enabled = True
    Else
        tmrIcon.Enabled = False
    End If
End Sub
```

THE *FORM_UNLOAD()* EVENT PROCEDURE

The `Form_Unload()` event procedure prompts the user to confirm ending the program. It also allows for the user to keep the CD running, if it is currently playing. Following is a listing of the `Form_Unload()` event procedure:

LISTING 27.13. MAIN.FRM, `Form_Unload()`.

```
Sub Form_Unload (Cancel As Integer)

    'declare variables
    Dim m$        'message constructor
    Dim res%      'holds results

    m$ = "Confirm Close!"
    res% = MsgBox(m$, 292, "Warning")
    If res% = IDNO Then
        Cancel = True
        Exit Sub
    End If

    'ask about keeping CD running, if currently playing
    If mmControl.Mode = MCI_MODE_PLAY Then
        m$ = "Keep CD running?"
        res% = MsgBox(m$, 292)
        If res% = IDNO Then
            'stop CD
            mmControl.Command = "Stop"
        End If
    End If

    'close device
    mmControl.Command = "Close"

    'end program
    End

End Sub
```

THE *MENU* OBJECT

The menu object is created by using Visual Basic's built-in menu editor. It has code associated with only one Click() event procedure. It is

◆ menu_about()

THE *MENU_ABOUT_CLICK( )* EVENT PROCEDURE

The menu_about_Click() event procedure simply shows the about form for program information. Following is a listing of the menu_about_Click() event procedure:

LISTING 27.14. MAIN.FRM, menu_about_Click().

```
Sub menu_about_Click ()

    frmAbout.Show MODAL

End Sub
```

THE MMCONTROL CONTROL

MMControl is the name of the actual multimedia MCI control, which is the heart of this application. It handles all communication to and from the CD player. The MMControl control has code in three event procedures. They are:

◆ MMControl_EjectCompleted()

◆ MMControl_PlayClick()

◆ MMControl_StatusUpdate()

 For more information on the audio portion of the MCI control, which is handled automatically, refer to Chapter 12, "Multimedia."

THE *MMCONTROL_EJECTCOMPLETED( )* EVENT PROCEDURE

The MMControl_EjectCompleted() event procedure clears all displays when eject is completed. Following is a listing of the MMControl_EjectCompleted() event procedure:

LISTING 27.14. MAIN.FRM, MMControl_EjectCompleted().

```
Sub MMControl_EjectCompleted (ErrorCode As Long)

    'make sure all displays are blank
    Call ClearAll

End Sub
```

611

THE *MMCONTROL_PLAYCLICK( )* EVENT PROCEDURE

The MMControl_PlayClick() event procedure makes sure the static displays are populated, and the variable displays are populated by issuing the Prev command. Following is a listing of the MMControl_PlayClick() event procedure:

LISTING 27.15. MAIN.FRM, MMControl_PlayClick().

```
Sub MMControl_PlayClick (Cancel As Integer)

    'populate all displays which only change with disc
    Call PopulateStaticDisplays

    'make sure track plays from beginning of track
    mmControl.Command = "Prev"


End Sub
```

THE *MMCONTROL_STATUSUPDATE( )* EVENT PROCEDURE

The MMControl_StatusUpdate() event procedure is invoked every second automatically. This procedure updates the displays during this time. The StatusUpdate() event procedure is the key to updating the displays on the form. This event is used to populate the displays individually. Refer to the comments in the following code for complete understanding. Following is a listing of the MMControl_StatusUpdate() event procedure:

LISTING 27.16. MAIN.FRM, MMControl_StatusUpdate().

```
Sub MMControl_StatusUpdate ()

    'declare variables
    Dim temp&        'temporary long
    Dim TempTotal&   'temporary to hold totals
    Dim loopcount%   'loop counting variable

    'Current Running Time
    temp& = mmControl.Position

    'add up time from first track to track just before this one
    TempTotal& = 0

    'handle error
    On Error GoTo subscripterror

    'total all tracks from beginning to previous track
    For loopcount% = 0 To mmControl.Track - 1
        TempTotal& = TempTotal& + TrackTime&(loopcount%)
    Next loopcount%
```

```
'convert from seconds only to minutes and seconds
ConvertToMMSS (ConvertToSeconds(temp&) - ConvertToSeconds(TempTotal&))

'populate display with new byte values(calculated in ConvertToMMSS)
PopulateDisplay PTIME, Format$(Trim$(Str(Byte1)), "00") + Format$(Trim$(Str(Byte2)),
"00") + Format$(Trim$(Str(Byte3)), "00") + Format$(Trim$(Str(Byte4)), "00")

'verify that the track displayed is actually the current track
Call CalculateTrack(ConvertToSeconds(temp&), ConvertToSeconds(TempTotal& +
TrackTime&(mmControl.Track)))

'track number
PopulateDisplay PTRACK, Str(mmControl.Track)

'track length
Unformat (mmControl.TrackLength)

'populate track length
PopulateDisplay PTRACKLENGTH, Format$(Trim$(Str(Byte1)), "00") +
Format$(Trim$(Str(Byte2)), "00") + Format$(Trim$(Str(Byte3)), "00")
'update static displays if stopped
'this allows for trapping the loading of a new CD
If MMControl.Mode = MCI_MODE_STOP then
Call PopulateStaticDisplays
End If

Exit Sub

subscripterror:
    Exit Sub
    'avoid errors
    Resume

End Sub
```

 For more information on how to calculate and decipher the StatusUpdate() event information, refer to Chapter 12, "Multimedia."

THE *TMRICON* CONTROL

tmrIcon is the name of the timer control that, when enabled, allows the minimized icon to appear animated. The tmrIcon control has code in only one event procedure. It is:

◆ tmrIcon_Timer()

THE *TMRICON_TIMER()* EVENT PROCEDURE

The tmrIcon_Timer() event procedure is invoked every second automatically. The event will only be generated (by setting the tmrIcon.enabled property to True) when the form is minimized. This procedure toggles the icon between two static icons loaded at design time so that it appears animated. Following is a listing of the tmrIcon_Timer() event procedure:

LISTING 27.17. MAIN.FRM, tmrIcon_Timer().

```
Sub tmrIcon_Timer ()

    'toggle icon picture
    If frmMain.Icon <> pictIcon(0).Picture Then
        frmMain.Icon = pictIcon(0).Picture
    Else
        frmMain.Icon = pictIcon(1).Picture
    End If
End Sub
```

    For more information on animating icons, refer to Chapter 5, "Graphics."

THE ABOUT.FRM FILE

ABOUT.FRM is the other form in this application. Figure 27.3 presents the form as it appears at runtime.

FIGURE 27.3.
*CD Player About
form at runtime.*

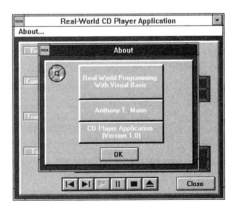

Fundamentally, there is no difference in the form at design time, so it is not presented. Table 27.2 lists all the relevant properties of each control on the form, which have been changed from their standard default values. The ABOUT.FRM file is contained on the CD accompanying this book in the CHAP27 subdirectory.

TABLE 27.2. PROPERTIES OF EACH CONTROL ON **ABOUT.FRM**.

Object	Control Type	Property	Value
frmAbout	Form	BackColor	&H00404000&
		Caption	"About"
		Height	3525
		Left	1035
		MaxButton	False
		MinButton	False
		Top	1140
		Width	4545
pnlMain	SSPanel	BackColor	&H00C0C0C0&
		BevelWidth	3
		Caption	""
		Font3D	None
		ForeColor	&H00C0C0C0&
		Height	2895
		Left	120
		RoundedCorners	False
		ShadowColor	Black
		Top	120
		Width	4215
pnl1	SSPanel	BackColor	&H00C0C0C0&
		BevelWidth	3
		Caption	"Real-World Programming With Visual Basic"
		Font3D	None
		ForeColor	&H0000FFFF&
		Height	975
		Left	960
		RoundedCorners	False
		ShadowColor	Black
		Top	120

continues

TABLE 27.2. CONTINUED

Object	Control Type	Property	Value
		Width	2415
pnl2	SSPanel	BackColor	&H00C0C0C0&
		BevelWidth	3
		Caption	"Anthony T. Mann"
		Font3D	None
		ForeColor	&H0000FFFF&
		Height	615
		Left	960
		RoundedCorners	False
		ShadowColor	Black
		Top	1080
		Width	2415
pnl3	SSPanel	BackColor	&H00C0C0C0&
		BevelWidth	3
		Caption	"CD Player Application (Version 1.0)"
		Font3D	None
		ForeColor	&H0000FFFF&
		Height	615
		Left	960
		RoundedCorners	False
		ShadowColor	Black
		Top	1680
		Width	2415
cmdOK	CommandButton	Caption	"OK"
		Height	375
		Left	1680
		Top	2400
		Width	1095
pictAbout	PictureBox	Autosize	True
		BackColor	&H00C0C0C0&

Object	Control Type	Property	Value
		BorderStyle	None
		Height	615
		Left	120
		Top	120
		Width	735

FUNCTION, SUBROUTINE, AND EVENT PROCEDURES

There are several procedures of code for each object(control) that comprise this form. Each is listed in the following sections.

THE (GENERAL) OBJECT

The (general) object contains only one procedure at the form level. You may notice that the MAIN.FRM file also has the same procedure, CenterForm(). This is because it is not advantageous to create a separate *.BAS file only for this one procedure. If this procedure had to be used by many files, that would be a different story. The procedure for the (general) object is:

- ◆ (declarations)
- ◆ CenterForm()

THE (DECLARATIONS) PROCEDURE

The (declarations) procedure contains only one line of declarations used in the form, ABOUT.FRM. It is only to allow for variable syntax checking and forcing the declaration of variables in each procedure. Following is a listing of the (declarations) procedure:

LISTING 27.18. ABOUT.FRM, (general) (declarations).

```
Option Explicit
```

THE CenterForm() PROCEDURE

The CenterForm() procedure simply centers the form in the client area upon form loading. The CenterForm() procedure accepts one argument, F. It is the actual form to be centered. You may notice that the code in the frmAbout.CenterForm() procedure is not the same as the frmMain.CenterForm() procedure. It performs exactly the same function; however, it is shown differently for informational purposes only. Following is a listing of the CenterForm() procedure:

LISTING 27.19. ABOUT.FRM,CenterForm().

```
Sub CenterForm (F As Form)

    'center the form
    F.Left = (Screen.Width - F.Width) / 2
    F.Top = (Screen.Height - F.Height) / 2

End Sub
```

 For more information on manipulating graphics and forms, refer to Chapter 5, "Graphics."

THE *CMDOK* CONTROL

cmdOK is the name of the command button control that, when clicked, closes the frmAbout form. The cmdOK control has code in only one event procedure. It is

◆   cmdOK_Click()

THE *CMDOK_CLICK()* EVENT PROCEDURE

The cmdOK_Click() event procedure simply unloads the form. Following is a listing of the cmdOK_Click() event procedure:

LISTING 27.20. ABOUT.FRM,cmdOK_Click().

```
Sub cmdOK_Click ()

    'unload
    Unload frmAbout

End Sub
```

THE *FORM* OBJECT

The Form object itself has code in only one event procedure. It is

◆   Form_Load()

THE *FORM_LOAD()* EVENT PROCEDURE

The Form_Load() event procedure centers the form and assigns an icon to the pictAbout control. Following is a listing of the Form_Load() event procedure:

LISTING 27.21. ABOUT.FRM, Form_Load().

```
Sub Form_Load ()

    'center form
    CenterForm Me

    'load icon
    pictAbout.Picture = frmMain.Icon

End Sub
```

THE CHAP27.ICO FILE

This file contains the icon that has been attached to the form at design time. It is only used so that this icon is displayed in the Program Manager. When the form is minimized, the CD1.ICO and CD2.ICO files are used. The CHAP27.ICO file is contained on the CD accompanying this book in the CHAP27 subdirectory.

FIGURE 27.4.
CD Player Program Manager icon.

THE CD1.ICO FILE

This file contains one of the icons used to simulate animation of the icons when the form is minimized. CD2.ICO is the other icon file used in the animation process. The CD1.ICO file is contained on the CD accompanying this book in the CHAP27 subdirectory.

FIGURE 27.5.
One of the icons used for animation.

THE CD2.ICO FILE

This file contains one of the icons used to simulate animation of the icons when the form is minimized. CD1.ICO is the other icon file used in the animation process. The CD2.ICO file is contained on the CD accompanying this book in the CHAP27 subdirectory.

FIGURE 27.6.
One of the icons used for animation.

THE 0.BMP FILE

This file contains the bitmap that represents the number 0 (zero) to be displayed in the CD player status area. The 0.BMP file is contained on the CD accompanying this book in the CHAP27 subdirectory.

FIGURE 27.7.
*Bitmap used to display
the number 0.*

     If you wish, you can alter the look and feel of these bitmaps to include in your application.

THE 1.BMP FILE

This file contains the bitmap that represents the number 1 to be displayed in the CD player status area. The 1.BMP file is contained on the CD accompanying this book in the CHAP27 subdirectory.

FIGURE 27.8.
*Bitmap used to display
the number 1.*

THE 2.BMP FILE

This file contains the bitmap that represents the number 2 to be displayed in the CD player status area. The 2.BMP file is contained on the CD accompanying this book in the CHAP27 subdirectory.

FIGURE 27.9.
*Bitmap used to display
the number 2.*

THE 3.BMP FILE

This file contains the bitmap that represents the number 3 to be displayed in the CD player status area. The 3.BMP file is contained on the CD accompanying this book in the CHAP27 subdirectory.

FIGURE 27.10.
Bitmap used to display
the number 3.

THE 4.BMP FILE

This file contains the bitmap that represents the number 4 to be displayed in the CD player status area. The 4.BMP file is contained on the CD accompanying this book in the CHAP27 subdirectory.

FIGURE 27.11.
Bitmap used to display
the number 4.

THE 5.BMP FILE

This file contains the bitmap that represents the number 5 to be displayed in the CD player status area. The 5.BMP file is contained on the CD accompanying this book in the CHAP27 subdirectory.

FIGURE 27.12.
Bitmap used to display
the number 5.

THE 6.BMP FILE

This file contains the bitmap that represents the number 6 to be displayed in the CD player status area. The 6.BMP file is contained on the CD accompanying this book in the CHAP27 subdirectory.

FIGURE 27.13.
Bitmap used to display
the number 6.

THE 7.BMP FILE

This file contains the bitmap that represents the number 7 to be displayed in the CD player status area. The 7.BMP file is contained on the CD accompanying this book in the CHAP27 subdirectory.

FIGURE 27.14.
*Bitmap used to display
the number 7.*

THE 8.BMP FILE

This file contains the bitmap that represents the number 8 to be displayed in the CD player status area. The 8.BMP file is contained on the CD accompanying this book in the CHAP27 subdirectory.

FIGURE 27.15.
*Bitmap used to display
the number 8.*

THE 9.BMP FILE

This file contains the bitmap that represents the number 9 to be displayed in the CD player status area. The 9.BMP file is contained on the CD accompanying this book in the CHAP27 subdirectory.

FIGURE 27.16.
*Bitmap used to display
the number 9.*

THE BLANK.BMP FILE

This file contains the bitmap that represents when the display is to be cleared. The BLANK.BMP file is contained on the CD accompanying this book in the CHAP27 subdirectory.

FIGURE 27.17.
*Bitmap used for a
blank display.*

THE COLON.BMP FILE

This file contains the bitmap that represents the colon between digits in the display. The COLON.BMP file is contained on the CD accompanying this book in the CHAP27 subdirectory.

FIGURE 27.18.
*Bitmap used to
display a colon.*

THE CHAP27.EXE FILE

This is the executable file that is distributable. If you distribute this application, you must include the following files:

- ◆ CHAP27.EXE
- ◆ MCI.VBX
- ◆ CMDIALOG.VBX
- ◆ COMMDLG.DLL
- ◆ VBRUN300.DLL
- ◆ THREED.VBX

The CHAP27.EXE file and source files are contained on the CD accompanying this book in the CHAP27 subdirectory, while all DLLs and VBXs are in the RESOURCE subdirectory.

RELATING THE CD PLAYER APPLICATION TO YOUR APPLICATION

The CD Player application shows how to create a basic CD player by using the MCI control. You could possibly create a more "realistic" CD player using a bitmap of an actual CD player and creating hotspots for the controls. In this case, you would have to have the MCI control hidden, and send commands to the control as the hotspots were clicked.

 For more information on hotspots, see Chapter 5, "Graphics," and the application in Chapter 25, "Dynamic Hotspot Application."

You can also enhance the CD Player as it is right now by adding a database so that the program appears to automatically detect which CD is in the player. Programs usually do this by calculating an algorithm by using the number of tracks, the total disc time, and other disc information.

FINAL NOTES

This application was created on a standard VGA display using 16 colors. Your particular hardware could have adverse effects on the code the way it is written. You may need to modify it slightly.

Also, depending on how your CD-ROM reacts with windows, you could experience problems with the MCI compatibility issues.

CHAPTER TWENTY-EIGHT

MAPI APPLICATION

THE MAPI APPLICATION WAS DESIGNED TO ALLOW YOU TO SEND A PRE-DETERMINED TYPE OF MESSAGE THROUGH A MAPI-COMPLIANT MESSAGING SYSTEM, SUCH AS MICROSOFT MAIL. *MAPI* IS AN ACRONYM FOR *MESSAGING APPLICATION PRO-GRAMMING INTERFACE*. IT IS A SET OF APIS USED TO SEND AND RECEIVE MESSAGES FROM PCS AND SERVERS. THE APPLICATION'S MAIN SCREEN USES A VISUAL BASIC FORM TO FORMAT THE MESSAGE TO SEND. THIS PARTICU-LAR FORM IS USEFUL IF YOU ARE A DEVELOPER WHO REGULARLY CREATES EXECUTABLE FILES AND COPIES THEM TO A FILE SERVER. THE APPLICATION ALLOWS YOU TO "FILL IN THE BLANKS" AND PRESS THE SEND BUTTON TO ALERT RECIPIENTS AS TO THE CHANGES IN THE EXECUTABLE FILE. IT SAVES A LOT OF TIME VERSUS HAVING TO COMPOSE A NEW MESSAGE MANU-ALLY EACH TIME YOU COMPILE A NEW EXECUTABLE FILE.

REM For you to use the application, you have to install a MAPI-compliant messaging system on your PC. Also, if you do not have a MAPI-compliant system installed, loading the source code from the CD accompanying this book will produce an error, indicating that the messaging system is not present. If you installed Windows for Workgroups, you probably have the necessary DLLs installed on your system to be able to load the source code, even if you cannot connect to a mail server.

Figure 28.1 shows the main screen (MAIN.FRM) at runtime.

FIGURE 28.1.
MAPI application at
runtime.

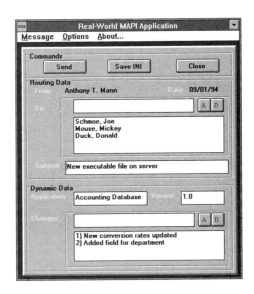

To use the application, all you have to do is fill in the different fields on the form and click on the Send button.

Upon startup, all fields are populated with the values stored in the CHAP28.INI file. Table 28.1 lists the possible key fields that could be used in this application. You can create the INI file using any text editor or by filling in the fields and clicking the SaveINI command button. If you create the INI file with a text editor, place all the keys under a section labeled [Initialization].

TABLE 28.1. POSSIBLE KEY FIELDS IN FILE CHAP28.INI.

Key	Purpose	Format
PollFreq	Number of seconds to wait before polling for new messages	number (stored as text)
LogonMessage	Boolean for retrieving messages upon logon	Boolean Text (TRUE/FALSE)

Key	Purpose	Format
Greeting	Opening line in message sent	Text
Closing	Closing line in message sent	Text
From	Static name for informational purposes. Not actually sent through MAPI	Text
To	Recipient List	Text, delimited by semicolons (;)
Subject	Subject of message	Text
Application	Application that has been updated	Text
Version	Version number	Text or number stored as text
Changes	List of changes made to application	Text, delimited by semicolons (;)

To add a new recipient, type the name of the recipient in the text box adjacent to the To: label. The A (add) command button will become enabled. Click on it to add to the list. You can also add recipients by selecting the Message->AddressBook menu option. Figure 28.2 shows what the address book looks like (using fictitious names) at runtime.

FIGURE 28.2.
MAPI Address Book
at runtime.

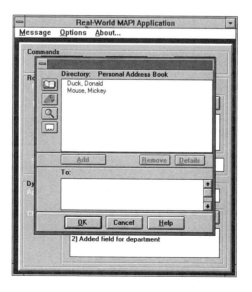

To delete a recipient, select the recipient to delete. The D (Delete) command button will become enabled. Click on it to delete the recipient.

The only required field to be filled in is the recipient. A message will actually be sent if only this field has been filled in; however, the message wouldn't make much sense. After you have filled in the fields on the form, click on the Send command button. If you have not logged into the MAPI-compliant system, it will prompt you to do so and advise that the message has been sent.

As long as you are logged into the MAPI system, if a message has been sent to you, one of two things will happen. If the MAPI application is minimized, the icon will change from a mailbox with the flag down to a mailbox with the flag up, indicating that mail is in. If the MAPI application is not minimized, a dialog box will indicate that a message has been sent to you. If you receive notification that a message has been sent to you, you must select the Message->Retrieve menu option to review the message.

REM   If the polling frequency is 0, you will not automatically receive notification of incoming messages. In this case, to receive messages, you must manually request messages by selecting the Message->Retrieve menu option.

Once the Message->Retrieve menu option is selected, if there are messages waiting, the frmInbox form is invoked. This form is used solely for the purpose of displaying messages. It cannot be used to send messages. Figure 28.3 shows a sample message at runtime that was actually sent from this application.

FIGURE 28.3.
MAPI frmInbox *form at runtime.*

From the frmInbox form, you can view each message by clicking on the message subject in the listbox. You can also use the menu options to delete the messages or attachments.

To change the polling frequency (time period to wait before checking to see if there are new messages), select the Options->Polling Frequency menu option. It will invoke the frmPoll form. Figure 28.4 shows the frmPoll form at runtime. Simply type in the new number (in minutes) for the polling frequency. The Save command button will enable the new request to take effect immediately. The change will not be saved to the INI file until you click the SaveINI command button on the main form.

FIGURE 28.4.
MAPI frmPoll form at runtime, with a polling frequency of two minutes.

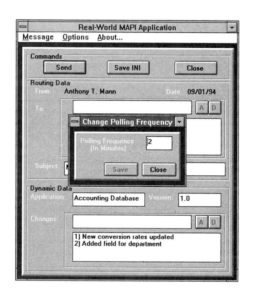

To change the greeting or closing, select the Options->Change Remarks menu option. This will invoke the frmRemark form. Figure 28.5 shows the Remark form at runtime. Making changes to the frmRemark form will not be saved to the INI file until you click the SaveINI command button on the main form.

 For more information on the MAPI application, refer to Chapter 13, "MAPI."

CODE LISTINGS

The MAPI application contains the following files and listings, if appropriate:

- ◆ CHAP28.MAK
- ◆ MAIN.FRM
- ◆ INBOX.FRM
- ◆ REMARK.FRM

+ POLL.FRM
+ ABOUT.FRM
+ CHAP28.BAS
+ CHAP28.INI
+ MAILIN.ICO
+ MAILOUT.ICO
+ CHAP28.EXE

FIGURE 28.5.
MAPI `frmRemark` *form*
at runtime.

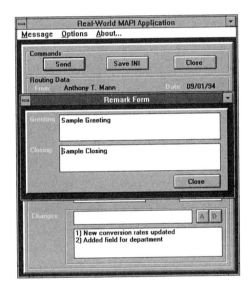

THE CHAP28.MAK FILE

CHAP28.MAK is the project file for the MAPI application, CHAP28.EXE. It contains a listing of all the files necessary to load the project into Visual Basic. The CHAP28.MAK file is contained on the CD accompanying this book in the CHAP28 subdirectory. The file listing is:

LISTING 28.1. CHAP28.MAK.

```
MAIN.FRM
INBOX.FRM
REMARK.FRM
POLL.FRM
ABOUT.FRM
CHAP28.BAS
THREED.VBX
MSMAPI.VBX
CMDIALOG.VBX
ProjWinSize=228,389,248,215
ProjWinShow=2
```

```
IconForm="frmMain"
Title="MAPI"
ExeName="CHAP28.EXE"
```

THE MAIN.FRM FILE

MAIN.FRM is one of five forms in this application. It is the startup form for the application, as well as the form used to construct and send a message through the MAPI-compliant message system. Figure 28.1 presented the main form as it appears at runtime. Figure 28.6 presents the form at design time. Table 28.1 lists all the relevant properties of each control on the form that have been changed from their standard default values. The MAIN.FRM file is contained on the CD accompanying this book in the CHAP28 subdirectory.

FIGURE 28.6.
MAPI application
MAIN.FRM at design
time.

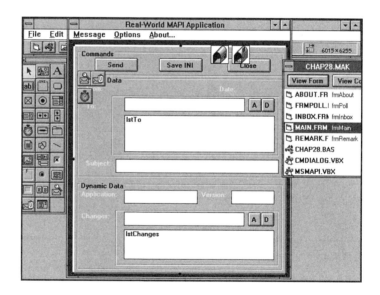

TABLE 28.2. PROPERTIES OF EACH CONTROL ON MAIN.FRM.

Object	Control Type	Property	Value
frmMain	Form	BackColor	&H00404000&
		Caption	"Real-World MAPI Application"
		Height	7125
		Icon	"MAILOUT.ICO"
		Left	1905

continues

TABLE 28.2. CONTINUED

Object	Control Type	Property	Value
		MaxButton	False
		Top	0
		Width	6330
Panel3D1	SSPanel	BackColor	&H00C0C0C0&
		BevelWidth	3
		Font3D	None
		ForeColor	&H0000FFFF&
		Height	6255
		Left	120
		Top	120
		Width	6015
pictMailOut	PictureBox	AutoSize	True
		Height	510
		Left	3960
		Picture	"MAILOUT.ICO"
		Top	120
		Visible	False
		Width	510
pictMailIn	PictureBox	AutoSize	True
		Height	510
		Left	4440
		Picture	"MAILIN.ICO"
		Top	0
		Visible	False
		Width	510
tmrPoll	Timer	Interval	1000
		Left	120
		Top	1200
MapiMessages1	MAPIMessage	Left	0
		Top	0

Object	Control Type	Property	Value
MapiSession1	MAPISession	Left	0
		Top	0
Frame3D3	SSFrame	Caption	"Commands"
		Font3D	None
		Height	735
		Left	120
		Top	120
		Width	5775
cmdClose	CommandButton	Cancel	True
		Caption	"Close"
		Height	375
		Left	4200
		TabStop	False
		Top	240
		Width	1215
cmdSave	CommandButton	Caption	"Save INI"
		Height	375
		Left	2280
		TabStop	False
		Top	240
		Width	1215
cmdSend	CommandButton	Caption	"Send"
		Height	375
		Left	480
		TabStop	False
		Top	240
		Width	1215
Frame3D2	SSFrame	Caption	"Dynamic Data"
		Font3D	None
		Height	2415
		Left	120

continues

TABLE 28.2. CONTINUED

Object	Control Type	Property	Value
		Top	3720
		Width	5775
Frame3D4	SSFrame	Font3D	None
		Height	1575
		Left	1080
		Top	720
		Width	4575
cmdChangeDelete	CommandButton	Caption	"D"
		Enabled	False
		Height	375
		Left	4080
		TabStop	False
		Top	120
		Width	375
cmdChangeAdd	CommandButton	Caption	"A"
		Enabled	False
		Height	375
		Left	3720
		TabStop	False
		Top	120
		Width	375
lstChanges	ListBox	BackColor	&H00FFFFFF&
		Height	810
		Left	240
		Top	600
		Width	3375
txtChanges	TextBox	BackColor	&H00FFFFFF&
		Height	375
		Left	240
		Top	120
		Width	3375

Object	Control Type	Property	Value
Panel3D8	SSPanel	Alignment	Left Justify - Middle
		BackColor	&H00C0C0C0&
		BevelOuter	None
		BevelWidth	0
		BorderWidth	0
		Caption	"Changes:"
		Font3D	None
		ForeColor	&H0000FFFF&
		Height	255
		Left	120
		Top	840
		Width	1095
Panel3D6	SSPanel	Alignment	Left Justify - Middle
		BackColor	&H00C0C0C0&
		BevelOuter	None
		BevelWidth	0
		BorderWidth	0
		Caption	"Application:"
		Font3D	None
		ForeColor	&H0000FFFF&
		Height	255
		Left	120
		Top	240
		Width	1095
txtApplication	TextBox	BackColor	&H00FFFFFF&
		Height	375
		Left	1320
		Top	240
		Width	2055
txtVersion	TextBox	BackColor	&H00FFFFFF&
		Height	375
		Left	4320

continues

635

TABLE 28.2. CONTINUED

Object	Control Type	Property	Value
		Top	240
		Width	1215
Panel3D5	SSPanel	Alignment	Left Justify - Middle
		BackColor	&H00C0C0C0&
		BevelOuter	None
		BevelWidth	0
		BorderWidth	0
		Caption	"Version:"
		Font3D	None
		ForeColor	&H0000FFFF&
		Height	255
		Left	3480
		Top	240
		Width	735
Frame3D1	SSFrame	Caption	"Routing Data"
		Font3D	None
		Height	2775
		Left	120
		Top	840
		Width	5775
cmdReceiptAdd	CommandButton	Caption	"A"
		Enabled	False
		Height	375
		Left	3840
		TabStop	False
		Top	120
		Width	375
cmdRecipientDelete	Command Button	Caption	"D"
		Enabled	False
		Height	375
		Left	4200

Object	Control Type	Property	Value
		TabStop	False
		Top	120
		Width	375
lstTo	ListBox	BackColor	&H00FFFFFF&
		Height	1005
		Left	360
		Top	600
		Width	4215
txtTo	TextBox	BackColor	&H00FFFFFF&
		Height	375
		Left	360
		Top	120
		Width	3375
lblDate	SSPanel	Alignment	Left Justify - Middle
		BackColor	&H00C0C0C0&
		BevelOuter	None
		BevelWidth	0
		BorderWidth	0
		Font3D	None
		ForeColor	&H00000000&
		Height	255
		Left	4560
		Top	240
		Width	1095
Panel3D7	SSPanel	Alignment	Left Justify - Middle
		BackColor	&H00C0C0C0&
		BevelOuter	None
		BevelWidth	0
		BorderWidth	0
		Caption	"Date:"
		Font3D	None
		ForeColor	&H0000FFFF&

continues

TABLE 28.2. CONTINUED

Object	Control Type	Property	Value
		Height	255
		Left	3960
		Top	240
		Width	615
Panel3D2	SSPanel	Alignment	Left Justify - Middle
		BackColor	&H00C0C0C0&
		BevelOuter	None
		BevelWidth	0
		BorderWidth	0
		Caption	"From:"
		Font3D	None
		ForeColor	&H0000FFFF&
		Height	255
		Left	240
		Top	240
		Width	735
Panel3D3	SSPanel	Alignment	Left Justify - Middle
		BackColor	&H00C0C0C0&
		BevelOuter	None
		BevelWidth	0
		BorderWidth	0
		Caption	"To:"
		Font3D	None
		ForeColor	&H0000FFFF&
		Height	255
		Left	240
		Top	720
		Width	735
Panel3D4	SSPanel	Alignment	Left Justify - Middle
		BackColor	&H00C0C0C0&
		BevelOuter	None

Object	Control Type	Property	Value
		BevelWidth	0
		BorderWidth	0
		Caption	"Subject:"
		Font3D	None
		ForeColor	&H0000FFFF&
		Height	255
		Left	240
		Top	2280
		Width	735
pnlFrom	SSPanel	Alignment	Left Justify - Middle
		BackColor	&H00C0C0C0&
		BevelOuter	None
		BevelWidth	0
		BorderWidth	0
		Font3D	None
		ForeColor	&H00000000&
		Height	255
		Left	1080
		Top	240
		Width	2655
txtSubject	TextBox	BackColor	&H00FFFFFF&
		Height	375
		Left	1080
		Top	2280
		Width	4575
menu_message	Menu	Caption	"&Message"
menu_address	Menu	Caption	"&Address Book"
menu_send	Menu	Caption	"&Send"
menu_retrieve	Menu	Caption	"&Retrieve"
menu_exit	Menu	Caption	"&Exit"
menu_options	Menu	Caption	"&Options"
menu_LogonMsg	Menu	Caption	"&Messages w/logon"

continues

TABLE 28.2. CONTINUED

Object	Control Type	Property	Value
menu_separator	Menu	Caption	"-"
menu_save	Menu	Caption	"&Save INI"
menu_remarks	Menu	Caption	"&Change Remarks"
menu_poll	Menu	Caption	"&Polling Frequency"
menu_about	Menu	Caption	"&About..."

FUNCTION, SUBROUTINE, AND EVENT PROCEDURES

There are several procedures of code for each object(control) that comprise this form. Each is listed in the following sections.

THE *(GENERAL)* OBJECT

The (general) object contains declarations and procedures at the form level. The procedures for the (general) object are:

- ◆ (declarations)
- ◆ BuildToList()
- ◆ Logoff()
- ◆ Logon()
- ◆ PopulateTo()

THE *(DECLARATIONS)* PROCEDURE

The (declarations) procedure contains only one line of code. All variable declarations are in CHAP28.BAS. Following is a listing of the (declarations) procedure:

LISTING 28.2. MAIN.FRM, (GENERAL)(DECLARATIONS).

```
Option Explicit
```

THE *BUILDTOLIST()* PROCEDURE

The BuildToList() procedure builds a list of MAPI recipients. This procedure deletes the list of recipients and then rebuilds the list to verify that it is current.

Following is a listing of the BuildToList() procedure:

LISTING 28.3. MAIN.FRM,BuildToList().

```
Sub BuildToList ()

    'declare variables
    Dim loopcount%   'loop counting variable
    Dim Temp$        'temporary string


    'first delete all recipients which might have been placed in the control
    'by the address book
    For loopcount% = 0 To MAPIMessages1.RecipCount - 1
        'assign recipient index
        MAPIMessages1.RecipIndex = loopcount%

        'delete
        MAPIMessages1.Action = RECIPIENT_DELETE
    Next loopcount%


    'next build new list of recipients
    'initialize index
    MAPIMessages1.RecipIndex = 0

    For loopcount% = 0 To lstTo.ListCount - 1

        'assign new recipient from "To" list box
        MAPIMessages1.RecipDisplayName = lstTo.List(loopcount%)

        'increment index-if not the last item
        If loopcount% < lstTo.ListCount - 1 Then
            MAPIMessages1.RecipIndex = MAPIMessages1.RecipIndex + 1
        End If

    Next loopcount%

End Sub
```

THE *LOGOFF()* PROCEDURE

The Logoff() procedure logs off the MAPI server. Following is a listing of the Logoff() procedure:

LISTING 28.4. MAIN.FRM,Logoff().

```
Sub logoff ()

    'logoff
    MAPISession1.Action = SESSION_SIGNOFF

End Sub
```

THE *LOGON( )* PROCEDURE

The Logon() procedure logs on to the MAPI server. Following is a listing of the Logon() procedure:

LISTING 28.5. MAIN.FRM, Logon( ).

```
Sub Logon ()

    'check if flag is set to check messages on logon
    If menu_LogonMsg.Checked = True Then
        MAPISession1.DownloadMail = True
    Else
        MAPISession1.DownloadMail = False
    End If

    'handle errors
    On Error GoTo LogonError

    'logon
    If MAPISession1.SessionID = 0 Then
        MAPISession1.Action = SESSION_SIGNON
    End If

    'assign mapi session id
    MAPIMessages1.SessionID = MAPISession1.SessionID

    'exit
    Exit Sub

LogonError:
    MsgBox Error$

    Exit Sub

    'avoid errors
    Resume

End Sub
```

THE *POPULATETO( )* PROCEDURE

The PopulateTo() procedure populates the lstTo listbox with the names of the recipients stored in the MAPIMessages1 control. Following is a listing of the PopulateTo() procedure:

LISTING 28.6. MAIN.FRM, PopulateTo( ).

```
Sub PopulateTo ()

    'declare variables
    Dim loopcount%      'loop counting variable

    'clear list box
    lstTo.Clear
```

```
'loop through all recipients and populate
For loopcount% = 0 To MAPIMessages1.RecipCount - 1
    'assign index
    MAPIMessages1.RecipIndex = loopcount%

    'add to name
    lstTo.AddItem MAPIMessages1.RecipDisplayName
Next loopcount%

End Sub
```

THE *cmdChangeAdd()* CONTROL

cmdChangeAdd() is the name of the command button control that, when clicked, adds the text in the txtChange textbox to the lstChange listbox. The cmdChangeAdd() control has code in only one event procedure. It is:

◆ cmdChangeAdd_Click()

THE *cmdChangeAdd_Click()* EVENT PROCEDURE

Following is a listing of the cmdChangeAdd_Click() event procedure:

LISTING 28.7. MAIN.FRM, cmdChangeAdd_Click().

```
Sub cmdChangeAdd_Click ()

    'add to list of changes
    lstChanges.AddItem txtChanges.Text

    'clear text
    txtChanges.Text = ""

    'set focus
    txtChanges.SetFocus

End Sub
```

THE *cmdChangeDelete()* CONTROL

cmdChangeDelete() is the name of the command button control that, when clicked, deletes the currently selected item from the lstChange listbox. The cmdChangeDelete() control has code in only one event procedure. It is:

◆ cmdChangeDelete_Click()

THE *cmdChangeDelete_Click()* EVENT PROCEDURE

Following is a listing of the cmdChangeDelete_Click() event procedure:

LISTING 28.8. MAIN.FRM,cmdChangeDelete_Click().

```
Sub cmdChangeDelete_Click ()

    'remove list item
    lstChanges.RemoveItem lstChanges.ListIndex

    'disable button
    cmdChangeDelete.Enabled = False

End Sub
```

THE *CMDRECIPIENTADD( )* CONTROL

cmdRecipientAdd() is the name of the command button control that, when clicked, adds the text in the txtTo textbox to the lstTo listbox. The cmdRecipientAdd() control has code in only one event procedure. It is:

◆ cmdRecipientAdd_Click()

THE *CMDRECIPIENTADD_CLICK( )* EVENT PROCEDURE

Following is a listing of the cmdRecipientAdd_Click() event procedure:

LISTING 28.9. MAIN.FRM,cmdRecipientAdd_Click().

```
Sub cmdReceiptAdd_Click ()

    'add to list of changes
    lstTo.AddItem txtTo.Text

    'clear text
    txtTo.Text = ""

    'set focus
    txtTo.SetFocus

End Sub
```

THE *CMDRECIPIENTDELETE( )* CONTROL

cmdRecipientDelete() is the name of the command button control that, when clicked, deletes the currently selected item from the lstTo listbox. The cmdRecipientDelete() control has code in only one event procedure. It is:

◆ cmdRecipientDelete_Click()

THE *CMDRECIPIENTDELETE_CLICK( )* EVENT PROCEDURE

Following is a listing of the cmdRecipientDelete_Click() event procedure:

LISTING 28.10. MAIN.FRM,cmdRecipientDelete_Click().

```
Sub cmdReceiptDelete_Click ()

    'remove item from recipient list
    If MAPIMessages1.RecipCount > 0 Then
        If MAPIMessages1.RecipIndex >= lstTo.ListIndex Then
            MAPIMessages1.RecipIndex = lstTo.ListIndex
            'if session is active-delete
            If MAPIMessages1.SessionID <> 0 Then
                MAPIMessages1.Action = RECIPIENT_DELETE
            End If
        End If
    End If

    'remove list item
    If lstTo.ListCount > 0 Then
        lstTo.RemoveItem lstTo.ListIndex
    End If

    'disable button
    cmdReceiptDelete.Enabled = False

End Sub
```

REM The If/Then branch at the beginning of the preceding code listing ensures that all recipients in the MAPI system are the same as that shown in the text box.

THE *cmdClose( )* CONTROL

cmdClose() is the name of the command button control that, when clicked, invokes closing the application by unloading the form. The cmdClose() control has code in only one event procedure. It is:

◆ cmdClose_Click()

THE *cmdClose_Click( )* EVENT PROCEDURE

Following is a listing of the cmdClose_Click() event procedure:

LISTING 28.11. MAIN.FRM,cmdClose_Click().

```
Sub cmdClose_Click ()

    'unload form
    Unload frmMain

End Sub
```

THE *cmdSave( )* CONTROL

cmdSave() is the name of the command button control that, when clicked, saves the configuration to the CHAP28.INI configuration file. The cmdSave() control has code in only one event procedure. It is:

◆ cmdSave_Click()

THE *cmdSave_Click( )* EVENT PROCEDURE

Following is a listing of the cmdSave_Click() event procedure:

LISTING 28.12. MAIN.FRM, cmdSave_Click().

```
Sub cmdSave_Click ()

    'save INI file
    Call SAVEINI

End Sub
```

THE *cmdSend( )* CONTROL

cmdSend() is the name of the command button control that, when clicked, sends a message through the MAPI-compliant system. The cmdSend() control has code in only one event procedure. It is:

◆ cmdSend_Click()

THE *cmdSend_Click( )* EVENT PROCEDURE

Following is a listing of the cmdSend_Click() event procedure:

LISTING 28.13. MAIN.FRM, cmdSend_Click().

```
Sub cmdSend_Click ()

    'declare varaibles
    Dim msg$            'message to print
    Dim loopcount%      'loop counting variable
    Dim m$              'message constructor
    Dim res%            'holds results

    If cmdChangeAdd.Enabled = True Then
        'user has not added change to lstChanges
        m$ = "Continue without adding last change?"
        res% = MsgBox(m$, 292, "Warning")
        If res% = IDNO Then Exit Sub
    End If

    If cmdReceiptAdd.Enabled = True Then
```

```
        'user has not added recipient to lstTo
        m$ = "Continue without adding recipient?"
        res% = MsgBox(m$, 292, "Warning")
        If res% = IDNO Then Exit Sub
    End If


    'test for recipients
    If lstTo.ListCount = 0 Then
        m$ = "There is no individual specified" + Chr$(13)
        m$ = m$ + "to receive the message!"
        MsgBox m$
        Exit Sub
    End If

    'logon
    Call Logon

    'set msgindex to enable compose buffer
    MAPIMessages1.MsgIndex = -1

    'clear compose buffer
    MAPIMessages1.Action = MESSAGE_COMPOSE

    'assign recipients
    Call BuildToList

    'allow mail system to resolve bad names
    MAPIMessages1.AddressResolveUI = True

    'assign subject
    MAPIMessages1.MsgSubject = txtSubject.Text

    'build message
    msg$ = frmRemark.txtGreeting.Text + Chr$(13)
    msg$ = msg$ + "APPLICATION:" + Chr$(9) + txtApplication.Text + Chr$(13) + Chr$(13)
    msg$ = msg$ + "VERSION:" + Chr$(9) + txtVersion.Text + Chr$(13) + Chr$(13)

    If lstChanges.ListCount > 0 Then
        msg$ = msg$ + "CHANGES:" + Chr$(9)
    End If

    'build list of changes
    For loopcount% = 0 To lstChanges.ListCount - 1
        If lstChanges.List(loopcount%) <> "" Then
            msg$ = msg$ + lstChanges.List(loopcount%) + Chr$(13)
            'if this is not the last item in the list, add 2 tabs to line up
            If loopcount% < lstChanges.ListCount - 1 Then
                msg$ = msg$ + Chr$(9) + Chr$(9)
            End If
        End If
    Next loopcount%

    'add new line before closing remark
    msg$ = msg$ + Chr$(13)

    'add closing string to message
```

continues

647

LISTING 28.13. CONTINUED

```
      msg$ = msg$ + frmRemark.txtClosing.Text

      'send actual text
      MAPIMessages1.MsgNoteText = msg$

      'change cursor
      screen.MousePointer = HOURGLASS

      'actually send message
      MAPIMessages1.Action = MESSAGE_SEND

      'change cursor
      screen.MousePointer = DEFAULT

      'show message
      MsgBox "Message Sent!"

End Sub
```

THE *FORM* OBJECT

The Form object has code in three event procedures. They are:

◆ Form_Load()

◆ Form_Resize()

◆ Form_Unload()

THE *FORM_LOAD()* EVENT PROCEDURE

The Form_Load() event procedure initializes, loads defaults from CHAP28.INI, and loads the main form. Following is a listing of the Form_Load() event procedure:

LISTING 28.14. MAIN.FRM, Form_Load().

```
Sub Form_Load ()

      'change cursor
      screen.MousePointer = HOURGLASS

      'center the form
      CenterForm Me

      'initialize
      Call GETINI
      lblDate.Caption = Format$(Now, "MM/DD/YY")

      'load remark form, but don't show
      Load frmRemark

      'change cursor
```

```
    screen.MousePointer = DEFAULT

End Sub
```

The reason the form is loaded but not shown is so its objects can be accessed from other forms.

THE *FORM_RESIZE( )* EVENT PROCEDURE

The Form_Resize() event procedure handles changing the icon to MAILOUT.ICO. Following is a listing of the Form_Resize() event procedure:

LISTING 28.15. MAIN.FRM,Form_Resize().

```
Sub Form_Resize ()

    'if form is minimized then assign out icon
    If frmMain.WindowState = 1 Then
        frmMain.Icon = pictMailOut.Picture
    End If

End Sub
```

THE *FORM_UNLOAD( )* EVENT PROCEDURE

The Form_Unload() event procedure prompts the user to confirm ending the program. Following is a listing of the Form_Unload() event procedure:

LISTING 28.16. MAIN.FRM,Form_Unload().

```
Sub Form_Unload (cancel As Integer)

    'declare variables
    Dim m$       'message constructor
    Dim res%     'holds results

    m$ = "Confirm Close!"
    res% = MsgBox(m$, 292)
    If res% = IDNO Then
        cancel = True
        Exit Sub
    End If

    'logoff
    Call logoff

    'close
    End

End Sub
```

THE *LSTCHANGES_CLICK( )* CONTROL

lstChanges is the name of the listbox control that lists all of the changes to an application's executable file. The lstChanges control has code in only one event procedure. It is:

◆ lstChanges_Click( )

THE *LSTCHANGES_CLICK( )* EVENT PROCEDURE

The lstChanges event procedure is used to enable the cmdChangesDelete command button. Following is a listing of the lstChanges_Click( ) event procedure:

LISTING 28.17. MAIN.FRM, lstChanges_Click( ).

```
Sub lstChanges_Click ()

    'enable delete button
    cmdChangeDelete.Enabled = True

End Sub
```

THE *LSTTO* CONTROL

lstTo is the name of the listbox control that lists all of the recipients to receive a MAPI message. The lstTo control has code in only one event procedure. It is:

◆ lstTo_Click( )

THE *LSTTO_CLICK( )* EVENT PROCEDURE

The lstTo_Click( ) event procedure is used to enable the cmdRecipientDelete command button. Following is a listing of the lstTo_Click( ) event procedure:

LISTING 28.18. MAIN.FRM, lstTo_Click( ).

```
Sub lstTo_Click ()

    'enable delete button
    cmdReceiptDelete.Enabled = True

End Sub
```

THE *MENU* OBJECT

The menu object was created by using Visual Basic's built-in menu editor. It has code associated with nine Click( ) event procedures. They are:

◆ menu_about( )

◆ menu_address( )

- ◆ menu_exit()
- ◆ menu_LogonMsg()
- ◆ menu_Poll()
- ◆ menu_remarks()
- ◆ menu_retrieve()
- ◆ menu_save()
- ◆ menu_send()

THE *MENU_ABOUT_CLICK( )* PROCEDURE

The menu_about_Click() procedure simply shows the about form for program information. Following is a listing of the menu_about_Click() procedure:

LISTING 28.19. MAIN.FRM,menu_about_Click().

```
Sub menu_about_Click ()

frmAbout.Show MODAL

End Sub
```

THE *MENU_ADDRESS_CLICK( )* PROCEDURE

The menu_address_Click() procedure invokes the MAPI-compliant address book. Following is a listing of the menu_address_Click() procedure:

LISTING 28.20. MAIN.FRM,menu_address_Click().

```
Sub menu_address_Click ()

    'logon
    Call Logon

    'change cursor
    screen.MousePointer = HOURGLASS

    'handle errors
    On Error GoTo AddressError

    'enable the To: box to be shown on address book
    MAPIMessages1.AddressEditFieldCount = 1

    'set index to -1 to enable saving of names chosen(automatically)
    MAPIMessages1.MsgIndex = -1

    'invoke address book
    MAPIMessages1.Action = MESSAGE_SHOWADBOOK
```

continues   651

LISTING 28.20. CONTINUED

```
    'populate "To" box
    PopulateTo

    'change cursor
    screen.MousePointer = DEFAULT

    'exit
    Exit Sub
AddressError:
    Resume Next

End Sub
```

THE *MENU_EXIT_CLICK( )* PROCEDURE

The `menu_exit_Click()` procedure starts the program exit procedure, invoked in the `Form_Unload()` event. Following is a listing of the `menu_exit_Click()` procedure:

LISTING 28.21. MAIN.FRM,menu_exit_Click().

```
Sub menu_exit_Click ()

    'unload form
    Unload frmMain

End Sub
```

THE *MENU_LOGONMSG_CLICK( )* PROCEDURE

The `menu_LogonMsg_Click()` procedure toggles the checked property on and off. Following is a listing of the `menu_LogonMsg_Click()` procedure:

LISTING 28.22. MAIN.FRM,menu_LogonMsg_Click().

```
Sub menu_LogonMsg_Click ()

    'toggle check
    If menu_LogonMsg.Checked = True Then
        menu_LogonMsg.Checked = False
    Else
        menu_LogonMsg.Checked = True
    End If

End Sub
```

THE *MENU_POLL_CLICK( )* PROCEDURE

The menu_poll_Click() procedure simply invokes the frmPoll form to change the polling frequency. Following is a listing of the menu_poll_Click() procedure:

LISTING 28.23. MAIN.FRM,menu_poll_Click().

```
Sub menu_poll_Click ()

    'show change polling frequency form
    frmPoll.Show

End Sub
```

THE *MENU_REMARKS_CLICK( )* PROCEDURE

The menu_remarks_Click() procedure simply invokes the frmRemark form to the greeting or closing remarks. Following is a listing of the menu_remark_Click() procedure:

LISTING 28.24. MAIN.FRM,menu_remarks_Click().

```
Sub menu_remarks_Click ()

    'show change remark form
    frmRemark.Show

End Sub
```

THE *MENU_RETRIEVE_CLICK( )* PROCEDURE

The menu_retrieve_Click() procedure requests the MAPI-compliant server for any messages for the given Login ID. Following is a listing of the menu_retrieve_Click() procedure:

LISTING 28.25. MAIN.FRM,menu_retrieve_Click().

```
Sub menu_retrieve_Click ()

    'declare variables
    Dim loopcount%        'loop counting variable

    'logon
    Call Logon

    'change cursor
    screen.MousePointer = HOURGLASS

    'set to fetch all messages
    MAPIMessages1.FetchUnreadOnly = False
```

continues

LISTING 28.25. CONTINUED

```
        If MAPISession1.SessionID <> 0 Then
          'fetch messages
          MAPIMessages1.Action = MESSAGE_FETCH

          If MAPIMessages1.MsgCount > 0 Then
              'there are messages waiting-show inbox form
              frmInbox.Show
              DoEvents

              'display number of messages
              frmInbox.pnlNumMsg.Caption = MAPIMessages1.MsgCount

              'clear list box
              frmInbox.lstMessage.Clear

              'populate messages
              For loopcount% = 0 To MAPIMessages1.MsgCount - 1

                  'change index
                  MAPIMessages1.MsgIndex = loopcount%

                  'get subject
                  frmInbox.lstMessage.AddItem MAPIMessages1.MsgSubject
              Next loopcount%
          Else
              MsgBox "No Messages"
          End If

        End If

        'change cursor
        screen.MousePointer = DEFAULT

End Sub
```

THE *MENU_SAVE_CLICK( )* PROCEDURE

The menu_save_Click() procedure simply calls the cmdSave_Click() procedure to invoke saving the configuration to the INI file. Following is a listing of the menu_save_Click() procedure:

LISTING 28.26. MAIN.FRM, menu_save_Click().

```
Sub menu_save_Click ()

    'invoke save ini routine
    cmdSave.Value = True

End Sub
```

THE *MENU_SEND_CLICK()* PROCEDURE

The menu_send_Click() procedure simply calls the cmdSend_Click() procedure to invoke sending a message through the MAPI-compliant message system. Following is a listing of the menu_send_Click() procedure:

LISTING 28.27. MAIN.FRM, menu_send_Click().

```
Sub menu_send_Click ()

    'invoke send routine
    cmdSend.Value = True

End Sub
```

THE *TMRPOLL* CONTROL

tmrPoll is the name of the timer control responsible for polling. The tmrPoll control has code in only one event procedure. It is:

◆ tmrPoll_Timer()

THE *TMRPOLL_TIMER()* EVENT PROCEDURE

The tmrPoll_Timer() event procedure is invoked every second automatically because the interval property is set to 1000 (1000 milliseconds, or 1 second) at design time. When the event fires a counter, IntervalCount&, is incremented. If the IntervalCount& equals the desired poll frequency, the action is called to fetch messages. Following is a listing of the tmrPoll_Timer() event procedure:

LISTING 28.28. MAIN.FRM, tmrPoll_Timer().

```
Sub tmrPoll_Timer ()

    'increment number of seconds in CurrentInterval&
    CurrentInterval& = CurrentInterval& + 1

    'check to see if polling time has elapsed
    If CurrentInterval& = DesiredInterval& Then
        If MAPISession1.SessionID <> 0 Then
            'fetch only new messages
            MAPIMessages1.FetchUnreadOnly = True

            'fetch messages
            MAPIMessages1.Action = MESSAGE_FETCH

            'test for new messages - this insures that the message will only be displayed
            'once, and not once each polling period!
            If MAPIMessages1.MsgCount > 0 And MAPIMessages1.MsgCount > NewMessages% Then
```

continues

LISTING 28.28. CONTINUED

```
                If frmMain.WindowState = 1 Then
                    'form is minimized then assign In icon
                    frmMain.Icon = pictMailIn.Picture
                Else
                    'advise about new message
                    MsgBox "You have new message(s)!"
                End If

                'increment number of new messages
                NewMessages% = NewMessages% + 1
            End If

            'set back to fetch all messages
            MAPIMessages1.FetchUnreadOnly = False

        End If

        'reset current interval&
        CurrentInterval& = 0
    End If

End Sub
```

The reason all the extra work is needed with the `CurrentInterval&` and `DesiredInterval&` variables is so you can poll at any frequency. The Visual Basic timer only allows for a maximum of 64 seconds. The code shown here allows you to get around this limitation.

THE *txtChanges* CONTROL

`txtChanges` is the name of the text box control that allows the user to enter a new change into the `lstChanges` listbox. The `txtChanges` control has code in only one event procedure. It is:

◆ `txtChanges_Change()`

THE *txtChanges_Change()* EVENT PROCEDURE

The `txtChanges_Change()` event procedure is invoked when the user types text into this text box. It is used to enable the `cmdChangeAdd` command button to add the text to the `lstChanges` listbox. Following is a listing of the `txtChanges_Change()` event procedure:

LISTING 28.29. MAIN.FRM, `txtChanges_Change()`.

```
Sub txtChanges_Change ()

    'enable/disable add button
    If Len(txtChanges.Text) > 0 Then
```

```
                cmdChangeAdd.Enabled = True
        Else
                cmdChangeAdd.Enabled = False
        End If

End Sub
```

THE *txtTo* CONTROL

txtTo is the name of the text box control that allows the user to enter a new recipient into the lstTo listbox. The txtTo control has code in only one event procedure. It is:

◆ txtTo_Change()

THE *txtTo_Change()* EVENT PROCEDURE

The txtTo_Change() event procedure is invoked when the user types text into this text box. It is used to enable the cmdRecipientAdd command button to add the text to the lstTo listbox. Following is a listing of the txtTo_Change() event procedure:

LISTING 28.30. MAIN.FRM,txtTo_Change().

```
Sub txtTo_Change ()

    'enable/disable add button
    If Len(txtTo.Text) > 0 Then
        cmdReceiptAdd.Enabled = True
    Else
        cmdReceiptAdd.Enabled = False
    End If

End Sub
```

THE INBOX.FRM FILE

INBOX.FRM is one of five forms in this application. It is used to display messages that have been sent to the user of this application (Incoming). Figure 28.3 presents this form as it appears at runtime. Figure 28.7 shows the form as it appears at design time. Table 28.3 lists all the relevant properties of each control on the form that have been changed from their standard default values. The INBOX.FRM file is contained on the CD accompanying this book in the CHAP28 subdirectory.

FIGURE 28.7.
*MAPI application
INBOX.FRM at
runtime.*

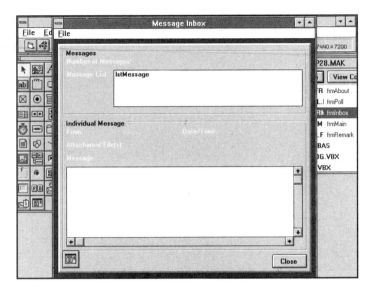

TABLE 28.3. PROPERTIES OF EACH CONTROL ON **INBOX.FRM**.

Object	Control Type	Property	Value
frmInbox	Form	BackColor	&H00404000&
		Caption	"Message Inbox"
		Height	7200
		Left	1005
		MaxButton	False
		Top	195
		Width	7440
Panel3D1	SSPanel	BackColor	&H00C0C0C0&
		BevelWidth	3
		Font3D	None
		ForeColor	&H00000000&
		Height	6255
		Left	120
		Top	120
		Width	7095
cmDialog	CommonDialog	Left	120
		Top	5640

Object	Control Type	Property	Value
Frame3D2	SSFrame	Caption	"Messages"
		Font3D	None
		Height	1815
		Left	120
		Top	120
		Width	6855
Panel3D2	SSPanel	Alignment	Left Justify - Middle
		BackColor	&H00C0C0C0&
		BevelOuter	None
		BevelWidth	0
		BorderWidth	0
		Caption	"Number of Messages:"
		Font3D	None
		ForeColor	&H0000FFFF&
		Height	255
		Left	120
		Top	240
		Width	2055
pnlNumMsg	SSPanel	Alignment	Left Justify - Middle
		BackColor	&H00C0C0C0&
		BevelOuter	None
		BevelWidth	0
		BorderWidth	0
		Font3D	None
		ForeColor	&H00000000&
		Height	255
		Left	2160
		Top	240
		Width	615
Panel3D3	SSPanel	Alignment	Left Justify - Middle
		BackColor	&H00C0C0C0&
		BevelOuter	None

continues 659

TABLE 28.3. CONTINUED

Object	Control Type	Property	Value
		BevelWidth	0
		BorderWidth	0
		Caption	"Message List:"
		Font3D	None
		ForeColor	&H0000FFFF&
		Height	255
		Left	120
		Top	600
		Width	1215
lstMessage	ListBox	Height	1005
		Left	1440
		Top	600
		Width	5295
Frame3D1	SSFrame	Caption	"Individual Message"
		Font3D	None
		Height	3615
		Left	120
		Top	2040
		Width	6855
pnlAttachFile	SSPanel	Alignment	Left Justify - Middle
		BackColor	&H00C0C0C0&
		BevelOuter	None
		BevelWidth	0
		BorderWidth	0
		Font3D	None
		ForeColor	&H00000000&
		Height	255
		Left	1800
		Top	600
		Width	4935

Object	Control Type	Property	Value
Panel3D7	SSPanel	Alignment	Left Justify - Middle
		BackColor	&H00C0C0C0&
		BevelOuter	None
		BevelWidth	0
		BorderWidth	0
		Caption	"Attachment File(s):"
		Font3D	None
		ForeColor	&H0000FFFF&
		Height	255
		Left	120
		Top	600
		Width	1695
pnlDateTime	SSPanel	Alignment	Left Justify - Middle
		BackColor	&H00C0C0C0&
		BevelOuter	None
		BevelWidth	0
		BorderWidth	0
		Font3D	None
		ForeColor	&H00000000&
		Height	255
		Left	4440
		Top	240
		Width	2175
pnlFrom	SSPanel	Alignment	Left Justify - Middle
		BackColor	&H00C0C0C0&
		BevelOuter	None
		BevelWidth	0
		BorderWidth	0
		Font3D	None
		ForeColor	&H00000000&
		Height	255
		Left	720

continues

TABLE 28.3. CONTINUED

Object	Control Type	Property	Value
		Top	240
		Width	2535
Panel3D6	SSPanel	Alignment	Left Justify - Middle
		BackColor	&H00C0C0C0&
		BevelOuter	None
		BevelWidth	0
		BorderWidth	0
		Caption	"Date/Time:"
		Font3D	None
		ForeColor	&H0000FFFF&
		Height	255
		Left	3360
		Top	240
		Width	975
Panel3D5	SSPanel	Alignment	Left Justify - Middle
		BackColor	&H00C0C0C0&
		BevelOuter	None
		BevelWidth	0
		BorderWidth	0
		Caption	"From:"
		Font3D	None
		ForeColor	&H0000FFFF&
		Height	255
		Left	120
		Top	240
		Width	615
Panel3D4	SSPanel	Alignment	Left Justify - Middle
		BackColor	&H00C0C0C0&
		BevelOuter	None
		BevelWidth	0
		BorderWidth	0

Object	Control Type	Property	Value
		Caption	"Message:"
		Font3D	None
		ForeColor	&H0000FFFF&
		Height	255
		Left	120
		Top	960
		Width	975
txtMessage	TextBox	BackColor	&H00FFFFFF&
		Height	2175
		Left	120
		MultiLine	True
		ScrollBars	Vertical
		Top	1320
		Width	6615
cmdClose	CommandButton	Caption	"Close"
		Height	375
		Left	6000
		Top	5760
		Width	975
menu_file	Menu	Caption	"&File"
menu_delete	Menu	Caption	"&Delete Message"
menu_delAttach	Menu	Caption	"Delete&Attachment(s)"
menu_print	Menu	Caption	"&Print"
menu_separator	Menu	Caption	"-"
menu_exit	Menu	Caption	"&Exit"

FUNCTION, SUBROUTINE, AND EVENT PROCEDURES

There are several procedures of code for each object (control) that comprise this form. Each is listed in the following sections.

THE *(GENERAL)* OBJECT

The (general) object contains form level declarations and two form level procedures. The procedures for the (general) object are:

- ◆ (declarations)
- ◆ FindAttachments()
- ◆ FindMessage()

THE *(DECLARATIONS)* PROCEDURE

The (declarations) procedure contains only one line of declarations used in the form, INBOX.FRM. It is only to allow for variable syntax checking and forcing the declaration of variables in each procedure. Following is a listing of the (declarations) procedure:

LISTING 28.31. INBOX.FRM, (general) (declarations).

```
Option Explicit
```

THE *FINDATTACHMENTS()* PROCEDURE

The FindAttachments() procedure builds a semicolon delimited string to list all attachments for a message. The procedure is a function that returns that string. Following is a listing of the FindAttachments() procedure:

LISTING 28.32. INBOX.FRM, FindAttachments().

```
Function FindAttachments () As String

    'declare variables
    Dim loopcount%  'loop counting variable
    Dim Attach$     'string holding attachments

    'find all attachments and build string
    For loopcount% = 0 To frmmain.MapiMessages1.AttachmentCount - 1

        'assign index
        frmmain.MapiMessages1.AttachmentIndex = loopcount%

        'assign name to string
        Attach$ = Attach$ + frmmain.MapiMessages1.AttachmentName

        'append semi-colon if not last item
        If loopcount% < frmmain.MapiMessages1.AttachmentCount - 1 Then
            Attach$ = Attach$ + ";"
        End If

    Next loopcount%

    'assign none if blank
```

```
    If Attach$ = "" Then Attach = "None"

    FindAttachments = Attach$

End Function
```

THE *FINDMESSAGE( )* PROCEDURE

The FindMessage() procedure finds the actual message text part of the message. This is necessary because if the message was sent from a Macintosh server to a PC, the subject, message, and so on will all be part of the message.

 The actual message will be separated from the headers by a series of 78 dashes. This procedure extracts only the message and returns that message. I have found that if a message was sent from a MAC file server, the text of the message will contain a string of 78 dashes. This is not documented anywhere, to my knowledge, but in actuality I've found this to be true.

Following is a listing of the FindMessage() procedure:

LISTING 28.33. INBOX.FRM, FindMessage().

```
Function FindMessage () As String

    'declare variables
    Dim pos%       'holds position of instr

    'test type of server by querying for 78 "-"'s
    pos% = InStr(frmmain.MapiMessages1.MsgNoteText, String$(78, "-") + Chr$(13))

    If pos% = 0 Then
        'this file came from a PC file server
        FindMessage = frmmain.MapiMessages1.MsgNoteText
    Else
        'this file came from a MAC file server
        FindMessage = Right$(frmmain.MapiMessages1.MsgNoteText,
Len(frmmain.MapiMessages1.MsgNoteText) - pos% - 79)

    End If

End Function
```

THE *FORM* OBJECT

The Form object has code in two event procedures. They are:

◆ Form_Load()

◆ Form_Unload()

THE *FORM_LOAD()* EVENT PROCEDURE

The Form_Load() event simply calls the routing to center the form. Following is a listing of the Form_Load() event procedure:

LISTING 28.34. INBOX.FRM, Form_Load().

```
Sub Form_Load ()

    'center the form
    CenterForm Me

End Sub
```

THE *FORM_UNLOAD()* EVENT PROCEDURE

The Form_Unload() event requests for confirmation to close the form. Following is a listing of the Form_Unload() event procedure:

LISTING 28.35. INBOX.FRM, Form_Unload().

```
Sub Form_Unload (cancel As Integer)

    'declare variables
    Dim m$        'message constructor
    Dim res%      'holds results

    m$ = "Confirm Close!"
    res% = MsgBox(m$, 292)
    If res% = IDNO Then
        cancel = True
        Exit Sub
    End If

End Sub
```

THE *CMDCLOSE* CONTROL

cmdClose is the name of the command button control that, when clicked, invokes closing the form by invoking the form_Unload event. The cmdClose control has code in only one event procedure. It is:

◆ cmdClose_Click()

THE *cmdCLOSE_CLICK( )* EVENT PROCEDURE

Following is a listing of the cmdClose_Click() event procedure:

LISTING 28.36. INBOX.FRM, cmdClose_Click().

```
Sub cmdClose_Click ()

    'unload form
    Unload frmInbox

End Sub
```

THE *lstMESSAGE* CONTROL

lstMessage is the name of the listbox control that lists all of the available message subjects. When clicked, the message and its attributes will be populated in the designated areas of the form. The lstMessage control has code in only one event procedure. It is:

◆ lstMessage_Click()

THE *lstMESSAGE_CLICK( )* EVENT PROCEDURE

Following is a listing of the lstMessage_Click() event procedure:

LISTING 28.37. INBOX.FRM, lstMessage_Click().

```
Sub lstMessage_Click ()

    'change cursor
    screen.MousePointer = HOURGLASS

    'change message index based on index of list box
    frmmain.MapiMessages1.MsgIndex = lstMessage.listindex

    'populate from
    pnlFrom.Caption = frmmain.MapiMessages1.MsgOrigDisplayName

    'populate date/time
    pnlDateTime.Caption = frmmain.MapiMessages1.MsgDateReceived

    'populate file attachments
    pnlAttachFile.Caption = FindAttachments()

    'populate message
    txtmessage.text = FindMessage()

    'change cursor
    screen.MousePointer = DEFAULT

End Sub
```

667

THE *MENU* OBJECT

The menu object was created using Visual Basic's built-in Menu editor. It has code associated with four Click() event procedures. They are:

- ◆ menu_delAttach()
- ◆ menu_delete()
- ◆ menu_exit()
- ◆ menu_print()

THE *MENU_DELATTACH_CLICK()* PROCEDURE

The menu_delAttach_Click() procedure deletes all attachments for a message. Following is a listing of the menu_delAttach_Click() procedure:

LISTING 28.38. INBOX.FRM, menu_delAttach_Click().

```
Sub menu_delAttach_Click ()

    'declare variables
    Dim m$          'message constructor
    Dim res%        'holds results
    Dim loopcount%  'loop counting variable

    'see if there are any attachments
    If frmmain.MapiMessages1.AttachmentCount = 0 Then
        m$ = "There are no attachments to delete!"
        MsgBox m$
        Exit Sub
    End If

    'build message
    m$ = "Are you sure you want to DELETE" + Chr$(13)
    m$ = m$ + "all attachments?"
    res% = MsgBox(m$, 292, "Warning")
    If res% = IDNO Then Exit Sub

    'change cursor
    screen.MousePointer = HOURGLASS

    'handle error
    On Error GoTo DelAttachError

    'loop through all attachments and delete
    For loopcount% = 0 To frmmain.MapiMessages1.AttachmentCount - 1
        'do delete
        frmmain.MapiMessages1.Action = ATTACHMENT_DELETE
    Next loopcount%

    'verify that there are no attachments-change caption
    pnlAttachFile.Caption = FindAttachments()
```

```
         'change cursor
         screen.MousePointer = DEFAULT

         'exit
         Exit Sub

DelAttachError:
         'show error
         MsgBox Error$
         Resume Next

End Sub
```

The *menu_delete_Click()* Procedure

The menu_delete_Click() procedure deletes the actual message. Following is a listing of the menu_delete_Click() procedure:

Listing 28.39. INBOX.FRM, menu_delete_Click().

```
Sub menu_delete_Click ()

    'declare variables
    Dim m$        'message constructor
    Dim res%      'holds results

    'test to see if there is a selection
    If lstMessage.listindex = -1 Then
        m$ = "You must select a message to delete!"
        MsgBox m$
        Exit Sub
    End If

    m$ = "Are you sure you want to DELETE" + Chr$(13)
    m$ = m$ + "Message: " + frmmain.MapiMessages1.MsgSubject + " ?"
    res% = MsgBox(m$, 292, "Warning")
    If res% = IDNO Then Exit Sub

    'change cursor
    screen.MousePointer = HOURGLASS

    'do delete
    frmmain.MapiMessages1.Action = MESSAGE_DELETE

    'remove item from lstMessage
    lstMessage.RemoveItem lstMessage.listindex

    'clear all areas in the individual message frame
    pnlFrom.Caption = ""
    pnlDateTime.Caption = ""
    pnlAttachFile.Caption = ""
    txtmessage.text = ""
```

continues

LISTING 28.39. CONTINUED

```
    'subtract one from number of messages
    pnlNumMsg.Caption = Trim$(Str$(Val(pnlNumMsg.Caption) - 1))

    'change cursor
    screen.MousePointer = DEFAULT

End Sub
```

THE *MENU_EXIT_CLICK( )* PROCEDURE

The menu_exit_Click() procedure closes the form by invoking the form_Unload event. Following is a listing of the menu_exit_Click() procedure:

LISTING 28.40. INBOX.FRM, menu_exit_Click().

```
Sub menu_exit_Click ()

    'unload form
    Unload frmInbox

End Sub
```

THE *MENU_PRINT_CLICK( )* PROCEDURE

The menu_print_Click() procedure prints the message using the Visual Basic standard Printer object. Following is a listing of the menu_print_Click() procedure:

LISTING 28.41. INBOX.FRM, menu_print_Click().

```
Sub menu_print_Click ()

    'declare variables
    Dim msg$                'message to print
    Dim m$                  'message constructor

    'test for selection
    If lstMessage.listindex = -1 Then
        m$ = "You must select a message first!"
        MsgBox m$
        Exit Sub
    End If

    'change cursor
    screen.MousePointer = HOURGLASS

    'start building of message
    msg$ = "FROM:" + Chr$(9) + Chr$(9) + pnlFrom.Caption + Chr$(13)

    'assign date/time
    msg$ = msg$ + "DATE/TIME:" + Chr$(9) + pnlDateTime.Caption + Chr$(13)
```

```
        'assign subject
        msg$ = msg$ + "SUBJECT:" + Chr$(9) + lstMessage.list(lstMessage.listindex) + Chr$(13)

        'assign message
        msg$ = msg$ + "MESSAGE:" + Chr$(13)
        msg$ = msg$ + txtmessage.text

        'print text and eject
        printer.Print msg$
        printer.EndDoc

        'change cursor
        screen.MousePointer = DEFAULT

        'exit
        Exit Sub

PrinterError:
        'show error
        MsgBox Error$

        'change cursor
        screen.MousePointer = DEFAULT

        'exit
        Exit Sub

        'avoid errors
        Resume

End Sub
```

THE REMARK.FRM FILE

REMARK.FRM is one of five forms in this application. It is used to enter or display the greeting or closing of a MAPI-compliant message to be sent. The greeting is the first part of the message to be sent, and the closing is, of course, the last. Figure 28.5 presents this form as it appears at runtime. It is fundamentally no different at design time, so it is not shown again. Table 28.4 lists all the relevant properties of each control on the form that have been changed from their standard default values. The REMARK.FRM file is contained on the CD accompanying this book in the CHAP28 subdirectory.

TABLE 28.4. PROPERTIES OF EACH CONTROL ON REMARK.FRM.

Object	Control Type	Property	Value
frmRemark	Form	BackColor	&H00404000&
		Caption	"Remark Form"
		Height	2940

continues

671

TABLE 28.4. CONTINUED

Object	Control Type	Property	Value
		Left	1110
		MaxButton	False
		Top	2340
		Width	6135
Panel3D1	SSPanel	AutoSize	AutoSize Child To Panel
		BackColor	&H8000000F&
		BevelWidth	3
		Font3D	None
		ForeColor	&H00000000&
		Height	2295
		Left	120
		RoundedCorners	False
		ShadowColor	Black
		Top	120
		Width	5775
cmdClose	CommandButton	Caption	"Close"
		Height	375
		Left	4200
		Top	1800
		Width	1335
Panel3D2	SSPanel	Alignment	Left Justify - Middle
		BackColor	&H00C0C0C0&
		BevelOuter	None
		BevelWidth	0
		BorderWidth	0
		Caption	"Greeting:"
		Font3D	None
		ForeColor	&H0000FFFF&
		Height	255
		Left	120
		Top	120

Object	Control Type	Property	Value
		Width	735
Panel3D9	SSPanel	Alignment	Left Justify - Middle
		BackColor	&H00C0C0C0&
		BevelOuter	None
		BevelWidth	0
		BorderWidth	0
		Caption	"Closing:"
		Font3D	None
		ForeColor	&H0000FFFF&
		Height	255
		Left	120
		Top	960
		Width	735
txtGreeting	TextBox	BackColor	&H00FFFFFF&
		Height	735
		Left	960
		MultiLine	True
		Top	120
		Width	4575
txtClosing	TextBox	BackColor	&H00FFFFFF&
		Height	735
		Left	960
		MultiLine	True
		Top	960
		Width	4575

FUNCTION, SUBROUTINE, AND EVENT PROCEDURES

There are several procedures of code for each object (control) that comprise this form. Each is listed in the following sections.

THE *(GENERAL)* OBJECT

The (general) object contains only one form level declaration and no form level procedures. The procedure for the (general) object is:

◆ (declarations)

THE *(DECLARATIONS)* PROCEDURE

The (declarations) procedure contains only one line of declarations used in the form, REMARK.FRM. It is only to allow for variable syntax checking and forcing the declaration of variables in each procedure. Following is a listing of the (declarations) procedure:

LISTING 28.42. REMARK.FRM,(general)(declarations).

```
Option Explicit
```

THE *CMDCLOSE* CONTROL

cmdClose is the name of the command button control that, when clicked, will hide the form, not unload it. It is hidden so that frmMain can still query its properties for sending a message and saving to an INI file. These could have been stored in variables, but it takes very little memory for a form of this size. The cmdClose control has code in only one event procedure. It is:

◆ cmdClose_Click()

THE *CMDCLOSE_CLICK()* EVENT PROCEDURE

Following is a listing of the cmdClose_Click() event procedure:

LISTING 28.43. REMARK.FRM,cmdClose_Click().

```
Sub cmdClose_Click ()

    'hide-don't unload
    frmRemark.Hide

End Sub
```

THE *FORM* OBJECT

The Form object has code in only one event procedure. It is:

◆ Form_Load()

THE *FORM_LOAD()* EVENT PROCEDURE

The Form_Load() event procedure simply centers the form. Following is a listing of the Form_Load() event procedure:

LISTING 28.44. REMARK.FRM, Form_Load().

```
Sub Form_Load ()

    'center the form
    CenterForm Me

End Sub
```

THE POLL.FRM FILE

POLL.FRM is one of five forms in this application. It is used to enter or display the time in minutes between polling cycles to determine if there are any new messages to receive. Figure 28.4 presents this form as it appears at runtime. It is fundamentally no different at design time, so it is not shown again. Table 28.5 lists all the relevant properties of each control on the form that have been changed from their standard default values. The POLL.FRM file is contained on the CD accompanying this book in the CHAP28 subdirectory.

TABLE 28.5. PROPERTIES OF EACH CONTROL ON POLL.FRM.

Object	Control Type	Property	Value
frmPoll	Form	BackColor	&H00404000&
		Caption	"Change Polling Frequency"
		Height	1965
		Left	1830
		MaxButton	False
		Top	1335
		Width	3360
Panel3D1	SSPanel	BackColor	&H00C0C0C0&
		BevelWidth	3
		Font3D	None
		Height	1335
		Left	120
		Top	120
		Width	3015
cmdSave	CommandButton	Caption	"Save"
		Enabled	False
		Height	375

continues

TABLE 28.5. CONTINUED

Object	Control Type	Property	Value
		Left	840
		Top	840
		Width	975
cmdClose	CommandButton	Caption	"Close"
		Height	375
		Left	1920
		Top	840
		Width	975
txtPoll	TextBox	Height	375
		Left	2040
		Top	120
		Width	735
Panel3D7	SSPanel	BackColor	&H00C0C0C0&
		BevelOuter	None
		BevelWidth	0
		BorderWidth	0
		Caption	"Polling Frequency (In Minutes)"
		Font3D	None
		ForeColor	&H0000FFFF&
		Height	495
		Left	120
		Top	120
		Width	1695

FUNCTION, SUBROUTINE, AND EVENT PROCEDURES

There are several procedures of code for each object (control) that comprise this form. Each is listed in the following sections.

THE (GENERAL) OBJECT

The (general) object contains only one form level declaration and no form level procedures. The procedure for the (general) object is:

676

◆ (declarations)

THE *(DECLARATIONS)* PROCEDURE

The (declarations) procedure contains only one line of declarations used in the form, POLL.FRM. It is only to allow for variable syntax checking and forcing the declaration of variables in each procedure. Following is a listing of the (declarations) procedure:

LISTING 28.45. POLL.FRM,(general)(declarations).

```
Option Explicit
```

THE *CMDCLOSE* CONTROL

cmdClose is the name of the command button control that, when clicked, unloads the form. The cmdClose control has code in only one event procedure. It is:

- ◆ cmdClose_Click()

THE *CMDCLOSE_CLICK()* EVENT PROCEDURE

Following is a listing of the cmdClose_Click() event procedure:

LISTING 28.46. POLL.FRM,cmdClose_Click().

```
Sub cmdClose_Click ()

    'declare variables
    Dim m$        'message constructor
    Dim res%      'holds results

    If cmdSave.Enabled = True Then
        m$ = "Close without saving changes?"
        res% = MsgBox(m$, 292, "Warning")
        If res% = IDNO Then Exit Sub
        'unload
        Unload frmPoll
    Else
        'unload
        Unload frmPoll
    End If

End Sub
```

THE *CMDSAVE* CONTROL

cmdSave is the name of the command button control that, when clicked, saves the new value into the DesiredInterval& variable. This allows the change to take effect immediately. The cmdSave control has code in only one event procedure. It is:

- ◆ cmdSave_Click()

THE *cmdSAVE_CLICK( )* EVENT PROCEDURE

Following is a listing of the cmdSave_Click() event procedure:

LISTING 28.47. POLL.FRM,cmdSave_Click().

```
Sub cmdSave_Click ()

    'assign the new value
    DesiredInterval& = Int(Val(txtPoll.Text) * 60)

    'disable save
    cmdSave.Enabled = False

End Sub
```

THE *FORM* OBJECT

The Form object has code in only one event procedure. It is:

◆ Form_Load()

THE *FORM_LOAD( )* EVENT PROCEDURE

The Form_Load() event procedure populates the text box and centers the form. The reason for the Populating% flag is so that the change event for the text box is ignored on population. Following is a listing of the Form_Load() event procedure:

LISTING 28.48. POLL.FRM,Form_Load().

```
Sub Form_Load ()

    'flag populating
    Populating% = True

    'populate text box
    txtPoll.Text = Trim$(Str$(Int(DesiredInterval& / 60)))

    'center the form
    CenterForm Me

    'unflag populating
    Populating% = False

End Sub
```

THE *TXTPOLL* CONTROL

txtPoll is the name of the text box control for entering a new polling frequency. The txtPoll control has code in only one event procedure. It is:

◆ txtPoll_Change()

THE *TXTPOLL_CHANGE()* EVENT PROCEDURE

The txtPoll_Change() event procedure simply enables the cmdSave command button. Following is a listing of the txtPoll_Change() event procedure:

LISTING 28.49. POLL.FRM, txtPoll_Change().

```
Sub txtPoll_Change ()

    'enable save button
    If Populating% = False Then
        cmdSave.Enabled = True
    End If

End Sub
```

THE ABOUT.FRM FILE

ABOUT.FRM is one of five forms in this application. It shows information about the application. Figure 28.8 presents the form as it appears at runtime. Fundamentally, there is no difference in the form at design time, so it is not presented. Table 28.6 lists all the relevant properties of each control on the form that have been changed from their standard default values. The ABOUT.FRM file is contained on the CD accompanying this book in the CHAP28 subdirectory.

FIGURE 28.8.
*MAPI application
About form at runtime.*

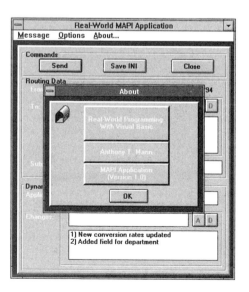

TABLE 28.6. PROPERTIES OF EACH CONTROL ON ABOUT.FRM.

Object	Control Type	Property	Value
frmAbout	Form	BackColor	&H00404000&
		Caption	"About"
		Height	3525
		Left	1035
		MaxButton	False
		MinButton	False
		Top	1140
		Width	4545
pnlMain	SSPanel	BackColor	&H00C0C0C0&
		BevelWidth	3
		Caption	""
		Font3D	None
		ForeColor	&H00C0C0C0&
		Height	2895
		Left	120
		RoundedCorners	False
		ShadowColor	Black
		Top	120
		Width	4215
pnl1	SSPanel	BackColor	&H00C0C0C0&
		BevelWidth	3
		Caption	"Real-World Programming With Visual Basic"
		Font3D	None
		ForeColor	&H0000FFFF&
		Height	975
		Left	960
		RoundedCorners	False
		ShadowColor	Black
		Top	120
		Width	2415
pnl2	SSPanel	BackColor	&H00C0C0C0&
		BevelWidth	3

Object	Control Type	Property	Value
		Caption	"Anthony T. Mann"
		Font3D	None
		ForeColor	&H0000FFFF&
		Height	615
		Left	960
		RoundedCorners	False
		ShadowColor	Black
		Top	1080
		Width	2415
pnl3	SSPanel	BackColor	&H00C0C0C0&
		BevelWidth	3
		Caption	"MAPI Application (Version 1.0)"
		Font3D	None
		ForeColor	&H0000FFFF&
		Height	615
		Left	960
		RoundedCorners	False
		ShadowColor	Black
		Top	1680
		Width	2415
cmdOK	CommandButton	Caption	"OK"
		Height	375
		Left	1680
		Top	2400
		Width	1095
pictAbout	PictureBox	Autosize	True
		BackColor	&H00C0C0C0&
		BorderStyle	None
		Height	615
		Left	120
		Top	120
		Width	735

FUNCTION, SUBROUTINE, AND EVENT PROCEDURES

There are several procedures of code for each object (control) that comprise this form. Each is listed in the following sections.

The (general) object contains only one form level declaration and no form level procedures. The procedure for the (general) object is:

◆ (declarations)

THE *(DECLARATIONS)* PROCEDURE

The (declarations) procedure contains only one line of declarations used in the form, ABOUT.FRM. It is only to allow for variable syntax checking and forcing the declaration of variables in each procedure. Following is a listing of the (declarations) procedure:

LISTING 28.50. ABOUT.FRM, (general)(declarations).

```
Option Explicit
```

THE *CMDOK* CONTROL

cmdOK is the name of the command button control that, when clicked, closes the frmAbout form. The cmdOK control has code in only one event procedure. It is:

◆ cmdOK_Click()

THE *CMDOK_CLICK()* EVENT PROCEDURE

The cmdOK_Click() event procedure simply unloads the form. Following is a listing of the cmdOK_Click() event procedure:

LISTING 28.51. ABOUT.FRM, cmdOK_Click().

```
Sub cmdOK_Click ()

    'unload
    Unload frmAbout

End Sub
```

THE *FORM* OBJECT

The Form object has code in only one event procedure. It is:

◆ Form_Load()

THE *FORM_LOAD( )* EVENT PROCEDURE

The Form_Load() event procedure centers the form and assigns an icon to the pictAbout control. Following is a listing of the Form_Load() event procedure:

LISTING 28.52. ABOUT.FRM, Form_Load( ).

```
Sub Form_Load ()

    'center form
    CenterForm Me

    'load icon
    pictAbout.Picture = frmMain.Icon

End Sub
```

THE CHAP28.BAS FILE

CHAP28.BAS is the module that contains application level variables and procedures. The CHAP28.BAS file is contained on the CD accompanying this book in the CHAP28 subdirectory.

FUNCTION, SUBROUTINE, AND EVENT PROCEDURES

There are several procedures of code for each object (control) that comprise this module. Each is listed in the following sections.

The (general) object contains application level variables and procedures. The procedures for the (general) object are:

- ◆ (declarations)
- ◆ CenterForm()
- ◆ GETINI()
- ◆ ParseList()
- ◆ PopulateList()
- ◆ SAVEINI()

THE *(DECLARATIONS)* PROCEDURE

The (declarations) procedure contains variables and API declarations used in the application. Following is a listing of the (declarations) procedure:

LISTING 28.53. CHAP28.BAS, (general) (declarations).

```
Option Explicit

'global varaibles
Global DesiredInterval&          'number of seconds before polling
Global CurrentInterval&          'number of seconds which elapsed
Global NewMessages%             'number of new messages-so new message message box
                                'won't display continuously
Global Populating%              'flag for populating text boxes


'API declares
Declare Function GetPrivateProfileString Lib "Kernel" (ByVal lpAppName As String, ByVal
lpKeyName As String, ByVal lpDefault As String, ByVal lpReturnedString As String, ByVal
nSize As Integer, ByVal lpFileName As String) As Integer
Declare Function WritePrivateProfileString Lib "Kernel" (ByVal lpApplicationName As
String, ByVal lpKeyName As String, ByVal lpString As String, ByVal lpFileName As String)
As Integer

'api constants
Const lpFile$ = "CHAP28.INI"
Const lpAppName$ = "Initialization"
Const lpKeyName1$ = "PollFreq"
Const lpKeyName2$ = "LogonMessage"
Const lpKeyName3$ = "Greeting"
Const lpKeyName4$ = "Closing"
Const lpKeyName5$ = "From"
Const lpKeyName6$ = "To"
Const lpKeyName7$ = "Subject"
Const lpKeyName8$ = "Application"
Const lpKeyName9$ = "Version"
Const lpKeyName10$ = "Changes"


'mousepointers
Global Const HOURGLASS = 11
Global Const DEFAULT = 0

'messageboxes
Global Const IDNO = 7


'----------------------------------------
' MAPI MESSAGE CONTROL Global Const ANTS
'----------------------------------------
'Action
Global Const MESSAGE_FETCH = 1           ' Load all messages from message store
Global Const MESSAGE_SENDDLG = 2         ' Send mail bring up default mapi dialog
Global Const MESSAGE_SEND = 3            ' Send mail without default mapi dialog
Global Const MESSAGE_SAVEMSG = 4         ' Save message in the compose buffer
Global Const MESSAGE_COPY = 5            ' Copy current message to compose buffer
Global Const MESSAGE_COMPOSE = 6         ' Initialize compose buffer (previous
                                         ' data is lost
Global Const MESSAGE_REPLY = 7           ' Fill Compose buffer as REPLY
Global Const MESSAGE_REPLYALL = 8        ' Fill Compose buffer as REPLY ALL
Global Const MESSAGE_FORWARD = 9         ' Fill Compose buffer as FORWARD
Global Const MESSAGE_DELETE = 10         ' Delete current message
```

```
Global Const MESSAGE_SHOWADBOOK = 11      ' Show Address book
Global Const MESSAGE_SHOWDETAILS = 12     ' Show details of the current recipient
Global Const MESSAGE_RESOLVENAME = 13     ' Resolve the display name of the recipient
Global Const RECIPIENT_DELETE = 14        ' Fill Compose buffer as FORWARD
Global Const ATTACHMENT_DELETE = 15       ' Delete current message
Global Const SESSION_SIGNON = 1
Global Const SESSION_SIGNOFF = 2
Global Const MODAL = 1



'---------------------------------------
'   ERROR Global Const ANT DECLARATIONS (MAPI CONTROLS)
'---------------------------------------
Global Const SUCCESS_SUCCESS = 32000
Global Const MAPI_USER_ABORT = 32001
Global Const MAPI_E_FAILURE = 32002
Global Const MAPI_E_LOGIN_FAILURE = 32003
Global Const MAPI_E_DISK_FULL = 32004
Global Const MAPI_E_INSUFFICIENT_MEMORY = 32005
Global Const MAPI_E_ACCESS_DENIED = 32006
Global Const MAPI_E_TOO_MANY_SESSIONS = 32008
Global Const MAPI_E_TOO_MANY_FILES = 32009
Global Const MAPI_E_TOO_MANY_RECIPIENTS = 32010
Global Const MAPI_E_ATTACHMENT_NOT_FOUND = 32011
Global Const MAPI_E_ATTACHMENT_OPEN_FAILURE = 32012
Global Const MAPI_E_ATTACHMENT_WRITE_FAILURE = 32013
Global Const MAPI_E_UNKNOWN_RECIPIENT = 32014
Global Const MAPI_E_BAD_RECIPTYPE = 32015
Global Const MAPI_E_NO_MESSAGES = 32016
Global Const MAPI_E_INVALID_MESSAGE = 32017
Global Const MAPI_E_TEXT_TOO_LARGE = 32018
Global Const MAPI_E_INVALID_SESSION = 32019
Global Const MAPI_E_TYPE_NOT_SUPPORTED = 32020
Global Const MAPI_E_AMBIGUOUS_RECIPIENT = 32021
Global Const MAPI_E_MESSAGE_IN_USE = 32022
Global Const MAPI_E_NETWORK_FAILURE = 32023
Global Const MAPI_E_INVALID_EDITFIELDS = 32024
Global Const MAPI_E_INVALID_RECIPS = 32025
Global Const MAPI_E_NOT_SUPPORTED = 32026

Global Const CONTROL_E_SESSION_EXISTS = 32050
Global Const CONTROL_E_INVALID_BUFFER = 32051
Global Const CONTROL_E_INVALID_READ_BUFFER_ACTION = 32052
Global Const CONTROL_E_NO_SESSION = 32053
Global Const CONTROL_E_INVALID_RECIPIENT = 32054
Global Const CONTROL_E_INVALID_COMPOSE_BUFFER_ACTION = 32055
Global Const CONTROL_E_FAILURE = 32056
Global Const CONTROL_E_NO_RECIPIENTS = 32057
Global Const CONTROL_E_NO_ATTACHMENTS = 32058



'---------------------------------------
'   MISCELLANEOUS Global Const ANT DECLARATIONS (MAPI CONTROLS)
'---------------------------------------
Global Const RECIPTYPE_ORIG = 0
Global Const RECIPTYPE_TO = 1
Global Const RECIPTYPE_CC = 2
```

continues

LISTING 28.53. CONTINUED

```
Global Const RECIPTYPE_BCC = 3

Global Const ATTACHTYPE_DATA = 0
Global Const ATTACHTYPE_EOLE = 1
Global Const ATTACHTYPE_SOLE = 2
```

REM There are constants presented in the preceding listing that are not necessarily used in this program. They are listed anyway to make it easier for you to modify and use this program for your needs.

THE *CENTERFORM( )* PROCEDURE

The CenterForm() procedure simply centers the form in the client area upon form loading. The CenterForm() procedure accepts one argument, .F.. It is the actual form to be centered. For more information on manipulating graphics and forms, refer to Chapter 5, "Graphics." Following is a listing of the CenterForm() procedure:

LISTING 28.54. CHAP28.BAS, CenterForm( ).

```
Sub CenterForm (F As Form)

    'center the form
    F.Left = (screen.Width - F.Width) / 2
    F.Top = (screen.Height - F.Height) / 2

End Sub
```

THE *GETINI( )* PROCEDURE

The GETINI() procedure finds the CHAP28.INI file and populates the appropriate areas of the application.

 For more information on INI files, refer to Chapter 7, "File Input/Output (I/O)."

Following is a listing of the GETINI() procedure:

LISTING 28.55. CHAP28.BAS, GETINI( ).

```
Sub GETINI ()

    'declare variables
    Dim res%         'holds results
    Dim Temp$        'temporary string$
Const INILENGTH = 1028
```

```
'get polling frequency
Temp$ = Space$(INILENGTH)
res% = GetPrivateProfileString(lpAppName$, lpKeyName1$, "", Temp$, INILENGTH,
lpFile$)
If res% > 0 Then
    'assign interval
    DesiredInterval& = Val(Left$(Temp$, res%))
End If

'get Boolean for getting messages at logon
Temp$ = Space$(INILENGTH)
res% = GetPrivateProfileString(lpAppName$, lpKeyName2$, "", Temp$, INILENGTH,
lpFile$)
If res% > 0 Then
    If UCase$(Left$(Temp$, res%)) = "FALSE" Then
        'uncheck menu
        frmMain.menu_LogonMsg.Checked = False
    ElseIf UCase$(Left$(Temp$, res%)) = "TRUE" Then
        'check menu
        frmMain.menu_LogonMsg.Checked = True
    End If
End If

'flag populating
Populating% = True

'get greeting
Temp$ = Space$(1028)
res% = GetPrivateProfileString(lpAppName$, lpKeyName3$, "", Temp$, 1028, lpFile$)
If res% > 0 Then
    frmRemark.txtGreeting.Text = Left$(Temp$, res%)
End If

'get closing
Temp$ = Space$(1028)
res% = GetPrivateProfileString(lpAppName$, lpKeyName4$, "", Temp$, 1028, lpFile$)
If res% > 0 Then
    frmRemark.txtClosing.Text = Left$(Temp$, res%)
End If

'unflag populating
Populating% = False

'get from
Temp$ = Space$(INILENGTH)
res% = GetPrivateProfileString(lpAppName$, lpKeyName5$, "", Temp$, INILENGTH,
lpFile$)
If res% > 0 Then
    frmMain.pnlFrom.Caption = Left$(Temp$, res%)
End If

'get to
Temp$ = Space$(INILENGTH)
res% = GetPrivateProfileString(lpAppName$, lpKeyName6$, "", Temp$, INILENGTH,
lpFile$)
If res% > 0 Then
    Call PopulateList(frmMain.lstTo, Left$(Temp$, res%))
```

continues

LISTING 28.55. CONTINUED

```
End If

    'get subject
    Temp$ = Space$(INILENGTH)
    res% = GetPrivateProfileString(lpAppName$, lpKeyName7$, "", Temp$, INILENGTH,
    lpFile$)
    If res% > 0 Then
        frmMain.txtSubject.Text = Left$(Temp$, res%)
    End If

    'get application
    Temp$ = Space$(INILENGTH)
    res% = GetPrivateProfileString(lpAppName$, lpKeyName8$, "", Temp$, INILENGTH,
    lpFile$)
    If res% > 0 Then
        frmMain.txtApplication.Text = Left$(Temp$, res%)
    End If

    'get version
    Temp$ = Space$(INILENGTH)
    res% = GetPrivateProfileString(lpAppName$, lpKeyName9$, "", Temp$, INILENGTH,
    lpFile$)
    If res% > 0 Then
        frmMain.txtVersion.Text = Left$(Temp$, res%)
    End If

    'get changes
    Temp$ = Space$(INILENGTH)
    res% = GetPrivateProfileString(lpAppName$, lpKeyName10$, "", Temp$, INILENGTH,
    lpFile$)
    If res% > 0 Then
        Call PopulateList(frmMain.lstChanges, Left$(Temp$, res%))
    End If

End Sub
```

REM   The reason for the `Populating%` flag is to have a way to indicate to the program that the user didn't change the value of the text boxes on the appropriate forms.

THE *PARSELIST( )* PROCEDURE

The `ParseList()` procedure searches through a listbox and builds a string of either recipients or changes, delimited by a semicolon (`;`). The procedure accepts a listbox control, `WhichList`, as an argument. The procedure is also a function and returns the string that is built. Following is a listing of the `ParseList()` procedure:

LISTING 28.56. CHAP28.BAS,ParseList().

```
Function ParseList (Whichlist As ListBox) As String

    'declare variables
    Dim loopcount%  'loop counting variable
    Dim Temp$       'temporary string

    'loop through each item in list box
    For loopcount% = 0 To Whichlist.ListCount - 1
        'add item from list box
        Temp$ = Temp$ + Whichlist.List(loopcount%)

        'if not last item, add semicolon
        If loopcount% < Whichlist.ListCount - 1 Then
            Temp$ = Temp$ + ";"
        End If

    Next loopcount%

    'return from function
    ParseList = Temp$

End Function
```

THE *POPULATELIST( )* PROCEDURE

The PopulateList() procedure populates a listbox, parsing a string delimited by semicolons. The procedure accepts two arguments. The first, WhichList, is the listbox to populate. The second, WithWhat$, is the string to parse and populate. Following is a listing of the PopulateList() procedure:

LISTING 28.57. CHAP28.BAS,PopulateList().

```
Sub PopulateList (Whichlist As ListBox, WithWhat$)

    'declare variables
    Dim pos%        'holds position of instr

    'assign pos% so that it goes into loop
    pos% = Instr (WithWhat$, ";")

    'loop while there are semicolons
    Do While (pos% > 0
        'determine position of semicolon
        pos% = InStr(WithWhat$, ";")

        If pos% > 0 Then
            'add to list box
            Whichlist.AddItem Left$(WithWhat$, pos% - 1)

            'assign new string
```

continues

689

LISTING 28.57. CONTINUED

```
            WithWhat$ = Right$(WithWhat$, Len(WithWhat$) - pos%)

        End If

    Loop

    'there may be text left
    If Len(WithWhat$) > 0 Then

        'add to list box
        Whichlist.AddItem WithWhat$

    End If

End Sub
```

THE *SAVEINI()* PROCEDURE

The SAVEINI() procedure saves the form configuration to the CHAP28.INI file. Following is a listing of the SAVEINI() procedure:

LISTING 28.58. CHAP28.BAS, SAVEINI().

```
Sub SAVEINI ()

    'declare variables
    Dim res%        'holds results
    Dim Temp$       'temporary string$

    'save polling frequency
    Temp$ = Trim$(Str$(DesiredInterval&))
    res% = WritePrivateProfileString(lpAppName$, lpKeyName1$, Temp$, lpFile$)

    'save Boolean for getting messages at logon
    If frmMain.menu_LogonMsg.Checked = False Then
        Temp$ = "FALSE"
    ElseIf frmMain.menu_LogonMsg.Checked = True Then
        Temp$ = "TRUE"
    End If
    res% = WritePrivateProfileString(lpAppName$, lpKeyName2$, Temp$, lpFile$)

    'save greeting
    Temp$ = frmRemark.txtGreeting.Text
    res% = WritePrivateProfileString(lpAppName$, lpKeyName3$, Temp$, lpFile$)

    'save closing
    Temp$ = frmRemark.txtClosing.Text
    res% = WritePrivateProfileString(lpAppName$, lpKeyName4$, Temp$, lpFile$)

    'save from
    Temp$ = frmMain.pnlFrom.Caption
    res% = WritePrivateProfileString(lpAppName$, lpKeyName5$, Temp$, lpFile$)

    'save to
```

```
Temp$ = ParseList(frmMain.lstTo)
res% = WritePrivateProfileString(lpAppName$, lpKeyName6$, Temp$, lpFile$)

'save subject
Temp$ = frmMain.txtSubject.Text
res% = WritePrivateProfileString(lpAppName$, lpKeyName7$, Temp$, lpFile$)

'save application
Temp$ = frmMain.txtApplication.Text
res% = WritePrivateProfileString(lpAppName$, lpKeyName8$, Temp$, lpFile$)

'save version
Temp$ = frmMain.txtVersion.Text
res% = WritePrivateProfileString(lpAppName$, lpKeyName9$, Temp$, lpFile$)

'save changes
Temp$ = ParseList(frmMain.lstChanges)
res% = WritePrivateProfileString(lpAppName$, lpKeyName10$, Temp$, lpFile$)

End Sub
```

THE CHAP28.INI FILE

This file contains the configuration to be used for default values to load into the application. This file is not necessary. If it is missing, all fields will be blank. The file can be created with a text editor, or by selecting the Save INI command button. The CHAP28.INI file is contained on the CD accompanying this book in the CHAP28 subdirectory. Following is a listing of the CHAP28.INI file:

LISTING 28.59. CHAP28.INI.

```
[Initialization]
PollFreq=120
LogonMessage=FALSE
Greeting=Sample Greeting
Closing=Sample Closing
From=Anthony T. Mann
To=Schmoe, Joe;Mouse, Mickey;Duck, Donald
Subject=New executable file on server
Application=Accounting Database
Version=1.0
Changes=1) New conversion rates updated;2) Added field for department
```

THE MAILIN.ICO FILE

This file contains the icon that is loaded into the picture box, pictMailIn (see Figure 28.9). Therefore, it can be copied to the form's icon property when minimized and new mail is received, and the user is logged in to the MAPI system. The MAILIN.ICO file is contained on the CD accompanying this book in the CHAP28 subdirectory.

FIGURE 28.9.
MAPI application
MAILIN icon.

THE MAILOUT.ICO FILE

This file contains the icon that has been attached to the form at design time (see Figure 28.10). It is also the file that is loaded into the picture box, `pictMailOut`, so that it can be copied to the form's icon property when minimized. The MAILOUT.ICO file is contained on the CD accompanying this book in the CHAP28 subdirectory.

FIGURE 28.10.
MAPI application
MAILOUT icon.

THE CHAP28.EXE FILE

This is the executable file that is distributable. If you distribute this application, you must include the following files:

◆ CHAP28.EXE

◆ CMDIALOG.VBX

◆ MSMAPI.VBX

◆ COMMDLG.DLL

◆ VBRUN300.DLL

◆ THREED.VBX

The CHAP28.EXE file and source files are contained on the CD accompanying this book in the CHAP28 subdirectory, while all DLLs and VBXs are in the RESOURCE subdirectory.

RELATING THE MAPI APPLICATION TO YOUR APPLICATION

The MAPI application shows how to send and receive MAPI messages. To do this, you need to call extended MAPI API functions.

You can also enhance this application by using Microsoft's E-Forms Designer. This is a development tool for Visual Basic that allows you to actually send a graphic of a form (not just text) to a recipient.

FINAL NOTES

This application was created on a standard VGA display using 16 colors. Your particular hardware could have adverse effects on the code the way it is written. You may need to modify it slightly.

Also, to implement this application, either runtime or design time, you must have a MAPI-compliant messaging system in place. If you load the Visual Basic project, CHAP28.MAK, and do not have a messaging system present, errors occur while trying to load the MSMAPI.VBX.

CHAPTER TWENTY-NINE

DYNAMIC DATA EXCHANGE (DDE) APPLICATION

DYNAMIC DATA EXCHANGE (DDE) IS ONE OF THE FIRST CONVENTIONS ADOPTED BY MICROSOFT TO ALLOW THE EXCHANGE OF DATA BETWEEN APPLICATIONS. THIS DDE APPLICATION SHOWS HOW TO RUN MICROSOFT EXCEL (IF IT IS NOT ALREADY RUNNING) AND FILL THE SPREADSHEET WITH DATA FROM A VISUAL BASIC GRID. THE REASON YOU WOULD POSSIBLY WANT TO DO THIS IS FOR FORMATTING PURPOSES. EXCEL HAS A MUCH EASIER AND BETTER PRINTOUT THAN THAT AVAILABLE IN VISUAL BASIC. EXCEL ALLOWS FOR SHADING AND BORDERS. IT IS POSSIBLE TO DO THIS IN VISUAL BASIC, BUT NOT WITHOUT A TREMENDOUS AMOUNT OF WORK. IT IS FAR EASIER TO INVOKE EXCEL AND LET IT DO THE WORK.

Unfortunately, DDE is not always reliable. This is largely due to timing issues between applications. You may experience some problems while running this application. A more reliable method of communicating between applications is *Object Linking and Embedding (OLE)*. For more information on DDE, refer to Chapter 14, "Dynamic Data Exchange (DDE)." For more information on OLE, refer to Chapter 15, "Object Linking and Embedding (OLE)" and the application in Chapter 30, "Object Linking and Embedding (OLE) Application."

This application allows for setting up a personal annual budget. The basic template is set up using the Visual Basic GRID.VBX control. You can then update Excel and either save or print the new budget.

Figure 29.1 shows the main screen (MAIN.FRM) at runtime.

FIGURE 29.1.
DDE application at runtime.

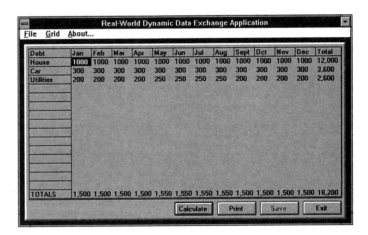

To use the application, select the File->Open menu option to open the file, or click on the Open command button. The file and password form appear. Type in the name of the file and password. The default file is "FINANCE.XLS" and the default password is "VBFINANCE." Note that this password is case sensitive. This loads Excel and populates the grid. This process could take a couple of minutes. Excel is populating 15 rows of data and 14 columns. This doesn't sound like a big deal but with DDE, it takes a while.

Once the grid is populated, you can make changes. To maintain integrity, Excel does all the calculations in the grid, which means that the DDE communication process has to take place all over again. To perform the calculations, select the Grid->Calculate menu option. It is probably a good idea to enter all the data at once, and then calculate.

 Even though you are presented a text box to specify the Excel filename, this box allows you to specify only a different path for the file. The program still expects the filename "FINANCE.XLS" to work properly.

696

You can save changes to the Excel spreadsheet by selecting the File->Save menu option, or by clicking the Save command button. This will actually save the spreadsheet, not the grid. Nothing is actually saved in Visual Basic.

You can also print the Excel spreadsheet by selecting the File->Print menu option or by clicking the Print command button. This printing is performed by Excel, not Visual Basic.

Since there is no way to put the focus on a cell in column 0 of the grid, you cannot click on a cell to label the debt. You must select the Grid->Label Debt menu option to do this through an InputBox() function.

CODE LISTINGS

The DDE application contains the following files and listings, if appropriate:

- CHAP29.MAK
- MAIN.FRM
- FILEPW.FRM
- ABOUT.FRM
- CHAP29.BAS
- FINANCE.XLS
- CHAP29.ICO
- CHAP29.EXE

THE CHAP29.MAK FILE

CHAP29.MAK is the project file for the DDE application, CHAP29.EXE. It contains a listing of all the files necessary to load the project into Visual Basic. The CHAP29.MAK file is contained on the CD accompanying this book in the CHAP29 subdirectory. The file listing is

LISTING 29.1. CHAP29.MAK.

```
MAIN.FRM
FILEPW.FRM
ABOUT.FRM
CHAP29.BAS
THREED.VBX
GRID.VBX
MSMASKED.VBX
ProjWinSize=152,402,248,215
ProjWinShow=2
IconForm="frmMain"
Title="DDE"
ExeName="CHAP29.EXE"
```

THE MAIN.FRM FILE

MAIN.FRM is one of three forms in this application. It is the startup form for the application as well as the form used to enter data into the grid to send to the Excel spreadsheet. Figure 29.1 presents the main form as it appears at runtime. Figure 29.2 presents the form at design time. Table 29.1 lists all the relevant properties of each control on the form that have been changed from their standard default values. The MAIN.FRM file is contained on the CD accompanying this book in the CHAP29 subdirectory.

FIGURE 29.2.
DDE application MAIN.FRM at design time.

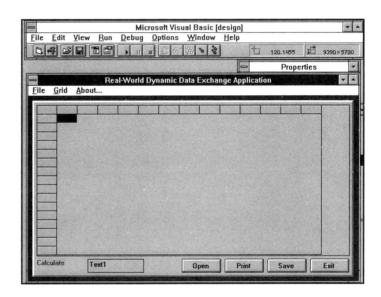

TABLE 29.1. PROPERTIES OF EACH CONTROL ON MAIN.FRM.

Object	Control Type	Property	Value
frmMain	Form	BackColor	&H00404000&
		Caption	"Real-World Dynamic Data Exchange Application"
		Height	5730
		Icon	"CHAP29.ICO"
		Left	0
		MaxButton	False
		Top	210
		Width	9390

Object	Control Type	Property	Value
Panel3D1	SSPanel	BackColor	&H00C0C0C0&
		BevelWidth	3
		Font3D	None
		ForeColor	&H0000FFFF&
		Height	4815
		Left	120
		Top	120
		Width	9015
cmdSave	CommandButton	Caption	"Save"
		Height	375
		Left	6600
		Top	4320
		Width	1095
cmdExit	CommandButton	Caption	"Exit"
		Height	375
		Left	7800
		Top	4320
		Width	1095
cmdPrint	CommandButton	Caption	"Print"
		Height	375
		Left	5400
		Top	4320
		Width	1095
cmdOpen	CommandButton	Caption	"Open"
		Height	375
		Left	4200
		Top	4320
		Width	1095

continues

TABLE 29.1. CONTINUED

Object	Control Type	Property	Value
Grid1	Grid	Cols	14
		Height	4120
		Left	120
		Rows	17
		Top	120
		Width	8790
Text1	TextBox	Height	375
		Left	1560
		Text	""
		Top	4320
		Visible	False
		Width	1575
lblCalculate	Label	BackColor	&H00C0C0C0&
		Caption	"Calculate"
		ForeColor	&H000000FF&
		Height	255
		Left	120
		Top	4320
		Width	975
menu_about	Menu	Caption	"&About"
menu_file	Menu	Caption	"&File"
menu_open	Menu	Caption	"&Open"
menu_print	Menu	Caption	"&Print"
menu_save	Menu	Caption	"&Save"
menu_exit	Menu	Caption	"&Exit"
menu_grid	Menu	Caption	"&Grid"
menu_label	Menu	Caption	"&Label Debt"
menu_calculate	Menu	Caption	"&Calculate"

Function, Subroutine, and Event Procedures

There are several procedures of code for each object(control) that comprise this form. Each is listed in the following sections.

The (general) Object

The (general) object contains declarations and procedures at the form level. The procedures for the (general) object are

◆ (declarations)

◆ PokeData()

◆ PokeLabel()

The (declarations) Procedure

The (declarations) procedure contains only one line of code. All variable declarations are in CHAP29.BAS. Following is a listing of the (declarations) procedure:

Listing 29.2. MAIN.FRM,(GENERAL)(DECLARATIONS).

```
Option Explicit
```

The PokeData() Procedure

The PokeData() procedure pokes data into Excel, one cell at a time. This procedure is necessary only to simulate pressing the Enter key. If this was not done, moving between cells with the mouse or arrow keys would not update Excel. The PokeData() procedure accepts two arguments. The first, ToRow%, is the row in the Visual Basic Grid to poke. The second, ToCol%, is the column in the Visual Basic Grid to poke. Following is a listing of the PokeData() procedure:

Listing 29.3. MAIN.FRM,PokeData().

```
Sub PokeData (ByVal ToRow%, ByVal ToCol%)

    If Populating% = True Then Exit Sub

    'no link
    text1.LinkMode = NONE

    'set topic
    text1.LinkTopic = "EXCEL¦FINANCE"

    'set cell location
    text1.LinkItem = "R" + Trim$(Str$(OldRow% + 4)) + "C" + Trim$(Str$(OldCol% + 1))
```

continues

701

LISTING 29.3. CONTINUED

```
            'set link to automatic
            text1.LinkMode = AUTOMATIC

            Populating% = True
            'move to old position
            grid1.Row = OldRow%
            grid1.Col = OldCol%

            text1.Text = grid1.Text

            'move to new position
            grid1.Row = ToRow%
            grid1.Col = ToCol%
            Populating% = False

            'poke new value
            text1.LinkPoke

            'handle error
            On Error GoTo pokeerror

            'set mode back to manual
            text1.LinkMode = NONE

            Exit Sub

    pokeerror:
            'display error
            MsgBox Error$

            'set mode back to manual
            text1.LinkMode = MANUAL

            'exit
            Exit Sub

            'avoid errors
            Resume

    End Sub
```

THE *PokeLabel( )* PROCEDURE

The PokeLabel( ) procedure pokes data into Excel, one cell at a time. This procedure is similar to the PokeData( ) procedure except that this procedure is called to populate every cell in the spreadsheet, one at a time. The PokeLabel( ) procedure accepts three arguments. The first, WhatData$, is the data to poke. The second, ToRow%, is the row in the Visual Basic Grid to poke. The third, ToCol%, is the column in the Visual Basic Grid to poke. Following is a listing of the PokeLabel( ) procedure:

Listing 29.4. MAIN.FRM, PokeLabel().

```
Sub PokeLabel (ByVal WhatData$, ByVal ToRow%, ByVal ToCol%)

    'no link
    text1.LinkMode = NONE

    'set topic
    text1.LinkTopic = "EXCEL¦FINANCE"

    'set cell location
    text1.LinkItem = "R" + Trim$(Str$(ToRow% + 4)) + "C" + Trim$(Str$(ToCol% + 1))

    'handle error
    On Error GoTo pokelinkerror

    'set link to automatic
    text1.LinkMode = AUTOMATIC

    'assign data to text control
    text1.Text = WhatData$

    'poke new value
    text1.LinkPoke

    'set mode back to manual
    text1.LinkMode = NONE

    Exit Sub

pokelinkerror:
    'display error
    MsgBox Error$

    'set mode back to manual
    text1.LinkMode = MANUAL

    'exit
    Exit Sub

    'avoid errors
    Resume

End Sub
```

The *cmdExit* Control

cmdExit is the name of the command button control that, when clicked, starts the exiting process by invoking the form_Unload() event. The cmdExit control has code in only one event procedure. It is

◆ cmdExit_Click()

THE *cmdExit_Click()* EVENT PROCEDURE

The cmdExit_Click() event procedure simply unloads the form, ending the application. Following is a listing of the cmdExit_Click() event procedure:

LISTING 29.5. MAIN.FRM,cmdExit_Click().

```
Sub cmdExit_Click ()

    'exit
    Unload frmMain

End Sub
```

THE *cmdOpen* CONTROL

cmdOpen is the name of the command button control that, when clicked, opens an Excel file via the frmFile form. The cmdOpen control has code in only one event procedure. It is

◆ cmdOpen_Click()

THE *cmdOpen_Click()* EVENT PROCEDURE

The cmdOpen_Click() event procedure allows the user to open an Excel spreadsheet file. Following is a listing of the cmdOpen_Click() event procedure:

LISTING 29.6. MAIN.FRM,cmdOpen_Click().

```
Sub cmdOpen_Click ()

    'declare variables
    Dim res%          'holds results

    If FirstTimeEnter% = False Then
        'user did not press enter after entering the last figures
        'simulate pressing enter now
        Call PokeData(grid1.Row, grid1.Col)

    End If

    If GlobalPassword$ = "" Or GlobalFileName$ = "" Then
        'no password or file name, but is finance running?
        res% = FindWindow(0&, "Microsoft Excel - FINANCE.XLS")
        If res% > 0 Then
            'the window is already open, don't ask for password
            Call OpenExcel
        Else
            frmFile.Show
        End If
```

```
    Else
        Call OpenExcel
    End If

End Sub
```

THE *cmdPrint* CONTROL

cmdPrint is the name of the command button control that, when clicked, prints an Excel file through Excel, not Visual Basic. The control has code in only one event procedure. It is

◆ cmdPrint_Click()

THE *cmdPrint_Click()* EVENT PROCEDURE

The cmdPrint_Click() event procedure allows the user to print the file through Excel. Following is a listing of the cmdPrint_Click() event procedure:

LISTING 29.7. MAIN.FRM,cmdPrint_Click().

```
Sub cmdPrint_Click ()

    'declare variables
    Dim cmd$          'command building string
    Dim m$
    Dim res%

    'check calculate label-if visible, printing won't be the
    'same as what the user sees on the screen
    If lblCalculate.Visible = True Then
        m$ = "You have not calculated!" + Chr$(13)
        m$ = m$ + "The printed spreadsheet will not" + Chr$(13)
        m$ = m$ + "be the same as what you see here." + Chr$(13)
        m$ = m$ + "          Continue anyway?"
        res% = MsgBox(m$, 292, "Warning")
        If res% = IDNO Then Exit Sub
    End If

    'no link
    text1.LinkMode = NONE

    'set topic
    text1.LinkTopic = "EXCEL¦FINANCE"

    'set arbitrary cell location, because VB needs it
    text1.LinkItem = "R1C1"

    'set link to automatic
    text1.LinkMode = AUTOMATIC

    'build print file string
    cmd$ = "[PRINT]"
```

continues

LISTING 29.7. CONTINUED

```
        'handle error
        On Error GoTo printerror

        'execute printing
        text1.LinkExecute cmd$

        'set mode back to manual
        text1.LinkMode = MANUAL

        Exit Sub

printerror:
    If Err <> 286 Then  'timeout
        'display error
        MsgBox Error$
    End If

        'set mode back to manual
        text1.LinkMode = MANUAL

        'exit
        Exit Sub

        'avoid errors
        Resume

End Sub
```

For more information about printing, refer to Chapter 6, "Printing."

THE *cmdSave* CONTROL

cmdSave is the name of the command button control that, when clicked, saves an Excel file through Excel, not Visual Basic. The cmdSave control has code in only one event procedure. It is

◆ cmdSave_Click()

THE *cmdSave_Click()* EVENT PROCEDURE

The cmdSave_Click() event procedure allows the user to save an Excel spreadsheet. Following is a listing of the cmdSave_Click() event procedure:

LISTING 29.8. MAIN.FRM, cmdSave_Click().

```
Sub cmdSave_Click ()

    'declare variables
    Dim cmd$          'command building string
```

```
    Dim m$
    Dim res%

    'check calculate label-if visible, printing won't be the
    'same as what the user sees on the screen
    If lblCalculate.Visible = True Then
        m$ = "You have not calculated!" + Chr$(13)
        m$ = m$ + "The printed spreadsheet will not" + Chr$(13)
        m$ = m$ + "be the same as what you see here." + Chr$(13)
        m$ = m$ + "          Continue anyway?"
        res% = MsgBox(m$, 292, "Warning")
        If res% = IDNO Then Exit Sub
    End If

    'no link
    text1.LinkMode = NONE

    'set topic
    text1.LinkTopic = "EXCEL¦FINANCE"

    'set arbitrary cell location, because VB needs it
    text1.LinkItem = "R1C1"

    'set link to automatic
    text1.LinkMode = AUTOMATIC

    'build save file string
    cmd$ = "[SAVE()]"

    'handle error
    On Error GoTo saveerror

    'execute saving file
    text1.LinkExecute cmd$

    'set mode back to manual
    text1.LinkMode = MANUAL

    'disable save
    cmdSave.Enabled = False
    menu_save.Enabled = False

    'exit
    Exit Sub

saveerror:
    If Err <> 286 Then 'timeout
        'display error
        MsgBox Error$
    End If

    'set mode back to manual
    text1.LinkMode = MANUAL

    'disable save
    cmdSave.Enabled = False
    menu_save.Enabled = False
```

continues   707

LISTING 29.8. CONTINUED

```
    'exit
    Exit Sub

    'avoid errors
    Resume

End Sub
```

THE *Form* OBJECT

The Form object has code in two event procedures. They are

◆ Form_Load()

◆ Form_Unload()

THE *Form_Load()* EVENT PROCEDURE

The Form_Load() event procedure initializes the grid and other controls, centers the main, and loads the main form. Following is a listing of the Form_Load() event procedure:

LISTING 29.9. MAIN.FRM,Form_Load().

```
Sub Form_Load ()

    'change cursor
    Screen.MousePointer = HOURGLASS

    'center the form
    CenterForm Me
    Const COLWIDTH = 555

    'initialize
    grid1.ColWidth(0) = 1185
    grid1.ColWidth(1) = COLWIDTH
    grid1.ColWidth(2) = COLWIDTH
    grid1.ColWidth(3) = COLWIDTH
    grid1.ColWidth(4) = COLWIDTH
    grid1.ColWidth(5) = COLWIDTH
    grid1.ColWidth(6) = COLWIDTH
    grid1.ColWidth(7) = COLWIDTH
    grid1.ColWidth(8) = COLWIDTH
    grid1.ColWidth(9) = COLWIDTH
    grid1.ColWidth(10) = COLWIDTH
    grid1.ColWidth(11) = COLWIDTH
    grid1.ColWidth(12) = COLWIDTH
    grid1.ColWidth(13) = 700

    cmdPrint.Enabled = False
    cmdSave.Enabled = False
    lblCalculate.Visible = False
    FirstTimeEnter% = True
```

```
        menu_calculate.Enabled = False
        menu_save.Enabled = False
        menu_print_enabled = False

        'change cursor
        Screen.MousePointer = DEFAULT

End Sub
```

The *Form_Unload()* Event Procedure

The Form_Unload() event procedure prompts the user to confirm ending the program. Following is a listing of the Form_Unload() event procedure:

Listing 29.10. MAIN.FRM, Form_Unload().

```
Sub Form_Unload (Cancel As Integer)

    'declare variables
    Dim m$          'message constructor
    Dim res%        'holds results
    Dim cmd$        'command building string
    Dim loopcount%  'loop counting variables

    If cmdSave.Enabled = True Then
        m$ = "Exit without saving changes?"
        res% = MsgBox(m$, 292, "Warning")
        If res% = IDNO Then Exit Sub
    End If


    m$ = "Are you sure you want to Exit?"
    res% = MsgBox(m$, 292, "Warning")
    If res% = IDNO Then
        Cancel = True
        'exit
        Exit Sub
    End If

    'find out if excel is loaded
    res% = FindWindow("XLMAIN", 0&)
    If res% = 0 Then
        'find out if excel is minimized
        res% = FindWindow("EXCEL>", 0&)
    End If

    If res% <> 0 Then
        'close down excel

        'no link
        text1.LinkMode = NONE

        'set topic
        text1.LinkTopic = "EXCEL¦FINANCE"
```

continues 709

LISTING 29.10. CONTINUED

```
            'set arbitrary cell location, because VB needs it
            text1.LinkItem = "R1C1"

            'handle error
            On Error GoTo exiterror

            'set link to automatic
            text1.LinkMode = AUTOMATIC

            'build quit string
            cmd$ = "[QUIT()]"

            'execute quitting
            text1.LinkExecute cmd$

        End If

        'end
        End

exiterror:

        'give enough time for excel to close
        For loopcount% = 0 To 25
            DoEvents
        Next loopcount%

        'even if there is an error, excel could have closed-check
        res% = FindWindow("XLMAIN", 0&)
        If res% = 0 Then
            'find out if excel is minimized
            res% = FindWindow("EXCEL>", 0&)
        End If

        If res% <> 0 Then
            MsgBox "Error Closing Excel-Close Manually!"
        End If
        End

        Resume

End Sub
```

THE *Grid1* CONTROL

Grid1 is the name of the Grid control used to enter and display data to and from Excel. The Grid1 control has code in two event procedures. They are

◆ Grid1_KeyPress()

◆ Grid1_RowColChange()

The *Grid1_KeyPress()* Event Procedure

The `Grid1_KeyPress` event procedure is used because, by default, the grid does not show any characters typed from the keyboard. There has to be code to update the current cell location. Following is a listing of the `Grid1_KeyPress()` event procedure:

Listing 29.11. MAIN.FRM, `Grid1_KeyPress()`.

```
Sub Grid1_KeyPress (KeyAscii As Integer)

    Select Case (KeyAscii)
        Case KEY_DOWN, KEY_UP, KEY_LEFT, KEY_RIGHT:
        Case 48 To 57:
            If FirstTimeEnter% = False Then
                'assign text + new text
                grid1.Text = grid1.Text + Chr$(KeyAscii)
            Else
                'assign new text
                grid1.Text = Chr$(KeyAscii)
                FirstTimeEnter% = False
            End If
            'show that calculate is needed
            lblCalculate.Visible = True
        Case KEY_RETURN:
            'flag for the next time entered
            FirstTimeEnter% = True
            'send the value of this cell to corresponding cell in excel
            Call PokeData(grid1.Row, grid1.Col)
        Case KEY_BACK:
            'test for length to avoid errors
            If Len(grid1.Text) > 0 Then
                grid1.Text = Left$(grid1.Text, Len(grid1.Text) - 1)
            End If
    End Select


    'memorize current positions and assign them to old positions
    OldCol% = grid1.Col
    OldRow% = grid1.Row

    'enable save
    cmdSave.Enabled = True
    menu_save.Enabled = True


End Sub
```

The *Grid1_RowColChange()* Event Procedure

The `Grid1_RowColChange` event procedure is used to alert the program that the user has left the current cell. This is significant because the application needs to know that a recalculation needs to take place. The user does not press enter. This event is generated by the system when the mouse

is clicked on a different cell, or the arrow keys are used. Following is a listing of the
Grid1_RowColChange() event procedure:

LISTING 29.12. MAIN.FRM, Grid1_RowColChange().

```
Sub Grid1_RowColChange ()

    If Populating% = True Then Exit Sub

    'flag first time
    FirstTimeEnter% = True

    If (grid1.Row = grid1.Rows - 1) Or (grid1.Row = 0) Then
        'positioned on totals row or headings row-not allowed
        grid1.Col = OldCol%
        grid1.Row = OldRow%

        'exit
        Exit Sub
    End If

    If (grid1.Col = grid1.Cols - 1) Or (grid1.Col = 0) Then
        'positioned on totals col or headings col-not allowed
        grid1.Col = OldCol%
        grid1.Row = OldRow%

        'exit
        Exit Sub
    End If

    'send the value of this cell to corresponding cell in excel
    Call PokeData(grid1.Row, grid1.Col)

End Sub
```

THE *menu* OBJECT

The menu object was created using Visual Basic's built-in Menu editor. It has code associated
with seven Click() event procedures. They are

- ◆ menu_about()
- ◆ menu_calculate()
- ◆ menu_exit()
- ◆ menu_label()
- ◆ menu_open()
- ◆ menu_print()
- ◆ menu_save()

The *menu_about_Click()* Event Procedure

The menu_about_Click() event procedure simply shows the about form for program information. Following is a listing of the menu_about_click() event procedure:

Listing 29.13. MAIN.FRM, menu_about_Click().

```
Sub menu_about_Click ()

    'show about form
    frmAbout.Show MODAL

End Sub
```

The *menu_calculate_Click()* Event Procedure

The menu_calculate_Click() event procedure re-calculates the values of the grid (through Excel) simply by calling the routine that opens the Excel spreadsheet. Following is a listing of the menu_calculate_Click() event procedure:

Listing 29.14. MAIN.FRM, menu_calculate_Click().

```
Sub menu_calculate_Click ()

    'open button is used for calculating also
    Call cmdOpen_Click

End Sub
```

The *menu_exit_Click()* Event Procedure

The menu_exit_Click() event procedure starts the program exit procedure, invoked in the Form_Unload() event. Following is a listing of the menu_exit_Click() event procedure:

Listing 29.15. MAIN.FRM, menu_exit_Click().

```
Sub menu_exit_Click ()

    'exit
    Unload frmMain

End Sub
```

The *menu_label_Click()* Event Procedure

The menu_label_Click() event procedure allows for the labeling of the grid column 0. This is necessary because you cannot click on this column to type the text directly. Following is a listing of the menu_label_Click() event procedure:

LISTING 29.16. MAIN.FRM, menu_label_Click().

```vb
Sub menu_label_Click ()

    'declare variables
    Dim Label$       'holds new label from inputbox
    Dim m$           'message constructor
    Dim prevcol%     'holds previous column

    If (grid1.Row = grid1.Rows - 1) Or grid1.Row = 0 Then
        m$ = "You cannot change the label " + Chr$(13)
        m$ = m$ + "for the first or last row!"
        MsgBox m$
        Exit Sub
    End If

    'flag populating
    Populating% = True

    'remember old col
    prevcol% = grid1.Col

    'move col to first position(where label will be)
    grid1.Col = 0
    If grid1.Text = "" Then
        m$ = "Current Label is not set" + Chr$(13)
    Else
        m$ = "Current Label is" + grid1.Text + Chr$(13)
    End If
    m$ = m$ + "Please enter new label"
    Label$ = InputBox$(m$)

    'set text
    grid1.Text = Label$

    'set back to old position
    grid1.Col = prevcol%

    'Unflag populating
    Populating% = False

    'poke data
    Call PokeLabel(Label$, grid1.Row, 0)

    'enable save
    cmdSave.Enabled = True
    menu_save.Enabled = True

    'enable calculate label
    lblCalculate.Visible = True

End Sub
```

THE *menu_open_Click()* EVENT PROCEDURE

The menu_open_Click() event procedure simply invokes the frmFile form to open the Excel file. Following is a listing of the menu_open_Click() event procedure:

LISTING 29.17. MAIN.FRM,menu_open_Click().

```
Sub menu_open_Click ()

    'open the file
    Call cmdOpen_Click

End Sub
```

THE *menu_print_Click()* EVENT PROCEDURE

The menu_print_Click() event procedure simply invokes the cmdPrint command button to print the Excel file. Following is a listing of the menu_print_Click() event procedure:

LISTING 29.18. MAIN.FRM,menu_print_Click().

```
Sub menu_print_Click ()

    'print the file
    Call cmdPrint_Click

End Sub
```

THE *menu_print_Click()* EVENT PROCEDURE

The menu_save_Click() event procedure simply invokes the cmdSave command button to save the Excel file. Following is a listing of the menu_save_Click() event procedure:

LISTING 29.19. MAIN.FRM,menu_save_Click().

```
Sub menu_save_Click ()

    'save the file
    Call cmdSave_Click

End Sub
```

THE FILEPW.FRM FILE

FILEPW.FRM is one of three forms in this application. It is used to open the Excel file. The default file name is "FINANCE.XLS." The default password expected by the file is "VBFINANCE." Figure 29.3 presents the form as it appears at runtime. Fundamentally, there is no difference in the form at design time, so it is not presented. Table 29.3 lists all the relevant properties of each control on the form that have been changed from their standard default values. The FILEPW.FRM file is contained on the CD accompanying this book in the CHAP29 subdirectory.

FIGURE 29.3.
DDE application
FILEPW.FRM at
runtime.

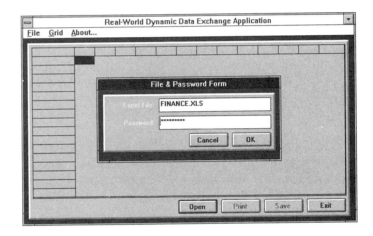

TABLE 29.2. PROPERTIES OF EACH CONTROL ON FILEPW.FRM.

Object	Control Type	Property	Value
frmFile	Form	BackColor	&H00404000&
		Caption	"File & Password Form"
		Height	2325
		Left	1680
		MaxButton	False
		MinButton	False
		Top	2955
		Width	5160
Panel3D1	SSPanel	BackColor	&H00C0C0C0&
		BevelWidth	3
		Font3D	None
		ForeColor	&H0000FFFF&
		Height	1575
		Left	120
		Top	120
		Width	4815

Object	Control Type	Property	Value
cmdCancel	CommandButton	Caption	"Cancel"
		Height	375
		Left	2400
		Top	1080
		Width	1095
cmdOK	CommandButton	Caption	"OK"
		Height	375
		Left	3600
		Top	1080
		Width	1095
mePassword	MaskEdBox	BackColor	&H00FFFFFF&
		Height	375
		Left	1560
		Mask	"-"
		MaxLength	1
		PromptChar	"_"
		Top	600
		Width	3135
txtFileName	TextBox	BackColor	&H00FFFFFF&
		Height	375
		Left	1560
		Top	120
		Width	3135
Panel3D3	SSPanel	Alignment	Right Justify - Middle
		BackColor	&H00C0C0C0&
		BevelOuter	None
		BevelWidth	3
		Caption	"Password:"
		Font3D	None
		ForeColor	&H0000FFFF&
		Height	375

continues

717

T ABLE 29.2. CONTINUED

Object	Control Type	Property	Value
		Left	120
		Top	600
		Width	1335
Panel3D2	SSPanel	Alignment	Right Justify - Middle
		BackColor	&H00C0C0C0&
		BevelOuter	None
		BevelWidth	3
		Caption	"Excel File:"
		Font3D	None
		ForeColor	&H0000FFFF&
		Height	375
		Left	120
		Top	120
		Width	1335

FUNCTION, SUBROUTINE, AND EVENT PROCEDURES

There are several procedures of code for each object(control) that comprise this form. Each is listed in the following sections.

THE *(general)* OBJECT

The (general) object contains form level declarations and no form level procedures. The procedure for the (general) object is:

◆ (declarations)

THE *(declarations)* PROCEDURE

The (declarations) procedure contains declarations used in the form, FILEPW.FRM. Following is a listing of the (declarations) procedure:

LISTING 29.20. FILEPW.FRM, (general) (declarations).

```
Option Explicit

'declare variables
Dim Password$          'holds unmasked password
```

THE *cmdCancel* CONTROL

cmdCancel is the name of the command button control that, when clicked, closes the form by invoking the form_Unload() event. The cmdCancel control has code in only one event procedure. It is

◆ cmdCancel_Click()

THE *cmdCancel_Click()* EVENT PROCEDURE

Following is a listing of the cmdCancel_Click() event procedure:

LISTING 29.21. FILEPW.FRM,cmdCancel_Click().

```
Sub cmdCancel_Click ()

    'unload form
    Unload Me

End Sub
```

THE *cmdOK* CONTROL

cmdOK is the name of the command button control that, when clicked, opens the specified Excel file by calling the OpenExcel() routine. The control has code in only one event procedure. It is

◆ cmdOK_Click()

THE *cmdOK_Click()* EVENT PROCEDURE

Following is a listing of the cmdOK_Click() event procedure:

LISTING 29.22. FILEPW.FRM,cmdOK_Click().

```
Sub cmdOK_click ()

    'declare variables
    Dim m$

    GlobalFileName$ = txtFileName.Text
    GlobalPassword$ = Password$

    If GlobalFileName$ <> "" And GlobalPassword$ <> "" Then
        'open excel and file
        Call OpenExcel
    Else
        m$ = "You must specify a FileName and Password!"
        MsgBox m$
    End If
```

continues

LISTING 29.22. CONTINUED

```
    'hide form
    frmFile.Hide

End Sub
```

THE *Form* OBJECT

The Form object has code in one event procedure. It is

◆ Form_Load()

THE *Form_Load()* EVENT PROCEDURE

The Form_Load() event simply calls the routing to center the form and initialize the text box. Following is a listing of the Form_Load() event procedure:

LISTING 29.23. FILEPW.FRM, Form_Load().

```
Sub Form_Load ()

    'center the form
    CenterForm frmFile

    'initialize
    txtFileName.Text = "FINANCE.XLS"

End Sub
```

THE *mePassword* CONTROL

mePassword is the name of the Masked Edit control that keeps track of the password but displays asterisks (*) instead of the actual characters being typed. The mePassword control has code in two event procedures. They are

◆ mePassword_GotFocus()
◆ mePassword_KeyPress()

THE *mePassword_GotFocus()* EVENT PROCEDURE

The mePassword_GotFocus() procedure re-initializes the control. Following is a listing of the mePassword_GotFocus() event procedure:

LISTING 29.24. FILEPW.FRM,mePassword_GotFocus().

```
Sub mePassword_GotFocus ()

    'initialize
    mePassword.Mask = ""
    mePassword.Text = ""
    Password$ = ""

End Sub
```

THE *mePassword_KeyPress()* EVENT PROCEDURE

The mePassword_KeyPress() procedure handles displaying the asterisk on the screen, while keeping track of the password. Following is a listing of the mePassword_KeyPress() event procedure:

LISTING 29.25. FILEPW.FRM,mePassword_KeyPress().

```
Sub mePassword_KeyPress (KeyAscii As Integer)

    Select Case (KeyAscii)
        Case 48 To 57:   'numbers
            If mePassword.Mask <> "-" Then
                mePassword.Mask = mePassword.Mask + "*"
            Else
                mePassword.Mask = "*"
            End If
            Password$ = Password$ + Chr$(KeyAscii)
        Case 65 To 90:   'Upper Case
            If mePassword.Mask <> "-" Then
                mePassword.Mask = mePassword.Mask + "*"
            Else
                mePassword.Mask = "*"
            End If
            Password$ = Password$ + Chr$(KeyAscii)
        Case 97 To 122:  'Lower Case
            If mePassword.Mask <> "-" Then
                mePassword.Mask = mePassword.Mask + "*"
            Else
                mePassword.Mask = "*"
            End If
            Password$ = Password$ + Chr$(KeyAscii)
        Case KEY_RETURN:
            'same as clicking on OK
            Call cmdOK_click
    End Select

End Sub
```

REM The reason for the identical code in the first three cases in the preceding code is because you are trying to trap only numbers and upper- and lowercase letters. While you would not normally have redundant code, it is presented for clarity.

THE ABOUT.FRM FILE

ABOUT.FRM is one of three forms in this application. It shows information about the application. Figure 29.4 presents the form as it appears at runtime. Fundamentally, there is no difference in the form at design time, so it is not presented. Table 29.4 lists all the relevant properties of each control on the form that have been changed from their standard default values. The ABOUT.FRM file is contained on the CD accompanying this book in the CHAP29 subdirectory.

FIGURE 29.4.
DDE application
ABOUT.FRM at
runtime.

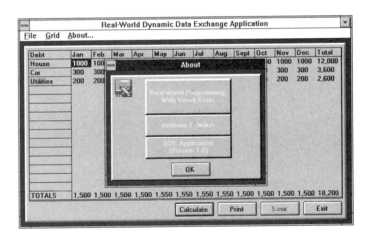

TABLE 29.3. PROPERTIES OF EACH CONTROL ON ABOUT.FRM.

Object	Control Type	Property	Value
frmAbout	Form	BackColor	&H00404000&
		Caption	"About"
		Height	3525
		Left	1035
		MaxButton	False
		MinButton	False
		Top	1140
		Width	4545

Object	Control Type	Property	Value
pnlMain	SSPanel	BackColor	&H00C0C0C0&
		BevelWidth	3
		Caption	" "
		Font3D	None
		ForeColor	&H00C0C0C0&
		Height	2995
		Left	120
		RoundedCorners	False
		ShadowColor	Black
		Top	120
		Width	4215
pnl1	SSPanel	BackColor	&H00C0C0C0&
		BevelWidth	3
		Caption	"Real-World Programming With Visual Basic"
		Font3D	None
		ForeColor	&H0000FFFF&
		Height	975
		Left	960
		RoundedCorners	False
		ShadowColor	Black
		Top	120
		Width	2415
pnl2	SSPanel	BackColor	&H00C0C0C0&
		BevelWidth	3
		Caption	"Anthony T. Mann"
		Font3D	None
		ForeColor	&H0000FFFF&
		Height	615
		Left	960
		RoundedCorners	False
		ShadowColor	Black

continues

TABLE 29.3. CONTINUED

Object	Control Type	Property	Value
		Top	1080
		Width	2415
pnl3	SSPanel	BackColor	&H00C0C0C0&
		BevelWidth	3
		Caption	"DDE Application (Version 1.0)"
		Font3D	None
		ForeColor	&H0000FFFF&
		Height	615
		Left	960
		RoundedCorners	False
		ShadowColor	Black
		Top	1680
		Width	2415
cmdOK	CommandButton	Caption	"OK"
		Height	375
		Left	1680
		Top	2400
		Width	1095
pictAbout	PictureBox	Autosize	True
		BackColor	&H00C0C0C0&
		BorderStyle	None
		Height	615
		Left	120
		Top	120
		Width	735

FUNCTION, SUBROUTINE, AND EVENT PROCEDURES

There are several procedures of code for each object(control) that comprise this form. Each is listed in the following sections.

The (general) object contains only one form level declaration and no form level procedures. The procedure for the (general) object is

◆ (declarations)

THE *(declarations)* PROCEDURE

The (declarations) procedure contains only one line of declarations used in the form, ABOUT.FRM. It is only to allow for variable syntax checking and forcing the declaration of variables in each procedure. Following is a listing of the (declarations) procedure:

LISTING 29.26. ABOUT.FRM, (general) (declarations).

```
Option Explicit
```

THE *cmdOK* CONTROL

cmdOK is the name of the command button control that, when clicked, closes the frmAbout form. The cmdOK control has code in only one event procedure. It is

◆ cmdOK_Click()

THE *cmdOK_Click()* EVENT PROCEDURE

The cmdOK_Click() event procedure simply unloads the form. Following is a listing of the cmdOK_Click() event procedure:

LISTING 29.27. ABOUT.FRM, cmdOK_Click().

```
Sub cmdOK_Click ()

    'unload
    Unload frmAbout

End Sub
```

THE *Form* OBJECT

The object itself has code in only one event procedure. It is

◆ Form_Load()

THE *Form_Load()* EVENT PROCEDURE

The Form_Load() event procedure centers the form and assigns an icon to the pictAbout control. Following is a listing of the Form_Load() event procedure:

LISTING 29.28. ABOUT.FRM,Form_Load().

```
Sub Form_Load ()

    'center form
    CenterForm Me

    'load icon
    pictAbout.Picture = frmMain.Icon

End Sub
```

THE CHAP29.BAS FILE

CHAP29.BAS is the module that contains application level variables and procedures. The CHAP29.BAS file is contained on the CD accompanying this book in the CHAP29 subdirectory.

FUNCTION, SUBROUTINE, AND EVENT PROCEDURES

There are several procedures of code for each object(control) that comprise this module. Each is listed in the following sections.

The (general) object contains application level variables and procedures. The procedures for the (general) object are

◆ (declarations)

◆ CenterForm()

◆ OpenExcel()

◆ PopulateGrid()

THE *(declarations)* PROCEDURE

The (declarations) procedure contains variables and API declarations used in the application. Following is a listing of the (declarations) procedure:

LISTING 29.29. CHAP29.BAS,(general)(declarations).

```
Option Explicit

'declare varibles
Global GlobalPassword$    'holds excel spreadsheet password
Global GlobalFileName$    'holds excel spreadsheet filename


Global Populating%    'flag for populating grid
Global OldCol%
Global OldRow%
```

```
Global FirstTimeEnter% 'variable flag which is true if this is the first key pressed
                       'this would effectively clear the text box before entering text

'mousepointers
Global Const HOURGLASS = 11
Global Const DEFAULT = 0

'messageboxes
Global Const IDNO = 7
Global Const IDYES = 6

'links
Global Const NONE = 0
Global Const MANUAL = 0      ' 0 - Manual
Global Const AUTOMATIC = 1 ' 1 - Automatic

'keys
Global Const KEY_LEFT = &H25
Global Const KEY_UP = &H26
Global Const KEY_RIGHT = &H27
Global Const KEY_DOWN = &H28
Global Const KEY_BACK = &H8
Global Const KEY_RETURN = &HD

'API declares
Declare Function FindWindow Lib "User" (ByVal lpClassName As Any, ByVal
 lpWindowName As Any) As Integer
Global Const MODAL = 1
```

The *CenterForm()* Procedure

The CenterForm() procedure simply centers the form in the client area upon form loading. The CenterForm() procedure accepts one argument, F. It is the actual form to be centered. Following is a listing of the CenterForm() procedure:

Listing 29.30. CHAP29.BAS, CenterForm().

```
Sub CenterForm (F As Form)

    'center the form
    F.Left = (screen.Width - F.Width) / 2
    F.Top = (screen.Height - F.Height) / 2

End Sub
```

For more information on manipulating graphics and forms, refer to Chapter 5, "Graphics."

THE *OpenExcel()* PROCEDURE

The OpenExcel() procedure starts Excel (if it is not already running) and opens the file specified in the FILEPW.FRM form. Following is a listing of the OpenExcel() procedure:

LISTING 29.31. CHAP29.BAS, OpenExcel().

```
Sub OpenExcel ()
    'declare variables
    Dim res%        'holds results
    Dim cmd$        'command building string

    'find out if excel is loaded
    res% = FindWindow("XLMAIN", 0&)
    If res% = 0 Then
        'find out if excel is minimized
        res% = FindWindow("EXCEL>", 0&)
    End If

    If res% = 0 Then
        'invoke excel
        res% = Shell("EXCEL.EXE")
    End If

    'no link
    frmMain.Text1.LinkMode = NONE

    'set topic so that excel comes up blank
    frmMain.Text1.LinkTopic = "EXCEL¦Book1"

    'set arbitrary cell location, because VB needs it
    frmMain.Text1.LinkItem = "R1C1"

    'handle error
    On Error GoTo linkerror

    'set link to automatic
    frmMain.Text1.LinkMode = AUTOMATIC

    'build open file string
    cmd$ = "[OPEN(" + Chr$(34) + GlobalFileName$ + Chr$(34) + ",0,FALSE,," + Chr$(34) +
    GlobalPassword$ + Chr$(34) + ")]"

    'execute opening file
    frmMain.Text1.LinkExecute cmd$

    'set mode back to manual
    frmMain.Text1.LinkMode = MANUAL

    'populate grid
    Call PopulateGrid

    'rename button, because it performs the calculation also
    frmMain.cmdOpen.Caption = "Calculate"
```

```
            'change menu options enabled properties
            frmMain.menu_calculate.Enabled = True
            frmMain.menu_open.Enabled = False

            'exit
            Exit Sub

    linkerror:
        Select Case (Err)
            Case 282:    'application didn't respond error, however, it probably did-check
                res% = FindWindow(0&, "Microsoft Excel - FINANCE.XLS")
                If res% > 0 Then
                    'change to manual link
                    frmMain.Text1.LinkMode = MANUAL

                    'populate grid headings
                    Call PopulateGrid

                    'rename button, because it performs the calculation also
                    frmMain.cmdOpen.Caption = "Calculate"

                    'change menu options enabled properties
                    frmMain.menu_calculate.Enabled = True
                    frmMain.menu_open.Enabled = False

                    'exit
                    Exit Sub

                Else
                    'window didn't exist-display error
                    MsgBox Error$
                    MsgBox "You may want to close Excel, if it is open!"
                End If
            Case Else
                    'display error
                    MsgBox Error$
        End Select

        'avoid errors
        Resume Next

    End Sub
```

THE *PopulateGrid( )* PROCEDURE

The PopulateGrid() procedure populates the grid with all data items from Excel that were opened using the preceding procedure, OpenExcel. Following is a listing of the PopluateGrid() procedure:

LISTING 29.32. CHAP29.BAS, PopluateGrid().

```
Sub PopulateGrid ()

    'declare variables
    Dim looprow%
    Dim loopcol%
    Dim pos%
    Dim lefttext$
    Dim righttext$

    'Flag populating
    Populating% = True

    'position to upper left corner
    frmMain.Grid1.Row = 0
    frmMain.Grid1.Col = 0


    'set topic
    frmMain.Text1.LinkTopic = "EXCEL¦FINANCE"


    'loop through all cells in each row, starting with row 4
    For looprow% = 4 To 20
        For loopcol% = 1 To 14
            'clear text box
            frmMain.Text1.Text = ""

            'no link
            frmMain.Text1.LinkMode = NONE

            'set cell location
            frmMain.Text1.LinkItem = "R" + Trim$(Str$(looprow%)) + "C" +
            Trim$(Str$(loopcol%))

            'set link to automatic
            frmMain.Text1.LinkMode = AUTOMATIC

            'increment grid1
            frmMain.Grid1.Col = loopcol% - 1
            frmMain.Grid1.Row = looprow% - 4

            'remove formatting
            pos% = InStr(frmMain.Text1.Text, "$")
            If pos% > 0 Then
                lefttext$ = Left$(frmMain.Text1.Text, pos% - 1)
                righttext$ = Right$(frmMain.Text1.Text, Len(frmMain.Text1.Text) - pos%)
                frmMain.Text1.Text = lefttext$ + righttext$
            End If

            'assign text
            frmMain.Grid1.Text = frmMain.Text1.Text

        Next loopcol%
    Next looprow%
```

```
        'enable buttons and menus
        frmMain.cmdPrint.Enabled = True
        frmMain.Menu_Print.Enabled = True

        'unflag
        Populating% = False

        frmMain.lblCalculate.Visible = False

End Sub
```

REM The looping starts with row 4 because it is the row where the data begins.

The FINANCE.XLS File

This file is the spreadsheet that contains the formatting and basic template for Excel to exchange data with Visual Basic and to provide formatted printing. The FINANCE.XLS file is contained on the CD accompanying this book in the CHAP29 subdirectory.

REM The password expected by this file is "VBFINANCE." Also note that the password is case sensitive. It is all uppercase.

The CHAP29.ICO File

This file contains the icon that has been attached to the form at design time. The CHAP29.ICO file is contained on the CD accompanying this book in the CHAP29 subdirectory.

FIGURE 29.5.
*DDE application
CHAP29 icon.*

The CHAP29.EXE File

This is the executable file that is distributable. If you distribute this application, you must include the following files:

- ◆ CHAP29.EXE
- ◆ FINANCE.XLS
- ◆ MSMASKED.VBX
- ◆ GRID.VBX

- ◆ THREED.VBX
- ◆ VBRUN300.DLL

The CHAP29.EXE file and source files are contained on the CD accompanying this book in the CHAP29 subdirectory, while all DLLs and VBXs are in the RESOURCE subdirectory.

RELATING THE DDE APPLICATION TO YOUR APPLICATION

The DDE application shows how to manipulate data using Dynamic Data Exchange methods. In the future, you will see very little of DDE. Applications will inter-communicate using Object Linking and Embedding (OLE). The reason that this application is presented is to allow for backward compatibility with existing DDE applications, for communication with applications that don't yet support OLE, and because it wasn't shown anywhere else! For more information on OLE, refer to Chapter 15, "Object Linking and Embedding (OLE)," and the application in Chapter 30, "Object Linking and Embedding (OLE) Application."

You could also enhance this application by actually converting it to OLE, which is more reliable.

FINAL NOTES

This application was only used and tested for Microsoft Excel, Version 5.0. It may or may not work with a previous version.

For this application to find Excel, it must be loaded in your path, or you must hard-code the path in the OpenExcel() procedure. If you have installed Microsoft Office and have elected to have your path updated, it has already been done for you.

OBJECT LINKING AND EMBEDDING (OLE) APPLICATION

THIS OBJECT LINKING AND EMBEDDING (OLE) APPLICATION USES OLE AUTOMATION TECHNIQUES TO INVOKE MICROSOFT WORD'S SPELL CHECKER, THESAURUS, AND GRAMMAR CHECKER FROM VISUAL BASIC. FOR MORE INFORMATION ON OLE, REFER TO CHAPTER 15, "OBJECT LINKING AND EMBEDDING (OLE)."

A FEW NOTES ABOUT THIS APPLICATION. THE GRAMMAR CHECKER WORKS ONLY ON THE ENTIRE TEXT IN THE TEXT BOX. IT DOES NOT CHECK TEXT THAT MAY BE SELECTED. THE THESAURUS MUST HAVE SELECTED TEXT TO CHECK. IT CANNOT CHECK THE ENTIRE TEXT. THE SPELL CHECKER WORKS ON EITHER THE ENTIRE TEXT OR SELECTED TEXT. THESE RULES ARE IMPOSED BY WORD.

The OLE Automation error, number 440, is used because an error is generated after the desired operation is completed.

For example, if you use the Spell Checker and replace a word, when you are finished, an error is produced, but it works fine. This is the reason that an error is handled as a "non-error" condition.

The code in this chapter could have been more proceduralized, but it is left in three manageable pieces. These pieces are for the Grammar Checker, Thesaurus, and Spell Checker. The main reason that the code is left "non-proceduralized" is so that you can cut and paste the code from a desired procedure into your application.

Figure 30.1 shows the main screen (MAIN.FRM) at runtime.

FIGURE 30.1.
*OLE application
at runtime.*

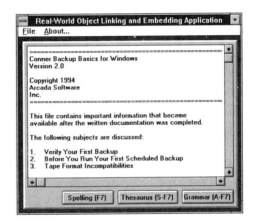

To use the application, you can either type text in the text box or open a text file using the File->Open menu option to enter text into the text box. Then click on the desired transaction: Spell Checker, Thesaurus, or Grammar Checker. You can also invoke these tools from the text box itself by pressing F7, Shift+F7, or Alt+F7, respectively.

CODE LISTINGS

The OLE application contains the following files and listings:

- ◆ CHAP30.MAK
- ◆ MAIN.FRM
- ◆ ABOUT.FRM
- ◆ CHAP30.ICO
- ◆ CHAP30.EXE

THE CHAP30.MAK FILE

CHAP30.MAK is the project file for the OLE application, CHAP30.EXE. It contains a listing of all the files necessary to load the project into Visual Basic. The CHAP30.MAK file is contained on the CD accompanying this book in the CHAP30 subdirectory. The file listing is

LISTING 30.1. CHAP30.MAK.

```
MAIN.FRM
ABOUT.FRM
THREED.VBX
MSOLE2.VBX
CMDIALOG.VBX
ProjWinSize=152,402,248,215
ProjWinShow=2
IconForm="frmMain"
Title="OLE"
ExeName="CHAP30.EXE"
```

THE MAIN.FRM FILE

MAIN.FRM is one of two forms in this application. It is the startup form for the application. Figure 30.1 presents the main form as it appears at runtime. Figure 30.2 presents the form at design time. Table 30.1 lists all the relevant properties of each control on the form that have been changed from their standard default values. The MAIN.FRM file is contained on the CD accompanying this book in the CHAP30 subdirectory.

FIGURE 30.2.
OLE application MAIN.FRM at design time.

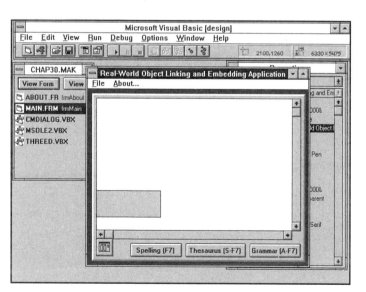

TABLE 30.1 PROPERTIES OF EACH CONTROL ON MAIN.FRM.

Object	Control Type	Property	Value
frmMain	Form	BackColor	&H00404000&
		Caption	"Real-World Object Linking and Embedding Application"
		Height	5475
		Icon	"CHAP30.ICO"
		Left	1485
		MaxButton	False
		Top	855
		Width	6330
Panel3D1	SSPanel	BackColor	&H00C0C0C0&
		BevelWidth	3
		Font3D	None
		ForeColor	&H0000FFFF&
		Height	4575
		Left	120
		Top	120
		Width	6015
cmdGrammar	CommandButton	Caption	"Grammar (A-F7)"
		Height	375
		Left	4440
		Top	4080
		Width	1455
cmdThesaurus	CommandButton	Caption	"Thesaurus (S-F7)"
		Height	375
		Left	2640
		Top	4080
		Width	1695
cmdSpell	CommandButton	Caption	"Spelling (F7)"
		Height	375
		Left	1080
		Top	4080
		Width	1455

Object	Control Type	Property	Value
txtOLE	TextBox	Height	3855
		Left	120
		MultiLine	True
		Scrollbars	Both
		Top	120
		Width	5775
cmDialog	CommonDialog	CancelError	True
		Left	120
		Top	3960
oleWord	OLE	Class	"Word.Document.6"
		Height	735
		Left	120
		SizeMode	AutoSize
		Top	2640
		Visible	False
		Width	1815
menu_file	Menu	Caption	"&File"
menu_open	Menu	Caption	"&Open"
menu_sep	Menu	Caption	"-"
menu_exit	Menu	Caption	"&Exit"
menu_about	Menu	Caption	"&About..."

REM It is important to note that you cannot simply type "Word.Document.6" in the Class property. You must select the ellipsis (...) on the Property sheet and select this class. Also, this class must be registered with Windows. For more information about registering, see the "Final Notes" section at the end of this chapter.

FUNCTION, SUBROUTINE, AND EVENT PROCEDURES

There are several procedures of code for each object(control) that comprise this form. Each is listed in the following sections.

THE *(GENERAL)* OBJECT

The (general) object contains declarations and procedures at the form level. The procedures for the (general) object are

- ◆ (declarations)
- ◆ CenterForm()

THE *(DECLARATIONS)* PROCEDURE

The (general) object contains declarations and procedures at the form level. You may notice that the ABOUT.FRM file also has a CenterForm() procedure. This is because it is not advantageous to create a separate *.BAS file only for this one procedure. If this procedure had to be used by many files, that would be a different story. The procedures for the (general) object are

LISTING 30.2. MAIN.FRM, (general)(declarations).

```
Option Explicit

'mousepointers
Const HOURGLASS = 11
Const DEFAULT = 0

'messageboxes
Const IDNO = 7
Const IDYES = 6

'key constants
Const KEY_F7 = &H76

' Shift parameter masks
Const SHIFT_MASK = 1
Const ALT_MASK = 4

'OLE Constants
Const OLE_ACTIVATE = 7
Const OLE_CLOSE = 9

'other options
Const MODAL = 1
Const DLG_FILE_OPEN = 1
```

THE *CENTERFORM()* PROCEDURE

The CenterForm() simply centers the form in the client area upon form loading. The CenterForm() procedure accepts one argument, F. It is the actual form to be centered.

For more information on manipulating graphics and forms, refer to Chapter 5, "Graphics."

Following is a listing of the `CenterForm()` procedure:

Listing 30.3. MAIN.FRM,`CenterForm()`.

```
Sub CenterForm (F As Form)

    'center the form
    F.Left = (Screen.Width - F.Width) / 2
    F.Top = (Screen.Height - F.Height) / 2

End Sub
```

The *cmdGrammar* Control

cmdGrammar is the name of the command button control that, when clicked, starts Microsoft Word's Grammar Checker. The cmdGrammar control has code in only one event procedure. It is

◆ cmdGrammar_Click()

The *cmdGrammar_Click()* Event Procedure

Following is a listing of the `cmdGrammar_Click()` event procedure:

Listing 30.4. MAIN.FRM,`cmdGrammar_Click()`.

```
Sub cmdGrammar_Click ()

    'declare variables
    Dim m$
    Dim LeftText$
    Dim RightText$
    Dim wordobj As Object

    'check to see if it's ok to go on
    If Len(Trim$(txtOLE.Text)) = 0 Then
        m$ = "You must insert text to check!"
        MsgBox m$
        Exit Sub
    End If

    'start OLE control
    oleWord.Action = OLE_ACTIVATE

    'assign wordobj with word basic
    Set wordobj = oleWord.Object.application.wordbasic

    'position to beginning of OLE document
    wordobj.startofdocument

    'position to end, selecting all in between
    wordobj.endofdocument (1)
```

continues

LISTING 30.4. CONTINUED

```
'clear selection
wordobj.editclear

'insert all text from VB Text box
wordobj.insert txtOLE.Text

'handle errors
On Error GoTo GrammarError

'check grammar
wordobj.ToolsGrammar

'all worked fine
MsgBox "Finished Checking Grammar!"
  'position to beginning
wordobj.startofdocument

'position to end, selection all in between
wordobj.endofdocument (1)

'cut selection to clipboard
wordobj.editcut

'nothing was selected, replace whole text
txtOLE.Text = clipboard.GetText(1)

'close ole object
oleWord.Action = OLE_CLOSE

'Make sure text box has focus
txtOLE.SetFocus

'exit
Exit Sub

GrammarError:
    Select Case (Err)
        Case 440 'OLE Automation Error
            MsgBox "Finished Checking Grammar!"

            'position to beginning
            wordobj.startofdocument

            'position to end, selection all in between
            wordobj.endofdocument (1)

            'cut selection to clipboard
            wordobj.editcut

            'nothing was selected, replace whole text
            txtOLE.Text = clipboard.GetText(1)

            'close ole object
            oleWord.Action = OLE_CLOSE

            'Make sure text box has focus
            txtOLE.SetFocus
```

```
    Case Else
        MsgBox "error " + Str$(Err)
End Select

'exit
Exit Sub

'avoid errors
Resume

End Sub
```

THE *CMDSPELL( )* CONTROL

cmdSpell() is the name of the command button control that, when clicked, starts Microsoft Word's Spell Checker. The cmdSpell() control has code in only one event procedure. It is

◆ cmdSpell_Click()

THE *CMDSPELL_CLICK( )* EVENT PROCEDURE

Following is a listing of the cmdSpell_Click() event procedure:

LISTING 30.5. MAIN.FRM,cmdSpell_Click( ).

```
Sub cmdSpell_Click ()

    'declare variables
    Dim Selected%
    Dim m$
    Dim LeftText$
    Dim RightText$
    Dim wordobj As Object

    'check to see if it's ok to go on
    If Len(Trim$(txtOLE.Text)) = 0 Then
        m$ = "You must insert text to check!"
        MsgBox m$
        Exit Sub
    End If

    'start OLE control
    oleWord.Action = OLE_ACTIVATE

    'assign wordobj with word basic
    Set wordobj = oleWord.Object.application.wordbasic

    'initialize flag
    Selected% = False

    'position to beginning of OLE document
    wordobj.startofdocument
```

LISTING 30.5. CONTINUED

```
    'position to end, selecting all in between
    wordobj.endofdocument (1)

    'clear selection
    wordobj.editclear
If txtOLE.SelText <> "" Then
        'flag selected
        Selected% = True

        'insert only selected text
        wordobj.insert txtOLE.SelText
    Else
        'insert all text from VB Text box
        wordobj.insert txtOLE.Text
    End If

    'handle errors
    On Error GoTo SpellError

    'check spelling
    wordobj.toolsspelling

    'all worked fine
    MsgBox "Finished Spell Checking!"

    'position to beginning
    wordobj.startofdocument

    'position to end, selection all in between
    wordobj.endofdocument (1)

    'cut selection to clipboard
    wordobj.editcut

    If Selected% = False Then
        'nothing was selected, replace whole text
        txtOLE.Text = clipboard.GetText(1)
    Else
        'text was selected, replace only selected text
        LeftText$ = Left$(txtOLE.Text, txtOLE.SelStart)
        RightText$ = Right$(txtOLE.Text, Len(txtOLE) - (txtOLE.SelStart +
        txtOLE.SelLength))
        txtOLE.Text = LeftText$ + clipboard.GetText(1) + RightText$
    End If

    'close ole object
    oleWord.Action = OLE_CLOSE

    'Make sure text box has focus
    txtOLE.SetFocus


    'exit
    Exit Sub
```

```
SpellError:
    Select Case (Err)
        Case 440 'OLE Automation Error
            MsgBox "Finished Spell Checking!"

            'position to beginning
            wordobj.startofdocument

            'position to end, selection all in between
            wordobj.endofdocument (1)

            'cut selection to clipboard
            wordobj.editcut

            If Selected% = False Then
                'nothing was selected, replace whole text
                txtOLE.Text = clipboard.GetText(1)
            Else
                'text was selected, replace only selected text
                LeftText$ = Left$(txtOLE.Text, txtOLE.SelStart)
                RightText$ = Right$(txtOLE.Text, Len(txtOLE) - (txtOLE.SelStart +
                txtOLE.SelLength))
                txtOLE.Text = LeftText$ + clipboard.GetText(1) + RightText$
            End If

            'close ole object
            oleWord.Action = OLE_CLOSE

            'Make sure text box has focus
            txtOLE.SetFocus

        Case Else
            MsgBox "error " + Str$(Err)
    End Select

    'exit
    Exit Sub

    'avoid errors
    Resume

End Sub
```

The *cmdThesaurus* Control

cmdThesaurus is the name of the command button control that, when clicked, starts Microsoft Word's Thesaurus. The cmdThesaurus control has code in only one event procedure. It is

◆ cmdThesaurus_Click()

The *cmdThesaurus_Click()* Event Procedure

Following is a listing of the cmdThesaurus_Click() event procedure:

LISTING 30.6. MAIN.FRM, cmdThesaurus_Click().

```
Sub cmdThesaurus_Click ()

    'declare variables
    Dim m$
    Dim LeftText$
    Dim RightText$
    Dim wordobj As Object

    'check to see if it's ok to go on
    If txtOLE.SelText = "" Then
        m$ = "There is no text selected"
        MsgBox m$
        Exit Sub
    End If

    'start OLE control
    oleWord.Action = OLE_ACTIVATE

    'assign wordobj with word basic
    Set wordobj = oleWord.Object.application.wordbasic

    'position to beginning of OLE document
    wordobj.startofdocument

    'position to end, selecting all in between
    wordobj.endofdocument (1)

    'clear selection
    wordobj.editclear

    'insert only selected text
    wordobj.insert txtOLE.SelText

    'handle errors
    On Error GoTo ThesaurusError

    'check thesaurus
    wordobj.toolsthesaurus

    'all worked fine
    MsgBox "Finished Checking Thesaurus"

    'position to beginning
    wordobj.startofdocument

    'position to end, selection all in between
    wordobj.endofdocument (1)

    'cut selection to clipboard
    wordobj.editcut

    'text was selected, replace only selected text
    LeftText$ = Left$(txtOLE.Text, txtOLE.SelStart)
    RightText$ = Right$(txtOLE.Text, Len(txtOLE) - (txtOLE.SelStart + txtOLE.SelLength))
    txtOLE.Text = LeftText$ + clipboard.GetText(1) + RightText$
```

```
    'close ole object
    oleWord.Action = OLE_CLOSE

    'Make sure text box has focus
    txtOLE.SetFocus

    'exit
    Exit Sub

ThesaurusError:
    Select Case (Err)
        Case 440 'OLE Automation Error
            MsgBox "Finished Checking Thesaurus"

            'position to beginning
            wordobj.startofdocument

            'position to end, selection all in between
            wordobj.endofdocument (1)

            'cut selection to clipboard
            wordobj.editcut

            'text was selected, replace only selected text
            LeftText$ = Left$(txtOLE.Text, txtOLE.SelStart)
            RightText$ = Right$(txtOLE.Text, Len(txtOLE) - (txtOLE.SelStart +
            txtOLE.SelLength))
            txtOLE.Text = LeftText$ + clipboard.GetText(1) + RightText$

            'close ole object
            oleWord.Action = OLE_CLOSE

            'Make sure text box has focus
            txtOLE.SetFocus

        Case Else
            MsgBox "error " + Str$(Err)
    End Select

    'exit
    Exit Sub

    'avoid errors
    Resume

End Sub
```

The *Form* Object

The Form object has code in two event procedures. They are

◆ Form_Load()

◆ Form_Unload()

THE *FORM_LOAD()* EVENT PROCEDURE

The Form_Load() event procedure simply centers and loads the main form. Following is a listing of the Form_Load() event procedure:

LISTING 30.7. MAIN.FRM, Form_Load().

```
Sub Form_Load ()

    'change cursor
    Screen.MousePointer = HOURGLASS

    'center the form
    CenterForm Me

    'change cursor
    Screen.MousePointer = DEFAULT

End Sub
```

THE *FORM_UNLOAD()* EVENT PROCEDURE

The Form_Unload() event procedure prompts the user to confirm ending the program. Following is a listing of the Form_Unload() event procedure:

LISTING 30.8. MAIN.FRM, Form_Unload().

```
Sub Form_Unload (Cancel As Integer)

    'declare variables
    Dim m$
    Dim res%

    m$ = "Are you sure you want to exit?"
    res% = MsgBox(m$, 292)
    If res% = IDNO Then
        'cancel
        Cancel = True

        'exit
        Exit Sub
    End If

End Sub
```

THE *MENU* OBJECT

The menu object was created using Visual Basic's built-in Menu editor. It has code associated with three Click() event procedures. They are

◆ menu_about()

◆ menu_exit()

◆ menu_open()

THE *MENU_ABOUT_CLICK()* PROCEDURE

The menu_about_Click() procedure simply shows the about form for program information. Following is a listing of the menu_about_Click() procedure:

LISTING 30.9. MAIN.FRM,menu_about_Click().

```
Sub menu_about_Click ()

    'show about form
    frmAbout.Show MODAL

End Sub
```

THE *MENU_EXIT_CLICK()* PROCEDURE

The menu_exit_Click() procedure starts the program exit procedure, invoked in the Form_Unload() event. Following is a listing of the menu_exit_Click() procedure:

LISTING 30.10. MAIN.FRM,menu_exit_Click().

```
Sub menu_exit_Click ()

    'exit
    Unload frmMain

End Sub
```

THE *MENU_OPEN_CLICK()* PROCEDURE

The menu_open_Click() procedure simply invokes the common dialog control to open a text file. Following is a listing of the menu_open_Click() procedure:

LISTING 30.11. MAIN.FRM,menu_open_Click().

```
Sub menu_open_Click ()

    'declare variables
    Dim Filename$
    Dim TheLine$
    Dim TotalText$

    'handle errors
```

LISTING 30.11. CONTINUED

```
    On Error GoTo OpenError

    cmDialog.Filter = "Text Files¦*.TXT"
    cmDialog.Action = DLG_FILE_OPEN

    Filename$ = cmDialog.Filename

   'open file
    Open Filename$ For Input As #1

   'Loop through file, while it doesn't find an End Of File marker
    Do While Not EOF(1)

        'Get a line
        Input #1, TheLine$

        'carriage return-add newline character
        TotalText$ = TotalText$ + TheLine$ + Chr$(13) + Chr$(10)

    Loop

    'assign text
    txtOLE.Text = TotalText$

    'Close Handle
    Close #1

    'exit
    Exit Sub

OpenError:
    'show error
    MsgBox Error$

    'exit
    Exit Sub

    'avoid errors
    Resume

End Sub
```

THE *TXTOLE* CONTROL

txtOLE is the name of the text box control that contains the text that Microsoft Word will act on. The txtOLE control has code in only one event procedure. It is

◆ txtOLE_KeyDown()

THE *txtOLE_KeyDown( )* EVENT PROCEDURE

The txtOLE_KeyDown event procedure is used so that the hotkeys F7, Shift+F7, and Alt+F7 can be used. Following is a listing of the txtOLE_KeyDown() event procedure:

LISTING 30.12. MAIN.FRM, txtOLE_KeyDown().

```
Sub txtOLE_KeyDown (KeyCode As Integer, Shift As Integer)

    'F7 is for Spell Checking
    'Shift-F7 is for Thesaurus
    'Alt-F7 is for Grammar Checker

    If KeyCode = KEY_F7 Then
        If Shift And SHIFT_MASK Then
            cmdThesaurus.Value = True
        ElseIf Shift And ALT_MASK Then
            cmdGrammar.Value = True
        Else
            cmdSpell.Value = True
        End If
    End If

End Sub
```

THE ABOUT.FRM FILE

ABOUT.FRM is the other form in this application. Figure 30.3 presents the form as it appears at runtime. Fundamentally, there is no difference in the form at design time, so it is not presented. Table 30.2 lists all the relevant properties of each control on the form that have been changed from their standard default values. The ABOUT.FRM file is contained on the CD accompanying this book in the CHAP30 subdirectory.

FIGURE 30.3.
OLE application ABOUT.FRM at runtime.

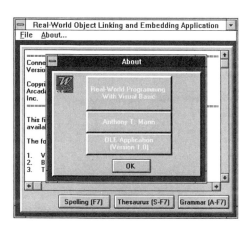

TABLE 30.2. PROPERTIES OF EACH CONTROL ON ABOUT.FRM.

Object	Control Type	Property	Value
frmAbout	Form	BackColor	&H00404000&
		Caption	"About"
		Height	3525
		Left	1035
		MaxButton	False
		MinButton	False
		Top	1140
		Width	4545
pnlMain	SSPanel	BackColor	&H00C0C0C0&
		BevelWidth	3
		Caption	""
		Font3D	None
		ForeColor	&H00C0C0C0&
		Height	2895
		Left	120
		RoundedCorners	False
		ShadowColor	Black
		Top	120
		Width	4215
pnl1	SSPanel	BackColor	&H00C0C0C0&
		BevelWidth	3
		Caption	"Real-World Program ming With Visual Basic"
		Font3D	None
		ForeColor	&H0000FFFF&
		Height	975
		Left	960
		RoundedCorners	False
		ShadowColor	Black
		Top	120
		Width	2415

Object	Control Type	Property	Value
pnl2	SSPanel	BackColor	&H00C0C0C0&
		BevelWidth	3
		Caption	"Anthony T. Mann"
		Font3D	None
		ForeColor	&H0000FFFF&
		Height	615
		Left	960
		RoundedCorners	False
		ShadowColor	Black
		Top	1080
		Width	2415
pnl3	SSPanel	BackColor	&H00C0C0C0&
		BevelWidth	3
		Caption	"OLE Application (Version 1.0)"
		Font3D	None
		ForeColor	&H0000FFFF&
		Height	615
		Left	960
		RoundedCorners	False
		ShadowColor	Black
		Top	1680
		Width	2415
cmdOK	Command Button	Caption	"OK"
		Height	375
		Left	1680
		Top	2400
		Width	1095
pictAbout	Picture Box	Autosize	True
		BackColor	&H00C0C0C0&
		BorderStyle	None
		Height	615

continues

TABLE 30.2. CONTINUED

Object	Control Type	Property	Value
		Left	120
		Top	120
		Width	735

FUNCTION, SUBROUTINE, AND EVENT PROCEDURES

There are several procedures of code for each object(control) that comprises this form. Each is listed in the following sections.

THE *(GENERAL)* OBJECT

The general object contains only one procedure at the form level. You may notice that the MAIN.FRM file also has the same procedure, `CenterForm()`. This is because it is not advantageous to create a separate *.BAS file only for this one procedure. If this procedure had to be used by many files, that would be a different story. The procedures for the (general) object are

◆ (declarations)

◆ CenterForm()

THE *(DECLARATIONS)* PROCEDURE

The (declarations) procedure contains only one line of declarations used in the form, ABOUT.FRM. It is only to allow for variable syntax checking and forcing the declaration of variables in each procedure. Following is a listing of the (declarations) procedure:

LISTING 30.13. ABOUT.FRM, (general)(declarations).

```
Option Explicit
```

THE *CENTERFORM()* PROCEDURE

The CenterForm() procedure simply centers the form in the client area upon form loading. The CenterForm() procedure accepts one argument, F. It is the actual form to be centered.

 For more information on manipulating graphics and forms, refer to Chapter 5, "Graphics."

Following is a listing of the CenterForm() procedure:

LISTING 30.14. ABOUT.FRM,CenterForm().

```
Sub CenterForm (F As Form)

    'center the form
    F.Left = (Screen.Width - F.Width) / 2
    F.Top = (Screen.Height - F.Height) / 2

End Sub
```

THE *CMDOK* CONTROL

cmdOK is the name of the command button control that, when clicked, closes the frmAbout form. The cmdOK control has code in only one event procedure. It is

◆ cmdOK_Click()

THE *CMDOK_CLICK()* EVENT PROCEDURE

The cmdOK_Click() event procedure simply unloads the form. Following is a listing of the cmdOK_Click() event procedure:

LISTING 30.15. ABOUT.FRM,cmdOK_Click().

```
Sub cmdOK_Click ()

    'unload
    Unload frmAbout

End Sub
```

THE *FORM* OBJECT

The Form object has code in only one event procedure. It is

◆ Form_Load()

THE *FORM_LOAD()* EVENT PROCEDURE

The Form_Load() event procedure centers the form and assigns an icon to the pictAbout control. Following is a listing of the Form_Load() event procedure:

LISTING 30.16. ABOUT.FRM,Form_Load().

```
Sub Form_Load ()

    'center form
    CenterForm Me
```

continues

LISTING 30.16. CONTINUED

```
'load icon
pictAbout.Picture = frmMain.Icon

End Sub
```

THE CHAP30.ICO FILE

This file contains the icon that has been attached to the form at design time. The CHAP30.ICO file is contained on the CD accompanying this book in the CHAP30 subdirectory.

FIGURE 30.4.
OLE application
CHAP30 icon.

THE CHAP30.EXE FILE

This is the executable file that is distributable. If you distribute this application, you must include the following files:

- ◆ CHAP30.EXE
- ◆ MSOLE2.VBX
- ◆ CMDIALOG.VBX
- ◆ THREED.VBX
- ◆ COMMDLG.DLL
- ◆ MSOLEVBX.DLL
- ◆ VBRUN300.DLL
- ◆ COMPOBJ.DLL
- ◆ OLE2.DLL
- ◆ OLECONV.DLL
- ◆ OLE2DISP.DLL
- ◆ OLE2NLS.DLL
- ◆ OLE2PROX.DLL
- ◆ STORAGE.DLL
- ◆ VBOA300.DLL
- ◆ OLE2.REG

The CHAP30.EXE file and source files are contained on the CD accompanying this book in the CHAP30 subdirectory, while all DLLs and VBXs are in the RESOURCE subdirectory.

RELATING THE OLE APPLICATION TO YOUR APPLICATION

The OLE application shows how to invoke Microsoft Word objects using OLE automation. This opens up the door to a world of possibilities. It is Microsoft's future to incorporate OLE into its products, languages, and even operating systems to ensure interoperability. With OLE, you can use virtually any objects exposed by the Server application to fit your own specific needs.

It used to be that if you wanted a spell checker, you needed to purchase a specialized spell checking custom control and spend a few hundred dollars. Now, with OLE, you can use many of the objects inside other OLE 2.x-compliant applications and save your money!

There are other commercial applications, such as Excel, which expose objects that allow you to access their properties. The theory is the same; however, in Word there is only one object exposed. It is WordBasic. This can be seen in the code in this chapter.

FINAL NOTES

This application was only used and tested for Microsoft Word, version 6.0. It may or may not work with a previous version.

For this application to find Word, it must be loaded in your path. If you have installed Microsoft Office, it is done for you.

It is important to note that for OLE communication to work, the OLE object must be registered with Windows. In most cases, this is done automatically when you load the application for the first time. If this is not done, you must either reinstall the application or register it yourself. This can be done by running the REGEDIT.EXE application that comes with Windows, but it is very tricky and beyond the scope of this book. There is not an icon for it. When you invoke this program, you must use the /V switch for Advanced mode.

DATA ACCESS APPLICATION

THE DATA ACCESS APPLICATION IS A SAMPLE APPLICATION THAT USES THE MICROSOFT ACCESS DATABASE FILE, CHAP31.MDB, FOR TRACKING A RUDIMENTARY INVENTORY. TABLE 31.1 LISTS THE COMPONENTS OF THE CHAP31.MDB DATABASE.

TABLE 31.1. COMPONENTS OF THE CHAP31.MDB DATABASE.

Table	Field	Data Type	Size	Primary Key
INVENTORY	product_id	Text	6	Y
	description	Text	50	N
	supplier_id	Text	6	N
	quantity	Double	8	N
SALES	product_id	Text	6	N
	staff_id	Text	6	N
	date_sold	Text	50	N
	quantity_sold	Double	8	N
STAFF	staff_id	Text	6	Y
	last_name	Text	25	N
	first_name	Text	25	N
SUPPLIER	supplier_id	Text	6	Y
	supplier	Text	50	N

The application allows for inserting, updating, and deleting of items in the database. One form, MAIN.FRM, is used to enter data into all four tables in the database. This saves on resources required for the application. To perform any operation in the database, you must search on the table first using the Search menu option. You can, however, run reports on the database without searching first.

Figure 31.1 shows the main screen (MAIN.FRM) at runtime.

FIGURE 31.1.
*Data Access application
at runtime.*

To use the application, search on one of the tables by using the Search menu options. Once a table is searched, the data is populated one record at a time in the four text boxes provided. Use the command buttons to browse through the individual records.

To insert another record, simply change any of the fields. Provided that there is a new primary key field, you can select the Records->Add New menu option. This will insert another record in the table.

To delete a record, select the Records->Delete Current menu option. You will be prompted for confirmation before deleting.

To update a record, change any of the fields and then select the Records->Update Current menu option. The record will be updated.

Once fields are entered, you can run any of three pre-canned reports—one each for Staff, Sales, and Inventory. To run a report, select the Reports menu option. This will invoke the CRYSTAL.FRM form. From the Crystal form, you can choose the report to run. Figure 31.2 shows the CRYSTAL.FRM form at runtime.

FIGURE 31.2.
*Data Access application
Crystal Report form at
runtime.*

To look up a particular ID number, if the lookup command button is enabled, select it to look up the ID number. The lookup command button will be enabled in one of the following situations:

◆ Searching the INVENTORY table, with the focus on supplier_id.

◆ Searching the SALES table, with the focus on product_id or staff_id.

Figure 31.3 shows the Lookup form at runtime while looking up a supplier_id.

 For more information about the SQL statements used in this chapter, refer to Chapter 18, "Structured Query Language (SQL)."

This chapter demonstrates two techniques. The first uses the Data Access control, and the second uses Data Access Objects (DAO). Your application may not need both, but they are presented for the sake of example.

 For more information about Data Access, refer to Chapter 16, "Data Access."

FIGURE 31.3.
*Data Access application
Lookup form at runtime.*

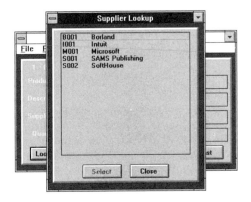

CODE LISTINGS

The Data Access application contains the following files and listings:

- ◆ CHAP31.MAK
- ◆ MAIN.FRM
- ◆ CRYSTAL.FRM
- ◆ LOOKUP.FRM
- ◆ ABOUT.FRM
- ◆ CHAP31.BAS
- ◆ CHAP31.MDB
- ◆ CHAP31.ICO
- ◆ CHAP31.EXE
- ◆ SALES.RPT
- ◆ STAFF.RPT
- ◆ INVENT.RPT

THE CHAP31.MAK FILE

CHAP31.MAK is the project file for the data access application, CHAP31.EXE. It contains a listing of all the files necessary to load the project into Visual Basic. The CHAP31.MAK file is contained on the CD accompanying this book in the CHAP31 subdirectory. The file listing is

LISTING 31.1. CHAP31.MAK.

```
MAIN.FRM
CRYSTAL.FRM
LOOKUP.FRM
```

```
ABOUT.FRM
CHAP31.BAS
THREED.VBX
CRYSTAL.VBX
CMDIALOG.VBX
ProjWinSize=152,402,248,235
ProjWinShow=2
IconForm="frmMain"
Title="Data Access"
ExeName="CHAP31.EXE"
```

The MAIN.FRM File

MAIN.FRM is one of four forms in this application. It is the startup form for the application as well as the form used for data entry and browsing. Table 31.2 lists all the relevant properties of each control on the form that have been changed from their standard default values. The MAIN.FRM file is contained in the CHAP31 subdirectory on the CD accompanying this book.

Table 31.2. Properties of each control on MAIN.FRM.

Object	Control Type	Property	Value
frmMain	Form	BackColor	&H00404000&
		Caption	"Real-World Data Access Application"
		Height	3840
		Icon	"CHAP31.ICO"
		Left	1425
		MaxButton	False
		Top	2325
		Width	6225
Panel3D1	SSPanel	BackColor	&H00C0C0C0&
		BevelWidth	3
		Font3D	None
		ForeColor	&H0000FFFF&
		Height	2895
		Left	120
		Top	120
		Width	5895

continues

761

TABLE 31.2. CONTINUED

Object	Control Type	Property	Value
txtLUCaption	TextBox	Height	375
		Left	120
		Text	"Lookup Caption"
		Top	720
		Visible	False
		Width	1575
txtField	TextBox	DataSource	"Data1"
		Height	375
		Index	0,1,2,3*
		Left	1320
		Top	480,960,1440,1920*
		Width	4455
pnlSearchLabel	SSPanel	BackColor	&H00C0C0C0&
		BevelOuter	None
		BevelWidth	3
		Font3D	None
		ForeColor	&H0000FFFF&
		Height	255
		Left	1320
		Top	120
		Width	4455
pnlRecordTotal	SSPanel	BackColor	&H00C0C0C0&
		BevelOuter	None
		BevelWidth	3
		Font3D	None
		ForeColor	&H0000FFFF&
		Height	255
		Left	840
		Top	120
		Width	495

Object	Control Type	Property	Value
Panel3D2	SSPanel	BackColor	&H00C0C0C0&
		BevelOuter	None
		BevelWidth	3
		Caption	"Of"
		Font3D	None
		ForeColor	&H0000FFFF&
		Height	255
		Left	600
		Top	120
		Width	255
pnlRecordNo	SSPanel	BackColor	&H00C0C0C0&
		BevelOuter	None
		BevelWidth	3
		Font3D	None
		ForeColor	&H0000FFFF&
		Height	255
		Left	120
		Top	120
		Width	495
pnlFieldLabel	SSPanel	BackColor	&H00C0C0C0&
		BevelOuter	None
		BevelWidth	3
		Font3D	None
		ForeColor	&H0000FFFF&
		Height	255
		Index	0,1,2,3*
		Left	120
		Top	480,960,1440,1920*
		Width	1095

continues

TABLE 31.2. CONTINUED

Object	Control Type	Property	Value
Data1	Data	Connect	""
		DatabaseName	""
		Exclusive	False
		Height	270
		Left	1320
		Options	0
		ReadOnly	False
		RecordSource	""
		Top	2160
		Visible	False
		Width	4455
cmdLookup	CommandButton	Caption	"Lookup"
		Enabled	False
		Height	375
		Left	240
		Top	2400
		Width	975
cmdLast	CommandButton	Caption	"Last"
		Enabled	False
		Height	375
		Left	4680
		Top	2400
		Width	975
cmdFirst	CommandButton	Caption	"First"
		Enabled	False
		Height	375
		Left	1440
		Top	2400
		Width	975

Object	Control Type	Property	Value
cmdNext	CommandButton	Caption	"Next"
		Enabled	False
		Height	375
		Left	3600
		Top	2400
		Width	975
cmdPrev	CommandButton	Caption	"Previous"
		Enabled	False
		Height	375
		Left	2520
		Top	2400
		Width	975
menu_file	Menu	Caption	"&File"
menu_exit	Menu	Caption	"&Exit"
menu_records	Menu	Caption	"&Records"
menu_new	Menu	Caption	"&Add New"
menu_update	Menu	Caption	"&Update Current"
menu_delete	Menu	Caption	"&Delete Current"
menu_search	Menu	Caption	"&Search"
menu_inventory	Menu	Caption	"&Inventory"
menu_sales	Menu	Caption	"&Sales"
menu_staff	Menu	Caption	"S&taff"
menu_suppliers	Menu	Caption	"S&uppliers"
menu_reports	Menu	Caption	"Re&ports..."
menu_about	Menu	Caption	"&About..."

* This control is a control array and these are the only properties that vary within the control. To save space, they were not listed separately.

FUNCTION, SUBROUTINE, AND EVENT PROCEDURES

There are several procedures of code for each object(control) that comprise this form. Each is listed in the following sections:

THE (GENERAL) OBJECT

The (general) object contains declarations and procedures at the form level. The procedures for the (general) object are

- ◆ (declarations)
- ◆ BlankFields()
- ◆ CheckButtons()
- ◆ ClearDataFields()
- ◆ EnableAll()
- ◆ EnableLookup()
- ◆ UpdateRecordCount()

THE (DECLARATIONS) PROCEDURE

The (general) object contains declarations and procedures at the form level. All global variable declarations are in CHAP31.BAS. Following is a listing of the (declarations) procedure:

LISTING 31.2. MAIN.FRM, (general) (declarations).

```
Option Explicit

'remember old text boxes for updating current record
Dim Text1$
Dim Text2$
Dim Text3$
Dim Text4$

'flags
Dim ChangeMade%        'flag for changing data
Dim Populating%        'flag when populating
```

THE BLANKFIELDS() PROCEDURE

The BlankFields() procedure tests if there are any blank fields that need to be filled in. The procedure is also a function that returns a Boolean value, True, if there are blank fields — False if not. Following is a listing of the BlankFields() procedure:

LISTING 31.3. MAIN.FRM, BlankFields().

```
Function BlankFields() As Integer

    'checks to make sure that there are no blank fields for any field
    'which is enabled

    'declare variables
```

```
    Dim loopcount%        'loop counting variable

    For loopcount% = 0 To 3
        If txtField(loopcount%).Enabled = True Then
            If Trim$(txtField(loopcount%).Text) = "" Then
                'blank field was found-return
                BlankField = True
                Exit Function
            End If
        End If
    Next loopcount%

    'no blank fields were found
    BlankField = False

End Function
```

THE *CheckButtons()* PROCEDURE

The CheckButtons() procedure enables and disables the appropriate command buttons. For example, if there is only one record, it will disable all buttons because you cannot browse anywhere. Following is a listing of the CheckButtons() procedure:

LISTING 31.4. MAIN.FRM, CheckButtons().

```
Sub CheckButtons ()

    'check first/previous buttons
    If Val(pnlRecordNo.Caption) <= 1 Then
        cmdFirst.Enabled = False
        cmdPrev.Enabled = False
    Else
        cmdFirst.Enabled = True
        cmdPrev.Enabled = True
    End If

    'check next/last buttons
    If Val(pnlRecordNo.Caption) < Val(pnlRecordTotal.Caption) Then
        cmdNext.Enabled = True
        cmdlast.Enabled = True
    Else
        cmdNext.Enabled = False
        cmdlast.Enabled = False
    End If

    'remember old text
    Text1$ = txtField(0).Text
    Text2$ = txtField(1).Text
    Text3$ = txtField(2).Text
    Text4$ = txtField(3).Text

End Sub
```

767

The reason why you need to remember the old fields is because if you perform an update, you must know the value of the old fields before they are changed. This allows only one row to be updated.

THE *CLEARDATAFIELDS()* PROCEDURE

The `ClearDataFields()` procedure clears the text from all data fields. Following is a listing of the `ClearDataFields()` procedure:

LISTING 31.5. MAIN.FRM, `ClearDataFields()`.

```
Sub ClearDataFields ()

    'clear all datafields
    txtField(0).DataField = ""
    txtField(1).DataField = ""
    txtField(2).DataField = ""
    txtField(3).DataField = ""

    'clear text from text box
    txtField(0).Text = ""
    txtField(1).Text = ""
    txtField(2).Text = ""
    txtField(3).Text = ""

    'refresh so that new fields take effect·
    Data1.Refresh

End Sub
```

THE *ENABLEALL()* PROCEDURE

The `EnableAll()` procedure simply enables all field text boxes. Following is a listing of the `EnableAll()` procedure:

LISTING 31.6. MAIN.FRM, `EnableAll()`.

```
Sub EnableAll ()

    'enable all text fields
    txtField(0).Enabled = True
    txtField(1).Enabled = True
    txtField(2).Enabled = True
    txtField(3).Enabled = True

End Sub
```

The *EnableLookup( )* Procedure

The EnableLookup() procedure checks to see if the focus is on a field that can be "looked up" in a table instead of having to memorize it. Following is a listing of the EnableLookup() procedure:

LISTING 31.7. MAIN.FRM, EnableLookup( ).

```
Sub EnableLookup (Index As Integer)
    'enables lookup button, if in certain fields,
    'while certain tables are searched

    'first disable lookup button
    cmdLookup.Enabled = False

    Select Case UCase$((pnlSearchLabel.Caption))
        Case "INVENTORY":
            'enable if Supplier ID is selected
            If Index = 2 Then          'supplier ID
                'enable lookup button
                cmdLookup.Enabled = True

                'change LUCaption to hold caption for lookup form
                txtLUCaption.Text = "Supplier Lookup"
            End If
        Case "SALES":
            'enable if Product ID or Staff ID is selected
            If Index = 0 Then          'product ID
                'enable lookup button
                cmdLookup.Enabled = True

                'change LUCaption to hold caption for lookup form
                txtLUCaption.Text = "Product Lookup"

            ElseIf Index = 1 Then       'staff ID
                'enable lookup button
                cmdLookup.Enabled = True

                'change LUCaption to hold caption for lookup form
                txtLUCaption.Text = "Staff Lookup"
            End If
    End Select

End Sub
```

The *UpdateRecordCount( )* Procedure

The UpdateRecordCount() procedure updates the pnlRecordTotal control with the number of records in the table. Following is a listing of the UpdateRecordCount() procedure:

LISTING 31.8. MAIN.FRM,`UpdateRecordCount()`.

```vb
Sub UpdateRecordCount ()

    'handle errors, in case there are no records
    On Error GoTo RecordError

    'move to last record to update record count
    Data1.Recordset.MoveLast

    'label number of records
    pnlRecordTotal.Caption = Data1.Recordset.RecordCount

    'move back to first
    Data1.Recordset.MoveFirst

    'label current record
    pnlRecordNo.Caption = "1"

    'enable delete menu
    menu_delete.Enabled = True

    'exit
    Exit Sub

RecordError:

    'label number of records
    pnlRecordTotal.Caption = "0"

    'label current record
    pnlRecordNo.Caption = "0"

    'disable delete menu
    menu_delete.Enabled = False

    'exit
    Exit Sub

    'avoid errors
    Resume

End Sub
```

THE *cmdFirst* CONTROL

`cmdFirst` is the name of the command button control that, when clicked, will move the record pointer to the first record in the table. The `cmdFirst` control has code only in one event procedure. It is

◆ `cmdFirst_Click()`

THE *CMDFIRST_CLICK()* EVENT PROCEDURE

The cmdFirst_Click() event procedure moves to the first record in the table. Following is a listing of the cmdFirst_Click() event procedure:

LISTING 31.9. MAIN.FRM,cmdFirst_Click().

```
Sub cmdFirst_Click ()

    'flag populating
    Populating% = True

    'move to first record
    Data1.Recordset.MoveFirst

    'label current record
    pnlRecordNo.Caption = "1"

    'enable command buttons, if appropriate
    Call CheckButtons

    'unflag populating
    Populating% = False

End Sub
```

REM The purpose of the Populating% flag is to have a way for the change event not to require you to save a change when simply populating a field.

THE *CMDLAST* CONTROL

cmdLast is the name of the command button control that, when clicked, will move the record pointer to the last record in the table. The cmdLast control has code in only one event procedure. It is

◆ cmdLast_Click()

THE *CMDLAST_CLICK()* EVENT PROCEDURE

The cmdLast_Click() event procedure moves to the last record in the table. Following is a listing of the cmdLast_Click() event procedure:

LISTING 31.10. MAIN.FRM,cmdLast_Click().

```
Sub cmdLast_Click ()

    'flag populating
    Populating% = True
```

continues

LISTING 31.10. CONTINUED

```
'move to last record
Data1.Recordset.MoveLast

'label current record
pnlRecordNo.Caption = pnlRecordTotal.Caption

'enable command buttons, if appropriate
Call CheckButtons

'unflag populating
Populating% = False

End Sub
```

THE *CMDLOOKUP* CONTROL

cmdLookup is the name of the command button control that, when clicked, will invoke the LOOKUP.FRM form. The cmdLookup control has code in only one event procedure. It is

◆ cmdLookup_Click()

THE *CMDLOOKUP_CLICK()* EVENT PROCEDURE

The cmdLookup_Click() event procedure simply shows the Lookup form. Following is a listing of the cmdLookup_Click() event procedure:

LISTING 31.11. MAIN.FRM, cmdLookup_Click().

```
Sub cmdLookup_Click ()

    'show lookup form
    frmLookup.Show

End Sub
```

THE *CMDNEXT* CONTROL

cmdNext is the name of the command button control that, when clicked, will move the record pointer to the next record in the table. The cmdNext control has code in only one event procedure. It is

◆ cmdNext_Click()

THE *CMDNEXT_CLICK()* EVENT PROCEDURE

The cmdNext_Click() event procedure moves to the next record in the table. Following is a listing of the cmdNext_Click() event procedure:

LISTING 31.12. MAIN.FRM, cmdNext_Click().

```
Sub cmdNext_Click ()

    'flag populating
    Populating% = True

    'move to next record
    Data1.Recordset.MoveNext

    'label current record
    pnlRecordNo.Caption = Trim$(Str$(Val(pnlRecordNo.Caption) + 1))

    'enable command buttons, if appropriate
    Call CheckButtons

    'unflag populating
    Populating% = False

End Sub
```

THE *cmdPrev* CONTROL

cmdPrev is the name of the command button control that, when clicked, will move the record pointer to the previous record in the table. The cmdPrev control has code in only one event procedure. It is

◆ cmdPrev_Click()

THE *cmdPrev_Click()* EVENT PROCEDURE

The cmdPrev_Click() event procedure moves to the preview record in the table. Following is a listing of the cmdPrev_Click() event procedure:

LISTING 31.13. MAIN.FRM, cmdPrev_Click().

```
Sub cmdPrev_Click ()

    'flag populating
    Populating% = True

    'move to previous record
    Data1.Recordset.MovePrevious

    'label current record
    pnlRecordNo.Caption = Trim$(Str$(Val(pnlRecordNo.Caption) - 1))

    'enable command buttons, if appropriate
    Call CheckButtons

    'unflag populating
    Populating% = False

End Sub
```

773

THE *FORM* OBJECT

The Form object has code in two event procedures. They are

- Form_Load()
- Form_Unload()

THE *FORM_LOAD()* EVENT PROCEDURE

The Form_Load() event procedure initializes, centers, and loads the main form. Following is a listing of the Form_Load() event procedure:

LISTING 31.14. MAIN.FRM,Form_Load().

```
Sub Form_Load ()

    'change cursor
    screen.MousePointer = HOURGLASS

    'center the form
    CenterForm Me

    GlobalDB = APP.Path = "CHAP31.MDB"

    'assign database
    Data1.DatabaseName = GlobalDB$

    'disable menu option
    menu_delete.Enabled = False

    'change cursor
    screen.MousePointer = DEFAULT

End Sub
```

THE *FORM_UNLOAD()* EVENT PROCEDURE

The Form_Unload() event procedure prompts the user to confirm ending the program. Following is a listing of the Form_Unload() event procedure:

LISTING 31.15. MAIN.FRM,Form_Unload().

```
Sub Form_Unload (cancel As Integer)

    'declare variables
    Dim m$
    Dim res%

    m$ = "Are you sure you want to exit?"
    res% = MsgBox(m$, 292)
```

```
        If res% = IDNO Then
            'cancel form unloading
            cancel = True

            'exit
            Exit Sub
        End If

        End

End Sub
```

THE *MENU* OBJECT

The menu object was created using Visual Basic's built-in Menu editor. It has code associated with ten Click() event procedures. They are

- ◆ menu_about()
- ◆ menu_delete()
- ◆ menu_exit()
- ◆ menu_inventory()
- ◆ menu_new()
- ◆ menu_reports()
- ◆ menu_sales()
- ◆ menu_staff()
- ◆ menu_suppliers()
- ◆ menu_update()

THE *MENU_ABOUT_CLICK()* EVENT PROCEDURE

The menu_about_Click() event procedure simply shows the about form for program information. Following is a listing of the menu_about_Click() event procedure:

LISTING 31.16. MAIN.FRM, menu_about_Click().

```
Sub menu_about_Click ()

    'show about form
    frmAbout.Show MODAL

End Sub
```

THE *menu_delete_Click()* EVENT PROCEDURE

The menu_delete_Click() event procedure deletes the current record. Following is a listing of the menu_delete_Click() event procedure:

LISTING 31.17. MAIN.FRM, menu_delete_Click().

```
Sub menu_delete_Click ()

    'declare variables
    Dim cmd$            'SQL building variable
    Dim m$              'message constructor
    Dim res%            'holds results

    'construct message
    m$ = "Are you sure you want to" + Chr$(13)
    m$ = m$ + "delete the current record?"

    'confirm deletion
    res% = MsgBox(m$, 292, "Warning")
    If res% = IDNO Then Exit Sub

    'open the database
    Set DB = OpenDatabase(GlobalDB$)

    Select Case UCase$((pnlSearchLabel.Caption))
        Case "INVENTORY":
            'create dynaset before deleting record
            cmd$ = "SELECT * FROM INVENTORY "
            cmd$ = cmd$ + "WHERE product_id = '" + txtField(0).Text + "' "
            cmd$ = cmd$ + "AND description = '" + txtField(1).Text + "' "
            cmd$ = cmd$ + "AND supplier_id = '" + txtField(2).Text + "' "
            cmd$ = cmd$ + "AND quantity = " + txtField(3).Text + " "
            Set DS = DB.CreateDynaset(cmd$)

            'tell the dynaset to delete current
            DS.Delete

            'unflag changes made
            ChangeMade% = False

            'repopulate
            Call menu_inventory_Click

        Case "SALES":
            'create dynaset before deleting record
            cmd$ = "SELECT * FROM SALES "
            cmd$ = cmd$ + "WHERE product_id = '" + txtField(0).Text + "' "
            cmd$ = cmd$ + "AND staff_id = '" + txtField(1).Text + "' "
            cmd$ = cmd$ + "AND date_sold = '" + txtField(2).Text + "' "
            cmd$ = cmd$ + "AND quantity_sold = " + txtField(3).Text + " "
            Set DS = DB.CreateDynaset(cmd$)

            If DS.RecordCount > 0 Then
                'move record pointer to the first occurrence of this combination of
                records
```

```
                DS.MoveFirst
            End If

            'tell the dynaset to delete current
            DS.Delete

            'unflag changes made
            ChangeMade% = False

            'repopulate
            Call menu_sales_Click

        Case "SUPPLIER":
            'create dynaset before deleting record
            cmd$ = "SELECT * FROM SUPPLIER "
            cmd$ = cmd$ + "WHERE supplier_id = '" + txtField(0).Text + "' "
            cmd$ = cmd$ + "AND supplier = '" + txtField(1).Text + "' "
            Set DS = DB.CreateDynaset(cmd$)

            'tell the dynaset to delete current
            DS.Delete

            'unflag changes made
            ChangeMade% = False

            'repopulate
            Call menu_suppliers_Click

        Case "STAFF":
            'create dynaset before deleting record
            cmd$ = "SELECT * FROM STAFF "
            cmd$ = cmd$ + "WHERE staff_id = '" + txtField(0).Text + "' "
            cmd$ = cmd$ + "AND last_name = '" + txtField(1).Text + "' "
            cmd$ = cmd$ + "AND first_name = '" + txtField(2).Text + "' "
            Set DS = DB.CreateDynaset(cmd$)

            'tell the dynaset to delete current
            DS.Delete

            'unflag changes made
            ChangeMade% = False

            'repopulate
            Call menu_staff_Click
        Case Else:
            'user did not search on any table yet
            m$ = "You must search on a table" + Chr$(13)
            m$ = m$ + "before you can delete a record!"
            MsgBox m$
    End Select

End Sub
```

 In actuality, the only fields necessary in the SQL WHERE clauses in the preceding code are any fields that make up the primary key. It is not wrong to leave the extra fields in, but it does lead to extra code. The fields were left in for example purposes.

THE *MENU_EXIT_CLICK()* EVENT PROCEDURE

The menu_exit_Click() event procedure starts the program exit procedure, invoked in the Form_Unload() event. Following is a listing of the menu_exit_Click() event procedure:

LISTING 31.18. MAIN.FRM, menu_exit_Click().

```
Sub menu_exit_Click ()

    'exit application
    Unload frmMain

End Sub
```

THE *MENU_INVENTORY_CLICK()* EVENT PROCEDURE

The menu_inventory_Click() event procedure searches on the INVENTORY table and populates the text fields with the first record. Following is a listing of the menu_inventory_Click() event procedure:

LISTING 31.19. MAIN.FRM, menu_inventory_Click().

```
Sub menu_inventory_Click ()

    'declare variables
    Dim m$       'message constructor
    Dim res%     'holds results

    If ChangeMade% = True Then
        'construct message
        m$ = "Re-populate without saving changes?"
        res% = MsgBox(m$, 292, "Warning")
        If res% = IDNO Then Exit Sub

    End If

    'flag no change
    ChangeMade% = False

    'flag populating
    Populating% = True

    'change cursor
    screen.MousePointer = HOURGLASS

    'label panel
    pnlSearchLabel.Caption = "Inventory"

    'enable all text boxes-so errors don't occur
    Call EnableAll
```

```
'assign table
Data1.RecordSource = "INVENTORY"

'clear all data fields
Call ClearDataFields

'assign captions
pnlFieldLabel(0).Caption = "Product ID"
pnlFieldLabel(1).Caption = "Description"
pnlFieldLabel(2).Caption = "Supplier ID"
pnlFieldLabel(3).Caption = "Quantity"

'enable text boxes
txtField(0).Enabled = True
txtField(1).Enabled = True
txtField(2).Enabled = True
txtField(3).Enabled = True

'assign fields to text boxes
txtField(0).DataField = "product_id"
txtField(1).DataField = "description"
txtField(2).DataField = "supplier_id"
txtField(3).DataField = "quantity"

'refresh so new parameters will take effect
Data1.Refresh

'enable command buttons
cmdFirst.Enabled = True
cmdlast.Enabled = True

'update number of records
Call UpdateRecordCount

'enable command buttons, if appropriate
Call CheckButtons

'set focus twice, so that enable lookup event is generated
txtField(1).SetFocus
txtField(0).SetFocus

'unflag populating
Populating% = False

'change cursor
screen.MousePointer = DEFAULT

End Sub
```

THE *MENU_NEW_CLICK( )* EVENT PROCEDURE

The menu_new_Click( ) event procedure inserts a new record in the currently selected table.
Following is a listing of the menu_new_Click( ) event procedure:

779

LISTING 31.20. MAIN.FRM,menu_new_Click().

```
Sub menu_new_Click ()

    'declare variables
    Dim cmd$        'SQL building variable
    Dim m$          'message constructor
    Dim res%        'holds results

    If BlankField() = True Then
        m$ = "You must fill in all fields which are enabled"
        MsgBox m$
        Exit Sub
    End If

    'open the database
    Set DB = OpenDatabase(GlobalDB$)

    Select Case UCase$((pnlSearchLabel.Caption))
        Case "INVENTORY":
            'ensure entity integrity by checking primary key of table
            cmd$ = "SELECT * FROM INVENTORY "
            cmd$ = cmd$ + "WHERE product_id = '" + txtField(0).Text + "' "
            Set DS = DB.CreateDynaset(cmd$)

            If DS.RecordCount > 0 Then
                'build message
                m$ = "Product ID " + txtField(0).Text + " already exists"
                MsgBox m$

                'exit
                Exit Sub
            End If

            'find out if this supplier exists
            cmd$ = "SELECT * FROM SUPPLIER "
            cmd$ = cmd$ + "WHERE supplier_id = '" + txtField(2).Text + "' "
            Set DS = DB.CreateDynaset(cmd$)
            If DS.RecordCount = 0 Then
                'this supplier doesn't exist in the database
                m$ = "Supplier ID " + txtField(2).Text + " doesn't exist in the supplier
                table"
                MsgBox m$
                Exit Sub
            End If

            'create dynaset for new record
            Set DS = DB.CreateDynaset("SELECT * FROM INVENTORY")

            'tell the dynaset to add a new record
            DS.AddNew

            'add individual fields
            DS("product_id") = txtField(0).Text
            DS("description") = txtField(1).Text
            DS("supplier_id") = txtField(2).Text
            DS("quantity") = txtField(3).Text
```

```
    'update dynaset
    DS.Update

    'unflag changes made
    ChangeMade% = False

    'repopulate
    Call menu_inventory_Click

Case "SALES":
    'there is no primary key for sales-can't check integrity,
    'but we need to find out if there is an employee with this ID
    ' and if there is enough of this item in inventory to sell

    'find out if this employee exists
    cmd$ = "SELECT * FROM STAFF "
    cmd$ = cmd$ + "WHERE staff_id = '" + txtField(1).Text + "' "
    Set DS = DB.CreateDynaset(cmd$)
    If DS.RecordCount = 0 Then
        'this person doesn't exist in the database
        m$ = "Staff ID " + txtField(1).Text + " doesn't exist in the staff table"
        MsgBox m$
        Exit Sub
    End If

    cmd$ = "SELECT quantity FROM INVENTORY "
    cmd$ = cmd$ + "WHERE product_id = '" + txtField(0).Text + "' "
    Set DS = DB.CreateDynaset(cmd$)
    If DS.RecordCount = 0 Then
        'this item doesn't exist in the database
        m$ = "Product ID " + txtField(0).Text + " doesn't exist in inventory"
        MsgBox m$
        Exit Sub
    Else
        'this product exists-check number in inventory
        If Val(txtField(3).Text) > DS.Fields(0) Then
            'build message
            m$ = "There are only " + Trim$(Str$(DS.Fields(0))) + " items in
            inventory." + Chr$(13)
            m$ = m$ + "Would you like to continue to update inventory anyway?"
            res% = MsgBox(m$, 292, "Warning")

            'user doesn't want to have negative inventory-exit
            If res% = IDNO Then Exit Sub
        End If

    End If

    'enter edit mode
    DS.Edit

    'update quantity fields
    DS("quantity") = DS.Fields(0) - Val(txtField(3).Text)

    'update quantity to reflect current inventory minus this sale
    DS.Update
```

continues

LISTING 31.20. CONTINUED

```
Set DS = DB.CreateDynaset("SELECT * FROM SALES")

'tell the dynaset to add a new record
DS.AddNew

'add individual fields
DS("product_id") = txtField(0).Text
DS("staff_id") = txtField(1).Text
DS("date_sold") = txtField(2).Text
DS("quantity_sold") = txtField(3).Text

'update dynaset
DS.Update

'unflag changes made
ChangeMade% = False

'repopulate
Call menu_sales_Click

Case "SUPPLIER":
    'ensure entity integrity by checking primary key of table
    cmd$ = "SELECT * FROM SUPPLIER "
    cmd$ = cmd$ + "WHERE supplier_id = '" + txtField(0).Text + "' "
    Set DS = DB.CreateDynaset(cmd$)

    If DS.RecordCount > 0 Then
        'build message
        m$ = "Supplier ID " + txtField(0).Text + " already exists"
        MsgBox m$

        'exit
        Exit Sub
    End If

    'create dynaset for new record
    Set DS = DB.CreateDynaset("SELECT * FROM SUPPLIER")

    'tell the dynaset to add a new record
    DS.AddNew

    'add individual fields
    DS("supplier_id") = txtField(0).Text
    DS("supplier") = txtField(1).Text

    'update dynaset
    DS.Update

    'unflag changes made
    ChangeMade% = False

    'repopulate
    Call menu_suppliers_Click
```

```
      Case "STAFF":
          'ensure entity integrity by checking primary key of table
          cmd$ = "SELECT * FROM STAFF "
          cmd$ = cmd$ + "WHERE staff_id = '" + txtField(0).Text + "' "
          Set DS = DB.CreateDynaset(cmd$)

          If DS.RecordCount > 0 Then
              'build message
              m$ = "Staff ID " + txtField(0).Text + " already exists"
              MsgBox m$

              'exit
              Exit Sub
          End If

          'create dynaset for new record
          Set DS = DB.CreateDynaset("SELECT * FROM STAFF")

          'tell the dynaset to add a new record
          DS.AddNew

          'add individual fields
          DS("staff_id") = txtField(0).Text
          DS("last_name") = txtField(1).Text
          DS("first_name") = txtField(2).Text

          'update dynaset
          DS.Update

          'unflag changes made
          ChangeMade% = False

          'repopulate
          Call menu_staff_Click
      Case Else:
          'user did not search on any table yet
          m$ = "You must search on a table" + Chr$(13)
          m$ = m$ + "before you can insert a new record!"
          MsgBox m$
  End Select

End Sub
```

REM
The Fields() property allows you to query the results of a specific column that was requested in a Recordset, without having to specify a column name. This makes for a more dynamic application.

THE *MENU_REPORTS_CLICK()* EVENT PROCEDURE

The menu_reports_Click() event procedure simply calls the CRYSTAL.FRM form. This form is used for invoking one of three pre-canned reports, using the CRYSTAL.VBX custom control. Following is a listing of the menu_reports_Click() event procedure:

LISTING 31.21. MAIN.FRM, menu_reports_Click().

```
Sub menu_reports_Click ()

    'show report form
    frmCrystal.Show

End Sub
```

THE *MENU_SALES_CLICK()* EVENT PROCEDURE

The menu_sales_Click() event procedure searches on the SALES table and populates the text fields with the first record. Following is a listing of the menu_sales_Click() event procedure:

LISTING 31.22. MAIN.FRM, menu_sales_Click().

```
Sub menu_sales_Click ()

    'declare variables
    Dim m$        'message constructor
    Dim res%      'holds results

    If ChangeMade% = True Then
        'construct message
        m$ = "Re-populate without saving changes?"
        res% = MsgBox(m$, 292, "Warning")
        If res% = IDNO Then Exit Sub

    End If

    'flag no change
    ChangeMade% = False

    'flag populating
    Populating% = True

    'change cursor
    screen.MousePointer = HOURGLASS

    'label panel
    pnlSearchLabel.Caption = "Sales"

    'enable all text boxes-so errors don't occur
    Call EnableAll

    'assign table
    Data1.RecordSource = "SALES"

    'clear all data fields
    Call ClearDataFields

    'assign captions
    pnlFieldLabel(0).Caption = "Product ID"
```

```
pnlFieldLabel(1).Caption = "Staff ID"
pnlFieldLabel(2).Caption = "Date Sold"
pnlFieldLabel(3).Caption = "Qty Sold"

'enable text boxes
txtField(0).Enabled = True
txtField(1).Enabled = True
txtField(2).Enabled = True
txtField(3).Enabled = True

'assign fields to text boxes
txtField(0).DataField = "product_id"
txtField(1).DataField = "staff_id"
txtField(2).DataField = "date_sold"
txtField(3).DataField = "quantity_sold"

'refresh so new parameters will take effect
Data1.Refresh

'enable command buttons
cmdFirst.Enabled = True
cmdlast.Enabled = True

'update number of records
Call UpdateRecordCount

'enable command buttons, if appropriate
Call CheckButtons

'set focus twice, so that enable lookup event is generated
txtField(1).SetFocus
txtField(0).SetFocus

'unflag populating
Populating% = False

'change cursor
screen.MousePointer = DEFAULT

End Sub
```

THE *MENU_STAFF_CLICK()* EVENT PROCEDURE

The menu_staff_Click() event procedure searches on the STAFF table and populates the text fields with the first record. Following is a listing of the menu_staff_Click() event procedure:

LISTING 31.23. MAIN.FRM, menu_staff_Click().

```
Sub menu_staff_Click ()

    'declare variables
    Dim m$      'message constructor
    Dim res%    'holds results
```

continues

LISTING 31.23. CONTINUED

```
If ChangeMade% = True Then
    'construct message
    m$ = "Re-populate without saving changes?"
    res% = MsgBox(m$, 292, "Warning")
    If res% = IDNO Then Exit Sub

End If

'flag no change
ChangeMade% = False

'flag populating
Populating% = True

'change cursor
screen.MousePointer = HOURGLASS

'label panel
pnlSearchLabel.Caption = "Staff"

'enable all text boxes-so errors don't occur
Call EnableAll

'assign table
Data1.RecordSource = "STAFF"

'clear all data fields
Call ClearDataFields

'assign captions
pnlFieldLabel(0).Caption = "Staff ID"
pnlFieldLabel(1).Caption = "Last Name"
pnlFieldLabel(2).Caption = "First Name"
pnlFieldLabel(3).Caption = ""

'enable text boxes
txtField(0).Enabled = True
txtField(1).Enabled = True
txtField(2).Enabled = True
txtField(3).Enabled = False

'assign fields to text boxes
txtField(0).DataField = "staff_id"
txtField(1).DataField = "last_name"
txtField(2).DataField = "first_name"

'refresh so new parameters will take effect
Data1.Refresh

'enable command buttons
cmdFirst.Enabled = True
cmdlast.Enabled = True

'update number of records
Call UpdateRecordCount
```

```
'enable command buttons, if appropriate
Call CheckButtons

'set focus twice, so that enable lookup event is generated
txtField(1).SetFocus
txtField(0).SetFocus

'unflag populating
Populating% = False

'change cursor
screen.MousePointer = DEFAULT

End Sub
```

THE *MENU_SUPPLIERS_CLICK( )* EVENT PROCEDURE

The menu_suppliers_Click() event procedure searches on the SUPPLIERS table and populates the text fields with the first record. Following is a listing of the menu_suppliers_Click()
event procedure:

LISTING 31.24. MAIN.FRM, menu_suppliers_Click().

```
Sub menu_suppliers_Click ()

    'declare variables
    Dim m$        'message constructor
    Dim res%      'holds results

    If ChangeMade% = True Then
        'construct message
        m$ = "Re-populate without saving changes?"
        res% = MsgBox(m$, 292, "Warning")
        If res% = IDNO Then Exit Sub

    End If

    'flag no change
    ChangeMade% = False

    'flag populating
    Populating% = True

    'change cursor
    screen.MousePointer = HOURGLASS

    'label panel
    pnlSearchLabel.Caption = "Supplier"

    'enable all text boxes-so errors don't occur
    Call EnableAll
```

continues

787

LISTING 31.24. CONTINUED

```
'assign table
Data1.RecordSource = "SUPPLIER"

'clear all data fields
Call ClearDataFields

'assign captions
pnlFieldLabel(0).Caption = "Supplier ID"
pnlFieldLabel(1).Caption = "Supplier"
pnlFieldLabel(2).Caption = ""
pnlFieldLabel(3).Caption = ""

'enable text boxes
txtField(0).Enabled = True
txtField(1).Enabled = True
txtField(2).Enabled = False
txtField(3).Enabled = False

'assign fields to text boxes
txtField(0).DataField = "supplier_id"
txtField(1).DataField = "supplier"

'refresh so new parameters will take effect
Data1.Refresh

'enable command buttons
cmdFirst.Enabled = True
cmdlast.Enabled = True

'update number of records
Call UpdateRecordCount

'enable command buttons, if appropriate
Call CheckButtons

'set focus twice, so that enable lookup event is generated
txtField(1).SetFocus
txtField(0).SetFocus

'unflag populating
Populating% = False

'change cursor
screen.MousePointer = DEFAULT

End Sub
```

THE *MENU_UPDATE_CLICK( )* EVENT PROCEDURE

The menu_update_Click() event procedure updates the current record in the currently selected table. Following is a listing of the menu_update_Click() event procedure:

LISTING 31.25. MAIN.FRM, menu_update_Click().

```
Sub menu_update_Click ()

    'declare variables
    Dim cmd$          'SQL building variable
    Dim m$            'message constructor
    Dim res%          'holds results

    If BlankField() = True Then
        m$ = "You must fill in all fields which are enabled"
        MsgBox m$
        Exit Sub
    End If

    'construct message
    m$ = "Are you sure you want to" + Chr$(13)
    m$ = m$ + "update the current record?"

    'confirm deletion
    res% = MsgBox(m$, 292, "Warning")
    If res% = IDNO Then Exit Sub

    'open the database
    Set DB = OpenDatabase(GlobalDB$)

    Select Case UCase$((pnlSearchLabel.Caption))
        Case "INVENTORY":

            'only check if this is the field being updated
            If Text1$ <> txtField(0).Text Then
                'ensure entity integrity by checking primary key of table
                cmd$ = "SELECT * FROM INVENTORY "
                cmd$ = cmd$ + "WHERE product_id = '" + txtField(0).Text + "' "
                Set DS = DB.CreateDynaset(cmd$)

                If DS.RecordCount > 0 Then
                    'build message
                    m$ = "Product ID " + txtField(0).Text + " already exists"
                    MsgBox m$

                    'exit
                    Exit Sub
                End If
            End If

            'only check if this is the field being updated
            If Text3$ <> txtField(2).Text Then
                'find out if this supplier exists
                cmd$ = "SELECT * FROM SUPPLIER "
                cmd$ = cmd$ + "WHERE supplier_id = '" + txtField(2).Text + "' "
                Set DS = DB.CreateDynaset(cmd$)
                If DS.RecordCount = 0 Then
                    'this supplier doesn't exist in the database
                    m$ = "Supplier ID " + txtField(2).Text + " doesn't exist in the
                        supplier table"
```

continues

LISTING 31.25. CONTINUED

```vbnet
                MsgBox m$
                Exit Sub
            End If
        End If

        'create dynaset from old data
        cmd$ = "SELECT * FROM INVENTORY "
        cmd$ = cmd$ + "WHERE product_id = '" + Text1$ + "' "
        cmd$ = cmd$ + "AND description = '" + Text2$ + "' "
        cmd$ = cmd$ + "AND supplier_id = '" + Text3$ + "' "
        cmd$ = cmd$ + "AND quantity = " + Text4$ + " "
        Set DS = DB.CreateDynaset(cmd$)

        'edit the dynaset
        DS.Edit

        'add individual fields
        DS("product_id") = txtField(0).Text
        DS("description") = txtField(1).Text
        DS("supplier_id") = txtField(2).Text
        DS("quantity") = txtField(3).Text

        'update dynaset
        DS.Update

        'unflag changes made
        ChangeMade% = False

        'repopulate
        Call menu_inventory_Click

    Case "SALES":
        'there is no primary key for sales-can't check integrity,
        'but we need to find out if there is an employee with this ID
        ' and if there is enough of this item in inventory to sell

        'find out if this employee exists
        cmd$ = "SELECT * FROM STAFF "
        cmd$ = cmd$ + "WHERE staff_id = '" + txtField(1).Text + "' "
        Set DS = DB.CreateDynaset(cmd$)
        If DS.RecordCount = 0 Then
            'this person doesn't exist in the database
            m$ = "Staff ID " + txtField(1).Text + " doesn't exist in the staff table"
            MsgBox m$
            Exit Sub
        End If

        cmd$ = "SELECT quantity FROM INVENTORY "
        cmd$ = cmd$ + "WHERE product_id = '" + txtField(0).Text + "' "
        Set DS = DB.CreateDynaset(cmd$)
        If DS.RecordCount = 0 Then
            'this item doesn't exist in the database
            m$ = "Product ID " + txtField(0).Text + " doesn't exist in inventory"
            MsgBox m$
            Exit Sub
        Else
```

```
            'this product exists-check number in inventory
            If Val(txtField(3).Text) > DS.Fields(0) Then
                'build message
                m$ = "There are only " + Trim$(Str$(DS.Fields(0))) + " items in
                    inventory." + Chr$(13)
                m$ = m$ + "Would you like to continue to update inventory anyway?"
                res% = MsgBox(m$, 292, "Warning")

                'user doesn't want to have negative inventory-exit
                If res% = IDNO Then Exit Sub
            End If

        End If

        'enter edit mode
        DS.Edit

        'update quantity fields
        DS("quantity") = DS.Fields(0) - Val(txtField(3).Text)

        'update quantity to reflect current inventory minus this sale
        DS.Update

        'create dynaset from old data
        cmd$ = "SELECT * FROM SALES "
        cmd$ = cmd$ + "WHERE product_id = '" + Text1$ + "' "
        cmd$ = cmd$ + "AND staff_id = '" + Text2$ + "' "
        cmd$ = cmd$ + "AND date_sold = '" + Text3$ + "' "
        cmd$ = cmd$ + "AND quantity_sold = " + Text4$ + " "
        Set DS = DB.CreateDynaset(cmd$)

        'edit the dynaset
        DS.Edit

        'add individual fields
        DS("product_id") = txtField(0).Text
        DS("staff_id") = txtField(1).Text
        DS("date_sold") = txtField(2).Text
        DS("quantity_sold") = txtField(3).Text

        'update dynaset
        DS.Update

        'unflag changes made
        ChangeMade% = False

        'repopulate
        Call menu_sales_Click

Case "SUPPLIER":
    'only check if this is the field being updated
    If Text1$ <> txtField(0).Text Then

        'ensure entity integrity by checking primary key of table
        cmd$ = "SELECT * FROM SUPPLIER "
        cmd$ = cmd$ + "WHERE supplier_id = '" + txtField(0).Text + "' "
```

continues

LISTING 31.25. CONTINUED

```
            Set DS = DB.CreateDynaset(cmd$)

            If DS.RecordCount > 0 Then
                'build message
                m$ = "Supplier ID " + txtField(0).Text + " already exists"
                MsgBox m$

                'exit
                Exit Sub
            End If
        End If

        'create dynaset from old data
        cmd$ = "SELECT * FROM SUPPLIER "
        cmd$ = cmd$ + "WHERE supplier_id = '" + Text1$ + "' "
        cmd$ = cmd$ + "AND supplier = '" + Text2$ + "' "
        Set DS = DB.CreateDynaset(cmd$)

        'edit the dynaset
        DS.Edit

        'add individual fields
        DS("supplier_id") = txtField(0).Text
        DS("supplier") = txtField(1).Text

        'update dynaset
        DS.Update

        'unflag changes made
        ChangeMade% = False

        'repopulate
        Call menu_suppliers_Click

    Case "STAFF":
        'only check if this is the field being updated
        If Text1$ <> txtField(0).Text Then

            'ensure entity integrity by checking primary key of table
            cmd$ = "SELECT * FROM STAFF "
            cmd$ = cmd$ + "WHERE staff_id = '" + txtField(0).Text + "' "
            Set DS = DB.CreateDynaset(cmd$)

            If DS.RecordCount > 0 Then
                'build message
                m$ = "Staff ID " + txtField(0).Text + " already exists"
                MsgBox m$

                'exit
                Exit Sub
            End If
        End If

        'create dynaset from old data
        cmd$ = "SELECT * FROM STAFF "
```

```
            cmd$ = cmd$ + "WHERE staff_id = '" + Text1$ + "' "
            cmd$ = cmd$ + "AND last_name = '" + Text2$ + "' "
            cmd$ = cmd$ + "AND first_name = '" + Text3$ + "' "
            Set DS = DB.CreateDynaset(cmd$)

            'edit the dynaset
            DS.Edit

            'add individual fields
            DS("staff_id") = txtField(0).Text
            DS("last_name") = txtField(1).Text
            DS("first_name") = txtField(2).Text

            'update dynaset
            DS.Update

            'unflag changes made
            ChangeMade% = False

            'repopulate
            Call menu_staff_Click
        Case Else:
            'user did not search on any table yet
            m$ = "You must search on a table" + Chr$(13)
            m$ = m$ + "before you can insert a new record!"
            MsgBox m$
    End Select

End Sub
```

THE *txtFIELD* CONTROL

txtField is the name of the textbox control array that is the entry into the CHAP31.MDB database. It also allows for browsing. The txtField control has code in two event procedures. They are

- ◆ txtField_Change()
- ◆ txtField_GotFocus()

THE *txtFIELD_CHANGE( )* EVENT PROCEDURE

The txtField_Change() event procedure is invoked every time the text is changed. Following is a listing of the txtField_Change() event procedure:

LISTING 31.26. MAIN.FRM, txtField_Change( ).

```
Sub txtField_Change (Index As Integer)

    'flagging change is invalid if populating
    If Populating% = True Then Exit Sub
```

continues

LISTING 31.26. CONTINUED

```
        'flag change
        ChangeMade% = True

End Sub
```

THE *txtField_GotFocus( )* EVENT PROCEDURE

The txtField_GotFocus() event procedure is invoked every time the textbox gets the focus. It is used to check if the lookup button can be enabled. Following is a listing of the txtField_GotFocus() event procedure:

LISTING 31.27. MAIN.FRM, `txtField_GotFocus( )`.

```
Sub txtField_GotFocus (Index As Integer)

    'check to see if the lookup button should be enabled
    Call EnableLookup(Index)

End Sub
```

THE CRYSTAL.FRM FILE

CRYSTAL.FRM is one of four forms in this application. It is used to select and display one of three types of Crystal Reports. They are Inventory, Sales, and Staff reports. These reports are possible because of the CRYSTAL.VBX custom control that comes with Visual Basic, Professional edition. Figure 31.2 presents this form as it appears at runtime. Figure 31.4 shows the form as it appears at design time. Table 31.3 lists all the relevant properties of each control on the form that have been changed from their standard default values. The CRYSTAL.FRM file is contained in the CHAP31 subdirectory on the CD accompanying this book.

 For more information about Crystal Reports, refer to Chapter 17, "Crystal Reports."

FIGURE 31.4.
*Data Access application
CRYSTAL.FRM at
design time.*

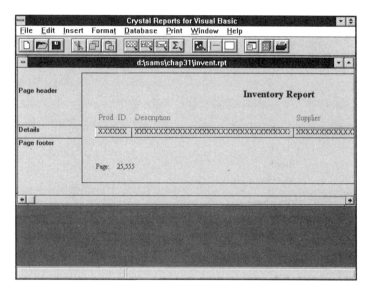

TABLE 31.3. PROPERTIES OF EACH CONTROL ON CRYSTAL.FRM.

Object	Control Type	Property	Value
frmCrystal	Form	BackColor	&H00404000&
		Caption	"Crystal Reports Form"
		Height	4005
		Left	2595
		MaxButton	False
		Top	1785
		Width	4500
Panel3D1	SSPanel	BackColor	&H00C0C0C0&
		BevelWidth	3
		Font3D	None
		ForeColor	&H00000000&
		Height	3375
		Left	120
		Top	120
		Width	4095

continues

T ABLE 31.3. CONTINUED

Object	Control Type	Property	Value
Frame3D2	SSFrame	Caption	"Select Destination"
		Font3D	None
		Height	1935
		Left	2040
		Top	240
		Width	1815
Frame3D1	SSFrame	Caption	"Select Report"
		Font3D	None
		Height	1935
		Left	240
		Top	240
		Width	1695
fmeDates	SSFrame	Caption	"Dates"
		Font3D	None
		Height	495
		Left	240
		Top	2280
		Visible	False
		Width	3615
optOther	SSOption	Caption	"Other"
		Font3D	None
		Height	255
		Left	1680
		Top	120
		Value	True
		Width	855
optToday	SSOption	Caption	"Today"
		Font3D	None
		Height	255
		Left	720
		Top	120
		Width	855

Object	Control Type	Property	Value
optPrinter	SSOption	Caption	"Printer"
		Font3D	None
		Height	255
		Left	120
		Top	960
		Width	1455
optFile	SSOption	Caption	"File"
		Font3D	None
		Height	255
		Left	120
		Top	1440
		Width	1455
optInventory	SSOption	Caption	"Inventory"
		Font3D	None
		Height	255
		Left	120
		Top	1440
		Width	1455
optSales	SSOption	Caption	"Daily Sales"
		Font3D	None
		Height	255
		Left	120
		Top	960
		Width	1455
optStaff	SSOption	Caption	"Staff"
		Font3D	None
		Height	255
		Left	120
		Top	480
		Value	True
		Width	1455

continues

TABLE 31.3. CONTINUED

Object	Control Type	Property	Value
optScreen	SSOption	Caption	"Screen"
		Font3D	None
		Height	255
		Left	120
		Top	480
		Value	True
		Width	1455
txtOther	TextBox	BackColor	&H00FFFFFF&
		Height	285
		Left	2520
		Top	120
		Width	975
cmdClose	CommandButton	Caption	"Close"
		Height	375
		Left	2160
		Top	2880
		Width	1455
cmdBegin	CommandButton	Caption	"Begin"
		Height	375
		Left	360
		Top	2880
		Width	1455
cmDialog	CommonDialog	CancelError	True
		Left	3600
		Top	360
rptCrystal	CrystalReport	Connect	""
		CopiesToPrinter	1
		Destination	Window
		GroupSelectionFormula	""
		Left	3600

Object	Control Type	Property	Value
		PrintFileName	""
		SelectionFormula	""
		SessionHandle	0
		Top	840
		UserName	""
		WindowBorderStyle	Sizable
		WindowControlBox	True
		WindowHeight	300
		WindowLeft	100
		WindowMaxButton	True
		WindowMinButton	True
		WindowParentHandle	0
		WindowTitle	""
		WindowTop	100
		WindowWidth	480

FUNCTION, SUBROUTINE, AND EVENT PROCEDURES

There are several procedures of code for each object(control) that comprise this form. Each is listed in the following sections.

THE (GENERAL) OBJECT

The (general) object contains form level declarations and two form level procedures. The procedures for the (general) object are

- ◆ (declarations)
- ◆ GetcmDialogFile()

THE (DECLARATIONS) PROCEDURE

The (declarations) procedure contains only one line of declarations used in the form, CRYSTAL.FRM. It is only to allow for variable syntax checking and forcing the declaration of variables in each procedure. Following is a listing of the (declarations) procedure:

LISTING 31.28. CRYSTAL.FRM, (general)(declarations).

```
Option Explicit
```

THE *GETCMDIALOGFILE( ) EVENT* PROCEDURE

The GetcmDialogFile() event procedure invokes the common dialog box. It is also a function that returns the file received by the common dialog control. Following is a listing of the GetcmDialogFile() event procedure:

LISTING 31.29. CRYSTAL.FRM, GetcmDialogFile( ).

```
Function GetcmDialogFile () As String

    'handle errors
    On Error GoTo cmDialogError:

    'set filter to all files
    cmDialog.Filter = "Text Files¦*.TXT"

    'invoke save as dialog box
    cmDialog.Action = DLG_FILE_SAVE

    'assign file
    GetcmDialogFile = cmDialog.Filename

    'exit
    Exit Function

cmDialogError:
    Select Case (Err)
        Case 32755: 'cancel-do nothing
        Case Else
            MsgBox Error$
    End Select

    'exit function
    GetcmDialogFile = ""
    Exit Function

    'avoid errors
    Resume

End Function
```

THE *CMDBEGIN* CONTROL

cmdBegin is the name of the command button control that, when clicked, will start the report specified by the option buttons. Figure 31.5 shows a crystal report (INVENTORY.RPT) at runtime. It is invoked by selecting the optInventory radio button.

The cmdBegin control has code only in one event procedure. It is

◆ cmdBegin_Click()

FIGURE 31.5.
Inventory report at runtime.

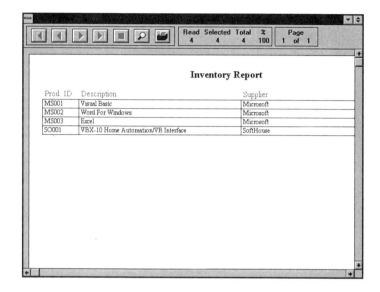

THE *CMDBEGIN_CLICK()* EVENT PROCEDURE

The cmdBegin_Click() event procedure starts the report running process. Following is a listing of the cmdBegin_Click() event procedure:

LISTING 31.30. CRYSTAL.FRM, cmdBegin_Click().

```
Sub cmdBegin_Click ()

    'declare variables
    Dim m$                 'message constructor
    Dim TempFileName$      'temp variable
    Dim TempFileLen&       'temporary length of file

    'check "SELECT REPORT" frame to see if selections are made
    If optStaff.Value = False And optSales.Value = False And optInventory.Value = False
    Then
        'build message
        m$ = "You must select a report first!"
        MsgBox m$

        'exit
        Exit Sub
    End If

    'check "SELECT DEST." frame to see if selections are made
    If optScreen.Value = False And optPrinter.Value = False And optFile.Value = False
    Then

        'build message
        m$ = "You must select a destination first!"
        MsgBox m$
```

continues

801

LISTING 31.30. CONTINUED

```
        'exit
        Exit Sub
    End If

    'determine which report to print
    If optStaff.Value = True Then
        rptCrystal.ReportFileName = "STAFF.RPT"
    ElseIf optSales.Value = True Then
        rptCrystal.ReportFileName = "SALES.RPT"

        'also send date to filter output of report
        If optToday.Value = True Then
            rptCrystal.Formulas(0) = "PrintDate = '" + Format$(Now, "MM/DD/YY") + "'"
        Else
            rptCrystal.Formulas(0) = "PrintDate = '" + txtOther.Text + "'"
        End If
    ElseIf optInventory.Value = True Then
        rptCrystal.ReportFileName = "INVENT.RPT"
    End If


    'determine where to print report
    If optScreen.Value = True Then
        rptCrystal.Destination = 0
    ElseIf optPrinter.Value = True Then
        rptCrystal.Destination = 1
    ElseIf optFile.Value = True Then
        rptCrystal.Destination = 2

        'file was selected-get file name
        TempFileName$ = GetcmDialogFile()

        'assign file name to crystal
        If TempFileName$ <> "" Then
            rptCrystal.PrintFileName = TempFileName$
        Else
            'build message
            m$ = "No Valid File Name" + Chr$(13)
            m$ = m$ + "Operation Cancelled!"
            MsgBox m$

            'exit
            Exit Sub
        End If
    End If


    'handle errors
    On Error GoTo FileError:

    'test for report file name to see if it exists
    TempFileLen& = FileLen(rptCrystal.ReportFileName)

    'start report
    rptCrystal.Action = 1
```

```
        'exit
        Exit Sub

FileError:
    Select Case (Err)
        Case 53:    'file not found
            'build message
            m$ = "File " + rptCrystal.ReportFileName + " doesn't exist!"
            MsgBox m$
        Case Else
            MsgBox Error$
    End Select

        'exit
        Exit Sub

        'avoid errors
        Resume

End Sub
```

 For more information about Crystal Reports, refer to Chapter 17, "Crystal Reports."

THE *cmdClose* CONTROL

cmdClose is the name of the command button control that, when clicked, simply closes the form. The cmdClose control has code in only one event procedure. It is

♦ cmdClose_Click()

THE *cmdClose_Click()* EVENT PROCEDURE

The cmdClose_Click() event procedure simply closes the form. Following is a listing of the cmdClose_Click() event procedure:

LISTING 31.31. CRYSTAL.FRM, cmdClose_Click().

```
Sub cmdClose_Click ()

    'unload report form
    Unload frmCrystal

End Sub
```

THE *FORM* OBJECT

The Form object has code in only one event procedure. It is

♦ Form_Load()

803

THE *FORM_LOAD()* EVENT PROCEDURE

The Form_Load() event simply calls the routine to center the form. Following is a listing of the Form_Load() event procedure:

LISTING 31.32. CRYSTAL.FRM, Form_Load().

```
Sub Form_Load ()

    'change cursor
    Screen.MousePointer = HOURGLASS

    'center the form
    CenterForm Me

    'change cursor
    Screen.MousePointer = DEFAULT

End Sub
```

THE *optINVENTORY* CONTROL

optInventory is the name of the radio button control that indicates that the user wants to run the Inventory report. It also hides the dates frame used only for the Sales report. The optInventory control has code in only one event procedure. It is

◆ optInventory_Click()

THE *optINVENTORY_CLICK()* EVENT PROCEDURE

The optInventory_Click() event procedure processes that the user wants to run an Inventory report. Following is a listing of the optInventory_Click() event procedure:

LISTING 31.33. CRYSTAL.FRM, optInventory_Click().

```
Sub optInventory_Click (Value As Integer)

    'hide dates frame
    fmeDates.Visible = False

End Sub
```

THE *optOTHER* CONTROL

optOther is the name of the radio button control that, when clicked, allows the user to report on a date other than the current date. This is only enabled for the Sales report. The optOther control has code in only one event procedure. It is

◆ optOther_Click()

THE *optOTHER_CLICK()* EVENT PROCEDURE

The optOther_Click() event procedure allows the user to input a different date other than the current date. Following is a listing of the optOther_Click() event procedure:

LISTING 31.34. CRYSTAL.FRM, optOther_Click().

```
Sub optOther_Click (Value As Integer)

    'show date text box
    txtOther.Visible = True

    'clear text
    txtOther.Text = ""

    'set focus
    txtOther.SetFocus

End Sub
```

THE *optSALES* CONTROL

optSales is the name of the radio button control that indicates that the user wants to run the Sales report. It also shows the dates frame that is used only for the Sales report. The optSales control has code in only one event procedure. It is

◆ optSales_Click()

THE *optSALES_CLICK()* EVENT PROCEDURE

The optSales_Click() event procedure processes that the user wants to run a Sales report. Following is a listing of the optSales_Click() event procedure:

LISTING 31.35. CRYSTAL.FRM, optSales_Click().

```
Sub OptSales_Click (Value As Integer)

    'show dates frame
    fmeDates.Visible = True
    optToday.Value = True

End Sub
```

THE *optSTAFF* CONTROL

optStaff is the name of the radio button control that indicates that the user wants to run the Staff report. It also hides the dates frame that is used only for the Sales report. The optStaff control has code in only one event procedure. It is

◆ optStaff_Click()

805

THE *optStaff_Click()* EVENT PROCEDURE

The `optStaff_Click()` event procedure processes that the user wants to run a Staff report. Following is a listing of the `optStaff_Click()` event procedure:

LISTING 31.36. CRYSTAL.FRM, `optStaff_Click()`.

```
Sub optStaff_Click (Value As Integer)

    'hide dates frame
    fmeDates.Visible = False

End Sub
```

THE *optToday* CONTROL

`optToday` is the name of the radio button control that, when clicked, allows the user to report based on today's date. This is only enabled for the Sales report. The `optToday` control has code in only one event procedure. It is

◆ `optToday_Click()`

THE *optToday_Click()* EVENT PROCEDURE

The `optToday_Click()` event procedure processes that the user wants to select today's date. Following is a listing of the `optToday_Click()` event procedure:

LISTING 31.37. CRYSTAL.FRM, `optToday_Click()`.

```
Sub optToday_Click (Value As Integer)

    'hide date text box
    txtOther.Visible = False

End Sub
```

THE LOOKUP.FRM FILE

LOOKUP.FRM is one of four forms in this application. It is used to lookup an ID number from a table in the CHAP31.MDB database. Figure 31.3 presents this form as it appears at runtime. It is fundamentally no different at design time, so it is not shown again. Table 31.4 lists all the relevant properties of each control on the form that have been changed from their standard default values. The LOOKUP.FRM file is contained on the CD accompanying this book in the CHAP31 subdirectory.

TABLE 31.4. PROPERTIES OF EACH CONTROL ON LOOKUP.FRM.

Object	Control Type	Property	Value
frmLookup	Form	BackColor	&H00404000&
		Height	4920
		Left	1035
		MaxButton	False
		Top	1140
		Width	4470
Panel3D1	SSPanel	BackColor	&H00C0C0C0&
		BevelWidth	3
		Font3D	None
		ForeColor	&H0000FFFF&
		Height	4215
		Left	120
		Top	120
		Width	4095
cmdClose	CommandButton	Caption	"Close"
		Height	375
		Left	2160
		Top	3720
		Width	1095
cmdSelect	CommandButton	Caption	"Select"
		Height	375
		Left	840
		Top	3720
		Width	1095
lstLookup	ListBox	BackColor	&H00C0C0C0&
		Height	3345
		Left	240
		Top	120
		Width	3615

FUNCTION, SUBROUTINE, AND EVENT PROCEDURES

There are several procedures of code for each object(control) that comprise this form. Each is listed in the following sections.

THE *(GENERAL)* OBJECT

The (general) object contains only one form level declaration and no form level procedures. The procedure for the (general) object is

◆ (declarations)

THE *(DECLARATIONS)* PROCEDURE

The (declarations) procedure contains only one line of declarations used in the form, LOOKUP.FRM. It is only to allow for variable syntax checking and forcing the declaration of variables in each procedure. Following is a listing of the (declarations) procedure:

LISTING 31.38. LOOKUP.FRM, (general)(declarations).

```
Option Explicit
```

THE *CMDCLOSE* CONTROL

cmdClose is the name of the command button control that, when clicked, simply closes the form. The cmdClose control has code in only one event procedure. It is

◆ cmdClose_Click()

THE *CMDCLOSE_CLICK()* EVENT PROCEDURE

The cmdClose_Click() event procedure simply closes the form. Following is a listing of the cmdClose_Click() event procedure:

LISTING 31.39. LOOKUP.FRM, cmdClose_Click().

```
Sub cmdClose_Click ()

    'unload
    Unload frmLookup

End Sub
```

THE *cmdSELECT* CONTROL

`cmdSelect` is the name of the command button control that, when clicked, populates the field on the MAIN.FRM form with the chosen selection. It also closes this form. The `cmdSelect` control has code in only one event procedure. It is

◆ cmdSelect_Click()

THE *cmdSELECT_CLICK()* EVENT PROCEDURE

The `cmdSelect_Click()` event procedure processes which report selection the user has chosen. Following is a listing of the `cmdSelect_Click()` event procedure:

LISTING 31.40. LOOKUP.FRM, `cmdSelect_Click()`.

```
Sub cmdSelect_Click ()

    'declare variables
    Dim TempID$        'temporary string
    Dim pos%           'holds position of tab character

    'find out which is selected
    TempID$ = lstLookup.List(lstLookup.ListIndex)

    'find tab
    pos% = InStr(TempID$, Chr$(9))

    'parse string to find out which is the specific ID
    TempID$ = Left$(TempID$, pos% - 1)

    'populate list box based on title of caption
    Select Case (UCase$(frmLookup.Caption))
        Case "PRODUCT LOOKUP":
            'this could have only come from SALES search, text box index 0
            frmMain.txtField(0).Text = TempID$
        Case "STAFF LOOKUP":
            'this could have only come from SALES search, text box index 1
            frmMain.txtField(1).Text = TempID$
        Case "SUPPLIER LOOKUP":
            'this could have only come from INVENTORY search, text box index 2
            frmMain.txtField(2).Text = TempID$
    End Select

    'close the form
    Call cmdClose_Click

End Sub
```

THE *FORM* OBJECT

The Form object has code in only one event procedure. It is

◆ Form_Load()

THE *FORM_LOAD( )* EVENT PROCEDURE

The Form_Load() event procedure centers the form and populates the list of available ID numbers. Following is a listing of the Form_Load() event procedure:

LISTING 31.41. LOOKUP.FRM, Form_Load( ).

```
Sub Form_Load ()

    'declare variables
    Dim cmd$         'SQL building string
    Dim loopcount%   'loop counting variable
    Dim RCount%      'holds record count

    'change cursor
    Screen.MousePointer = HOURGLASS

    'change caption, based on operation selected
    frmLookup.Caption = frmMain.txtLUCaption.Text
    DoEvents

    'center the form
    CenterForm Me

    'open the database
    Set DB = OpenDatabase(GlobalDB$)

    'clear the list box
    lstLookup.Clear

    'populate list box based on title of caption
    Select Case (UCase$(frmLookup.Caption))
        Case "PRODUCT LOOKUP":

            'build SQL for dynaset
            cmd$ = "SELECT product_id,description FROM INVENTORY "
            cmd$ = cmd$ + "ORDER BY product_id "

            'create the dynaset
            Set DS = DB.CreateDynaset(cmd$)

            'move to last record-to auto calculate recordcount
            DS.MoveLast

            'assign Record count
            RCount% = DS.RecordCount

            'move to first record
            DS.MoveFirst

            'loop through all items in dynaset and populate list box
            For loopcount% = 1 To RCount%
                lstLookup.AddItem DS.Fields(0) + Chr$(9) + DS.Fields(1)
```

```
                       'move to next record
                        DS.MoveNext
                 Next loopcount%

        Case "STAFF LOOKUP":

                 'build SQL for dynaset
                 cmd$ = "SELECT staff_id,last_name,first_name FROM STAFF "
                 cmd$ = cmd$ + "ORDER BY staff_id "

                 'create the dynaset
                 Set DS = DB.CreateDynaset(cmd$)

                 'move to last record-to auto calculate recordcount
                 DS.MoveLast

                 'assign Record count
                 RCount% = DS.RecordCount

                 'move to first record
                 DS.MoveFirst

                 'loop through all items in dynaset and populate list box
                 For loopcount% = 1 To RCount%
                        lstLookup.AddItem DS.Fields(0) + Chr$(9) + DS.Fields(1) + ", " +
                        DS.Fields(2)

                        'move to next record
                        DS.MoveNext
                 Next loopcount%
        Case "SUPPLIER LOOKUP":

                 'build SQL for dynaset
                 cmd$ = "SELECT supplier_id,supplier FROM SUPPLIER "
                 cmd$ = cmd$ + "ORDER BY supplier_id "

                 'create the dynaset
                 Set DS = DB.CreateDynaset(cmd$)

                 'move to last record-to auto calculate recordcount
                 DS.MoveLast

                 'assign Record count
                 RCount% = DS.RecordCount

                 'move to first record
                 DS.MoveFirst

                 'loop through all items in dynaset and populate list box
                 For loopcount% = 1 To RCount%
                        lstLookup.AddItem DS.Fields(0) + Chr$(9) + DS.Fields(1)

                        'move to next record
                        DS.MoveNext
                 Next loopcount%
End Select
```

continues

LISTING 31.41. CONTINUED

```
'disable select button
cmdSelect.Enabled = False

'change cursor
Screen.MousePointer = DEFAULT

End Sub
```

THE *lstLookup* CONTROL

lstLookup is the name of the listbox that holds all of the ID numbers for the given table. When clicked, it simply enables the Select command button. When double-clicked, it will act the same as the Select command button. The lstLookup control has code in two event procedures. They are

- lstLookup_Click()
- lstLookup_DblClick()

THE *lstLookup_Click()* EVENT PROCEDURE

The lstLookup_Click() event procedure acts the same as clicking the Select button. Following is a listing of the lstLookup_Click() event procedure:

LISTING 31.42. LOOKUP.FRM, lstLookup_Click().

```
Sub lstLookup_Click ()

    'enable select button
    cmdSelect.Enabled = True

End Sub
```

THE *lstLookup_DblClick()* EVENT PROCEDURE

Following is a listing of the lstLookup_DblClick() event procedure:

LISTING 31.43. LOOKUP.FRM, lstLookup_DblClick().

```
Sub lstLookup_DblClick ()

    'same as single click then clicking on select button
    Call cmdSelect_Click

End Sub
```

THE ABOUT.FRM FILE

ABOUT.FRM is one of four forms in this application. It shows information about the application. Figure 31.6 presents the About form as it appears at runtime. Fundamentally, there is no difference in the form at design time, so it is not presented. Table 31.5 lists all the relevant properties of each control on the form that have been changed from their standard default values. The ABOUT.FRM file is contained in the CHAP31 subdirectory on the CD accompanying this book.

FIGURE 31.6.
Data Access application
About form at runtime.

TABLE 31.5. PROPERTIES OF EACH CONTROL ON ABOUT.FRM.

Object	Control Type	Property	Value
frmAbout	Form	BackColor	&H00404000&
		Caption	"About"
		Height	3525
		Left	1035
		MaxButton	False
		MinButton	False
		Top	1140
		Width	4545
pnlMain	SSPanel	BackColor	&H00C0C0C0&
		BevelWidth	3
		Caption	""
		Font3D	None
		ForeColor	&H00C0C0C0&
		Height	2895
		Left	120

continues

TABLE 31.5. CONTINUED

Object	Control Type	Property	Value
		RoundedCorners	False
		ShadowColor	Black
		Top	120
		Width	4215
pnl1	SSPanel	BackColor	&H00C0C0C0&
		BevelWidth	3
		Caption	"Real-World Programming With Visual Basic"
		Font3D	None
		ForeColor	&H0000FFFF&
		Height	975
		Left	960
		RoundedCorners	False
		ShadowColor	Black
		Top	120
		Width	2415
pnl2	SSPanel	BackColor	&H00C0C0C0&
		BevelWidth	3
		Caption	"Anthony T. Mann"
		Font3D	None
		ForeColor	&H0000FFFF&
		Height	615
		Left	960
		RoundedCorners	False
		ShadowColor	Black
		Top	1080
		Width	2415
pnl3	SSPanel	BackColor	&H00C0C0C0&
		BevelWidth	3
		Caption	"Data Access Application (Version 1.0)"

Object	Control Type	Property	Value
		Font3D	None
		ForeColor	&H0000FFFF&
		Height	615
		Left	960
		RoundedCorners	False
		ShadowColor	Black
		Top	1680
		Width	2415
cmdOK	CommandButton	Caption	"OK"
		Height	375
		Left	1680
		Top	2400
		Width	1095
pictAbout	PictureBox	Autosize	True
		BackColor	&H00C0C0C0&
		BorderStyle	None
		Height	615
		Left	120
		Top	120
		Width	735

FUNCTION, SUBROUTINE, AND EVENT PROCEDURES

There are several procedures of code for each object(control) that comprise this form. Each is listed in the following sections.

The (general) object contains only one form level declaration and no form level procedures. The procedures for the (general) object are

◆ (declarations)

THE (DECLARATIONS) PROCEDURE

The (declarations) procedure contains only one line of declarations used in the form, ABOUT.FRM. It is only to allow for variable syntax checking and forcing the declaration of variables in each procedure. Following is a listing of the (declarations) procedure:

LISTING 31.44. ABOUT.FRM, (general)(declarations).

```
Option Explicit
```

THE *CMDOK* CONTROL

cmdOK is the name of the command button control that, when clicked, closes the frmAbout form. The cmdOK control has code in only one event procedure. It is

◆ cmdOK_Click()

THE *CMDOK_CLICK()* EVENT PROCEDURE

The cmdOK_Click() event procedure simply unloads the form. Following is a listing of the cmdOK_Click() event procedure:

LISTING 31.45. ABOUT.FRM, cmdOK_Click().

```
Sub cmdOK_Click ()

    'unload
    Unload frmAbout

End Sub
```

THE *FORM* OBJECT

The Form object has code in only one event procedure. It is

◆ Form_Load()

THE *FORM_LOAD()* EVENT PROCEDURE

The Form_Load() event procedure centers the form and assigns an icon to the pictAbout control. Following is a listing of the Form_Load() event procedure:

LISTING 31.46. ABOUT.FRM, Form_Load().

```
Sub Form_Load ()

    'center form
    CenterForm Me

    'load icon
    pictAbout.Picture = frmMain.Icon

End Sub
```

The CHAP31.BAS File

CHAP31.BAS is the module that contains application level variables and procedures. The CHAP31.BAS file is contained on the CD accompanying this book in the CHAP31 subdirectory.

Function, Subroutine, and Event Procedures

There are several procedures of code for each object(control) that comprise this module. Each is listed in the following sections.

The (general) object contains application level variables and procedures. The procedures for the (general) object are

- ◆ (declarations)
- ◆ CenterForm()

The *(declarations)* Procedure

The (declarations) procedure contains variable declarations used in the application. Following is a listing of the (declarations) procedure:

Listing 31.47. CHAP31.BAS, (general)(declarations).

```
Option Explicit

'mousepointers
Global Const HOURGLASS = 11
Global Const DEFAULT = 0

'messageboxes
Global Const IDNO = 7
Global Const IDYES = 6

Global DB As database
Global DS As dynaset
Global GlobalDB$
Global Const MODAL = 1
Global Const DLG_FILE_SAVE = 2
```

The *CenterForm()* Procedure

The CenterForm() procedure simply centers the form in the client area upon form loading. The CenterForm() procedure accepts one argument, F. It is the actual form to be centered. For more information on manipulating graphics and forms, refer to Chapter 5, "Graphics." Following is a listing of the CenterForm() procedure:

LISTING 31.48. CHAP31.BAS, CenterForm().

```
Sub CenterForm (F As Form)

    'center the form
    F.Left = (Screen.Width - F.Width) / 2
    F.Top = (Screen.Height - F.Height) / 2

End Sub
```

THE CHAP31.ICO FILE

This file contains the icon that has been attached to the form at design time. The CHAP31.ICO file is contained in the CHAP31 subdirectory on the CD accompanying this book.

FIGURE 31.7.
Data Access application
CHAP31 icon.

THE CHAP31.EXE FILE

This is the executable file that is distributable. If you distribute this application, you must include the following files:

- ◆ CHAP31.EXE
- ◆ CMDIALOG.VBX
- ◆ CRYSTAL.VBX
- ◆ THREED.VBX
- ◆ COMMDLG.DLL
- ◆ VBRUN300.DLL
- ◆ CRPE.DLL
- ◆ PDIRJET.DLL
- ◆ PDBJET.DLL
- ◆ MSAJE110.DLL
- ◆ MSAES110.DLL
- ◆ MSABC110.DLL
- ◆ CTL3D.DLL
- ◆ SALES.RPT
- ◆ STAFF.RPT
- ◆ INVENT.RPT

There may be other files required if you distribute a database that is not an Access database (for example, SQL Server and Oracle).

The CHAP31.EXE file and source files are contained in the CHAP31 subdirectory on the CD accompanying this book, while all DLLs and VBXs are in the RESOURCE subdirectory.

RELATING THE DATA ACCESS APPLICATION TO YOUR APPLICATION

The Data Access application shows how to create a multi-table Access Database. This opens the door to a variety of different databases. You can enhance this application by making it a full-fledged inventory tracking database. You can also extend it to track appointments and perform scheduling.

FINAL NOTES

This application was created on a standard VGA display using 16 colors. Your particular hardware could have adverse effects on the code the way it is written. You may need to modify it slightly.

MULTIMEDIA PLAYER
APPLICATION

THE MULTIMEDIA PLAYER APPLICATION ALLOWS YOU TO PLAY MANY TYPES OF MULTIMEDIA FILES. THESE FILE TYPES ARE MUSICAL INSTRUMENT DIGITAL INTERFACE—MIDI (*.MID), WAVE (*.WAV), AUDIO/VIDEO INTERLEAVE (*.AVI), AND MULTIMEDIA MOVIES (*.MMM).

Selecting a file with one of the file extensions listed in parenthesis above will instruct the multimedia player application to play in the appropriate mode. For example, if an AVI or MMM file is selected, a picture box is shown and initialized. If a MID or WAV file is selected, the box is invisible and the form is resized accordingly. This is made possible with the MCI.VBX control that comes with the Professional Edition of Visual Basic version 3.0.

Figure 32.1 shows the main screen (MAIN.FRM) at runtime.

FIGURE 32.1.
Multimedia Player at runtime, showing an AVI file.

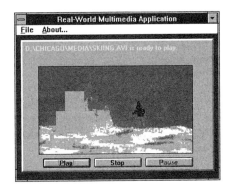

To use the application, open the appropriate file by selecting one of the file types listed earlier. By default, the common dialog file filter is set to All files. If you wish, you can choose a filter corresponding to a file extension supported by this application.

Once a file is chosen, if the appropriate drivers are in place to play the file, the MCI control is then enabled. Use the standard VCR-like controls to play the file.

 For more information on multimedia drivers, refer to Chapter 12, "Multimedia."

 For more information, refer to Chapter 5, "Graphics," and Chapter 11, "Audio."

CODE LISTINGS

The multimedia player application contains the following files and listings:

- ◆ CHAP32.MAK
- ◆ MAIN.FRM
- ◆ ABOUT.FRM
- ◆ CHAP32.ICO
- ◆ CHAP32.EXE

THE CHAP32.MAK FILE

CHAP32.MAK is the project file for the Multimedia Player application, CHAP32.EXE. It contains a listing of all the files necessary to load the project into Visual Basic. The CHAP32.MAK file is contained on the CD accompanying this book in the CHAP32 subdirectory. The file listing is

LISTING 32.1. CHAP32.MAK.

```
MAIN.FRM
ABOUT.FRM
THREED.VBX
MCI.VBX
CMDIALOG.VBX
ProjWinSize=152,402,248,215
ProjWinShow=2
IconForm="frmMain"
Title="Multimedia"
ExeName="CHAP32.EXE"
```

THE MAIN.FRM FILE

MAIN.FRM is one of two forms in this application. Figure 32.1 presents the form as it appears at runtime. Figure 32.2 presents the form at design time. Table 32.1 lists all the relevant properties of each control on the form that have been changed from their standard default values. The MAIN.FRM file is contained on the CD accompanying this book in the CHAP32 subdirectory.

FIGURE 32.2.
Multimedia Player at design time.

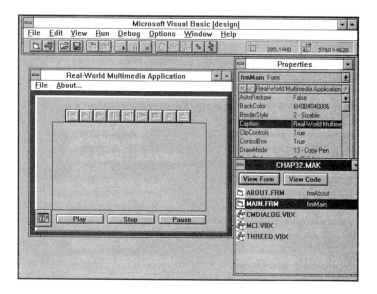

TABLE 32.1. PROPERTIES OF EACH CONTROL ON **MAIN.FRM**.

Object	Control Type	Property	Value
frmMain	Form	BackColor	&H00404000&
		Caption	"Real-World Multimedia Application"
		Height	4620
		Icon	"CHAP32.ICO"
		Left	2100
		MaxButton	False
		Top	2040
		Width	5760
pnlMain	SSPanel	BackColor	&H00C0C0C0&
		BevelWidth	3
		Font3D	None
		ForeColor	&H0000FFFF&
		Height	3735
		Left	120
		Top	120
		Width	5415
cmdPause	CommandButton	Caption	"Pause"
		Height	255
		Left	3480
		Top	3240
		Width	1325
cmdStop	CommandButton	Caption	"Stop"
		Height	255
		Left	2040
		Top	3240
		Width	1325
cmdPlay	CommandButton	Caption	"Play"
		Height	255
		Left	600
		Top	3240
		Width	1325

Object	Control Type	Property	Value
pictVideo	PictureBox	Height	2415
		Left	480
		Top	720
		Width	4325
pnlStatus	SSPanel	Alignment	Left Justify-Middle
		BackColor	&H00C0C0C0&
		BevelOuter	None
		BevelWidth	3
		Font3D	None
		ForeColor	&H0000FFFF&
		Height	255
		Left	120
		Top	120
		Width	5175
cmdialog	CommonDialog	Left	0
		Top	3120
mmControl	MMControl	Height	375
		Left	840
		Top	360
		Visible	False
		Width	3540
menu_file	Menu	Caption	"&File"
menu_exit	Menu	Caption	"&Exit"
menu_about	Menu	Caption	"&About"

FUNCTION, SUBROUTINE, AND EVENT PROCEDURES

There are several procedures of code for each object(control) that comprise this form. Each is listed in the following sections.

THE (GENERAL) OBJECT

The (general) object contains declarations and procedures at the form level. You may notice that the ABOUT.FRM file also has a CenterForm() procedure. This is because it is not advantageous to create a separate *.BAS file only for this one procedure. If this procedure had to be used by many files, that would be a different story. The procedures for the (general) object are

- ◆ (declarations)
- ◆ CenterForm()
- ◆ CloseDevice()
- ◆ EnablePicture()
- ◆ EnableSound()

THE (DECLARATIONS) PROCEDURE

The (declarations) procedure contains variable declarations used in the form, MAIN.FRM. Following is a listing of the (declarations) procedure:

LISTING 32.2. MAIN.FRM, (general)(declarations).

```
Option Explicit

'mousepointers
Const HOURGLASS = 11
Const DEFAULT = 0

'messageboxes
Const IDNO = 7

'MCI control
Const MCI_MODE_NOT_OPEN = 524
Const MCI_MODE_PAUSE = 529
Const MCI_MODE_STOP = 525

Const MODAL = 1
Const DLG_FILE_OPEN = 1
```

THE CENTERFORM() PROCEDURE

The CenterForm() procedure simply centers the form in the client area upon form loading. The CenterForm() procedure accepts one argument, F. It is the actual form to be centered. Following is a listing of the CenterForm() procedure:

LISTING 32.3. MAIN.FRM, CenterForm().

```
Sub CenterForm (F As Form)

    'center the form
    F.Move (Screen.Width - F.Width) / 2, (Screen.Height - F.Height) / 2

End Sub
```

For more information on manipulating graphics and forms, refer to Chapter 5, "Graphics."

THE *CLOSEDEVICE( )* PROCEDURE

The CloseDevice() procedure simply closes the MCI control. Following is a listing of the CloseDevice() procedure:

LISTING 32.4. MAIN.FRM, CloseDevice().

```
Sub CloseDevice ()

    'close device
    mmControl.Command = "Close"

End Sub
```

THE *ENABLEPICTURE( )* PROCEDURE

The EnablePicture() procedure enables the picture box that will play the MCI control's picture file. It also resizes the form accordingly. Following is a listing of the EnablePicture() procedure:

LISTING 32.5. MAIN.FRM, EnablePicture().

```
Sub EnablePicture ()

    'this routine prepares the form by enabling the picture box
    'and moving the controls to play sound and pictures

    'change 3D panel to full height
    pnlMain.Height = 3615

    'show picture box
    pictVideo.Visible = True

    'move the buttons
    cmdPlay.Top = 3240
    cmdStop.Top = 3240
    cmdPause.Top = 3240

    'change height of form
    Me.Height = 4620

    'center the form
    CenterForm Me

End Sub
```

THE *ENABLESOUND()* PROCEDURE

The EnableSound() procedure disables the picture box because there will be no picture file playing, only sound. It also resizes the form accordingly. Following is a listing of the EnableSound() procedure:

LISTING 32.6. MAIN.FRM, EnableSound().

```
Sub EnableSound ()

    'this routine prepares the form by disabling the picture box
    'and moving the controls to play sound only

    'change 3D panel to full height
    pnlMain.Height = 735

    'hide picture box
    pictVideo.Visible = False

    'move the buttons
    cmdPlay.Top = 360
    cmdStop.Top = 360
    cmdPause.Top = 360

    'change height of form
    Me.Height = 1650

    'center the form
    CenterForm Me

End Sub
```

THE *OPENDEVICE()* PROCEDURE

The OpenDevice() procedure opens the MCI control. Following is a listing of the OpenDevice() procedure:

LISTING 32.7. MAIN.FRM, OpenDevice().

```
Sub OpenDevice ()

    'open the device
    mmControl.Notify = False
    mmControl.Wait = True
    mmControl.Shareable = False
    mmControl.Command = "Open"

End Sub
```

THE *CMDPAUSE* CONTROL

cmdPause is the name of the command button control that, when clicked, pauses the multimedia file that is currently playing. The cmdPause control has code in only one event procedure. It is

◆ cmdPause_Click()

THE *CMDPAUSE_CLICK()* EVENT PROCEDURE

The cmdPause_Click() event procedure puts the MCI control in Pause mode. Following is a listing of the cmdPause_Click() event procedure:

LISTING 32.8. MAIN.FRM,cmdPause_Click().

```
Sub cmdPause_Click ()

    'pause file
    mmControl.Command = "Pause"

    'enable stop button
    cmdStop.Enabled = True

    'enable play button
    cmdPlay.Enabled = True

    'disable pause button
    cmdPause.Enabled = False

End Sub
```

THE *CMDPLAY* CONTROL

cmdPlay is the name of the command button control that, when clicked, plays the selected multimedia file. The cmdPlay control has code in only one event procedure. It is

◆ cmdPlay_Click()

THE *CMDPLAY_CLICK()* EVENT PROCEDURE

The cmdPlay_Click() event procedure puts the MCI control in Play mode. Following is a listing of the cmdPlay_Click() event procedure:

LISTING 32.9. MAIN.FRM,cmdPlay_Click().

```
Sub cmdPlay_Click ()

    If mmControl.Mode <> MCI_MODE_PAUSE Then
        'make sure file pointer is set to beginning
        mmControl.Command = "Prev"
    End If
```

continues

829

LISTING 32.9. CONTINUED

```
'play file
mmControl.Command = "Play"

'disable play button
cmdPlay.Enabled = False

'enable stop button
cmdStop.Enabled = True

'enable pause button
cmdPause.Enabled = True

End Sub
```

THE *CMDSTOP* CONTROL

cmdStop is the name of the command button control that, when clicked, stops the selected multimedia file from playing and resets it to the beginning of the file. The cmdStop control has code in only one event procedure. It is

◆ cmdStop_Click()

THE *CMDSTOP_CLICK()* EVENT PROCEDURE

Following is a listing of the cmdStop_Click() event procedure:

LISTING 32.10. MAIN.FRM, cmdStop_Click().

```
Sub cmdStop_Click ()

    'stop file
    mmControl.Command = "Stop"

    'disable stop button
    cmdStop.Enabled = False

    'enable play button
    cmdPlay.Enabled = True

    'clear picture display
    pictVideo.Picture = LoadPicture("")

End Sub
```

THE *FORM* OBJECT

The Form object has code in two event procedures. They are

- Form_Load()
- Form_Unload()

THE *FORM_LOAD()* EVENT PROCEDURE

The Form_Load() event procedure enables the multimedia player to play a sound file, initializes controls, and loads the main form. Following is a listing of the Form_Load() event procedure:

LISTING 32.11. MAIN.FRM, Form_Load().

```
Sub Form_Load ()

    'change cursor
    Screen.MousePointer = HOURGLASS

    'center the form
    CenterForm Me

    'change cursor
    Screen.MousePointer = DEFAULT

    'disable buttons
    cmdPlay.Enabled = False
    cmdStop.Enabled = False
    cmdPause.Enabled = False

    'setup form
    Call EnableSound

End Sub
```

THE *FORM_UNLOAD()* EVENT PROCEDURE

The Form_Unload() event procedure prompts the user to confirm ending the program. Following is a listing of the Form_Unload() event procedure:

LISTING 32.12. MAIN.FRM, Form_Unload().

```
Sub Form_Unload (cancel As Integer)

    'declare variables
    Dim m$       'message constructor
    Dim res%     'holds results

    m$ = "Are you sure you want to exit?"
    res% = MsgBox(m$, 292)
    If res% = IDNO Then
```

continues

LISTING 32.12. CONTINUED

```
        'cancel form unloading
        cancel = True

        'exit
        Exit Sub
    End If

    'close the device
    Call CloseDevice

    'exit
    End

End Sub
```

THE *MENU* OBJECT

The menu object was created using Visual Basic's built-in Menu editor. It has code associated with three event procedures. They are

- menu_about_Click()
- menu_exit_Click()
- menu_open_Click()

THE *MENU_ABOUT_CLICK()* EVENT PROCEDURE

The menu_about_Click() event procedure simply shows the about form for program information. Following is a listing of the menu_about_Click() event procedure:

LISTING 32.13. MAIN.FRM, menu_about_Click().

```
Sub menu_about_Click ()

    'show about form
    frmabout.Show MODAL

End Sub
```

THE *MENU_EXIT_CLICK()* EVENT PROCEDURE

The menu_exit_Click() event procedure starts the program exit procedure, invoked in the Form_Unload() event. Following is a listing of the menu_exit_Click() event procedure:

LISTING 32.14. MAIN.FRM, menu_exit_Click().

```
Sub menu_exit_Click ()

    'close application
    Unload frmMain

End Sub
```

THE *MENU_OPEN_CLICK()* EVENT PROCEDURE

The menu_open_Click() event procedure opens the common dialog box for selecting a file to play. Following is a listing of the menu_open_Click() event procedure:

LISTING 32.15. MAIN.FRM, menu_open().

```
Sub menu_open_Click ()

    'declare variables
    Dim m$          'message constructor

    'set filter
    cmDialog.Filter = "Wave Files¦*.WAV¦MIDI Files¦*.MID¦AVI Video¦*.AVI¦Movie
    Files¦*.MMM¦All Files¦*.*"

    'set filter index for files
    cmDialog.FilterIndex = 5

    'flag for errors
    cmDialog.CancelError = True

    'handle errors
    On Error GoTo openerror

    'invoke open option
    cmDialog.Action = DLG_FILE_OPEN

    'check mode-if open, then close device
    If mmControl.Mode <> MCI_MODE_NOT_OPEN Then
        Call CloseDevice
    End If

    If cmDialog.Filename <> "" Then
        'determine which type of media to play
        Select Case UCase$((Right$(cmDialog.Filename, 3)))
            Case "WAV":
                'set device type
                mmControl.DeviceType = "WaveAudio"

                'setup form
                Call EnableSound
            Case "MID":
                'set device type
                mmControl.DeviceType = "Sequencer"
```

continues   833

LISTING 32.15. CONTINUED

```
                  'setup form
                  Call EnableSound
             Case "AVI":
                  'set device type
                  mmControl.DeviceType = "AVIVideo"

                  'assign handle of window to display video
                  mmControl.hWndDisplay = pictVideo.hWnd

                  'setup form
                  Call EnablePicture
             Case "MMM":
                  'set device type
                  mmControl.DeviceType = "MMMovie"

                  'assign handle of window to display movie
                  mmControl.hWndDisplay = pictVideo.hWnd

                  'setup form
                  Call EnablePicture
             Case Else:
                  'construct message for bad file type
                  m$ = "Cannot recognize file type!" + Chr$(13)
                  m$ = m$ + "It must be (*.WAV),(*.MID),(*.AVI),(*.MMM)"
                  MsgBox m$
                  Exit Sub
        End Select

        'assign file name
        mmControl.FileName = cmDialog.Filename

        'open the device
        Call OpenDevice

        'check status
        If mmControl.Mode = MCI_MODE_NOT_OPEN Then
             m$ = "Cannot open device"
             MsgBox m$

             'change caption
             pnlStatus.Caption = ""

             'disable all buttons
             cmdPlay.Enabled = False
             cmdStop.Enabled = False
             cmdPause.Enabled = False

             'exit
             Exit Sub
        Else
             'show status
             pnlStatus.Caption = mmControl.FileName + " is ready to play."

             'enable play button
             cmdPlay.Enabled = True
        End If
```

```
      End If

      'exit
      Exit Sub

openerror:
   Select Case (Err)
      Case 32755:
         'cancel was selected-do nothing
      Case Else:
         MsgBox Error$
   End Select

      'exit
      Exit Sub

      'avoid errors
      Resume

End Sub
```

The *MMControl* Control

MMControl is the name of the actual multimedia MCI control that is the heart of this application. It handles all communication to and from the Windows multimedia system. The MMControl control has code in only one event procedure. It is

◆ MMControl_Done()

 For more information on the audio portion of the MCI control, which is handled automatically by the MCI control, refer to Chapter 11, "Audio," and Chapter 12, "Multimedia."

The *MMControl_Done()* Event Procedure

The MMControl_Done() event procedure clears all displays when eject is completed. Following is a listing of the MMControl_Done() event procedure:

Listing 32.16. MAIN.FRM,MMControl_Done().

```
Sub mmControl_Done (NotifyCode As Integer)

   'if stopped, enable/disable buttons
   If mmControl.Mode = MCI_MODE_STOP Then
      cmdPlay.Enabled = True
      cmdStop.Enabled = False
      cmdPause.Enabled = False

      'clear picture
```

continues

835

LISTING 32.16. CONTINUED

```
        pictVideo.Picture = LoadPicture("")
    End If

End Sub
```

THE ABOUT.FRM FILE

ABOUT.FRM is the other form in this application. Figure 32.3 presents the form as it appears at runtime. Fundamentally, there is no difference in the form at design time, so it is not presented. Table 32.2 lists all the relevant properties of each control on the form that have been changed from their standard default values. The ABOUT.FRM file is contained on the CD accompanying this book in the CHAP32 subdirectory.

FIGURE 32.3.
*Multimedia Player
About form at runtime.*

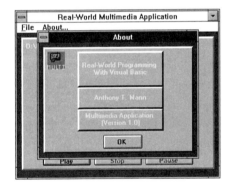

TABLE 32.2. PROPERTIES OF EACH CONTROL ON ABOUT.FRM.

Object	Control Type	Property	Value
frmAbout	Form	BackColor	&H00404000&
		Caption	"About"
		Height	3525
		Left	1035
		MaxButton	False
		MinButton	False
		Top	1140
		Width	4545
pnlMain	SSPanel	BackColor	&H00C0C0C0&
		BevelWidth	3

Object	Control Type	Property	Value
		Caption	""
		Font3D	None
		ForeColor	&H00C0C0C0&
		Height	2895
		Left	120
		RoundedCorners	False
		ShadowColor	Black
		Top	120
		Width	4215
pnl1	SSPanel	BackColor	&H00C0C0C0&
		BevelWidth	3
		Caption	"Real-World Programming With Visual Basic"
		Font3D	None
		ForeColor	&H0000FFFF&
		Height	975
		Left	960
		RoundedCorners	False
		ShadowColor	Black
		Top	120
		Width	2415
pnl2	SSPanel	BackColor	&H00C0C0C0&
		BevelWidth	3
		Caption	"Anthony T. Mann"
		Font3D	None
		ForeColor	&H0000FFFF&
		Height	615
		Left	960
		RoundedCorners	False
		ShadowColor	Black
		Top	1080
		Width	2415

continues

TABLE 32.2. CONTINUED

Object	Control Type	Property	Value
pnl3	SSPanel	BackColor	&H00C0C0C0&
		BevelWidth	3
		Caption	"Multimedia Player Application (Version 1.0)"
		Font3D	None
		ForeColor	&H0000FFFF&
		Height	615
		Left	960
		RoundedCorners	False
		ShadowColor	Black
		Top	1680
		Width	2415
cmdOK	CommandButton	Caption	"OK"
		Height	375
		Left	1680
		Top	2400
		Width	1095
pictAbout	PictureBox	Autosize	True
		BackColor	&H00C0C0C0&
		BorderStyle	None
		Height	615
		Left	120
		Top	120
		Width	735

FUNCTION, SUBROUTINE, AND EVENT PROCEDURES

There are several procedures of code for each object(control) that comprise this form. Each is listed in the following sections.

THE (GENERAL) OBJECT

The (general) object contains only one procedure at the form level. You may notice that the MAIN.FRM file also has the same procedure, CenterForm(). This is because it is not advantageous to create a separate *.BAS file only for this one procedure. If this procedure had to be used by many files, that would be a different story. The procedures for the (general) object are

- (declarations)
- CenterForm()

THE *(DECLARATIONS)* PROCEDURE

The (declarations) procedure contains only one line of declarations used in the form, ABOUT.FRM. It is only to allow for variable syntax checking and forcing the declaration of variables in each procedure. Following is a listing of the (declarations) procedure:

LISTING 32.17. ABOUT.FRM, (general)(declarations).

```
Option Explicit
```

THE *CENTERFORM()* PROCEDURE

The CenterForm() procedure simply centers the form in the client area upon form loading. The CenterForm() procedure accepts one argument, F. It is the actual form to be centered. You may notice that the code in the frmAbout.CenterForm() procedure is not the same as the frmMain.CenterForm() procedure. It performs exactly the same function; however, it is shown differently for informational purposes only. Following is a listing of the CenterForm() procedure:

LISTING 32.18. ABOUT.FRM, CenterForm().

```
Sub CenterForm (F As Form)

    'center the form
    F.Left = (Screen.Width - F.Width) / 2
    F.Top = (Screen.Height - F.Height) / 2

End Sub
```

 For more information on manipulating graphics and forms, refer to Chapter 5, "Graphics."

THE *CMDOK* CONTROL

cmdOK is the name of the command button control that, when clicked, closes the frmAbout form. The cmdOK control has code in only one event procedure. It is

- cmdOK_Click()

THE *cmdOK_Click()* EVENT PROCEDURE

The cmdOK_Click() event procedure simply unloads the form. Following is a listing of the cmdOK_Click() event procedure:

LISTING 32.19. ABOUT.FRM,cmdOK_Click().

```
Sub cmdOK_Click ()

    'unload
    Unload frmAbout

End Sub
```

THE *FORM* OBJECT

The Form object has code in only one event procedure. It is

◆ Form_Load()

THE *FORM_LOAD()* EVENT PROCEDURE

The Form_Load() event procedure centers the form and assigns an icon to the pictAbout control. Following is a listing of the Form_Load() event procedure:

LISTING 32.20. ABOUT.FRM,Form_Load().

```
Sub Form_Load ()

    'center form
    CenterForm Me

    'load icon
    pictAbout.Picture = frmMain.Icon

End Sub
```

THE CHAP32.ICO FILE

This file contains the icon that has been attached to the form at design time. The CHAP32.ICO file is contained on the CD accompanying this book in the CHAP32 subdirectory.

FIGURE 32.4.
Multimedia Player
Program Manager icon.

THE CHAP32.EXE FILE

This is the executable file that is distributable. If you distribute this application, you must include the following files:

- CHAP32.EXE
- MCI.VBX
- CMDIALOG.VBX
- COMMDLG.DLL
- VBRUN300.DLL
- THREED.VBX

The CHAP32.EXE file and source files are contained on the CD accompanying this book in the CHAP32 subdirectory, while all DLLs and VBXs are in the RESOURCE subdirectory.

RELATING THE MULTIMEDIA PLAYER APPLICATION TO YOUR APPLICATION

The Multimedia Player application shows how to play different types of multimedia files. These procedures can be used to incorporate audio and/or video into your own applications either in its entirety or in pieces.

 For more information on audio, refer to Chapter 11, "Audio." For more information on multimedia, refer to Chapter 12, "Multimedia."

FINAL NOTES

This application was created on a standard VGA display using 16 colors. Your particular hardware could have adverse effects on the code the way it is written. You may need to modify it slightly.

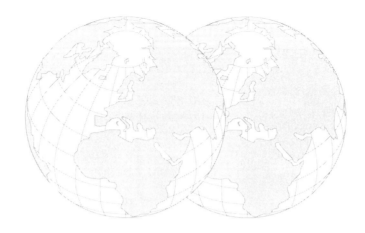

INDEX

B

849

Add to Your Sams Library Today with the Best Books for Programming, Operating Systems, and New Technologies

The easiest way to order is to pick up the phone and call

1-800-428-5331

between 9:00 a.m. and 5:00 p.m. EST.

For faster service please have your credit card available.

ISBN	Quantity	Description of Item	Unit Cost	Total Cost
0-672-30467-8		Sybase Developer's Guide (Book/Disk)	$40.00	
0-672-30440-6		Database Developer's Guide with Visual Basic 3.0 (Book/Disk)	$44.95	
0-672-30160-1		Multimedia Developer's Guide (Book/CD-ROM)	$49.95	
0-672-30364-7		Win32API Desktop Reference	$49.95	
0-672-30338-8		Inside Windows File Formats	$29.95	
0-672-30308-6		Tricks of the Graphics Gurus (Book/Disk)	$49.95	
0-672-30507-0		Tricks of the Game-Programming Gurus (Book/CD-ROM)	$45.00	
0-672-30362-0		Navigating the Internet	$24.95	
0-672-30481-3		Teach Yourself NetWare in 14 Days	$29.95	
0-672-30413-9		Multimedia Madness! Deluxe Edition (Book/2 CD-ROMs)	$55.00	
0-672-30448-1		Teach Yourself C in 21 Days, Bestseller Edition	$24.95	
0-672-30465-1		Developing PowerBuilder 3 Applications	$45.00	
0-672-30621-2		How to Create Real-World Applications with Visual Basic (Book/CD-ROM)	$39.99	
0-672-30456-2		The Magic of Interactive Entertainment (Book/CD-ROM/3D-Glasses)	$39.95	
❏ 3 ½" Disk		Shipping and Handling: See information below.		
❏ 5 ¼" Disk		TOTAL		

Shipping and Handling: $4.00 for the first book, and $1.75 for each additional book. Floppy disk: add $1.75 for shipping and handling. If you need to have it NOW, we can ship product to you in 24 hours for an additional charge of approximately $18.00, and you will receive your item overnight or in two days. Overseas shipping and handling adds $2.00 per book and $8.00 for up to three disks. Prices subject to change. Call for availability and pricing information on latest editions.

201 W. 103rd Street, Indianapolis, Indiana 46290

1-800-428-5331 — Orders   1-800-835-3202 — FAX   1-800-858-7674 — Customer Service

Book ISBN 0-672-30619-0

HOME AUTOMATION!

Now that you have a handle on how to write specialized, highly productive applications, why not extend Visual Basic to control your home or office with the VBX-10$_{TM}$ home-automation custom control? It was written by Anthony T. Mann, author of *Real-World Programming with Visual Basic* and founder of SoftHouse®, to allow you to send and receive industry standard X-10$_{TM}$ based signals from your Visual Basic application.

Using the control is as easy as setting a few properties. Then you're on your way to writing a custom application in Visual Basic that can communicate with lights, appliances, and special devices throughout your home or office. Product includes required hardware. Complete hardware and software cost only $139.95 plus $5.00 shipping/handling. Visa and MasterCard are accepted.

To order, simply fill out the form below and mail, fax, or E-mail information to SoftHouse®. For faster service, phone in your order.

Mail To:	SoftHouse
	5000-B University Parkway
	Suite 19
	Winston-Salem, NC 27106
Phone/Fax:	(800) 5-OK-4-X-10 (800-565-4910)
E-mail:	CompuServe 75141,2522

Ship To:

Name:_____

Address:_____

City/State/Zip:_____

Country:_____

Phone/Fax:_____

Payment Method:

☐ Check enclosed (payable to SoftHouse)

☐ Visa/MC Card #:_____

  Exp. Date:_____

  Authorized Signature:_____

PLUG YOURSELF INTO...

MACMILLAN INFORMATION SUPERLIBRARY™

que NRP SAMS PUBLISHING alpha books Hayden Books Brady que COLLEGE ADOBE PRESS

THE MACMILLAN INFORMATION SUPERLIBRARY™

Free information and vast computer resources from the world's leading computer book publisher—online!

FIND THE BOOKS THAT ARE RIGHT FOR YOU!

A complete online catalog, plus sample chapters and tables of contents give you an in-depth look at *all* of our books, including hard-to-find titles. It's the best way to find the books you need!

- **STAY INFORMED** with the latest computer industry news through our online newsletter, press releases, and customized Information SuperLibrary Reports.

- **GET FAST ANSWERS** to your questions about MCP books and software.

- **VISIT** our online bookstore for the latest information and editions!

- **COMMUNICATE** with our expert authors through e-mail and conferences.

- **DOWNLOAD SOFTWARE** from the immense MCP library:
    - Source code and files from MCP books
    - The best shareware, freeware, and demos

- **DISCOVER HOT SPOTS** on other parts of the Internet.

- **WIN BOOKS** in ongoing contests and giveaways!

TO PLUG INTO MCP: ➜ WORLD WIDE WEB: **http://www.mcp.com**

GOPHER: gopher.mcp.com

FTP: ftp.mcp.com

Home Page What's New Bookstore Reference Desk Software Library Macmillan Overview Talk to Us

What's on the Disc

The companion disc contains the source code for all complete programs presented in the text. The disc also contains third-party tools and multimedia files.

REM To install files from the CD-ROM, youll need at least 8.2 MB of free disk space on your hard drive.

Software Installation Instructions

1. Insert the CD-ROM disc into your CD-ROM drive.

2. From File Manager or Program Manager, choose **R**un from the **F**ile menu.

3. Type `<drive>INSTALL` and press Enter, where `<drive>` corresponds to the drive letter of your CD-ROM. For example, if your CD-ROM is drive D:, type `D:INSTALL` and Press Enter.

4. Follow the on-screen instructions in the installation program. Files will be installed to a directory named \RWPROGVB, unless you choose a different directory during installation.

To conserve space on your hard drive, bonus multimedia .AVI and .WAV files are not copied to your hard disk by the install program. These files can be played directly from the CD by using the multimedia browser program discussed in Chapter 32.